In this book Rudolf Tőkés offers a comprehensive overview of the rise and fall of the Kádár regime in Hungary between 1957 and 1990. The approach is interdisciplinary, reviewing the regime's record with emphasis on politics, macroeconomic policies, social change, and the ideas and personalities of political dissidents and the regime's "successor generation." The study provides a fully documented reconstruction of the several phases of the *ancien régime*'s road from economic reform to political collapse, based on interviews with former top party leaders and transcripts of the Party Central Committee. Tőkés gives an in-depth account of the personalities and issues involved in Hungary's peaceful transformation from one-party state to parliamentary democracy, and a comprehensive assessment of Hungary's postcommunist politics, economy, and society.

HUNGARY'S NEGOTIATED REVOLUTION

Cambridge Russian, Soviet and Post-Soviet Studies: 101

Cambridge Russian, Soviet and Post-Soviet Studies, under the auspices of Cambridge University Press and the British Association for Slavonic and East European Studies (BASEES), promotes the publication of works presenting substantial and original research on the economics, politics, sociology and modern history of Russia, the Soviet Union and Eastern Europe.

Cambridge Russian, Soviet and Post-Soviet Studies

Series list continues after index

HUNGARY'S NEGOTIATED REVOLUTION

Economic reform, social change,
and political succession, 1957–1990

RUDOLF L. TŐKÉS

CAMBRIDGE
UNIVERSITY PRESS

Published by the Press Syndicate of the University of Cambridge
The Pitt Building, Trumpington Street, Cambridge CB2 1RP
40 West 20th Street, New York, NY 10011–4211, USA
10 Stamford Road, Oakleigh, Melbourne 3166, Australia

First published 1996

Printed in Great Britain at the University Press, Cambridge

A catalogue record for this book is available from the British Library

Library of Congress cataloguing in publication data
Tőkés, Rudolf L., 1935–
  Hungary's negotiated revolution: economic reform, social change, and
political succession, 1957–1990 / by Rudolf L. Tőkés.
    p.   cm. – (Cambridge Russian, Soviet and post-Soviet studies; 101)
    ISBN 0 521 57044 1 (hbk) 0 521 57850 7 (pbk)
1. Hungary – Politics and government – 1945–1989. 2. Hungary – Social
conditions – 1945–1989. 3. Hungary – Economic policy – 1945– 4. Dissenters –
Hungary. 5. Post-communism – Hungary. I. Title. II. Series.
JN2066.T58   1966
943.905'3–dc20   95–48155 CIP

.• ISBN 0 521 57044 1 hardback
ISBN 0 521 57850 7 paperback

For Mary, Anne, and Adam

Contents

Tables

Preface and acknowledgments

This book is the result of many years of thinking, reflection, and intellectual soul-searching about my native land, which I, then a third-year law student, left in November 1956. After an extremely rewarding twenty-year detour of studying, teaching, and writing about Soviet and East European politics and comparative communist studies, in 1981 I decided that I was ready to sort out what has become of Hungary since the heady days of the 1956 revolution. Several short trips, five extended visits, hundreds of conversations, and about two dozen publications later I can now report on what I found out.

Major road markers of my rediscovery of Hungary were the summers of 1982 and 1983 spent at the University of Debrecen with groups of exceptionally talented American graduate students and the *crème de la crème* of the Hungarian reform intelligentsia, who shared their wisdom and personal beliefs with my students and me. My late friend Professor György Ránki was responsible for the arrangements and for much of what we learned about Hungarian history. Both Ránki and his distinguished colleagues – Professors Domokos Kosáry, Iván T. Berend, Zsuzsa L. Nagy, Tibor Hajdu, Géza Jeszenszky, Márton Tardos, Tamás Bácskai, Csaba Csáki, Elemér Hankiss, Kálmán Kulcsár, Zsuzsa Ferge, Pál Tamás, and Zoltán Kárpáti – showed us that there was *another*, intellectually vibrant and increasingly restless, Hungary beneath the bland façade of the late Kádár era.

In the next five years I had the good fortune to meet with many scholars and politicians from both sides of the political fence. Conversations with leaders of the democratic opposition – especially János Kis, Miklós Haraszti, and György Konrád; meetings with the reform socialists András Hegedüs and Pál Demény; long discussions with Professors Mihály Bihari, György Csepeli, István Schlett, Csaba Gombár, László Kéri, Mária Csanádi, László Bruszt, and the late Zsolt Papp; and serendipitous encounters with members of the Fidesz leadership greatly enriched my understanding of what the regime's critics had in mind about a post-Kádár democratic Hungary. Similar and equally frank exchanges of ideas with Imre Pozsgay, Rezső Nyers, and György Aczél made me aware of what the regime's top ideologues thought of the coming crisis and possible transformation of Hungary in the late 1980s. Consultations with some of the party's leading foreign policy experts, particularly Csaba Tabajdi and Imre Szokai, and discussions with other staff members of the party Central Committee served as important "reality checks" as to what Hungary's foreign policy options were in the last two years of Soviet rule in Eastern Europe.

With these experiences behind me, I was privileged to witness some of the key events of the "year of miracles" in Hungary: the deliberations of the ruling party's last congress in October 1989, the electoral campaign of February–March 1990, the first free elections in late March and early April, and the installation of the first postcommunist government in May 1990. In the following year I was honored to have been asked to serve for six months as *pro bono* senior advisor to the foreign minister. It was an interesting experience – both in the traditional and in the Chinese sense of the word. It was also a "reality check" of another kind that became essential to my appreciation of the obstacles that any postcommunist government must overcome to make its way in the world while trying to build democracy at home.

Next, I should like to acknowledge my indebtedness to several friends and colleagues who were kind enough to read and comment on parts or the entire text of this study. Professors Tibor Hajdu and György Csepeli read and provided incisive critiques of the entire manuscript. Professors George Schopflin, Elemér Hankiss, Paul Marer, Polly Allen, Walter D. Connor, and László Vass and Messrs János Barabás and László Lengyel read parts of the manuscript and gave helpful advice on methodology, substance, and factual details. Dr. Péter Tölgyessy, MP, Mr. László Vitézy, Professor György Vukovich, and Dr. István Harcsa gave me access to valuable source material with which to document my case. Dr. László Soós and his colleagues in the Hungarian National Archives were generous with their time in providing access to the Archives' holdings on the HSWP. I am also grateful to the publisher's anonymous referees for their thorough review of the material. My sincere thanks to them all – as well as to those who also helped, but asked not to be named.

Special thanks are due to graduate students in my East European Politics and Transitions to Democracy seminars. As the first and, in my view most important, readers of several chapters, they were tough, yet thorough, critics of my work in progress. Their ideas, in one way or another, are in this book.

My research for this study has benefited from many kinds of support in the past several years. These include grants from the Fulbright-Hays program, the International Research and Exchange Board, the United States Information Agency, the Konrad Adenauer Stiftung-Forschungsinstitut, the Danubia Research Foundation, and the National Endowment for the Humanities, and from the steadfast supporter of in-house faculty research, the University of Connecticut Graduate Research Foundation. My special thanks to the program officers of these funding agencies, as well as to Deans Hugh Clark, Julius A. Elias and Thomas Giolas of my university.

I am also indebted to Professor George Cole and the staff of the Political Science department for his support and their cheerful help with this project, to Mrs. Betty Seaver for her crisp and thoughtful copyediting of the manuscript, and to Mr. Victor Chudowski for his assistance with the preparation of the index. As is appropriate, I wish to accept responsibility for any and all errors of fact and interpretation that the reader might find in this work.

Finally, I would like to thank my wife and children for putting up with me while this project was on the top of the family agenda. It is to them that this book is affectionately dedicated.

Chronology of key events in Hungary, 1956–1990

1956

October 23 to
November 4   Revolution in Hungary.

November 4   Armed intervention by the USSR; establishment of
the Hungarian Revolutionary Workers' and
Peasants' Government under János Kádár.

1957

May 27   Agreement on the legal status of Soviet troops
stationed in Hungary signed.

June 27–29   National conference of the HSWP reconfirms János
Kádár's position as the party's leader.

1958

April 2–11   Khrushchev–Kádár agreement on the long-term
stationing of Soviet troops in Hungary.

June 16   Execution of Imre Nagy and codefendants; other
defendants receive long-term prison terms.

1959

December 5   HSWP 7th congress; beginning of the
recollectivization of agriculture.

1960

April 4   Partial amnesty of political prisoners sentenced for
five years or less.

1961

February 22   Completion of the recollectivization of agriculture.

1962

January 1   Kádár's New Year message: "he who is not against
us is with us."

August 19	Mátyás Rákosi, Ernő Gerő, and twenty-three Stalinists expelled from the HSWP.
November 20–24	HSWP 7th congress: "95 percent of those sentenced for participation in the 'October events' are being released from detention."

1965
November 18–20	Report by János Kádár and Rezső Nyers to CC, HSWP on the Guiding Principles of the New Economic Mechanism (NEM).

1967
September 6–9	Twenty-year Treaty of Friendship, Cooperation and Mutual Assistance between Hungary and the USSR signed.

1968
January 1	Inauguration of the NEM.
August 21	Hungary joins the Soviet-led invasion of Czechoslovakia.

1971
September 28	Agreement between Hungary and the Vatican on Cardinal József Mindszenty's departure from Hungary.

1972
November 14–15	CC, HSWP "midterm" meeting; implementation of first of several anti-NEM measures by regime.

1973
December 20	Establishment of full diplomatic relations with the Federal Republic of Germany.

1974
March 21	Resignation of leading reformers Rezső Nyers as secretary of CC, HSWP, and of Lajos Fehér as deputy prime minister.

1975
May 15	Resignation of pro-reform Jenő Fock as prime minister.
August 1	Kádár signs, on Hungary's behalf, the Helsinki Final Act.

August 4	First substantial price rise of consumer goods.
1977	
January	Members of the Hungarian democratic opposition sign statement in support of Charter '77.
June 7–9	Kádár visits Italy and meets Pope Paul VI.
1978	
January 6	US delegation led by Secretary of State Cyrus Vance returns the Crown of St. Stephen to Hungary.
February–March	HSWP Politburo decision to revive the NEM process.
April 19–20	Hardliner Béla Biszku dismissed as CC secretary and retires from party work.
1979	
July 22	Major price rises of food and consumer goods announced.
1980	
March	HSWP 12th congress; leadership renewal postponed.
November	The samizdat *Bibó Memorial Book* by seventy-six authors published.
1981	
November	First issue of samizdat journal *Beszélő* published; Hungary seeks admission to the International Monetary Fund and the World Bank.
December 15	Hungarian government endorses the Polish martial law regime.
1982	
May 25	János Kádár is 75 years old.
June	Imre Pozsgay named secretary general of Patriotic People's Front.
1983	
September–October	Mikhail Gorbachev visits Hungary.
1984	
February	Prime minister Margaret Thatcher visits Hungary.

April 17-20	Meeting of CC, HSWP: instead of further economic reforms, Kádár endorses a "new development path" for Hungary.
December 6	Károly Grósz named first secretary of the Budapest party organization and is coopted to membership in the Politburo.

1985

March 25–28	HSWP 13th congress; ambitious plan targets are announced.
April 26	Hungary's membership in the Warsaw Treaty Organization is renewed for twenty years.
June 8	Multicandidate elections for the Parliament and the local governments.
December 13–15	Patriotic People's Front, 8th congress; first public criticism of HSWP's congressional plan targets.

1986

March 15	Young demonstrators attacked by police riot squads.
June 8–11	Mikhail Gorbachev's first visit to Hungary as Soviet leader.
October 22	Conference of Catholic bishops: "military service is patriotic duty."
November 19–20	Meeting of CC, HSWP: "congressional plan targets are unattainable."
December 28	Miklós Németh named head of Department of Economic Policy, CC, HSWP.

1987

June 10	Samizdat "Social Contract" says "Kádár must go!"
June 23–26	Károly Grósz named prime minister, János Berecz elected to the Politburo, Miklós Németh named CC secretary for economic policy; Kádár takes on Miklós Lázár as deputy secretary general, but refuses to step down as party leader.
September 27	Founding conference of the HDF.

1988

January 29	HDF-sponsored public debate on democratization and political pluralism.
March 15	15,000 demonstrators demand democracy and human rights.

April 9	Four reform intellectuals expelled from the HSWP.
May 20–22	*"Putsch* of the apparat"; Kádár and four associates leave the Politburo; Károly Grósz elected secretary general; reform leaders Imre Pozsgay and Rezső Nyers join the Politburo; Pozsgay named minister of state.
June 16	Peaceful commemoration of Imre Nagy and associates dispersed by the riot police.
June 27	30,000 demonstrate in Budapest to protest violations of human rights by the Ceauşescu regime.
July 19–30	Károly Grósz visits the United States.
August 28	Grósz and Ceauşescu meet in Arad.
September 3	HDF declares itself as a "democratic spiritual–political movement."
October 2	First congress of the League of Young Democrats (Fidesz).
November 13	The Alliance of Free Democrats (AFD) is established.
November 24–26	Miklós Németh named prime minister.
November 29	First HSWP Reform Circle founded in Szeged; Grósz speaks of the specter of "white terror" in Hungary.

1989

January 24	Caucus of nonparty MPs established in Parliament.
January 29	Imre Pozsgay: "there was a popular uprising in 1956."
February 10–11	CC, HSWP endorses political pluralism in Hungary.
March 15	Public celebration of national holiday.
March 19	AFD becomes a political party.
March 24	Opposition Roundtable convened.
April 12	Christian Democratic People's Party (CDPP) established.
April 25	Beginning of Soviet troop withdrawals from Hungary.
May 8–9	HSWP surrenders its *nomenklatura* rights to the government.
June 14	Beginning of the National Roundtable (NRT) negotiations.

June 16	Ceremonial reburial of Imre Nagy, his codefendants, and the "unknown freedom fighter of 1956."
June 24	HSWP taken over by a four-man presidency and a 21- person Political Executive Committee.
July 6	János Kádár dies.
July 11–13	Visit of U.S. President George Bush in Budapest.
July–August	HDF candidates win at four parliamentary by-elections.
September 10	Hungarian government opens the Iron Curtain and permits departure of 12,000 East German tourists for the West.
September 18	NRT Agreement signed by regime and opposition.
October 6–10	Last congress of HSWP; founding congress of the Hungarian Socialist Party (HSP).
October 23	Hungarian People's Republic renamed the Republic of Hungary; Hungarian army seizes weapons of the Workers' Guard.
November 26	"Four-question" referendum thwarts Imre Pozsgay's candidacy for president of Hungary.
1990	
February 1 to March 24	Electoral campaign.
March 25, April 8	First and second round of democratic Hungary's founding elections.
April 29	Political agreement between the HDF and the AFD.
May 22	Installation of Hungary's freely elected government.

Abbreviations

AFD	Alliance of Free Democrats (SZDSZ)
CC	Central Committee
CC, AP	CC Department of Agitation and Propaganda
CC, CE	CC Department of Educational, Scientific, and Cultural Affairs
CC, EP	CC Department of Economic Policy
CC, FA	CC Department of Foreign/International Affairs
CC, PA	CC Department of Law and Public Administration
CC, PMO	CC Department of Party and Mass Organizations
CCC	Central Control Commission
CDPP	Christian Democratic People's Party (KDNP)
CMEA	Council of Mutual Economic Aid and Assistance
CPSU	Communist Party of the Soviet Union
CSCE	Commission for Security and Cooperation in Europe
DUSC	Democratic Union of Scientific Workers (TDDSZ)
EBZSS	Endre Bajcsy-Zsilinszky Society
FYP	Five-Year Plan
HAS	Hungarian Academy of Sciences (MTA)
HCC	Hungarian Chamber of Commerce (MKK)
HCP	Hungarian Communist Party (MKP)
HDF	Hungarian Democratic Forum (MDF)
HSDP	Hungarian Social Democratic Party (MSZDP)
HSP	Hungarian Socialist Party (MSZP)
HSWP	Hungarian Socialist Workers' Party (MSZMP)
HWP	Hungarian Workers' Party (MDP)
ILF	Independent Lawyers' Forum
IMF	International Monetary Fund
ISP	Independent Smallholders' Party
LYD	League of Young Democrats (Fidesz)

MP	Member of Parliament
NAC	National Alliance of Cooperatives (KISOSZ)
NCAC	National Council of Agricultural Cooperatives (TOT)
NEM	New Economic Mechanism
NFI	Network of Free Initiatives (*Hálózat*)
NMF	New March Front
NPO	National Planning Office (OT)
NRT	National Roundtable
ORT	Opposition Roundtable
PB	Politburo (Politikai Bizottság)
PD	People's Democratic Platform
PEC	Political Executive Committee
PP	People's Party
RA	Reform Alliance
RC	Reform Circle
TUF	Trade Union Federation (SZOT)
TYP	Three-Year Plan
WTO	Warsaw Treaty Organization
YCL	Young Communist League (KISZ)

Introduction
The mainsprings of political change in Hungary

Hungary's journey from totalitarian dictatorship to parliamentary democracy commenced on October 23, 1956. The Hungarian revolution, the nation's short-lived bid for freedom from Stalinist dictatorship and Soviet rule, began on that day. The next milestone on the road to national independence and political democracy was the installation, on May 22, 1990, by Hungary's freely elected national legislature, of the coalition government of prime minister József Antall. The general time frame of the narrative falls between these two dates. The principal objective of this study is to analyze the issues, identify the participants, and reconstruct the linkages between antecedent events and key turning points of the terminal phase (1984–90) of Hungary's epic journey from revolution to liberty.

What follows is neither a comprehensive history of the Kádár era nor a technical treatise on the many facets of what academic observers called "the Hungarian model," Kádár's internal conservative critics labeled "Frigidaire socialism," and Nikita Khrushchev dubbed "goulash communism." Though each of these terms tends to capture one or another aspect of Hungarian realities of the 1960s and the 1970s, none of them can explain the institutional dynamics, ideational complexity, social milieu, and political outcomes of the entire period. The writing of a definitive account of the politics of the Kádár era in Hungary, however desirable it may be for scholars and the Hungarian people alike, must await publication of memoirs and unrestricted access to the holdings of the Hungarian Socialist Workers' Party (HSWP) and state archives. Full disclosure and the scholarly review of signed policy directives on internal security matters, strategic resource allocations decisions, and top-level personnel choices are not possible as long as Hungary's new and old political elites feel vulnerable to potentially embarrassing evidence from such sources.

In developing my case, I shall endeavor to test, with the help of parsimonious selection of analytical tools, the validity of evidence and interpretation from all sources. The necessary methods and concepts will be drawn from the Western academic literature on socioeconomic change and political development in communist states, as well as from selected works on political leadership, decision- and policy-making, macroeconomic analyis, social mobility and stratification, and elite circulation. Empirical evidence and social science theorizing will be augmented with biographic sketches throughout the narrative. I believe it is essential to account for the personalities and the ideas of political actors who played key roles during the Kádár era. In my view, three scores of politicians and intellectuals were, as much as the people for whom they spoke, responsible for what took place in Hungary between 1970 and 1989.

The Kádár regime's key domestic policy dilemmas were those of political legitimacy, resource allocation, social engineering, political steering, and ideological congruence.[1] Most of these, particularly ideological preferences that may be inferred from official statements and published party documents, are demonstrable with a remarkable degree of precision.[2] Thus, with the exception of arcane, albeit crucial, details of party and government personnel decisions and international (Hungarian–Soviet; Warsaw Treaty Organization) and internal security (mainly secret police) affairs, internal documents on the rest of the ruling party's policy record are generally accessible to scholarly scrutiny.[3]

Evidence derived from hitherto top-secret transcripts of leadership deliberations in the Politburo (PB) and the Central Committee (CC) is helpful to corroborate or to refute the received wisdom of Western views on the issues, the available policy choices, and the rationale for key decisions made during the Kádár era. Data of this kind, though unavailable on internal security, personnel, and HSWP–Communist Party of the Soviet Union (CPSU) operative relationships, should help enhance the accuracy of analytical judgments about how Hungary was actually ruled by Kádár and his associates.[4]

Fundamentally, there is a story to tell about the recent history of the people of an East Central European country and the way political, economic, and social forces shaped their destiny in the second half of the twentieth century. My purpose is to show that what took place in Hungary, particularly during the eventful "year of miracles," 1989, was not a miracle at all but the consequence of specific policies and statistically documentable socioeconomic processes that the political regime and its key incumbents had set into motion since the communist takeover of Hungary in 1947–8.

The title and the subtitle of this study are broadly indicative of what I plan to discuss. In general, I intend to isolate and analyze the dynamics of Hungary's political transformation and to explain the reasons for the collapse and, since 1990, partial survival of the developmental dilemmas and social values of the Kádár regime. Though much of the narrative will focus on sociopolitical change, the elements of continuity, particularly that of political culture, economic constraints, and social dynamics, will form an essential subtext of my case. My approach to these matters is presented in six propositions that address what I believe are the core issues behind Hungary's political transformation in 1989–90.

The propositions are: (1) The antinomies and ideologies of nationalism and modernization in Hungary; (2) the phenomenon of negotiation and legal traditions of peaceful conflict resolution in Hungarian elite political culture; (3) the role of terror, coercion, and persuasion during the Kádár era; (4) the personality, ideological motivations, and political style of János Kádár; (5) the structural and situational constraints on, and the evolving leadership styles of, the ruling HSWP; and (6) the international context in which the Hungarian transition took place in the late 1980s. The hypotheses are summarized below in the form of six paired propositions and arguments.

(A) Nation and progress: six ideas in search for survival and change

Proposition: The ideas for political democracy, rule of law, economic transformation, and social justice of the political elites that came to power in Hungary in 1990 had been rooted in, and were informed by, those of historic Hungarian intelligentsia debates on strategies of national survival and socioeconomic development.[5] The record and the outcome of these debates are instructive and are also useful for the placing of the new Hungarian elites' policy agenda in a historically valid context. The perception that some observers of Hungary's postcommunist politics share by viewing the principal ideological cleavages underlying policy debates of the early 1990s in terms of "liberal/conservative," "urbanist/Populist," and "Marxist internationalist/native socialist" dichotomies is misleading and tends to obscure the common intellectual origins of these labels.[6] I submit that each of these ideological postures takes its departure from the ideas of traditional Hungarian intelligentsia politics – that of a search for answers to questions of national identity and of the imperatives of modernization.

Argument: Hungary's evolution toward modern statehood, economic development, the reception of values of civil society, and quest for a permanent place in the community of European nations, has been shaped by many factors. Among these, the Hungarian people's chronic sense of existential insecurity due to the country's geostrategic vulnerability (to be discussed below), economic backwardness, delayed social and political modernization, and the elites' beliefs of cultural identity and national destiny are most pertinent to the matter at hand. The factors were not unique to Hungary, but were parts of the regional predicament of small East European nations over the past two centuries.[7] They were also of paramount concern for the region's intellectuals – whether from communities, in Herder's phrase, with a "history" of independent statehood or those without one.[8]

The Hungarian elites' programmatic responses to the nation's developmental dilemmas have taken many forms since the onset of the "Age of Reforms" (1790–1848). Though this proposition vastly oversimplifies the rich diversity of their ideas, the leaders (István Széchenyi, Lajos Kossuth, Ferenc Deák, and many others) of Hungary's "first reform generation" conceptualized these problems in terms of "nation and progress."[9] Since then, these notions have been posed in both a complementary and an antithetical sense. In terms of these statesmen's philosophical legacy, by "nation" I understand the community of people and its elites and their capacity to share values and aspirations for political citizenship, equality under the law, good society, economic opportunities, and a secure place for Hungary in the world. By "progress" I refer to choices, as mediated by an elite-led national consensus, about the ways and means of promoting institutional change, economic development, societal *rapprochement*, and cultural advancement.

The reconciliation, in political terms, of the intrinsically clashing requisites for "Hungary as it is" and "Hungary as it ought to be" and the manner in which backwardness in its various manifestations might be overcome has been played out in the realm of political ideas as periodically recurring choices between reform and revolution.[10] As a rule, proponents of either alternative sought to address a dual agenda of domestic and foreign policy issues. The reformers (some of whom became revolutionaries) spoke for incremental change and peaceful consensus-building at home and for a semisovereign Hungary and a pragmatic accommodation of the regional hegemon. The revolutionaries have typically argued for radical action; they have ended up on the gallows, or have chosen exile, or have become reformers. Initially however, they have pressed for the mass mobilization of the people and sought the immediate gratification of demands that neither the society (as in the case of full political emancipation in 1848–9, or the dictatorship of the proletariat in 1919) nor the regional hegemons have been prepared to accept.

To each of these postures and personal fates one could attach a long list of names and a somewhat shorter one for ideological labels to views that were propounded by Hungary's reformers and revolution-aries in the past two centuries. However, taxonomical exercises will not advance my arguments. The point, as will be shown in the chapter on dissident and regime ideologies in the 1980s, is that all political actors in Hungary, except the vanished breed of Marxist international-ists have, since 1988–90, made claims as the proper, and often sole, heirs to both the revolutionary and reformist intellectual legacies of Hungarian history. The task at hand is not to prove or disprove the "truth in labeling" of hastily improvised party programs of the transition period. Rather, it is to identify the political-economic trade-offs that we might infer from the three paired ideological dichotomies as policy alternatives for addressing the challenge of "nation and progress" in Hungary in the 1990s.

During the "Age of Dualism" (1867–1918) the ideas of classical liberalism dominated Hungarian politics: the liberal governments' Praxis of "nation" stood for the rule of the landed nobility together with co-opted professionals and wealthy enterpreneurs; the denial of political access and cultural autonomy to the ethnic communities that resisted policies of forced assimilation into the "Hungarian nation"; a combination of *laissez-faire* economics and state intervention; and the indefinite deferral of social reforms.[11] In the realm of foreign relations, liberalism amounted to ritualized feuds with Austria over budgetary policies and full support for the monarchy's imperial designs for territorial aggrandizement.

The regime of Admiral Miklós Horthy (1920–44) has been variously characterized as "conservative," "Christian-national," "authoritarian," and "fascist." The first three adjectives are accurate, but the fourth is not.[12] At any rate, the ideologies and the policy positions of Hungary's interwar politics that are of interest during the tenure of the first postcommunist conservative Christian democratic government of József Antall (1990–3) include the following: the enshrining of the political system and the incumbent government as the heir to traditions of Hungary "as a thousand-year-old Christian kingdom"; the perception of liberalism – in both its "Dualist" and "Wilsonian" versions – as alien to the nation's values and institutions; continued postponement of overdue social legislation, particularly that for land reform; the emergence of the state as the principal promoter of economic modernization; preoccupation with the recovery of people and territories lost to Romania, Czechoslovakia, and Yugoslavia; and a fatal vulnerability to the appeals of the revanche-driven policies of fascist Italy and National Socialist Germany.[13]

In the original sense, "urbanism" is understood to denote the views of the liberal, Western-orientated, and, to a substantial extent, culturally assimilated, Jewish intelligentsia of Budapest of the interwar (1920–39) period. My use of this term also includes the ideas of the similarly urban "second reform generation" of 1890–1914, and subsumes both under the label "modern liberalism."[14] The positive reception of ideas of modernity and the vigorous advocacy of reforms to reshape Hungary's political institutions, electoral laws, the governments' social policies – particularly those pertaining to ethnic and religious minorities – and the promotion of values of modern culture, science, and the arts may be a fair way to summarize the liberals' policy platform. However, in its subsequent configurations, "urbanism" also denotes the Budapest intellectuals' battles on two fronts: against the radical Right of the Horthy era and the regime's alliance with fascist Italy and Nazi Germany, and against the radical Left of both radical Populist and Marxist–Leninist persuasion.

In terms of its intellectual origins, Populism was a protest movement of members of the provincial intelligentsia.[15] Their targets were the political, economic, and social injustices that had befallen the people of rural Hungary. To overcome these, they advocated values of a yet-to-be-born modern native intelligentsia-led peasant society. Questions of land reform, the creation of a prosperous farm economy, and a search for foreign models for a drastic socioeconomic transformation of Hungary were the main components of the Populist agenda. Populists sought to distance themselves from the totalitarian essence of fascism and Stalin's brand of socialism and remained rather oblivious to the appeal of Western-style liberal democracy. Instead, they endeavored to embark on a Hungarian "third road": a program of radical reforms that proposed to incorporate the "best" and rejected the "worst" features of fascism and communism.[16]

Marxist-internationalist ideologies and programs dominated Hungarian politics in two specific periods: the 133-day-long Hungarian

Soviet Republic of 1919 led by Béla Kun, and the phase of "mature Stalinism" (1948–56) under the leadership of Mátyás Rákosi and his Muscovite associates. The common agenda of both leaders was the revolutionary transformation of Hungary from a traditional and, after the Second World War, potentially liberal democratic state into a Leninist–Stalinist soviet republic and a People's Democracy, respectively. Apart from its Soviet-inspired policy agenda, the Marxist internationalist model was also notable for its vigorous pursuit of Hungary's cultural modernization. Kun's and Rákosi's "cultural revolutions" tended to confer considerable powers to the ideologically converted intellectuals. In fact, it may not be far-fetched to argue that Kun's and Rákosi's policies ought to be seen as foreign-inspired "shock therapies" to address the dilemma of "nation and progress" – albeit in a highly coercive fashion and at the expense of democracy, freedom, and human rights.[17]

The Hungarian elites' "native socialist" ideas consist of a complex mixture of foreign and indigenous left-wing intellectual traditions and political programs. Ideas of Austro-German social democracy, agrarian socialism, left-wing Populism, "native" communism, revisionist Marxism, and low-key Hungarian nationalism are parts of this ideological hybrid. In policy terms, many components of this eclectic package had, as mediated through the impeccably orthodox rhetoric of the political leadership, become from the 1970s on, the *de facto* ideological foundations of the Kádár regime in Hungary.[18]

In sum, ideas do matter in Hungary. They have a life of their own and have a remarkable capacity to shape national history. My arguments focus on six selected and, of necessity, highly condensed ideological paradigms that helped define political outcomes in a small Central European country. Each searched for and proposed answers to questions posed by the dilemma of "nation and progress" in the past two centuries. Many of the answers emerged as government programs, opposition platforms, or revolutionary manifestos; some have lain dormant for many years to await the arrival of freedom and national indepence in Hungary.

(B)   Compromise and survival

Proposition: The adjective "negotiated" (*kialkudott*), or "made a deal at the end of protracted bargaining," in Hungarian; (*verhandelt* in German) rather than "peaceful," "consensual," or "pacted," to characterize the manner of Hungary's political transformation from posttotalitarian dictatorship to parliamentary democracy seeks to convey an image not merely of a nonviolent, and essentially elite-brokered, process of political bargaining that took place between early 1989 and May 1990 but much more.[19] In my view, negotiation as an instrument of choice for the reconciliation of seemingly intractable differences in political beliefs and interests has well-established historic and contemporary precedents in Hungary.

Traditionally, in Hungary it was public law – an unstructured aggregate of royal edicts, István Werbőczy's *Tripartitum Corpus Juris* of 1514–17, acts of the Diet that constituted Hungary's unwritten constitution, and, even more, political customs derived from laws – that informed the language, defined the terms, and set the structure of negotiations and the manner of compliance with political agreements of all kinds.[20] Latin was the official written language of public administration until 1841. Although the formal reception of Roman law never materialized in Hungary, its language and spirit deeply penetrated the substance and idiom of elite discourse on political affairs. Be these decades-long litigation over obscure land titles, protracted disputes between self-governing towns and counties and the Hapsburg monarchy's central bureaucracy in Vienna, or the terms of *rapprochement* betwen the indigenous elites and their foreign overlords, it was the classical principles of the law that provided the principles and shaped the outcomes of negotiations of all kinds. Hungary used to be called a "country of lawyers." Although this epithet was not meant to flatter, it is the combination of pragmatic instincts for the "art of the deal" and the intellectual rigor of legal analysis as the essential prerequisite of a well-made contract that has been the hallmark of pragmatic Hungarian-style negotiations in the last four centuries.

Argument: Hungary's geographic location, the size of its Magyar-speaking population, and the political and cultural elites' traditional preoccupation with questions of national survival have been the causes and effects of the nation's profound vulnerability to foreign influences of all kinds. Hungary's existential need over the centuries to overcome adverse external realities gave birth to a desperate cycle of national history: pursuit of security through territorial aggrandizement, confrontations with adversaries of superior strength, military defeat, foreign occupation, coming to terms with the conqueror, national rebuilding, and national uprising to regain independence.[21]

When seen in its historic dimension, the vehicle of negotiations between the native elites and the nation's foreign conquerors (and their native collaborators) has been a traditional component of the indigenous elites' survivalist political culture that played a crucial role in shaping the form and substance of Hungary's recent transition from one political system to another. The elites' pragmatic mind-set and, when all else failed, willingness to come to terms with adversity were rooted in the similarly pragmatic, perhaps fatalistic, values of Hungary's traditional peasant society.

As the poet Mihály Babits put it in a poignant essay written on the eve of the Second World War:

> The Hungarian nation would have perished long ago if its political wisdom had not succeeded in preserving it ... In a strange way this squabbling and impetuous people had ensured the survival and the development of its country more by its sense of reality than by the military exploits imposed upon it by external necessities or by its bravery ... It is very characteristic that it is by giving up the battle that it in fact consolidated its situation and possibilities in Europe ... And since then the whole existence of this people is only a series of lucid compromises, an uninterrupted meditation on actual possibilities.[22]

Indeed, Hungary's history is rich in precedents of quixotic bids for national independence that were followed by devastating defeats and "negotiated" settlements with foreign overlords. Several historical examples should help illustrate and, to some extent, explain the embedded nature of "limited sovereignty with economic prosperity and personal autonomy through negotiations" as a positive value in the national psyche.

Upon the crushing defeat of the Hungarian forces by the Ottoman army of Suleyman the Magnificent, at the Battle of Mohács in 1526, the country became divided into Ottoman-, Austrian-, and Hungarian-controlled parts. For the next 150 years, the Principality of Transylvania remained Hungarian, but was caught "between two [Ottoman and Austrian] heathens." The art of survival and the preservation of national identity through constant negotiations with the enemy, as practiced by the Hungarian rulers of Transylvania, offer one model of survival and modest prosperity through pragmatic adaptation to adverse political realities.[23]

Prince Ferenc Rákóczi's campaign (1703–11) for the liberation of Hungary from Hapsburg rule, though defeated, led to the Pragmatic Sanction Act of 1722. The codification of a negotiated political *modus vivendi* with Austria gave the country – just emerging from the ravages of Turkish occupation of 165 years – and the nobility a much-needed respite to rebuild and to live to fight another day.[24]

Hungary's next bid for freedom and national independence came in 1848–9.[25] The uprising was crushed by the combined forces of Russia and Austria. The revolutionary leaders either were executed, as were prime minister Lajos Batthyány and thirteen generals of the revolutionary army on October 6, 1849, or were driven into exile, as were Lajos Kossuth (a lawyer) and his followers. Yet, eighteen years later another group of Hungarian politicians, led by Ferenc Deák (another lawyer), found a way to come to terms with the conqueror and helped forge the Compromise of 1867 with the Hapsburg monarchy.[26]

Although nominally in control of the Hungarian half of the Dual Monarchy, the Hungarian ruling elites failed to extend the benefits of compromise and fair accommodation of interests, such as cultural and administrative autonomy, to the millions of Slovaks, Romanians, Serbs, and Croats living in the territory of "historic Hungary." Their settling for quasi-sovereignty from Austria without negotiating similar agreements for some kind of power sharing with the ethnic minorities meant that the fruits of the Compromise of 1867 – most prominently, a period of unprecedented economic growth in Hungarian history – were swept away by the forces of resurgent nationalism at the end of the First World War.[27]

The Peace Treaty of Trianon of 1920 was a diktat that left no room for negotiations of any kind. This was also true of the postwar politics of Hungary. In the aftermath of a "red" revolution of 1919 and a "white" counterrevolution of 1919–20, and upon the loss of two-thirds of the national territory and one-third of the Hungarian-speaking population, "negotiation" and "liberal democracy" became discredited terms in the nation's political vocabulary. The recovery, by means fair or foul, of people and territory lost to the neighboring states became the centerpiece of the interwar governments' political agenda.[28] Hungary's alliance with Nazi Germany and fascist Italy was the logical consequence of this policy, as were the country's subsequent crushing military defeat, the death of one million people (more than half a million in the eastern front or in Soviet POW camps, and 450,000 Jews in Nazi extermination camps), and the Soviet occupation of Hungary in 1944–5.[29]

The Allied victory over Germany brought the rebirth of political pluralism and free elections, and offered, for the first time in modern Hungarian history, the hope of parliamentary democracy, a market economy, and the restoration of individual freedoms. However, the postwar democratic elites, though beneficiaries of a landslide electoral victory in the fall of 1945, were gradually driven, at Soviet gunpoint, into increasingly hopeless negotiations by the Muscovite Mátyás Rákosi-led Left Bloc of communists, renegade social democrats, and fellow-traveling urban and rural intellectuals. Attempts at constructive compromises between the democrats and the Left Bloc rapidly degenerated into the elimination of naysayers and, from there, to communist tyranny and the establishment, in 1948–9, of a Soviet-style totalitarian dictatorship.[30]

The time for national rebirth came in October 1956.[31] The revolution, though crushed by the Soviet Red Army, left in its wake a political regime that tried but could never fully overcome the burden of its illegitimate origins. János Kádár, of whom much will be said in the narrative, was a quisling, albeit a pragmatic one. His oft-quoted *bon mot* "He who is not against us is with us" was a clever slogan but not a binding proposal for a social contract between the regime and the people. Nevertheless, the need to overcome the intolerable political and psychological burden of the bloody suppression of the revolution and the public revulsion over the judicial murder on June 16, 1958 of its leader, Imre Nagy, and his codefendants, was central to the subsequent inauguration of a twenty-year (1968–88) period of consensus-seeking behavior by the regime.

With the passage of time, particularly after 1968, a growing number of Hungary's economic, cultural, and social elites either were co-opted into the ruling establishment or, in exchange for political passivity, were granted substantial personal autonomy. The absence of overt conflicts between the people and the regime in Hungary, from the early 1960s on, gave the appearance of political stability, which, in turn, helped establish Kádár's credentials with his Soviet masters. Indeed, in retrospect it appears that Hungary's spurious tranquility between the early 1960s and the late 1970s might have been the product of not one but two sets of mutually reinforcing informal understandings: one between János Kádár and Moscow, and the other between the regime and the people. The terms of each will be discussed in the narrative.

In any event, the erosion, from the mid-1970s on, of the regime's economic legitimacy helped create a new correlation of political and social forces in Hungary. The growing gap between the ruling party's ideological pretensions and its mismanagement of the country's economic, human, and environmental resources was the main reason for the gradual destabilization and the accelerated dichotomization of the thitherto stable relationship between the rulers and the ruled. The most striking manifestation of the new relationship was the emergence, as an unintended consequence of economic reforms, of an astonishing range of formal and informal bargaining and interest-adjudication environments between the people and the regime. These could be found in factories and enterprises, in government offices, at universities and research institutes, at professional associations, at county and city party headquarters, and, from the mid-1980s on, at editorial offices of the media.

From the mid-1970s on, in these places of work one found sets of paired opponents, one member pitted against the other, as negotiating partners with increasingly comparable leverage: workers/managers; farmers/local bureaucrats; enterprise managers/the supervisory ministries; corporatist entities/the state; artists, writers, scholars/cultural watchdogs, editors and censors; and citizens/tax collectors.[32] The ostensible subjects of negotiations were wages, vegetable prices, modified plan targets, state subsidies, artistic and intellectual autonomy, freedom of information, and fair taxation. However, the hidden agenda was political power. The real stakes were the recovery of personal, local, regional, and quasi-corporatist autonomy, the restoration of civil society, and the emancipation of Hungary from foreign rule.[33]

The regime's record of initial success until the early 1970s, its subsequent underperformance, and the corrosive effects of citizen and elite assertiveness on the political incumbents' sense of self-confidence were causally linked with the collapse of the once-monolithic Hungarian party state in 1989. The time was April–May, and the issue was the government's right to act as it saw fit – even against the publicly stated wishes of the party's leader. At that point, the principal negotiators were prime minister Miklós Németh's "government of reform communist experts" and secretary general Károly Grósz's "lame-duck" but nominally still ruling party.[34] The government won the showdown, but the price, as an inevitable consequence, was the commencement, in June, of the old regime's negotiated liquidation by the incoming and outgoing elites of Hungary.

The Hungarian National Roundtable (NRT) discussions of June–September 1989 represented a historic opportunity for a negotiated settlement of the people's demands for freedom, human rights, and civil society and the incumbent elites' asking price of guarantees for a sheltered exit from the political arena. With respect to the crucially important details of its political agenda, the NRT was the scene of negotiations between two teams of lawyers. The first was the Independent Lawyers' Forum (ILF), which contributed members and advisers to the eight-party Opposition Roundtable (ORT). The other consisted of legal experts from the Ministry of Justice who worked for the HSWP delegation, as well as of the politically less consequential "third side" of trade unions and other political interest groups.

The critical difference between these and all previous negotiations over the country's political destiny was that, for the first time in Hungarian history, these took place solely among the native elites rather than between them and the representatives of a foreign power.[35] The outcome was a peaceful transition and the affirmation of time-tested national traditions of nonviolent conflict resolution between political adversaries.

(C)   Revolution or evolutionary change?

Proposition: What happened in Hungary between October 23 and November 4, 1956, was a revolution. It was not a shouting match between the natives and the invaders, or an organized but nonviolent outburst of popular anger, or a combination of the two that took place in Czechoslovakia and Poland in 1968 and 1981, respectively. Therefore, the Hungarian October must be seen for what it was: a spontaneous national uprising that rapidly escalated into a revolutionary yet highly self-conscious armed collective action on behalf of a people's yearning for freedom and national independence – waged regardless of the cost and the extent of human sacrifice of taking on 2,000 tanks and 150,000 Red Army soldiers in Budapest and the provincial towns.

Argument: The Kádár regime was born from the ashes of a defeated popular revolution. The insurgents were armed workers, working-class teenagers, patriotic soldiers and officers, and unarmed students and intellectuals. It was these people, perhaps not more than 35,000 nationwide, who stood up to the old regime's "Revolutionary Battalions" and its armed *Lumpenproletariat*, the *pufajkások*, and also fought their protectors in Soviet uniforms. The human toll of the Hungarian people's armed struggle with their oppressors was – on the Hungarian side – 2,502 dead, and 19,226 wounded and hospitalized. On the Soviet side there were 669 dead, 1,450 wounded, and 51 who "disappeared without a trace." Of the number of Hungarians who died during the revolution, the Kádár regime declared that 242 of its own had been killed in action or lynched by the insurgents.[36] In the aftermath, 211,000 people fled to the West (of whom about 45,000 eventually returned).

Between November 4, 1956 and July 31, 1957, approximately 28,000 people were arrested and tried in the Hungarian courts for "counter-revolutionary crimes." Of these, 6,321 were found guilty. Eight hundred were sentenced to death and at least 600 were executed between late 1956 and August 1961. These numbers do not include those who fell victim to summary executions by the regime's para-military vigilante squads and to the unrecorded settling of scores by the secret police, and those who lost their lives while trying to cross the border in the winter of 1956–7. The rest of those detained were either sent to internment camps (including 1,074 people shipped in cattle cars, for a short period of time, to Ukraine) or received terms ranging from a few months to life imprisonment.[37]

At the time of its outbreak, the Hungarian revolution was a unique event in the history of twentieth-century European revolutions. Unlike the Bolshevik-led Petrograd uprising of October 1917, which was destined to degenerate into a tyranny of the Communist Party apparat, the Hungarian "little October" embraced an agenda of national emancipation, human rights, workers' self-management, and multi-party democracy. Thirteen days of freedom were insufficient for the Imre Nagy-led government, the reborn political parties, and the nascent economic and political interest groups to build a record from which one might infer the future shape of Hungary's postrevolutionary politics. However, it is incontestable that it was the ideas of modern nationalism, transnational citizenship, democratic socialism, and liberal democracy that formed the philosophical foundations of the Hungarian October.

The precedent of the Hungarian revolution was rightly seen by Moscow and its East European allies as a viable and therefore in terms of its emancipatory message menacing alternative political model that posed an unacceptable threat to the stability of the regional political status quo. In other words, while the memory of the Hungarian events soon receded, as a kind of troublesome episode in East–West relations, into the background of global concerns of the 1950s and the 1960s, for the Soviets and their Hungarian surrogates the events of 1956 became a traumatic lesson in political steering and system management.

It is axiomatic that whoever was appointed by Moscow to rule Hungary after the bloody suppression of the revolution, he and his counterrevolutionary regime would be bereft of even the kind of ersatz "legitimacy through longevity" that the despots of the neigh-borhood – Josip Broz Tito, Antonin Novotný (and later Gustáv Husák), Gheorge Gheorghiu-Dej (and later Nicolae Ceauşescu), and

Todor Zhivkov – enjoyed in the next three decades. From Moscow's viewpoint, Hungary – albeit not a part of the Warsaw Treaty Organization's (WTO) strategically critically important "northern tier" force structure – was important enough to merit particular attention and warrant special handling. New evidence unearthed from the archives of the former Communist Party of the Soviet Union (CPSU) indicates that Moscow was sufficiently impressed by what the then Soviet ambassador Yuri Andropov and, at various times, special emissaries Anastas Mikoyan, Mikhail Suslov, Georgi Malenkov, KGB chief Ivan Serov, and at the end Nikita Khrushchev reported to the Soviet Politburo to make special provisions for the political management of Hungary.[38]

Moscow's eventual solution to the Hungarian problem may be summarized as the systematic deployment of a combination of conflict-prevention policy tools. These may, in a summary fashion and in the sequence of utilization, be called "political shock therapy," "military presence," "agents-in- place," "longer leash by way of enhanced local autonomy," and "economic dependency." Of these, the deployment of locally available coercive resources and capabilities is of special interest for a realistic appreciation of the role that nonviolent policy tools, particularly ideological manipulation, persuasion, incentives, and informal negotiation, came to play in keeping the Kádár regime afloat.

The ruthless elimination of the remnants of the revolution in the winter of 1956–7, the subsequent roundup and imprisonment of tens of thousands of people and the judicial murder of Imre Nagy and his comrades were not merely panicky reactions of this insecure regime. Rather, these measures must be seen as premeditated acts of state terrorism against the Hungarian people under the joint leadership of János Kádár, Ferenc Münnich (a veteran Hungarian communist and a senior official of the Soviet military intelligence), Géza Révész (another Soviet-trained military commander), and a team of holdover apparatchiki, such as György Marosán, Béla Biszku, Lajos Czinege, and others from the Rákosi regime.[39]

With the gradual receding of overt terror, such measures were gradually replaced by a host of standby coercive institutions such as the Workers' Guard, paramilitary volunteer groups, and networks of police informers. The embedding of Soviet and Hungarian internal security agents-in-place throughout the party, the government, the military, the police, the media, and the full range of "transmission-belt" agencies such as the Trade Union Federation (TUF), the Young

Communist League (YCL), the Patriotic People's Front (PPF), and other mass organizations completed this process.[40]

The genius of the Kádár regime lay in its capacity for the adroit utilization of unorthodox and at times audacious strategies of political management. Common to these were the emphasis on the ruling party's national identity and the deliberate pragmatic downplaying of Marxist–Leninist ideology, the Soviet model, and everything else that could appear as a reminder of the essential continuity between the discredited Rákosi regime and its presumably chastened, and therefore reformed, successor.

Whereas demagoguery and blunt carrot-and-stick methods may have sufficed to keep the average Hungarians in line, the chronically discontented and potentially rebellious intellectuals required more sophisticated techniques of political manipulation. With the selectively designated intellectual culprits sent to the gallows or safely ware-housed in jails, the regime mounted a complex three-decades-long campaign to reward, neutralize, or, if need be, punish the artists, writers, and humanistic intellectuals. Though the results fell short of the intention, the fact remains that the vast majority of yesterday's rebels eventually came to terms with the party, the censors, and the regime's ideological watchdogs.

Kádár kept an eye on the "men on the street," and his ideological-cultural deputy György Aczél orchestrated, quite brilliantly, the score, the players, and the instruments of the cultural scene. The policies of the "three t's" (*tiltás* [ban], *tűrés* [toleration], *támogatás* [support]) paid the expected dividends. Though dissonant tunes and defiant voices could never be eliminated, the policies worked well enough, that is, until the late 1970s. And even then, it was mainly groups of disenchanted post-Marxist philosophers, economists, sociologists, the journalists, rather than the self-appointed keepers of the nation's conscience, the writers and the poets, who were the first to raise their voices for radical change.

However, behind the façade of mass propaganda and cultural manipulation lay a well-entrenched and instantly available systemic capability for the prevention of the Kádár regime's ultimate nightmare, that is, the recurrence of the 1956 revolution. A confrontation of this magnitude was never a realistic possibility at any time during the next thirty-three years. Still, the very existence of this apocalyptic precedent offers an important clue to the nature of the regime's approach to its balancing act between coercion and appeasement throughout its tortured path between Hungary's two revolutions.

(D)   János Kádár: personality and political leadership

Proposition: Between 1956 and 1988 the name of János Kádár became synonymous with the political regime that ruled Hungary. Therefore, explanations seeking to account for the reasons for the regime's slow-motion decline and eventual collapse must be informed by what one might call the "Kádár factor" in Hungarian politics.[41]

Argument: The facts of the case are fairly straightforward and may be summarized as follows:

From 1929 on, when he first joined the outlawed communist movement, János Csermanek – "Kádár" was an underground name that he assumed in 1945 – was a rank-and-file activist who, upon the arrest of scores of higher-ranking cadres above him, in 1943 became a secretary of the party's Central Committee. Although he too had served two prison terms for his party work, the most memorable activity associated with him was, inspired by vaguely understood Comintern directives but at his initiative, the decision to disband the party and subsequently reconstitute it under a different name.

Kádár was one of the few hundred "native" party militants who survived the war. In 1945 he was co-opted by the party's Muscovite leadership (Mátyás Rákosi, Ernő Gerő, József Révai, Mihály Farkas, and Imre Nagy) into Politburo membership. Over the next six years Kádár, as a faithful Rákosi loyalist, served in several top leadership capacities. Probably the best remembered of these was that of emissary from Rákosi to persuade the imprisoned top native communist László Rajk to confess falsely to being a Titoist renegade, a Western spy, and a traitor to the party. Rajk was executed on October 15, 1949.

Kádár's turn to be arrested came in April 1951. He too was coerced to confess to treasonable activities in the prewar communist movement, and on December 26, 1952, was sentenced to life imprisonment. He was released on July 22, 1954, and promptly "rehabilitated" as an innocent victim of Stalinist excess.[42] Shortly thereafter (October 9, 1954), at Rákosi's behest, he assumed the position of secretary of the Budapest 13th district party committee. A year later (September 6, 1955) he was promoted to first secretary of the Pest county party committee with the right to attend, as a nonmember, the meetings of the party's Central Committee.

In terms of his political career, Kádár was probably the main Hungarian beneficiary of Nikita S. Khrushchev's secret speech on Stalin's cult of personality at the 20th congress of the CPSU in February 1956. As one of the surviving party-elite victims of Stalinist repression in Hungary, he demanded (but only within party circles) that his case and that of Rajk's be reviewed and the culpability of those responsible established. The showdown between Kádár and Rákosi came at the July 18–21, 1956, meeting of the CC, Hungarian Workers' Party (HWP), where the forced resignation of Rákosi was brought about with the assistance of CPSU special emissary Anastas Mikoyan. Kádár was not only readmitted to the CC but was elected as a CC secretary and Politburo member as well. Although he was bested by Mikoyan's nominee Ernő Gerő as Rákosi's successor, Kádár's candidacy for the position of first secretary was supported by a remarkable 10 percent of the traditionally docile CC membership.[43]

On October 25, 1956, two days after the outbreak of the revolution, Gerő was dismissed and Kádár elected as the new first secretary of the by then virtually extinct HWP. Five days later he and his anti-Rákosi colleagues on the party's Presidium dissolved the HWP and founded its successor, the Hungarian Socialist Workers' Party (HSWP). Kádár initially supported Imre Nagy and his critical stance on the Soviets' armed interference with the revolution. He was also in favor of the reestablishment of a multiparty system in Hungary. However, on November 1 Kádár and Münnich left for a meeting to "confer with Soviet Ambassador Yuri Andropov" and vanished from Hungary.

The full details of Kádár's clandestine trip to Moscow on a Soviet military plane, and of the specifics of his negotiations with the Soviet party leaders during his short stay there in early November 1956, are only now beginning to emerge from Soviet army and party archives. According to the recollections of his Soviet military escort, Kádár boarded a Soviet military plane and arrived in Moscow on November 2. The following day Kádár, Ferenc Münnich, and minister of defense István Bata met with members of the CPSU Politburo to discuss the particulars of a political declaration that Kádár was to broadcast upon his return to, and the Soviet Army reoccupation of, Hungary. The text had been drafted by Rákosi and Gerő. According to his Soviet interpreter, Kádár rejected the original version and demanded inclusion of a passage that fixed the blame on Rákosi, Gerő, and Farkas for the outbreak of the October uprising in Hungary. In the end, the Soviet leadership conceded the point. Thereupon Kádár, as the newly designated head of the "Worker-Peasant Revolutionary Government," and that of the HSWP, returned to Hungary.[44]

This thumbnail sketch of Kádár's early career will be expanded at several points throughout the narrative. The purpose of this biographical outline is to offer a general background against which his subsequent record as Hungary's principal political leader, authoritative international spokesman, dominant ideologue and ultimate economic decision-maker may be assessed by the readers.

János Kádár's various leadership roles were inextricably interwoven with the kinds of political, security, economic, and ideological challenges that he was compelled to confront and sought to overcome between 1956 and 1988. A preliminary, and of necessity tentative assessment of Kádár's personality and politics might proceed from the proposition that the man and the public roles he came to play may be divided into two parts. To the first belong personality traits that can be inferred from his family background, childhood, and adolescent socialization and political preferences that can be attributed to workplace experiences and exposure to prewar left-wing – social democratic and communist – politics. To the second, one might assign those characteristics that can be inferred from his conduct as a senior official (1945–51, 1954–6), then leader (1956–88) of a ruling communist party.

Born in 1912 to an unmarried, young, peasant cleaning-woman in Fiume (now Rijeka, Croatia), Kádár endured a childhood of deprivation, hard work, and loneliness. He was brought up by foster parents, a Calvinist farming family in a small village in southwestern Hungary. Subsequently, he moved to his mother in Budapest, where he completed eight grades before learning the trade of typewriter repair. Unemployed on and off during the Great Depression (his last full-time job was that of a delivery man at a Budapest umbrella factory), the well-spoken young man was discovered by one of the underground Communist Party's "talent spotters." Before he knew what he was about, Kádár was picked up by the police and, just like everyone else in the underground party under similar circumstances, told the authorities all he knew.[45]

Because he persisted as a Young Communist League activist, Kádár was arrested again and sentenced to a prison term of two years, which he served in the premier *Csillag* jail for political detainees. This is where he met Mátyás Rákosi and many of the people with whom he was to work after the war. From these and other wartime experiences of underground work, another jail term, and in the fall of 1944 a harrowing escape *en route* to a German death camp, Kádár emerged as a prize candidate for a leadership position in Rákosi's party in 1945.

His contemporaries describe the young Kádár as a low-key introvert, a moderate drinker, a chess player of some promise, and an avid physical fitness enthusiast with a flair for making a lasting impression on his female comrades in the communist youth movement.[46] By his own admission, his Marxist theoretical education consisted of reading – it took him a year – Engels' *Anti-Dühring*, which, much to his credit, he never claimed to have understood. The wartime activist Kádár is remembered as a reserved, secretive, and self-effacing person who, unlike many of his contemporaries, had no intellectual and ideological pretensions of any kind. Again, unlike many of the querulous militants of the faction-ridden Hungarian underground party, this modest man was well liked by his comrades, who saw him as an individual of honesty and personal integrity.

Kádár's years in power as a junior adjunct member of the Muscovite "foursome" (Mátyás Rákosi, Ernő Gerő, József Révai, Mihály Farkas) and the "odd man in and out" Imre Nagy obviously left a lasting imprint on his thinking and behavior. Though a part of the party hierarchy, Kádár was never the initiator or the maker of strategic decisions. Given his total loyalty to Rákosi and the Soviet strategic priorities that the Hungarian Stalinists spoke for, it is inconceivable that Kádár, though nominally their equal as a Politburo member, ever contradicted, let alone opposed, Rákosi's policies. In fact, he willingly performed the ultimate act of self-abasement, when agreeing to betray his friend László Rajk by urging him, in an uncharacteristically thuggish manner, to incriminate himself as an enemy agent.[47] Kádár's deferential petitions from prison to the party's general secretary went unanswered. His loss of political innocence – if he still had any illusions left after his own incarceration and possible physical mistreatment – was completed when he confronted, and in the end bowed to, the unrepentant Rákosi in the summer of 1954.

Kádár's decision to return as a mid-level official to Rákosi's apparat rather than, say, taking a managerial appointment in industry, hints at motivations that a complex pathology of "party discipline, sense of duty," and a kind of "Stockholm syndrome" of continued ideological attachment to one's captors might help explain. Another explanation might take its departure from looking at Kádár as a "born follower" with a deep-seated need to look up to and obey authority figures such as Rákosi and Khrushchev. As a person with little formal education but that of on-the-job experience as a party official, Kádár seemed singularly vulnerable to being guided by ideological abstractions such as "the party," "the Soviet Union, the birthplace of socialism," "the working class," and "proletarian internationalism."

A third type of motivation might have been the compulsion in Kádár to remain in the party apparat "to serve and excel" as an honest and unselfish wielder of power and influence. An ancillary hypothesis to the notion of "excellence" is the proposition that in the given context, that is, in a ruling communist party in which Kádár sought to excel, personal ruthlessness in the elimination of one's competitors was a Leninist, therefore necessary and ethically correct, way of serving the working class. Kádár's role in the judicial murder of his party's two prominent leaders, László Rajk in 1949 and Imre Nagy in 1958, seems to support the latter proposition. The former was a friend and a possible rival, the latter was a senior colleague who became a political adversary. The party that Kádár served sent both to the gallows.[48]

In the foregoing discussion I sought to alert the reader to the range of possible interpretations of Kádár's motivations as a high-ranking official (and victim) of the Stalinist Rákosi regime in Hungary. As I see it, Kádár's personal background and political record were attributes and dispositions – particularly manifested in both the ethical choices he made under stressful circumstances, and his apparent need for authority figures and ideological maxims to guide and justify his actions – that made him eminently eligible to play the role into which his Soviet masters cast him in 1956–7. On the other hand, "dispositions," however well embedded in the mind of a 45-year-old Hungarian communist official, did not necessarily determine the direction and the policy substance of Kádár's own path as the country's paramount leader over the next thirty-two years.

The "second" type of Kádár – the eligible, and then the subsequently chosen leader – was born in July–October 1956. His political comeback was, somewhat paradoxically, accelerated by the political rehabilitation and ceremonial reburial of László Rajk in early October and, more logically, by the party's collapse and the dismissal of Ernő Gerő, the last Muscovite political boss of the old regime. Rajk's martyrdom tended to benefit "fellow-victim" Kádár – but only up to a point. A voice recording and the transcript of a prison conversation featuring Kádár in the act of attempting to talk Rajk into falsely confessing to betraying his party were evidence that any political rival might have used to impugn Kádár's credentials as an anti-Stalinist.

Upon Kádár's return on November 4, 1956 to Hungary from his meeting with the Soviet Politburo, it became apparent that Imre Nagy, the revolution's leader, unless somehow neutralized, could become such a political rival. On November 11, at the first meeting of the Provisional Executive Committee of the HSWP, Kádár stated: "I am personally convinced that Imre Nagy, Géza Losonczy and the other comrades who were members of the government did not wish to aid the counterrevolution."[49] However, in less than two weeks Kádár actively plotted with his Soviet mentors to entice, with promises of safe conduct, Imre Nagy and his associates to give up their asylum at the Yugoslav Embassy and walk into the waiting arms of the Soviet security organs for shipment to Romania.[50]

To compound Kádár's difficulties, neither during his Romanian exile nor in Hungarian prison did Nagy agree to submit his resignation as prime minister of the last legitimate government of Hungary. In this sense, Kádár was – and remained in the public eye – a usurper of Nagy's lawful position as Hungary's leader. In sum, the coincidence of Moscow's strategic interests in maintaining communist rule in Hungary and Kádár's need to cover up his betrayal of his "native" comrades set the stage for, and helped define the limits of, János Kádár's political destiny.

Kádár's years in power may be analyzed by viewing his conduct through a prism of constantly evolving and chronologically overlapping leadership roles he played between late 1956 and May 1988. In my view, the essential attributes of Kádár's changing public persona might be described in the following terms:

"Reluctant hostage" (1956–63). The term denotes Kádár's utter dependency on Khrushchev's support and on that of the Stalinist cadres he inherited from the Rákosi regime to consolidate communist power in Hungary. However, it also hints at his desperate attempts to become, partly on Soviet and partly on his own terms, master of his political fiefdom. The execution of Imre Nagy and the continued stationing of Soviet troops on Hungarian soil was the price Kádár had to pay to keep Rákosi in Soviet exile and himself in power as the titular ruler of Hungary.

"Risk-taking reformer" (1963–71). Here the emphasis shifts from the coercive consolidation of the political regime to the courageous implementation of an unorthodox strategy of relegitimation through depoliticization, consumerism, and economic reforms. The launching and assumption of political responsibility for – in face of Soviet misgivings – the Hungarian New Economic Mechanism (NEM), and, after the crushing of the Czechoslovak reform movement of 1968, the stonewalling, to a degree, of growing Soviet, East German, Czechoslovak, Polish, and Romanian opposition to reform experiments in Hungary were Kádár's finest achievements as a *Hungarian* politician.

"Good king" (1972–80). The political payoff of consumerism and the regime's sensibly low-key steering of public affairs, as well as representing the manifest political payoff of consumerism, was the wide-

spread public acceptance of, and growing respect for, Kádár as a benevolent *national* leader. Modest prosperity, declining coercion, and Kádár's self-effacing anti-"cult-of-personality" style of leadership also marked the beginning of his gradual withdrawal, as hands-on manager, from the political scene.

"Enfeebled autarch" (1981–8). Kádár's declining health, the growing burden of policy-making responsibilities, and the diminishing range of ideologically correct economic and political choices available to him helped undermine public confidence in his leadership. Kádár and his similarly aged Politburo colleagues' refusal to make provisions either for drastic policy correction or for leadership succession yielded a political stalemate of epic proportions. Kádár's exit from politics in 1988 came six to eight years too late to prevent the paralysis and subsequent collapse of the regime he created from the ashes of the Hungarian revolution.

The above discussion on János Kádár's personality, leadership style, and political legacy sought to offer a set of propositions with which to distance my views on this remarkable communist politician from those of certain Western analysts and Hungarian apologists alike. Western explanations seeking to account for Hungary's gradual transformation into a semiautonomous and quasi-sovereign Central European state in the 1980s tended to credit János Kádár and his leaderhip skills for these positive results. The unchallenged proliferation of journalistic clichés such as "the Kádár mystique" as tentative explanations for what Hungary had accomplished in the preceding twenty-five years counsels caution and requires the careful reexamination of the evidence. Shorthand explanations of this kind are akin to the now *passé* academic "Gorbymania" to which some Western Sovietologists succumbed in lieu of performing a rigorous autopsy on the less accessible innards within the political cadaver of the former USSR.

The old regime fell, but Kádár's legacy is still a significant factor with demonstrated political salience in Hungary today. This is to suggest that until and unless the full documentary evidence on Kádár's stewardship in key policy areas of the preceding three decades is open to scrutiny – and possibly not even then – his ideological heirs in and out of Hungary's freely elected Parliament will be, as they have been, tempted to promote their own interpretation of the record. The object is to profit from nostalgic yearnings for the "good king's" legacy of "little freedoms," egalitarian wage policies, and guaranteed employment for all Hungarian citizens.[51] For these reasons, János Kádár's role will be a recurring theme throughout this study. The man and the system he wrought might be inseparable, but the task at hand is to assess the contribution of each to the outcomes of 1989–90.

(E)   The HSWP: constraints and leadership styles

Proposition: With János Kádár at the helm until May 1988, the HSWP was the ultimate source of political authority in Hungary. The party's power, however, was limited by various constraints, thereby compelling its leaders to adopt different styles of political steering to overcome the challenges of systemic change. The main argument of this study is that the root causes of the regime's political collapse in 1989 were structural and situational.[52] In both cases we are addressing the issue of external and internal constraints on a Marxist–Leninist regime's political will and organizational capability to manage systemic change. As a related proposition, and as a partial explanatory device, I shall offer an informal typology of styles of organizational leadership that the Hungarian ruling party adopted during its relatively short existence between 1945 and 1989.

Argument: My case addressing the issue of policy constraints and the Hungarian party's adaptative responses thereto is presented in two parts. In the first, I shall briefly describe the the nature of obstacles that helped attenuate the party's overall performance. In the second, I shall outline the specifics of the changing styles of organizational leadership that the HSWP adopted over time.

Structural and situational constraints

By "structural" constraints I understand the political, economic, ideological, and social impediments that prevented the leaders of the East European communist regimes from making effective use of the available resources of the state to preserve political stability. Structural constraints were of two kinds. The first can be derived from Hungary's membership in the Soviet alliance system. These consisted mainly of expectations, ideological guidance, and explicit instructions that were communicated to Hungary through state-to-state, party-to-party, and first secretary-to-first secretary formal and informal channels. The "message," be it the CPSU's "general line" handed down at party congresses, the Soviet first secretary's key policy statements, "recommendations" for military budgetary outlays from the WTO High Command, or "comradely advice" conveyed over secure KGB-monitored telephone lines to Kádár or to his deputy, must be seen for what it was: a decisive constraint on the Hungarian regime's ability to act as its leaders saw fit.

The second kind of structural constraint may be inferred from the flawed, to use Martin Malia's apt phrase, "genetic code" of a ruling communist party state.[53] The party-state's commitment to the voluntaristic legacy of Marxism–Leninism, to the application of Soviet policy precedents, and to the top cadres' patently inadequate managerial competence were additional factors that prevented the Hungarian regime from making optimal use of the political, economic, and human resources under its nominal control.

The political consequences of the extrinsic and intrinsic constraints on the regime's managerial performance were twofold. In the international realm, these entailed (a) the subordination of Hungary's national interests to those of the USSR and Moscow's security needs in Europe; (b) the making of strategic decisions on economic development, particularly industrial policies, and foreign trade hostage to the requisites of Soviet policy priorities for its domestic economic development and regional economic integration; and (c) the accumulation of economic and political opportunity costs of timely adaptation to the new political-economic realities of postwar Europe. These included Hungary's inability to benefit, as Yugoslavia did from the 1960s on, from vigorous interaction with processes of European economic integration, from a better utilization of regional trading links with neighboring states and from periodic diplomatic opportunities to come to terms with Romania, Yugoslavia, and Czechoslovakia about the status of their Hungarian ethnic minorities.

In the domestic realm, the constraints, particularly the "genetic" kind, were manifest by (a) the handing down of Delphic Politiburo decrees in lieu of clearly articulated action programs; (b) the making of budgetary decisions by ideological criteria; and (c) the perception of society and social change in abstract terms of class struggle and the habit of justifying voluntaristic policy goals by obscure agitprop slogans. All these were symptoms of the underlying malaise that beset the East European states of "existing socialism" from the early 1970s on.[54]

At a certain point, which economists call the exhaustion of the growth potentials of the "extensive mode of economic development," another process begins. It is marked by the accumulation of adverse results due to chronic economic underperformance, bureaucratic inertia, and hastily improvised measures, such as reckless borrowing from Western lending institutions to keep stagnant living standards and the regimes' shrinking legitimacy afloat.

By "situational" constraints I understand circumstances that might be seen, to whatever extent, as unique to Hungary during the Kádár era. These include the complex legacy of the 1956 revolution, Hungary's increasingly anomalous position in the Soviet bloc, and the leader's personality, ideological preferences, and management style. The regime's early commitment to economic reforms and its methods of crisis prevention and conflict management are also parts of the picture – as were the top cadres' political culture and the "fit," however tenuous, between the regime's developmental objectives and the indigenous intellectual elites' ideologies of modernization and social change.

The confluence, in the early 1980s, of the Hungarian regime's structural and situational problems yielded policy paralysis and a significantly reduced range of options to effect changes needed to facilitate a smooth transition from a totalitarian to a posttotalitarian (consensual, elite-cooptative, and noncoercive) style of political management.

The main phases and the essential components of the entire process that took place in a given party state may be reconstructed from a critical review of the political leadership's strategic decisions, an evaluation of the party's organizational structure, and an assessment of the regime's policy responses to challenges of adaptation to changes in the domestic and international environment. These matters will be discussed in the next chapter.

Three styles of political leadership

The communist party, as Lenin never ceased to assert, was a party of the "new type." It was an "organizational weapon" in the hands of professional revolutionaries to overthrow the old regime, to institute the dictatorship of the proletariat, and to embark on the enterprise of building socialism in one, then in several, and, at the end, perhaps in all countries of the world. The centrality of the communist party to processes of political transformation, economic development, and the reshaping of the society according to preconceived formulae is axiomatic. And so is the way the party seeks to implement its ideological agenda over time.[55]

Leadership is a critically important element for the management of an organization and the attainment of its strategic objectives. Different types of organizations have different kinds of indicators with which to measure their performance. A business firm measures its success by profits, growth, and market share; a public bureaucracy, by the scope of its jurisdiction, the growth in personnel and the size of budgetary allocations it obtains; a ruling communist party by the fulfillment of plan targets, positive feedback from the population, and the stability of institutions and personnel under its direct control.

To succeed in any of these environments, a leader must overcome bureaucratic inertia, external competitors, and other kinds of resistance to the organization's values and strategic goals. There are many ways to lead, but only few yield the desired results. The *virtú* of leadership and the *fortuna* of policy exigencies are at work here. Therefore, at issue is the style and substance of leadership and the manner in which a leader and the organization make use of their resources and adapt to changes in the external environment.[56]

These propositions might be better explicated by the introduction of a related theme of inquiry concerning the evolving manner – "vanguard," "system management," and "rearguard" – in which a ruling communist party seeks to exercise its leadership over time.[57]

Whether it came to power in the wake of an "authentic" or a "derivative" revolution (the Russian Bosheviks on the one hand, and the Hungarian party and its Central European neighbors, except Yugoslavia, on the other, offer examples of each),[58] a Marxist–Leninist party begins its reign in the "vanguard" mode of dominance under the leadership of professional revolutionaries. The historic project of overcoming political adversaries and assuming direct control over, in Lenin's words, the "commanding heights of power," took three tries for the Hungarian communists. The first lasted 133 days before it was quashed in 1919; the second began in 1948, came to a halt with the launching, soon after Stalin's death, of the "New Course" in 1953, and finally collapsed in October 1956. The third was initiated by János Kádár in late 1956 and was more or less completed in 1962–3.

In the "vanguard mode" the party's principal tasks are the consolidation of political power, the drastic realignment of property relations, the mobilization of the society, and the systematic deployment of the coercive resources of the state to obtain public compliance with the leadership's policy objectives. The regime's use of force contributes to the "primitive accumulation of legitimacy." As Alfred Meyer explains, "It is a desperate attempt to transform power into authority as quickly as possible ... against great obstacles."[59] This is augmented by vigorous campaigns of political reeducation and the promotion of the leader's cult of personality. As a rule, the "vanguard" style of leadership is prone to strategic miscalculations and false starts. What is at issue here is how the leaders might proceed after a Soviet New Economic Policy, a Hungarian New Course, a Chinese "Hundred Flowers Campaign," or a debacle of the magnitude of the Hungarian October.

The doctrinal justification of Kádár's "third try" was in the December 5, 1956, decision of the Provisional Central Committee (CC herafter) of the HSWP.[60] In it the leadership held the disastrous policies of the "Rákosi–Gerő clique," the "seditious conduct of the Nagy–Losonczy group," "agents of the [prewar] Horthy regime," and the forces of "international imperialism" responsible for the "counter-revolution." Apart from the propaganda rhetoric about domestic subversives and enemy agents, what mattered was that the party went on record distancing itself from the excesses of its Stalinist predecessor.

Pursuant to this objective, and also in hopes of erecting a fragile ideological shelter to ward off Soviet attempts to meddle in Hungarian affairs, for the next fifteen years the HSWP took great pains to endorse the "spirit of the 20th CPSU congress." In retrospect, the notion might seem naïve, but in Kádár's mind the 20th CPSU congress was perceived as a ruling communist party's saying "nay" and "never again" to Stalinism and the affirmation of the *political* and the rejection of administrative-coercive measures as ways to address and resolve domestic and international conflicts.[61] In doing so, Kádár laid the groundwork for the subsequent introduction of a different kind of political leadership in Hungary.

The "system-management" mode of political leadership in Hungary was inaugurated in the early 1960s. Transition from the previous phase was effected in three successive steps. First came the restoration of political power, the partial reorganization of the party, and the rebuilding of the shattered institutions of public administration, particularly the police and the judiciary. The second step was the resuscitation of the "transmission-belt" mass organizations (the Trade Union Federation, the Young Communist League, and so on), the coercive recollectivization of agriculture, and the purging of left-wing extremists from public life. And finally, with the courageous spokesmen of the revolution safely behind bars, came the silencing, then the selective co-optation, of writers, journalists, and academic intellectuals who agreed to serve the new regime with their pens and professional skills. With these accomplished, the party embarked on the system-management phase that lasted until the late 1970s.

The party's role as "system manager" takes its departure from an established set of institutions, routinized procedures of policy-making and policy implementation, and personnel stability – at least at the level of senior and mid-level *nomenklatura* officials.[62] In the economic sphere, the central planning bureaucracy, the economic regulatory mechanisms, and the hierarchy of production units are all in place. The society, though still perceived in terms of class and social origin, is on the mend and begins coalescing along lines of position, status, formal education, place of residence, and the like. Mass coercion is beginning to subside and is replaced by more sophisticated methods of political behavior modification with emphasis on incentives and disincentives of the economic rather than the administrative-repressive kind.

The essential hallmark of the system-management mode of leadership is the process of functional differentiation between the party and the state. In a systemic context, this process first surfaced in the Soviet Union in the 1950s as the beginning of what may be called "postmobilization etatism."[63] For reasons of organizational self-preservation, as much as a gesture to the requisites of rational political steering, the party's direct management functions are gradually handed over to the state, which becomes the principal executor of the party's political will. Although the party, at least in the Hungarian case, still retains hands-on control over foreign, security, cultural and ideological affairs, it is the state and its specialized administrative agencies that, as they did from the mid-1970s on, assume the role of visible and high-profile managers of the economy and the social-welfare aspects of public policy. The party's political control of the state is preserved by the *nomenklatura* system, as well as by overlapping memberships of key cadres at corresponding administrative levels of party and state bodies.

One of the important consequences of the system-management mode of leadership is the large-scale recruitment of specialist elites, lower-level "production leaders," and, to buttress the leaders' ouvrierist pretensions, masses of blue-collar workers to party membership. At this point the party ceases to be a tight-knit community of militant cadres (which it may have been in early 1957 but certainly was not after 1970), begins to lose its vanguard character, and becomes a catch-all mass organization. As a result, the intensity of the average party member's identification with the party's ideological objectives begins to subside and, in a remarkably short period of time, the rank-and-file members' views are no longer distinguishable from those of the population at large.

A similar process of devolution takes place at the state level. It is marked by the entry into the process of policy implementation, initially in a consultative and subsequently in a comanagerial capacity, of a growing number of state nomenclature notables, such as managers of large enterprises and leaders of "transmission-belt" corporatist entities. Once ensconced in the Central Committee, county party executive committees, or as members of policy advisory committees, these raiders of the once-monolithic commanding heights of economic and administrative power begin making claims on the state's decision- and rule-making prerogatives. The end result is incipient but steadily growing administrative pluralism and the subtle erosion of the party's power and ideological authority.[64]

The political viability of the system-management mode of party leadership is predicated on adequate systemic performance with respect to economic growth, positive trends in personal consumption, and the continued internalization and acceptance of the regime's founding myths and currently operative legitimating ideologies by members of the society. When, for any reason, these success indicators fail to develop in the desired direction, the regime's political legitimacy is at risk. The appropriate response to such danger signs can be either a return to a vanguard mode of mass mobilization and coercion or a tactical retreat into yet another style of leadership.

If for historic reasons (as in Hungary), relapse into the leadership style of the Rákosi years or that of the postrevolutionary period are not feasible policy options, token reforms of various kinds are introduced. When reforms fail as well to restore political stability, cadre loyalty, and ideological coherence, and to recapture decision-making power lost to nonparty actors in the state sector, the only remaining choice – short of a drastic change at the top – is a retreat into a "rearguard" mode of political leadership. Other than adapting to new political realities and thus displaying Leninist flexibility in face of adversity, the immediate objective of the change in leadership style is to free the party from the burden of public dissatisfaction with the regime's performance by shifting the responsibility for the inadequate delivery of goods, services, and living standards to the state.

The transfer of most – save a cluster – of strategic policy decisions to the state bureaucracy is justified on ideological grounds. Strenuous efforts are made to square the circle by redefining the party's role from that of omnicompetent hands-on decision-maker to that of a behind-the-scenes quasi-apolitical "hegemonic" leader and an impartial arbiter of conflicting state and public interests.[65] However, a Marxist–Leninist party does not voluntarily surrender its power, and if need be, suitable measures are taken to preserve its ultimate decision-making authority.

Rearguard leadership consists of a series of stopgap policy measures and is designed to gain time for organizational self-examination, policy reassessment, and the orderly redeployment of the party's personnel resources to nonparty entities.[66] The success of these moves depends on many factors, of which at least three are critical to the eventual outcome.

The first factor is bold, preferably charismatic, leadership to obtain prompt and supportive compliance with the multitude of corrective policy decisions handed down from above. The second is organizational adaptation for the facilitation of the party's retreat from the political scene as direct manager of public policies. The rejuvenation and professional upgrading of the party apparat and the routinization, possibly institutionalization, of consultative relationships with hitherto excluded interest groups and policy lobbies – thereby enriching the political decision-making process – are key elements of this new leadership strategy. The third factor is the process whereby the party center embarks on a new path of offering political partnership to those at the bottom of the *nomenklatura*, the rank-and-file party activists, and the nonparty experts and intellectuals.

Throughout, the hidden agenda is the establishment of the party center's privileged access to its cadres, field workers and the nonparty majority of the population. They are to be the centerpiece of the party's rearguard strategy and are to serve as a political counterweight to the state. The autonomist aspirations of the latter – realized mainly through the budgetary redistribution process – pose a threat to the party as the sole originator of strategic decisions on matters outside its managerial competence. The outcome of the hidden tug-of-war between the party and the state is decided, ironically enough, by the people themselves. Their daily existence, job security, and ultimately escape from the past all hinge on the only remaining credible source of power: the state itself.

In the end, the party becomes a helpless captive of a system of its own creation. The party center's relentless backward march to retain its hold on, if nothing else, its proprietary levers of power, that is, cadre affairs and domestic and foreign security policies, begins to yield diminishing returns. Expertise now outweighs party membership. The military – never comfortable under party domination – shifts its loyalty to the state, and foreign policies are now more likely to be driven by export–import balance sheets than by the ideological imperatives of socialist internationalism.

Leadership in a regional context

National scenarios of changes in leadership styles varied widely in Soviet-dominated Eastern Europe.[67] These ranged from those of the time-warped Albanian party and the septuagenarian knights of the Berlin Wall to the feeble posturing and rapid collapse of the Husák–Jakes regime in Prague and the virtually soundless implosion of Kádár's HSWP. For rather different reasons, the Polish party also became a victim of the "etatist" thrust of General Jaruzelski's martial law regime – yet it too expired in early 1990. Another scenario and the same outcome obtained in Romania, where the enraged masses and the patently disloyal army both deposed and exterminated the Ceau-şescus, though leaving the old regime – save a few designated scapegoats – largely intact. In any case, the Hungarian party, for reasons that will be explained below, had been over the preceding thirty years out of sync with the rest of the fraternal parties of the region. Still, at the end, all ruling communist parties, including the Hungarian, had to go.

In sum, the factors that contributed to the downfall of the old regime in Hungary were both structural and situational. Changing leadership styles were as much causes as effects of this process. However, in attempting to explain the Hungarian case, one must be aware of at least three potential analytical pitfalls that, unless controlled for, could lead to misleading conclusions. These are (a) the drawing of unwarranted inferences from, and attributing systemic salience to, the policy record of one ruling communist party; (b) the eulogization of János Kádár as a benevolent leader and a helpless victim of tragic circumstances rather than seeing him for what he was: a shrewd politician, a wily manipulator of people and ideas, and a tenacious survivor; and (c) the succumbing to the temptation, in the words of Peter Wiles, of "capitalist triumphalism" by viewing the Hungarian, East European, and Soviet political outcomes of 1989–91 as having been made inevitable by the inherent wickedness of communism and the superiority of capitalism and liberal democracy.[68] I shall attempt to show in this study that neither proposition is necessarily true.

(F)   Hungary's transformation in an international perspective

Proposition: The principal lesson of the 1956 revolution was that Hungary's national independence and the restoration of political democracy could not be won by unilateral actions such as the declaration of neutrality or the peremptory abandonment of the Soviet-led military alliance to which, by valid treaty, Hungary belonged. External realities, specifically the regional security constraints provided for by the postwar "Yalta regime," set firm limits for domestic political experimentation in all of Eastern Europe, including Hungary.[69]

Argument: Until Mikhail Gorbachev's explicit abandonment of the Brezhnev doctrine and the subsequent dissolution of the Warsaw Treaty Organization on February 25, 1991, Hungary had been a part of a Soviet-led international system of semi-sovereign states. The continuous presence of Soviet troops on Hungarian soil since 1944 was a visible reminder of the subordination of Hungary's interests to those of the USSR. The overwhelming influence of the regional hegemon imposed limits on the extent of systemic change in Hungary. Some of the "limits" were spelled out in official statements; others were simply understood as the *modus operandi* of a Soviet-led alliance system. In any event, the unequal relationship was flexible enough to permit cosmetic changes within the existing system, including modest experimentation, from the early 1980s on, with Hungary's financial and trading links with the West. However, any policy innovation that raised the specter of change *of* the system was promptly rebuffed by Moscow.

At issue is the relationship between the unfolding Hungarian domestic developments, particularly the economic reforms since 1968, and the transformation of the country's external political, economic, and security environment. The Kádár regime, however disorientated and unpopular it became in the late 1980s, was not destined to collapse under the weight of its economic underperformance and congenital political illegitimacy. The regime's adaptive foreign policy moves, from 1977 on, to seek an enhanced role and to reinforce it in the post-*détente* world of East–West relations, helped establish an early economic and political foothold (US–Hungarian and German–Hungarian ties, Hungary's IMF membership, and so on) for the benefit of the regime and Hungarian consumers alike. On the other hand, it is axiomatic that the regime's inertia-driven staying power owed some of its apparent stability to one old and one new external factor. One was Moscow's regional hegemony, particularly Hungary's ideologically hostile regional environment that helped reinforce it. The second was the post-*détente* East–West security stalemate that created new diplomatic and economic opportunities for Hungary.[70]

The Helsinki process, the Polish example, the shortlived tenures of Yuri Andropov and Konstantin Chernenko, and Gorbachev's ascendance in the USSR, the challenge of Western European integration, the collapse of Moscow's Third World adventures, and irresistible Western – mainly American – pressures on behalf of human rights in communist-dominated states were responsible for the drastic changes in the international context in which the *ancien régime* in Hungary came to an end. Thus, it was the favorable correlation of forces in Hungary's international and regional environment that helped shape the necessary conditions for the recapture of national sovereignty and the peaceful transformation of the old political system into a parliamentary democracy.

The political system that had arisen in Hungary after the free elections of March–April 1990 and the social-liberal government that followed it four years later have been perceived as legitimate by not only the Hungarian people but the international community as well. The coincidence of domestic legitimacy and virtually unanimous positive international endorsement of the new political status quo is a "first" in modern Hungarian history. It also helps explain why the sum total of internal and external changes that have affected Hungary between 1988 and 1990 could be seen as the results of not one but possibly two "negotiated revolutions."

The first "revolution" was facilitated by the two superpowers and set the stage for the strategic withdrawal of the USSR from its militarily overextended global, and its politically increasingly untenable East European, positions.[71] Hungary and its East European neighbors were the most immediate beneficiaries of this process. The second "revolution," though aided immensely by the rapid transformation of the Polish political scene, and later by the collapse of the old regimes in Czechoslovakia, East Germany, and Romania, was managed and brought to fruition by both the outgoing and the incoming political elites of Hungary. Its political substance consists of a carefully crafted hybrid of indigenous libertarian ideas, continental European constitutional traditions, and Western, to a modest extent Anglo-Saxon, liberal democratic institutions. The combined results of the two negotiated revolutions constitute the substantive foundation for Hungary's quantum, and in my view revolutionary, leap from posttotalitarian communism to parliamentary democracy.

PART I

Systemic change: adaptation and transformation

1 From vanguard to rearguard: the rise and decline of a ruling communist party, 1957–1980

The first political victim of the Hungarian revolution was the ruling Hungarian Workers' Party (HWP). In less than a week, its membership of 859,000 (January 1956) collapsed into scattered groups of diehard Stalinists at home and discredited party leaders (Rákosi, Gerő, Révai, András Hegedüs, and a few others) whom the Soviets quickly airlifted, at the end of October, to Moscow.[1] On October 30 the HWP was formally dissolved and members of the regional party apparat were dismissed.[2] On November 1 the successor Hungarian Socialist Workers' Party was founded.[3] Its charter members were János Kádár, as first secretary, prime minister Imre Nagy, Géza Losonczy (both executed in 1958), Ferenc Donáth, Sándor Kopácsi (both sentenced to life imprisonment in 1958), György Lukács and Zoltán Szántó (both exiled to Romania, and upon their return to Hungary, expelled from the party).[4]

In the next thirty-three years, from a "party of one," the HSWP grew into a mass organization with 860,000 (1987) members, and about 10,000 part- and full-time central, regional, and local officials. During this time the party's formal decision-making bodies held 1,270 Politburo meetings, 260 Central Committee meetings, seven party congresses, and two national party conferences. Each passed resolutions, decisions, theses, and advisory opinions and issued thousands of public and secret operative directives in aid of building socialism in Hungary. Over the years the party also became the legal owner, or *de facto* possessor, of 2,400 buildings and other assets, such as bank accounts, vacation resorts, publishing houses, several journals, one national and twenty- one regional newspapers.[5]

The party's slow rise from the ruins of the revolution and the twists and turns of the regime's efforts to reassert its control over Hungary are well documented in the recently published annotated transcripts of the HSWP's Provisional Executive Committee (Politburo) and Central

Committee for November 11, 1956 to January 14, 1957.[6] These months also witnessed the transformation, in the course of leadership deliberations, of "comrades" such as Imre Nagy to "traitors," and of "honest Hungarian citizens" and "idealistic insurgents" to "fascists" and "counterrevolutionary rubble."

The initially shell-shocked and temporarily chastened members of the Provisional Politburo were at first contemplating everything from Yugoslav-style neutrality to the wholesale withdrawal of the party from daily political decision-making and the drastic downsizing of the bloated party apparat. Thanks to the reassuring presence of the Soviet military and shipments of food, raw materials, and equipment, and a great deal of political pressure from the USSR, China, East Germany, and Romania, such panicky reactions soon gave way to the logic of the dictatorship of the party apparat.

At the end what mattered was that with Soviet help, in early November 1956 Kádár formed a "Workers' and Peasants' Revolutionary Government" and, in the next three months, extinguished the last vestiges of overt mass resistance to the Soviet occupation of the country. With the government in place, as Ágnes Ságvári, a retired senior Central Committee staff member, put it in her memoirs, Kádár, as a kind of afterthought, turned to the task of "putting together a party to back up the existing government."[7]

(A)   Decision-making in a ruling party

In what follows I will propose a selective overview of the Hungarian party's record between 1956 and the 1970s as it may be gleaned from János Kádár's strategic policy decisions, the roles that the HSWP Politburo and the Central Committee Secretariat played in formulating policies, and the contributions of the Central Committee and the party congresses to the promotion of the party's values and policy objectives. As the first step, one must make a distinction between the party's official decision-making hierarchy, as it is specified in the party statutes, and the actual loci of decision-making power in a Marxist–Leninist ruling party.

The HSWP, just like its Soviet model, the CPSU, was run by the PB, the CC Secretariat, and its departments, rather than by the CC or by the delegates of the party's quinquennial congresses. The party's decision-making praxis, therefore conferred exceptional, and often extrastatutory, powers to individuals, particularly the first secretary and key members of the PB and the Secretariat, over elected bodies from the party congress and the CC down to the lowest elected party assembly.

The next step is to assess the performance of the principal actors and the party's official decision-making bodies in terms of the quality of decisions made by the "executive" (the PB and the CC Secretariat) and "legislative" (the CC and the party congress) branches of the ruling party. To make my case, I will draw on some of the propositions that Yehezkel Dror advanced in his studies on public policy-making and on "policy-making under adversity."[8]

Let us first specify the terms of the argument by making a distinction between "decision making" and "policy-making." According to Richard Snyder, as summarized by James A. Robinson, "decision-making is a social process that selects a problem for decision (i.e. choice) and produces a limited number of alternatives from among which a particular alternative is selected for implementation and execution."[9] Harold Laswell divides this process into separate components: "since an official decision or a private choice is a problem-solving activity, five intellectual tasks are performed at varying levels of insight and understanding: clarification of goals; description of trends; analysis of conditions; projection of future developments; and invention, evolution and selection of alternatives."[10]

Whereas decision-making is a discrete process with readily identifiable stages and components, the term "policy-making," especially "public policy-making," in my view, denotes a more comprehensive activity. As Dror explains, "Public policy-making is a very complex, dynamic process whose various components make different contributions to it. It decides guidelines for action directed at the future, mainly by governmental organs."[11]

In Dror's view, the efficacy of public policy can be evaluated by several criteria. These are "its clarity; its internal consistency; its comparability with other public policies; its scope, in terms of values and the time-span it is concerned with; its comprehensiveness, in terms of the variety of activities it deals with; and its operationability, in the sense of being concrete enough to be a meaningful guide for action."[12]

The party's adequacy for the task of system management can be measured by the "net output" – that is, "public interest realized minus the cost of achieving it" – of its policy-making activities.[13] However, a ruling communist party is neither a Weberian legal-rational bureaucracy nor a democratically accountable public problem-solving agency. Rather, it is the embodiment of the political will of an ideologically committed active minority. Moreover, at least until termination of the vanguard mode of leadership, the party's policy-makers perceive themselves not as civil servants but as militant builders of a new socioeconomic order and the executors of the party's ideologically postulated long-term policy goals.

The party's record of decision- and policy-making should, at first, be analyzed on its own terms. The objective is to determine the appropriateness of the decision-making means to achieve the stated policy ends. In what follows, the discussion will focus on four actors or agencies of policy-making in Hungary. These are first secretary, later secretary general, János Kádár, the Politburo and the Secretariat, the CC, and the party congress.

(B)   Strategic decisions: the Kádár record, 1958–68

At the April 17, 1984 session of the HSWP Central Committee, first secretary János Kádár sought credit, and took responsibility, for four strategic decisions he had made in the preceding twenty-eight years. In his words, these were
1 the capturing and consolidation of political power for the working class,
2 the establishment of stable public order, economy and cultural life,
3 the socialist reorganization of agriculture,
4 the reform of the economic guidance system.[14]

The list of these accomplishments, though accurate, is incomplete, because it fails to account for the entire post-1956 record of Kádár's stewardship. The full record is complex and, in one way or another, includes virtually all decisions made by the regime between 1956 and 1988. Of these, I elected to discuss four key decisions in the areas of military security, agriculture, leadership stability, and foreign policy made between 1958 and 1968.

The stationing of Soviet troops in Hungary

Kádár's affirmative decision on this matter was made during the April 2–9, 1958 official visit of a Khrushchev-led Soviet party delegation in Hungary.[15] The main item on the agenda was the laying out of a comprehensive framework for long-term cooperation between the two states. The occasion also served to convey Moscow's reconfirmation of Kádár as the authoritative leader of Hungary.

To strengthen bilateral ties, an economic package of aid programs, trade protocols, and other cooperative projects were agreed upon by the two sides. With respect to security matters, Khrushchev offered, and Kádár agreed to, the withdrawal of Soviet advisors from government ministries.[16] Khrushchev also offered to withdraw several army divisions. Kádár "vehemently objected," saying that the long-term presence of Soviet forces in Hungary enabled the Hungarian regime to "continue its internal experimentation."[17] In the end, a compromise was reached. The formula endorsed the continued presence of Soviet forces on Hungarian soil "due to the complex international situation." Kádár's decision benefited himself – and, as discussed below, perhaps Hungary as well. Moscow's reconfirmation of his leadership undermined the prospects of Rákosi – thitherto Moscow's standby alternative to Kádár – for a political comeback in Hungary.[18] It also kept the HSWP's holdover cadres from the HWP at bay, thus permitting Kádár to relinquish the security branches of the government to Ferenc Münnich and to devote more time to the task of reshaping the party in his own image.[19] Because the Soviets (rightly) viewed the Hungarian military "unfit" to cooperate with the Red Army, the outcome gave Kádár much-needed time to create an army that was more loyal to him than to Moscow.[20]

The costs of agreeing to keep Hungary under direct Soviet military control of indefinite duration are still difficult to estimate. The expression of "reorganization under a court-appointed guardian" comes close to describing the political liabilities that Kádár incurred with this decision. One of these was the further deterioration of Hungary's international standing – already at a low point after the crushing of the 1956 revolution – as a sovereign state.[21] Another, and far more substantial, cost was Kádár's consent to Hungary's long-term integration with the Soviet and the CMEA economies. Kádár had no choice but to buy into the Soviet economy. In doing so, he effectively mortgaged Hungary's future economic policy choices to the long-term viability of the Soviet economy.

Over the years the decision for the stationing of Soviet troops on Hungarian soil lost some of its initial rationale. What remained valid was Kádár's hunch that with Soviet troops already in place, Hungary would be seen by Moscow as an adequate safeguard against a possible reenactment of October 1956. And he also guessed right in sensing that bayonets were excessively blunt instruments to thwart incremental changes of the nonpolitical kind. In any case, the renewal, in 1968, of the twenty-year Treaty of Friendship and Cooperation with the USSR was still a political necessity.

The topic of Hungary's military relations with the USSR warrant extended analysis. From the perspective of four decades what stands out is the way the wily Kádár turned the misfortune of the Soviet military presence in Hungary into political strength. To forestall the rise of an institutional rival that might threaten the party's monopoly of power, in 1960 Kádár found a singularly untalented, corrupt, but unambitious party cadre, Lajos Czinege, whom he appointed to serve as minister of defense. In the next twenty-four years (it was said to be a global longevity record at that time) Czinege's job was to humor the WTO High Command and stonewall Soviet demands for ever-higher military outlays by Hungary. Czinege, sober or drunk, did exactly what he was told. For this, the usually puritanical Kádár rewarded him with ironclad job security and chose to tolerate his scandalous lifestyle. Kádár's payoff was having the "cheapest army in Europe" and the rechanneling of the savings, such as these were, to support Hungarian living standards from 1968 on.[22]

The second collectivization in Hungary

The transformation, through radical land reforms, of Hungary from a country of large estates into one of small farmers was the Hungarian communists' first, and by far the most successful, policy initiative. The land reform of 1945–6 was implemented under the leadership of Imre Nagy, but its benefits were soon retrieved by the party when it embarked on a path of forcible collectivization between 1948 and 1950. In fact, of all of Rákosi's policies, the regime's campaign to liquidate the Hungarian kulaks "as a class" was the most coercive aspect of the HWP's political record.

In 1953 it was again Imre Nagy and the inauguration of his New Course that came to the aid of the beleaguered peasantry. By permitting the partial decollectivization of the farm sector, Nagy helped defuse political tensions in the Hungarian countryside. Ironically, his policies worked well enough to keep the rural response – apart from isolated confrontations and the settling of scores in some villages – to the events of October 1956 at best lukewarm, and at worst indifferent.[23] Still, much of the collective farm sector collapsed after 1956 and left Kádár with a policy dilemma of considerable magnitude. On the one hand, he was enough of a Leninist not to tolerate the existence of an independent agricultural sector with its potential of giving, as Lenin put it, "daily birth and rebirth of capitalism in the countryside." On the other hand, he could ill afford to alienate yet another, thus far politically complacent, segment of Hungarian society.

Kádár's response to this policy dilemma may be gleaned from five Central Committee decisions and one Politburo decision on agriculture between December 7, 1958 and February 17, 1961.[24] The CC was divided on this issue. Of the three contending groups, he sided with those who emphasized persuasion and material incentives to obtain the peasantry's rejoining "voluntarily" the agricultural cooperatives.[25] Though not free of strong-arm methods and widespread psychological intimidation, the process of agricultural recollectivization was brought to a successful conclusion in less than three years. According to the CC's communiqué of February 17, 1961, 75 percent of the country's arable land now belonged to the "socialist cooperative sector."[26]

The immediate political costs of pressuring hundreds of thousands of small farmers to join the agricultural cooperatives were, by all appearences, relatively low. The farmers who brought land to the cooperative were given an annual user fee according to acreage contributed to the common property. With the introduction of the "Nádudvar plan" in 1966, each member was given an allotment for a household plot, as well as the use, for a nominal payment, of the cooperative's equipment for the cultivation of the same.[27] Although some cooperative farm chairmen were incompetent political hacks, some turned out to be shrewd entrepreneurs who brought prosperity for the membership.

Kádár's pragmatic approach to the rural economy yielded substantial political and economic dividends in the years to come. As beneficiaries, from the late 1960s on, of sizeable state investments in modern agricultural technology and trained labor, the cooperatives repaid the politicians by making Hungary – alone in Eastern Europe – self-sufficient in food production. Though the agricultural operations were not particularly efficient by Western European standards, the basic staples, rain or shine, were always there in the well-stocked Hungarian food stores. Whereas periodic meat and food shortages helped, from time to time, destabilize some regimes of the region, the "goulash" part of Hungary's communism became a model of consumerist legitimacy under state socialism.

The long-term political consequences of bringing the rural economy back into the socialist fold were contradictory. On the one hand, the appointment and often decade-long tenure of county HSWP first secretaries and those of their state administrative opposite numbers, the county council chairmen, created a semblance of political stability. On the other hand, the situation thus created was ready-made for the rise of semiautonomous fiefdoms of the county and small-town party apparat. Together with clientelist management and an astonishing range of corrupt practices, there also developed a new provincial society with political, economic, and ideological interests of its own.

To succeed, particularly to deliver on plan targets, over the years many of the "little tyrants" (*kiskirályok*) of the counties had no choice but to "go native" and become lobbyists for local interests with little regard for those of the political center.[28] Tensions inherent in the clashing interests of the political center and the political periphery were further exacerbated by the emergence of policy lobbies speaking for the interests of agriculture and industry. As a consequence, in the next two decades, the Budapest party headquarters and its provincial prefects' local political machines grew apart. Each had an agenda of its own that became irreconcilable by the early 1980s.

The "cult of personality": political showdown and leadership consolidation

In October 1961, János Kádár, his deputy György Marosán, and the Comintern veteran PB member Dezső Nemes represented the Hungarian party at the 22nd congress of the CPSU. At the congress Khrushchev denounced and called for the expulsion from the party of Georgy Malenkov, Vyacheslav Molotov, and several others for their complicity in the crimes associated with Stalin's cult of personality. Though aware of Khrushchev's own rising cult of personality, Kádár found in Moscow's new anti-Stalin campaign the needed opportunity to finish off his left-wing opponents in the HSWP.

On November 11, 1961, the PB appointed a three-man committee under Béla Biszku to review the thus-far-unexamined record of the Rákosi regime's crimes against leading party members between 1949 and 1956.[29] As far as these can be reconstructed from published documents, transcripts of secret CC meetings, and György Marosán's 1989 memoirs, Kádár had several goals in mind. These, in summary form, were:

1 the removal of Soviet military-intelligence veteran Ferenc Münnich as prime minister and the reassertion of his (Kádár's) complete personal control over the regime by the assumption of that office;

2 the political liquidation of Rákosi and his still-active followers in Hungary;

3 the firm establishment of the primacy of a handpicked PB over the potentially unpredictable, therefore unreliable, CC;

4 the elimination, by nonreappointment, of several incumbent CC members prior to the party's then-forthcoming 7th congress in November 1962;

5 the revamping and professionalization of the central party apparat and the appointment of department heads and line CC secretaries of proven personal loyalty to him.

Kádár's ambitious scenario worked well up to a point. The August 14–15, 1962 meeting of the CC heard the results of the Biszku committee's review of the major Stalinist show trials of 1949–52, as well as of the trials of an additional 898 individual victims of Rákosi's purges.[30] The report, notwithstanding the same body's previous unanimous support of these criminal acts, exonerated the incumbent CC of any responsibility for Rákosi's record. In doing so, the report made the holdover members from the HWP CC political hostages to Kádár's goodwill. After all, incriminating but currently then-suppressed evidence could, if need be, be recovered from the archives and used as and when Kádár deemed appropriate. Party gossip had it that Kádár's personal safe was the ultimate repository of such documents on key personnel. Most of these vanished somehow in the spring of 1989.[31] In any event, for their complicity in the execution or imprisonment of 382 and the internment of 336 top cadres, in addition to the exiled Rákosi, several of his close associates and twenty-two other high-ranking officials were expelled from the party.[32]

Neither at the meeting nor in the closing communiqué was anything said about the matter of political or legal responsibility for the fate of the nonparty victims of Stalinism in Hungary. Rákosi's secret police had an active file on approximately 1.5 million Hungarian citizens. About half of them ended up in court, were sent to prison and internment camps, or were deported from the cities into backward rural regions of Hungary between 1950 and 1953.[33]

The immediate outcome of this CC meeting may have satisfied Kádár. However, it prompted several blistering letters and a long political statement from his deputy György Marosán. In a hitherto top-secret eighty-one-page letter to Kádár, Marosán gave a devastating account of his comrade's petty manipulation of people, ideas, and issues for his personal benefit. Kádár, as depicted by Marosán, was a temperamental and vindictive tyrant, a jealous boss, an anti-Semite who actively recruited subservient Jews to run key CC departments, and an ungrateful colleague whom he had saved from a 1958 apparat *Putsch*. Perhaps his most damning accusation was that Kádár had been seeking to impose his will on the CC by transferring its decision-making prerogatives to his hand-picked PB.[34]

Marosán's high visibility in Hungarian politics, his newly found sense of due process in party affairs, and his refusal to play the role of a "tame Social Democrat" – such as Sándor Rónai, Rezső Nyers, and many others in the years to come – in Kádár's party were handicaps that he could not overcome. On October 12, 1962, he resigned his membership in the PB and the CC and his government job as minister of state. Three years later, he gave up his party membership as well.[35]

With two of his former deputies, Marosán and Münnich, out of the way, Kádár set out to consolidate his personal power. Learning from the Marosán affair, particularly the way the latter had gotten strange ideas while accompanying Kádár to the 22nd CPSU congress, Kádár resolved never again to take his party deputy to Moscow.[36] At the party headquarters his immediate entourage was enlarged to include such loyalists as Jenő Fock, Sándor Gáspár, Béla Biszku, Károly Németh, Zoltán Komócsin, Dezső Nemes, István Szirmai, and Rezső Nyers.[37] These people, with periodic promotions, demotions, retirements, and the co-optation of new cadres, were Kádár's political shield, and at times pawns, for the next two decades. Kádár's inner circle included old chess, card-playing, and hunting cronies and his personal staff, whom he affectionately called the "iron brigade." Members of these two groups made up the Praetorian guard that served as his first line of defense against his enemies, personal and political, domestic and foreign.[38]

That it was not the "restoration of socialist legality" but that of his authority that motivated Kádár may be surmised from the fact that in the next five years up to 7,600, virtually all nonparty, people were tried and sentenced to prison terms for "antistate activities" of various kinds.[39] Thus, by the end of the 1960s the unfinished business of "restoring the people's power" was finally completed in Hungary.

The main objective of Kádár's "struggle on two fronts," that is, against Stalinist intraparty opponents and thousands of innocent Hungarians, was the imposition of his will, his policy agenda, and his political style on the party, the government and the people of Hungary. He never fully achieved this goal, but the personnel outcomes of the 1962 August–October PB and CC decisions gave him enough staying power to weather the next ten years without significant internal challenges to his leadership and political power.

János Kádár and the invasion of Czechoslovakia, January–August 1968

In mid-July 1968, Kádár made a tentative decision to commit Hungarian military forces in support of a Soviet-led invasion of Czechoslovakia before the end of August 1968. A reconstruction of issues and events that led up to, and followed from, this decision presents the observer with an unique opportunity to examine Kádár's conduct as Hungary's principal policy-maker under complex and stressful international conditions.[40]

Leadership changes between December 1967 and January 1968, in Czechoslovakia from the Stalinist Antonin Novotný to the young reformer Alexander Dubček could not have come at a less opportune time for Kádár and his proreform colleagues in the Hungarian leadership. As the Hungarians saw it, Brezhnev's reply, "It is your business," when asked for advice on the impending removal of Novotný as the head of the Czechoslovak party in December 1967, was welcome evidence of Soviet noninterference in East European party affairs. On the other hand, young Dubček – though "Kádárist" enough to have supported the Soviet invasion of Hungary in 1956 – was an unknown quantity who was bound to cause unpredictable changes in Czechoslovakia that might spill over into Hungary.[41]

Hungary's situation was precarious in the international realm. In an effort to accommodate Moscow's wishes for the holding of a "great conference" of ruling and nonruling communist parties of the world, the HSWP had agreed to serve as the convenor and principal organizer of that event. The conference would have provided Moscow with the opportunity to expel or isolate further the Chinese and their assorted followers in the international communist movement. In either case, Kádár's reward would have been an enhanced role of the HSWP as an honest broker and peacemaker in the troubled world of communist interparty relations.

Kádár, his chief economist Rezső Nyers, and CC foreign secretary Zoltán Komócsin had yet another and, from an economic viewpoint, far more important project in mind. The issue at hand was the normalization of Hungary's political ties and a significant expansion of its trading ties with the Federal Republic of Germany (FRG). It was axiomatic that the NEM could not be sustained without an appreciable growth in Hungary's Western exports, as well as in its imports of modern Western agricultural and industrial technology. The HSWP's foreign policy team sought to find a way between the East Germans' and the Poles' adamant refusal to have anything to do with the FRG and the tempting examples of Yugoslavia and Romania, which had found a way around Moscow's – as it turned out two to three years later, temporary – rejection of the Hallstein Doctrine and its ban on normalization of ties with the FRG.

Kádár's first meeting with Dubček as the newly elected head of the Czechoslovak party took place in mid-January, 1968. The two men hit it off extremely well. As Kádár reported to his PB colleagues:

> He made a very good impression on me. There is no sense of triumphalism or haughtiness about him. In fact, quite the opposite. He is very distressed about having been elected [as first secretary]. He is conscious of the problems and he is suffering. My view and judgment is that in all respects comrade Dubček's position is that of a totally principled communist.[42]

At this meeting Dubček gave Kádár an exceptionally candid account of his policy dilemmas and personal frustrations. As Dubček explained, there were Novotný and his conservative cronies in the leading party organizations seeking to thwart his efforts to unite the party behind him. Moreover, from the Prague conservatives' perspective, anything he hoped to accomplish in Slovakia branded him as a "Slovak nationalist." Kádár counseled Dubček to avoid a showdown with the conservatives, "bury the hatchet" in the Czechoslovak PB, "submit new proposals and see how the members vote on them." Dubček wanted to have his house in order before going to introduce himself in Moscow. He also cited to Kádár Novotný's parting advice: "Follow Kádár's example." It was unclear whether Novotný had in mind Kádár the ruthless "consolidator" of 1956–57 or Kádár the "deal-maker" and the man of communist *Realpolitik*.[43]

The next Dubček–Kádár meeting, in early February, marked the beginning of a deeper "older brother–younger brother" relationship between the two men. Komócsin, who had witnessed the first meeting, was persuaded that Dubček was "personally attached to comrade Kádár." Apart from personal empathy, Kádár was pleased to learn that his young colleague, Moscow's misgivings notwithstanding, planned to authorize the opening of a West German trade office in Prague and to initiate discussions between Czechoslovakia and the Common Market. While these initiatives seemed very promising, Kádár felt duty-bound to remind his PB that of the six points of a 1967 WTO policy declaration on West Germany, "there is one that practically demands that a Soviet Republic be set up in the FRG."[44] Kádár's initial misgivings were further reinforced by the report of a Rezső Nyers-led PB fact-finding mission to Czechoslovakia. The report spoke of the immense political burdens of Czechoslovakia's "still unresolved Stalinist past" and of "the challenge of overcoming such obstacles as political infighting, economic disarray, the explosive discontent of the intelligentsia and the Novotný regime's suppression of the Slovak problem."[45]

The Kádár–Dubček political honeymoon came to an end in the middle of March. By then Kádár had grown extremely concerned by the Prague reformers', to him alarming, proclivity to issue "action programs of all sorts," and by Dubček's suspected inability to keep things under control. In any event, while Kádár was busy helping Dubček, he was rudely reminded by his own, normally tame, CC that some of Dubček's ideas might be worth adopting in the HSWP. The matter had surfaced at the February 8–10, 1968 meeting of the CC in PB member Béla Biszku's report on the "working methods of the higher organs of the HSWP." It appeared that some of the would-be reformers in the party apparat recommended that the scope of the PB's and the CC secretaries' decision-making authority be reduced to the benefit of the CC as an autonomous decision-making body; that the membership of the latter become privy to the PB's secret "operative decisions" (that is, over 70 percent of PB decisions); and that the CC "have a foreign affairs committee of its own."[46] Though these heretic recommendations were promptly dismissed by Kádár's loyal PB, he could not help being concerned about the unpredictable ripple effects of the Czechoslovak ideological contraband in his own party.

Questions of ideological heresy of a different kind were articulated at a significantly higher level and in a more menacing tone by the East German and Polish participants in the March 23, 1968 Dresden meeting of the five most closely involved ruling parties. Walter Ulbricht and Władisław Gomułka spoke of the situation as "resembling the prologue to the Hungarian counterrevolution," Kádár and the Bulgarian delegate urged restraint and noninterference in internal Czechoslovak affairs, while Brezhnev appeared to be both concerned and noncommittal. Yet, the initial version of the meeting's official communiqué amounted to, as PB member and Hungarian prime minister Jenő Fock put it, "the Czechoslovaks' burial." Apparently, Kádár's forceful intervention and concessions from Brezhnev saved Dubček from the wrath of Ulbricht and Gomułka.[47] Under the circumstances, the noninvited Romanians would have been most welcome to give a hand to Kádár, but as he explained it in his report to the PB: "we dared not broach the matter of Romanian participation."[48]

The Hungarian party's position and foreign policy hopes were further eroded by a proposal by Kosygin and Gomułka for the tightening of ranks among members of the Council for Mutual Economic Aid and Assistance (CMEA) and consequent thwarting of Czechoslovak and Hungarian plans for expanding their respective trading ties with the West. Indeed, it seems that Fock's commentary on the Dresden meeting touched on the heart of the matter: "There is something more behind the Kosygin plan. We must be prepared for it."[49]

As the events, or more specifically the full ideological and political dimensions, of the Prague Spring unfolded, Kádár's self-appointed role as a go-between and an honest broker seeking to assuage Brezhnev's worry, and later undisguised anger, at Dubček and his fellow reformers, and to urge, with a growing sense despair, Dubček to contain "political anarchy" in Czechoslovakia, brought diminishing returns. At the stormy May 28, 1968 five-party meeting in Moscow, Brezhnev warned that the Soviet Union would take "any step to contain the Czechoslovak situation." Kádár, by then the only voice counseling patience, asked for a "more circumspect" evaluation of the Czechoslovak events. To this he added: "One cannot settle matters by calling Mao Zedong and his associates crazy, Castro petty bourgeois, Ceauşescu nationalist, and the Czechoslovaks lunatics. If we must criticize individuals, let us begin with comrade Novotný, rather than with comrade Dubček."[50]

From the Hungarian PB's perspective, the end-game phase of Hungary's role as an effective moderating force in the four-party (Soviet, East German, Polish, and Bulgarian) dispute with the Prague reform communists commenced with the June 11, 1968 meeting of the PB. Of the two main reports presented, the first dealt with "current questions of foreign policy." In a tour-of-the-horizon kind of review of Hungary's relations with the socialist world, the report found Hungary to be very different from its near and far, moderate and dogmatic, nationalist and pseudorevolutionary (this epithet pertained to Cuba) fraternal allies in the community of ruling communist parties.

With all its unresolved problems, Czechoslovakia under Dubček was seen in Budapest as the nearest to Hungary's way of building socialism. Indeed, as Kádár stated in the follow-up discussion, "When we next meet with the Czechoslovak comrades, I cannot imagine saying anything else but that we are fully supportive '*teljes mértékben szolidárisak'* of them."[51] As for the Western world, the report supported the Soviet–East German line "with reservations." Because all internal HSWP deliberations, including the substance of PB debates, were either leaked to Moscow or directly communicated to Moscow, the otherwise sensible report paid homage to the Soviets by reciting the hoary golden rule of interparty relations: "The touchstone of internationalism is one's relationship to the Soviet Union."[52]

The HSWP's brave posturing came to an end during the June 27–July 4, 1968 official Hungarian party-state visit in the Soviet Union. The prospects of a bad harvest prompted the Hungarian delegation to request Soviet aid; therefore, Kádár had no choice but to appear receptive to Brezhnev's gloomy assessment of the Czechoslovak scene and its security implications for the Soviet alliance system. Still, perhaps hoping against hope, Kádár declared: "Whatever we do, it must be done together with the Czechoslovaks ... [in a way that] should help, rather than harm our [common socialist] cause."[53]

By mid-July it was clear in Budapest that drastic measures would be taken to salvage the "socialist foundations" of Czechoslovakia. The PB set up an *"ad hoc* operative committee" of the Foreign and the Agit-Prop Departments to keep an eye on regional developments and to prepare the Hungarian public for the inevitable. In its first report, the committee cited the Hungarian party membership's fears of the country's international isolation. They asked: "only five of us are left [to take on Czechoslovakia]?"[54]

At the end, Kádár asserted that he had no choice but to wash his hands of the eventual fate of the Czechoslovak reformers. Speaking at the August 7, 1968 meeting of the CC, he stated: "The situation has changed – everything is adrift in Czechoslovakia. The Czechoslovak party might cease to be a revolutionary vanguard at the next party congress. Should this happen, there will be a real danger of them calling some kind of national elections [where] all kinds of political forces will be given the green light."[55]

At the July 14, 1968 five-party meeting in Moscow, Kádár found himself totally isolated in his continued support of a political solution for Czechoslovakia. As he explained to the HSWP CC, "in Moscow the other parties disagreed with what I had to say. This has not happened in the last twelve years," and added, "We can hardly expect to have any influence over the events. We could have said that we would not participate in the planned military alert [read: preparations for an invasion]. But what would have been the outcome?" If Hungary balked, the rest of the parties "would have acted in an unpredictable manner."[56] Or, as Ulbricht put it at the Warsaw meeting: "After Czechoslovakia, Hungary will be the next."[57]

Kádár's concluding remarks at the August CC meeting offer a credible summary of his long and ultimately futile efforts to come to terms with the foreseeable consequences of the Czechoslovak reform movement. As he saw it, "a Masaryk-type bourgeois democracy may be seen as progressive when compared to [Admiral] Horthy's fascism, but it is nothing but reactionary and counterrevolutionary when compared to a socialist republic." Moreover, Kádár submitted, "there can be even a greater tragedy – that of Czechoslovakia ceasing to be a socialist republic. I would choose the lesser tragedy rather than the greater one."[58]

On August 21, 1968 the "lesser tragedy," in the form of a Soviet-led five-nation invasion of Czechoslovakia, materialized. Because of the apparent unavailability of the transcript of the HSWP PB's meeting of August 20, 1968, we do not know how the members of that body voted on Hungary's participation in the crushing of the Czechoslovak reform movement. On the other hand, the tone of deliberations of the CC's first postinvasion secret meeting – in fact, so secret, that two CC members rather than the usual clerical staff took notes and prepared the minutes – may be characterized as somber and imbued with a deep sense of shame over Hungary's involvement in the affair.[59] Although Kádár went through the motions of trying to blame the victim for the crime, the real agenda was that of domestic and international damage control and search for ways to extricate the regime from the political quagmire of the postinvasion scene.

On the face of it, the muted domestic reaction – confidential letters of protest from the philosopher György Lukács and the former prime minister András Hegedüs, a letter of resignation from András Tömpe, then Hungarian ambassador to the GDR (he subsequently committed suicide over the invasion), and open letters of protest from two groups of Marxist philosophers and sociologists – was a small price to pay for the HSWP's complicity in the rape of the Czechoslovak people's hopes for a better life under democratic socialism.[60] On the other hand, as the embittered Jenő Fock – who had somehow vanished rather than accompany Kádár to the August 18 five-party meeting in Moscow that gave the final go-ahead for the military – put it, "[I]f we took a secret vote after August 21st, several million no's would have come in." He concluded by saying "it is not good enough to say that the [Populist writer] László Németh was in favor and András Hegedüs was opposed." Indeed, the real issue was not the Hungarian people's and the cultural elites' shellshocked immediate reaction but, as the PB's September 17 position paper on Czechoslovakia put it, "the growing [public] concern about the preservation of the ... confidence [in the regime] ... and of the achievements of the last twelve years."[61]

In Kádár's view, the Soviets badly mishandled the Czechoslovak situation. Throughout, it was a botched operation. Moreover, to add insult to injury, the HSWP ended up supporting, in Kádár's words, the "Slovak nationalist Husák" and the Slovak party against Dubček and Prague. To make matters worse, on the international scene the HSWP found itself in the dubious company of a handful of proinvasion communist parties and on a collision course with forty-five others that denounced the invasion as a gross violation of Marxist principles.[62]

Twenty-one years after the fact, Alexander Dubček, in an interview with a Western scholar, called Kádár's decision to have Hungary take part in the invasion of Czechoslovakia a "tragic mistake."[63] In my view, this summary judgment is both unfair and, in light of Kádár's conduct in the months preceding that event, historically inaccurate.

As shown above, the facts of the case were as follows. Apart from sympathizers in nonruling communist parties and occasional self-serving comments of support by Tito and Ceauşescu, Kádár was the only leader of a ruling party who stood up for Dubček in 1968. Whereas Kádár had a great deal to lose (including his job) and relatively little to gain from speaking for moderation in the face of Moscow's growing hostility toward Dubček, neither the "autonomist" Ceauşescu nor the "nonaligned" Tito came forth to aid a fellow reformer when such support might have stayed Moscow's hand for either a few months or perhaps years. In any case, it is fair to say that all three – Kádár, Ceauşescu, and Tito – were motivated by their respective states' national interests, rather than by politically suicidal impulses of ideological solidarity with the Dubček team's open-ended and not particularly well-managed agenda of political democratization, "socialism with a human face," and prospects of free elections and a multiparty system in a WTO member state.

When placed in a domestic context, Kádár's conduct and eventual decision are open to various interpretations. On the one hand, as will be shown in the next chapter, there is sufficient circumstantial evidence to suggest that in the early days of the NEM the matter of augmenting the economic reforms with cautiously designed but potentially substantive political-institutional reforms was still an open issue. Therefore, the Dubček program, if permitted to unfold in a gradual and tightly controlled fashion, was bound to give new impetus for –

admittedly less ambitious – changes in Hungary. On the other hand, it may be argued that the logic of the Hungarian situation, particularly the precarious balance of pro- and antireform forces in the HSWP would, sooner or later, have compelled Kádár to part ways with his younger and more courageous northern neighbor. For these reasons, Dubček's historic second-guessing, however understandable from his personal perspective, is substantially off the mark. The real decisions were made in Moscow rather than in Budapest, Bratislava, and Prague. It was also where Czechoslovakia's and Hungary's oil, natural gas, and raw materials, and Prague's grain supplies came from.

The long-term effects of Kádár's decision were of two kinds. In the international context, the Hungarian regime was rewarded by Moscow with the holding of a 1969 conference on European security issues. This, in turn, laid the groundwork for the East–West *détente*-driven process that culminated with the Helsinki Conference on Security and Cooperation in Europe (CSCE) in 1975. Hungary's vigorous role in pre-Helsinki deliberations and the preparatory work that led to the 1975 East Berlin conference of European communist parties could be seen as compensatory efforts to make amends for Hungary's role in the Czechoslovak invasion.

The domestic consequences of the invasion are difficult to sort out. Kádár's solidarity with Brezhnev bought him time to get on with the NEM and also kept the HSWP hardliners at bay for the next two to three years. On the other hand, Kádár's orthodox ideological stance gave a new lease of life to conservatives throughout the party apparat. The latter – mainly in the provincial party organizations – had been bloodied, but not defeated, in the 1962 purges and were biding their time to settle scores with the HSWP center. Other conservative constituencies were also threatened by the "Czechoslovak model." The political influence of the internal security organs, the "red barons" of the large industrial enterprises, and the Trade Union hierarchy was greatly enhanced by Hungary's participation in the invasion of Czechoslovakia. All this left Kádár with a diminished range of options to make headway in the economic sphere while preserving his hold on the political levers of power in Hungary.

In sum, Kádár's four strategic decisions affected issues of foreign policy, socioeconomic engineering, and leadership consolidation. In each case, Kádár made choices among structurally and situationally constrained policy alternatives. In the foreign policy area the defining condition was Hungary's membership in the Warsaw Treaty Organization (WTO). To make the most of Hungary's limited sovereignty,

Kádár agreed to trade-offs between short-term sacrifices, such as the continued Soviet military presence in Hungary and the abandonment of a fellow reformer abroad, and hopes of long-term benefits of improved *Spielraum* in international affairs.

The anguish of the second collectivization was to be offset by long-term economic incentives, hence a new kind of political stability for rural Hungary. The 1962 anti-Stalinist purges, though they temporarily destabilized the party apparat, helped to put in place a cohesive management team under a moderate, yet purposeful, leader. In any case, if we define "public interest" in terms of the Hungarian people's desire to be left alone to get on with their lives after the trauma of a defeated revolution, then, the regime's incapacities notwithstanding, the "net output" of these decisions was somewhere on the plus side of the ledger. If nothing else, the people and the regime gained time to try to work out their differences among themselves.

(C)   The Politburo and the Secretariat

The Politburo, a select group of senior party officials, is said to be the ultimate decision- and policy-making body in a communist party state. This proposition is derived as much from the party's statutes, from the organizational principles of democratic centralism, and from the pyramidal structure of party organizations from the local cells to the highest body as from the widely held belief in the omnicompetence of this secretive group of communist politicians. Attempts thus far to make sense of the workings of this body, particularly the dynamics of interpersonal relations therein, have yielded useful, but partial, explanations of the PB's "operational code," the principal actors' personal motivations, their policy preferences, and the indigenous political traditions that shaped leadership behavior in a ruling communist party.

In terms of the leaders' longevity of service in the PB, the Hungarian party might be likened to the Ulbricht–Honecker, the Brezhnev, and the Zhivkov PBs. The length of Kádár's tenure of thirty-two years at the helm was bested only by Josip Broz Tito, Enver Hoxha, and Todor Zhivkov in the European part of the socialist camp. Moreover, as the top policy-making body of a ruling Marxist–Leninist party, the Hungarian PB fell victim to the same incapacities as did, at one time or another, the rest of the ruling parties. Some of these, in Ezra Vogel's terminology, were due to "communist universals," and others to local exigencies of policy resources and leadership judgment.[64]

However, beyond similarities of command structure, there were important national differences that affected the ruling parties' policy-making performance. The exalted role of the military in the Chinese and the Yugoslav parties, the ethnic clan-based oligarchies in the Albanian party, the familialist quasi-monarchic ruling style and the idiosyncratic recruitment of top cadres in the Romanian and the North Korean parties, the ethnic conflicts in the Czechoslovak party, and the "Muscovite"–"native" clashes in the Polish party are examples of national differences, in terms of policy veto groups, ruling styles, ethnic-regional, and ideological cleavages, that shaped the makeup and policy-making performance of ruling PBs.

Unless still in the midst of an unresolved succession struggle – in which case he may be only the "first among equals" – the first secretary, or general secretary, is the ex officio chair of the PB and is the chief executive officer of the Secretariat. The simultaneous holding of positions in both bodies by other senior cadres could, under certain conditions, diminish the leader's freedom of action in policy areas that are not under his immediate administrative oversight. However, it is also true that in the history of ruling communist parties, "collective leadership" has been the exception rather than the rule. In any case, in the system-management phase, the requisites of leadership stability and those of an unambiguous command structure confer on the incumbent leader exceptional positional advantages to promote his policy agenda.

The study of the HSWP PB's policy-making record is a difficult undertaking. As András Nyirő, one of the four young Hungarian sociologists who prepared the *Handbook for the Study of the Politburo*, submitted, "what can be known about the Politburo is not worth knowing; what is worth knowing is [locked up] in the heads of the Politburo members."[65] However, after the fall of the Kádár regime, some of these locked-up heads began talking; they have given inter-views and parliamentary testimonies, and published memoirs of varying degrees of reliability. In any case, the editors of the handbook made good use of this new evidence in empirical studies on the leading organs of the HSWP.[66] These data and interpretation, when combined with partial transcripts of ninety-three CC and eighty-seven PB meetings held between 1958 and 1989 that I reviewed at the Hungarian National Archives, seem sufficient for the making of some generalized statements about the "operational code" of these policy-making bodies.

Personnel and structural characteristics

Between 1957 and 1988 thirty-three senior party officials served on the PB (Appendix 1.1). Those who were born before 1927 may be characterized either as "professional revolutionaries" or "early joiners" with party membership of the 1944–5 vintage. Apart from the four former Social Democrats who joined the party in 1948, in terms of formative experiences the rest may be called either "Rákosi's children" or children of the postrevolutionary consolidation period of 1957–66. Typically, the older members were trade-school graduates with considerable on-the-job experience as party officials. The younger ones had either Hungarian or Soviet university or higher party-school diplomas and job training in the YCL apparat.[67]

During the Kádár years the average size of the PB was twelve and that of the Secretariat seven. Of the latter, the staff/line secretaries in charge of the Departments of Party and Mass Organizations (PMO), Public Administration (PA), Agitation and Propaganda (AP), and Economic Policy (EP) were always PB members. The line, or direct command, responsibilities of the four senior CC departments amounted to the hands-on daily management of several government agencies.

1 The Department of PA controlled the Ministries of Defense, Interior (including liaison with the Soviet military and the KGB), Justice, the procuracy, the court system, the Office of the Parliament, and the domestic (and probably foreign) intelligence operations.
2 The Department of AP oversaw the the party's internal indoctrination programs, the print and electronic (Hungarian Radio and Television) media, the party press (*Népszabadság* was under direct PB supervision), the State Office of Church Affairs, the National Peace Council, the official news agency, and the publishing industry.
3 The Department of CE managed the Ministry of Culture, the Ministry of Health, the Academy of Sciences, the National Sports Office, and the National Youth Committee.
4 Beyond intraparty administration and cadre affairs, the Department of PMO ran the Young Communist League, the Trade Union Federation, the Patriotic People's Front, and the Workers' Guard.
5 In addition to liaison with ruling and nonruling foreign communist parties, the Department of FA supervised, both directly and through the CC-member foreign minister, the Ministry of Foreign Affairs and the special party committee in Moscow for Hungarians working and studying in the USSR.[68]

With the exception of György Aczél (four terms), István Szirmai (1959–1966), János Berecz, and Imre Pozsgay (one and one-half terms and one term, respectively) no ideological secretary was permitted to join the PB. Similarly, with the exception of Zoltán Komócsin (three terms) no foreign secretary was admitted to the PB. Except for the four-year (1957–61) tenure of Béla Biszku as minister of interior and the token attachment, as candidate member, of minister of defense Lajos Czinege (1960–1970), the ministers of defense and interior were permanently exluded from the PB.[69]

Cadre stability was an important characteristic of the Hungarian PB in the Kádár era. With the exception of Kádár (thirty-two years at the helm), and the marathon-length services of Sándor Gáspár (twenty-nine years), Károly Németh (twenty-five years), Jenő Fock (twenty-three years), and Gyula Kállai (twenty years), the average length of a PB member's tenure was three terms, or about fifteen years. Under Kádár, only six PB members were removed "out of cycle" from this body and transferred to nonparty positions or pensioned off: György Marosán in 1962, Lajos Fehér and Rezső Nyers in 1975, Béla Biszku in 1978, István Huszár in 1980, and Lajos Méhes in 1985.

The rest of the PB members died of natural causes or were allowed to retire "with recognition" of their "merits." The pattern of gradual senior cadre turnover was broken only once, in May 1988, when Kádár and five of his senior colleagues fell victim to a "*Putsch* of the apparat" and lost their seats in the PB.[70] Personnel turnover in the Secretariat – the party center's main administrative agency that was usually staffed by younger people – was somewhat more volatile. Between 1957 and 1988 only in two instances were more than three individuals leaving and joining this body at the same time.[71]

If the PB is seen as a corporate board of directors, then Kádár and the four senior secretaries in charge of the departments of PMO, PA, AO, and EP formed the executive committee. These five, the prime minister, the foreign secretary, with staff support from the ministries of Defense, Interior, and Foreign Affairs, formed the regime's *de facto* "national security council."[72] The rest of the PB consisted of "ex officio" members, such as the prime minister, the first secretary of the Budapest party organization, and, from the late 1960s on, the heads of the YCL and the TUF; the titular head of state (chairman of the Presidential Council), such as Pál Losonczi for three terms between 1975 and 1987; and the token woman member, Valéria Benke, between 1970 and 1985.

The organization of the central party apparat in the mid-1980s is shown in Appendix 1.2. Though the four core CC departments remained in place throughout, the number of CC departments and of standing committees was changed eleven times between 1970 and 1989. The size of the central party apparat fluctuated between 270 and 350 professional positions.[73] Of the CC departments, the PMO, with fifty-six authorized positions, apportioned among three sections, was the Secretariat's largest operating unit in 1977.[74] Also counted as parts of the central apparat were 200 researchers, speech writers, historians, and ideologues employed at the CC's Institute for the Social Sciences, the Institute of Party History (archives), and the editorial offices of *Társadalmi Szemle*, the party theoretical monthly.

The work of the central staff was assisted and its decisions were executed by the HSWP's regional, political military, police, and local apparat. The party center took considerable pride in having reduced the number of its full- time political workers from a July 1, 1956 high of 11,491 to 7,321 on July 1, 1970.[75] However, contrary to the party's claims of financing its operations solely from the members' dues, well over one-third of the apparat was supported by the Ministries of Defense and Interior and by the agricultural cooperatives. In addition to the 2,084 full-time party workers on the security ministries' payroll, the government budget also supported much of the apparat – about 20,000 cadres – of the "transmission-belt" organizations (TUF, YCL, PPF, Workers' Guard, and so on) and paid the salaries of tens of thousands of people dispatched to short- and long-term programs of political education. Thus, the actual size of the full-time party and transmission-belt apparat – and the corresponding burden on the state's resources – was at least four times that shown in the party's internal statistics.

Decision- and policy-making

Except in the summer months, the PB met fortnightly under the chairmanship of Kádár or his general deputy. Between 1957 and 1988 the latter position was held by György Marosán, Béla Biszku, Károly Németh, and György Lázár. Prior to each meeting, Kádár reviewed and approved the guest list and the proposed agenda. Non-PB members of the Secretariat were permitted to attend and to take part in the discussion but had no right to vote. From the early 1980s on, editors in chief of the party press, trade union chiefs, YCL and PPF leaders, and invited CC members were also in attendance.

Topics for deliberation and action reached the PB through three channels: (a) the Secretariat (as a collective decision-making body at the weekly conference of all staff and line secretaries), (b) individual CC departments, standing committees, and working groups, either directly or through the office of the appropriate CC secretary, and (c) PB-commissioned special task forces that reported directly to the PB. As the chair of the PB and the head of the Secretariat, Kádár was free to place any item, at any time, on the agenda.

The party's direct management of four "security" (Foreign Affairs, Defense, Interior, and Justice) ministries and one "ideological" (Education and Culture) ministry imposed significant decision-making burdens on the PB. In addition to the problem of decision overload, the process was wasteful because it duplicated and probably confused the government's routine decision-making work as well. The PB and the Council of Ministers devoted comparable amounts of time to international affairs, social welfare, and economic policies (see Tables 1.1 and 1.2).

Table 1.1   *HSWP Politburo meeting subject matter, January 1, 1967–July 31, 1970*[76]

Subject matter	Frequency		Percentage	
Party affairs		118		24.3
International affairs		172		35.3
International workers' movement	77		15.8	
Foreign policy of the Hungarian state	37		7.6	
Party and state international links	58		11.9	
Economic issues		59		12.1
Economic policy	51		10.5	
Specific issues	8		1.6	
Sociopolitical issues		27		5.4
Education, science, cultural affairs		14		3.0
Work of other organs		54		11.1
State organs	40		8.2	
Social organizations	14		2.9	
Other matters		43		8.8
Protocol matters	24		4.9	
Domestic travel scheduling	16		3.2	
Total		487		100.0

Table 1.2   *Council of Ministers meeting agendas, subject matter, January 1, 1967–July 31, 1970*[77]

Subject matter		Frequency	Percentage
State business			
(Council of Ministers, individual ministries)		264	23.5
International affairs		323	28.8
Foreign policies of the state	311		27.7
International links of party and the state	12		1.1
Economic issues		305	27.2
Economic policy	122		10.9
Specific measures	183		16.3
Sociopolitical issues		75	6.7
Education, science, and cultural affairs		80	7.1
Other		76	6.8
Total		1,123	100.0

Under the rubric of "work of other organs," the PB devoted at least 8.2 percent of its time to discussing the work of "state organs," that is, military and internal security affairs. Perhaps because Kádár was absent from that PB meeting, prime minister Jenő Fock felt free to observe: "We must change the way the Council of Ministers conducts its business. Five ministries have been taken out of the hands of the Council of Ministers. From the viewpoint of daily management, five ministers report to the party."[78] Indeed, it was testimony to the central party apparat's tightly compartmentalized way of doing business that members of the task force to study the agendas of the PB and the Council of Ministers had been unaware of this practice.

As may be inferred from Table 1.1, about half the submissions for PB decision originated with the Departments of PMO and AP.[79] Though less frequently, the standing Committee for Economic Policy and the Department of PA also contributed lengthy policy documents for PB review. Personnel decisions imposed heavy burdens on the PB. Of the five spheres (the CC proper, the PB, the Secretariat, the individual secretaries, and the CC departments) of the party headquarters' "decisional competency," the PB acted on the biweekly share of its own quota of positions (169), screened and preapproved the CC's quota (95), and reviewed the Secretariat's (387) and the individual secretaries' (458) cadre decisions.[80] Based on a review of the agendas of eighty-seven PB meetings for 1958–89, it appears that most of the cadre decisions did reach the formal sessions of the PB and were discussed by those present. Here again, on all key appointments, Kádár's was the first and the last word.

From a comparison of the drafts and the final – published or unpublished – texts of the eventually adopted decisions (including resolutions, advisory opinions, and expressions of concurrence), one can conclude that a very high percentage, perhaps all, of the PB's and the Secretariat's draft decisions, resolutions, and the like were precleared by Kádár himself. Indeed, other than minor editorial changes, in most cases the two sets of texts were virtually the same.

The Politburo at work: Kádár at the helm

Between 1956 and October 1989 the party's central decision-making bodies were the source of 677 published policy statements of all kinds. Of the ten principal topics, party management, agitation and propaganda, and economic issues received the greatest attention (see Table 1.3).

Because of the enormously time-consuming chore of nomenclature management, it is doubtful that the senior policy-makers had sufficient time and energy to address policy questions that affected the well-being of the country rather than that of the party elite. Given the estimated number of annual personnel turnover at about 1,000 and the number of published personnel decisions – 164 made by the party center and, within it, 65 by the PB in *thirty-two years* – one might suppose that the published numbers represent less than one-half of 1 percent of cadre decisions made by the "executive branch" of the HSWP.

In view of the party center's obsession with secrecy and Kádár's habit of sharing information on the narrowest possible "need-to-know" basis, it is fair to assume that the actual volume of policy documents was significantly higher than the 5,000 printed pages from which the contents of Table 1.3 have been extracted. The party's conspiratorial traditions and the habit of seeking to obliterate one's role, hence responsibility, in the chain of decision-making, were responsible for the policy-makers' preference for verbal communications over leaving a paper trail of verifiable evidence.

Table 1.3   *HSWP policy statements by source and subject matter, 1956–89*[81]

Subject matter (N=677)[*]	Source					
	PB[**]	CC[**]	Secr.[**]	Working Committee	Unspecified	Total
Party management	65	62	17	18	2	164
Individual personnel decision	–	21	–	–	–	21
Guidance for non-party organizations	43	8	18	16	2	87
State, general public administration	40	33	4	6	1	84
Economic policy: general assessment; budget or annual or FYP	28	95	6	6	2	137
Economic policy: implementation	12	18	–	6	–	36
Agit-prop. ideology, science, education	57	33	7	64	10	171
Social welfare, youth and women's affairs	33	21	–	17	–	71
Foreign affairs	4	81[***]	–	1	1	87
Security affairs	3	3	–	1	–	7
Total:	285	375	52	135	18	865[****]

Notes:
[*] Includes resolutions, decisions, declarations, guiding principles, theses, and statements.
[**] PB=Politburo; CC=Central Committee; Secr.= CC Secretariat.
[***] All but seven are condensed reports by line secretaries for foreign affairs for routine acceptance by the Central Committee.
[****] Some policy statements are listed under two or more subject matters.

These traditions were kept alive, above all, by Kádár himself. When greeting the newly co-opted members of the PB at the June 30, 1987 session of that body, Kádár took pains to keep the newcomers in line. As he explained,

> the PB's decision-making process is not public information. Information about the contributions to [our] deliberations and the identity of persons speaking for or against a proposal cannot be divulged ... The decision itself can, and should be publicized, but the way we arrived

at a decision, must not [be leaked] because it will put an end to ...
responsible discussions ... Any public reference to what transpired
here is absolutely impermissible. This is where party unity begins.[82]

The thus silenced key policy-makers were, however, free to consult
with non-PB-member CC secretaries and with the heads of CC departments under their – at times only nominal – supervision. The influence
of the CC's senior staff members and that of the party center's lower-
ranking political officers is difficult to estimate. As a collective entity,
they were the "voice" and the "ideological conscience" of the party
apparat. Moreover, as managers of internal paper flow at the party
center, they were political gatekeepers and, as such, a critically
important counterweight to Kádár and the PB. Therefore, the central
apparat was both a quasi-autonomous internal bureaucratic interest
group and the embodiment of hidden "checks and balances" within
the regime's decision-making hierarchy.

It should be apparent from the foregoing that the necessary policy
knowledge, that is, policy precedents and verifiable information on the
"net output" of previous decisions, was locked up in the tribal
memory of two clusters of central policy-makers and policy initiators.
These were the longest-serving members of the PB that constituted an
informal "Executive Committee" and the twenty-three men who
served as heads of key CC departments and were the ultimate gatekeepers of the decision-making process between 1957 and 1988.[83]

Decision-making at the party center may be characterized as a
mixture of intense bureaucratic infighting that yielded both well-
argued policy papers and Delphic compromise documents, and idiosyncratic decisions by Kádár. In any case, when an issue finally took
the shape of a predecisional policy brief, the paperwork landed on
Kádár's desk. The processes of prioritization and "preemptive clear-
ance" were, for the most part, informal and, depending on Kádár's
sense of the necessary gestation period, took from a few weeks to
several years.[84]

Kádár was not a gambler but a cautious chess player. Before making
his move and committing himself to a policy, he made use of three
types of opportunities for preliminary policy assessment:
1 informal soundings, usually after-hours, with CC staff members
  who were still in their offices long after the end of the workday;
2 following the morning review of the latest opinion polls, the holding
  of the Friday afternoon "tea parties" with CC secretaries and CC
  department heads on pending matters;

3 individual discussions with fellow PB members, CC secretaries, and randomly selected lower-level party officials.

As the recipient of daily foreign and domestic intelligence briefs, personal communication from heads of other ruling parties, and hundreds of petitions from Hungarians in all walks of life, Kádár was a well-informed decision-maker. However, as one who insisted on writing his own speeches and personally reviewing and anno- tating hundreds of policy briefs, he was also a poor manager of his time, energy, and the policy-making resources that were available to him.

Well into the 1980s, when the infirmities of age caught up with him (such as falling asleep at the end of the first hour of a meeting), Kádár tried to keep the PB on a tight leash. Because he placed a firm ban on any kind of predecisional lobbying even by those few with whom he was on a first-name basis, it was probably only Kádár's wife – his sole trusted advisor – who knew how he would vote at the next PB meeting.[85]

As his PB colleagues recall, Kádár steered the group's deliberations toward the desired outcome in one or more of three ways: (a) Kádár stated his position at the outset, thus leaving to the rest of the PB the task of making minor amendments and editorial changes in the text at hand; (b) if additional persuasion was needed, he took an active part in the debate and reiterated his original position; (c) if that did not work, then at the end Kádár summed up the discussion and simply told the PB what *it* had decided.[86] Sometimes Kádár softened the blow by sending back the text for departmental redrafting or dispatched a PB subcommittee to produce a compromise version by a specific, usually two-week, deadline.

All topics but two had a chance of receiving free airing at a regular PB meeting. Soviet party relations, particularly Kádár's frequent tele- phone consultations with Khrushchev, Brezhnev, and their successors, and Hungarian military and internal security affairs were Kádár's personal domain. Though it was never registered in the Hungarian Constitution, as first secretary of the HSWP – "the leading force of the society" – Kádár was the commander in chief of the Hungarian military. These levers of power were further augmented by other personal and proprietary leadership resources.

Whereas when operating in a Politburo environment, Kádár was handicapped by his limited understanding of technical details of economic policy, international finance, legal analysis, and foreign affairs in general, he had a sure grasp of cadre management and unrivaled mastery of manipulating his associates into untenable positions from which only he could extricate them. Perhaps the best example is Kádár's custom prior to each party congress, or "midterm" CC meeting, to request his PB colleagues and fellow secretaries to prepare written evaluations of their own and their colleagues' work in the preceding period. Self-incriminated by their "critical self-critical" assessments, Kádár's senior associates were always on probation and served at the pleasure of the "Old One."[87]

The term *gazda* (the Russian word *khoziain* is an accurate translation, but the word "boss" a misleading one), which the younger apparatchiki used to refer to Kádár among themselves, was probably an affectionate appellation. In the context of Hungarian rural, say, small-village, authority relationships, the connotation was that of benign but firm paternal authority. However, judging from the occasionally bitter recollections of his senior colleagues, to them Kádár was a tough taskmaster, a bully, and a ruthless infighter with an elephantine memory for political offenses and perceived personal slights, whether they occurred a week or twenty-five years ago.[88]

Over the years, both Kádár and his PB grew older. Despite the occasional infusion of new blood in the 1980s, the average age of the PB increased from 48.8 years in 1957 to 61.1 years in early 1988 (see Table 1.4).

Together with ageing and the debilitating workload on the senior policy-makers, the PB was also confronted, particularly after the inauguration of the NEM in 1968, with a daunting and increasingly complex range of policy issues. Decision overload, restricted channels for the flow of policy-relevant information, and idiosyncratic leadership behavior made for policy-making of declining quality.

As Laswell and Dror remind us, at the heart of decision- and policy-making lies the task of making *choices* among policy alternatives. The selection of choices in an organizational environment makes contestation, the clash of opposing views, and the internal and external mobilization of support by proponents of policy alternatives inevitable parts of this process.

When the needed articulation of clashing interests is preempted and rechanneled to obtain the appearance of unanimity, the leader's will prevails, but the process is deprived of its vital element. The naysayers and the policy innovators are gradually eliminated from the party center. Or, as former PB member Miklós Óvári put it in a moment of disarming candor: "the way it worked out after 1956 was that smart

Table 1.4 *HSWP Politburo membership, average age, 1957–89.*[89]

Party congress/Conference/Year		Average age in years
Conference 6/1957		48.8 (n=12)
7th	1959	52.2 (n=12)
8th	1962	53.0 (n=13)
9th	1966	50.9 (n=11)
10th	1970	53.1 (n=13)
11th	1975	55.1 (n=14)
12th	1980	56.8 (n=14)
13th	1985	59.6 (n=13)
	May 1988	61.1 (n=13)
Conference 5/1988		52.7 (n=11)
Presidium 6/1989		55.5 (n=4)

people *'okos emberek'* left and right fell by the wayside and that left my generation [in power]."[90]

Hungarian party insiders credit György Aczél with exceptional influence on strategic decisions during the Kádár era. This has been an unexamined proposition that warrants a brief detour on the politics and personality of this remarkable individual. Aczél was born into a Jewish working-class family in 1917. He joined the underground party in 1935 and was active in the wartime resistance movement, including that of the Budapest Jewish community for survival under German occupation in 1944. After the war he joined the party apparat and worked both in a Budapest district and in two county (Zemplén and Borsod) party organizations. On July 11, 1949 he was arrested on trumped-up charges as a supporter of László Rajk. He was released from prison on July 22, 1954.

Aczél became a member of HSWP CC in November 1956. From 1957 on he served in the state's cultural administration as deputy, and later first deputy minister of culture. On April 12, 1967, he was elected as CC secretary for cultural affairs and in 1970 he was elected for membership in the PB. In March 1974 he was removed as CC secretary and appointed as deputy prime minister. In 1982 he was reappointed as CC secretary for cultural and ideological affairs but lost this position in March 1985. In May 1988 he chose not to seek reelection to the PB. His last official position was that of director-general of the HSWP's Institute for the Social Sciences. He died in 1991.

This biographical summary seems to describe a fairly typical career path of a senior Hungarian party offical of the Kádár era. However, neither Aczél nor his career was typical in any sense of this word. Whether due to shared adversity as victims of Stalinism or to unusual personal empathy between two communist politicians, the fact remains that Aczél was Kádár's principal political advisor – though perhaps not his closest personal friend. As indicated in the Introduction, Aczél's main responsibility was that of keeping Hungary's restless intellectuals in line. Though a man with at best a secondary school education, Aczél was a formidable student of Hungarian literature and the arts.

As a senior policy-maker and manager of cultural policies, Aczél could cite from the writings of fifth-rate poets – and first-rate writers such as László Németh and Gyula Illyés – and simply overwhelm (and charm) those who had doubts about the party's ideological line. Although a loyal communist, Aczél never wholeheartedly embraced the Soviet Union and Soviet culture. In literary matters he was an incurable elitist with a close afffinity to the writings of leading Western leftist and fellow-traveler authors. On the other hand, as a cultural manager, Aczél was always close to the regime's internal security organs and occasionally made use of them to punish some recalcitrant intellectuals. Aczél's political fortunes rose and fell together with those of Kádár. By all accounts, he was a vigorous supporter of economic reforms – and an equally vigorous opponent of intellectual autonomy and political dissent. Above all, as a practicing politician he was an unsurpassed manipulator of people, ideas, and bureaucratic procedures. In the tribal world of Hungarian communist politics, to the "village elder" Kádár, Aczél was the "village shaman" – a man with a mind, a will, and a vision of his own.[91]

The foregoing discussion on the *modus operandi* of the HSWP's central decision and policy-making institutions – the first secretary, the PB, the Secretariat, and the party's *eminence grise* – sought to provide a first-approximation kind of description and assessment of how public policies and specific decisions were made at the party headquarters. Kádár's hands-on management style obtained roughly until the late 1970s. From then on the core decision-making institutions remained the same, but the influence of internal advisory bodies changed dramatically. And so did the number of policy lobbies in the party, the government, and the economy with direct access to the central policy-makers.

The making of authoritative decisions and the issuing each day of dozens of policy directives, advisory opinions, and micromanagerial decisions from the center, was only half, in fact the *only* manageable part, of the process of translating the leadership's political will into concrete action. Policy implementation was the other half. This is where the prescience of those making strategic choices and the quality of deliberations behind each decision are tested in the public arena. At the end, ambitious policy decrees handed down by the party center yielded diminishing returns with respect to the sum of the equation of "public interest realized minus the cost of achieving it."

(D)   The "legislative branch": the Central Committee and Party Congress

According to the HSWP statutes, between two party congresses the CC "directs the work of all party organs and institutions; speaks for the party in its relations with the government, social organizations and represents [the HSWP] in the international sphere." The CC had other prerogatives, such as the election of the PB, the CC Secretaries, heads of standing committees and working groups, those of the party institutions, and the editors in chief of the party press.[92]

The Central Committee: policy-making forum, or a well-tempered orchestra?

With the exception of three relatively brief periods of time, in the late 1950s and in 1988–89, when the respective issues of political consolidation, agricultural collectivization, and the HSWP's impending collapse were vigorously debated in the CC, the body was not a policy-maker but a rubber stamp for PB decisons and policy initiatives. The HSWP CC was a carefully screened assembly of Kádár loyalists: central and regional party officials, state bureaucrats, industrial and agricultural executives, and representatives of transmission-belt mass organizations. These core constituencies were augmented by a handful of military people, cultural-scientific notables, and a dozen or so token "direct production managers" of workers and peasants.

Of the 345 individuals who were CC members between November 1956, and October, 1989, thirty-four, including Kádár and several of his senior associates, had also served in Rákosi's CCs between 1945 and 1956.[93] Throughout, members of the full-time central and regional party apparat had a comfortable majority in this body. Other than the apparat's own voting bloc, there were present in the CC no other distinct constituencies, such as clusters of military, agricultural, or industrial managerial delegates as spokesmen of such policy lobbies. Until the early 1980s views and policy preferences of these groups were, as a rule – sometimes after intense infighting between the affected CC departments and subdepartments – sorted out by Kádár and the Secretariat well before such sectoral interests could form alliances and, as a voting bloc, force a showdown in the CC.

Unlike the Soviet *obkom* party chiefs with their formidable presence in the CPSU CC, only a relatively few of the nineteen Hungarian county first secretaries and the five major city ("with county rights") party bosses were elected to serve in the HSWP CC at any time. (Their interests were said to have been represented by two to three former county first secretaries promoted to membership in the PB.) In any case, these twenty-four party field commanders were not even allowed to meet as a group except when called to do so by the CC secretary supervising the Department of PM, or another designated PB member, to be briefed at the end of that body's four annual meetings.[94] The exclusion of these key party officials from the CC's deliberations was partly responsible for the growing gap between the micromanaged, and essentially unresponsive, central policy-making forum and the urgent, and too often ignored, problems of the four-fifths of Hungary outside Budapest.

Until the mid-1980s CC members were rarely consulted in advance about any major policy or personnel decisions. They were also cut off from highly classified information about foreign policy, relations with other "fraternal parties," security issues, and economic, especially budgetary, matters that was routinely available to all full-time personnel in the Secretariat. Because of Kádár's morbid preoccupation with unauthorized leaks of policy plans, and the likelihood of the people's hearing about these first from Radio Free Europe, instead of the party daily *Népszabadság*, CC members were often presented with voluminous documentation on the day's business only thirty minutes before the meeting commenced. As a result, the most that an average member could contribute to the discussion were some editorial changes and pro forma endorsement of PB decisions.

As Rezső Nyers explained to me in 1984, as a "simple CC member" – though a former CC secretary and key policy-maker until 1974 – he had no access to confidential background material of any kind.[95] Such essential policy information was in the hands of CC departments, working committees, task forces, and similar *ad-hoc* groups. The latter, though nominally chaired by CC members, were, in fact, run by designated mid- or low-level members of the central apparat – often at the level of Secretariat subdepartment heads and *their* personal staff.

The level of the average CC member's participation at formal, most often two- but sometimes three-day meetings was relatively low. The number of speakers who signed up to participate in open debates rarely exceeded twenty to twenty- five. The CC's work sessions were chaired by the CC secretaries, who oversaw the active involvement of three kinds of speakers. These were the PB's political heavyweights (who set the tone for the deliberations); party, or government, experts on the topic at hand (offering support and occasional editorial changes); and, once in a while, "rogues" with views that were very much their own. The last, with a growing number of exceptions after June 1987, were almost invariably tough-minded party pensioneers in their last term in the CC or cashiered but still CC members: former PB potentates, such as Jenő Fock, Lajos Fehér, and Rezső Nyers after 1975; István Huszár after 1980; György Aczél and Ferenc Havasi after May, 1988; and János Berecz and several others after April, 1989.

From the viewpoint of the average CC member, his (there were very few women in the CC) chances of making a contribution to the drafting, predecisional deliberations, and actual substance of any policy decision put before this body by the party leadership were extremely remote indeed. Being thus deprived of a meaningful participatory role in CC-level decision-making, a member could articulate his concerns about matters on which he had been allowed to vote but not to speak in the CC only by making use of his *line* position for this purpose.

Until the mid-1980s János Kádár was the director, producer, chief scenario writer, and principal conductor of CC deliberations. As an active participant in all discussions and in sole control of the concluding part of the proceedings, he prevailed in the CC until the Grósz team of government technocrats came on board in the fall of 1987. To keep the CC at bay, yet seem responsive to the party membership's growing resentment of the central apparat's high-handed methods of suppressing local initiatives, the PB kept producing policy papers – about one every third year between 1968 and 1985 – on the "improvement of working methods of the leading organs of the HSWP."[96] Each of these documents is a testimony to the hidden power struggle between the self-appointed and self-perpetuating central apparat and the party's elected bodies from the CC down to local party assemblies.

The stake in these long-simmering disputes was not only power to make autonomous decisions but gaining access to factual information about the economy, particularly the well-hidden details of budgetary allocations for prestige projects and privileged industries. Vast disbursements for such undertakings – most often under the personal control of the CC head of Department of EP – helped syphon off funds originally earmarked for housing construction, hospitals, schools, and annual wage hikes that the local party organizations desperately needed to shore up their positions in their home districts.

Membership in the Central Committee, though bereft of substantive policy-making powers, entailed significant personal authority and various important perquisites for the incumbents. Through the Office of the CC, members were provided weekly information digests from the foreign press and other, not particularly sensitive, confidential information (delivered by special couriers) of the kind to which an attentive Western reader of the national press had free access with his or her morning coffee.

Moreover, each CC member had total immunity from arrest (for *any* alleged crime or infraction) until he was "released" to the authorities by CC vote. As parts of the top *nomenklatura*, they had access to amenities ranging from the use of official automobiles, preferential housing, and the use of party recreation facilities and of high-quality medical care in the top government hospital. As CC members, they also had the right to demand a written response to any query, criticism, or policy recommendation they made to any government and lower-level party agency.

Kádár took great pride in the HSWP's "humane methods" of managing the personnel affairs of the senior nomenclature. From 1962 on, he sharply distanced himself from the Soviet methods of "today a hero, tommorow a bum" (or worse) type of cadre policies. As he put it to Brezhnev in May 1965, "[The Soviet] way of treating [their demoted] leaders is totally unacceptable west of the USSR."[97] Nonreappointed CC members were, as a rule, looked after well by the party center. Well-paying sinecures, royalties from the publication of collected ghost-written speeches and memoirs, medals, generous pensions, first-class geriatric care, splendid funerals and well-tended cemetery lots (arranged for by the CC "piety commission," *kegyeleti bizottság*), and jobs for widows and children were the rewards of "disciplined party-like conduct" of the retired denizens of Kádár's political machine.

It appears that these modest powers and generous fringe benefits were quite sufficient for all concerned to keep saying aye when the presiding officer asked for a vote in the CC. In the Kádár years, of the 345 CC members only two (József Köböl and Antal Gyenes in 1957) found it necessary to resign from that body "for reasons of conscience."

In sum, the Central Committee, though very much the PB's junior partner as a policy-making body, fulfilled several useful functions in

Hungarian politics. As the nominally supreme decision-making body, the CC helped legitimate the party's leading role over the government and the daily lives of citizens. As the statutory recipient of periodic progress reports from the party center, the CC helped create a semblance of normalcy and of the party's responsiveness to rank-and-file demands for leadership, economic stability, and cultural conformity. And third, the CC as a "parallel legislature," through the persons of its individual members, was widely used by party members and nonmembers alike as go-betweens to wrest favors from the government bureaucracy and unresponsive public officials.

As will be shown in Chapters 6 and 7, the CC had great difficulties in defining its political mission in the "rearguard" mode of political leadership. Although Kádár was nominally in charge until May 1988, toward the end his aspiring successors fought their battles outside this profoundly corrupt and politically discredited body. In their pursuit of power and to find a way out of the Kádárist quagmire, Károly Grósz sought to harness the government bureaucracy; Imre Pozsgay made use of the PPF and the reform intelligentsia's lobbies; János Berecz tried to garner support from the police and the conservative party apparat; and Rezső Nyers endeavored to create new extraparty forums. Without an established sounding board, such as the CC, the contenders for Kádár's mantle would have been cut off from their party constituencies and thus tempted, as Grósz was, between December 1988 and April 1989, to bypass the CC and make a bid for the restoration of order by way of a martial law regime, or worse.

Though none of this came to pass, by mid-1989 the CC became an obstacle to the negotiated transformation of Hungarian politics from a one-party to a multiparty system. On June 24, 1989, within a few days after the ceremonial reburial of Imre Nagy and his fellow victims, the CC, though not formally disbanded, was replaced, by yet another coup of the apparat: a twenty-one-person Political Executive Committee and a four-man party Presidium. Their task was to oversee businesslike preparations for the party's burial at the forthcoming 14th congress of the HSWP. True to form, with but a handful of dissenting votes, the CC bowed to the inevitable and consented to its own demise.[98]

Relegitimation and political theatre: congresses and conferences of the HSWP, 1957–89

The purpose of holding a party congress, or of convening a party conference, in a communist party-state was either to renew the incumbent leaders' political mandate or to break a policy deadlock in the Central Committee with the help of delegates from local party constituencies. During Kádár's tenure the HSWP held seven congresses and two conferences. As will be shown in Chapter 7, that four-day affair in early October 1989 was neither a congress nor a conference but improvised political theatre for the hasty internment of the remains of the HSWP.

Party congresses held between 1965 and 1985 were symbolic participatory opportunities for the party constituencies that normally did not have any say about policy planning or policy-making in Hungary. (On this, see Appendix 1.3.) The essential objective of these periodic gatherings of the extended party *nomenklatura* was not policy-making but the confirmation and the elevation to the rank of operative ideology of the party leadership's strategic priorities. A related goal was the demonstration of the party's continued vitality as a political movement and as a broadly inclusive social force for "nation and progress."

A routine party congress in the 1960s and the 1970s was designed to promote five political objectives:

1 To provide a public accounting of the party's stewardship in the preceding period, as measured by tons of coal and steel produced, wheat harvested, numbers of houses built and percentages of increases in real wages.

2 To demonstrate the party's continued growth in terms of membership statistics, participation in ideological indoctrination programs, and routine leadership turnover.

3 To obtain external affirmation, primarily through the message of the principal Soviet guest speaker, of the HSWP's good standing in the Soviet bloc and of Kádár's credentials as Hungary's trusted leader.

4 To present the party as the guardian of the nation's cultural traditions and demonstrate its commitment to intellectual excellence by the prominent showcasing of invited nonparty cultural notables, such as the Populist fellow-traveler writers László Németh and Gyula Illyés; the Populist-turned-communist Ferenc Erdei; cultural icons, such as Zoltán Kodály; and assorted "peace" clergy and sports heroes.

5 To renew and reaffirm János Kádár's mandate as the nation's benevolent leader and authoritative spokesman in national and international affairs.

For the people of Hungary, it was Kádár's closing congressional speech rather than the rituals of that pseudoevent that represented the gist of the entire affair. From a closer reading of seven such homilies that Kádár gave over twenty-five years, toward the end there emerges an image of a modest man, a down-to-earth socialist, and, as György Aczél put it in 1988, an earnest "day laborer of [political] compromises." Kádár was a poor public speaker and, as an orator, the subject of much ridicule by the intellectuals. Yet despite, or perhaps because of, his fractured grammar, confused syntax, and poker-faced and transparently unconvincing recitals of ideological pieties, the average Hungarian found it easy to accept him as a man of common sense and personal decency. The party propagandists' wistful slogan in the early 1980s, "May he live to be 120," was a sentiment that was shared by many in Hungary at that time.

The June 1957 and the May 1988 party conferences symbolized the beginning and the end of the Kádár era in Hungary. The first was called together to put a veneer of political legitimacy on the restoration of the old order by the half-Stalinist and half-reformed Communist Party and to anoint Kádár as Hungary's leader. This conference became notorious for having laid the foundations for a two-year wave of police terror, the crushing of intellectual resistance, and Imre Nagy's judicial murder in June 1958. The absence of foreign guests made the 1957 conference the apparat's "family affair" and, in a historical sense, the apparat's crime against the best of its sons.

As will be shown in Chapter 6, the May 1988 party conference was another family affair – this time in the form of patricide rather than fratricide. The apparat's generational revolt sought to save the party by casting off those most responsible for the political bankruptcy of the regime. The conference, as engineered by an improbable alliance of Károly Grósz, Imre Pozsgay, and their respective clients in the party, the government, and the provincial *nomenklatura*, claimed no lives, only the power of Kádár and that of his thirty-six senior CC colleagues.

(E)   The HSWP as system manager

The foregoing narrative sought to present partial evidence on the performance of the ruling party and its leader, János Kádár, as principal managers of Hungary's political, economic, and human resources between 1956 and the late 1970s. The purpose of the discussion was to develop an informal analytical framework with which to assess the policy- and decision-making performance of János Kádár and the HSWP in the "system-management" phase of their rule in Hungary.

As system managers, Kádár and the party's central policy-making institutions were handicapped by various structural and situational constraints that limited their freedom of action to implement the regime's policy objectives. The terms of Hungary's political, economic, and military ties to the USSR isolated and, up to the early 1970s, sheltered the regime from the economic exigencies of its international environment and permitted it to focus on its domestic agenda. On the other hand, the task of orderly recovery from the political ruins of the 1956 revolution called for a long-term strategy of consensus building through incremental change. This, in turn, necessitated the inauguration of new methods of political steering.

The regime's choice of reforms to effect needed changes entailed the gradual replacement of traditional leadership techniques of coercion, command, and mobilization with those of persuasion, material incentives, and official tolerance of apolitical behavior. By the late 1960s the HSWP's pursuit of accommodation with the people yielded a new correlation of political forces between the rulers and the ruled in Hungary.

Rezső Nyers' *bon mot*, "In the last twenty years we have been trying to dance with our feet shackled," was close to the mark in describing the HSWP's balancing act between the party conservatives' ideological impulses for rapid change and the reformers' pragmatic instincts of self-preservation by yielding to public pressures for political stability and economic prosperity.[99] In any case, the PB's inherent incapacities as an omnicompetent policy-maker were balanced and often overcome (or exacerbated) by János Kádár and his prudent managerial instincts for conflict avoidance and interest reconciliation. On the other hand, the PB's authority was both enhanced and attenuated by the Byzantine politics of the central party apparat. When the latter perceived the PB as a promoter of its interests, certain kinds of strategic decisions – such as the counterreforms of 1972–5 – the apparat threw its weight behind such measures. However, when the apparat felt threatened by its perception of weak leadership above – as in 1987–8 – the key staffers switched their loyalties and supported Kádár's aspiring successor, Károly Grósz.

János Kádár's larger-than-life-size role as the ultimate, and often sole, policy-maker tended to monopolize and personalize, and to some extent paralyze, the policy process. In doing so, Kádár and his PB unwittingly preempted whatever administrative rationality the government apparat, as designated submanagers of strategic decisions, might have developed if it had been permitted to act on its own. The party leadership's preoccupation with nomenclature management and recurring jurisdictional disputes with the CC and the regional apparat caused the central policy-makers to lose administrative control over the unintended consequences of the regime's reform programs. The most important of these were the growing autonomy of the state, particularly the economic ministries, the central planning and financial institutions, the military–industrial complex, and regional party organizations.

The party that Kádár had fabricated in the fall of 1956 from the wreck of the old regime to "back up the existing government" thirty-two years later had become an entity alien to the new constellation of political, economic, and social forces. By early 1988 the PB had become a victim of ideological bankruptcy and bureaucratic entropy. In the end, this body was more of a private domain, and a kind of institutionalized conspiracy of a few tired and bewildered communist politicians, than an effective manager of political adaptation and systemic change.

Appendix 1.1   *Full members of the Politburo, HSWP, 1957–88*

Name	Birth date	1957	1959	1962	1966	1970	1975	1980	1985	1988
APRÓ, Antal	1913	+	+	+	+	+	+	–	–	–
BISZKU, Béla	1921	+	+	+	+	+	+	–	–	–
FEHÉR, Lajos	1917	+	+	+	+	+	–	–	–	–
FOCK, Jenő	1916	+	+	+	+	+	+	–	–	–
KÁDÁR, János*	1912	+	+	+	+	+	+	+	+	–
KÁLLAI, Gyula	1910	+	+	+	+	+	–	–	–	–
KISS, Károly	1903	+	+	–	–	–	–	–	–	–
MAROSÁN, György	1908	+	+	–	–	–	–	–	–	–
MÜNNICH, Ferenc	1886	+	+	+	–	–	–	–	–	–
RÓNAI, Sándor	1892	+	+	+	–	–	–	–	–	–
SOMOGYI, Miklós	1896	+	+	+	–	–	–	–	–	–
KOMÓCSIN, Zoltán	1923	**	**	+	+	+	–	–	–	–
NEMES, Dezső	1908	**	+	+	+	+	–	–	–	–
NYERS, Rezső	1923	–	–	*	+	+	–	–	–	+
SZIRMAI, István	1906	–	**	+	+	–	–	–	–	–
GÁSPÁR, Sándor	1917	–	**	+	+	+	+	+	+	–
ACZÉL, György	1917	–	–	–	–	+	+	+	+	–
BENKE, Valéria	1920	–	–	–	–	+	+	+	–	–
NÉMETH, Károly	1922	–	–	**	**	+	+	+	+	–
LÁZÁR, György	1924	–	–	–	–	–	+	+	+	–
MARÓTHY, László	1942	–	–	–	–	–	+	+	+	–
ÓVÁRI, Miklós	1925	–	–	–	–	–	+	+	+	–
SARLÓS, István	1921	–	–	–	–	–	+	+	+	–
HUSZÁR, István	1927	–	–	–	–	–	+	–	–	–
HAVASI, Ferenc	1929	–	–	–	–	–	–	+	+	–
KOROM, Mihály	1927	–	–	–	–	–	–	+	–	–
LOSONCZI, Pál	1919	–	–	–	–	–	+	+	+	–
MÉHES, Lajos	1927	–	–	–	–	–	–	+	–	–
GRÓSZ, Károly	1930	–	–	–	–	–	–	–	+	+
HÁMORI, Csaba	1948	–	–	–	–	–	–	–	+	+
SZABÓ, István	1924	–	–	–	–	–	–	–	+	+
BERECZ, János	1931	–	–	–	–	–	–	–	–	+
CSEHÁK, Judit	1940	–	–	–	–	–	–	–	–	+
IVÁNYI, Pál	1942	–	–	–	–	–	–	–	–	+
LUKÁCS, János	1935	–	–	–	–	–	–	–	–	+
NÉMETH, Miklós	1948	–	–	–	–	–	–	–	–	+
POZSGAY, Imre	1933	–	–	–	–	–	–	–	–	+
TATAI, Ilona	1935	–	–	–	–	–	–	–	–	+
Total:		11	12	13	11	13	14	13	13	11

Notes: + = member; − = nonmember.
* First secretary, 10/56–3/85; secretary general, 3/85–5/88; chairman, 4/88–4/89.
** Candidate member. This category of Politburo membership was abolished at the 10th HSWP Congress in 1970.
Sources: HSWP Seventh, Eighth, Ninth, Tenth, Eleventh, Twelfth, and Thirteenth Congress; and stenographic minutes of the HSWP National Conference, May 20–22, 1988.

Appendix 1.2 *Hungarian Socialist Workers' Party: organization of the Party Center in 1986*

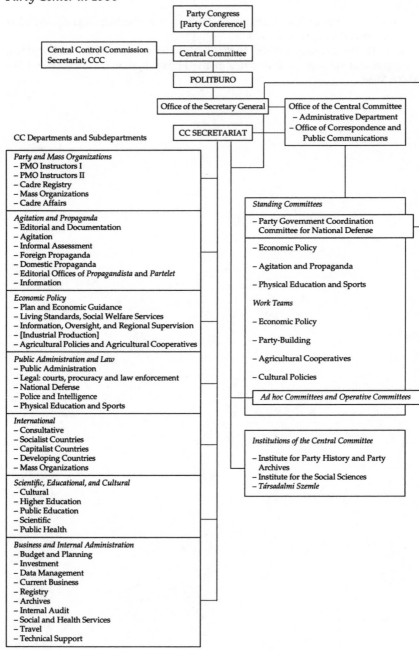

Appendix 1.3   *Speakers at HSWP congressional debates, by place in party and state hierarchy, 1970–85*

Speakers	10th	11th	12th	13th	Avg.	%
	\[Party Congress\]					
National party leaders	10	10	6	6	8	13.5
Regional and local party executives	9	17	18	12	14	23.6
State administration National-level executives	2	4	5	3	3.5	5.9
Regional and local executives	2	0	3	2	1.7	2.9
Culture, science, education	12	8	6	6	8	13.5
Mass organizations	5	4	3	10	5.5	9.3
Local production (industrial and agricultural manuals and managers at all levels)	17	18	17	22	18.5	31.3
Total	57	61	58	61	59.2	100.0

Source: HSWP Tenth, Eleventh, Twelfth, and Thirteenth Congress

2   Economic reforms: from plan to market

In this chapter I will present evidence on the origins, evolution, and periodic crises of the Hungarian command economy and discuss the ways in which the political leadership sought to overcome the country's economic difficulties that arose in the system-management (1963–80) phase of Kádár's rule in Hungary. The principal subject of the following discussion is the New Economic Mechanism (NEM) of 1968 and its short- and long-term impact on Hungary. In terms of its intended and unintended consequences, the inauguration of the NEM was by far the most significant policy decision made by the Kádár regime during its thirty-three-year reign in Hungary. The NEM unleashed a wide array of thitherto latent political and social forces and also set in motion a process of complex systemic change that the regime could neither foresee nor control.

The policy intent behind the introduction of economic reforms in communist party states was to overcome the intrinsic limitations of the classical Stalinist plan-driven command economy. These limitations become manifest upon the exhaustion of the internal resources (capital, material, and labor) of the extensive mode of a communist party state's economic development. Declining rates of growth and productivity, diminishing yields from additional material and labor inputs, and the ideologically constrained inelasticity of the available wage incentives were the most tangible manifestations of this process.

Pressures for economic reforms arise when the existing political and institutional guidance mechanisms of the state are seen by the party leadership as inadequate for the promotion of further economic development and the preservation of political legitimacy. From the early 1960s on, economic reforms of various kinds were introduced throughout the Soviet bloc. Although each of the national reform programs was different in terms of scope, depth, and duration, all began (and often ended) with the addressing of the symptoms rather than the ideological and structural causes of the underlying malaise. Reforms of this kind generally consisted of the ruling parties' cautious tinkering with the administrative structures of the existing programs rather than of radical changes in resource-allocation priorities, industrial decentralization, and the introduction of new wage incentives in the workplace.[1]

To introduce drastic changes in economic policies is a politically risky proposition. To the extent that such measures, say, as the decentralization of economic decision-making tend to confer a degree of autonomy on regional and local managers of enterprises, the integrity of the political regime's vertical command structure may be jeopardized by unauthorized local initiatives.[2] In this and in many similar cases when the hitherto sovereign central decision-makers delegate substantial authority to nonparty subordinates, two principles – those of the Leninist primacy of politics and of cost-benefit-conscious economic rationality are on a potential collision course.

Radical economic reforms inevitably affect the existing power relationships of a communist regime. Over time jurisdictional conflicts develop between the political center and the regime's local officials. Moreover, the implementation of reform measures tends to upset the traditional distribution of power and authority among the party and the state and the various bureaucratic entities that are entrusted with the direct management of new reform programs. To gain rank-and-file support for drastic policy innovations, the political leadership must propose some kind of doctrinal justification of its new policies.[3]

Reform measures also impinge upon the basic terms of the unwritten social contract between the regime and the people. The "quid" of the reform-generated social-welfare package must be acceptable to the intended recipients as fair exchange for the "quo" of continued citizen compliance with the laws, informal rules, and expectations of the political incumbents. Therefore, the new party line should seek to preserve existing loyalties yet contain provisions to accommodate the interests of the nonparty majority. Drastic economic reforms pose several short-term risks but offer few and uncertain long-term benefits.

(A)   From traditional economy to Stalinist shock therapy, 1938–53

On the eve of the Second World War Hungary was economically a less-developed European country. By "less developed" I refer to Hungary's relative position, with its 1937 per capita national income of $120, in a European continuum between Great Britain ($440) and

Greece ($92). In this regard the countries closest to Hungary were Czechoslovakia ($170), Italy ($135), Poland ($100), Spain ($95), Portugal ($93), and Greece ($92). However, unlike Czechoslovakia and Austria, which derived 52/33 and 43/35 percent of their respective national income from industry and agriculture, these percentages were 36/37 for Hungary.[4]

In structural terms, the prewar Hungarian economy was rather similar to those of its East European neighbors. The national economy rested on five fragile pillars: 1. a large, undercapitalized, and inefficient agricultural sector; 2. privately owned light and manufacturing industries; 3. state-owned and -managed telecommunications, transportation, and related mining and equipment-fabrication industries; 4. a substantial agricultural cooperative marketing arrangement and a well-developed commercial and retail sector; and 5. a partly foreign-controlled and relatively weak private banking sector.[5]

Because of the country's size, location, and relatively high dependence on foreign trade, the economy was vulnerable to external exigencies, such as the Great Depression in the early 1930s, as well as to politically motivated autarkic constraints on regional trade. Moreover, chronic shortages of domestic investment capital necessitated the large-scale influx of foreign, mainly German, but also French, Italian, and British investment in Hungarian banks and light industries.

Although still a predominantly agricultural economy, with one-half of the labor force employed (in 1941) in agriculture and one-fourth in industry, Hungary had a more than adequate infrastructure, relatively modern transportation and communications networks, and sufficient health, social service, educational, and technological resources to provide for a balanced, if slow, growth of the economy. Given these constraints on economic capabilities, the governments of the day and the business elites and, later on, communist economic planners had two basic options for the attainment of higher rates of economic growth.

The first might be conceptualized as a combination of a mixed economy that involved an economically active state and a vigorous private sector, aided by a substantial participation of foreign investment capital. With the confiscation of German assets in Hungary by the Soviet Union, the nationalization of all foreign assets, and the communist regime's rejection of assistance from the Marshall Plan, such external resources were unavailable until the late 1950s. The second and, with the onset of the Cold War, the only other option was a state-sponsored thoroughgoing mobilization of the country's human and material resources for economic revitalization and higher rates of growth.

With respect to strategies for the promotion of rapid economic development, one must call attention to the essential continuity of such policies in pre- and postwar Hungary. In 1937 the Darányi government launched a major program of public works and of the targeted development of defense industries. Here the dual objective was to overcome the still-lingering effects of the Great Depression and to make preparations for the coming war.[6] The postwar coalition government had, in effect, continued the Darányi program – this time to rebuild a war-devastated national economy. With the communist takeover the initially noncommunist Three Year Plan (TYP)[7] of reconstruction and economic revitalization was promptly transformed into yet another crash program of economic development, the first FYP.[8] Although the communist-sponsored FYPs were qualitatively different from similar undertakings that had been mounted by their bourgeois predecessors, all three programs sought solutions to the same generic problems of economic backwardness, underindustrialization, and scarcity of domestic investment capital.

In addition to severe losses in human lives, Hungary also sustained extremely high material losses during the war. The extent of damage in buildings and equipment was valued at 40 percent of all national assets, or about 500 percent of Hungary's 1938 national income of Hungarian Pengő (HP) 5.5 Bn, which, with the 1938 exchange rate of 1 US\$ = 5 HP, amounted to US\$ 5 Bn.[9] War reparation payments to the USSR, Czechoslovakia, and Yugoslavia absorbed one-third of all government expenditures between 1945 and 1949. Contributions to the cost of maintaining the Soviet occupational forces placed additional burdens on the economy.[10]

The first postwar years witnessed a series of economic changes of unprecedented scope and intensity. These included the comprehensive land reform of 1945–6 that prompted the distribution of approximately 6 million hectares to more than 400,000 new small farmers;[11], the hyperinflation, then of world-record dimensions, of 1945–6; and the massive transfer of Hungary's manufacturing, mining, and commercial (all wholesale and some retail) enterprises and rental housing assets from private to state ownership. By the end of 1949 the state became virtually the sole owner of the bulk of Hungary's industry, transportation, banking, and commerce (see Table 2.1).

The nationalization of key industrial assets, such as mines, steel mills, and railroads, was a widespread trend in postwar Europe. Given

Table 2.1   *State ownership in Hungary, Three Year Plan of 1947–9*[12]

Economic sector	7/1947 %	7/1948 %	12/1948 %	12/1949 %
Mining	91	91	91	100
Industry	38	80	87	100
Transportation	98	98	98	100
Commercial banking	–	95	95	95
Commerce (wholesale)	–	16	75	100
Commerce (retail)	–	–	20	30

the East European states' traditional position as owners of significant industrial resources, the communist-sponsored drive for the socialization of the "means of production" may be seen as a natural, albeit ideologically exaggerated, extension of this process. However, what actually took place in Hungary and elsewhere in East Europe may be explained by the local communists' sense of urgency to consolidate their political positions and by the regimes' efforts to satisfy Moscow's demands for assistance in the rebuilding of the war-shattered Soviet economy.

The main driving force behind the sweeping economic changes that were inaugurated by the constantly upwardly revised TYP was the Hungarian Workers' Party (HWP) or, more specifically, the political will of Mátyás Rákosi, Ernő Gerő, and the rest of the party leadership, which also included Imre Nagy and János Kádár. The Rákosi–Gerő team pursued three ambitious and, in terms of feasibility, utterly unrealistic goals. Briefly, these were: (1) the radical structural transformation, in less than five years, of Hungary from a semiagrarian into a predominantly industrialized economy and the targeting of industrial production to dovetail with the immediate needs of the Soviet crash program of rearmament and preparations for a war with the West; (2) in addition to the complete collectivization of agriculture, the "total liquidation of [the] backwardness" of the agricultural sector; and (3) the radical 50 percent increase in living standards and commensurate improvement in the delivery of educational, health, and cultural services by the end of the first FYP. As Rákosi exlained at the December 14, 1950, meeting of the HWP CC: "(a) good plan is a taut plan ... it is one that you can reach only on your tiptoes."[13]

Hungary's industrial investments in percentages of national income were higher than those committed by Bulgaria, Czechoslovakia, Poland, and, for its first FYP, by the USSR (see Table 2.2). Moreover,

Table 2.2   *Socialist industrialization programs: resource commitments by seven states*[14]

State	Investments in percentage of national income	Industrial investments as percentage of all investments	Heavy and construction industry investments as percentage of industrial investments
Bulgaria, 1st FYP	19.6	43.1	83.5
Czechoslovakia, 1st FYP	22.3	40.6	78.1
Poland, Six Year Plan	21.6	45.4	75.0
Hungary, 1st FYP	25.2	51.7	92.1
GDR, 1st FYP	–	53.9	75.2
Romania, 1st FYP	–	53.4	82.6
USSR, 1st FYP	–	49.1	85.7
USSR, 2nd FYP	–	47.8	83.1
USSR, fulfillment of investment plan for 1946–50	21.0	–	–

war damages notwithstanding, the level of Hungary's industrial development in 1949 was higher than that of Bulgaria, Romania, and Poland and even that of the USSR in the mid-1920s. Therefore, investment rates of the Hungarian magnitude may have caused even more severe socioeconomic dislocations than did those that materialized in the course of similar undertakings in these four countries.

The victims of Rákosi's reckless experiment in social engineering and rapid industrialization were the Hungarian people and the Hungarian economy. The regime promised a 50 percent increase in living standards, but this failed to materialize until the end of the 1950s. Indeed, in the fourth year (1953) of the first FYP the population's share (food, shelter, clothing) from the redistribution of the national income was still the same as it had been in 1949. On the other hand, "other consumption," that is, material inputs into the investment-hungry industrial–military sector, were up by 462 percent.

The first FYP left a burdensome long-term macroeconomic legacy that Rákosi's successors were compelled to address in the coming decades. The most important aspects of Hungary's Stalinist economic heritage were structural imbalance, misplaced investment priorities, and the cumulative growth of opportunity costs of repairing the initial damage to the long-term viability of the economy. Indeed, it may not be idle speculation to suppose that had Kádár inherited a less devastated and misaligned economy, he, like his "revolution-free" neighbors, might have opted for incremental changes rather than embarking on an open-ended program of radical economic reforms.

(B)   Resource allocation for economic development – investment cycles and diminishing returns

Standard pathologies of development strategies in Soviet-type command economies tend to emphasize themes of relative economic backwardness, underdeveloped industries and weak infrastructure, inefficient agriculture, and surplus unskilled labor as partial explanations for the "constrained choices" made by communist economic policy-makers. Such diagnoses are further refined by references to Marxist–Leninist ideological biases and the precedent-setting nature of the Soviet scenario.[15]

Diagnostic literature of the "what went wrong?" kind on the Hungarian regime's economic performance that appeared in the early 1980s sought to transcend the limitations of previous self- and regime-censored writings and raised new questions about the political leadership's economic policy-making record since 1949. As a noneconomist, *my* purpose in considering this literature is to identify and make use of objective data and interpretation to determine the proper place of the NEM within the broader matrix of Hungary's postwar economic development. In so doing, I am seeking to embed the "NEM experience" not as a series of serendipitous events but as an organic component of longitudinal trends in patterns of resource allocation and economic policy-making in Hungary.[16]

The general thrust of the Hungarian investment-cycle literature is that the country's postwar economic development is divisible into seven discrete "macrocycles." These are the periods between (1) 1945–52, (2) 1953–8, (3) 1959–64, (4) 1966–72, (5) 1973–9, (6) 1980–6, and (7) 1987–94(?). Each odd-numbered cycle – that is, 1945–52, 1959–64, and so on – is inaugurated by political mobilization and major structural changes in the economy. In terms of resource-allocation priorities, these periods are characterized by high levels of investments – mainly into the "sector A" category of raw-material extraction and heavy-industry projects. The needed investment resources are derived primarily from funds diverted from agriculture, public consumption, and infrastructure.[17]

Each odd-numbered cycle terminates with declining growth rates and renewed grassroots pressures for higher living standards. The even-numbered cycles are devoted to efforts for the consolidation of previous quantitative gains and to the restoration, mainly by increased public consumption, of sociopolitical stability. In the end, and depending on how well the leadership's learning curve works at that juncture, preparations are made for a (somewhat modified) resumption of the regime's ideologically imprinted program of intensive development.

The longitudinal evolution of these cycles may best be demonstrated by juxtaposing several indices of Hungary's economic development between 1945 and 1989 (see Table 2.3).

Next to the astonishingly high rate of 40 percent net annual accumulation in the initial period 1945–52, there are three other noteworthy aspects of these data. First, that in odd-numbered intensive-growth cycles the rate of accumulation invariably exceeds that of investment. In other words, units of investment above and beyond those that may be effectively utilized in production yield declining rates of output. Second, that with a thirty-year annual average rate of growth of 3.6 percent of public consumption (versus 5.1 percent of net annual accumulation), the principal victim of the regime's "taut" FYPs and program of forced economic development was the Hungarian public.

Another way of assessing the record of the regime's resource-allocation priorities between 1950 and 1987 is to consider the intensity of the economy's structural transformation in each investment cycle. By juxtaposing the share of industry and construction in the capital stock of the economy at the beginning of each cycle (it was 13 percent in 1950) and this sector's share in the total capital investments of this period (50 percent), we arrive at an index of "investment intensity" by dividing the latter by the former. Thus, $50 \div 13 = 3.85$. When the same calculation is performed for agriculture, infrastructure, and total material production in each investment cycle, we obtain a compelling macroperspective on the Hungarian Stalinist and post- Stalinist leaderships' investment policies for the past four decades (Table 2.4).

The policy of deliberately withholding investment resources from the infrastructural and, to a lesser extent, from the agricultural sectors is evident, and its consequences will be discussed at a later point. However, what is of considerably greater importance are the compounding effects, over time, of the regime's resource commitments to industry and construction. Indices of lesser magnitude, such as 2.53 for 1959–65 and 1.62 for 1966–72, are calculated on the basis of cumulative relative capital stock ratios of industry and construction; therefore,

Table 2.3   *Hungarian national income: production, domestic utilization, accumulation, public consumption, and imports, 1945–89*[18]

Years	Average annual increase				
	Production %	Domestic utilization %	Net accumulation %	Public consumption %	Imports %
1945–52	14.1	14.8	40.0	6.0	14.4
1953–8	4.9	4.3	2.2	7.2	5.1
1959–65	5.2	5.8	10.9	4.0	13.2
1966–72	6.5	6.3	8.3	5.5	9.8
1972–9	4.9	5.3	9.9	4.0	12.7
1980–7	1.0	−1.4	−12.0	1.2	5.8
1949–89	4.6	4.1	5.1	3.6	10.8

Table 2.4   *Indices of change in structure of capital assets, Hungary, 1950–87*[19]

Years	Industry and construction	Agriculture	Infrastructure	Total material production
1950–8	3.85	1.00	0.54	2.85
1959–65	2.52	1.29	0.53	2.21
1966–72	1.62	1.48	0.62	1.52
1973–9	1.14	1.08	0.92	1.13
1980–7	1.07	1.00	0.95	1.05
1950–87	2.85	1.35	0.61	1.68

these seemingly more moderate outlays of investment resources were only marginally effective in restoring the equilibrium of capital stocks for balanced, let alone structurally flexible, growth.

In the early 1980s agreement was prevalent among Hungarian economists that the regime's economic difficulties had been rooted in the Stalinist political leadership's unwise investment decisions for the first FYP.[20] There is considerable merit to this proposition in so far as the initial outlays on capital-intensive but expensive-to-maintain low- and medium-technology industries and gigantic – at least on the Hungarian scale – prestige projects were concerned. After 1955 each successive Politburo and government was confronted with two capital investment alternatives: writing off misplaced investments in plant and equipment or "throwing good money after bad" – making the most of what there was and, at a minimum, keeping afloat the loss-making monuments of socialist industrialization with additional infusions of scarce investment capital.

(C)   The NEM: controlled experiment or commitment to radical change?

Continuity of embedded ideological priorities, political and economic institutions, and government personnel were the main political characteristics of the process of "recapturing and consolidating the people's power" in Hungary. The elimination of both reformers (Imre Nagy) and Stalinists (Ernő Gerő) from the political leadership gave Kádár an opportunity to replace the economic planning government apparat with cadres who shared his political preference for gradual change.

Political continuity and economic change

Senior Central Committee staff member Ágnes Ságvári's memoirs speak of the party's "unsmiling reserves," particularly of the heavy-industry lobby in 1957.[21] The latter consisted of cadres from the county party committees, the economic branch ministries, the National Planning Office and the Trade Union Federation. Throughout the party and government apparat, members of this group chose not to remember what had happened in October 1956 and kept vetoing proposals for cutbacks in large investments and price supports. Of the government's eleven economic ministries, only in *one* (Finance) were there more than one or two ministerial changes between 1957 and 1967.[22] In any event, *all* of the incumbent senior government bureaucrats had served in similar or identical positions in the Rákosi era.

Between 1958 and 1965 the regime initiated two national economic plans: the second TYP (1958–60) and the second FYP (1961–5). The near-doubling in the course of the second TYP of industrial production was more than matched by the more than fourfold increase of real wages – albeit at the expense of agricultural production and the fivefold increase of imports (see Table 2.5).

It was at this point, that is, between 1958 and 1960, when the regime implemented a new strategy for the better utilization of productive capacities that had been created by previous investments and for the accelerated development of selected priority industries in Hungary. Pursuant to the Khrushchev–Kádár agreements of March 1958, the

Table 2.5   *Second Three Year Plan, 1958–60, projections and actual rates*[23]

Category	Rate of growth	
	Plan %	Fact %
National income	14.0	25.0
Industrial output	22.0	39.0
Agricultural output	12.0	3.0
Construction	20.0	51.0
Real wages	2.5	11.0
Imports	−8.0	43.0
Exports	38.0	79.0

Hungarian regime's next step was deeper and wider integration with the Council for Mutual Economic Aid and Assistance (CMEA), as well as with the Soviet economy. Prospects of a greatly increased volume of (mainly barter) trade with CMEA partners and those of the opening of the vast Soviet market seemed irresistible to the PB's economic sages and, to use Khrushchev's phrase, to the "Hungarian metal-eaters" as well.

These optimistic expectations received new impetus from the resolutions of the 21st CPSU congress of 1958, particularly the commitment (or slogan?) to "catch up and surpass" (*dognat' i peregnat'*; DIP) the West within the next twenty years.[24]

The regime's ideological euphoria was vigorously articulated in several party documents and reached a new high at the 8th HSWP congress in November 1962. With reference to economic development, the congress decided that

> between 1960 and 1980 we shall shall have a fourfold increase in the national income ... industrial output will increase fivefold ... [and] the majority industrial products will be of high technology in origin ... By 1980 the per capita consumption will be higher in Hungary than in the developed capitalist countries ... [and] by overfulfilling the [the targets] of our 15-year program of housing construction, we shall, within the next ten years, provide housing for every family...[25]

This rhetoric was just that, rather than a serious commitment to the prompt commencement of a "long march" to laying, within twenty years, the "material-technical foundations" for the building of communism. The regime's real priorities may be gleaned from Kádár's testy

rejoinder to a proposal that, in view of its rapid all-around development, Hungary should be renamed and called a socialist republic. As
Kádár put it, "There is a People's Republic that renamed itself and two
years later it is worse off than before. Let us not rush things."[26] Kádár
had Czechoslovakia in mind and, as Prague's economic, then political,
troubles kept mounting in the next six years, he proved to be right in
counseling patience to his party's ideological hotheads.

Data on annual changes in the utilization of national income
between 1962 and 1965 (not shown here) offer additional evidence for
raising questions about the meaning of the HSWP's economic
rhetoric.[27] With respect to the average annual rates of growth in
national income and in investments, Hungary's performance, similar
to that of its neighbors for 1961–5, showed unmistakable signs of rapid
decline (see Table 2.6). Whether this trend was due mainly to

Table 2.6   *Average annual rate of growth in national income and in
investment, CMEA states, 1951–65*[28]

State	National income			Investment		
	1951–5	1956–60	1961–5	1951–5	1956–60	1961–5
Bulgaria	12.2	9.6	6.7	12.3	17.7	7.9
Czechoslovakia	8.1	7.0	1.9	9.6	13.1	2.0
Poland	8.6	6.6	6.2	11.2	8.9	7.0
Hungary	5.7	6.0	4.1	11.1	13.1	4.7
GDR	13.1	7.1	3.4	17.7	14.6	5.0
Romania	14.2	6.6	9.1	18.3	13.6	11.2
USSR	11.3	9.2	6.5	12.1	13.1	5.5

exhaustion of the growth potentials of these countries' capital-intensive
transition from a semiagricultural to a relatively mature industrialized
stage of development or to the failure of the political regimes to make
better use of human and material resources for continued growth was
the question that confronted the political leaders and economic planners of the Soviet bloc in the early 1960s.[29]

*Reform options: preparations, decision-making, and policy
implementation*

The intellectual origins of the NEM reforms may be traced back to 1953
when prime minister Imre Nagy (an agricultural economist by
training) inaugurated his "New Course" reform policies. Early expert

commentaries on the desirability of changes in the "economic mechanism" (the phrase apparently was a Hungarian invention) touched on questions of bureaucratic guidance, excessive centralization, planning methods, quantitative versus qualitative success indicators, enterprise costs and profits and the like.[30]

Although DIP-inspired resource-allocation policies helped postpone the renewal of academic debate on reform options, in 1961, as Rezső Nyers recalled it in 1988, there had been a "hidden turn" in favor of proreform elements in the party.[31] One might surmise that this turn was due to Kádár's taking on the additional position of prime minister in September 1961.

It is still unclear whether Nyers' appointment at the 8th HSWP congress in November 1962 as a candidate member of the PB and CC secretary for economic policy was the result of routine rotation of key personnel and the replacement of the "rogue" former Social Democrat György Marosán with a "tame" one with no political ambitions or an opening gambit in Kádár's chess game for the revamping of the Hungarian economy.[32] One suspects the latter because in less than one year, Nyers – also the chair of the CC Standing Committee for the State Economy – began recruiting a "brains trust" (agytröszt) to explore ways to reform the economic guidance system in Hungary. This effort, as a follow-up to the CC's highly critical assessment of the results to date of the second FYP, received formal CC authorization in December 1964.[33]

Nyers' case for comprehensive economic reforms was first submitted to the November 18–20, 1965 meeting of the HSWP CC.[34] His main point was that both society and the economy had become too complex to respond to traditional methods of administrative guidance by the state and that such measures ought to be replaced by a complex set of economic policy tools to produce the desired results of economic growth and the democratization of public life.[35] The reasons, even from a perspective of three decades, for the bold coupling of these two objectives are still somewhat obscure.

In Nyers' version, as subsequently amplified by Kádár, by "democratization" the reformers initially understood the creation of new economic and political incentives to promote the hitherto passive lower-level middle managers' and local bureaucrats' active involvement in the implementation of reform measures. In any case, Nyers submitted,

> What would happen if we recommended and implemented only partial measures instead of comprehensive reforms? Our economic

life surely would not collapse. Improvements in methods of guidance could help enhance economic performance ... However, should we choose not to act now, this most certainly would not make reforms unnecessary, but merely postpone [needed action]. The main economic drawback [of delays] would be the narrowing of [the range of] choices and the opting for the "lesser evil." Then the choice will be between rapid, but unbalanced, economic growth and a balanced, but ever-decelerating, economic development. With the help of reforms we can do better ... Moreover ... the delayed solution of well-known economic problems could lead to political tensions.[36]

To persuade the skeptics, Nyers sought to demonstrate what the reforms would *not* do: the party cadres would not be replaced with experts and the enterprises would not be "self-managed," Yugoslav-style, but run by party-approved directors. Nyers insisted that by preserving the system of overall state regulation, "no concessions will be made to the spontaneity of the market." And, to square the circle, he assured his audience that reforms would usher in an age of "democratic centralism in the economy."[37]

As Nyers summarized it, the four main policy objectives of the proposed reforms were achievement of "economic development and balanced growth"; the improvement of the technological standards of production; improvement of the efficiency of foreign trade to help redress the adverse balance of payments; and, above all, improvement of the living standards of the working people.

Kádár reiterated Nyers' theme of "there is no alternative to reforms" and also put the matter in a broader perspective. He submitted that "our decision will determine the direction of Hungary's economic development, as well as the social issues for the next 15 years." He also reminded the CC that the radical rhetoric of the 1962 party congress, with its ambitious timetable of rapid transition to "full socialism" in twenty years, was a thing of the past.[38]

The CC, though undoubtedly torn by severe misgivings about the radical changes, unanimously approved the draft proposal for the introduction of the NEM on January 1, 1968.[39] Kádár put his full political authority on the line on behalf of his party's leap to a "more prosperous" and "more democratic" stage of building socialism in Hungary. The final version of the NEM reform package was submitted by Nyers to the May 25–27, 1966 meeting of the CC for discussion and formal approval.[40]

Upon a careful review of what Kádár and Nyers actually proposed under sixteen specific headings of this document, one wonders whether even they realized the magnitude, let alone the full political implications, of the changes they recommended. Administrative action on *any* of the affected policy areas would have had significant ripple effects on the rest of the political and economic system. Simultaneous action, if taken on all these matters, would have amounted to nothing less than a reinvention of the entire system.

Nyers took great pains to explain that the leadership was not about to legislate itself out of existence and would preserve, notwithstanding the NEM, all of its prerogatives of power. As Nyers explained, the state would remain the owner or, in case of agricultural land, the *de facto* possessor of all means of production; the government's right to make strategic investments, levy taxes, and control the distribution of social incomes would be preserved, as would its authority to issue decrees and to define budgetary parameters for allocations among the productive branches of the economy.

Moreover, the central planning agencies would remain intact and be entrusted with new responsibilities of priority setting and policy oversight. Concerning the latter, the most important lever – that of central control of personnel decisions – would remain firmly in the party's hands.[41] However, what mattered most to his listeners, the apparat, particularly the regional and local party committees, would still retain their powers "as defined by the [currently] authorized scope of their decisional competency."[42]

Economic reforms: the more things change the more they remain the same?

The technical details and some of the more obvious political and economic consequences of the initial NEM package are well described in the standard literature and therefore will not be discussed here.[43] Instead, I shall consider the policy implications of several items of the reform agenda that had a critical bearing on the mid- and long-term political stability of the Hungarian regime.

Reform of the price system was intended to compel the enterprises to make better use of productive assets and to bring their costs closer to market prices. Because 70 percent of goods and services were still sold at state-controlled prices, enterprise profitability had to be measured more by the success of internal juggling of accounts, depreciation schedules, tax liabilities, and the still largely fixed labor costs than by the production and marketing skills of the management. Industry-wide cost/price inequalities were further exacerbated by state preferences (loans and price subsidies) granted to priority dollar and ruble export industries and defense-related enterprises.

Kádár wanted to put an end to the "ignoble competition for investment funds" and replace it with "noble socialist competition for investment resources."[44] However, given the chaos in cost and price policies, enterprise managers had no choice but to ignore the, to them, undoubtedly incomprehensible ethical difference between these two ways of garnering needed investment funds from the supervisory ministries.

Incomes policies spawned by the NEM reforms were the most volatile aspect of the entire proposition. At issue was, on the one hand, the balancing act between egalitarian and achievement-based wage policies, and on the other, that of the differentiated compensation of the top and middle enterprise management and the workers on the shop floor. The regime's incomes policies provided for a complex system of cash and in-kind payments (see Table 2.7). Whereas the employees – human nature being what it is – took their entitlements and fringe benefits for granted, it was the threat of reform-induced differentiation in take-home pay and the thitherto guaranteed annual rises in the same that proved to be the eventual political undoing of *this* aspect of the NEM.

Closely linked to blue-collar and managerial incomes was the compensation of those working in the agricultural sector. Kádár may have sounded reassuring to the CC when saying that "we represent the interests of the working class together with those of the peasantry but, if we must, against the peasantry."[45]

The agricultural workers' inclusion in the state retirement system was a useful step, but insufficient to make up for the average 10 percent difference between the living standards of the cooperative peasantry and the blue-collar workers. The proposed solution of permitting the fuller utilization of household plots and the marketing of the products of the same was helpful, at least in the short run. The authorization of the agricultural cooperatives' embarking on profit-making off-season nonagricultural entrepreneurial activities (equipment repair, small-scale manufacturing, and contract labor) was the first step toward restoration of private enterprise in the Hungarian countryside. In less than five years average agricultural incomes, particularly those of the dual-income "peasant workers," matched and exceeded average industrial wages (see Table 2.8).

Table 2.7   *Growth in per capita real income 1961–90 (in constant [Hungarian Forint] prices)*[46]

Year	Cash income %	Of which: FW %	FSB %	LIK %	DI %	SBIK %	ADI %	Of which: FW %	FSB %
1961	1.5	nd	7.4	−3.3	0.5	2.9	0.8	−0.2	4.6
1962	5.1	nd	6.5	−3.3	3.4	7.5	3.9	3.0	7.1
1963	7.4	nd	9.4	−2.1	5.6	8.1	5.9	5.2	8.6
1964	7.3	nd	6.9	−1.2	5.8	5.7	5.8	5.2	6.2
1965	2.0	0.9	8.6	−7.7	0.4	2.7	0.7	−0.7	5.0
1966	5.6	4.2	15.4	4.7	5.4	2.4	5.1	4.3	7.7
1967	7.2	7.5	9.0	3.8	6.7	4.2	6.4	6.7	6.3
1968	8.1	7.5	9.4	−2.0	6.5	4.6	6.3	5.8	6.7
1969	7.4	7.1	7.2	−2.7	5.9	5.7	5.9	5.4	6.4
1970	8.4	7.2	12.2	0.8	7.4	6.8	7.3	6.1	9.2
1971	5.4	4.4	7.3	−3.3	4.2	4.7	4.2	3.1	6.0
1972	3.8	3.0	9.4	−2.6	3.0	5.7	3.3	2.1	7.6
1973	5.8	4.5	13.9	−4.4	4.5	5.8	4.7	3.2	10.0
1974	7.6	6.0	14.3	−3.5	6.4	5.3	6.2	4.8	10.1
1975	5.0	3.8	12.9	−3.5	4.2	5.8	4.4	2.9	9.8
1976	0.5	−0.9	7.9	−1.5	0.3	4.6	0.9	−1.0	6.5
1977	5.2	5.3	6.0	3.8	5.0	4.1	4.9	5.1	5.1
1978	2.9	3.0	2.7	−1.9	2.4	5.4	2.9	2.5	4.1
1979	−0.5	−2.4	7.3	−1.6	−0.5	2.5	−0.2	−2.3	5.2
1980	0.0	−1.6	5.5	−1.4	−0.1	3.8	0.4	−1.6	4.8
1981	3.1	2.3	3.3	0.5	2.9	3.9	3.0	2.1	3.6
1982	0.5	0.0	2.1	−1.0	0.4	4.6	1.0	−0.1	3.2
1983	1.4	0.4	2.2	−1.3	1.2	1.6	1.2	0.2	1.9
1984	1.2	1.3	3.9	−0.1	1.1	1.9	1.2	1.2	3.0
1985	2.4	3.0	2.0	−4.7	1.9	3.0	2.1	2.2	2.4
1986	3.1	3.7	3.1	−3.9	2.6	2.5	2.6	3.0	2.9
1987	0.3	0.1	1.6	6.6	0.7	2.9	1.0	0.6	2.2
1988	−1.2	−7.0	9.9	3.3	−0.9	−1.9	−1.0	−6.1	4.9
1989	2.6	−0.7	6.6	4.4	2.7	4.2	2.9	−0.4	5.6
1990	−1.1	−1.9	−2.2	3.4	−1.2	−3.8	−1.5	−1.5	−2.9

Note: FW = from work; FSB = from social benefits; LIK = labor income in kind; DI = disposable income; SBIK = social benefits in kind; ADI = adjusted disposable income

Table 2.8 *Per capita annual income of social groups, by source, 1965–70*[47]

Social group	Income from work and other sources		Social benefits				Total	
			cash		in kind			
	1965	1970	1965	1970	1965	1970	1965	1970
Workers	11,129	15,035	1,041	1,915	1,813	2,547	13,983	19,497
White collar	14,652	20,428	1,349	2,212	2,586	3,563	18,586	26,203
Peasants	11,172	16,621	565	981	1,291	1,862	13,028	19,464
Dual income	11,808	15,533	681	1,126	1,279	1,856	13,768	20,289
Independent	13,726	18,654	452	857	1,577	2,159	15,755	21,661
Pensioneers	4,148	5,721	4,895	6,827	1,996	2,803	11,039	15,351
Average for all recipients	11,364	15,818	1,239	2,135	1,782	2,541	14,385	20,494

Note: In current Hungarian Forints

A new relationship between the enterprises and the state's agencies of administrative-fiscal oversight (the National Planning Office, the Ministry of Finance, the economic branch ministries, the Hungarian National Bank, and the banking system) was to be the centerpiece of the NEM. On the one hand, the directors general and managers of trusts and enterprises were endowed with a great deal of formal autonomy. On the other hand, they were the administrative creatures of the supervisory ministry and the political pawns of the county or major city party committees. They acted as provisional caretakers of state-owned assets, and their executive powers – be these the organization of production, the maintenance of labor discipline, fiscal planning, pricing, and marketing – were severely circumscribed by laws, decrees, administrative regulations, trade union prerogatives, and formal and informal political pressures and expectations.

Disparities in managerial ability to promote the enterprise's goals in a sheltered business environment were exacerbated by the regime's policies of industrial recentralization in the 1960s. With the incorporation of many small and medium-size enterprises into large trusts, or as subsidiaries of major enterprises, the average manager, if his firm was taken over by a trust or a conglomerate, got another bureaucratic layer over his head.

Regime rhetoric to the contrary, the enterprise directors' real goal of "management by objective" was not profits and market share but political survival by getting along in the impenetrable jungle of constantly shifting political power relationships. As János Kornai explained,

> The firm's manager watches the customer and the supplier with one eye and his superiors in the bureaucracy with the other eye. Practice teaches him that it is more important to keep the second eye wide open: managerial career, the firm's life and death, taxes, subsidies and credit, prices and wages, all financial "regulators" affecting the firm's prosperity, depend more on the higher authorities than on market performance.[48]

Traditionally, the trade unions were the enterprise managers' partners rather than adversaries in socialist party states. In their role as the "best friends of the management" the unions had shared interests in seeing the enterprise prosper and even make profits from the fruits of "wage labor." On the other hand, the endorsement of differentiated wage policies, including the introduction of performance-linked large bonuses to upper and middle management, called for abandonment of its essential blue-collar constituency, particularly the "core group" (törzsgárda) of middle-aged and older workers with substantial seniority on the shop floor. As a group, these skilled and semiskilled workers were the social backbone of one-party rule and the intended beneficiaries of the "dictatorship" that the regime asserted it had exercised on their behalf.

The accommodation of this key constituency's interests in total job security, guaranteed pay raises, and the "we are paddling in the same boat" mentality toward attempts at income differentiation by performance and quality skills inputs into production was a daunting challenge to the party and the unions. The problem was further exacerbated by the influx, since the early 1960s, of hundreds of thousands of commuting peasant workers from the countryside. By 1970 every fifth industrial and every third construction worker was a peasant-worker commuter.[49]

These new arrivals came to make money rather than to become parts of the enterprise community. They sought to supplement their incomes from household plots and owed no loyalty to the incumbent törzsgárda. Moreover, albeit at the cost of eighty-hour workweeks at home and factory, these "dual-income" workers earned more than did their "7-to-3" coworkers at the enterprise. The implementation of new policies of wage differentiation tended to isolate and alienate the conservative blue-collar labor force and made the issue of higher earnings by dual-income types a crucial ideological debating point, as well as a mobilizable political counterweight, against the reformist party center for the opponents of the NEM.

The party's role in the NEM was that of "political guidance, coordination, and control." According to the CC's policy guidelines, the party organs were not "anywhere and at any time" to assume direct management of economic activities.[50] The Nyers-led reform initiative permitted the entry, and was responsible for the growing influence, of a new breed of economists, technocrats, and assorted reform ideologues in the policy process. These newcomers, including some resuscitated New Course (1953) reform economists, argued for new standards of policy-making rationality.[51]

Those segments of the apparat that had been excluded, even in a consultative sense, from preparations leading to the enactment of the CC's reform decisions had a legitimate grievance over the party center's secretive deliberations and the PB's habit of policy-making by fiat. These concerns, as much as the anticipated adverse outcomes of NEM policy initiatives, were responsible for the surfacing of open discontent and recurring demands of the "improvement of the working methods" of the party's leading organs, particularly those of the PB.[52] As will be discussed below, the informal antireform coalition of conservative apparatchiki remained, well into the 1980s, a permanent undercurrent in the party's internal life.

The NEM: an interim balance sheet

Let us next consider the NEM in terms of its positive short- and long-term accomplishments. In the most general sense, it was hope – for a better life and perhaps a modest expansion of the sphere of "small freedoms" – that the reforms promised to most Hungarians. It seemed to many that a decade after the 1956 revolution the regime was ready to begin to deliver on its part of the unwritten social contract. In this respect, the record is fairly unambiguous.

The second main accomplishment of the NEM was the initiation of a process of the regime's institutional devolution. The formal endowment of the government and the state agencies with substantial decision-making responsibilities for the execution of reform measures was the first step toward the functional differentiation between, and eventual separation, of the party and the state.

The process of institutional hybridization did not end there. The party's upgrading of the political status of "mass organizations," such as the TUF, the YCL, the National Council of Agricultural Cooperatives (TOT), the National Alliance of [industrial and service] Cooperatives (KISOSZ), the Hungarian Academy of Sciences (MTA), and the Hungarian Chamber of Commerce, to assist with the realization of reform policies also conferred on them legitimate standing as institutional representatives of specific constituency interests.[53]

The NEM: retrenchment and policy drift

The first phase of the NEM came to an end at the November 1972 "mid-term" plenary session of the CC. The stated purpose was to review the implementation of the policy decisions of the 10th party congress of November 1970. However, the real agenda was the halting, drastic revamping and partial salvaging of the NEM.[54]

Western and Hungarian commentaries, both contemporary and recent, on the regime's sudden turnabout and the apparent abandonment of its bold reform program cite five reasons for this unexpected turn of events:

1 economic constraints on the fulfillment of plan targets in terms of industrial output, supply of consumer goods, growth of living standards, and the balance of payments;

2 internal political pressures, particularly from the trade unions and the heavy-industry lobby on behalf of blue-collar constituencies and large unprofitable enterprises, respectively;

3 pressures from the conservative regional party apparat seeking to recapture its influence over enterprises that had been lost to the economic branch ministries (ágazati minisztériumok) of the government;

4 pressures from central planning agencies seeking to regain control over the, to them inherently inimical, forces of the market and enterprise autonomy;

5 external pressures, mainly from Moscow, but also from the GDR, Czechoslovakia, and Bulgaria, that had been motivated by the NEM's perceived negative effects on the political and ideological coherence of the socialist camp.[55]

Although the published evidence supports all of these explanations, they are incomplete in three respects. First, they fail to account for the full range of internal constituency pressures on the HSWP PB; second, they fail to identify the policy and personality context of an aborted Soviet attempt to remove Kádár and replace him with a less independent leader; and third, they tend to overstate the dimensions of Kádár's retreat from his original reform agenda.

The arduous preparatory work, the "selling" of the NEM to the apparat, and the implementation of reform measures took a heavy toll on the health of Hungarian leaders and party workers alike. Jenő Fock and Béla Biszku suffered nervous breakdowns and had to be hospitalized in the mid-1960s.[56] According to reports from various county party committees, over one-third of full-time party workers required medical care owing to overwork and nervous exhaustion.[57] From the apparat's perspective, the NEM's incomes policies posed new threats to the party workers' sense of financial security and psychological well-being. Specifically, the party's new emphasis on expertise was perceived by many less-well-educated cadres as a threat to their job security.

As Zoltán Komócsin explained to the PB, "as the NEM progresses, [the apparat's] relative financial position will decline. Right now, I cannot find enough qualified candidates for full-time party work ... this is simply an existential matter." To this György Aczél added, "few younger people aspire for party work ... we have created titles, scientific degrees and have conferred honors [on such people], while [similar incentives] are unavailable to the leading and coordinating forces of our society."[58] For want of instant remedies, Mátyás Tóth, head of the CC Department of Party and Mass Organizations, recommended that government civil service equivalencies be developed between the party apparat and the state administration. "We might call it a social rank ladder," he added.[59] Although the PB vetoed the proposal recommending extension of the military/police early-retirement plan (at the age of 45) for the benefit of deserving party employees, measures were taken to transfer overworked cadres into less-demanding and better-paying positions in the state administration.[60]

Unlike the problem of apparat burn-outs who could be transferred to government jobs, the financial problems of the military and the internal security organs posed a qualitatively different kind of challenge to the leadership. According to Károly Csémi, the much-decorated veteran commander of the 1956–7 campaign to hunt down suspected counterrevolutionaries, "Our military pay scales are 25 to 30 percent behind" the comparable civilian pay scales. For this reason, "it is difficult to recruit good students to military academies," and this is why "non-commissioned officers go to work in industry rather than re-enlist in the military."[61]

As far as it can be ascertained from perusal of the Soviet press in the mid-1960s, the inauguration of the Hungarian NEM was received in guarded, but on the whole positive, terms.[62] However, such commentaries on the Hungarian reforms tended to link proposed policy changes with expressions of confidence in the person of János Kádár. *Pravda, Izvestiya,* and *Voprosy Ekonomiki* commentaries on the Hungarian NEM were still positive in 1968–9.[63] Hungary's involvement in the invasion of Czechoslovakia helped shelter the ongoing NEM experiment for several months from Soviet, though not necessarily from East German and Bulgarian, criticism.

However, as Károly Németh, then PB member and first secretary of the Budapest party committee, recalls, by 1969 the "Soviets were banging on the table" protesting the confusion and potential ideological contraband to which the NEM had given rise in Hungary. Németh was probably also right in saying that "other than a few reform economists and an occasional political leader, the Hungarian reforms never had any support in the USSR."[64]

Moscow's main problem with Kádár was that he had become too well ensconced in the Hungarian party. The eligible successors Béla Biszku and Zoltán Komócsin were ideologically sound and loyal to the Soviet Union, but neither had a substantial following in the rejuvenated Kádárite apparat. For a starter, the Kremlin called attention to "nationalist manifestations" and "Zionist intrigues" in Hungary that, as a February 3, 1972 *Pravda* report hinted, the Kádár team seemed unable to contain.[65] These potshots may have been sufficient to cast aspersions on the Jewish György Aczél and Lajos Fehér but not credible enough to dislodge the demonstratively pro-Soviet first secretary. If not removal, then an intensive "comradely consultation" seemed to be in order in early 1972.

Kádár's flying visit to Moscow (he preferred trains) and several meetings with Brezhnev between February 11 and 14, 1972 may have settled some matters but, judging from the disappointing results of prime minister Jenő Fock's negotiations with Alexei Kosygin six weeks later, not all was well between Moscow and Budapest.[66] Fock was seeking additional raw-material deliveries but had no luck "as to what proposals we could make that would greatly interest our Soviet comrades and would not only be good for the Soviet Union, but also useful and necessary for Hungary."[67]

Kádár wasted no time in responding to Soviet pressures. On May 10, 1972 he sent a letter to the HSWP PB in which he referred to his forthcoming sixtieth birthday (May 26, 1972) and asked that body's consent to his request to retire and relinquish his position as first secretary of the HSWP. In this, and in a follow-up letter to the PB, he asked to be relieved of his duties in early 1973. As he explained, "whether I like it or not, I must realistically face the fact that I have reached the age when one's capacity for work no longer increases; on the contrary, with the passage of time, it gradually decreases from year to year."[68]

Jenő Fock, who chaired the June 15, 1972 secret session of the CC, conveyed the PB's unanimous decision to reconfirm János Kádár's position as the party's first secretary. In an emotionally charged speech Kádár explained that he wanted out while the situation was stable in Hungary, but his PB colleagues convinced him to stay at the helm. Without debate, the CC unanimously endorsed the PB's decision. The subject of Kádár's voluntary retirement was thus laid to rest until June 1987.

Why did Kádár offer his resignation in the spring of 1972? Béla Biszku, who together with Károly Németh and Zoltán Komócsin had been suspected in party circles of being members of a Moscow-endorsed alternative leadership, flatly denied this accusation and proposed a different explanation for Kádár's actions. "I must admit that for the longest time I did not understand why he did it. No one tried to remove him. On the contrary, Komócsin, [Sándor] Gáspár and I talked him into staying at his post. What he really wanted was to strengthen his position by being reconfirmed by the CC."[69]

It appeared that Kádár's *fait accompli* checkmated what was widely rumored to have been Mikhail Suslov's initiative to remove him from power. The immediate results seemed to vindicate Kádár and possibly the ideological correctness of the NEM. On the occasion of his sixtieth birthday he was awarded the Order of Lenin and when Brezhnev came to visit in November of that year, the Soviet general secretary heaped effusive praise on Kádár as "an outstanding personality of the international communist movement." The evidence, however, suggests a rather different outcome that may, at best, be called a stalemate – and a short-lived one, at that.

Whether it was due to irresistible Soviet pressures or an impending mutiny of the senior apparat, or both, the fact remains that the outcome of the November 14–15, 1972 CC plenary session resulted in the leadership's halting, drastic revamping, and partial salvaging of the NEM.

By all appearances, the party conservatives and their Soviet sponsors won the battle: in the coming months many economic reform measures were rescinded; intraenterprise wage differentials were reduced; free-wheeling entrepreneurship was reined in, and bourgeois tendencies of profiteering and selfish individualism came under strong attack. Wage rises for blue-collar workers were freed from the constraints of productivity and enterprises profitability, and were increased by an unprecedented 5 percent, effective March 1, 1973.

As the unrepentant Sándor Gáspár explained in 1991, "I was a trade union leader and demanded that even at unprofitable enterprises there should be wage increases. To have a profitable enterprise with 15 percent pay hikes alongside a state-subsidized [loss-maker] with no pay raise was unacceptable."[70] According to Béla Biszku, Kádár, too, came to share Gáspár's views. When visiting the Ikarus bus factory, Kádár was appalled to learn that the "core workers" were earning 14 Forints an hour, while temporary contract workers from the agricultural cooperatives were costing the factory 25 Forints an hour.[71]

The next three years witnessed a further regression of economic policies into pathologies of the pre-NEM era. As shown in Tables 2.3 and 2.4, the "odd-numbered" cycle of investment patterns was revived; hundreds of agricultural cooperatives were merged into larger entitites; trade deficits and hard-currency indebtedness grew and the blue-collar workers benefited from yet another round of unearned wage hikes. Profit-making was "out," "socially useful" unpaid volunteer labor and "socialist work competition" were "in." Chairmen of successful agricultural cooperatives, particularly those with thriving industrial contract-labor operations, were hauled before the courts on suspicion of corruption and embezzlement.[72]

The party's ideological vigilantes finally had their turn: muckraking sociologists, revisionist philosophers, and signatories of abortion-on-demand petitions were sacked from their jobs, were pressured to leave the country, and were reprimanded, respectively.[73] The ideological impulse to "shoot the bearers of bad tidings" might be credited to the "workers' opposition" within the central apparat and their allies throughout the party. The size of this group cannot be determined, but sources indicate that Béla Biszku, Árpád Pullai, Sándor Jakab, Imre Párdi, and, although he denies it, Károly Grósz, then deputy head of the CC Department of Agitation and Propaganda, were leading members of this contingent.[74] Through the offices of these key party officials "came a weekly flood of confidential information indicating widespread opposition to [the party's] economic policies."[75] As Nyers saw it, internal information flows were "manipulated" by a "hidden organized opposition to show the need for central intervention."[76]

Judging from his contributions to internal PB and CC discussions on the "wild offshoots" of the NEM gone astray, Kádár also endorsed the party's ouvrierist or, as Nyers sarcastically put it, *munkásista*, hard line.[77] As the consequence of Kádár's distancing himself from the NEM, the reformers' situation became untenable by the end of 1973. As Nyers recalled, during a three-day visit to Moscow in that year, his customary Soviet party and state negotiating partners refused to see him. A line secretary of a ruling party is not supposed to be treated that way.[78]

In the spring of 1974, a year before the next scheduled (11th) party congress, Rezső Nyers and the party's reformist agricultural expert Lajos Fehér were dismissed.[79] Nyers lost his party position in the Secretariat and Fehér lost his government position as deputy prime minister. A year later both lost their seats in the PB, though they were allowed to remain members of the CC. Upon the departure of his closest political allies, Jenő Fock also resigned as prime minister, though he retained his seat in the PB for one additional term.[80] Their replacement with the Kádárist Károly Németh as CC secretary for economic affairs, with the former Central Planning Office bureaucrat György Lázár as prime minister, and with a few quickly promoted younger apparatchiki, marked the completion of Kádár's payment on his end of the political-ideological bargain with Brezhnev.

Kádár's retreat was not a rout, though it seemed so to many at that time, but a temporary setback that left him with sufficient resources to get even with his internal opponents. Whether it was in response to another botched Brezhnev initiative to replace Kádár or it just happened, the fact remains that between the end of 1976 and April 1978, Árpád Pullai, Imre Párdi, and Béla Biszku lost their party positions. However, most of their clients in the party apparat escaped Kádár's wrath at that time.[81] With the ideological purists of the "workers' opposition" out of the way, Kádár's position in the party was safe again for the time being.

(D)   "Escape forward": economic adaptation and policy constraints

Political damage control and the purge of disloyal associates were manageable propositions for the head of a ruling party with twenty-two years of on-the-job seniority. However, the adverse economic effects of earlier Hungarian–Soviet trade agreements and CMEA commitments of 1958, 1964–6, and 1969–71 could not be overcome by administrative fiat. Nor was it possible to retrieve, short of a declaration of economic exigency, the vast amounts of misallocated funds spent on yet another set of "priority projects," on the keeping of the fifty largest loss-making industrial enterprises afloat, and on (largely unearned) higher wages and social benefits for the restless labor force.

As was shown in Table 2.7, the regime's retreat from the NEM yielded extreme fluctuations in wages and social benefits. In a political system where the workers had been led by the party and the trade unions to expect nothing less than a 3–4 percent annual increase in real wages, any shortfall was perceived by the blue-collar labor force in apocalyptic terms. It did not take long for the party leadership to realize that financially disastrous foreign trade policies could not be sustained without incurring the danger of political instability. The coincidence, in the mid-1970s, of higher energy costs with declining Western demand for Hungarian exports further exacerbated the regime's economic prospects.

Renewed pressures for "odd cycle" investments, increased consumer demand for imports, and higher energy costs resulted in staggeringly high trade deficits. The sum of these for 1971 through 1979 was HUF 101.3 billion, or about $4 billion at the current rate of exchange.[82] To finance trade deficits, Hungary sought relief by borrowing the needed funds mainly from Western commercial banks. As a result, the nation's net external debt in convertible currencies increased from $848 million (1971) to $7,320 million (1979). An additional one-third to one-half of the latter sum was owed to the USSR and CMEA trading partners by the end of the 1970s.[83] Thus, caught between the hard constraints of exponentially growing external indebtedness and the "soft" budgetary constraints that the party and the government dared to impose on enterprises and the restless consumers, Kádár had no choice but to revive the reform process in 1978.[84]

The Hungarian regime's actions, to the extent that these may be inferred from the published evidence, are fully discussed in the Western literature of economic reforms in Hungary.[85] However, a careful review of this analytical-descriptive material reveals certain gaps that, in the light of newly available internal HSWP material, warrant further discussion. These include: (a) the domestic political opportunity costs that the party incurred during the years of "counter-reforms"; (b) the changed international context, particularly the sharp deterioration of Hungarian–Soviet economic relations, that the regime was forced to confront in the late 1970s; and (c) the internal adminis-trative and ideological obstacles that the party leadership faced in trying to restart the NEM process.

The politics of "counterreforms"

The Central Committee's November 1972 decisions entailed political consequences that for the next several years impaired the leadership's ability to respond in a timely and effective manner to unexpected economic difficulties such as the global energy crisis and growing foreign trade deficits. The main obstacle to rapid policy adaptation to resource constraints was Kádár's "birthday gift" that unconditionally committed the party and the government to the delivery of higher living standards. By putting the regime's political legitimacy on the line, primarily for the benefit of the least efficient (unskilled and semiskilled blue-collar) workers, Kádár thwarted the emergence of the society's latent productive capabilities for overcoming external eco-nomic constraints from internal resources.

Another political consequence of the "counterreforms" was the nearly complete loss of the party's expert oversight of branch-ministry, trust, and enterprise performance and of the actual implementation of central policy directives. The party center may have had the personnel to keep in touch with the fifty top-priority enterprises of Hungary. However, the real issue was the ability of the HSWP apparat's 218 full-time economists to oversee the conduct of Hungary's 35,776 top- and middle-level enterprise executives and that of the additional thousands of planning agency and ministry bureaucrats.[86]

The original NEM scenario placed unusually strong emphasis on professional skills and called on nonparty experts to become actively involved in fulfilling Hungary's share of the Soviet bloc's "scientific-technical revolution." The 1973 crackdown on party intellectuals was an unambiguous signal that the regime's "reds" intended to manip-ulate rather than cooperate with Hungary's "experts." Such measures evoked the specter of the Rákosi regime's presumably discarded inquisitorial practices and helped strengthen the nonparty intellectuals' alienation from the political system.[87]

Economic reforms: the external dimensions

The NEM, and particularly Hungarian industrial policies, had been predicated on the unlimited availability of Soviet energy and raw-material supplies at or below world market prices, or against the delivery of Hungarian agricultural products and low- and medium-technology manufactured goods. From 1974–5 on, not only did the price of Soviet energy imports increase, albeit in a gradual manner, but the traditional terms of barter arrangements changed as well. Whereas both contributed to growing trade deficits in ruble terms, Soviet demands for higher-quality Hungarian imports necessitated further increases in the "dollar content" of Hungarian deliveries to the USSR.

As may be reconstructed from a secret joint report of the National Planning Office and the CC Standing Committee for Economic Policy (CEP) to the PB, Brezhnev, in a personal letter to Kádár, had agreed to the conversion of Hungary's short-term trade deficits that might develop between 1976 and 1980 into a ten-year low-interest loan.[88] However, eighteen months later, Moscow switched signals on its Hungarian partner by saying that the USSR was willing to convert into a long-term loan only a fraction of the anticipated 2.5 billion Ruble trade deficit for this period. As the report explained,

> From the Soviet side [there have been] incessant demands for additional Hungarian imports. According to the Soviet side, some of the Hungarian enterprises have surplus production and shipping capacity and believe [that the interests of both sides] are best served by the cutting of our trade deficit with additional imports. For this reason, the Soviet side gave up its previous [selective trade] preferences and is willing to accept all types of [Hungarian] imports.
>
> The Hungarian position is that additional export capacity is not merely a function of production capabilities of a given enterprise, but that of the related burdens on the [Hungarian] economy [in terms of] additional inputs, additional resource commitments and the redirection of production originally intended for capitalist export to the Soviet Union. Therefore, the only feasible solution is the mutual expansion of trade. [The Soviet side] neither appreciates, nor considers [our position] to be correct.[89]

The joint committee's concluding draft resolution for the PB spoke of the necessity to overcome the Soviet side's "discriminative monopolistic pricing practices" by a combination of short- and long-term loans and some Hungarian concessions on the volume of exports to the USSR.

The drastically changed behavior of the USSR from that of a tough but on the whole accommodating trading partner to that of a ruthless economic adversary contradicted and helped invalidate the policy premises of Kádár's consumerist strategy for Hungary. The regime's search for Western and Third World trade alternatives was bolstered by Kádár's image as a moderate communist politician and by Hungary's record of economic reforms.

Much of the burden of struggling with the "gnomes" of Tokyo, Frankfurt, and Moscow in the complex world of East–East and East–West international banking and economic relations fell on János Kádár. His periodic pilgrimages to the USSR to plead with Brezhnev for the continued deferral of payments on Hungary's debts and his several trips to Western Europe to seek tariff reductions and improved access to markets were key components of the leadership's "escape forward" strategy in search of help from friends and foes to shore up the domestic political status quo.

The normalization of US–Hungarian relations, the initiation of a pragmatic dialogue with the Vatican, and Hungary's constructive involvement in the Helsinki process were important elements in the regime's new trade-driven foreign policy agenda. Still, none of these steps, however useful they became in the long run, afforded immediate relief to the debt crisis at hand.

The task of selling these new initiatives to the concerned and disoriented CC was another challenge that Kádár had to overcome to obtain support for his unusual activities abroad. As he explained,

> there are different opinions about our western relations. I am thinking mainly about opinions in the party. On the one hand ... there are those who think that our economic links with the Soviet Union and the socialist states are [based on] inequality ... and that our difficulties are due to us trading with them. But there are those, [in fact] quite a few comrades, who say: "What's in it for us from cooperating with the capitalist world? We are importing the capitalists' inflation from the west." I think we need to clear up a few things ...
>
> [F]or us to exist, we must import ... a tremendous amount ... of raw materials, energy carriers, semi-finished goods, equipment etc. What we cannot buy from the Soviet Union, we buy from the socialist countries, and what we cannot get there, we must buy from the west.[90]

In sum, whether or not one agreed with Kádár's optimistic assessment, the externalization of Hungary's economic difficulties created a new set of policy dilemmas for the political leadership. The choices were limited and the likely outcomes were, at best, uncertain. On the one hand, too much time, effort, and political legitimacy had been invested in the NEM, which, even in a truncated form, was the only policy that kept the regime afloat. On the other hand, a high-profile inauguration of a "NEM II" was bound to give rise to unrealistic expectations for a rapid improvement of the economy. The solution, in typical Kádár fashion, was a compromise between the NEM and a "NEM II."

NEM redivivus: the anatomy of a decision

The main pillars of the NEM were the state-owned industrial sector, the cooperative agricultural sector, the cooperative service sector, and the (barely tolerated) private agricultural, handicraft, and illegal personal service sector. The *mechanizmus*, albeit performing well below capacity, served the regime's purposes up to a point. However, given Hungary's growing economic difficulties, the liberation and the energizing of the productive potentials of the second economy became an absolute necessity. The latter sector offered the only chance for the revitalization, from hitherto untapped human resources, of the Hungarian economy.

What became a protracted 46-month-long party and government decision-making process that ultimately gave legal recognition to the second economy began in February 1978 with an informal PB decision to expand and legitimize the private service sector. The matter surfaced with passing mention of "better utilization of internal capabilities and ... of internal resources" among the several tasks that the April 18–20, 1978 CC meeting resolved to see accomplished in the next two years.[91] As the Hungarian political scientist Judit Fekete explained, the party's intent was to overcome economic difficulties by "more intensive work, the better utilization of leisure time and improvements in the area of the delivery of [needed] services."[92]

It is still unclear what, if any, urgency the PB chose to attach to this matter. Long lead-times between decisions and policy implementation were customary in the party-state's bureaucracy. For example, within the party there were at least *four* levels: (a) county, "cities with county rights," and security-ministry (Defense, Interior and Foreign Affairs) party committees; (b) district and provincial city committees; (c) small city, major enterprise, and other "third level" party executive committees; (d) local party organizations of consultative opportunities. In a typical government ministry, or "institution with national jurisdiction," such as the National Planning Office, there were *nine* levels from the minister (chairman) down to the last desk officer, with each taking eight to ten days to move a file, up or down, in the administrative hierarchy.[93]

The leadership realized that to put across a major policy innovation – particularly one that evoked the specter of "capitalist restoration" in the economy – must be handled with the exclusion of traditional venues of decision-making. The path of least resistance lay in restricting the relevant participants to those in the top layer of the party and the state. The thus expedited procedure began with the April 1978 CC meeting and ended *four years later* when the decision was actually implemented in early 1982.

This is what happened between these two dates. The National Planning Office (NPO) was tasked to develop a feasibility study on the economic ramifications of the privatization of service industries. The NPO thereupon appointed an expert committe to study the matter. The report was sent on to the CC's Standing Committee on Economic Policy and, from there, to the PB. The PB then passed its recommendations on to the CC Secretariat. The Secretariat, in turn, forwarded the material to several top government agencies for comment. Feedback from the government bureaucracy landed on the desk of Ferenc Havasi, the CC secretary for economic policy. Havasi thereupon appointed yet another expert committee to study the matter. The final report was forwarded to the Council of Ministers. The Council then appointed an Interagency Operative Committee to make policy recommendations for government action. These recommendations were reviewed by the prime minister and handed back to the Council of Ministers for the drafting of enabling legislation. The text of the latter was sent to the CC's department of AP for the development of a publicity campaign to "sell" the regime's new policies to the party membership and the public at large.

The completion of the sequence of problem identification (preliminary assessment), internal and external expert review and recommendations (interim assessment), identification of policy-relevant line agencies (preliminary policy formulation), senior review (policy drafting), formal policy decision (policy selling) involved twelve top-level party and state agencies and officials and took *forty-six months*.

The foregoing summary of the key turning points in implementation of the CC's April 1978 decision tells a great deal about the adequacy of the HSWP to the task of system management and about its capacity to respond in a timely manner to economic threats to the regime's political stability. The decision to expand the scope of the second economy was of a landmark magnitude and had profound political, economic, and social consequences for Hungary in the coming years. In any event, it is worth noting that this was a *crash program* that had been facilitated by a series of administrative *faits accomplis* to bypass the established, and known to be inefficient, channels of policy-making and policy implementation.

Confusing signals from above, restricted flows of information, and a widely shared sense of ideological ambivalence and often outright hostility to drastic changes of *any* kind were the principal characteristics of this process. The hierarchical structure of the personnel involved, the web of mutual distrust among various layers of the apparat and their fear of the rank-and-file party membership are the main elements of an answer to the question of the regime's adequacy for effective governance through timely adaptation to changes in the international and domestic economic-policy environment.

Conclusions

The Hungarian NEM was a remarkable attempt by the leadership of a ruling communist party to preserve political stability by way of bold experiments with unorthodox economic policies. The credit for initiating changes and staying the course of reforms belongs to János Kádár – a typewriter repairman by original occupation. As Kádár's principal advisors, members of the PB deserve credit and blame for what the NEM did and did not accomplish. Still, considering the key PB policy-makers' humble backgrounds – Rezső Nyers, typesetter; Lajos Fehér, high-school teacher; Jenő Fock, mechanic; Sándor Gáspár, a sixth-grade dropout; Károly Németh, butcher; Béla Biszku, locksmith; Ferenc Havasi, stone mason; Gyula Kállai, journalist, György Aczél, bricklayer – it is astonishing that these men had the common sense to make the right decision when it mattered.

By contrast, one needs only to envision a group of opinionated academic intellectuals (such as the governments of József Antall and Péter Boross of 1990–4), instead of these self-made, or rather "party-made," working-class politicians, at the helm to appreciate the accomplishments, such as they were, of the Kádár team in Hungary between 1964 and 1980. To be sure, both Kádár and his postcommunist successors were, above all, politicians. The visceral impulses of *both* have been those of crisis avoidance, and their strategy of rolling over intractable economic problems, particularly the long-term burdens of financing the costs of current social stability, at the expense of future generations, was the same.

When the record is considered in terms of the originally envisaged and ultimately obtained macroeconomic results, the NEM was, and could not have been anything else but, a failure. After all, one is still dealing with a typically mismanaged communist regime, reformist or not, with a centrally planned economy and 98 percent of the "means of production" in the hands of the state. On the other hand, the on-and-off suppressed "democratization" half of the original NEM package succeeded far beyond the most optimistic expectations of its original proponents – whoever they might have been in the central party apparat in the 1960s.

This part of the NEM was responsible for the gradual emancipation from the direct tutelage of the party of the state, public administration, the local governments, the judiciary, the electoral process, the mass organizations, and the economic policy lobbies. The results should be seen as evidence not of democratization but of institutional protopluralism. The commencement in the early 1970s of formal and informal interactions within the bowels of the party-state and among semiautonomous policy lobbies and interest groups in processes of predecisional consultations, decision-making, and policy implementation marked the end of the Stalinist political model and the birth of a new kind of politics in Hungary.

The NEM's greatest achievements were the unintended restoration of individual initiative through the vehicle of private enterprise and the consequent corrosive effects of the second economy on the social cohesion of the regime's core political constituencies. The impact of consumerism helped sever the ties between the state's redistribution mechanisms and the party members, the new rural and urban middle class, and the blue-collar labor force. Though the "market," as an operative economic reality, was nowhere in evidence until the late 1980s, its dynamic elements, such as wage bargaining, had fully penetrated the realm of private and employee–employer relations well before the regime's collapse.

From 1979 on the NEM was no longer a "mechanism" but a set of improvised political fire-fighting measures to keep Hungary from sinking under the combined burdens of the state's external indebtedness and the party's failure to deliver on the terms of its social contract with the people. The regime's "escape forward" strategies sought to externalize its domestic policy problems by Western borrowing and by the intensification of Hungary's involvement in East–West trade. These measures bought time and a semblance of political stability. However, these new external linkages came with strings attached. The most important were the incurring of crushing short- and long-term financial obligations of debt servicing and that of heightened Western expectations for the regime's compliance with the new "Helsinki" standards of human rights in Hungary.

In the end what mattered was that the genie of the "Hungarian reform imperatives" had been released from the bottle and it, too, tried to "escape forward."[94] The details of these propositions will be discussed in Parts II and III of this study.

3   Social change: from latent pluralism to civil society

The subject of this chapter is the transformation of Hungarian society between 1949 and 1989. Social and cultural modernization, social mobility and restratification, generational change and new elite dynamics were the main components of this process. The object of the inquiry is to present evidence to gain a better understanding of the nature of individual, group, and societal interests that helped shape the political outcomes of 1989–90. The following discussion seeks tentative answers to simple questions that should be, but have not yet been, raised by academic analysts of the East European scene.

The issue at hand is that of making factual judgments about the accomplishments of four and a half decades of communist rule in Hungary. The central themes are social continuity and social transformation. Two questions ought to be posed in this regard. Should the tenure of the Rákosi and Kádár regimes be seen merely as a tragic historic interlude that helped, for a time, derail Hungary from the path toward modernity and social progress? Should we dismiss forty-five years of communist rule as an unfortunate but readily reversible experience in misdirected social transformation? As I see it, the answer to each question is a definite no. Mine is a dissenting view that runs counter to those held by many Hungarian intellectuals. The issue may be resolved by a careful review of the record, particularly the empirical evidence, on the dynamics of social change in Hungary in the past half-century.

The unexamined past is a dangerous commodity that sooner or later encroaches on the present. As an illustration, let us consider the case of traditional political beliefs in Eastern Europe after the fall of communism. We know that, profound social changes notwithstanding, the intensity of the Hungarians' and their neighbors' hitherto suppressed sense of ethnic, linguistic, and national identity has not diminished with the onset of democracy in that part of the world.[1] Yet we also

117

know that as winners or losers of the old regimes' economic, social, welfare, cultural, and educational policies, most people who speak for and against such traditional values still are, in many disturbing ways, creatures of a coercively imposed political system and the official ideologies of what used to be called "existing socialism."[2]

In an economic and psychological sense, most Hungarians and East Europeans have been beneficiaries or victims of the *nomenklatura* system and of previous policies of positive and negative discrimination on grounds of social origin, political adaptability, religious beliefs, age, gender, and place of residence. The same is true for the willing and unwilling subjects of the Kádár regime's economic reforms and occasional maladroit attempts at social engineering. Both kinds of policies yielded winners and losers. In either case, the eventual outcome serves as compelling evidence of the people's astonishing capacity to endure, and ultimately to prevail.

(A)   Modernization, regime performance and social change

Historically, communist regimes have been compelled to make difficult choices between investments in material and in human resources. As shown in the previous chapter, the imperatives of military security, rapid industrialization, and rural economic transformation required vast outlays. These measures also necessitated large-scale mobilization of the society. The choices between guns and butter and the consequent resource-allocation outcomes were always the same. The deferred gratification, beyond the bare necessities of food, clothing, and shelter, of public wants was justified by the regimes on grounds of national security, ideology, and economic backwardness.

However, upon attainment of a modest plateau of industrial maturity of the "smokestack" kind in the late 1950s in the USSR and much of East Central Europe in the late 1950s and, about fifteen years later, in the Balkans, traditional resource-allocation priorities were modified and legitimated by national variants of a "social contract." Its terms sought to accommodate conflicting and largely incompatible requirements of political stability, ideological continuity, ouvrierist egalitarianism, controlled consumerism, upward social mobility, and cultural development. The gist of the process may be summed up as a social contract that consisted of an "exchange between regime and society . . . [for the delivery] of political goods valued by the other."[3]

The concept of a "contract" can be useful in so far as it helps reduce the political dimensions of resource allocation choices to issue- and time-specific "pressure decision points" of the leadership's preventive, or reactive, policy outputs to a transactive framework of regime–society relationships.[4] On the other hand, the implications of the term can be misleading. The notion of a "them-and-us" dichotomous relationship tends to obscure the multitude of "subcontracts" between semiautonomous interest groups, policy lobbies, regional governments, and their respective constituencies. The object of subcontracts is the satisfaction not of societal but of particular group interests. Subcontracts modify and attenuate the never clearly articulated policy intent of the central "master contract."[5]

The Hungarian case takes its departure from that country's radical rejection of Rákosi's social contract – such as it was – and from Kádár's subsequent policies of social appeasement of the people. The "little October" of 1956 was not a "Hungarian Kronstadt" of idealist leftist workers and soldiers taking up arms to restore a "revolution betrayed" but a forceful negation of the communist revolution itself. Thus, Kádár's main social policy objective was the amelioration of the regime's congenital illegitimacy through the transformation of the non-elites' *contingent* compliance with the party-state's watered-down ideological expectations and key policy outputs into *consensual* support; or, failing that, at least into passive toleration of the political status quo. For this reason, terms such as "informal understandings," "*ad hoc* trade-offs," and "protracted noninstitutionalized bargaining" seem to be more accurate descriptions of the operative characteristics of people–regime relationships in the Kádár era than is "social contract," which is a quasi-legal, albeit attractive, paradigm of dubious precision.

As paired concepts, modernization and social change denote a causal relationship. On the one hand, "modernization ... is a process of social change in which development is the economic component."[6] This generic formulation clearly posits the phenomenon of social change as a dependent variable of politically motivated human actions to effect desirable changes in the material environment. On the other hand, if the object of change is rapid economic development, then the means of forced industrialization could, as shown below, entail a wide range of intended and unintended social outcomes.

The record shows that attempts by political regimes at social engineering according to *a priori* formulae for the realization of teleological objectives, that is, those of a classless society under full communism, must be seen as efforts to promote such goals as *ancillary* – always subordinated to the political and economic exigencies of the communist system-building process. The Rákosi and Kádár regimes had ideologues but, to Hungary's great fortune, neither social engineers nor politically influential social visionaries. József Révai was a journalist and a literary critic; György Aczél was a cultural puppet master; and György Lukács had no influence beyond the circle of a dozen fellow philosophers.

It is axiomatic that nationalism and a heightened sense of historic, cultural, and linguistic identity, rather than millennial notions of socialism, have been the mainsprings of the Hungarian people's political beliefs.[7] The regime, if it so chose, could easily have put it in the service of socialist system building in Hungary. Instead, all manifestations of nationalism were harshly suppressed – in fact, far more so than anywhere else in communist Eastern Europe. On the other hand, under Kádár the people were spared Maoist "Great Leaps," Ceauşescu-style "systematization," Zhivkov's ethnic–cultural revivalism, and of a local version of the Honecker regime's promotion of a Frederick the Great–Bismarck kind of latter-day Prussian ideological *Gestalt*.[8] As the result, processes of social change in Hungary were driven mainly by the consequences of forced economic development and occasionally political serendipity rather than by ideological blueprints.

Modernization and social change: internal migration

Hungary's postwar social transformation from a predominantly rural and traditional society into a mainly urbanized and largely modern society began with an immense social deficit. The war, the Holocaust, the flight of the *ancien régime*'s civil servants, and the expulsion of ethnic Germans deprived Hungary of important human resources. The effects, even fifty years later, still have not been fully overcome. War casualties and deaths in Soviet POW camps deprived the country of a half-million workers and farmers in the prime of life. The destruction of much of the Jewish community – virtually all from villages and provincial towns – stripped the nation of a great human reservoir of talent, as well as much of its rural middle class. Whereas the old regime's adherents were not irreplaceable, the quarter-million expelled ethnic Germans (most of them model farmers) were a keenly felt loss to the economy and the civic culture of rural Hungary.

A review of demographic data on the distribution of the population among the capital city and other towns with more than 5,000 inhabitants, reveals important trends and anomalies. The change in the respective population ratios for communities with fewer than 5,000 inhabitants from 43.7 percent (1949) to 30.5 percent (1990) and the corresponding growth of larger communities from 56.3 percent to 69.5 percent in this period represents the overall trend of the rural exodus to the cities. The net beneficiaries of this process have been the mid-size, 50,000 to 100,000, and the large, more than 100,000, cities that grew two- and fourfold, respectively, between 1950 and 1990.[9]

In the same period the number of farmers in the labor force declined from 53.6 percent to 22.3 percent. Some of the rural migrants settled in towns and cities and became unskilled or semiskilled workers in factories and at construction sites; some settled in the new "socialist" industrial centers. An elusive component of the rural population cluster was the growing army of commuting peasant workers. The process of daily or weekly commuting from villages to urban centers began with the economic refugees of the regime's first collectivization drive in the early 1950s. However, the movement of rural people gained momentum from an annual number of 638,000 (1960) to 977,000 (1970) and 1,218,000 (1980).[10] This mobile labor force mainly of people under 40 (68.2 percent of commuters in 1970) gave the initial impetus to the birth of the second economy in Hungary. Savings from work in factories were invested in new village houses and in small-business ventures like vegetable-growing greenhouses and contract lifestock raising. Indeed, as shown by Iván Szelényi and associates, these village entrepreneurs catalyzed the rebirth of rural civil society in the 1970s and the 1980s.[11]

The unresolved conflict of interests between the capital and the counties had a decisive bearing on the relationship between the central and the provincial party apparat. The main countertrend to Budapest's economic and cultural domination was the dynamic increase in population from 6.4 percent (1949) to 19.3 percent (1990) of provincial cities with more than 50,000 inhabitants. In these rapidly growing communities, probably more so than elsewhere, the state was always behind with the delivery of essential resources.[12] Therefore, this was where the communities' unmet needs (housing, services, and consumer goods) and the local elites' demands for discretionary resource allocations coalesced over time and helped shape local and regional political agendas in the multicandidate parliamentary elections in 1985.

Modernization and social change: occupational stratification

The longitudinal trends in the transformation of Hungary's occupational structure generally have been consonant with the general indices of economic modernization in East Central Europe in the past half century.[13] The fivefold increase from 1.8 percent to 9.5 percent in the number of executives and intellectuals between 1949 and 1984 seems roughly commensurate with the specialist labor requirements of the rapidly growing economic, administrative, and service sectors of Hungary in the 1980s. The comparable numerical growth from 6.8 to 20.1 percent of the white-collar, by the 1980s mainly female, cluster seems to be evidence more of bureaucratic overstaffing than of a balanced distribution of modestly educated personnel among the main branches of the national economy. On the other hand, the mere doubling, from 11.2 percent to 25.2 percent over thirty-five years, of the number of skilled workers seems to indicate major flaws in the regime's policies of technical–industrial modernization with reference to the quality and distribution of labor inputs, particularly into technology-sensitive industries.[14]

Among all occupational groups by far the greatest discrepancies lie in the eightfold decrease in the number of persons in the agricultural (10+ *hold*) and small business sectors from 20.2 percent in 1949 to 2.5 percent in 1984. In sum, with the exception of the – at least statistically – nearly eliminated entrepreneurial cluster, the distribution of skills within the occupational structure seems appropriate for Hungary's level of development, such as it was, in the past four decades.

Modernization and social change: educational development

In terms of educational attainment, Hungarian society was quite backward at the time of the communist takeover. To be sure, this dismal situation was wholly congruent with the cultural matrix – a small educated elite and a large poorly educated mass component – of prewar Hungary. Indeed, in 1949, 69.7 percent of the 15–29 age group had formal education of less than eight grades. By 1980 this figure had declined to 5.1 percent. Against this background of humble beginnings, the regime's educational record has been quite impressive. In 1980, of the 15–29 age group, 37.9 percent completed only eight grades; 30.7 percent vocational high school; 29.5 percent academic high school, and 9.8 percent, university or college as their highest level of formal education. In fact, in 1981, of the under-30 population, 46.1 percent were enrolled as full-time students from kindergarten through to university level – for a 1984 total of 2,387,400.[15]

The population's continued upgrading of educational qualifications continued unabated thrugh the 1980s. The virtual elimination of illiteracy (the 93,100 "unschooled," most likely rural Gypsy, cluster is the sole exception) and the growth in the number of high-school and postsecondary-school graduates to 6.7 and 2.9 percent, respectively, are solid evidence of progress in this area.

Thanks to the regime's policies that granted equal access to higher education for men and women, the number of female professionals increased fifteenfold between 1949 and 1990. In fact, at most of the fifty-seven faculties of Hungary's universities in the 1980s, the majority of students were women.[16] Although women were still kept out of high positions in the party and government, several professions, including law, medicine, the humanities, and many fields of science and engineering, became feminized to a considerable extent.

The Educational Reform Law of 1961 established a three-tier system of secondary education and two main tracks of higher education. At the age of 14 and upon completion of eighth grade, a student could continue in (a) an academic high school (referred to as *gimnázium* in Hungarian), (b) a vocational – trade or commercial – high school, or (c) an industrial or agricultural vocational secondary school, or they could (d) stay at home and start working at the age of 16.

A graduate of an academic high school was eligible to apply for admission to any university or college. A graduate of a vocational high school *could not* enter a university, but only a college (*főiskola* or college). His or her alternative option was to take a job as a skilled worker's apprentice and join the blue-collar labor force.

The reason for spelling out the gatekeeping functions of the Kádár regime's educational policies is to call attention to the hybrid "populist–elitist" premises of the political leadership's strategies of career development and elite formation in socialist Hungary. There were substantial differences between the "academic-merit" scores of students entering regular (daytime) university programs and those admitted to regular programs or evening and correspondence courses of (mainly technical–vocational) colleges and (primary and preschool) teacher-training programs. The graduates of *all* programs were deemed to be holders of diplomas, hence, for statistical purposes, were counted as members of the "intelligentsia."[17]

A politically much more important, and for the bona fide intellectuals extremely threatening, dilution of the cohort of university and college graduates was the development of a parallel system of party-sponsored political education. By 1985, 4 percent, or about 35,000 party members, were holders of educational credentials that had been earned at "higher party schools" (see Table 3.6). Some of these had been earned at two- or three-year Soviet, but mainly Hungarian, party schools. The curricula of these institutions were concerned more with the mysteries of Marxism–Leninism, political economy, and Soviet history than with the science of modern management or with mass communication.

The holders of such *foxi-maxi* (the reference here is to the cartoon character Mickey Mouse) credentials (including Politburo members Sándor Gáspár and Ferenc Havasi) and their lower-ranking colleagues in the party and government apparat tried to pass – and were so treated by the regime – as "expert" diploma-holding intellectuals. The proposition that the animus behind the Hungarian nonparty elites' opposition to the Kádár regime had more to do with frustrations on this score than with any other reason may not be entirely fatuous.[18]

Socialist redistribution: wages and fringe benefits

Citizens of communist party states were recipients of a combination of economic and social benefits, including cash income, in-kind compensation, and a wide range of free or heavily subsidized services. In assessing the regime's income policies, one is confronted with a vast array of contradictory official statements, government decrees, statistical data, sociological treatises, and personal accounts of the "way things actually were."[19] What emerges from these sources is an image of the party and government officials' permanent preoccupation with dilemmas of ideological preferences and workplace realities, and with the reconciliation of long-term planning and hands-on micromanagement of incomes, food prices, housing quotas, university admissions, and trivia – such as the cost of admission to village cinemas, a subject to which Rezső Nyers devoted several minutes at a 1967 PB meeting.[20]

The matter of incomes may be analyzed in several ways. In the most general sense, one can consider the longitudinal data (in Table 2.3) on utilization of the national income for "public consumption" (versus investments) or those (in Table 2.7) on the average increase of the same for the whole span of the communist regime in Hungary. In any case, minor fluctuations notwithstanding, the annual growth of the Hungarian wage earner's adjusted disposable income averaged 4.5 to 5 percent in the 1960s, about 3.5 percent in the 1970s, and about 0.3 percent in the 1980s.

Next to the unambiguous overall trend of modestly increasing, then stagnant, and in the end declining incomes between 1960 and 1990, what is of equal interest are the ratios of cash and in-kind incomes throughout the entire period. In-kind incomes constituted about 30

Table 3.1   *Social and private consumption, Eastern Europe, 1983*[21]

Country	Social consumption	Private consumption
Bulgaria	119.6	111.9
Czechoslovakia	115.2	110.0
GDR	122.9	112.6
Hungary (1981)	128.3	113.2
Poland	114.3	98.9
Romania	104.3	115.3

Note: 1977 = 100.

percent of the total work compensation package (see Table 2.8). This was one, quite telling, indicator of the overwhelmingly egalitarian thrust of the regime's income policies.

The advantage of making generous provisions for social incomes or, in Western political parlance, "social entitlements," is that in the absence of market prices for social services, these were likely to foster greater public dependency on the political regime and cause less controversy than would merit-based pay raises for selected members of the workforce. Indeed, the astonishingly high, 13.9, 14.3, and 12.9 percent increments in social benefits in 1973–5 (see Table 2.7), and the intriguingly timed giveaways of 9.9 and 6.6 percent increases – after seven lean years of 2 to 3 percent annual increments in the first part of the 1980s – in the same kinds of benefits in 1988 and 1989, respectively, are evidence of political manipulation rather than of periodic booms in the national economy.

Although comparative data are relatively difficult to obtain, it appears that as late as 1981, Hungary led the way in East Europe in the growth of social consumption of assorted benefits, while the rate of private – cash-based – consumption showed a more modest rate of growth between 1977 and 1983 (see Table 3.1).

Data on wages and salaries according to age and occupational status afford another way of looking at the regime's incomes policies. The disparity between average agricultural manual earnings and average top executive salaries (ratio, 1:1.7) – even factoring in such aspects of the total compensation package benefits as managerial bonuses, enterprise or government perquisites, and preferential access to low-cost rental housing – was extremely narrow.[22] From the perspective of social tensions and subsequent political outcomes, the nonexistent difference between the average salaries of such statistical categories as "managers and other experts" and "skilled workers" is of utmost importance. In a country where the average income of an "other expert" medical-school graduate took fifteen years to catch up with the wages of a skilled manual worker, there could not have been any kind of societal consensus behind the regime's class-differentiated incomes policies.

The wage system also discriminated against women and young people in general. As a rule, women doing work of "comparable worth" were underpaid by 16 to 23 percent.[23] Moreover, 53.2 percent of young men and women under 35 did not earn enough to move out of the parental home into a place of their own.

The central policy intent behind the official structure of material incentives in the state sector's wage- and salary-based "first economy" was the provision of basic financial security for all middle-aged heads of households. The level of compensation, until the needed budgetary resources became exhausted, was aimed at keeping the salary structure closely clustered around that of the regime's ideological icon – that is, the skilled factory worker – the pillar of the "core group" at the heavy industrial and manufacturing fortresses of socialism in Hungary.

The social safety net: housing and social-welfare benefits

The planned construction of 1.5 million apartments between 1960 and 1975 was the centerpiece of the Kádár regime's program to provide the working people of Hungary with affordable modern housing. The scarcity of available housing, particularly for people under 35, was a burning issue for members of the post-1956 generation.[24]

Of the four possible ways – rental from the local council, a service flat from one's place of employment, building and purchase of an apartment or a one-family house, and inheritance – of acquiring a roof over one's head, the first two were the most frequent solutions. However, both placed the aspiring tenant or homeowner in the position of deferential petitioner vis-à-vis the local authorities, the immediate employer (together with the workplace party and trade union secretaries), who were empowered to assign housing, or to approve requests for interest-free loans for the applicant.[25]

In addition to age – and probably more so than party membership – position in the occupational hierarchy was a critical factor that helped improve one's access to housing. It appears that the less costly solution, that is, the acquisition of a rent-controlled apartment from the local council, was more readily available to executives and intellectuals than to those at the bottom of the occupational hierarchy (see Table 3.2).

Table 3.2 *Family entitlement to housing, by occupation or profession of principal breadwinner, Hungarian provincial cities, 1968*[26]

Occupation or profession	Independent leaseholder	Owner of apartment	Neither owner nor leaseholder	Sample families
	N = 956	N = 943	N = 242	N = 2,141
Executive	58.9	34.4	6.7	90
Mid-level white-collar	59.4	31.2	9.4	128
Technician	46.9	44.5	8.6	254
Office worker	53.7	34.6	11.7	112
Service sector employee	50.6	34.4	15.0	73
Skilled worker	40.1	48.7	11.2	474
Semiskilled worker	40.6	46.8	12.6	271
Unskilled worker	35.8	52.1	12.1	217
Agricultural manual	8.4	91.6	0.0	36
Retired white-collar	58.5	32.3	9.2	99
Retired manual	44.7	48.6	6.7	387
Percentage	44.7	44.0	11.3	—

Note: Cities, Pécs and Szeged.

Data presented in György Konrád and Iván Szelényi's pioneering study on housing conditions in four provincial cities in the late 1960s demonstrate the endemic nature of bureaucratic maldistribution of publicly owned housing resources by criteria that were very different from those propounded by the political regime. In any case, most younger people, of whom 62.9 percent had no "independent entitlement" to housing, as well as half of the "over-40" age cohort, had to make do, often well into their 50s, with living in their parents' home.[27]

In sum, the regime's promise to provide state-built housing to 1.5 million Hungarian families by 1975 never materialized. Instead, from the very beginning the regime relied on private individuals to meet its commitment. The respective numbers of dwelling units built by the state and by private individuals speak for themselves: 1971–80: 311,000/580,000; 1982: 19,000/56,000; 1984: 10,000/60,000; 1986: 8,000/62,000; and 1988: 5,000/45,000.[28] Although state loans were essential to private construction, none of this would have been possible without personal sacrifices such as overtime, weekend work, second jobs, and risk-taking entrepreneurship in the second economy.

Social and health service entitlements: promise and performance

Between 1960 and 1989 the number of Hungarians receiving retirement pay increased by 323 percent.[29] Because life expectancy remained the same – in fact, for males it declined between 1975 and 1988 – the reasons for the rapid growth in the number of pensioners must be sought elsewhere.[30] The most obvious explanations are policies that set the low retirement age of 55 for women and 60 for men and the inclusion – from the 1960s on – of people in the agricultural cooperative sector in the state retirement system.

The removal, through retirement, of large numbers of people from the active labor force created an increasingly difficult situation both for the government and the recipients of pensions. On the one hand, the regime was "contract-bound" to honor its liberal retirement, and maternal and sickness leave policies, as well as those, from the late 1960s on, for a five-day workweek. On the other hand, these measures created a vast army of aid-dependent citizens that the economy was less and less able to support. For most retirees the reduced income and other job-related benefits proved to be barely sufficient to get by. In fact, the majority of the pensioners, particularly the remarkably high 25-plus percent on medical disability,[31] found themselves at or below the never fully defined "poverty line."[32]

The Hungarian sociologist Ágnes Bokor's major study on poverty in Hungary makes several important distinctions between "traditional poverty," that is, conditions that had been experienced by Hungary's rural and, to a lesser extent, urban underclass of "three million beggars" of the prewar years, and the new forms of poverty that she defines as affecting those who are "deprived," or simply poor, and those who are "at risk" of sliding into poverty. According to Bokor, in the early 1980s, about 11 and 20 percent of the Hungarian population fell into the "deprived" and "at-risk" categories, respectively.[33]

In addition to the elderly, the most severely affected by penury were those at the lowest rungs of the occupational hierarchy, active wage earners with three or more children, female heads of single-parent households, and young school dropouts. Of the "deprived" category, 56 percent were persons 60 years of age or older; of the "at-risk" category, 42 percent were 60 years of age or older.[34]

There was disparity between the reform-generated high hopes and expectations – including the regime's tacit encouragement of *enrichez vous* of the Hungarian population through the second economy – and the citizens' unequal access to new economic opportunities. One's ability to benefit materially from the reforms had far more to do with inherited educational advantages, professional skills, and entrepreneurial risk-taking ability than with the state's egalitarian redistribution of its economic largesse through the bureaucratic channels of the regime's social welfare system.

Whereas the term "quality of life" is notoriously difficult to quantify, the overall impact of unmet expectations and that of the stress of daily life under conditions of existing socialism in Hungary on the mental hygiene of the population may be measured with a degree of precision.[35] The doubling of the estimated number of alcoholics and the 75 percent increase in the number of alcoholics treated in welfare centers and psychiatric hospitals between 1980 and 1989 were warning signs that the regime chose not to heed.[36]

The underserved and systematically shortchanged recipients of the social-welfare delivery system – the old, the disabled, the uneducated, single parents, people in small villages, and the victims of alcohol abuse – were the unintended, but inevitable, losers of the economic reform process in Hungary. Their woes were of interest mainly to political dissidents, courageous journalists, muckraking sociologists, and the recipients, at the CC's Department of AP, of top-secret reports on the increasingly disenchanted rank-and-file views on the regime's shortcomings.

(B)   Social transformation: intergenerational and educational mobility

Social mobility is a key element in the overall process of modernization. Economic development is the principal structural cause "driving" social mobility – "creating space" in blue-collar occupations by means of the development of industry; in white-collar administrative, technical, and professional job strata by means of the need for a larger administrative/expert stratum; and typically reducing the need, relative and absolute, due to mechanization, for labor in agriculture and so on.

From the time it came to power in 1948–9, the Hungarian party sought to restructure the society to make it more responsive to the regime's developmental goals and political-ideological objectives. The massive promotion of additional blue-collar workers, 60,000 in 1948 alone, and by the early 1980s 210,000, to executive and managerial positions were important steps in the forty-year process of creating a new ruling elite that was both "red" and "expert."[37]

The initial losers in this process of the large-scale upward social mobility of one social class were members of another. Between 1949 and 1954 over 300,000 familes of entrepreneurs, small businessmen, farmers, and middle-class professionals were deprived of their property, jobs, higher education opportunities, and often their homes as well.[38]

Following the 1956 revolution the regime needed a highly skilled labor force to supply industry, agriculture, science, education, trade, commerce, and public administration with specialists and skilled workers of all kinds. The political leadership's solution to the dilemma of "modernization versus security" was ingenious. A key element in Kádár's break with Stalinist precedents was the implementation of the partial, and later complete, removal of class background as a decisive factor in the admission policies of universities and colleges. In doing so, the regime made amends for the sins of the Rákosi era and laid the groundwork, from the mid-1960s on, for the restoration of merit-based mobility opportunities for all Hungarians.

As Walter Connor explained, "education has been central in the process of status inheritance and attainment."[39] According to a 1973 survey of students in three types of secondary schools by father's occupation and secondary-school background before and after 1941, one discerns evidence of both continuity and change.[40] Those belonging to the top executive and intellectual occupational categories had preserved their traditional share in high-quality academic high-school programs; those at the lower rungs of the occupational hierarchy had made remarkable progress.

According to another, 1977 survey on the participation of 20-year-olds in higher education according to father's occupation, much of the socially more diversified pattern of secondary-school enrollments spilled over into the higher-education category as well.[41] Because this survey made no distinction between universities and the admittedly less demanding colleges, one may assume that most of those from culturally disadvantaged social backgrounds ended up in colleges rather than universities. These changes were evidence of the significant expansion of the pool of highly trained personnel and ultimately for the breakdown of the traditional intelligentsia's overwhelmingly favorable mobility opportunities. Withal, the children of those without inherited educational advantages still faced significant handicaps in the early 1970s.

The results of a 1977 national survey (see Table 3.3) bespeak much progress and new opportunities for offspring of nonintelligentsia and

Table 3.3   *Young person's chance of entering into the upper-white-collar (intelligentsia) group, by parental social status*[42]

Father's social status in 1938	Offspring's chance				
	in 1939	in 1949	in 1957	in 1963	in 1975
Men					
Executive and upper white-collar	107.4	73.4	23.8	17.1	19.5
Other white-collar	31.2	24.8	9.9	8.2	8.8
Craftsman, small businessman	5.6	5.0	3.1	2.6	2.9
Skilled worker	2.8	3.0	2.9	2.7	3.4
Semiskilled worker	1.6	3.1	1.8	1.6	1.8
Unskilled worker	1.8	2.1	0.9	0.8	0.8
Women					
Executive and upper white-collar	308.8	273.0	61.0	28.7	25.0
Other white-collar	49.0	38.0	20.0	10.7	10.9
Craftsman, small businessman	12.0	20.0	6.8	5.0	4.8
Skilled worker	8.0	4.0	4.8	3.9	4.1
Semiskilled worker	3.0	4.0	3.8	2.3	2.4
Unskilled worker	1.0	8.0	2.8	1.7	1.8

Note: Chance of a female child of an unskilled worker in 1939 = 1.

white-collar groups. Apart from the general tendency of enhanced mobility opportunities, that is, of chances of becoming a diploma-holding intellectual, for children of blue-collar families, women made important strides toward overcoming traditional handicaps due to gender and social origin.

Social mobility: occupational

The reopening in the mid-1960s of the gates of institutions of higher education to the offspring of the traditional intelligentsia helped improve the balance between the "merit"- and "equality"-based official policies of educational and occupational mobility. Well into the 1970s, there was still enough "room at the top" to accommodate educationally well-qualified people with both intellectual white-collar and manual-occupation family backgrounds.

According to a 1973 survey on the intergenerational mobility of wage-earning males by father's place in the occupational hierarchy in 1938, the high-level outflow of men from executive or intelligentsia backgrounds into the same categories, this cohort accounted for less than one-sixth of executives and intellectuals.[43]

In substantive terms, data shown in the 1973 mobility survey ought to be perceived as both the result and the terminal point of large-scale changes in occupational mobility since 1948–9. The onset of slowdown actually occured in 1962–4. In temporal terms, the slowdown and consolidation of mobility outflows coincided with the end of the extensive (capital-intensive and labor-extensive) phase of Hungary's economic development. With the rural migrants already absorbed into the industrial sector, women were the only available source of labor to take advantage of the (leftover) opportunities for occupational mobility.

Thanks to the regime-sponsored breakthrough of educational advancement for women, the 1962–4 share of females among executives and intellectuals increased from 19.7 percent to 36.6 percent in 1973.[44] During the Kádár era children of all three types – skilled, semiskilled, and unskilled – of blue-collar workers made remarkable headway in becoming parts of the top occupational category.[45] Here again, one may assume that women did progressively better than men in acquiring positions at the top.

The history of postwar occupational mobility in Hungary is divisible into three, more or less distinct, periods. The first, between 1948 and 1964, was marked by major structural and considerable intergenerational mobility, together with elements of circulation of the downward kind prior to 1962.

The second, between 1964 and 1973, was marked by the beginning of the coalescence of structural, intergenerational, and intragenerational elements of mobility, together with the rapid across-the-board mobility of women. In less than ten years women came to occupy a significant portion of skilled-worker, most of the white-collar, and a decisive share of rural second economy occupational sectors and made appreciable gains in the executive-intelligentsia job categories as well.

The third, between 1973 and 1989, may be characterized as continued diminution of structural changes and by the gradual – as much intergenerational as intragenerational – forward movement of much of the labor force. Circulation mobility consisted of the male intelligentsia's and white-collar offspring's choice of lower-prestige but better paying jobs; of the exit of males from white-collar positions to the second economy; and of the growing occupational marginalization of unskilled workers and of the majority, in Szelényi's phrase, of "proletarianized" agricultural manuals.[46]

On balance, it appears that the Kádár regime, except in the areas noted below, delivered on its part the educational and occupational mobility aspects of the unwritten social contract. Over the period of thirty years many hundreds of thousands of secondary-school and higher-education diplomas were awarded, and a multitude of new occupational positions were created. It is indisputable that the majority of occupationally mobile social clusters could not have gotten that far and as rapidly under the Horthy regime. For most of them, the changes tended to confer higher occupational status, though neither necessarily commensurately differentiated incomes nor, as shown below, changes in social prestige.

Those who failed to benefit from these positive trends in social mobility were the unintended losers of the economic reforms; scores of intelligentsia victims – mainly dissidents – of politically motivated blacklisting and those, most prominently Gypsies and the new *Lumpen-proletariat* of school-dropout working-class youths, who were beyond the pale of the official welfare system.

Social inequality: class and status

The Communist Party's traditional image of the socialist society as an agglomerate of two, worker and peasant, classes and one "stratum" – that is, a mixture of intellectuals, white-collar employees, and "others" – never corresponded to social realities. This was particularly true for the inner dynamics of social stratification, patterns of equality and inequality, and such matters as social status and lifestyles. Early critics, such as Milovan Djilas, spoke of a "new class," others of the "*nomenkla-tura* bourgeoisie," and still others of the rise of new technocratic, administrative, and intelligentsia elites.[47]

At issue is the "fit" of these groups in the officially endorsed models of acceptable social differences under socialism. The "fit," such as it was, promptly disintegrated with the introduction of economic reforms and, for many people, the opening up of the second economy. From this it follows that the extent to which the ideological foundations of the regime's social policies failed to correspond to new socio-economic realities, tensions – whether labeled as manifestations of "relative deprivation," "status inconsistency," or "cognitive disso-nance" – arose among members of the society. The consequent political difficulties had their roots in uncertainties and anxieties concerning the citizens' social status, cultural identity, and personal space in the official and in private realms of social life.[48]

To overcome the ambiguities inherent in the "two-classes-and-one-stratum" model, Hungarian sociologists sought to devise empirical referents with which to explain (a) the "social distance" between specific social layers; (b) the relative "social status," as derived from income and education, of incumbents of several occupational titles in the occupational hierarchy; (c) inequalities with respect to housing, ownership of durable consumer goods, and cultural consumption; (d) differences in lifestyles and material well-being among members of various occupational groups; (e) the stratification of society according to "status groups"; and (f) the perceived social prestige of persons at various levels of the occupational hierarchy.[49]

These scholarly inquiries unearthed evidence showing the birth of a complex, multilayered, highly stratified, and, in my view, essentially *new* society in Hungary in the mid-1970s. This society, in various and occasionally contradictory ways, incorporated many elements of the country's traditional social structure, of which the continued presence and visibility of the traditional scientific, technocratic, and literary intelligentsia were the most notable. Yet, there was also compelling evidence of a vast structural and intergenerational inflow of upwardly mobile and socially newly – at least nominally – empowered formerly low-status masses of people.

Between 1970 and 1980 the number of white-collar employees in the Hungarian labor force increased by 27 percent. By 1980 8.1 percent of *all* wage earners were university or college graduates, as were 27.6 percent of all white-collar employees.[50] Because of the magnitude of changes in the occupational structure of the wage-earning population, it may be argued that a new "critical social mass" came into being in the 1970s. This, for want of a better term, may be called the new posttotalitarian middle class.

Most of the educated individuals of the new middle class were beneficiaries of intergenerational mobility. It was a process that, in terms of *status*, helped to preserve and only marginally alter the traditional "privileged, less privileged, and underprivileged" hierarchical structure of Hungarian society. Status, moreover, conferred on nonparty elites neither commensurate income nor the capability to influence (inherently political) decisions affecting their jobs, occupational mobility, and, in the final analysis, personal autonomy as professionals and citizens.

Concerning the relationship between party membership and the relative position – as measured by a composite index consisting of variables such as job title, educational background, occupation, and age – of people belonging to twelve "status groups," it appears that party membership was responsible for at least one-third of the difference between well-off and less well-off cohorts within *each* of the status groups. Not surprisingly, party members were ahead of nonparty members in every category.[51]

At its inception the new Hungarian middle class was a heterogenous entity. Its cohesion hinged, to a large extent, on the successful routinization of interaction between the *nomenklatura* elite and the rapidly growing cluster of well-educated people who called themselves the "intelligentsia." Until the surfacing of the new entrepreneurial elites in the late 1970s, these two – one "in" and one "out" of power – elites had been the principal authorized players in Hungarian public life.

In terms of economic well-being and leisure consumption, there were several subtle, but important, differences between the lifestyles of the two elites. Virtually the entire (97.1 percent) of the *nomenklatura* elite lived in well-equipped homes, as did 86.3 percent of the intelligentsia. Similar ratios of patterns of consumption obtained in reading journals, newspapers, and books, spending weekends away from home, vacation travel abroad, ownership of a summer home, and ownership of an automobile.[52]

The proximity of the two patterns of consumption is misleading because it fails to account for the enormous differences of power wielded by members of the two elites. By "power," in the sense of one of the key variables used in Hungarian surveys, that is, an individual's "capacity for the realization of one's interests" (CRI), the existence of an embedded counterforce is also understood. The latter consisted of the top political elites' monopoly access to the coercive resources of the state and of their exclusive authority to allocate, by voluntaristic ideological criteria, or for any other reason, the economic and cultural resources of the state. The opening of the second economy served, for a time, to disguise these discrepancies and defuse tensions on the societal level.

Social inequality: income and consumption

The regime's economic reforms helped expand the sphere of citizens' economic activity from the "first" to the "second economy." The latter included a wide range of money-making opportunities in the nonstate sector. Overtime work, within-enterprise (and -agricultural cooperative) after-hours quasi-entrepreneurial activity were also parts of the unofficial economic realm.[53]

The most common motivation for participation in the second

economy was the supplementing of inadequate cash incomes earned from one's "first job" in the first economy. However, if the main object was fulfillment of traditional social ambitions, that is, that of "keeping up with (or getting ahead of) the Kovács," and thus the enhancement of one's social status, the second economy could serve as the appropriate venue. Moreover, whereas "merit," in the form of intellectual, artistic, or other form of marketable talent, might or might not have been rewarded in the first economy by the powers that be, such personal assets were, in many cases, readily convertible on the "market" into wealth and an improved quality of life. In the Kádár era the second economy was a political safety valve rather than a vehicle for the conversion of socioeconomic gains into political power.

The citizens' involvement in the second economy did not, *eo ipso*, help restructure the society. However, patterns of participation and nonparticipation by members of certain clusters yielded important changes in the social status of at least three main social groups. As shown under the categories of "housing," "cultural life style," "finances," and "capacity to realize – *inter alia* economic – interests," some citizens were much better off than others. The main beneficiaries of the second economy were members of the elite, the urban and rural upper groups, and the urban and rural (skilled) "affluent workers."

In sum, the range between the top "elite" and the bottom "deprived" status groups, when juxtaposed to seven social-status indicators, yields a picture of rich social diversity among people during the late Kádár years (see Table 3.4). Even if one disregards the generally unhelpful labels that the authors of this survey used to identify various status groups, one is impressed by the conflict potentials among those with different capabilities to "realize their interests" (CRI).

The elite families were at the top in all but one respect; with a CRI index of 5.6, the elites were still far from full possession of power in the noneconomic realm. Moving down the column of this criterion, one detects one or more flaws, such as inadequate housing for the "urban upper" intellectuals, poor infrastructure for the "rural upper" cluster, political powerlessness for the "affluent urban" and "affluent rural" workers, and multiple handicaps for families in the three social-status groups at the bottom. It appears that only two: that is, the sixth and the seventh, status groups (17 percent of the families) benefited from a balanced mix of status indicators. Therefore, if we accept the Hungarian sociologists' reasoning, the sixth and seventh groups were the

Table 3.4   *Hungarian family status, by criteria of material well-being, position, and power, 1981–2*[54]

Status group	Share among families	Consumption	Cultural lifestyle	CRI *	Housing	QRE **	Money	Position in occupational hierarchy
Elite	7.2	4.9	6.0	5.6	6.0	5.7	5.4	5.8
Urban upper	10.1	4.1	4.7	5.3	3.3	5.4	4.5	4.4
Rural upper	7.3	4.1	4.6	5.3	5.7	3.1	4.9	4.5
Consumer middle	4.6	5.0	4.6	3.4	4.9	4.9	3.3	4.6
Urban "affluent"	7.1	3.8	4.2	3.2	6.3	5.7	4.9	4.0
Poor middle	8.1	2.5	3.6	3.7	4.0	4.8	3.1	4.1
Rural middle	8.9	4.0	3.6	4.3	2.6	2.6	3.7	3.8
Better of rural lower	9.9	2.0	2.4	4.0	2.8	2.3	3.2	3.1
Affluent rural lower	6.5	2.8	2.4	1.6	3.0	3.3	5.5	2.8
Urban lower	7.4	2.1	2.1	1.6	3.6	5.4	2.2	3.0
Somewhat deprived	8.4	3.2	2.2	1.8	3.6	2.8	2.4	3.3
Deprived	14.4	1.6	1.5	1.6	1.7	2.4	1.9	2.5

Notes: N = 8,695 families. Numbers in each criterion are averages, arrived at from cluster analysis of several indicators.
* CRI = "personal capacity for the realization of interests" in a situational context, typically in dealings with those in positions of authority.
** QRE = "quality of residential environment," ranging from environmentally superior green-belt suburban to heavily polluted industrial slums, and access to – from very good to poor – infrastructural services.

least vulnerable to "status inconsistency" as a source of grievances against the regime's domestic shortcomings.[55]

Social inequality: prestige and power

The foregoing discussion on the distribution of status groups sought to present an empirical map on patterns of inequality and social distance in Hungarian society in the early 1980s. Though the data seem reliable and the methods of analysis are "state-of-the-art" in quality, these findings require corroboration. This may be attempted by considering the way in which sociologically inferred patterns of inequality were

Table 3.5 *Perceptions of occupations' prestige, income potential, level of knowledge, degree of power, and usefulness in Hungary, 1983*[56]

Occupation	General prestige	Money	Knowledge	Power	Usefulness
		Prestige attributes			
Deputy minister	3.63	3.03	4.64	2.62	9.61
Hospital doctor	3.66	4.50	2.77	3.98	2.98
Hospital director	3.67	4.40	3.39	3.05	7.54
Family doctor	3.86	4.43	2.37	4.41	4.00
University professor	3.93	6.17	2.57	4.72	4.93
Dentist	4.56	4.31	3.42	6.39	5.25
Factory manager	4.79	4.14	4.71	2.63	9.93
Lawyer	5.15	5.03	3.78	4.60	10.03
Chairman, county council	5.53	4.87	8.07	2.57	13.31
Teacher	6.28	12.56	4.64	6.96	5.94
Ministry official	6.30	6.73	8.71	4.37	12.90
Economist	7.34	9.50	5.69	6.26	9.26
Village mayor	7.40	7.83	9.76	3.08	14.07
Elementary-school teacher	8.06	15.71	7.19	8.53	6.37
Journalist	8.29	10.76	8.33	5.93	12.62
Actor	8.80	8.49	6.65	10.67	15.14
Communist Party county secretary	9.23	6.86	15.05	4.15	18.00
Army officer	10.01	8.38	10.85	5.22	17.21
Sociologist	10.24	12.35	8.50	10.74	15.44
Personnel officer	11.56	15.22	13.54	7.82	19.13
Priest	11.92	16.21	9.14	9.39	17.62
TV repairman	12.33	10.06	10.21	13.00	12.54
Local govt executive	12.44	16.41	9.14	9.39	17.62
Communist Party first secretary at an enterprise	12.54	10.68	17.01	6.23	20.34
Small businessman	13.29	9.42	16.44	13.72	15.76
Pro soccer player	13.96	9.47	19.24	15.89	23.64
Librarian	14.10	21.31	13.15	16.60	17.39
Policeman	14.26	13.65	17.30	6.62	14.44
Cab driver	15.43	11.64	18.73	14.94	18.21
Independent farmer	18.52	14.30	19.95	20.68	15.03
Mailman	20.06	21.79	21.99	18.85	17.48
Street sweeper	27.89	28.18	29.04	27.18	24.32

Note: N = +/- 7,500 males; high–low scale, 1–30.

perceived by the subjects of inquiry. The matter might be addressed by an assessment of public perceptions of the social prestige of incumbents positioned at various points in the occupational hierarchy. On this, see Table 3.5.

As William H. Form explained, "each society tends to assume that its occupational structure represents a hierarchy of skills socially legitimized by appropriate economic prestige and other rewards."[57] The difficulty of endowing with legitimacy the existing occupational structure of a communist state, such as Hungary, where the incumbents in several occupational positions owed their appointments solely to political reasons, is axiomatic. On the other hand, if the survey questionnaire seeks responses not only about prestige but also about other criteria, such as income, knowledge, power, and social usefulness, the issue becomes not one of legitimacy but that of the registering of public views. These concern perceptions of social, economic, and political *realities* and value judgments on the social usefulness of incumbents in the occupational hierarchy. The entire process may be perceived as a social plebiscite in which judgments of fact (money, knowledge, and power) and of value (general prestige and social usefulness) coalesce into a societal consensus on the way the regime's occupational reward structure works, or ought to work.

The data, in Table 3.5, were extracted from a list of 156 occupations listed in the survey and offer a combination of pragmatic-factual (money, knowledge, and power), "traditional deferential" (general prestige), and critical views on the incumbents of this sample. Noteworthy are the answers to the "factual" questions – particularly on the "power" of deputy ministers, factory managers, the county and enterprise party secretaries, chairmen of county councils and village mayors – and the discrepancy between the "power" and "social usefulness" ratings of these officials. Top intellectuals are seen as both useful and powerful, and sociologists, clergymen, and actors as neither powerful nor particularly useful.

Responses to the entire sample may be further analyzed by showing the correlation coefficients (Pearson's r) between four pairs of variables of this occupational prestige survey.[58] The values were as follows:

Between	Correlation coefficients
prestige and money	0.7774
prestige and knowledge	0.9767
prestige and power	0.9479
prestige and social usefulness	0.8228

Knowledge and power attributed to the incumbents seem to be the primary criteria for perceptions of occupational prestige. Lower significance attached to social usefulness and money might be explained by the respondents' understanding of the term "social," as to its applicability to themselves as individuals or to the larger community of which they were a part, and also by their confusion over the notion of income as derived from social entitlements, wages, and invisible earnings from the second economy. On the other hand, the public displayed very accurate understanding, though not necessarily support, of the officially concealed inequalities that characterized Hungary's social stratification in the early 1980s.

In a less direct way, the respondents also identified the types of elites whose knowledge and, by inference, educational background and occupational status qualified them to serve as an alternative meritocratic leadership of the community. As will be shown in Chapters 6 and 8, it was precisely the incumbents of such occupational positions who were elected as independent candidates both in the 1985 and, in far greater numbers, in the 1990 parliamentary elections.

(C)   Reds and experts: apparatchiks, technocrats, and bureaucrats

Within Hungarian society there was another "society" – the 800,000-odd strong Hungarian Socialist Workers' Party – to which every eighth adult belonged. Being a mass party with the declared ambition of becoming an "all-peoples' party," the HSWP was a somewhat skewed but nevertheless representative cross-section of the country's population. Party members were visible members of the "first," or official, society in that they, whether high officials or humble rank and file, were duty-bound to uphold the regime's values and to promote its policies. On the other hand, the party members, just like any ordinary citizen, "bled" when "pricked" by high prices, poor housing, and the general malaise that beset Hungary from the mid-1970s on.

Two societies

The task at hand is a brief examination of the party members' "fit" with the demographic, economic, educational, and occupational structure of Hungarian society. Data in Table 3.6 on the HSWP membership might be summarized as follows.

1 Women were underrepresented – though over time the women:men

ratio improved – and men in the 30–39 and 40–59 age cohorts were overrepresented in the party by a factor of two. However, the oldest cohort (60-plus) did catch up with the national average by the late 1980s.

2 The rank-and-file party members were significantly less well educated than were comparable cohorts in the national sample. The most important difference, as shown by the respective ratios of white-collar people in the two samples, lay in the party's ability to recruit university and college graduates far above the national average.

3 The overrepresentation of "intellectuals" in the party, though finessed in party statistics with emphasis on their social origin, was a practical necessity for managing the commanding heights of power in Hungary.

4 The contrast, in 1974, between the 59.8 percent of party members with educational background of eight grades or less and the rest with secondary- and higher-educational credentials, speaks of the coexistence of two to three "societies" with potentially clashing economic interests and widely different opportunities under the roof of the political house that Kádár built.

5 As indicated by the remarkably low rates of party affiliation among people under 29, the HSWP was an organization with a predominantly middle-aged, and gradually ageing, membership. It appears that only 1.6 percent of the approximately 100,000 students at higher-educational institutions and a similar percentage of young army draftees chose to join the HSWP.

Table 3.6 *Department of party and mass organizations, CC, HSWP, statistics on the sociopolitical attributes of party members, 1974, 1976, 1980, 1985*[59]

	12/31/1974 N=754,353 %	12/31/1976 N=761,184 %	1/1/1980 N=811,833 %	1/1/1985 N=870,992 %
Gender				
Male	73.5	72.7	71.7	69.5
Female	26.5	27.3	28.3	30.5
Age				
> 26	6.6	6.1	4.1	3.4
27–29	5.8	6.0	5.1	4.1
30–39	26.0	25.6	25.5	26.0
40–49	30.6	29.4	26.6	25.5
50–59	18.0	20.2	23.9	23.0
60+	13.0	12.7	14.8	18.0
Education				
> eight grades	18.8	15.8	11.5	7.9
Eight grades	41.0	41.2	25.4	21.5
Secondary school	25.5	27.0	45.5	49.3
University or college	14.5	15.8	17.4	21.0
Scientific degree	0.2	0.2	0.2	0.3
Joined party in				
Before 1944	1.1	1.0	0.8	0.5
1944–5	10.0	8.9	7.4	5.3
1946–56	22.1	20.4	17.8	13.9
1957–70	50.4	47.0	42.3	35.3
since 1971	16.4	22.7	–	–
1971–79	–	–	31.7	28.2
since 1979	–	–	–	16.8
Party schooling				
Higher party school	1.4	1.9	2.6	4.0
Mid-level party school	8.7	10.0	12.2	14.2
Lower-level party school	22.0	26.6	27.7	26.8
No party schooling	67.9	61.5	57.5	55.0
Original occupation				
Worker	59.2	60.6	62.4	62.3
Peasant	13.0	12.2	10.8	8.9
Intellectual/white collar	8.9	9.1	9.2	10.2
Employee	16.3	15.8	16.1	17.0
Other	2.4	2.0	1.0	0.8
Student	0.2	0.3	0.5	0.8
Current occupation				
Manual (including retired)	38.8	35.1	36.5	35.5
Foreman	6.1	6.7	7.0	7.1
Agricultural manual (including retired)	6.7	6.7	6.7	6.3
Agricultural foreman	–	–	1.4	1.5
White-collar (including retired)	40.0	40.8	41.0	42.4
Other	8.4	7.9	7.4	7.2

Nomenklatura *elites in the 1970s: stratification and diversity*

The HSWP's *nomenklatura* system covered, at its widest dispersal, approximately 450,000 jobs. Most of these, or about 380,000, fell under the jurisdiction of the local party organizations, 60,000 to 65,000 under that of the regional party committees; and the rest belonged to the CC's central personnel pool. The party, government, and economic elites shown in Table 3.7, were partly central but mainly regional party appointees.

The samples of thirteen elites cover 38,586 persons. These, with allowance made for modest overlaps between the CC *nomenklatura* list and the rest of the categories, may be divided into five clusters. Each cluster has different socioeconomic and political characteristics.

1 The *nomenklatura* appointees (column 5) were highly educated middle-aged people of worker or white-collar backgrounds (with no time for political education) and party membership of recent (1969 or later) and "Kádárite" (post-1957) vintage.

2 The incumbents of this category (column 6) were parts of the 11,816–strong party and mass organizations' cluster of appointees (1974), and represented the HSWP's full-time professional personnel.[61] On the whole, members of the party apparat were significantly *less* well educated than were their ministry counterparts – let alone most of the regional *nomenklatura* appointees whom they politically supervised.

3 The ministry executives and those at the twenty-odd administrative agencies "with national jurisdiction" (columns 1, 11, and 12) were highly educated experts. It was they who kept the state and the economy afloat. One-fourth to one-third were nonparty members; they showed remarkably little interest (58, 46.2, and 64 percent, respectively) in political education, and had mainly nonproletarian (71.7, 66.6, and 76.1 percent, respectively) social backgrounds.

4 The economic executives (colums 7 through 10) were both "red" and "expert." Virtually all enterprise and factory CEOs were party members (94 and 95.9 percent), but 42.1 and 37.9 percent of their (engineering, financial and marketing) expert deputies were *not*. The latter (columns 8 and 10) were as well educated or marginally better educated than were their bosses and showed pronounced disinterest (60.2 and 56.7 percent) in benefiting from political education. Executives of small enterprises and cooperatives (column 2) were a mixed bag of politically largely inconsequential, mainly college graduates

Table 3.7 Department of party and mass organizations, CC, HSWP, executives in public administration, industry, agriculture, commerce, party and local governments, by organizational affiliation, job category, 1973[60]

	Ministry or national agency executive	Executive in industry or service sector	Executive, in agriculture or industry	Executive, local government	CC, HSWP nomenklatura appointees	HSWP full-time central, regional and local apparat	Factories CEO	Factories Deputy CEO	Enterprises CEO	Enterprises Deputy CEO	Ministry or national agency MDPH**	Ministry or national agency DPYH***	City, town or village mayor
	(1)	(2)	(3)	(4)	(5)	(6)	(7)	(8)	(9)	(10)	(11)	(12)	(13)
	(%)	(%)	(%)	(%)	(%)	(%)	(%)	(%)	(%)	(%)	(%)	(%)	(%)
N=	1,396	6,590	13,675	4,141	1,488	3,736	1,022	1,818	1,461	2,253	303	703	1,764
Of these, women: (%)	8.1	5.8	11.3	16.4	9.5	22.2	3.0	10.3	2.7	5.7	6.9	10.5	6.6
	(%)	(%)	(%)	(%)	(%)	(%)	(%)	(%)	(%)	(%)	(%)	(%)	(%)
Age													
>30	0.3	1.4	10.9	8.7	1.6	6.8	0.5	3.4	0.2	0.7	—	0.6	4.0
31–40	8.4	15.5	28.1	25.3	12.2	39.0	15.0	22.9	7.7	15.2	3.6	11.5	20.0
41–50	49.8	49.2	37.4	44.6	53.8	45.4	49.5	50.2	47.6	49.7	50.8	50.0	50.0
51–55	23.8	23.7	16.1	16.7			26.0	17.2	31.1	23.4	27.8	22.6	21.5
55+	17.7	10.2	7.5	4.7	32.4	8.8	9.0	6.3	13.4	11.0	17.8	15.3	4.5
Party membership													
Before 1948	39.3	28.3	7.3	21.5	60.2	29.1	42.4	10.2	53.2	19.8	53.4	29.3	25.0
1949–56	14.7	14.7	11.0	24.9	21.8	26.7	21.7	11.0	20.9	10.6	17.2	13.8	31.1
Since 1957	21.1	30.5	41.0	41.1	13.7	44.2	29.9	36.7	21.8	31.7	14.2	24.1	40.5
Not party member	24.9	26.5	40.7	12.5	4.3	—	6.0	42.1	4.1	37.9	15.2	32.8	3.4
Education													
University/college	89.4	65.4	27.9	37.6	87.8	57.8	63.5	63.0	65.8	67.5	91.4	86.2	19.7
Secondary school	9.8	31.6	50.3	39.6	8.6	32.5	33.9	33.7	30.5	30.2	7.3	13.0	42.1
Elementary school	0.8	3.0	21.8	22.8	3.6	9.7	2.6	3.3	3.7	2.3	1.3	0.8	38.2
Political education													
Higher level	14.5	9.7	3.3	8.0	25.9	29.8	11.3	3.5	19.9	7.2	20.4	10.9	6.8
Mid-level	20.0	28.1	14.4	32.5	20.1	36.6	37.1	22.2	34.7	24.7	22.4	18.0	39.4

Table 3.7 (contd)

	Ministry or national agency executive	Executive in industry or service sector	Executive in agriculture or industry	Executive local government	CC, HSWP nomenklatura appointees	HSWP full-time central, regional and local apparat	Factories CEO*	Factories Deputy CEO	Enterprises CEO	Enterprises Deputy CEO	Ministry or national agency MDPH**	Ministry or national agency DPYH***	City, town or village mayor
	(1)	(2)	(3)	(4)	(5)	(6)	(7)	(8)	(9)	(10)	(11)	(12)	(13)
Lower level	7.5	13.3	24.1	31.6	12.5	14.1	15.8	14.1	14.0	11.4	11.0	7.1	33.3
No political education	58.0	48.9	58.2	27.9	41.5	19.5	35.8	60.2	31.4	56.7	46.2	64.0	20.5
Original occupation													
Worker	27.2	37.4	22.6	35.4	49.3	44.2	58.4	28.2	55.0	23.9	32.1	22.9	45.9
Peasant	1.1	2.3	22.1	12.7	0.9	9.2	4.5	2.2	2.2	1.4	1.3	1.0	17.8
Intellectual and white-collar	36.2	24.6	22.0	9.3	30.8	22.7	21.0	26.6	19.0	28.3	36.3	36.0	7.9
Other	35.5	35.7	33.3	42.6	19.0	23.9	16.1	43.0	23.8	46.4	30.3	40.1	28.4
In present position since													
1945–56	6.4	10.6	7.9	13.1	5.4	2.6	11.5	10.1	11.9	10.0	9.5	7.2	12.0
1957–68	42.0	46.0	50.9	44.8	48.1	40.2	45.9	40.0	52.7	46.3	50.1	38.5	46.5
1969–	51.6	43.4	41.2	42.1	46.5	57.2	42.6	49.9	35.4	43.7	40.4	54.3	41.5
Transferred to present position from/as													
Party apparat	5.2	3.8	1.7	6.2	nd	—	7.3	0.3	9.7	1.0	7.6	2.3	8.7
State administration	37.0	12.7	9.9	50.3	nd	21.6	8.4	5.2	23.0	13.8	40.6	33.7	35.0
Mass organization	2.4	1.7	1.2	1.7	nd	21.3	1.8	0.2	5.0	0.7	2.7	2.6	2.8
Economic manager	29.0	64.8	35.8	11.0	nd	28.1	69.0	75.3	46.6	66.2	24.4	32.3	16.1
Other institutions	11.0	3.1	2.5	5.6	nd	15.1	1.2	2.5	3.5	4.4	12.9	9.8	6.8
Manual worker	1.7	2.0	13.7	11.1	nd	4.3	2.9	1.3	3.0	1.4	0.9	2.3	16.7
Other	13.7	11.9	35.2	14.1	nd	9.6	9.4	15.2	9.2	12.5	10.9	17.0	13.9

Note: N = 38, 586;   *CEO = Director-General;   **MDPH = Main Department Head;   *** = DPYH = Deputy Department Head

who toiled in the small manufacturing, construction, transportation, and service sectors.

5 Local government bureaucrats, and municipal and village mayors (columns 4 and 13) had much in common. This included modest-to-middling educational backgrounds, high ratios of party members, substantial involvement in political education, worker or peasant social background, and previous job experience as local administrators, "manual workers," or officers at "other institutions."

In sum, the "reds" were located in cluster (b), and occupied one-half and one-third of cluster (c), one-half of (d), and the entire cluster of (e). The "experts" were located in clusters (c) and (d). Those who were both – that is, the highly educated minority with university degrees – were the central *nomenklatura* appointees and much of the party apparat proper.

From these data one can draw guarded inferences about the dynamics of the parallel, yet overlapping, political and meritocratic occupational hierarchies in Hungary in the early 1970s. With the prudent use of such evidence, one can identify areas of relative political and professional autonomy – as well as loci of nascent political proto-pluralism – within the state administrative sector.

Data in Table 3.7 can also serve as a point of departure for the "before" part of a "before-and-after" kind of longitudinal comparison of elite stratification and mobility between the early (1973) and late (1983–7) years of the Kádár regime. In my view, questions of "class rule of the intelligentsia," "second society," and the sociopolitical consequences of economic reforms may best be addressed by a study of elite mobility and social restratification in this crucial period of economic crisis, social instability, and political decline.

Hungarian elites in the 1980s: generational change, professional autonomy, and political exit

Elite mobility in the 1980s was driven by three main determinants: political criteria in the selection of personnel, processes and outcomes of generational change, and the internal realignment of elite groups. The regime's criteria of occupational advancement were political reliability, educational qualifications, and leadership skills. The salience of each to appointments, transfers, and promotions varied according to the place and distance from political power of a given position in the occupational hierarchy. Village clerks need not have been university graduates; ministry deputy main department heads, deputy enterprise CEOs for engineering, and museum directors, though *nomenklatura* appointees, need not have been party members.

In the age of "diploma inflation" in Hungary, the possession of formal educational credentials by prospective appointees for executive and managerial positions could be taken for granted. However, "leadership skills," whether or not buttressed by diplomas, were judged by the permissive standards of the regime's semi-Balkanic administrative culture.[62] In a political system where in 1987 only nineteen of 14,416 permanent senior civil servants were facing state disciplinary action, the standards of professional conduct could not have been particularly rigorous.[63]

By generational change I refer to the large-scale exit of the 20- to 30-year-olds of 1945–9, that is, those now 60 and older, and their replacement by the 20- to 30-year- olds of 1960; that is, the 40- to 50-year old cohort that came to occupy 42 percent of the elite positions in the 1980s. Except for the tenacious 50-year-old or older survivors at the top of the occupational hierarchy, for the younger professionals of the "reform era," and for recent university graduates of the post-1975 period, the doors at the top were generally closed.

The realignment of elite groups between 1975 and 1985 was the result of changes due to (a) continued improvements in educational qualifications and the highly differentiated inflow and horizontal mobility of university and college graduates into various elite categories; (b) significant inroads made by women into several elite but less prestigious occupational groups; (c) transfers of personnel from the party apparat, mass organizations, and the military into targeted elite occupational groups; and (d) the growing social and professional homogeneity of several elite occupational clusters.

In discussing each of these matters, I am seeking to test propositions that I submitted in the Introduction about (a) the Hungarian party elites' declining functional adequacy to tasks of system management in the economy, public administration, and the delivery of other – cultural, educational, legal, health, and other infrastructural, that is, local government – services; (b) the increasing differentiation between the party and the state, and the growing autonomy of the latter in the area of policy implementation and, albeit gradually, in that of policy-making as well; and (c) the HSWP's declining authority and, as a consequence, the exit of the educated party cadres from the party, mass organizations, and the military into selected clusters of the state bureaucracy.

In my view, answers to (a) may be obtained by examining the mobility outcomes, particularly in terms of the presence or absence of professional skills throughout the elite hierarchy. Answers to (b) may be gleaned from trends in the social and educational *homogeneity* of the specific elite groups employed in the state bureaucracy with emphasis on their increasing "differentness" from the comparable attributes of the party and mass organization apparat. And answers to (c), from the degree of highly specialized elite groups' *permeability* to transfers from the party and mass organization apparat and from the *occupational destinations* of well-educated refugees from the party apparat. Thus, the themes of "professional autonomy," and "apparat conversion" seem to be the appropriate venues of inquiry for the study of the changing Hungarian administrative elites of the 1980s.

There are two sets of data from which to derive evidence for the analysis of generational change and elite mobility in the 1980s. These are party- and government-sponsored national surveys in 1983 and 1987, with samples of 14,000 to 15,000 each, on twenty occupational elite groups; and a sociological study with statistical information on the socioeducational attributes of 5,600 members of the HSWP apparat in 1981 and 1989.[64] Each data base brings us closer to tentative answers to questions and propositions advanced above.

Bureaucrats at the crossroads: professional autonomy and political exit

From the early 1970s on, the state and its upper-echelon bureaucracy gradually went from co-managers to the *de facto* administrative executors of the regime's political will. Implementation of the economic reforms, by way of hands-on management of the state's resources and all, except the top *nomenklatura*, of its personnel, imparted a remarkable amount of discretionary authority to low-and mid-level bureaucrats. Because the party center was increasingly preoccupied with strategic macroeconomic, top cadre, and foreign policy issues, the regime's administrative prefects in charge of regional county and municipal resource management enjoyed growing decision-making autonomy over their respective areas of jurisdiction. Thus, there emerged, within the bowels of the party-state, a new counterforce with a will and interests of its own.

The party- and Council of Ministers-commissioned surveys of 1983, 1984, and 1987 on the political, social, and economic attributes of the *nomenklatura* elites were highly specific in scope and covered in each year 14,000 to 15,000 individuals in twenty occupational categories. The following discussion will draw on the published findings of the

1983 and 1987 surveys, as well as on the initial results that emerged from the processed contents of this data base.[65] Explicit comparisons, however desirable, between the results of these surveys and the data in Table 3.7 are possible only to a limited degree. The samples are different, the data base for the 1973 survey is unavailable, and, as shown below, there is only partial information on the social and educational attributes of the party apparat in the 1980s.

The results of these surveys generally confirm the essential findings of the 1980 and 1990 censuses on educational background and occupational stratification.[66] However, the survey data at hand do permit the making of important distinctions among the incumbents of twenty elite occupational clusters. Each cluster is an aggregate of 1 to 47 civil service occupational titles among the 228 included in the sample. (The range is roughly equivalent to US Civil Service ranks from G-11 down to G-77.) The data in Table 3.8 are particularly useful in shedding light on trends in elite mobility during the last four years (1983–7) of the old regime's rule. The description and coding of the clusters are given in Appendix 3.1.

The extent of *professional autonomy* and degree of cohesion of incumbents who belonged to specific occupational elite groups may be measured in various ways. Given the high shares of party members (78.5 and 80.5 percent) in the 1983 and in the 1987 samples, the first step will be the determination of the educational qualifications of each cluster's incumbents and, within each, the ratios of less well-skilled high-school and college graduates, and the better-educated university graduates.

The data in Table 3.8 can be rearranged according to shares of university graduates in the 1987 sample to generate three layers with several occupational clusters in each.

To the first layer we can assign clusters with shares of university graduates from 80 to 98.9 percent, thus obtaining a layer consisting of incumbents of STADM I and II, COUNCIL I, ENT I, and II, and the nongovernmental CULTED, HEALTH, and LAW clusters.

To the second layer belong the clusters with shares of university graduates from 60 to 79 percent. From this we thus obtain a layer consisting of incumbents of the STADM II., COUNCIL II, ENT II, INT, and BANK clusters.

To the third layer belong the clusters with shares of university graduates from 9.7 to 58.4 per cent. From this we obtain a layer consisting of incumbents of the COUNCIL IV, AGCOOP I and II, and MEDIA clusters.

Table 3.8 *Executives and senior managers among state administrative, economic, and nongovernmental occupational clusters, by education, 1983, 1987*[67]

Occupational cluster*	N		Education (in % of cohort)					
			High school		College		University	
	1983	1987	1983	1987	1983	1987	1983	1987
STADM I	121	127	5.0	2.4	9.1	5.6	86.0	92.1
STADM II	1,311	1,440	6.5	11.1	11.7	12.6	81.8	76.3
STADM III	737	735	9.2	6.5	10.9	9.3	79.9	84.2
COUNCIL I	110	106	3.6	1.9	18.2	13.2	78.2	84.9
COUNCIL II	238	321	6.7	6.2	15.5	21.5	77.7	72.3
COUNCIL III	509	303	8.8	4.1	18.9	14.2	72.3	81.7
COUNCIL IV	2,681	2,597	27.4	24.6	64.4	65.7	8.2	9.7
ENT I	718	480	7.4	4.4	12.5	13.8	80.1	81.9
ENT II	1,258	2,473	8.5	7.1	12.9	12.2	78.6	80.8
ENT III	1,326	1,255	14.2	13.1	21.7	22.2	64.1	64.4
AGCOOP I	770	685	20.1	20.0	29.4	21.6	50.5	58.4
AGCOOP II	733	699	24.3	24.5	32.1	25.1	43.7	52.8
ISCOOP I	373	316	56.6	37.0	20.4	34.2	23.1	28.8
ISCOOP II	233	231	67.8	54.1	15.9	25.1	16.3	20.8
INT	127	114	28.3	10.5	13.4	25.4	58.3	64.0
CULTED	712	766	3.1	1.6	8.8	8.4	88.1	90.1
HEALTH	115	140	7.8	5.0	5.2	5.0	87.0	90.0
MEDIA	426	488	27.7	20.5	17.1	21.1	55.2	58.4
LAW	731	723	0.5	0.3	0.7	0.8	98.8	98.9
BANK	184	328	24.5	8.2	11.4	16.8	64.1	75.0

Note: 1983 N = 15,278; 1987 N = 14,416; * For description of occupational titles in each occupational cluster, please see Appendix 3.1 below.

In quantitative terms, the three layers, when each is rearranged by the above criteria, form a pyramidal structure that roughly duplicates the hierarchical division of administrative, particularly resource-allocation, power within the state structure. Although such was to be expected, this static scheme does not, in and of itself, explain the professional autonomy that one is inclined to attribute to the top three (CULTED, HEALTH, and LAW) professional clusters. Moreover, this scheme fails to address the issue of the growing influence and *de facto* policy-veto power of organizations – the TUF, the YCL, the PPF, the NCAC, the Chamber of Commerce, and the assorted national associations of the technocratic intelligentsia – whose executives belonged to

INT. To a lesser extent, the same is probably true for the financial executives of BANK.

To augment these initial findings, I subjected the clusters to a test of *permeability* by considering the respective shares of cadre inflows into each cluster from the party apparat, the mass organizations, and the military in 1983 and 1987. For the sake of manageability, I divided the institutional sources of personnel inflows into the following categories: "first-job" new entrants and those coming from the HSWP, the mass organizations, and the military; state and local administrations (seven clusters); the economic bureaucracy (seven clusters); and three professional clusters collapsed into one.

The data, as shown in Table 3.9, on political cadre inflows into various aggregates of elite occupational clusters are self-explanatory and are also suitable for an informal test of "cluster permeability."

As measured by shares of political entrants into various clusters, one may distinguish among three layers of recipient clusters. To the first layer belong COUNCIL I with 39.1 (1983) and 34.9 (1987) percent intake; to the second, the clusters with 1983 and 1987 intake ratios of 20 to 29 percent (STADM I and COUNCIL II); and to the third, the clusters with 1983 and 1987 intake ratios of 1.3 to 6.7 percent, such as STADM III, COUNCIL IV, ENT I, II, and III, ISCOOP II, CULTED, HEALTH, LAW, and BANK.

What changed between 1973 and the mid-1980s was the apparat's virtual occupation of all levels (STADM I–III) of the Budapest municipal government and that of the nineteen main administrative regions (counties). The media and the interest groups have been customary career destinations for cashiered agit-prop types from the the HSWP apparat. On the other hand, the invasion by scores of keen apparatchiki of the high-cash-flow and half-second economy ISCOOP I cluster, hints at sensible trade-offs between money and administrative power. The same was probably true for those who saw new opportunities in the nearly doubled (1983–87) BANK cluster. In any case, from the declining rates of political entrants to the "red barons'" turf (ENT I), one might surmise that apparat castoffs were no longer welcome as CEOs by deficit-ridden large enterprises in the late 1980s.

The traditional intelligentsia enclaves of CULTED, HEALTH, and LAW with 95-plus percent professional incumbents came close to having an "apparatchik-free" personnel environment.

Another way of looking at the data might be by approaching the issue of *corporate autonomy* by measuring the inflow ratios from within the same, or functionally closely related, clusters. The highest ratios

Table 3.9 *Executives and senior managers among state administrative, economic, and nongovernmental occupational clusters, by place of previous employment, 1983, 1987 (by percentage of cohort[68]*

Occupational cluster	First job		HSWP, Mass org. Military		STADM I–III, COUNCIL I–IV		ENT I–III AGCOOP I–11 ISCOOP I–II		CULTED Other* HEALTH MEDIA	
	1983	1987	1983	1987	1983	1987	1983	1987	1983	1987
STADM I	4.1	4.8	21.5	22.2	41.3	30.2	22.3	31.7	10.7	11.1
STADM II	7.9	10.6	10.8	17.3	34.8	26.9	35.4	32.8	10.8	12.4
STADM III	9.9	14.4	6.1	5.6	28.1	26.5	40.3	39.0	15.3	14.1
COUNCIL I	3.6	2.8	39.1	34.9	30.9	32.1	20.0	22.6	6.4	7.5
COUNCIL II	2.1	3.1	15.5	15.3	51.7	56.7	23.5	19.0	7.1	5.9
COUNCIL III	2.0	2.8	23.4	21.4	41.8	44.0	20.6	20.6	12.0	11.2
COUNCIL IV	3.8	3.1	5.0	5.4	49.9	50.7	35.2	33.8	5.7	6.9
ENT I	11.8	16.9	7.2	4.6	11.1	10.6	66.9	66.3	2.4	1.7
ENT II	11.0	12.6	7.1	5.3	16.1	10.8	62.6	67.7	3.2	3.2
ENT III	7.8	16.3	5.1	5.4	13.8	13.0	68.4	61.2	4.0	3.7
AGCOOP I	9.9	9.1	5.3	3.8	9.7	5.8	71.0	77.5	2.1	2.2
AGCOOP II	13.2	12.7	2.0	1.3	8.0	5.4	73.4	78.0	1.6	2.0
ISCOOP I	4.3	9.1	13.4	12.0	5.9	6.3	70.5	67.7	2.1	1.9
ISCOOP II	4.3	7.4	6.4	4.8	7.3	8.2	79.4	76.2	2.1	2.0
INT	2.4	2.6	16.5	20.2	20.5	22.8	40.9	33.3	18.1	18.4
CULTED	12.1	13.1	4.1	3.7	21.9	16.4	15.9	18.9	45.0	47.4
HEALTH	4.3	5.0	1.7	4.3	15.7	14.3	4.3	5.0	73.0	71.4
MEDIA	11.3	15.8	15.7	12.7	11.3	8.6	18.8	19.5	42.5	40.8
LAW	35.7	33.5	3.8	4.0	34.1	35.3	20.5	21.4	4.4	5.0
BANK	19.6	23.8	13.6	6.7	25.0	20.4	39.1	45.7	2.7	3.0
Average	9.5	11.6	7.8	7.7	26.9	24.0	45.4	46.2	9.8	10.1

Note: 1983 N = 15,278; 1987 N = 14,416. * The category "other" in the original table has been omitted; its average value for the 20 clusters was 1.06 and 1.03 for 1983 and 1987, with the largest deviations being 3.8 and 3.8 (both for ISCOOP I) in 1983 and 1987 respectively. STADM I, COUNCIL I and II have no one from the "other" category in either year.

were those of the seven economic and industrial-service cooperatives, and that of the HEALTH cluster. In the municipal, county, sub-county, and village government sectors the trend toward greater circulation of same-sector bureaucrats was also apparent.

Elites "in place" in the 1980s were also displaying signs of self-confidence and growing *political autonomy*. Eighty percent of the incumbents of the 1983 sample held their appointments on the strength of routine "supplemental," rather than a more comprehensive "basic," job evaluation. This ratio, notwithstanding the major turn-overs since 1981, remained the same (81.9 percent) in 1987. The administrative elites' *de facto* job tenure thus became a *de jure* reality, and one that was guaranteed by the newly amended Hungarian Labor Code. The political regime could collapse, as it did in 1989, but the administrative, economic, and corporatist elites were firmly in place by the mid-1980s.

The option of a quiet exit from the party apparat for the state or for another sector was, at least in theory, open to all full-time party employees. As Károly Grósz explained in a 1992 interview, in September 1988 (then serving as secretary general and prime minister) he had held an informal Sunday meeting for a group of HSWP line secretaries – probably from the municipal and county apparats. "I told them that we, as leaders, will pay for the political and moral cost of [political] restructuring. He who cannot make this sacrifice, should leave now ... and he will be well looked after ... Everyone stayed."[69] We might ask why.

According to the Hungarian sociologist Ferenc Gazsó's empirical study on the party and state elites, the main source of the (remaining) apparat's difficulties in effecting a suitable transfer, without loss of income or equivalent administrative rank, from the party to the state lay in the lack of the would-be migrants' "convertible" qualifications.[70] There were significant disparities between the two, party and state, cohorts' respective "convertible" qualifications (see Table 3.10). Although Gazsó did not specify the attributes of "convertibility," one assumes that in addition to foreign languages, educational credentials, and previous professional experience, the term also included leadership and entrepreneurial skills that could be utilized either in the second, or later in an actual, market economy.

Therefore, most of Grósz's colleagues, especially those from the county apparat, had nowhere else to go (see Table 3.11). They had no choice but to accept whatever fate the hoped-for "change of the model" and, eventually, the change of the political system handed to

Table 3.10 *Educational qualifications of Hungarian party and state elites, 1981 and 1989*[71]

Qualification	Party elites		State elites	
	1981 (N=5,845) %	1989 (N=4,989) %	1981 (N=748) %	1989 (N=431) %
University or college degree	44.2	57.1	77.5	92.8
University diploma work (MA)	5.4	7.8	19.1	26.5
Postgraduate or higher academic degree	2.7	4.7	14.6	18.9
Knowledge of a foreign language	15.4	19.2	53.7	69.4
Knowledge of two or more foreign languages	4.7	7.1	28.5	43.6
Substantial previous professional experience	22.3	27.8	39.4	55.5
Convertible intellectual qualifications	17.6	28.5	49.6	71.4

Table 3.11 *Educational qualifications of HSWP apparat, 1980s*[72]

Qualification	Party apparat level[*]		
	Central %	Budapest %	County %
University or college degree	79.3	50.1	53.5
University diploma work (MA)	19.0	7.1	6.5
Postgraduate or higher academic degree	9.7	2.5	3.0
Knowledge of foreign language(s)	50.6	24.7	12.6
Substantial previous professional experience	44.3	17.9	26.9
Convertible intellectual qualifications	48.9	25.9	29.0

Note: [*] N = approximately 5,500.

them. At the end, whether as CC members or as the regime's provincial prefects and their local lieutenants, these victims of miseducation and obsolescent skills were not in a position to prevent the party's demise at the last congress of the HSWP in October 1989. Eighty-two percent of the 1,279 voting delegates were university and college graduates.[73] Most of them had skills that were readily convertible to executive and managerial positions and business opportunities in the postcommunist era. They arrived just in time to occupy, then promptly sink with all hands on board, the Kádár regime's derelict political flagship, the Hungarian Socialist Workers' Party.

The intellectuals: insurgents and the incumbents

Every third Hungarian university and college graduate was a party member in the 1980s, but all graduates were parts of the various layers of *nomenklatura* elites that ran Hungary on the regime's behalf. These people and the not-yet-elite but increasingly prosperous rural and urban entrepreneurs of the second economy constituted the new Hungarian middle class. To assess the contribution of new and old social forces to political outcomes, one must briefly consider the role that this amorphous social formation, particularly the intelligentsia, played in the transformation of the political system.

It is axiomatic that classes, *qua* classes, do not transform and replace political regimes; elites and active minorities do. Therefore, the task is to identify the active minorities that, in political terms, were or might have been salient to what took place in the waning years of the Kádár era in Hungary.

The sociologist Iván Szelényi and the writer György Konrád proposed in their influential (samizdat, but widely read) (1974) study, *The Intellectuals on the Road to Class Power*, that the logic of "rational redistribution," that is, the growing indispensability of highly trained specialist elites to policy-makers in the party apparat, would inevitably lead to the large-scale co-optation of the former by the latter.[74] In the end, the "intellectuals," particularly the technical and scientific types, with the humanistic intellectuals in tow, would take over the apparat, though still permit the political elite to wield power, albeit in an indirect, or "hegemonic" way.

This proposition, if one somehow still believed in the reformability of existing socialism in the 1970s, seemed plausible in the early 1970s. Its inherent flaw was that it overlooked the nascent autonomy of the state, that of the newly empowered interest groups and the already visible power of the rural second economy in Hungary. The barter of "brains for power" that Szelényi and Konrád proposed in 1974 posed no threat to the authoritarian essence of the political status quo. The logic of the Szelényi–Konrád agenda, to use Zygmunt Bauman's devastating insight on the Russian and East European intellectuals' actual motivations behind their "proselytism, moral mission and cultural crusade," called only for "the exchange of an enlightened despot for the despotism of the enlightened."[75] Ironically, this partnership, had it been accepted by Kádár and his PB, might have stabilized the regime for some time to come. However, this was not to be.

Whereas Stalin shot or imprisoned his troublesome intellectuals, Kádár only distrusted and, by all acounts, despised them. Instead of a partnership with the intelligentsia, he tried, or went along with ill-advised policies, to "reproletarianize" the apparat and keep the intellectuals in their tribal reservations at the Writers' Union and the Academy of Sciences. This solution passed the litmus test of ideological orthodoxy but failed the test of cost-effective management. The apparat, which was handicapped, to use Gazsó's phrase, by its "educational deficit" thus bereft of intellectual authority, deserted the party for positions in the state and for new opportunities in the second economy. All of this left the intellectuals high and dry or, as Szelényi and Konrád had characterized their original predicament, "marginalized."

In retrospect, the intellectuals' aborted raid on, and their exclusion from, the fortresses of the party apparat was a blessing in disguise. Instead of confronting, or being co-opted by, the party, the critical intelligentsia was compelled to fight its battles with the political and economic incumbents from within the political system. As expert consultants to CC policy advisory committees, or as authors of – ironically enough, many of them HSWP-commissioned – published studies on social stratification, poverty, and legal and economic reforms, the intellectuals contributed much more to the regime's demise than they might have as, inevitably junior, partners of the party apparat.[76]

Instead of the acquisition of "class power," it was their brainpower and success in raising doubts in books, journals, newspaper articles, and the electronic media, about the regime's right to rule that politicized the Hungarian middle class and helped them accept the eventual terms of an uncontested divorce from the old regime. Under economically and politically unstable conditions public perceptions do acquire political salience in helping strengthen or paralyze, in Harry Eckstein's terminology, the "insurgents'" and the "incumbents'" self-confidence.[77] Becoming society's "early warning system" – an honorable tradition of men and women of ideas everywhere – was the intellectuals' principal contribution to their and the society's eventual emancipation from communist rule.

Elite pluralism: towards a civil society?

Much of the above discussed intraelite competitive relationships and the reemergence of various semiautonomous bureaucratic interest groups making claims on the political incumbents may be seen as partial evidence for the birth of a new context for societal interaction and enhanced political self-awareness in Hungary. The political scientist Csaba Gombár called the outcome a politically differentiated society in which latent but distinct group interests could not find political expression or benefit from equitable interest adjudication by the powers that be.[78]

The sociologist Elemér Hankiss, in his important study *The East European Alternatives*, called this new context the "second society."[79] In Hankiss' conceptualization the new entity was much more than the social analogue of the second, or unofficial, economy. The term denoted the diverse results of an initially latent but, by the early 1980s, semivisible process of social restratification and the people's psychological transformation that had been taking place partly within the confines of, and partly outside, Hungary's first, or "official," society. As Hankiss explained,

> The first society and the second society were not two distinct groups of people; they were only two dimensions of social existence governed by two different sets of organizational principles. Everybody in Hungary, or at least most of its citizens, belonged to, and moved around in, both of these dimensions; in both of these "societies."[80]

The second society differed from the first in several respects. Hankiss offered nine criteria for distinguishing between the two. Of these, the processes of differentiation and integration, horizontal patterns of organization, the upward flow of power and influence, movement toward individual and group autonomy, the primacy of social and economic over political factors, the predominance of nonstate ownership, and the coexistence of several "alternative" values and ideologies were the most important.

Throughout, the political regime had a choice whether to resist or accommodate the autonomist aspirations of the new Hungarian middle class. Had accommodation been the chosen strategy, it could have taken the form of *controlled* generational, institutional, and, at the end, leadership change some time between 1978 and 1982. This, as will be shown in Chapters 6 and 7, was not and could not have been the regime's choice. In his last ten years in power Kádár and the elders of his PB opted for a policy of piecemeal concessions and protracted "house-to-house" rearguard action to postpone the day of reckoning with the new social forces whose time came in 1989.

Conclusions: a society in transition

In the foregoing discussion I sought to assess the impact of political mobilization, economic modernization and the development of new, and the revival of old, social forces on the Hungarian society in the Kádár era. The objective was to present evidence and to raise questions about the dimensions and inner dynamics of Hungary's social development under communist rule. The terms of inquiry focused on trends of continuity and change and on such dichotomies – intended versus unintended outcomes, promise versus performance and "trans-contractual" issues of elite circulation – as seemed useful to formulating hypotheses about the dynamics of social change in Hungary.

Some of my hypotheses about general social trends and outcomes have been borne out by the evidence presented in the narrative. These included (a) the role that the regime's developmental imperatives played in restoring the traditional elites' privileged access to educational and occupational mobility; (b) the primacy of social "subcontracts" over the regime's "master contract" and the way it contributed to group autonomy; (c) the interpenetration, due to vast inflows of first-generation university graduates into mid-level and top occupational positions, of the old intelligentsia and the new elites and the consequent birth of a new socialist middle class, and (d) the ambiguous "fit" of various layers of HSWP members in the larger nonparty community.

On the other hand, the hypothesized dichotomy of "reds" and "experts," on grounds of party membership and the implicit attribution to party members of ideological orthodoxy and political loyalty to the regime, never materialized in the age of reforms in Hungary. The distinction between "reds" and "experts" may have been useful as a first-approximation kind of taxonomical device for the classification of elites in cadre parties of the Chinese People's Republic and the USSR. However, in Kádár's "all-people's" mass party, the internalization of the regime's official mantra was, by special dispensation from the pragmatic leader, a private option for most of the elites.

In Hungary clashes over political and social issues arose *not* along ideological (reds versus experts), but functional (party versus state), redistributional (industry versus agriculture or infrastructure), spatial (center versus periphery), professional (educated versus less well-educated), and generational (younger versus older) lines of interest articulation and interest aggregation by members of the affected occupational clusters. Whereas party membership had high salience for recruitment into the *nomenklatura* elite, for higher educational background, and for incomes from the first economy, it became largely irrelevant in the context of the competitive relationship between the state bureaucracy and the party apparat – and even more so to the inner workings of traditional intelligentsia occupational clusters in the 1980s.

The second economy had a major influence on the formation and realignment of social-status groups in Hungary. The citizens' incomes from the second economy helped create new cross-cutting cleavages in the society. In the villages, the second economy restratified the local society into entrepreneurs, bureaucrats, and economic marginals; in factories the labor force became divided among commuters, intraenterprise entrepreneurs, and young, female, and unskilled hourly paid workers; and the university and college graduates were split between those with "convertible" skills and those without access to the second economy. Yet, as testimony to the persistence of traditional perceptions of social prestige, "money" as such played a secondary role to "knowledge" and "power" in determining occupational prestige in the 1980s. Therefore, it was the community notables – the local doctors, lawyers, and teachers – rather than the parvenu millionaire entrepreneurs who became the people's choices as parliamentary deputies in 1985 and 1990.

The invisible hand of the second economy contributed in subtle ways to special outcomes in social and occupational mobility. Although in terms of upward social mobility the winners greatly outnumbered the losers, few people in Hungary were free from frustrations of status inconsistency and from various pathologies of relative deprivation. Some of the causes were rooted in reasonable grievances over the state's delivery of health, education, and social welfare services; some may be attributed to the irreconcilability of public expectations for ever-increasing living standards and the government's finite resources to provide the same.

Public responses to real and perceived regime shortcomings became, in statistically demonstrable terms, manifest in the form of exits from the first economy and the first society. The commuting peasant-worker put in his hours at the factory but saved his energy for his household plot back in his village; the underpaid white-collar worker took a second job; young people quit dead-end jobs and, if they could, left for the second economy; the providers of professional services – doctors, lawyers, and those in the applied technical fields – had the least trouble in effecting their respective exits from the first economy of low salaries yet agreeably flexible work rules to the world of gratuities and high incomes. However, the unskilled worker, the rural laborer, the poor, and the sick had no choice, but to seek refuge in absenteeism from the workplace, in alcohol, or in the ultimate exit – suicide.

The party apparat's exit had been driven by an interesting version of Gresham's Law: the apparat's well-entrenched underachievers drove their comrades with convertible skills out into the state administration or to the second economy. The would-be refugees took a hard look at themselves, their colleagues, their leaders, and their take-home pay and promptly traded their political appointments for tenured positions in the state bureaucracy. However, unlike the peasant workers, the white-collar types, the young, the professionals, and the apparatchiki, the intellectuals, bereft of marketable skills, were on the spot and had nowhere to go.

The structure of Hungarian society in the 1980s had little in common with the regime's founders' "two classes – one stratum" ideological blueprint. As shown above, over the years the society had become sharply differentiated according to formal education, place in the occupational hierarchy, income, consumption, social status, access to housing, health care, and involvement in the second economy. Moreover, instead of a small monolithic ruling elite, toward the end of the Kádár era the by then mature *nomenklatura* elite was divided into hierarchically differentiated semiautonomous occupational clusters that were kept together more by a combination of inertia and their emerging sense of corporatist identity than by loyalty to the political incumbents.

Appendix 3.1

Executives, public administration, industry, agriculture, industrial, agricultural, and service cooperatives, interest groups, education, culture, health services, law and banking, Hungary, 1987

1. State administration I (STADM I);^{**}
   N = 121 (1983), 126 (1987).
   Presidential Council, Secretariat, Council of Ministers, Secretariat, Parliament (? positions);^{***}
   Government ministries (4 positions);
   Ministries and agencies with national jurisidiction (5 positions).
2. State administration II (STADM II);
   N = 1,311 (1983), 1,440 (1987).
   Presidential Council (? positions);
   Government ministries and agencies with national jurisdiction (9 positions);
   Branch offices of government ministries (5 positions).
3. State Administration III (STADM III);
   N = 737 (1983), 735 (1987).
   Ministries and agencies with national jurisdisdiction, department heads (1 position).
4. City and county councils I (COUNCIL II);
   N = 110 (1983), 106 (1987).
   Mayor, deputy mayors;
   Secretary, Executive Committee, Budapest;
   Mayors and secretaries of Executive Committees of other cities with county rights;
   Chairmen, deputy chairmen, and secretaries of Executive Committees of county councils (6 positions).
5. City and county councils II (COUNCIL II);
   N = 238 (1983), 321 (1987).
   Budapest municipal government;
   Main department heads and deputy heads, mayors and secretaries of Executive Committees of other cities (4 positions).
6. City and county councils III (COUNCIL III);
   N = 509 (1983), 393 (1987).
   Deputy heads of Budapest, county, and district local governments;
   Chairmen and executive secretaries of Budapest city districts (5 positions).

7. Village councils (COUNCIL IV);
    $N = 2,681$ (1983), 2,597 (1987).
    Mayors and secretaries of Executive Committees of villages (4 positions).
8. Major firms and enterprises (ENT I);
    $N = 718$ (1983), 480 (1987).
    Executives (CEO and deputy CEO) of major firms;
    Hungarian National Railway;
    Hungarian Postal Service (18 positions).
9. Medium-size firms and enterprises (ENT II);
    $N = 1,258$ (1983), 2,473 (1987).
    Senior executives and production managers of medium-size firms and enterprises (19 positions).
10. Smaller firms and enterprises (ENT III);
    $N = 1,326$ (1983), 1,255 (1987).
    Senior executives and production managers of smaller firms and enterprises (15 positions).
11. Large agricultural cooperatives (AGCOOP I);
    $N = 770$ (1983), 685 (1987).
    Chairmen and deputy chairmen of large agricultural cooperatives (2 positions).
12. Smaller agricultural cooperatives (AGCOOP II);
    $N = 733$ (1983), 699 (1987).
    Chairmen and deputy chairmen of smaller agricultural cooperatives (2 positions).
13. Industrial and service cooperatives I (ISCOOP I);
    $N = 373$ (1983), 316 (1987).
    Chairmen and deputy chairmen of industrial and service cooperatives (2 positions).
14. Industrial and service cooperatives II (ISCOOP II);
    $N = 233$ (1983), 231 (1987).
    Head accountants at industrial and service cooperatives (1 position).
15. Social organizations and policy lobbies (INT);
    $N = 127$ (1983), 114 (198).
    Chairman, secretary general, deputy chairman, key secretaries of mass organizations and policy lobbies (5 positions).
16. Top cultural and educational executives (CULTED); $N = 712$ (1983), 766 (1987).

Executives at cultural and educational institutions (including libraries, museums, colleges, universities, theatres, and so on) (43 positions).

17. Health administrators and senior physicians (HEALTH);
    $N = 115$ (1983), 140 (1987).
    Senior health administration and health care personnel (3 positions).

18. Agitprop and communications (MEDIA);
    $N = 426$ (1983), 488 (1987).
    Executives (senior editors, department heads, managers) in the print and electronic media (27 positions).

19. Judges and prosecutors (LAW);
    $N = 731$ (1983), 723 (1987).
    Senior personnel at the courts and the state procuracy (28 positions).

20. Bankers (BANK);
    $N = 184$ (1983), 328 (1987).
    Senior executives in financial institutions (7 positions).

Note: $N = 14,416$ (1987).

[*] Survey was designed and commissioned by the Department of PA, CC, HSWP and the Executive Secretariat of the Council of Ministers and administered by the National Statistical Office in 1983, 1985, and 1987.

[**] Taxonomy of occupational clusters adopted from the NSO coding instructions for the 1983 and 1987 surveys.

[***] $N = 228$ positions/job titles.

PART II

Elite politics: the insurgents and the incumbents

4   Opposition and dissent: ideas, personalities, and strategies

Hungary's political transformation from a postcommunist state to a parliamentary democracy was facilitated by people and their ideas for change. By "people" I mean professional political, academic, and literary elites and unattached intellectuals. They met at the National Roundtable in June, 1989, to craft a historic compromise for a peaceful transition from a politically bankrupt regime to a legitimate one of popular sovereignty, parliamentary democracy, and national independence. By "ideas" I refer to individual opinions and shared views and policy preferences that were brought to the negotiating table by the opposition and the political incumbents.

The ideas were those of the democratic opposition, the Populist-nationalist dissidents, the reform socialist wing of the ruling party, the "third side" of regime-coopted social interest groups and of the officials, mainly lawyers and economists, of Miklós Németh's "government of experts." Dissatisfaction with the old regime and a shared commitment to negotiated solutions for the prevention of Hungary's drift toward economic collapse and political anarchy were the principal motivations of the participants. As designated and self-appointed – incumbent and aspiring – representatives of the political community, all sides had a common interest in securing a sheltered exit for the incumbents and safe transit for the political newcomers. The coincidence of these interests was further strengthened by both elites' – publicly never stated – apprehensions about the Hungarian people's unpredictable, possibly radical, behavior during the forthcoming transition to a new political system. As the key participants saw it, a negotiated agreement, however imperfect, was preferable to chaos and civil disorder.

The purpose of the following discussion is to reconstruct the path, to identify the personalities, and to analyze the political objectives of each of the groups that first met on June 14, 1989 in the Hungarian

Parliament to salvage what they could and build what they might from the ruins of existing socialism. This chapter focuses on the record of those groups and individuals who might, for the want of a more precise term, be called "dissidents" and critics of the political incumbents.

In the most general sense, dissent in a communist one-party state may be conceptualized as a special kind of interest articulation with normative content. Dissent, when so defined, can be postulated as an illegitimate (suppressed) or semilegitimate (tolerated) dimension within the broader universe of interest-group politics in a communist polity. In this context, the articulation of dissident values and interests is perceived and acted upon by the political incumbents in ascending order in terms of threat posed to the political status quo, as one of three types: instrumental-pragmatic, moral-absolutist, and anomic-militant.[1]

All three kinds of dissidents were, in Frederick Bargoorn's terminology, "within-system" critics – not of János Kádár, the ruling party as such, or the top political leadership, but of the perceived shortcomings of existing socialism in Hungary.[2] Prior to 1987 none of the dissidents sought to change the one-party system, nor did they demand the prompt liquidation of central planning and its replacement with a free-enterprise-based market economy. Moreover, none of the dissidents demanded official guarantees of the free exercise of *collective* political rights – such as freedom of assembly and the right to form *political* organizations – beyond those *individual* human rights that had been specified in Basket Three of the Helsinki Final Act of 1975, to which Hungary was a signatory. For these reasons, such terms as "para-opposition" – as George Schopflin called some Hungarian naysayers of the 1970s – and "semicoopted," "self-limiting," and essentially "tolerated" opposition (my characterization) seem to be appropriate, albeit nonheroic, terms to denote the conduct of "otherwise-thinking" (in Russian: *inakomysliashchie*) courageous intellectuals in the late Kádár era in Hungary.[3]

In terms of issue preferences, manner of interest articulation, and location in the political-ideological map of Hungary, we can distinguish among three principal clusters of social, cultural, and political dissent between 1962 and 1988.

1 The Populist-nationalist group of literati, most prominently the writer-poet-playwright Gyula Illyés, the essayist-playwright László Németh, and a long list of writers, poets and provincial intellectuals;
2 The "democratic opposition" of former Marxist and non-Marxist, essentially Budapest-based, urban liberal academic intellectuals

associated with the samizdat journal *Beszélő* under the leadership of János Kis, György Bence, Miklós Haraszti, Ferenc Kőszeg, Ottilia Solt, László Rajk, György Konrád, Tamás Bauer, Miklós Gáspár Tamás, and their numerous followers among the Hungarian urban intelligentsia;

3 The Marxist, and subsequently "post-Marxist," reform socialist intellectuals, such as former prime minister András Hegedüs, the philosophers Ágnes Heller, György Márkus, Ferenc Fehér, the critical sociologists István Kemény and Iván Szelényi and, from the late 1970s on, social scientists at the HSWP's Institute for the Social Sciences (Zsolt Papp, Csaba Gombár, Ferenc Gazsó, Mihály Bihari) and scores of prominent economists, sociologists, and legal scholars at the Hungarian Academy of Sciences (HAS) and on the faculties of Hungary's major universities.

(A)   Dissent and policy-making

Dissent can take many forms in a communist state. What is of interest in the present context is the way in which the articulation of dissident opinions might have influenced party and government policies in Hungary. For this purpose, I will offer a set of propositions concerning the policy-making potentials of dissident views regarding desirable changes in politics, law, economics, ideology, and culture. The argument rests on the demonstrated fact that the posttotalitarian state cannot carry out economic reforms, let alone effect needed institutional change, without significantly enlarging the circle of decision-makers and accommodating a far more diverse set of policy inputs from the elites than before. The issue here is the regime's willingness to adopt, to tolerate, or to reject new ideas – including those coming from unconventional participants with critical views of the existing state of affairs.

Table 4.1 was developed by me to aid theorizing about the policy-making potentials of various dissident groups in the USSR in the 1970s.[4] While preserving the basic taxonomy of the original scheme, I converted the language of several categories to describe Hungarian conditions in the late Kádár era.

As shown above, I make certain assumptions about party and government elite perceptions with respect to the political costs and benefits to the regime of new, particularly of critical, ideas introduced by new entrants into the policy-making process. Much of the scheme is derived from Robert Dahl's reasoning on the conditions, characteristics,

Table 4.1   *Regime perceptions of dissident interest articulation in posttotalitarian Hungary: a heuristic model*

Official perception	Legitimate (supported)	Semilegitimate (tolerated)	Illegitimate (suppressed)
Label	Instrumental-pragmatic	Moral-absolutist	Anomic-militant
Issue area	Developmental rationality	Human rights, "socialist legality" Artistic freedoms Censorship Religious autonomy	October 1956 as revolution Imre Nagy's legacy Anti-Soviet agitation Strikes, other organized labor protest Clandestine activity of any kind
Target	Only to proper authorities (Kádár, party or government officials and agencies)	Proper authorities plus dissemination to unauthorized recipients (including foreign media)	Others – "the people," samizdat, and so on
Affective content	Legitimacy-supportive ("constructive," in "party" or "patriotic" spirit	Policy-legitimacy critical	Antiregime, "anti-Soviet," "subversive" "nationalist"
Style of articulation	Pragmatic-bargaining deferential, "correct" petitions	Uncompromising, "ultimatum-style" demands	"Militant," "verbally aggressive"
Mode of aggregation	Unorganized individuals	*Ad hoc* groups organized to promote one issue	Multi-purpose organization (frequent and routinized interaction)
Agent	High status in *nomenklatura* (economists, scientists, prominent nonparty intellectuals)	High- and medium-status intellectuals, retired party officials well-connected nonparty elites	Low status unattached intellectuals, young people, religious activists, former political prisoners

and developmental variables that determine the relationship between a political regime and its oppponents. Dahl proposed that "the likelihood that a government will tolerate an opposition increases as the expected costs of toleration decrease," and that "the likelihood that a government will tolerate an opposition increases as the expected costs of suppression increase."[5]

It is assumed that the incumbents are more inclined to consider and adopt policy inputs on "developmental" issues, such as economic reforms, than on abstract ideological questions, such as political democracy; that – everything being equal – the rulers could be persuaded to abide by their own formal legality and forgo the discretionary use of power; that recommendations forwarded through proper channels stand a better chance of receiving "open-minded" or at least serious official attention than do the contents of clandestine leaflets or samizdat sent to Radio Free Europe; that conciliatory and deferential language gets better results than do *ad hominen* denunciations of "malfeasance in high places" and so on.

Rezső Nyers' planning group in the early 1960s made full use of the ideas of scores of officially sidelined "reform economists." Official discussions on the social aspects of the yet-to-be inaugurated NEM took into account studies of former prime minister and, by then, "reform sociologist" András Hegedüs on enterprise management and workplace conditions; in 1974 the CC's Agit-Prop Department made use of a major study on rural society and the second economy by the (then-dissident) sociologist Iván Szelényi and his research team; throughout the 1970s the CC's Department of Economic Policy was a steady consumer of commissioned (and most frequently critical) studies on economic issues by senior staff members at the HAS Institute for Economics, and so on. In fact, CC secretary Ferenc Havasi's "in-house" seminar of 1982–4 on economic policy options consisted of a series of pro- and antireform presentations of orthodox and liberal, including semidissident, economists.[6]

However, when some of the initially discreet critics chose to "go public" and thus trespassed on the "semilegitimate" terrain of public policy, the official retaliation, albeit carefully measured to fit circumstances, was swift and ruthless. When György Lukács, András Hegedüs, and five philosophers sent letters to the CC to protest against the invasion of Czechoslovakia, they were reprimanded but did not lose their jobs. Four years later when their continued critical writings forced the regime's hand, they were expelled from the party and dismissed by their respective institutes.[7] At least initially, the same was true for István Kemény, Iván Szelényi, and György Konrád. Although expelled from the Philology Faculty of the Loránd Eötvös University for his involvement in a nebulous Maoist movement in the 1960s, Miklós Haraszti was left alone until he began circulating his explosive exposé on working conditions in a factory where he had been employed for a year.[8] His celebrated – several times postponed, yet inconclusive – trial that culminated in an official warning and a suspended sentence brought together on his behalf a stellar assembly of such character witnesses as the widows of Count Michael Károlyi (the President of the Hungarian Republic in 1918–19), László Rajk, and several leading intellectuals.

The regime's dilemmas on ways to manage dissent of various types in the early 1970s may best be illustrated by citing, *in extenso*, János Kádár's uncharacteristically vehement outburst at the November 28, 1973 meeting of the CC. As Kádár explained,

> The last time I was at the Technical University I said calmly: yes, there is an opposition in Hungary, Maoists, or whatever, but I would sign a ten-year contract with the class enemy that things would stay this way! I proceeded from realities – these are not serious things on a societal scale. However, there are symptoms that should be considered as warning signals!
>
> By now the March 15th nationalist demonstrations have become institutions! Nationalistic demonstrations! We had one this year, too. There were about 3–4 thousand people. We had 2,500 observers ... a few hundred social and official observers and 5–600 nationalist demonstrators. Of these there were a few hundred well-meaning idiots out for a "rumble" and the [showing] of the national colors – however, somebody had to organize it in the first place. And it is quite possible for three–four scoundrels to get together and, before you know it, it is in the world press that there is an annual nationalist demonstration in Hungary ...
>
> The other thing is the Haraszti affair. Everyone knows what it is, if no other way than from the handouts of the MTI (Hungarian Telegraph Agency), because the Hungarian press made no mention of it, but those present here are familiar with the story. There is a man whom I can hardly describe as a writer ... they printed his writings in ten or more copies and, at the end, there was a trial. In addition to this hostile phenomenon and the fact that they have become quite impertinent, another characteristic of this case is that it helped unite all opponents of the regime – leftist and rightist – as I will illustrate it for you. About the Haraszti affair: ... he had been a Maoist student for which he was kicked out of the university. This is how he became a worker. He was forced to become a worker ... At his trial [the

philosophers Ágnes] Heller, [Ferenc] Fehér, [Mihály] Vajda – the so-
called Lukács students – [András] Hegedüs, and [also there were] god
only knows what kinds of sociologists and a bunch of more Rightist
than Leftist sectarians. Then there were Mrs Rajk and Mrs Mihály
Károlyi. They were all in the same courtroom – the full spectrum of
the rainbow ...
     We have dealt with population problems, including the regulation
of abortion [on demand]. We were discussing it in the PB and
decided, in principle, that in the future the right to abortions would
be limited to a certain extent. Shortly thereafter Comrade Antal Apró
[chairman, Hungarian Presidential Council] receives a petition with
1,550 signatures in which one finds some sensible and correct sugges-
tions. However ... the gist of the petition was that we should not
regulate [the granting of] abortions. I assume that most signers were
people of goodwill who did not even realize what they were signing.
Among the signers I see less well-known actresses ... doctors ... but,
as you know, the organizers included a Maoist named György Pór ...
his wife and, as consultants, Ferenc Fehér, Ágnes Heller, András
Hegedüs ... and Mrs Károlyi, though no one expects her to give birth
to more children ... Moreover, and this is a far more serious matter,
there were several party members among the signatories! Now, no
party member should tell me that she does not know where to turn
with her problems instead of signing petitions written by unknown
authors![9]

The Kádár statement – one of a few in the 1970s and the 1980s on the
subject of dissent before the CC – affords a unique insight into the
leadership's problems of managing dissent in Hungary. Kádár's
message was that dissent posed no threat to the regime. This belief
generally defined the limits of coercive reactions to various manifestations of critical opinion in Hungary. Rebellious intellectuals, such as
Haraszti – partly because leftist deviation was more of a pardonable
sin than was the other kind – with quasi-Establishment supporters and
the world press on their side, were to be treated with kid gloves. Or, as
the party legend had it in the 1980s with reference to the dissident
young László Rajk, "He may be a son of a bitch, but he is the pup of
our bitch."
     Others, with less distinguished political pedigree and social status,
received considerably harsher treatment by the authorities. The March
15, 1972 demonstrators – who would become, at a significantly more
muted level, annual reminders of youthful patriotism in the Kádár era
– were mainly exuberant high-school and university students who
were, at least until 1988, vastly outnumbered by plainclothesmen and
party vigilantes. However, on March 15, 1988 the police intervened –

first with loudspeakers and later with rubber truncheons – and broke up the young people's peaceful march. The "battle of the Chain Bridge" was clear evidence of police brutality and official panic. The regime's image of paternalism and prudent toleration of nonviolent mass behavior was shattered beyond repair.

The environmental activists of the 1980s – concerned mainly about the ill-conceived Hungarian–Czechoslovak Gabčikovo-Nagymaros water-diversion project – though never exempt from police harassment and internal security surveillance, were treated with a measure of official ambivalence. Not even the PB diehards cared much either for Husák or for his "hydro-maniac" nationalist brethren in the Slovak party apparat. Similarly, small groups of unofficial Hungarian peace activists were seen by the regime more as a nuisance than as a threat to political stability.

Much of the above-discussed kinds of dissent fell into the instru-mental-pragmatic and moral-absolutist categories. In both cases, the regime's policies adhered to Dahl's axioms. Thus, the authorities chose to micromanage – as much by György Aczél's far-flung cultural-ideological apparat as by his well-spoken internal security officers – rather than to squash the middle-class and high-social-status bearers of critical messages.

Potentials for anomic-militant dissent in Hungary had been thwarted at the outset – by the hangman's noose, torture, imprisonment, and house arrest – between 1957 and the mid-1960s. With Cardinal Mind-szenty as an unwanted guest at the US Embassy, and outspoken clergymen behind bars or as blue-collar workers without parishes, the regime's Office of Religious Affairs – itself an operational arm of the CC's Agit-Prop Department – had no difficulties in finding willing collaborators from among the Catholic hierarchy.

Informal arrangements between the regime and the Catholic Church were subsequently firmed up by Kádár's "private concordat" with the pope during his visit in Italy in 1977. The regime's cozy relationship with, as Kádár put it, "our bishops" continued well into the 1980s. The Catholic hierarchy denied requests to lend support to Catholic con-scientious objectors who refused to perform military service. In return, the Office of Church Affairs stood by Cardinal László Lékai in his dispute with priests associated with the "basic communities" of grass-roots religious activists in Hungary.[10]

The hierarchy of the major Protestant denominations was also cooperative – as was their international body, the New York-based World Council of Churches. Their reward was the granting of exemption from military service to members of small Protestant groups, such as the Nazarenes. All of this left control of the (invariably nonviolent) followers – mainly conscientious objectors – of smaller religious sects, such as the Jehovah's Witnesses, as the only, and easily manageable, aspect of "anomic-religious" dissent.

Work stoppages and wildcat strikes in mines and large factories did occur now and then, but any attempt to resuscitate the revolutionary worker–intelligentsia alliance of 1956 was nipped in the bud by the vigilant authorities. After the Haraszti affair, the intellectuals were free to sign petitions, publish samizdat, and send letters to Western newspapers as long as they stayed away from the otherwise not particularly discontented blue-collar workers. Or, as Kádár put it at the December 9, 1980 meeting of the PB, "should the opposition try to link up with the workers, then all bets are off [akkor minden pardon megszünik], for no one can act against the Hungarian People's Republic and remain unpunished."[11] When all else failed, the low-status types were locked up for "hooliganism," the white-collar troublemakers were dispatched to psychiatric institutions, and prominent intellectuals with Western contacts were issued one-way passports for the desired destinations.[12]

(B)   Dissent: populist, "democratic," and socialist

On September 8, 1957, the "Declaration of Writers" appeared in the Hungarian press.[13] The statement, endorsed by 216 signatories, called on the "writers of the world" to accept them as "loyal citizens of the Hungarian People's Republic," to support the results of the newly restored public order, and to reject views of "renegades" who fled the country after the "tragic events of October 1956." The latter, according to the signers, had been the result of "imperialist meddling," "stirred up fascism," and "white terror." No one knew how many writers refused to sign the statement, but thirty-four years later, of those who did, only a handful would recall having done so.[14]

Statements signed under duress by intimidated people cannot serve as evidence by which to judge their political beliefs. On the other hand, there is no doubt that many, perhaps the majority, signed the statement voluntarily rather than out of fear. The list of signers was headed by the authors of luminous prose, such as that of the celebrated essay "The Emerging Nation" (László Németh), and stirring poems, such as "One Sentence on Tyranny" (Gyula Illyés), both of which had inspired pride and patriotism in the Hungarian people in October 1956.

The separation of the disheartened intellectual "sheep" from the already slaughtered or jailed "wolves" centered on the leading noncommunist literati of Hungary. The main targets were the leading Populist writers László Németh, Gyula Illyés, Géza Féja, János Kodolányi, József Erdélyi, Áron Tamási, and István Sinka, and some younger ones, such as Sándor Csoóri, and their followers among the intelligentsia. Kádár's and György Aczél's task was to persuade, cajole, or bludgeon into submission these spokesmen of the revolution and obtain their support for the regime's efforts at rebuilding and consolidation.

What happened? To begin at the end: in less than four years the Populists made their peace with the regime. Most of them endorsed its political goal of "consolidation," its economic policies of central planning and agricultural recollectivization, and the restoration of party control over the arts, sciences, and literature. By the time the amnestied – mainly non-Populist – writers were set free in 1962–3, the CC's Agit-Prop Department and the Writers' Union, led by the former Populist József Darvas, were back in business as if nothing had happened in 1956.

The regime's recapturing of the writers' allegiance was a complex and, for many, a deeply anguishing process. However, what is at issue here is whether these self-appointed moral guardians of the community had "betrayed the revolution" – as some believed at that time – or remained faithful to their original agenda. In my view, the second explanation is the correct one. Concerning the Populists, my reasoning may be summarized as follows:

1 The Hungarian Populists who first appeared on the public scene in the 1930s were *not* Russian Narodnik-type urban visionaries bound on a mission to enlighten, or to learn from, the rural poor. They were educated and self-educated provincial intellectuals from humble social backgrounds who sought to "discover," understand, and socially and culturally uplift the "three million beggars" of rural Hungary. The "Village Explorers" were young sociologists, journalists, economists, and fledgling authors of prose and poetry. Each, in his own way, was a radical and a critic of the Horthy regime's official Christian-national ideologies and authoritarian politics.[15]

2 Populist blueprints for rapid modernization, social justice, and the political enfranchisement of provincial Hungary were articulated by the movement's leading thinkers: László Németh, Ferenc Erdei, Gyula Illyés, Imre Kovács, Péter Veres, Gyula Kodolányi, and István Sinka. Their views, though these might be positioned along a left-to-right ideological continuum, were unanimous in denying the legitimacy of

the Horthy regime and in promoting radical solutions to overcome what all saw as economic injustice, social backwardness, and lack of feasible alternatives to the status quo.

3   In one way or another, all Populists endorsed an eclectic utilization of left- and right-wing modernization scenarios and preservation of the cultural authenticity of rural Hungary. They were ambivalent toward communism (Béla Kun's anti-peasant policies were still living memories), fascism, and National Socialism. The Populists were put off by right-wing militarism but were intrigued by notions of a Hungarian *Herrenvolk*. In any case, they all had deep doubts, bordering on outright rejection, about liberal democracy – the Treaty of Trianon was seen by many as Wilson's "gift" to Hungary. From a perspective of six decades these were the negative aspects of Populist ideologies. At any rate, the shorthand term "Third Road" which has been used to describe the Populists' "neither capitalist, nor communist" approach to modernization and national emancipation, was a misnomer. The label tended to obfuscate the elitist, authoritarian, and culturally intolerant nativist thrust of these provincial radicals' policy agenda.

4   When historically confronted with choices between incremental and rapid change, between evolutionary and radical transformation, between consensual agreements and elite-brokered fiats imposed from above, the Populists invariably chose the second alternative. Moreover, the Populists tended to be oblivious to ideological labels and sought help for their cause from whoever ruled Hungary: in 1935 they volunteered to form a "New Spiritual Front" with the radical rightist prime minister Gyula Gömbös; in 1937, more or less on the rebound from the political Right, they launched the March Front – this time with the help of native and Muscovite communists.[16] In 1945–7, when the leading Populists helped found the Peasant Party, some of them became "T" (secret) members of the Communist Party; the rest (Illyés, Veres, and several others) drifted along toward the, to them inevitable, communist takeover of Hungary. At the end, a few, such as Péter Veres and József Darvas, became public partners in Rákosi's Stalinist enterprise to build socialism in Hungary.

5   The Populists, the – by the 1960s, increasingly urbanized – rural poor, and the provincial lower middle class for whom they spoke were potentially eligible and indispensable allies of the Kádár-led "domesticist" HSWP. In retrospect both the regime and the Populists saw the 1956 uprising as a false dawn. For the Populists, Kádár's narrow path between "left-wing sectarianism" and "right-wing revisionism"

amounted to a viable national "Third Road" between the equally unpalatable alternatives of Soviet Stalinism and Western capitalism. The latter, with its commercialized mass culture, the attachment of the society to material possessions, and low public esteem enjoyed by cultural notables, was just as repugnant as had been the dictatorship of the antipeasant and predominantly Jewish Rákosi leadership. Thus, the Populists "bet the farm," as it were, and with it the country's future on János Kádár – a man of humble rural origin, a fellow victim of Stalinism, and yet the undisputed strongman of Hungary.

In sum, the Populists – though they abandoned their ideal of independent statehood and accepted Soviet overlordship – were not traitors but victims of their ill-starred origins and cultural insularity. They meant well for their people but were fearful of the coming of a modern Hungarian society of autonomous, and very likely "cosmopolitan," individuals with no need for writers and poets as moral guardians. For Zoltán Kodály, Gyula Illyés, László Németh, and the rest of the regime's designated "national, but socialist" cultural icons, playing second fiddle in Aczél's cultural orchestra was vastly preferable to becoming political anachronisms in a modern Hungary.

The regime's terms for a communist–Populist strategic partnership were spelled out in a "Resolution of the Cultural-Ideological Work Team of the CC, HSWP, on the 'Populist' Writers" which appeared – just in case anyone missed the point – in June 1958 to coincide with the secret trial and execution of Imre Nagy and some of his codefendants.[17] The resolution, as augmented by similar declarations in the next several years, spelled out the "encouraged" and "tolerated" limits of Populist conduct in the Kádár era.

The Populists' response, although undoubtedly not authorized by his fellow writers, was formulated in 1962 by László Németh in the private hundred-page "Letter to a Cultural Politician," that is, to György Aczél, then deputy minister of culture and the party's designated watchdog of the literary community. In the letter Németh outlined his vision of a "society of [socialist] intellectuals" made up of regime-educated young people of peasant, worker, and lower-middle-class background who would become the "yeast" of a new Hungary. He also argued for vast subsidies for elite and mass education, the official encouragement of *local* patriotism, more flexible censorship, and more subtle methods of political manipulation of the creative intelligentsia. A part of the Németh epistle on the "writer's freedom" alluded to the incorrigibles who wanted to undermine the regime's stability. "What would I say to them [in your place]?" Németh asked.

"I would give them a passport for two years abroad" was his own obliging response.[18]

The regime's subsequent adoption of many of Németh's proposals as its *modus operandi* of intellectual deviation control helped neutralize nationalist dissent in Hungary for the next two decades. In a broader sense, the precedent of the informal communist–Populist pact also served twenty-five years later as the political foundation to facilitate the regime's last-ditch attempt to salvage what it could of its remaining power and politically uncompromised leadership for the postcommunist era. Indeed, the basic terms of the reform communist (Pozsgay)–Populist partnership at the founding Lakitelek meeting of the Hungarian Democratic Forum had been set *not* on September 27, 1987, but in 1937, 1945–7, 1957, and in 1962.

The democratic opposition: from Marx to Monor

Hungarian and East European intelligentsia movements have traditionally begun with shared ideological dilemmas and small groups of people talking, writing, and, at the end, doing something about them. The time was the mid-1960s and the dilemma of the decade was that of the relevance of Marxism to the unfolding process of the building of socialism by a bureaucratic, albeit ostensibly reformist, political elite that called itself Marxist–Leninist. The small groups of people were three generations of Hungarian Marxist intellectuals that included György Lukács and his circle of middle-aged (György Márkus, Ágnes Heller, Ferenc Fehér, Mihály Vajda, Vilmos Sós) and young (János Kis, György Bence, Sándor Radnóti, Mihály Hamburger) philosophers; former primer minister (later "reform sociologist") András Hegedüs and his young associates; and a handful of young to very young ultraleftist activists (György Pór, Miklós Haraszti, Gábor Révai, and György Dalos). With Lukács' notable exception – his father had been an ennobled Jewish investment banker – the rest came mainly from urban middle and lower middle-class Jewish families with close ties to left-wing, particularly communist, causes.

Each of these groups had an agenda and made a contribution to the ideological ferment of the pre-NEM and early-NEM years in Hungary. The role of András Hegedüs – marked by his appointment in 1955 at the age of thirty-three, as Hungary's youngest prime minister in history; his signing, on Hungary's behalf, the Warsaw Treaty and also a letter inviting the Soviet military to put down the revolt on October 26, 1956; and his two-year exile in the USSR – warrants detailed discussion.[19] And so does the story of his Saul-to-Paul conversion to democratic socialism, his important contributions to the reform debates of the 1960s, and his courageous protest against the invasion of Czechoslovakia in 1968.[20] Because of limitations of space, his role in the pre-history of instrumental-pragmatic dissent in Hungary cannot be accommodated within the confines of this study.

The Budapest School of Marxism

Let us begin with György Lukács. This giant of twentieth-century Marxist philosophy and aesthetics was at one time (1928–9) the leader of the "native" faction of the underground Hungarian Communist Party. He was one of the party's top cultural ideologues until silenced by the Stalinists in 1949. In 1956 he served as a somewhat reluctant member of Imre Nagy's short-lived government, for which he was expelled from the party that he was permitted to rejoin only in 1967, four years before his death.[21]

The old Lukács was an admirer of Solzhenitsyn, a supporter of the Prague Spring and of the libertarian aspirations of the New Left in both halves of Europe. He maintained that man's alienation from his work and the political system around him could not be overcome by simply declaring an established state to be "socialist." The regime, he argued, because of the ruling party's preoccupation with power and system management through its new bureaucracy, actually reproduced the very circumstances that had made for alienation under capitalism. By assigning to the intellectuals the responsibility to become spokesmen for the average person, Lukács consciously encouraged elite criticism of the party apparat.[22]

One might submit, as did Iván Szelényi in a commentary on the Budapest School, that it was bad politics to attack the NEM before the regime had a chance to implement it.[23] Probably so, but from the perspective of almost four decades what matters is that the party's best theoreticians had gone on record as early as 1965–8 warning the regime not only that a one-dimensional reform program would not work but, unless political reforms were introduced as an integral part of the overall reform package, that such half-hearted innovations were doomed to failure.

The rest of the written output of the Budapest School – though challenging central aspects of the regime's ideological legitimacy – is of interest mainly to connoisseurs of modern critical Marxist philosophy. However, to place the personalities and the political legacy of Márkus,

Heller, Fehér, and the others in a proper perspective, two points should be made.

First, that these intellectuals and András Hegedüs were the only ones in Hungary who publicly protested against the Soviet invasion of Czechoslovakia, and for this courageous gesture they were promptly expelled from the party. Five years later, with Kádár's approval, they were all dismissed from their jobs as well. The Populists, much to Kádár's relief, remained silent in 1968 – and, with few exceptions, such as Sándor Csoóri – they remained so in 1977, 1979, and 1981.

Second, thanks to their mentors, the empirical branch – young sociologists, economists, and investigative journalists – of the Budapest School and the followers of András Hegedüs, István Kemény, and Iván Szelényi were remarkably well equipped to play the role of "instrumental pragmatic" critics of the regime. They had both the motivation and the mastery of the necessary problem-solving analytical tools with which to query and challenge the regime's policy dogmas in the years to come.

The democratic opposition: formative years

The foregoing discussion on the personalities and the ideas of the Budapest School and its intellectual environs sought to provide the background to introduce two of the youngest but, for our purposes, most important personalities of what was to become the Hungarian democratic opposition. János Kis (b. 1943) and György Bence (b. 1941) were, more than anyone else, responsible for the transformation of the Budapest School from an esoteric philosophical debating society into what became by far the most influential political opposition movement of the late Kádár era.

The terms "generational awakening," "moral reappraisal," and "personal commitment" might best describe the intellectual and personal transformation between 1968 and 1979 of Kis and Bence from star pupils of the Lukács school into principal ideologists of the democratic opposition. Though equal partners in philosophy and politics, Kis and Bence parted ways in 1981, and it was the former who came to play a more visible role in the 1980s. Therefore, the following comments will focus on Kis rather than his colleague Bence.

János Kis was born to a family of Jewish middle-class communists.[24] The Holocaust claimed the lives of his father and two uncles. His mother survived, and it was in the home of a dedicated communist mother and her second husband that Kis grew up as a privileged youngster. He attended the exclusive Gorky School for apparat children – the language of instruction was partly Russian and partly Hungarian – and, upon graduation from yet another high school, he enrolled as a Hungarian literature–philosophy major at the Loránd Eötvös University. A brilliant student, and a voracious reader of philosophy and history, and highly aware of political trends, Kis' own political views were greatly influenced by the 22nd CPSU congress and the "second wave" of de-Stalinization in the USSR and Hungary.

Each generation of intellectuals has an opportunity to rethink and, if need be, challenge the accepted wisdom of its academic discipline. For Kis, Bence, and their university mentor György Márkus, the events of the late 1960s in Hungary, Czechoslovakia, and the West compelled reflection on what they perceived as logically and morally untenable contradictions between Marx as a philosopher and Marx as an economist. The product of this joint enterprise was a closely reasoned 542–page manuscript and an intellectual *tour de force* with the intriguing title "How Can There Be a Critical [political] Economy?"[25] As Kis explained:

> Our point of departure was that Marx's original intentions and values were different from the socioeconomic institutional structure that [was created] to realize these original intentions. In Marx's view, socialism was to implement the economic foundations for a society of free and equal people in which people [are empowered to] supervise the processes of production and consumption. However, the logic of the economic system that Marx devised for the realization of these objectives totally contradicted these intentions and yielded results that were inimical to the freedoms of [people] – both as producers and as consumers. We tried to show that while Marx's basic values might not be realized in full, one ought to strive for better compromises [between theory and practice]. For this, however, not Marx's non-market and centralized *Naturwirtschaft* economy but a regulated market economy is necessary.[26]

These, as the designated discussants of the March 28, 1973 special meeting of a HSWP–Hungarian Academy of Sciences ideological kangaroo court pointed out, were heretical thoughts with dangerous political implications. Such notions as the persistence of "reification and alienation" in the socialist planned economy, the proposed revival of the market and the *de facto* acceptance of "labor as commodity" under socialism, and the continued (and growing) role of the state along with the prognosticated rise of social control of the state by "democratic associations of producers" were irreconcilable with the regime's ideological posture.[27]

Bence and Kis' decision to become full-time political dissidents was not a choice freely made by either of the two. Rather, as the first young Establishment victims of the official ban on employment, they were on their own and in the unusual position to observe and to reflect on the society, the regime, and the regional political environment in which they lived. Between 1973 and 1977, under the pseudonym Marc Rakovski, Bence and Kis published a series of essays in French journals that were later published in Hungarian samizdat under the title "Soviet-type Society from a Marxist Perspective." In a sense, the title was misleading because, as the authors explained in the book's English-language edition,

> After the events of Gdansk ... and the establishment of KOR ... we realized that what ... [we stood for] was radical reformism. This, in turn called into question the political substance of our Marxism. As long as [our Marxism] had been devoid of political substance we, upon diligent analysis, might have refilled it [with political meaning]. Now that we [have] found a very substantive (and, to us, acceptable) political posture, we find that there is nothing in it that one might consider Marxist. Therefore, we must acknowledge ... that our position may be Marxist only in a derivative sense.[28]

By the mid-1970s, Bence and Kis' "derivative Marxism" became a widely shared position among the leftist Hungarian reform intelligentsia. This, in turn, was only a short step away from reflecting and acting on the message of the Helsinki Final Act of 1975 and the example of the Polish dissident movement of 1975–6. As Kis saw it, the Polish example offered a model for a new *modus vivendi* for the incumbents and the dissidents in both Poland and Hungary.[29] Compromises and mutual guarantees were the essence of the new relationship: the dissidents would refrain from attacking the regime's institutions and the state's subordination to the interests of the USSR. In exchange, the regime would relinquish its control over civil society and cease interfering with the citizens' rights to free expression and "self-organization" at the grassroots level.

The unstated premise of Kis' post-Marxist position on trade-offs between society and the political incumbents was that the existing socialist states and societies were there to stay. The Kádár regime, for all its flaws, seemed unshakeable from within. However, as George Schopflin points out: "Yes, the socialist state was there to stay, but the Kis–Bence position was riven by a contradiction. If their indirect and explicit vision of a social order based on 'self-organization' and regime self-limitation were to be implemented, the system would no longer be socialist."[30]

The external environment – East–West *détente*, nuclear stalemate, and all-European security interests – promised no immediate relief. Therefore, the dissidents' political objective was not the overthrow but the transformation, through internal reforms, of the socioeconomic structures of the existing socialist state. This reasoning became the political foundation for strategies of the Hungarian democratic opposition until 1981. At that point, the Polish and Hungarian incumbents began to lose ground, and beliefs in the regimes' stability and that of the Soviet bloc ceased to be axiomatic propositions for the Hungarian dissident community.

The politics of samizdat: from Bibó to Beszélő

Samizdat, or the unauthorized publication of uncensored material for the purpose of illegal dissemination, and the Hungarian democratic opposition as an *organized* protest movement were born in January 1977. In a sense, both had been occasioned by the Czechoslovak Charter '77 manifesto and the letter of support signed by thirty-four Hungarian intellectuals. As János Kenedi, one of the most active organizers of samizdat projects at that time, recalled, the dissidents had struck outsiders as a clannish lot intent on recruiting people to support noble causes abroad but oddly disinterested in social problems at home and in Hungarian ethnic minority rights in Romania and Slovakia. Moreover, the dissidents had nothing to say about the 1956 revolution.[31]

Indeed, compared with fellow dissidents in the USSR, Poland, and Czechoslovakia, the Hungarians were late starters. Some of this was due to the Kádár regime's "repressive tolerance," some to the absence of visible high-status victims, and some to the lack of politically committed activist leadership among the Hungarian intelligentsia. However, judged by the volume and range of issues that one finds in samizdat publications that appeared between 1977 and 1980, the critical intellectuals of Budapest were catching up fast with their dissident brethren elsewhere in Central Europe.[32]

The death of István Bibó in April 1979 became the defining event that helped reshape the dissident movement from a loose intelligentsia network into a new coalition of democratic opposition in Hungary. Bibó (b. 1911) was a legendary figure of postwar Hungarian politics.

Originally a law professor at the University of Szeged and active in the wartime resistance movement, he joined the National Peasant Party in 1945 and became its prominent spokesman on issues of coalition politics. Bibó's writings on public administration, party politics, the evolution of democracy in Eastern Europe, and the Jewish question still stand as classics of liberal democratic thinking in Hungarian intellectual history.[33]

Like his party, Bibó was swept aside after the commmunist takeover, demoted from the rank of academician to that of an assistant librarian at a university. In October 1956 Imre Nagy asked him to join his government as the Petőfi Party representative with the rank of Minister of State. When the Soviet invasion came on November 4, Bibó was the only member of the government who did not flee the Parliament building. Unmolested by the Soviet troops who took him for a lowly clerk, he stayed there for two days typing protest documents and appeals for nonviolent resistance and noncooperation with the invaders. For some reason, he was not arrested until May 1957, but at his trial a year later he received a life sentence. He was amnestied in 1963 and permitted to hold the job of a librarian at the National Statistical Office until his retirement in 1971.[34]

Bibó's funeral serendipitously united everybody who was anybody in the intellectual community and prompted many – whether out of friendship, respect, or guilt – to agree to cooperate on a major samizdat project, the *Bibó Memorial Book*. The 1,001-page volume that emerged a year later featured seventy-six authors ranging from Ferenc Donáth, an agricultural expert and a codefendant at Imre Nagy's trial, through young dissidents, some Populists such as Gyula Illyés, to nondissident historians.[35] In most contributions the common thread was Bibó's philosophical legacy and its applicability to Hungary in the age of economic and the much-hoped-for political reforms.

The regime took a differentiated view of the significance of the *Bibó Memorial Book*. When the text was submitted for publication to one of the official publishing houses, the party commissioned a detailed evaluation by one of the apparat's top sociologists.[36] It appears that the party was at first inclined to authorize publication provided that five essays by hard-core dissidents were dropped. When that was rejected by Donáth and his ten-man editorial board, an intraparty debate followed that climaxed in a PB decision of December 10, 1980, requesting the CC Department for Science, Education and Culture to prepare a report on the manuscript for the CC Department of AP. Excerpts from the report were leaked to the dissidents and the Western media. These afford glimpses at the incumbents' perceptions of the personalities and message of their critical opponents. According to the report:

> A Bibó-type intelligentsia attitude and lifestyle seemed appropriate for the opposition to embrace as a model [of public conduct]. [Bibó's] example may be likened to a posture that acknowledges the positive results of socialist development but maintains a critical, yet constructive, attitude toward existing realities. On the other hand, the Bibó model is also compatible with beliefs about the total autonomy of nonhostile intelligentsia thought and action; thus, it is suitable for the building of a kind of consensus among various strata of the intelligentsia.[37]

Precisely. The dissidents' choice of Bibó as symbol and as an inspiration for a new antiregime "Popular Front" was also apparent in the report's assessment of the contents of the entire volume. As the cultural apparat saw it, with respect to their attitudes toward the existing political system in Hungary, the contributors were divisible into eight categories. The classification was totally accurate in sorting out the activist ideologues and "single-issue" (that is, 1956 and prison memoirs) authors from apolitical scholars and cautious "fellow-traveler" dissidents. In conclusion, Mihály Kornidesz, the head of the responsible CC department, and his deputy András Knopp, the author of the report recommended that the regime itself sponsor publication of two of Bibó's books "as a way of taking a more offensive stance toward an illegal Bibó book that will be published in the West."[38]

The legacy of István Bibó had many uses that the Kádár regime's opponents could utilize for their own purposes. The dissident "hard core's" emphasis on Bibó's most prominent intellectual posture, civil courage, and on what they saw as the essence of his politics – nonviolence, pragmatism, and the art of coming to terms with difficult political realities – became the operative guidelines of the democratic opposition for the rest of the 1980s in Hungary.

Democratic opposition: interest articulation and coalition building, 1981–5

The Polish events of 1980–1, particularly the Gdansk Agreement of August 1980 and the transformation of Solidarity into a national movement, compelled the Hungarian dissident community to enter the political arena in a new role: sounding board for thitherto latent political concerns and proponent of ideas for change. The principal vehicle for the articulation of new ideas and policy proposals was the samizdat journal *Beszélő*.[39] As the lead editorial of the first issue explained,

> *Beszélő* ["Speaker"] is going to speak about "irregular" events: a person, or a few people together violate the unwritten rules of the relationship between those who govern and those who are governed; people who resist unlawful orders, people who pressure their superiors ... We also would like to find out what kinds of resources the rulers deploy to have things return to "normal" and how conflicts are born and become resolved between the two sides. How outsiders behave when something unusual happens. We would like to record these events and experiences so people would know more about one another.
>
> [I]t is not our purpose to put out some kind of opposition journal. Instead, we would, our modest resources permitting, like to help so that the quiet multitude of people could form an opinion for themselves – people over whose heads two dwarf-like (*törpe*) minorities [a backhanded reference to Kádár's characterization of the opposition as "dwarf-like"], the opposition and the national leadership, quarrel loudly with one another.[40]

According to Kis, the *de facto* editor in chief of *Beszélő* and one of the five editors of the journal, the editors took the Soviet samizdat *Chronicle of Current Events* as their model in two respects: the editors' names, addresses, and telephone numbers were prominently displayed, and the journal's main function was defined as the dissemination of uncensored news. However, unlike the *Chronicle*, which did not have editorials or feature programmatic statements on behalf of the entire dissident community, *Beszélő* did both.

The 180-odd items that appeared in the first fifteen issues reported events that the media chose not to cover. And the half dozen major editorials, by Kis – each a gem of lucid prose and careful reasoning – were written for two audiences and two basic objectives. One audience was the dissident community and the approximately 7,000 to 10,000 regular readers. There was another audience of 1 to 2 million, ranging from mildly curious to passionately interested Hungarian listeners to Radio Free Europe broadcasts. The main objective was to overcome the regime's monopoly over the printed and electronic media. A related concern was reaching and influencing the already politicized intelligentsia.

The vigorous proliferation of critical intelligentsia groups in Hungary strengthened the hands of what the opposition called "the party of order" in the HSWP. Confiscation of samizdat products, widespread and often brutal harassment of younger and low-social-status dissidents including – as a kind of compensatory outlet for police frustrations – the roundup of social marginals not involved in "socially useful labor," and the harsh persecution of rural Gypsies were signs of growing official apprehensions about suspected subversive behavior.

Moreover, the Hungarian dissidents could expect no support from the outside, not even from the "Helsinki process." Miklós Haraszti, commenting on the CSCE-sponsored European Cultural Forum of November 1985 held in Budapest, put it bluntly:

> What kind of forum is this? A splendid example of Orwellian News-peak. It was a forum for a strictly controlled question and answer format of socialist TV, rather than an *agora* where everyone can speak his mind. There was not a single western delegation to take up the demands ... of the Hungarian opposition, or to read [into the record] a letter from Charter '77.[41]

Faced with these discouraging developments, the democratic opposition was compelled to rethink its strategies. As Kis explained in another *Beszélő* editorial, regime concessions, mainly in the second economy, had preserved social stability and made Hungary stand out in Eastern Europe as an island of political moderation and modest, albeit rapidly deteriorating, economic stability. Thus, for want of grass-roots support, a Solidarity-type mass movement was not an option – nor was open confrontation with the Kádár regime. The remaining choice was "quiet development through controlled changes." As Kis saw it, there were large and thitherto untapped potential constituencies in Hungary on behalf of issues of human rights, liberal democracy, ethnic autonomy, and self-governing socialism.[42]

Democratic opposition: programs and strategies

In substantive terms, in 1984–5 the Hungarian democratic opposition was confronted with three kinds of political challenges and opportunities.

1 To survive as a viable political movement, the small band of radical intellectuals of the Budapest-based samizdat network had to link up with the increasingly frustrated groups of young writers and Populist critics of the regime's apparent indifference to the fate of Hungarian ethnic minorities in Romania and Slovakia. However, the main objective of the initiatives to build a Popular Front-style coalition with the Populists and the emerging constituency of nationalist

provincial intellectuals was to prevent the incumbents, especially György Aczél's cultural apparat, from dividing the regime's critics into "urbanist" and "Populist" camps.

2 To keep the senior party apparat on the defensive and preoccupied with the regime's central legitimacy dilemma, the thitherto taboo subject of the 1956 revolution had to be revived, mainly as a *moral* issue, with which to appeal to the latent anticommunist sentiments of those who had not – or thought they had not – benefited from the "Kádár compromise" and the regime's reform policies to date. This issue was also helpful for driving wedges between the top incumbents with personal responsibility for the crushing of the revolt and the visibly restless successor generation of party elites with no personal culpability for past political repression, particularly the judicial murder of Imre Nagy.

3 The democratic opposition had to find ways to take advantage of the "rearguard" leadership's reactive-adaptive policy concessions to elite and grassroots pressures for a greater say about workplace conditions, community affairs and the officials' management of social welfare issues.[43]

The implementation of opposition strategies of coalition building, moral delegitimation, and the political empowerment of average Hungarians was a complex task with a slim chance of success in the mid-1980s. Yet, much to the credit of the *Beszélő* group, positive steps were taken in each of these areas.

From 1983 on, every issue of the journal gave prominent coverage to matters of Populist interest and paid substantial attention to regional concerns, including instances of regime censorship of provincial literary journals and of abuses of power by the "little tyrants" (*kiskirályok*) of the local party apparat. Publication of the leading Populist Sándor Csoóri's strongly worded introduction to a samizdat volume by Miklós Duray, the prominent Hungarian civil rights activist in Slovakia, and the coverage of the Transylvanian scene were major confidence-building steps toward the forging of a political alliance between the Hungarian urban and rural critical intelligentsia.

The first parliamentary elections – with two or more candidates in each electoral district – of the Kádár era were held on June 8, 1985. The preelection campaign marked the opposition's debut as prospective participants in the political process. The elections, the often stormy nominating meetings, and instances of official interference with the process of candidate selection were fully covered in the Western press and in the Hungarian samizdat.[44]

All told, 154 officially unauthorized "spontaneously nominated" candidates entered the electoral process. Of these, seventy-one stood for election and thirty-five were actually elected to the Parliament.[45] None of the dissidents managed to advance beyond the rigged nominating meetings. Neither the regime nor the conservative participants in the party apparat-stacked nominating meetings were ready to support the dissidents' well-reasoned campaign platforms for radical reforms.

The democratic opposition's efforts at coalition and consensus building among the various segments of the dissident community climaxed in a three-day conference at a campsite in Monor (about 20 miles from Budapest) on June 14–16, 1985. The forty-five invited participants included people from the democratic opposition, the Populists, reform socialists, and several well-known artists, writers, and academic intellectuals. The agenda consisted of four formal presentations by the Populist writers István Csurka and Sándor Csoóri, the economist Tamás Bauer, and János Kis, and comments by designated discussants of similar stature in the intellectual community.[46]

As Ferenc Donáth, the conference convenor, put it in his introductory comments, it was the Hungarian intellectuals' fear of a political crisis because of declining living standards and intractable economic problems that brought the participants to Monor. Csurka and Csoóri spoke, in moving terms, of the moral decline and cultural crisis of the society in the era of "soft dictatorship." Csurka saw the solution in moral renewal and in development of individual life strategies "without reference to daily politics." In Csoóri's view, the central issue was preservation of the national cultural identity and heightened awareness of the sufferings of ethnic Hungarians beyond the national boundaries.

Tamás Bauer, speaking as an economist and author of earlier critical policy recommendations addressed to the party leadership, called attention to several flaws in the regime's latest attempts to come to grips with the ailing national economy. However, as Mihály Laki, the designated discussant of the presentation, pointed out, "This is an agitative and analytical writing that mirrors Bauer's ambivalent position. On the one hand, he wrote a letter ... addressed to [indifferent] officials in charge of economic policies [and received no answer from them]. On the other hand, he seems to feel that the government is still committed to reforms."[47]

By contrast, Kis' address, "On Our Constraints and Opportunities," discussed the issues that separated and those that could unite the regime's critics into a political movement. He argued that the Populists' preoccupation with questions of culture, moral decline, national identity, and ethnic minorities did not square with their apparent lack of interest in social welfare issues, human rights, peace, environment, and institutional guarantees for the rule of law. Moreover, neither the Populists nor the democratic opposition had a credible and comprehensive plan to address *both* kinds of priorities. As Kis put it, "let us not look for cracks and gaps but focus on legal and institutional constraints" on the fulfillment of citizen aspirations for a better life.[48]

Reform socialists: dissent from within

Intellectuals whom I call reform socialists were younger people, mainly in their thirties and early forties, in the regime's political, administrative, and scientific bureaucracy. All of them had sound (that is, not evening or party school) academic credentials in economics, sociology, law, or philosophy. Most were employed as staff members at the CC's Institute for the Social Sciences, at the ministries, at the universities, and in research institutes of the HAS. Several worked as expert advisors, as authors of policy papers, or as speechwriters for the *nomenklatura* notables. Most came from peasant, working-class, or lower-middle-class social backgrounds. Virtually all were party members and had previous membership in the Young Communist League.

The formative university experiences of the young intellectuals had been exposure to academic debates over economic reforms and to works by Western sociologists, New Left ideologues, and Hegedüs, Kemény, Szelényi, and the Budapest School. If they had attended the Karl Marx University for Economics, as many had, chances were that they had taken economics courses from professors with one or more years of postdoctoral work or teaching experience at Western European and US universities. The same was true for other social science disciplines both at Karl Marx University and at the several faculties of Loránd Eötvös University of Budapest. Some of those who chose to stay in academia were, as was Miklós Németh, picked up by the party's talent spotters and co-opted into the central or regional apparat.

These young experts were the "regime's own" who had grown up and came of age in the Kádár era. They considered themselves members of the successor generation who would eventually inherit the regime's key positions in the party, state administration, and academia. Unlike their elders, they were largely free from the kinds of traumatic psychological and intellectual experiences that shaped the thinking of those who had been exposed to the Rákosi era and the 1956 revolution. Self-confidence, a sense of professional competence, and, as insiders, the tendency to treat politically sensitive questions as routine matters were unique attributes that neither the political incumbents nor the Populist and liberal dissidents possessed in the 1970s and the 1980s in Hungary.

Some of the leading reform socialists, such as Mihály Bihari (lawyer and political scientist), Ferenc Gazsó (sociologist), and Zoltán Biró (cultural historian), began their careers in the party apparat but moved on to the Ministry of Education and Culture when Imre Pozsgay took over that ministry in the late 1970s. Zsolt Papp (philosopher) and Csaba Gombár (political scientist) were senior researchers at the CC's Social Science Institute. László Lengyel and Erzsébet Szalai (both economists) were on the staff of the Ministry of Finance's in-house research institute. János Kornai, Rezső Nyers (between 1975 and 1988), Márton Tardos, Attila Károly Soós, Tamás Bauer, and scores of younger reform economists were based at the HAS's Institute for Economics. Zsuzsa Ferge, Julia Szalai, and their junior colleagues were located at the Institute of Sociology. This list of "reform socialists" is incomplete, for much of the under-35 generation of academic social scientists belonged to this category. Legal scholars, such as Jenő Széll, István Schlett, István Kukorelli, and Tamás Sárközy, and such key facilitators of reform dialogues as László Levendel (a leading clinical physician) were also parts of this cluster.

What these leading intellectuals had in common was a solid mastery of their respective academic disciplines and, from the 1980s on, a shared commitment to change, by way of drastic reforms, the existing political, social, and economic system. They all agreed that comprehensive reforms were necessary if the system was to survive the consequences of regime mismanagement and popular resistance to change, both of which threatened the modest achievements of economic reforms since 1968 and posed impediments to needed change. These men and women were, to use Mihály Bihari's phrase, "heroes with a dual commitment."[49] As scholars and experts, they were bound to advocate policies that were seen as "too drastic," "inexpedient," or politically risky. On the other hand, as university or HAS employees, they felt compelled to protect, even at the cost of compromises with their scholarly conscience, the limited autonomy of their institutions against the ideological and administrative encroachment by the powers that be.

The roles of reluctant upholder of the political status quo and of critic of the same, though inherently unstable in relation to each, were not necessarily incompatible when they coalesced into a collective elite posture of what Csaba Gombár called "logocracy." The term denoted an intellectual of a new type: that of thinker, policy consultant, and behind-the-scenes gatekeeper of public discussion on reform proposals.[50] A "logocrat" seemed to be the 1980s equivalent of Szelényi's and Konrád's co-opted apolitical technocrats,[51] with the major difference that the former were now making an explicit bid for a share of decision-making authority and offering their services for the proper implementation of the regime's reform policies.

Whereas Gombár's attempt to insert "logocracy" as a new entrant in the sheltered domains of "partocracy," "bureaucracy," and "technocracy" might be dismissed as an example of intelligentsia hubris, the fact remains that the reform socialists' immense written output on reform issues fully preempted and overwhelmed the "rearguard" rhetoric of the regime's apologists. From 1984 on, the public discourse on current policy options in Hungary was virtually dominated by the regime's internal critics.[52] Indeed, well before anyone heard about *glasnost'* and Gorbachev, the professional journals and, in a reactive sense, the party's ideological media had been inundated by reform writings of various kinds.

The practitioners of the newly authorized disciplines of political science and public law took it upon themselves to discuss several highly sensitive issues of public policy in Hungary. The principal topics were political culture, political participation, political legitimacy, the division of powers in the political system, and the *raison d'être* of the ruling party *vis-à-vis* the executive and the legislative branches of the government.

1 With respect to political culture, the reformers submitted that, notwithstanding the regime's efforts to keep the average Hungarian in a state of dependency and political infantilism, the people were conscious of their values and were fully aware of their interests. What they needed was not official tutelage but political democracy.[53]

2 Concerning the people's right to make autonomous choices between two or more candidates for a public office, the reform socialists called attention to the question of accountability of elected officials. They were particularly concerned about the ambiguous status of the Parliament as an institution with the (never exercised) constitutional right of oversight with respect to the state bureaucracy.

3 As the critics saw it, it was not good enough to say that the political

system was legitimate "because it was there and it was there to stay."[54] In their view, the regime's legitimacy ought to rest on *performance* and fulfillment of the incumbents' promises for an overall improvement in the quality of life.[55] Having defaulted on the unwritten social contract, the regime must put its house in order by restoring, as the essential first step, the rule of law. Notions of "community power" and of the autonomy of nascent civil-society-type social entities also occupied an important place on the legal reformers' agenda for the restoration of political legitimacy.[56]

4   "Respect your own laws" had been one of the key demands of instrumental-pragmatic dissidents in the USSR, Poland, and Czechoslovakia in the 1970s. A remarkable feature of the Hungarian reform debates was the unprecedented unanimity between reformers and conservatives concerning the chaotic conditions that characterized the daily operations of the quasi-legislative, executive, and judiciary branches of the government. In 1985 the Constitutional Council was formed to study the situation and make recommendations for remedial action.[57]

5   Since 1950 the law-making functions of the Parliament had been preempted by the Presidential Council; 95 percent of "decrees with the force of law" were the work of the latter body, which often neglected to inform the legislature of its actions. Moreover, the council had failed to exercise its duties of constitutional oversight regarding the prodigious decree- and rule-making activities of the Council of Ministers, individual ministries, and other agencies, such as the National Planning Office, with national jurisdiction.[58]

6   The Council of Ministers was found wanting on at least two counts. On the one hand, it had become a victim, to the point of near paralysis, of self-generated decision overload. The time span between identification of a policy problem and issuance of corrective decrees and enabling regulations had become unacceptably long. This state of affairs prompted some reformers to speak of a "war communism model" of public administration – a peculiar anachronism in the fortieth year of communist rule.[59]

7   The Parliament, though responsible for the enactment of laws – particularly those affecting the rights and duties of citizens – had passed fewer than 200 laws since 1950. This number represented less than 3 percent of the approximately 6,000 "decrees with the force of law" and other regulations issued by the Presidential Council and the Council of Ministers. Most of the decrees, in one way or another, *had* affected the citizens' rights and duties.[60]

None of the reform socialist critics was in a position to make a direct impact on major policy decisions at the PB level, yet their ideas deeply penetrated the thinking of party and government elites. The latter in particular were favorably disposed toward the étatist and implicitly antiparty thrust of critical reform writings on the party's "leading role." The "rearguard" party leadership's unwillingness to accept political responsibility for its disastrous policies strengthened the position of experts against the fumbling incumbents. The programmatic foundations for Miklós Németh's "government of experts" of April 1989 had been laid by the old regime's reform socialist critics well before Kádár's exit in May 1988. In the meantime, the critical "logocrats" were ready to advise and assist anyone who embraced their ideas and had a chance to replace Kádár at the helm.

(C)   Opposition and dissent in the mid-1980s: confrontation or collaboration?

According to the party center's assessment of the status of political dissidence in Hungary, in 1986 it ceased to be the "opposition" (*ellenzék*) and became a "hostile" (*ellenséges*) antiregime movement. In the judgment of the authors of a "strictly confidential" report that the CC Department for Science, Education and Culture submitted to the PB, the "bourgeois radical" and "radical nationalist" branches of the dissident movement had been coordinating their activities since 1982.[61] Although this certainly had not been the case, the policy paper took great pains to depict the democratic opposition, particularly its "hard core," that is, the *Beszélő* group, as the source of significant threat to the regime.

Political dissent: a moving target

The confidential report dismissed the Populists as a single-issue literary lobby preoccupied with the human rights of Hungarian ethnic minorities. On the other hand, the "bourgeois radicals" were seen as a politically subversive force whose leaders were active on many fronts. As alleged recipients of financial support from Western, most prominently US, "special services," the democratic opposition was portrayed as the Hungarian version of the (US-supported) Polish Solidarity movement. Moreover, they were perceived as the main source of antiregime influence over the intelligentsia and university youth.

The most plausible explanation for the resuscitation of ideological vigilantism *cum* "administrative measures" might be that of György Aczél's dismissal as CC secretary for ideology at the March 1985 HSWP congress. Kádár's brilliant cultural-ideological puppet master had been allowed to keep his seat in the PB but was exiled to the CC's Institute for the Social Sciences as its director general. He told me in June 1988 that he was pleased to run the institute and did not mind presiding over this hotbed of reform socialist dissent.[62]

What he did not mention was that he had lost the administrative resources – literary prizes, well-paying jobs, publishing contracts, approval of travel abroad, and other perquisites as the regime's chief censor – with which to manipulate dissident behavior. His maladroit successors in charge of ideology and culture – János Berecz was Aczél's *bête noir* – saw treason in cases that, in Aczél's day, had been handled as instances of minor political indiscretion. On the other hand, the state of the economy had been better, the public mood more optimistic, and critical intellectuals' influence over the society less pervasive during Aczél's watch than what they became by 1986–7 in Hungary. Though Aczél was "out," he had enough influence left to manipulate party policies until the very end, as will be shown below.

Populist dissent: independent critics or the regime's silent partners?

With the death of Gyula Illyés in 1983, the leadership of the Populist intellectuals passed on to the "second" (Sándor Csoóri, István Csurka, Gyula Fekete, Lajos Für) and the "third" (Csaba Gy. Kiss, Sándor Lezsák, Dénes Csengey, Zoltán Bíró) generations of writers, poets, and cultural historians.[63] Unlike Németh and Illyés, these younger intellectuals had never rated dinner invitations from Aczél. However, commensurate with their more modest talents, Csoóri and Csurka received their share of lesser literary prizes from the cultural bureaucracy. As Zoltán Bíró recalled, members of these groups had met regularly in beer halls, restaurants, and coffee houses since the late 1960s to talk about literature and politics. Their shared concerns were those of the traditional Populist agenda. Like all intellectuals, they were critical of the regime but let their leaders – first Illyés, then his heir apparent Sándor Csoóri – fight for their beliefs in the public arena.

According to Bíró, in late 1984 he and eighteen of his friends wrote a petition to the PB in which they requested permission to establish a Gábor Bethlen Foundation, to publish a journal, to publish a work on the history of Transylvania, and to initiate TV programming for Hungarians living beyond the national boundaries, and also asked that a senior government position on ethnic minority affairs be created. The party's response was both prompt and positive. The petitioners were invited to the party headquarters where they were met by Aczél, Kádár's personal secretary, and András Knopp, the CC's trouble-shooter for dissident affairs. Other than the new government position, the rest of the group's requests were approved by the party.[64]

In early 1987 the Populists made another attempt to resume coopera-tion with the *Beszélő* group by way of holding a "Monor II" conference later in the year. With the appearance of *Társadalmi Szerződés* (Social Contract) – a major policy statement by the democratic opposition that will be discussed below – the two groups, as representatives of social movements, never met again. According to Bíró, the "other side's" *Social Contract* had been prepared "behind our backs" and was nothing but an attempt to impose on the Populists the democratic opposition's radical agenda. János Kenedi's account of this event, however harsh, seems to be rather persuasive.

> In my view, the psychological reason for upsetting the applecart could be found in the Populist writers' inferiority complex, which they sought to overcome with a "Berecz and Grósz therapy": [that is,] to fill the intellectual void with [political] power. The Populist writers aspired to lead the nation but were unable to produce the kind of economic and social program that even the editors of *Beszélő* could slap together. This disadvantage could be turned around – and that was the political reason for quitting [the dialogue]. Für and Csurka failed to recognize that they were only pawns in the game that led to Kádár's ouster at the [May 1988] party conference. In the summer of 1987, Grósz and Berecz ... probably with Pozsgay's help ... were busy organizing the palace revolution for which they needed the support of nonparty intellectuals.[65]

Although Berecz was probably only a minor player in the anti-Kádár cabal, the rest of Kenedi's partisan account is accurate up to a point. In any case, following this fiasco the Populists had no choice but to explore the possibility of a tactical alliance with the party's young Turks. They approached Imre Pozsgay – then the secretary general of the PPF and Bíró's close friend – to lend a hand to the Populists' own effort to organize a Monor-style intelligentsia summit in September of that year.

The Lakitelek conference of September 27, 1987 was an important event, as well as the subject of subsequent myth-making and political reinterpretation.[66] The facts of the case are fairly unambiguous. A small organizing committee, consisting of Bíró, Lezsák, Für, and, on

Pozsgay's behalf, Mihály Bihari, invited 181 intellectuals (mostly Populists and Populist sympathizers with a few reform socialists) for an exchange of ideas about national concerns. The principal speakers were Imre Pozsgay, István Csurka, Mihály Bihari, Csaba Gombár, and two lesser lights. The formal presentations were followed by thirty or so comments, the passing of a political declaration, and the issuance of a closing communiqué.

Pozsgay began by "discharging a political commission," conveying prime minister Grósz's greetings to the conference: "We are willing to engage in a dialogue and work with those with a constructive approach to [political] stability and [national] recovery."[67] The rest of Pozsgay's message can be characterized as a strongly critical summary of the current state of affairs and a campaign speech calling for allies to launch a national movement to clear the road for drastic institutional and political reforms. He argued for a fresh start and radical innovations. Pozsgay's political message, "the political conditions ... for the realization of new reforms are in the making" (kialakulóban vannak), and his call for a "new national coalition" to spearhead the way toward a "democratic and socialist" Hungary, were clear and to the point.[68]

Bihari took the argument a step further by urging those present "to distinguish among those in power and decide as to who can or cannot be trusted." "[I]t is essential that with the proper deployment of political forces [those in] the reform movement make use of the existing institutions to help those who represent their interests to acquire positions in the political power structure."[69] Gombár added that the short-term political objective ought to be "transitional political pluralism." By this he meant a loose bipolar party system having the democratized and decentralized HSWP with several caucuses and policy platforms at one end, and a social movement of the reform intelligentsia at the other.

With the exception of two non-Populists, most of the discussants were in favor of these notions and further embellished the hosts' "popular-national" (népi-nemzeti) message. The dissenters were the novelist György Konrád and the reform economist László Lengyel. Konrád objected to the socialist-Populist two-party scheme and insisted that "pluralism implies [not a one- or a two-but] a multiparty system in which Hungary's political traditions ... are articulated, more or less the way they had been in 1947–8."[70] Lengyel was less diplomatic: "Where are those who for years had spoken up for the cause of Hungarian democracy and the rights of Hungarian citizens? Where are the János Kis'? I miss them!"[71] The organizers' lame response – "This is a gathering of friends" – must have sounded unconvincing to the many scores of participants who had never met before this event.

The political declaration registered the "present unavailability of opportunities for the free and independent expression of views" and recommended establishment of the Hungarian Democratic Forum (HDF) as the venue for an "ongoing and public" exchange of views. The declaration also envisaged the launching of an "independent publication" operating "within the existing constitutional framework."[72] The closing communiqué affirmed the group's commitment to "democracy, socialism, and the future of Hungary" and paid homage to the regime's proreform politicians. On the other hand, as promoters of "democratic socialism," the authors of the communiqué distanced themselves from those of "the worse, the better" persuasion and their attempts at "clique-style isolationist" tactics.[73]

The Lakitelek conference was a landmark event: the public renegotiation of the terms of the Kádár–Aczél–Populist compromise of 1958–62. The old regime had defaulted on its commitments to Németh, Illyés, and their ideological heirs. This, in turn, presented the reform communists, particularly Pozsgay, with the opportunity to revise the terms of the relationship to their political benefit. The recruitment of Populists for participation in a "democratic socialist" partnership with the political incumbents was an example of communist "rearguard" *Realpolitik* at its best.

The Populists' enthusiastic endorsement of the terms of Grósz's proposal helped drive a wedge between the democratic opposition and the nationalist intelligentsia. As the Populists saw it, Pozsgay's involvement as a trusted middleman between the regime and the intellectuals committed to values of "people and nation" held the promise of a Popular Front-type "democratic socialist" party pluralism. Prospects of peaceful power sharing by emerging constituencies, such as new clubs and associations, with the regime's PPF seemed irresistible to the "founding fathers" of the MDF in the fall of 1987.

The pact, such as it was, helped upgrade the Populist politicians' status from that of powerless petitioners to politically sheltered auxiliaries of the ruling party's nascent reform wing. The Populists got their Gábor Bethlen Foundation; their journal (with much delay); official permits to hold (unpublicized) meetings and to organize (with police protection) a large demonstration on June 27, 1988 in support of human rights in Transylvania; and direct access to the party's rising star, Imre Pozsgay.[74] Moreover, as Károly Grósz explained to me, they had been also in intermittent contact with his office "about certain long-term issues" until September 1988.[75] The Populists came back from the wilderness and regained their foothold in Hungarian politics.

Democratic opposition at the crossroads: the "social contract" reconsidered

Major personnel changes in the party and the government in June 1987, particularly Grósz's appointment as prime minister, marked the beginning of the endgame for the Kádár regime in Hungary. As shown above, Grósz and the reform advocate Pozsgay – and, behind the scenes, Aczél as well – tried to explore ways to reach accommodation with the dissident community. Morever, Pozsgay's reform-socialist supporters were on the move searching for ways out of the economic crisis. Caught between new pressures and new opportunities, the still loosely organized dissident movement was in danger of losing momentum or worse – succumbing to offers of co-optation by the regime or by its "human face," Imre Pozsgay.

The democratic opposition's response to these challenges was the publication, in mid-June 1987, of a special issue of *Beszélő* entitled *Társadalmi Szerződés – a politikai kibontakozás feltételei* (loosely translated: Social Contract – the requisites of political crisis management).[76] The closely argued sixty-page document consisted of a preamble, a five-part political action program, and closing arguments on the international context of Hungarian politics in the 1980s.

The preamble began with the new strategic message of the democratic opposition: "Kádár must go!" Although this succinct statement had been the hidden agenda of all political discourse in and out of the ruling party during the preceding decade, it took exceptional courage to drop this bombshell and call it a feasible solution to the present crisis. On the other hand, bringing the issue of political succession into the public arena could, as it did, serve as a catalyst to accelerate latent processes of change in public opinion, elite behavior, and the realignment political forces in the ruling party.

The main object of this document was to force the incumbents to act – without, however, engulfing the country in a potentially disastrous struggle for political succession.

Beszélő's case for Kádár's removal was blunt, yet prudently articulated. In answer to the question "New personalities, or new politics?" the authors submitted:

János Kádár used to be the symbol of the "golden mean" in Hungary. Unlike Rákosi, he did not try to impose on the people ambitious programs of social transformation. Unlike Imre Nagy, he was unwilling to accept limitations on the party's rule. Yet, as virtual possessor of the monopoly of political power, he refrained from trampling upon the interests of groups that had the capacity to articulate openly their grievances. He was content with changes by the spoonful. He let those who lost [material possessions as a result of communist rule] to compensate themselves the best they could ... Kádár is personally responsible for the paralysis of leadership. It was he who declared in 1983: there will be no second reforms. In 1984 he pressed for the irresponsible policy of economic revitalization through the 7th Five Year Plan. He was the master conductor of the 1985 [13th] party congress that promised higher investments, higher consumption, improved balance of payments, and the moderation of inflation at the same time ... Kádár's departure, however, will solve nothing. If his successors try to rectify the "mistakes" of the last few years and return to the "proven policies of the last thirty years," the crisis will go on unabated ... There must be a radical political change in Hungary.[77]

The five-part program submitted a list of urgent political demands and policy proposals on censorship, employees' rights, social welfare issues, and procedural guarantees for the protection of individual civil rights.

As the authors explained, Hungary had three possible escape routes from the political quagmire. The first was reenactment of the Romanian scenario: a combination of Stalinist and nationalist demagoguery, political mobilization and a regime-led "restoration of order." The second was the South Korean option: a police state *cum* free market economy. The third was public renegotiation of the unwritten social contract between the people and the regime. The Hungarian people, at least the politically conscious intelligentsia, were ready for a dialogue. Therefore, it was the regime that had to be pushed to the negotiating table.

As *Beszélő* saw it, implementation of needed economic reforms was inconceivable without a program of political transformation. Its main components were a multiparty system and parliamentary democracy; self-government in the communities and at the workplace; rule of law; and national self-determination and a declaration of neutrality as the mainstay of foreign policy.

These proposals were those of the editors of *Beszélő*, rather than of the entire democratic opposition. The foreign policy parts of the program devoted considerable attention to the issue of Hungarian ethnic minorities.[78] However, instead of yet another recitation of ethnic grievances and the use of Lakitelek-style emotionally charged prose, the *Beszélő* program outlined a prudent scenario of foreign policy options to address this festering problem. In fact, these proposals came very close to what the CC's Foreign Department (Mátyás Szűrös, Gyula Horn, Csaba Tabajdi, and Imre Szokai) and the Foreign Ministry under their control had been trying to do since the early 1980s.

The reform socialists: the limits of instrumental-pragmatic dissent in the late 1980s

According to the HSWP Statutes of March 28, 1985, "those party members who violate the party's norms [are subject to] disciplinary action by their local party organization ... by higher party organs, or by the Central Control Commission" (CCC).[79] Historically, the CCC had been a shadowy body of conservative party pensioners, Kádár loyalists, and faceless cadres dedicated to stamping out (mainly local) corruption and political misconduct in the party. Although it was subordinate only to the party congress, as a practical matter, its decisions were subject to PB approval. With these facts in mind, let us consider an announcement in the April 9, 1988 issue of *Népszabadság*:

> Pursuant to a decision of the CCC, HSWP, because of their behavior and [political] activities [the following individuals] were expelled from the party: Zoltán Biró, senior scientific associate, the National Széchenyi Library; Dr Mihály Bihari, professor at the Faculty of Law, University of Budapest; Zoltán Király, editor-reporter at the Szeged regional studio of the Hungarian TV; and Dr László Lengyel, senior scientific associate at the Financial Research, Inc. These party members have held views that were at variance with the party's policies and articulated these for some time at nonparty forums. They chose to misinterpret the party's Statutes, refused to abide by party discipline, and have harmed the party's unity.[80]

The expulsion from the party of four nationally known reform socialists was a major milestone in the history of instrumental-prag-matic dissent in the late Kádár era. It was also a test of the ruling party's capacity to accommodate internal pressures for change. More-over, the "gang of four" – as Budapest wit had it – were thought to have been protected auxiliaries of Pozsgay and, in a more tenuous fashion, of Grósz as well. Apart from the the "high politics" of the affair, let us briefly consider exactly *what* these reform socialists had done to merit the supreme political punishment for their actions.[81]

The "gang of four": profiles in reform socialist dissent

László Lengyel's career began as a researcher at the Finance Ministry's in-house think tank, the Institute of Financial Research. The ministry was one of the few government agencies where full and factual information was available on the Hungarian economy. In 1981 the government created the Economic Mechanism Coordinating Commission to consider expert recommendations on needed changes and new reform measures. The institute's contribution, "Debates on the Reform of the Economic Mechanism," was the product of a team effort by young economists (Lengyel, István Csillag, György Matolcsy, Erzsébet Szalai, and others) who came to play a decisive role in economic policy debates in the coming years. The report called for radical reforms, marketization, and an end to "cadre bargains," that is, the mutual accommodation of political interests between the party apparat and the antireform economic elites at the expense of efficiency and balanced growth.[82]

The message of the institute and that of many others addressed to the Coordinating Commission, senior politicians, the April 1984 meeting of the CC, and even to the 1985 party congress were either swept aside or were ignored by the recipients.[83] In the end, the frustrated young reform advocates turned to a fellow economist and CC member Rezső Nyers and the noneconomist, but committed reformer, Imre Pozsgay. Whereas Nyers could offer only moral support, Pozsgay had the resources with which to promote and publicize innovative reform proposals. The chosen vehicle to sponsor study groups and publications was the newly created Council for Social Policy of the PPF.

With Pozsgay's authorization in hand, the economists embarked on a project entitled *Fordulat és reform* (Turnabout and reform).[84] Its study became the key economic reform document of the decade and acquired a life of its own over the next two years. Apart from the document's substantive merits, what is of interest here is that it involved twenty-nine authors and fifty-eight discussants from as many as twenty-three research institutes, government agencies, and even the party's own Institute for the Social Sciences. The regime's ban on publication was of no avail, for both in a samizdat and in a printed version, the study became a rallying point for the Hungarian intelligentsia. At the end, the regime had no choice but to authorize publication of a "sanitized" version of *Fordulat és reform* in the June 1987 issue of *Közgazdasági Szemle*.[85]

Mihály Bihari represented another kind of challenge to the party apparat. Coming from an underprivileged working-class background, this extremely gifted law graduate was promptly recruited to the CC's ideological apparat in the early 1970s as one of Pozsgay's assistants in the editorial office of the party's theoretical monthly *Társadalmi Szemle*. He also served as an expert legal consultant for the CC's Department of PA. From the late 1970s on, Bihari published sophisticated but highly critical treatises on the structural flaws of the political system. Subsequently, he joined Pozsgay's Ministry of Education and Culture as head of the main department in charge of higher education. His critical public statements on the regime's inadequate budgetary commitments to education and research led to a showdown with the CC's cultural apparat and to his return to the Law Faculty as the head of (Hungary's first) Department of Political Science.[86]

Bihari "crossed the Rubicon" as the author of *Reform és demokrácia* (Reform and democracy) which he wrote at Pozsgay's request for the PPF's Council for Social Policy.[87] This study thoroughly examined the hidden administrative and legal dimensions of public administration in Hungary and proposed a specific legislative agenda to effect overdue institutional reforms. The problem, as with similar but less-publicized reform proposals at that time, was that Bihari chose not to sidestep the sensitive topic of the party's role in public life, calling it the main obstacle to meaningful institutional reforms. As one of the featured speakers at the Lakitelek meeting, Bihari was also deemed guilty of transgressing the limits of academic theorizing and of entering the ranks of an organized nonparty political movement. His expulsion from the party was a message to the social scientists: "Stay out of politics."

Zoltán Bíró was a literary historian who began his career at the Ministry of Culture in 1971 as an official in the department for literary policies. An early associate and then friend of Pozsgay's, he had a major role in the coordination of cultural organizations, particularly in the provincial cities and towns. In a way, Bíró's job in the late 1970s was to link Pozsgay with the national network of ministry-funded local cultural and educational elites and writers who spoke for the traditional values of Hungary.

Bíró, too, lost his ministerial position after Pozsgay left for the PPF in 1982, yet he remained in contact with his old Populist writer friends.

Although in his memoirs he shies away from admitting the obvious, it appears, however, that his role as one of the convenors of the Lakitelek conference had been that of Pozsgay's political emissary rather than of the Populist ideologue that he became in the late 1980s.[88] Biró's expulsion from the party served several purposes. It was a warning to the restless Populists to refrain from taking sides in the party's internal affairs. It was also a potshot at Pozsgay – already in trouble with the CCC for having gone public with the text of the Lakitelek closing communiqué in November 1987 – and those who had compromised their party membership by formal affiliation with a pseudolegal political movement.[89]

Zoltán Király, a popular local TV reporter in Szeged, in May 1985 found himself nominated and then elected as a parliamentary deputy, as he explained, "by accident."[90] While covering the proceedings of a stalemated nominating meeting – the choice was between two creatures of the local apparat – he had been nominated from the floor and subsequently went on to win in the Szeged third district's seat.

As a newly minted legislator, Király enjoyed the enviable record of having bested retired county first secretary Mihály Komócsin – the former first secretary of what his critics called "Pol Pot [Csongrád] county" – who had the disconcerting habit of asking questions of cabinet ministers from the floor of the "Esteemed House." He tried to introduce reform measures, proposed cuts in the defense budget, and led the parliamentary fight against the government's support of the controversial Gabčikovo-Nagymaros Hungarian–Czechoslovak water diversion project. Thanks to the occasional TV coverage of parliamentary sessions, Király became a nationally known reform politician.

As far as the CCC was concerned, Király was a bad influence on his fellow legislators. Thanks to Király, some developed the habit of voting with him and against the socialist government. His fellow MP János Kádár's pained expression on the TV screen at seeing Király in action manifested his distress. Obviously, Király was not worthy of membership in Kádár's party.

Conclusions

In Hungary patterns of interaction between the political incumbents and the dissidents were substantially different from those elsewhere in communist Eastern Europe and in the USSR. Self-limitation and accommodation-seeking behavior were the key characteristics of dissident interest articulation.[91] Moreover, almost to the very end, the dissidents' strategic goal was changes *in* the existing system rather than a change *of* systems.

The regime's congenital legitimacy defects, Kádár's strategic priorities, and his changing leadership styles help explain the indigenous characteristics of the Hungarian case. A combination of these factors yielded a unique style of conflict management and helped shape the regime's policies toward unauthorized expressions of political beliefs.

Between the early 1960s and 1988, dissent took various forms and dissident spokesmen advocated different priorities over time. Initially it was the NEM and its economic and societal impact that prompted criticism by András Hegedüs, György Lukács, and members of the Budapest School. In the 1970s the main concerns of political dissent were censorship and human rights, particularly the personal autonomy of the intellectuals. In the next decade, thanks to the *Beszélő* group and the spread of samizdat, the scope of the dissidents' targets became much wider. The new agenda addressed a broad range of regime policies from those on economic reforms to social welfare matters and the political empowerment of citizens.

The democratic opposition's involvement in the 1985 parliamentary elections was a quantum leap, and so were the dissidents' attempts to close ranks and propose alternative policy platforms to the incumbents. At the end, the regime's very existence – its laws, institutions, and the competency of the top office holders – came under fire. What had begun two decades earlier as quixotic individual acts of ideological defiance by 1988 became a coherent, albeit uncoordinated, radical national reform movement and a political factor in the terminal phase of the *ancien régime*.

Kádár tolerated his reformist critics in and out of the HSWP, provided that they kept their distance from the blue-collar workers. This attitude may have stemmed from his belated recognition of the folly of outlawing all noncommunist political parties in early 1957. His reports to the CC on his recent trips abroad – for example, to Finland and Britain – were peppered with wistful comments about the usefulness of having "correct" opposition parties in an efficient political system. The kind of ersatz multiparty safety valve of having three or four noncommunist parties in the legislature that served Kádár's Polish, East German, and Czechoslovak colleagues well, was unavailable in Hungary.

Although Kádár took pains to have at least a token "Social Democrat" (Marosán, Nyers, Sarlós, and Lázár) in the PB for one reason or another, eventually he had to dispense with their services. In the early

1970s Kádár's opponents tried to make use of the TUF as an antireform "workers' party." However, the apparat, the security organs, and, for lack of alternatives, the Soviets also stood by Kádár. As will be shown in the next chapter, in the 1980s, the Imre Pozsgay-led PPF and the restless apparatchiki of the YCL had ambitions to pose as a "party of nonparty members" and a party of the young generation, respectively. Both were too late to influence political outcomes in one way or another.

Up to a point, and each in its own way, the Populists, the reform socialists, and the democratic opposition were useful for Kádár's purposes. The presence of domestic critics was helpful to cite in negotiations with Moscow as evidence of internal constraints on Hungary's ability to comply with Soviet demands for additional resource commitments for military and other purposes. Having the dissidents around was essential to Kádár for steering a "middle course" between the party conservatives and the regime's "right-wing" opponents. The dissidents were not "rightists" but an essential and partly manipulated political counterweight to keep the party's troglodytes at bay.

The regime's harsh methods of postrevolutionary political consolidation and Kádár's and Aczél's working relationship with the Populist elites basically eliminated the anomic-militant and moral-absolutist dimensions of political dissent in Hungary. This left the instrumental-pragmatic cluster, which became manifest in the ideas and programs of the reform socialists and those of the democratic opposition. However, neither the ideas nor the ideologically divided leading dissident personalities posed any immediate threat to the regime's political stability. Adjustive concessions and diversionary mechanisms were readily available policy tools to promote desirable political behavior among potential troublemakers. Indeed, as long as the Populists and the urban radicals were kept apart and at each other's throats, the principal challenge was not their suppression, but sensible utilization of their ideas.

From a review of topics under PB consideration between 1970 and 1988 and of unsolicited dissident "policy inputs" over time, it appears that the top incumbents not only were *au courant* with what their critics had to say but tried to be responsive to the critics' demands. Or, as Kádár put it at the April 17, 1984 CC meeting, "to the extent it is possible, we try to follow and adapt to public opinion."[92]

By far the most effective form of dissident interest articulation was that which originated with the reform socialists. With only slight exaggeration it could be argued that from 1977 on the regime's macroeconomic policies, particularly the implementation of the same, were driven as much by the reform economists' policy preferences as by those of the incumbent decision-makers. A similar case can be made for the policy-drafting process that led to the holding of the multi-candidate elections of 1985. In fact, much of the comprehensive administrative-legislative reform package that served as the center-piece of National Roundtable deliberations in 1989 had originated from experts' reform proposals on subjects ranging from the office of the President of the Republic to the establishment of the Constitutional Court.[93]

Each of the dissident groups made important contributions that were essential to the collapse of the old regime, as well as to a negotiated and peaceful transition to a postcommunist political system in Hungary. The Populist agenda emphasized nationalism and national identity. As Kádár put it, "the most potent weapon against socialism is nationalism."[94] The message of the Lakitelek manifesto, however ambivalent toward socialism, did respond to the long-suppressed nationalist beliefs of the average Hungarian. The avail-ability of the "Populist alternative" was indispensable to the fall of the old regime.

The democratic opposition was responsible for the introduction into reform debates among the intellectuals of liberal values of human rights and civil society. These were effective, but nonrevolutionary, ideas and programs that captured the allegiance of the young genera-tion and the urban intelligentsia. However, it was not the nationalist and the liberal dissidents but the reform socialists who were the ultimate guarantors of peaceful transition and negotiated political outcomes. It was their administrative experience and policy knowledge that enabled them to bore from within and ultimately demoralize the incumbent party and government apparat. These internal critics also supplied ready-made solutions to the National Roundtable negotiators in the summer of 1989. The three sides were handed polished drafts of bills and policy papers that required only editing and choices among alternative versions to serve as a joint incumbent–insurgent platform on which to build a postcommunist political system.

To say nay or to ask why in a communist state – even in a posttotalitarian one – takes courage and deeply held personal convic-tions. There was a great deal more to dissent in Hungary than the articulation of critical opinions about the political regime. With the inclusion into the narrative of biographical sketches on several leading dissidents, I have sought to illuminate the human dimensions of opposition and dissent in Hungary. István Bibó, György Lukács, János Kis, György Bence, Sándor Csoóri and some of the Populist writers, scores of samizdat authors, and many reform socialists were the main protagonists in a thirty-year process of saying nay and asking why of the powers that be.

The dissidents' ideas and personal dignity under political and economic pressure still stand out as examples of intellectual integrity and nonviolent resistance to dictatorship and psychological intimidation. Not all of these people were saints or knights in shining armor. Nor was their progress from "there" to becoming intellectual progenitors of democracy in Hungary either linear, or free of false starts and compromises with political exigencies. "Warts and all," they were men of intellect and of goodwill. Whether they knew it or not, as Central European intellectuals, they were the community's self-appointed guardians on a mission of cultural enlightenment, social emancipation, and national independence. Without them Hungary would not be a democracy today.

5   Party elites in transition: the successor generation

The regime's dissident critics were instrumental in Hungary's political transformation between 1987 and 1990. The political leadership was divided on ways to respond to public pressures. Most Hungarians yearned for a return to the "good old days" of the 1970s, yet they also craved freedom, national independence, and closer ties with the West. The elites and the intellectuals clamored for radical reforms. These were signs of disorientation above and of public distrust below. Both were manifestations of the concurrent crises of authority and of public confidence in the incumbent political leadership. In 1987–8 the question of leadership succession became the central issue on Hungary's political agenda.

János Kádár was 75 years old on May 26, 1987. It was time for him to step down, yet he refused to name a successor. A year later he was removed from power by his younger colleagues. Károly Grósz, Imre Pozsgay, János Berecz, Miklós Németh, and their allies in the party and the government were the principal organizers of the May 1988 *Putsch* of the apparat. Who were they and what did they want? Were they, as the conservative Kádár loyalists declared, ruthless opportunists, traitors to the working people, the gravediggers of socialism in Hungary? Or were they courageous reformers who tried to salvage the positive accomplishments of the past forty years and lead the nation toward a social market economy, rule of law, and political democracy? These questions are still being debated in Hungary in the 1990s. Some of the answers are available as parts of the public record, some came to light only recently, and the rest must await the publication of new memoirs and the release of new documentary evidence on the personalities and politics of the transition period.[1]

In this chapter I shall explore the human and ideological dimensions of political succession in Hungary by reconstructing the life histories, careers, and political beliefs of the organizers of the events of May 1988 and other members of the party's "successor generation." The narrative will focus on the political career and intellectual development of Kádár's heirs from their entry into politics in the early 1950s until June 1987, when Károly Grósz became prime minister and the *in petto* designated successor of Kádár.[2]

The discussion will consider questions of political succession, elite mobility, and Kádár's style of cadre selection and personnel management; the characteristics of "political generations" in Hungarian society and in the ruling party; and an examination of the "parallel lives" and careers of Imre Pozsgay, János Berecz, and Károly Grósz from their youth to their arrival in 1987 as key political actors in Hungary.

Pozsgay's, Berecz's and Grósz's political strategies, alliance policies, and individual roles in the political outcomes of 1988–90 will be discusssed in Part III.

(A)   Political succession in a communist party-state

As a ruling communist party, the HSWP was a complex organization in which individual political actors were parts of a bureaucratic hierarchy. Their capacity to articulate personal opinions was circumscribed by seniority, rank, and access to the narrow circle of top political decision-makers. They functioned in an organizational environment in which a premium was placed on the preservation, as well as on the appearance, of stability. Both were essential to institutional survival in all modes of political leadership.

Political stability and the preservation of normalcy were the regime's principal policy objectives: however, their achievement was predicated on people rather than on institutions. The *nomenklatura* system rested on an inherently unstable personalistic network of clientelist (vertical) and spatial and generational (horizontal) alliances of upper- and lower-level officials. These alliances were components of an interlocking party-state directorate that created a system vulnerable to corruption, administrative inertia, and institutional entropy.[3] To prevent or to overcome internal decay, the periodic turnover of key personnel became a matter not of choice but of necessity. Changes, particularly in the top leadership, tended in turn to destabilize the affected clientelistic networks at all levels of the party hierarchy.

The situation becomes even more complex in cases of large-scale turnover of senior officials at the top. Changes of such magnitude entail risks of instability for some parts of the political power structure. With respect to its potential ripple effects on systemic stability, the departure of a long-serving first secretary is a qualitatively different proposition from any other personnel change. In such cases, what is at issue is the suitability not only of a successor but the party's "general line," the regime's legitimacy, and potentially survival of the political system itself.

The voluntaristic organizational culture of a ruling Marxist–Leninist party is inimical to the institutionalization of orderly change in key personnel. The history of cadre mobility, patterns of transfer, promotion, demotion, co-optation, and on-the-job longevity in ruling parties offers partial evidence on certain national differences in the management of cadre policies. The European and the Asian, the Soviet and the Chinese, and the Central European and the southeast European ruling parties approached personnel matters in different ways. Among them one finds a wide repertory of methods to effect cadre changes. These ranged from violent showdowns to Byzantine intrigues and complex multiplayer scenarios of musical chairs.

According to János Kádár, as cited in Gyula Horn's memoirs, "we have never consulted with Brezhnev about the makeup of our PB."[4] This statement was made in 1970 and it may have been true at that time. However, as shown in Chapter 2, two years later Kádár's *own* position was sufficiently threatened by the same Brezhnev to require a political showdown with Moscow to clear up his status as the party's leader. On the other hand, after 1974, when he had to bow to Moscow's demands to demote four senior associates, Kádár appears to have had sufficient authority to make his own appointments without fear of being second-guessed by the CPSU.[5] In any case, the point that must be made is that from very early on the HSWP's cadre policies were different from those of the CPSU and the rest of the ruling parties in Eastern Europe.

The Hungarian case may be explained by citing three indigenous factors that influenced cadre policies after 1957: the party's history, Kádár's previous political experience, and his administrative style as party leader.

1 The Hungarian party's history is a record of bruising clashes between the young activists at the bottom and the middle-aged and old cadres at the top of the organizational hierarchy. Interviews with party veterans help explain the evolution of the Hungarian communist movement from Béla Kun and the ultraleft young terrorists of 1919 to Kádár and his troubles with the party's young professionals in the 1970s and 1980s.[6] The process may be characterized as a series of intergenerational confrontations and uneasy truces between showdowns.

Some of the more notorious instances of intraparty splits were those between the Trotskyites/Bukharinites and the Stalinists in the 1920s; the native leftist intellectuals and the Muscovite apparatchiki in the 1930s; the old Moscow hands of Rákosi, Gerő, Révai, and Farkas and young natives such as Rajk, Kádár, and others in 1949–50; the established party apparat and the young radicals of the People's Colleges (NÉKOSZ) movement in the late 1940s; the old Stalinists and the Imre Nagy-led young revisionist intellectual rebels in 1953–6.

These confrontations demonstrated that: the nature of intraparty power struggles had been as much intergenerational as ideological; the younger cadres were invariably defeated by the older, more experienced, and politically more conservative apparat; and intergenerational co-optation and recruitment into the senior levels, either as a matter of routine rejuvenation of the top ranks with young cadres or as preparation for leadership succession, were marked by severe conflicts in the Hungarian party prior to 1957.

2   János Kádár had been a victim of Stalinist cadre policies. His transit from party deputy secretary general to prison inmate was both abrupt and humiliating. While he was in prison, his wife was denied employment and decent housing.[7] (The executed László Rajk's child was taken away from his mother and put into an orphanage under a different name.) The survivors, such as György Aczél and the rest of Rákosi's high-ranking party victims, fared the same way.[8]

Whether the exercise of leadership responsibilities was acts of political dissembling or evidence of concern for the well-being of fellow communists, the fact remains that the making of major personnel decisions was an anguishing and time-consuming chore for Kádár. He insisted that the retired top cadres would depart "with recognition" of their merits. For those who fell foul of political exigencies, Kádár saw to the making of provisions for a cushioned landing after they left the apparat.

3   As top personnel manager, Kádár was a firm yet paternalistic *gazda* ("chief," or "village elder") who displayed uncharacteristic patience with bright and hard-working young men from peasant or blue-collar-worker backgrounds who rose high enough in the apparat to earn a position at party headquarters. As shown below, the screening process was long and arduous.[9] The requisites of career advancement in the HSWP were years of hard work, the finding of senior sponsors (the operative word was *keresztapa* [godfather] in the apparat), and a certain amount of good luck at being in the right place and at the right time.

Once these young people proved themselves and kept out of trouble, they were given powerful positions in the party and the government. In making his appointments Kádár also relied on the advice of trusted PB colleagues, particularly Aczél and Miklós Óvári, the head of Kádár's personal secretariat. The only unofficial participant of Kádár's inner council was his wife, a tough yet whimsical judge of political fitness and personal character.[10]

"Tribal memory" and lifelong psychological (and physical) scars of intergenerational clashes in the Hungarian party counseled against premature promotion of young cadres to key positions. Over the years the senior incumbents – though on rather superficial personal terms with one another – became accustomed to doing business Kádár's way. The intrusion of better-educated, well-spoken, and most likely opinionated younger cadres was both a nuisance and a threat to the somnolent tranquility of the PB in the late Kádár years.

Unlike his Romanian, Bulgarian, and North Korean colleagues, the childless Kádár had no dynastic ambitions. To Hungary's good fortune, there were no Elena and Nicu Ceauşescus, Ludmilla Zhivkovas, and "Dear Leader" kinds of heirs apparent in the HSWP. On the other hand, Kádár and his wife were always on the lookout for a "political godson." Zoltán Komócsin, though he may have been a disappointment as one of the alleged anti-Kádár plotters of 1970–2, died of cancer in 1974 at the age of 51. László Maróthy – co-opted into the PB in 1975 at the age of 33 – was the next one, but this dutiful young man was also a disappointment. János Berecz, who undoubtedly aspired to the role, was for different reasons vetoed by Mrs Kádár.[11] Thus, the sole gatekeeper of political succession and generational change was János Kádár. The eventual choices of this lonely man would determine the future shape of Hungarian politics.

(B)   New party elites in Hungary: formative experiences and career patterns

Generational change is an elusive concept.[12] In a political sense, the term may be understood as the coexistence and interaction of political actors with different formative experiences and different motivations and opportunities for becoming professional politicians.[13] At the end of March 1985 the HSWP PB included members of six political generations.[14] These were the professional revolutionaries (János Kádár); underground and wartime resistance veterans (György Aczél and Sándor Gáspár); "forty-fivers," that is, those who joined the party in 1945 (Pál Losonczi, Valéria Benke, Károly Németh and Miklós Óvári); (former) "Social Democrats" (István Sarlós and György Lázár); and career apparatchiki (Ferenc Havasi, István Szabó, László Maróthy, Csaba Hámori, and Károly Grósz).[15] The terms are self-explanatory in denoting the nature of formative experiences and the chronological sequence of the coming to power of each party elite cohort.

Each of these leadership types implies many similar and some idiosyncratic personal preferences with respect to ideological stance, risk-taking ability, and capacity to adapt to changes in the political environment. In one way or another, they were survivors of severe personal hardships and decades of political infighting. However, as a group, the HSWP leadership was a product of and in many ways captive to Kádár's political record. As long as he was at the helm and enjoyed Moscow's support as Hungary's leader, the final say on cadre policies and leadership renewal was Kádár's prerogative.

On the other hand, however much he tried to isolate himself from Hungary's, to him increasingly incomprehensible, social environment of the 1980s, Kádár could not remain unaffected by the world around him. Although he was largely unaware of his younger colleagues' generational values and personal beliefs, decisions had to be made and people selected to run the party and the government. As will be shown in the next chapter, the bewildered autarch could not bring himself to make these decisons and was thus denied a graceful exit from Hungarian politics.

Political generations and generational change in Hungary

In a perceptive essay on generations and political values in Hungary in the 1980s, the political scientist Tamás Fricz developed a typology with which one might approach the matter of generational change in the ruling party. By "political generations" Fricz meant a combination of political events and dominant intellectual trends in which politically aware 20–year-old Hungarians came of age since 1945.[16] He proposed the following typology:

1 The "generation of bright winds" (entry into politics between 1944 and 1948; commitment to national and socialist values and demands for an active role in politics);

2 The "generation of bargain makers" (those who chose to come to terms with the results of the post-1956 political consolidation and accepted the conditions of the "Kádár compromise");

3 The "beat generation" of the early 1970s (those who distanced
   themselves from the materialistic values of the NEM and retreated
   into a private world of alternative culture and values);
4 The "generation of the prematurely old" young people of the late
   1970s (apolitical participants in the second economy and new
   entrants into the state bureaucracy);
5 The "crisis generation" of the middle to late 1980s (deprived of
   prospects of economic advancement and career opportunities, many
   of them embraced postmaterialist values and became eligible to
   participate of the "new politics" of the transition period).

In terms of chronologically eligible age cohorts, the rejuvenation of
the HSWP's top 60- to 75-year-old leadership was possible mainly by
the promotion of the 50- to 60-year-old members of the first two
postwar political generations. Of these, only the generation of "bargain
makers" fared well in the succession sweepstakes of 1985–9. What
happened to the first postwar political generation?

The words "Our flags fly in bright winds" are from a popular
marching song of the People's Colleges movement of the early postwar
years. The movement had been an outgrowth of a Populist and left-
wing radical initiative – backed by an improbable alliance of Catholic
and Protestant clergymen and progressive government officials – in
the late 1930s to promote educational opportunities for young people
from peasant and working-class backgrounds.[17] The goal was to break
the traditional middle and upper classes' monopoly on access to higher
education and to create a new educated elite committed to national
and socialist values.[18] The movement gained momentum after the war.
By 1948 there were as many as 160 People's Colleges with 7,000 to
8,000 – of whom about 2,000 university-age – young people aspiring to
earn a professional position in the new society of a democratic
Hungary. Many, though not all, of the colleges (these were residential
facilities with in-house learning and political programs) were commu-
nist-led, but all of them felt free to define their political mission in
generational terms.[19] In 1949 the Rákosi regime cracked down and
disbanded the People's Colleges.

A few of the promising alumni, such as András Hegedüs, were
recruited into the party apparat; the rest were suspected of nationalist
deviation and became victims of Stalinist repression. Some of those
still in public life came to support Imre Nagy's New Course and were
politically active in October 1956. Thus, the young people of Hungary's only authentic peasant and working-class intellectual successor
generation were deemed guilty of nationalism and "petty bourgeois

radicalism" and became disqualified from political advancement in Kádár's Hungary.[20]

The word *kontraszelekció* (counterselection) has been a traditional part of the Hungarian political vocabulary. It denotes the process of political and job recruitment and promotion characterized by conformism, deference to authority, and intellectual mediocrity. These were positive personality attributes for the cadre managers of Kádár's "democratic centralist" party. As a generation, the "bargain makers" of the post-1956 period seemed to fit the bill.

Imre Pozsgay, János Berecz, and Károly Grósz: parallel lives

The names of and the public roles played by Imre Pozsgay, János Berecz, and Károly Grósz in Hungarian politics are inseparable from and essential to an understanding of what took place between 1987 and 1990 in Hungary. All three men were widely perceived as Kádár's potential successors. Each was well positioned to influence events and determine the outcome of leadership succession in the HSWP. Pozsgay was 53, and Berecz and Grósz were 55 years old in 1985. All three were members of the CC. Pozsgay was secretary general of the Patriotic People's Front, the largest mass organization in Hungary, with a national newspaper and hundreds of local organizations throughout the country. Berecz had just been appointed ideological secretary of the CC. As Aczél's successor, he controlled the regime's media and the resources at his disposal to manipulate the behavior of the intelligentsia. Grósz was promoted to the PB, but retained his powerful position as first secretary of the Budapest party committee. With one-fourth of the HSWP membership of 860,000 under its jurisdiction, the Budapest committee was the most influential regional party organization in Hungary.

In what follows I shall endeavor to reconstruct the careers, intellectual development, and personality characteristics of the three men. As will be shown below, as members of the same political generation, the men had much in common. They were born to poor peasant and worker families, joined the party at an early age, excelled as students, and were exceptionally skilled in adapting to and benefiting from political challenges and career opportunities in whatever positions they occupied in the state and party bureaucracy.[21] They were the regime's creatures; however ambitious and talented, without the party and Kádár, Pozsgay might have become an agricultural engineer, Berecz a village elementary-school teacher, and Grósz a typesetter.

Whatever they had – power, creature comforts, and a great deal of personal autonomy – they owed to the regime.

To develop my case, the following narrative will address four topics in a chronological sequence: formative experiences, education, and the personal impact of the 1956 revolution; apprenticeship and early career; three cadres on the "fast track"; and strategies and political choices in the 1980s.

Formative experiences and the 1956 revolution

Imre Pozsgay was born on November 26, 1933, in Kóny, a small village in western Hungary. His father, the eighth child of a farming family, was a tailor and an active member of the village's Catholic community. His early death left his widow with three children: the 5-year-old Imre, a younger brother, and a newborn sister. Pozsgay's mother took the children to the home of their paternal grandfather, a well-read and respected farmer and village elder of another small community in the Lake Balaton region. The most enduring memories of Pozsgay's childhood were evening prayers with his family, hard work around the farm, helping his mother (she became a seamstress), and voracious reading of whatever there was to read in the village. He finished the first six grades in the local one-room Catholic elementary school and was a commuter (a walk of 10 kilometers each day) to a nearby middle school. For a time he considered entering a Catholic seminary to study for the priesthood. However, his mother vetoed the idea, and in 1948 Pozsgay enrolled in a vocational high school that specialized in horticulture and forestry. Although he enjoyed schoolwork, he was more interested in politics and soon became the head of his school's student organization. He also embarked on a program of political self-education that consisted of indiscriminate reading of works by Marx, Engels, and Lenin – of which he understood very little at that time.

In 1949 his "political awakening" prompted him alone, among the four hundred students at his school, to refuse to attend religious instruction, and by the time he graduated from school he had joined the Communist Party at the age of 17. In 1950 the local party organization sponsored his application for admission and a scholarship at the newly established Lenin Institute in Budapest. Although he did not realize it at that time, the institute – itself an off-campus branch of the Faculty of Letters of the Loránd Eötvös University in Budapest – was the Rákosi regime's answer to the People's Colleges. It was an academically demanding and politically orthodox training program and a finishing school for talented and politically ambitious young cadres from working-class and poor peasant backgrounds.[22]

Pozsgay was a shy and unsophisticated village lad, and his adjustment to college life was a slow process. As a student, however, he thrived on the intellectual challenge of the institute's program. In addition to excellent Russian-language training, the institute hosted several top Soviet visiting professors and distinguished lecturers from the university. His schoolmates included people who later became leading politicians (János Berecz) and writers (Sándor Csoóri and György Konrád) in the Kádár era. The intensely politicized atmosphere compelled the students to take part (and sides) in discussion on daily politics. Pozsgay must have passed scrutiny; he was elected to various party committees, though he declined opportunities for leadership positions.

As Pozsgay recalled, during his years at the institute his loyalties were torn between his family and village – where the granaries had been stripped bare by Rákosi's collectivization drive – and the values of his school community. Imre Nagy's New Course reform program pleased him as a man of his village, but Rákosi's return to power and especially Khrushchev's secret speech on the crimes of the Stalin era were like a "knife stab" for the communist Pozsgay. To escape from these dilemmas, he buried himself in his studies; in fact, he did well enough to be nominated by the institute's Rector as tutor to the young son of Ernő Gerő, the second man in the party and, after July 1956, Rákosi's short-lived political successor.[23] This job lasted until mid-October 1956, when, as a graduating senior, he was offered a position by the the Bács-Kiskun county party committee in Kecskemét – a provincial city about 40 miles south of Budapest – as director of its Marxist–Leninist Evening University.

The October revolution found Pozsgay in Kecskemét, where his priorities were far different from those consuming most other Hungarians. He was preoccupied with locating his fiancée in Budapest and making arrangements for their wedding on October 29. The wedding did take place, on November 2, but in all the excitement Pozsgay – one might say providentially – played no role one way or another in the tumultuous events of those days.

János Berecz was born on September 18, 1930, in Ibrány, a small village in northeastern Hungary. His father was a part-time shoe repairman and day laborer, the owner of a three-acre plot. The family, parents and three sons, lived in a small thatched-roof cottage with an earthen floor. Berecz's mother was a devout Protestant.[24] He attended the local elementary school and learned about politics while sitting in a corner of the family's one-room house and listening to the politicking of his father and his customers. Upon completing middle school, in 1947 Berecz was sent to the nearby Sarospatak *kollégium*, a venerable Calvinist boarding school of national renown. The cost of his tuition was 600 kilograms of wheat – about half the yield of one acre of spring wheat and an obvious economic hardship to the family.

In 1951 Berecz enrolled in the University of Debrecen as a literature major but ended up studying Marxism–Leninism and political economy. As a top student and volunter activist for the Young Communist League (YCL), he soon became a prominent student politician and was active on many fronts on campus and off. In the following year Géza Kassai, founder and the first rector of the Lenin Institute, persuaded him to transfer there. In 1952 he joined the Communist Party. Within a year the dynamic, or as Pozsgay put it "careerist," Berecz rose high in the institute's party organization and became its secretary in 1954. There is no information on Berecz's reaction to Imre Nagy's political vicissitudes, or to a crisis of beliefs stemming from Khrushchev's secret speech.

Upon graduation from the institute Berecz married a classmate, Anna Lőwinger.[25] His first job was at the University Department of the Budapest YCL organization where he had special responsibility for YCL activities in the schools of drama and fine arts. He was also active in the Petőfi Circle – then the center of anti-Stalinist dissent among the Hungarian intelligentsia.

The October revolution found Berecz at the YCL headquarters. When he and his colleagues asked for party guidance and weapons to defend the "people's power," they were told to go home and lie low. He kept visiting his office on Köztársaság Square, and on October 30 he missed by fifteen minutes the siege of the building and the subsequent lynching of some party officials and the uniformed (enlisted) secret policemen who guarded that facility.[26] In any case, Berecz did not take part in any street fighting but, as instructed, went into hiding to await the return of the Soviet troops and, with them, Kádár's Revolutionary Workers' and Peasants' Government.

In mid-November 1956 the YCL leadership gave Berecz the assignment of joining the new (noncommunist) Federation of University Students (MEFESZ) to dissuade that radical organization from criticizing the Kádár regime. He must have been successful in his mission because in mid-March 1957 he fell under suspicion by his political masters as a possible rogue who might have switched sides in the previous five months. It took Berecz a great deal of time to clear his name and be permitted to return to the one, and eventually the only, youth organization in Hungary: the YCL.[27]

The 1956 revolution came to play an important role in Berecz's future career, although he had been essentially a bystander during that event. He must have been sufficiently impressed, or possibly disturbed, by what he had seen in October–November 1956 to propose a "scientific exploration" of those events as the topic of his candidate of historical sciences dissertation at the Social Science Academy of the CC, CPSU, which he attended in the 1960s. Twenty years later, as the HSWP CC's ideological secretary, he staked his career on an ultraleftist interpretation of the 1956 revolution. He had bet right in the 1960s in Moscow. His second bet, in 1986, cost him the chance to become an eligible successor to Kádár.

Károly Grósz was born on August 31, 1930, in the northeastern industrial city of Miskolc, into a family of third-generation industrial workers. His father, a machinist at the nearby Diósgyőr steel mill, had been a member of the underground Communist Party before 1945. His mother, a worker in a print shop, was of Slovak origin; his father was of ethnic German background, with family roots in the Passau region of eastern Bavaria. After middle school, the young Grósz began working as an apprentice at the steel mill in 1944. The next year he switched jobs, becoming an apprentice and subsequently a skilled printer. Although most of his coworkers were Social Democrats, he chose to join the Communist Party at 15.[28]

Grósz's political career began in 1949, when he worked briefly at the national YCL headquarters and later at the CC's Department of AP in Budapest. Upon being drafted into the army, he was soon recognized as a promising young cadre and sent to the Petőfi Military Academy for political officers. The top graduate of his class, he was commissioned as an officer with the rank of first lieutenant. As he recalled, his job as a political officer was "very difficult." Indeed, it must have been hard to persuade young draftees of rural background that the party's agricultural policies somehow benefited their (often starving) families at home. In any event, the well-indoctrinated young officer did not think much of Imre Nagy and his reform program. It dawned on him only in late 1955 that Rákosi's "mistakes" had outweighed his accomplishments since 1948.

At the end of 1954, Grósz received an honorable discharge from the army and was sent to work at the Borsod county party committee as a political instructor of party organizations at factories and mines in the

Miskolc region. While there, he completed a three-year commercial high school evening program. As a civilian, Grósz was no longer sheltered from the working people. When he and his father learned about the innocence of László Rajk of the charges for which he had been hanged in 1949, Grósz wanted to quit the party and return to his trade. His father, however, persuaded him not to relinquish his membership.

Borsod was an unusual county in October 1956. Unlike most of his fellow county party chiefs elsewhere in Hungary who went into hiding after October 23, Rudolf Földvári, the first secretary of the Borsod county party committee, tried to negotiate and, whenever possible, accommodate the insurgents and accede to their demands. As one of Földvári's emissaries, Grósz tried but failed to dissuade Miskolc university students from printing and distributing radical manifestos. Moreover, a demonstration on October 24 ended with a siege of police headquarters and the lynching of a man (who happened to be Grósz's personal friend) whom the miners in the crowd mistook for a secret police officer.

As Grósz's luck would have it, Földvári authorized the printing of a radical manifesto in the county's daily newspaper and appointed Grósz (without his knowledge) as the paper's new editor. At that point, all the party bosses fled, leaving Grósz to keep the remaining apparat together. This he did, in fact well enough to be elected, at the age of 26, by his fellow apparatchiki as the new first secretary of Borsod county.

When the dust settled, Földvári was fired, arrested, tried, and given a life sentence for his unusual conduct in the fall of 1956. To save himself, Földvári asserted in a long petition to Kádár that it was Grósz who had led him astray in October.[29] At any rate, when the Soviet troops arrived in November 1956, Grósz was briefly detained then released when he signed a pledge to support the new government. As an alleged culprit in the Földvári affair, Grósz found his party membership suspended, and then he was expelled from the party. He must have done an effective job in rebutting Földvári's charges because later he was exonerated and his party membership was restored.[30] Well after the local (mainly absent) heroes of the "antirevolutionary struggles of 1956" received their medals, Grósz, too, was recognized as a loyal member of the Borsod apparat.

Apprenticeship and early career

Pozsgay's first job as director of the Bács-Kiskun county party committee's Evening University positioned him as a junior ideologue and intellectual-in-residence in the county apparat. The first secretary (Frigyes Molnár) was, by Pozsgay's account, a decent man and a supportive boss. Pozsgay's job of recruiting students, teaching, and overseeing the administration of the instructional program for three hundred students was time consuming but left him enough leisure to write occasional pieces for the county's daily newspaper and to embark on a program of reading and intellectual self-improvement. Most of the twenty-six articles he wrote for *Petőfi Népe* between 1957 and 1968 were routine agit-prop trivia. However, an article published in December 1957 deserves mention. It dealt with the "counterrevolution" of 1956 in language that was on a par with the worst propaganda drivel of the contemporary Hungarian media.[31] In his autobiography Pozsgay called this piece a "crime" of which he was "still ashamed."[32]

Over the years Pozsgay became a respected member of the county's political establishment: he was invited in 1964 to join the county notables' hunting club; he was promoted to agit-prop secretary of the city's party committee (by the end of the 1960s he held the same position at the county committee); and he made friends, such as István Horváth, who would play a decisive role in his political life in the 1980s. Because he had support from above, Pozsgay took the lead in transforming Kecskemét, already the home of the famous Kodály School of Music, into an important regional cultural center. He enticed Budapest theatrical companies to perform in Kecskemét (mainly plays that could not be put on in the capital), and artists to exhibit their politically unorthodox works. Politically banned movies were shown, and a literary quarterly was launched in the city during Pozsgay's tenure. The future minister of culture certainly made his mark in Bács-Kiskun county in the 1960s.

In 1965 Pozsgay submitted an application to the Hungarian Academy of Sciences for a graduate scholarship to study and to write his candidate of science dissertation on an appropriate topic. Upon successful completion of the qualifying examinations, he was given a year's leave of absence to work under Sándor Lakos, director of the HSWP CC's Institute for the Social Sciences.

Pozsgay's somewhat ponderously titled dissertation, "Some Questions of the Further Development of Socialist Democracy and of Our Political System," is a major political document that ought to be seen as the ideological foundation of subsequent reform socialist dissent in the HSWP.[33] Once one cuts through the obligatory smoke screen of ideological pieties on the dictatorship of the proletariat, the party's leading role, and the like, Pozsgay's real agenda surfaces. His central point – "reform of the economic mechanism presupposes the further development of other, relatively autonomous elements in the [political system's] structure, such as the state, political organizations and institutions" – was *the* hidden agenda of the NEM policy debates in 1967–9.[34]

As Pozsgay saw it, management of systemic change must take its departure from new methods of decision-making, enhanced information flows, and active involvement of the public. "People," he submitted, "approve of political stability, but an increasing number wish to supplement it with the further growth of personal freedoms, that is, democracy."[35] Because the average citizen lacked a sense of political efficacy, the political institutions, particularly the nonelected bodies [that is, the apparat], "must be made accountable to those below."[36]

Perhaps the most provocative and in many ways prophetic aspect of Pozsgay's treatise was his treatment of public opinion, "openness," and political steering.

> Any kind of democratization must begin with public opinion ... We must shape public opinion. [However] ... for this task we have created a bureaucratic-manipulative system that, instead of shaping, obliterated public opinion ... There is more to public opinion than the constant [official] expectation of the public's affirmation of the current political line.[37]

To obtain positive feedbacks from the public, not the people but the authorities had to change. Or, as Pozsgay put it, "it all depends on whether the party and state organs are prepared to function with the maximum degree of openness."[38]

The rest of Pozsgay's dissertation abounds in such intriguing notions as the "separation of the party from the state," the "granting of legitimacy to group interests," the institutionalization of officials' public accountability, the formal representation of (corporatist) interests at the regional level, and plebiscites to decide certain national issues. It concludes with an idea that seems to be a great deal closer to Jefferson than Lenin:

> We must create institutions to master the practice of democracy and must teach our people [about] democracy. This entails risks but requires us to accept decisions that have been democratically arrived at, even though these may not be the optimal solutions.[39]

A look at the sources Pozsgay cited helps explain the origin of some of his ideas. Next to the obligatory Marxist classics, one finds the works of Rosa Luxemburg, Edvard Kardelj, Serge Mallet, André Gorz,

Zygmunt Bauman, the Czechoslovak reform ideologues, and András Hegedüs. Echoes of the Yugoslav ideological debates, and the ideas of the Prague Spring and those of the Budapest School are all in evidence in this bold yet carefully argued study by the 36-year-old provincial ideological apparatchik Imre Pozsgay.

Although the dissertation was accepted and its author soon promoted to head of the press subdepartment of the CC's Department of AP, the work was put on the restricted shelves of the Academy library for the next twenty years. In any event, there is considerable merit to Pozsgay's retrospective assessment of this work: "there were several propositions in my study that, after the crushing of Prague, were first articulated by me from among the political incumbents in Eastern Europe."[40]

Credit for being the first in Hungary to develop a coherent argument for *glasnost*'; for proposing a systematic cost-benefit analysis on the relationship between political stability and direct democracy; and for recommending recognition and the according of legitimacy to partial interests in a quasi-pluralistic institutional framework belongs to Imre Pozsgay. His political "godfathers" (Pál Romány and probably György Aczél) and "godmother" (Valéria Benke, editor of the party's theoretical monthly *Társadalmi Szemle*) either did not read the work, or if they did, chose to overlook the heretical message of Pozsgay's earnest policy recommendations.

Upon his return to the YCL central apparat in the fall of 1957, *Berecz* was assigned to the University and High School Department. His first important mission was carried out when he was appointed one of the leaders of the YCL delegation to the 1960 festival of the World Federation of Democratic Youth in Moscow. Apparently, he did a good job in trying to persuade the young Western and Third World participants that in 1956 there had been a counterrevolution in Hungary, because he was promoted to the headship of his department.[41]

Infusing political life into the lethargic YCL organizations at the universities must have been a frustrating assignment. Moreover, Berecz struck some of his party elders, including some powerful county first secretaries, as being "too independent" – "arrogant" is the word that occurred to his contemporaries – and as one who acted like an "intellectual." Árpád Pullai, his boss at the YLC, was definitely not an intellectual but a tough conservative. In the end, Berecz found a way to escape from his dead-end job: he applied for a four-year scholarship at the Social Science Academy of the CPSU. His patron, now PB member, Zoltán Komócsin – himself a 1953 graduate of the very same academy – endorsed the idea, and in the fall of 1963 Berecz left for Moscow.

As Berecz recalled, he was placed under the aegis of the academy's Department for International Working Class Movements, which was, in his words, "the most enlightened" of the institution's instructional units. The presence of several former Gulag inmates on the instructional staff helped Berecz see Soviet history in a more realistic perspective. Berecz's approved dissertation topic, "Problems of Peaceful Coexistence, 1955–1960," proposed a general review of East–West relations. However, when given access to restricted material in the Lenin Library, he became interested in studying the events of 1956 in Hungary. His interest subsequently evolved into an ideologically correct reconstruction of the history of the 1956 "counterrevolution," with emphasis on Rákosi's mistakes as the main precipitant. However, his Soviet academic mentors kept pressuring him to downplay the role of Rákosi and Stalinism in Hungary and make a case for an imperialist conspiracy as the main cause.

In addition to a retelling of what had happened in 1956 in Hungary, some of Berecz's professors – and one assumes *their* political superiors – wanted an account of how young people felt about the Kádár regime since 1956. In the end, his question "What kind of socialism was there in Hungary that it took ten Red Army divisions to put down a few imperialist agents?" helped checkmate this line of inquiry. Although Berecz's dissertation was put on the shelf for the next three years, the re-publication in 1986 of his notorious 1969 book *Counterrevolution with Pens and Weapons* made a case that could not have been very different from the one that his Soviet professors expected of him in the 1960s.[42]

In the spring of 1966 Komócsin – his new position was CC secretary for international affairs – called Berecz in Moscow and told him to finish his work at the Academy and return to Hungary to take up the position of secretary of party committee in the Ministry of Foreign Affairs. It was a major career move that elevated Berecz to membership in the regime's foreign-policy-planning *troika*. The foreign minister János Péter – CC member and former Protestant bishop – Komócsin and Berecz were the principals of the team. Their assignment was to find a way out from Hungary's international isolation and to develop a sheltered position for the regime from its antireform critics in the Soviet bloc. Involvement in exploratory talks for the establishment of diplomatic relations with the FRG, preinvasion (that is, of Czechoslovakia) negotiations with the affected WTO states, damage control among the nonruling communist parties after August 21, and liaison with the Soviet Foreign Ministry were some of Berecz's major assignments. He must have done well because in the fall of 1972 Komócsin appointed him deputy head of the CC's international department. With this move, Berecz became a middle-level policy manager at the party center and, as such, one of the few with prospects of eventual membership in the CC.

With his political credentials restored, *Grósz* returned to the Borsod county party committee in the fall of 1957. He was appointed editor of the county's daily newspaper, where he worked for the next two years. In 1960 he was dispatched to enroll, as a full-time student, in the HSWP's Political Academy.[43] Upon graduation, Grósz served a brief stint as party secretary at a chemical plant and another as a low-level staffer at the CC's Department of AP.[44] However, his turn came in 1962 when he was appointed full-time secretary of the Hungarian radio and TV party organization. Overseeing the political activities of 3,500 journalists, broadcasters, and professional propagandists was a highly sensitive task,[45] which makes it remarkable that Grósz still found time to complete a five-year university (evening) program and earn a diploma from the Department of Scientific Socialism of the University of Budapest.[46]

Grósz's ultimate political superior was György Aczél – a man with ideas about everything from programming to personnel. The relationship between the blunt and outspoken Grósz and the suave ideologue Aczél was rocky, and it remained so for the next twenty-five years. The two started out on the wrong foot: in 1963 Grósz was instructed by Aczél to fire forty people from among radio and TV personnel. He demanded an explanation and was told by Aczél, "there are too many Jews there. If we want to shelter our best people, we must let go of others." Grósz took the case to Kádár, who countermanded Aczél's instructions.[47]

As the political supervisor of radio and TV programming and personnel, Grósz presided over the management of the regime's most valuable communications resource. By the early 1970s there were millions of TV sets in Hungary, and radio and TV media were the party's principal propaganda tool. Grósz's job also entailed disbursement of vast sums of money for the Hungarian literary intelligentsia and the *Lumpenintelligenz* alike. Being the political paymaster of writers of Illyés' stature down to fifth-rate agit-prop poets conferred on Grósz a great deal of power and, as may be judged from his comments about the literary intelligentsia in the 1980s, a sense of contempt for the wielders of the pen.

Grósz's duty ended in 1972 with his transfer to the party center, and promotion to deputy head of the Department of AP. Thus, Grósz, just like Pozsgay and Berecz, and about the same time, found himself on the "fast track."

Three cadres on the fast track

In terms of Hungarian party and state protocol, a CC department head outranked a cabinet minister, unless the latter was a CC member. The deputy department heads, though possibly on a par with senior government officials, in fact, controlled political resources far in excess of those available to top government bureaucrats. Deputy heads were the primary recipients of most written communications from the party and the government. They screened the upward flow of paperwork and were, in turn, the dispatchers of instructions and decisions from the Secretariat and the PB. These key staff members were the leadership's eyes and ears and, thanks to their access to the reigning decision-makers, they were in the position to make or break a party or government official below the rank of county first secretary or cabinet minister.[48] Pozsgay, Berecz, and Grósz were handed a great deal of power in 1971–2.

Shortly after his arrival as the new press chief in the Department of AP, *Pozsgay* was appointed deputy editor of the party's theoretical monthly *Társadalmi Szemle.* The editor, a onetime village grade-school teacher and a long-serving member of the apparat, was Valéria Benke. She must have had confidence in Pozsgay, because she authorized him to publish twelve major policy essays in the next four years. Some of these were watered-down portions of his embargoed dissertation, but the most important ones dealt with the social and the ideological consequences of the NEM.[49]

The most striking aspect of Pozsgay's reform essays was his ability to smuggle into the texts all kinds of provocative ideas. On closer reading, many of these had originated with the internal proreform arguments and writings of Rezső Nyers, Jenő Fock, and the head of the party's agricultural lobby, PB member Lajos Fehér. On the other hand, some of the essays, such as the one that appeared in the February 27, 1972 issue of *Népszabadság* on the "conflict and reconciliation" of social interests, could be read *both* ways: in support of further reforms and in opposition to reforms that might get out of hand.[50] In addition to these successful experiments of walking across ideological minefields without touching ground, Pozsgay's *real* interests gradually drifted in the direction of (low-key) philosophy and cultural policy.[51]

Pozsgay's adroit maneuvering between the pro- and antireform forces was made possible in part by his emerging public persona as a scholar, highly visible cultural spokesman, and public speaker. Armed with his freshly minted doctorate in political sociology, Pozsgay gave seminars on sociological theory and contemporary philosophy at the University of Budapest. One of his former students (now a faculty member at a top German university) called him the best instructor he ever had at the university. Pozsgay also found a way to become the host of a TV talk show on current affairs. His TV appearances gave him national visibility, which, in turn, yielded invitations for speeches, lectures, and consultations with intelligentsia groups.

Effective oral communication is valued more highly in Hungary than a well-written statement. The art of speech making and of rousing political rhetoric had fallen victim to Rákosi's heavily accented spoken Hungarian and to Kádár's poor diction and fractured grammar. In any case, Imre Pozsgay was a superb public speaker. When speaking – usually without notes – his precise syntax, wide vocabulary, and delivery were remindful of the celebrated oratory of nineteenth-century Hungarian politicians – or that of a spellbinding Calvinist minister. For the first time in many years, Pozsgay's audiences were treated to speeches by a politician who sounded like a *Hungarian* intellectual. When performing before party audiences, Pozsgay was the only top apparatchik who could, at length and always in the proper context, cite Marx, Engels, Lenin, Lukács, Gramsci, and, if need be, the Scriptures – and still finish his sentence in the correct tense.[52]

It was inevitable that Aczél would try to make use of Pozsgay's talents for his purposes. He needed someone whom he could deputize to manage the regime's on-and-off dialogue with the provincial intelligentsia, the Populist writers, and members of the young generation. Judging from his meteoric rise (deputy minister of culture in 1976 and minister of culture a year later), Pozsgay was eager to accept Aczél's sponsorship, as well as the – to outsiders still unfathomable – terms of their political partnership.

Pozsgay broadly hinted in his memoirs that as minister he had been in a position to build a national constituency for himself. Resources for new or refurbished schools, museums, theatres, houses of culture; subsidies for books and journals; literary prizes; and scholarships abroad were some of the largesse that a minister of culture (especially with the backing of a key PB member) could distribute among the deserving intelligentsia.[53] It appeared that Pozsgay was the designated facilitator of the regime's *rapprochement* with the intellectuals, a policy that Kádár had inaugurated in 1978.

In the meantime, much to Aczél's growing dismay, Pozsgay, in his pursuit of popularity with the humanistic and the provincial intelligentsia, was "going native." By this I refer to subtle but important changes in emphasis in his speeches and writings. The same man who in 1957–8 had written thundering articles against nationalism and nationalists was beginning to sound like a nationalist himself.[54] In the midst of his voluminous writings and published interviews, the themes of "nation," "traditional culture," "patriotism" – local and otherwise – appeared with increasing frequency. His conspicuous championship of the political rehabilitation of the People's Colleges movement and his open friendship with Populist writers were signs of ideological change and of his search for allies among the nonparty majority of Hungary.[55]

Pozsgay's political career reached a turning point at the 12th HSWP congress in March 1980. Neither a congressional delegate nor an incumbent member of the CC, he attended the meetings as a government official and the party's guest. On the last day a closed session was held at which Pozsgay was elected to membership in the CC. The last item on the agenda was the nomination of candidates for election to the PB and the Secretariat. A one-man nominating committee, the former Muscovite but staunch Kádár loyalist Dezső Nemes, presented the list of nominees.[56]

When Nemes asked for comments, Lajos Fehér rose and submitted the name of Imre Pozsgay as his nominee for membership in the PB and the Secretariat. Although Pozsgay's memoirs are silent about this, Fehér's nomination was promptly seconded by another veteran CC member, Jenő Fock. At a loss for words, Nemes yielded the rostrum to Kádár. He, in turn, applauded the motion and further extolled the candidate's merits but felt that the nomination was "premature." With this, Pozsgay's bid for a seat in the party's ultimate decision-making body remained in a limbo for the next eight years.

János Berecz's tenure as the new deputy head of the CC's international department commenced under rather inauspicious circumstances. Because of illness, his political patron, Zoltán Komócsin, relinquished his position as foreign secretary and was replaced, on a pro tem basis, by Árpád Pullai, Berecz's old antagonist from YCL days. Apparently, Berecz managed to weather these changes, because he was promoted to head of his department in 1974.[57]

With Komócsin's departure and the appointment of political light-weight András Gyenes as his successor, the foreign policy field became a poorly guarded turf that the conservative Biszku and Pullai tried to occupy for their own purposes. These hard-liners viewed diplomacy as a vehicle for aggressive foreign intelligence operations rather than as an instrument to promote Hungary's interests in the new world of East–West *détente*. At this point Kádár stepped in and, as Berecz explained, for the next several years personally managed the conduct of all aspects – party-to-party and state-to-state – of Hungarian foreign policy.

Berecz's department was assigned responsibility for several portions of Kádár's foreign policy program. These included:

1 cultivation of western European, though mainly the West German, social democratic parties, and, the search for an active role in preparatory work for the 1976 East Berlin conference of European ruling and nonruling communist parties;

2 work on the coordination of positions among the East European ruling parties prior to the 1975 Helsinki Conference on Security and Cooperation in Europe;

3 laying the groundwork for Kádár's visits to Germany, Austria, Finland, Italy, and France in the late 1970s and in the early 1980s;

4 cultivation of personal ties with the younger (and more liberal) members of the CPSU central apparat in the department for liaison with ruling parties (an important part of this enterprise was to allay Soviet suspicions about the normalization of Hungary's ties with the United States);

5 winning Moscow's consent to the HSWP's serving as the Soviet bloc's designated liaison with some of the Eurosocialist and Euro-communist parties (according to Berecz, somewhat to Moscow's dismay, the Hungarian party's ties with the Berlinguer's PCI became exceptionally strong);

6 initiation in 1978 of nongovernmental contacts with the United States to pave the way for an official invitation (much coveted by Kádár) of the HSWP's first secretary to Washington (this project came to naught because, as Averell Harriman explained to Berecz during his visit in 1978, the United States still had strong feelings about the Hungarian revolution, whereas Ceauşescu's visits were a matter of American *Realpolitik*).[58]

János Berecz's high-profile activities were noticed by friends and foes alike in the central apparat. Although the former seemed to have been in a distinct minority, they included Károly Grósz, a fellow executive and ideological soulmate. As Berecz explained, he and Grósz were different from their colleagues in some important ways. Both hailed from northeastern Hungary. Both had considerable experience in the art of political communication: Grósz dealt with crafty media editors, Berecz with even more slippery communist and Western diplomats. And neither of them cared for the incompetent time servers at party headquarters.

In any case, both Berecz and Grósz were nominated for membership in the CC at the party's congress in 1975, but neither was elected. It appears that for once the Biszku–Pullai group joined forces with Aczél's network to prevent the early promotion of these upstarts. In April 1978 at the "half-time" meeting of the CC, the results were the same, even though (or because) the "youth package" also included the name of Imre Pozsgay. In the fall of 1978, as a reward for his useful report on his American trip, Kádár explained to Berecz that he and "his friend" had conducted themselves unwisely, though they still enjoyed the first secretary's confidence. However, Grósz's explanation of the reasons for these false starts was more specific. According to him, in 1975 he and Berecz had a dinner meeting with a Soviet diplomat and made some critical comments about the Hungarian party's senior leadership. Kádár was promptly notified by Brezhnev, but, true to form, he sat on the damning evidence for the next three years.[59]

In March 1980 Berecz was finally elected to membership in the CC, but his position remained the same in the apparat. Although Berecz is less forthcoming on this subject, it appears that the job of having been Kádár's international troubleshooter engendered considerable jealousy among Berecz's less well traveled colleagues in the apparat. One could always go to the Crimea for the summer, but trips to the West were not readily available perquisites at the party center.[60] Moreover, his preoccupation with foreign affairs cut Berecz off from various party constituencies whose support (or the withholding of a veto) was essential for advancement to leading positions in the party.

In 1982 Kádár conducted an informal poll among senior CC staffers as to their opinion on Berecz's qualifications for a higher position in the apparat. The outcome: two for, eighteen against. Instead of the coveted job of CC secretary for international affairs (it went to Kádár's former personal secretary Péter Várkonyi), then, Berecz was offered a choice between running the Department of AP and the editorship of Népszabadság. When he chose the latter, Kádár's parting words were, "we will not forget about you, comrade Berecz."[61] Thus, Berecz's career was, as the local Kremlinologists had it, "put in a parking orbit" for the next three years.

Károly Grósz's arrival in the party headquarters as deputy head of the Department of AP in 1972 placed him in the middle of a political tug-of-war between the proreform minority and the antireform majority of the HSWP apparat. His department's task was to sell the leadership's ambiguous policies to the perplexed party membership.

In career terms, his agit-prop assignment created a "no-win" situation for Grósz. On the one hand, he was deeply disturbed by what he called Kádár's vacillation between "continuity and change." As Grósz saw it, "changes were needed" – he did not explain what kind – yet Kádár "insisted on continuity" and on doing more of the same. On the other hand, there was a tough "can-do" contingent of seasoned cadres in the party center who shared Grósz's concerns about the political dangers of equivocation on needed changes in economic and cadre policies. Although Grósz denied the existence of a "workers' opposition" – he declared that he first heard this term from Kádár himself – he freely admitted that his closest friends had been Béla Biszku, Árpád Pullai, Sándor Jakab, and several others whom Kádár considered as his leftist critics.[62] In any case, a new deputy department head should have known better than to join an antireform and anti-Kádár cabal. Whereas leftist Suslov-sympathizing PB members and CC secretaries were untouchable in the early 1970s, Grósz was an expendable pawn in the antireformers' chess game with the wily first secretary.

In October 1973, after less than a year in the agit-prop department, Grósz was abruptly sent to the politically less important Fejér county as first secretary. As he explained, "János Kádár and his closest associates were hypersensitive to criticism." He might have added that they did not bear grudges for very long: Grósz's exile and stormy tenure in Fejér county lasted for only ten months.[63]

Grósz's return to the party center as head of the Department of AP coincided with the fall of the reform team of Nyers, Fehér, Fock, and others, and the shortlived ascendance of Biszku and his colleagues in the party apparat. Although Grósz weathered his friends' subsequent elimination from the leadership, the challenge he could not overcome was his department's task of neutralizing adverse public opinion about worsening economic conditions. As Grósz saw it, Kádár's insistence on making the party the hands-on manager of everything in Hungary "doubled the size of the party apparat and created parallel decision-making mechanisms" at the expense of timely action and administrative efficiency. Moreover, as Grósz kept arguing "at every party forum," direct "party control of the economy" was "nonsense."[64]

Although Grósz chose to portray himself as a committed reformer as early as 1970, his close ties to the party's *ouvrierists* tend to raise doubts on this score. On the other hand, his harsh words about vacillating leadership, sloppy management, and lack of follow-up to policy decisions ring true, for these shortcomings would become the main targets of his government's program of economic recovery in the fall of 1987. In any case, Grósz insists that in the 1970s he was the "only one" at the party headquarters who "consistently spoke up" for his, then unpopular, beliefs.[65]

János Kádár, though probably displeased with this in-house bearer of bad tidings, apparently respected Grósz's candor and trusted his political judgment. Whether as a reward or just to have him out of the way, in November 1979 Kádár appointed Grósz as first secretary of the Borsod county party committee. This was a major promotion, because it conferred on Grósz the leadership of Hungary's second most important political fiefdom. The city of Miskolc, the Lenin Works in Diósgyőr, and scores of coal mines were the centerpieces of the regime's industrialization program. In the HSWP, where the importance of a county first secretary was measured by the number of blue-collar-worker party members in his district, Borsod led the way. In career terms, it was a natural springboard to the party's top leadership.

Candidates for leadership: strategies and political choices, 1980–7

The 12th HSWP congress of March 1980 left the issue of Kádár's succession unresolved. As Berecz recalled, the example of Brezhnev and the sight of an ambulance at the end of the motorcade during his visit in 1979 in Hungary was not much of a morale booster for the apparat.[66] Moreover, the unfolding of Polish events, particularly the fall of Edward Gierek and the quick exit of his successor Stanisław Kania, were reminders that the age of stable leadership had ended in the Soviet bloc. For the next seven years a series of incremental personnel changes took place in the Hungarian party and the government. These, as the party cognoscenti put it, were "fleet movements," rather than evidence of purposeful policies to affect generational change. As will be discussed below, Berecz, as the editor of the party's daily, and Pozsgay, as secretary general of the PPF, were constantly in the political limelight. Grósz, on the other hand, was safely ensconced in his Borsod fiefdom and, as it turned out, very wisely, eschewed publicity and tended to the affairs of his county.

Although unsuccessful in his initial bid for entry into the PB, *Pozsgay* was riding high in Hungarian public life. In addition to constant exposure in the electronic media, Pozsgay published a book and twenty-one newspaper and journal articles in 1980–1.[67] His coopera- tion with Aczél seemed to be on track and, as managers of cultural policies, the two formed a "good cop/tough cop" kind of team that got results and satisfied Kádár at the same time.

However, with the passage of time, Aczél became concerned about the freewheeling ways of his young protégé and decided to clip Pozsgay's wings by creating an *ad hoc* party-government group for the implementation of cultural policies.[68] It was at this juncture that Pozsgay realized that he had to make a choice: he could either remain Aczél's junior deputy in the cultural apparat or try an endrun around Aczél and the PB behind him. As long as he was regarded as an ideologue and a cultural bureaucrat, he could not expect to be taken seriously by the leadership. As can be reconstructed from his autobio- graphy, he embarked on a program of self-education in economic policy to take on the PB in a policy field where the regime was most vulnerable to internal criticism.[69]

Pozsgay gave his maiden speech on a general policy issue at the December 3, 1981 meeting of the CC. As a gesture to Aczél, Pozsgay had forwarded to him a summary of his forthcoming presentation that offered a scathing critique of many aspects of the regime's policies in the preceding twelve years. However, he dropped some of the most offending items from the CC speech itself. In any case, as a reciprocal gesture of sorts, Aczél prudently absented himself from the December 3 session.[70]

In his speech, and in uncharacteristically blunt language, Pozsgay made three points. (1) His ministry's budget had been cut from HUF 43 billion to 31 billion since 1978. This, he submitted, had created disastrous conditions throughout Hungary's educational system. (2) While endorsing the primacy of politics and the necessity of discre- tionary resource allocations to maintain living standards so as to preserve social stability, he accused the investment-hungry heavy- industry lobby of forcing the economy into higher foreign indebted- ness, thereby totally invalidating not only the 1982 plan targets but those of the current Five Year Plan as well. (3) He insisted that the regime's systematic neglect of infrastructral needs, such as invest- ment in human resources, research and development, and the cultural sector, would result in economic collapse and political crisis.[71]

Although Kádár quickly dispatched two speakers to refute Pozsgay's arguments by calling them a case of special pleading by a government bureaucrat and an amateur economist, he understood the message. A few days later Kádár invited Pozsgay to his office and suggested that he join Ferenc Havasi's newly created Consultative Group for Economic Policy. This, as Kádár explained, "will give you a chance to articulate your views on economic policies and acquire information that might change your opinions." Pozsgay accepted the offer.[72]

Pozsgay soon found out that one does not challenge the cherished policy beliefs of a ruling communist party's first secretary without paying a political price. In April 1982 he was asked to meet with prime minister György Lázár and Kádár's deputy Károly Németh. Their message was that as a part of a top-level personnel reshuffle ("routine cadre rotation," he was assured), Aczél would move from the position of deputy prime minister to CC secretary for ideology; PB member and PPF secretary general István Sarlós would take Aczél's place; and Pozsgay was being offered Sarlós' job. Pozsgay refused the offer and asked for Aczél's former job, saying that if "Comrade Kádár had a better idea" he would like to hear about it.

Following a six-week campaign of "half of the PB coming to see me trying to pressure me to accept the offer," Pozsgay relented, but he demanded a face-to-face meeting with Kádár. The meeting – possibly the last substantial conversation between the two men – yielded the desired outcome and also Kádár's consent personally to nominate Pozsgay for secretary general at the next plenary session of the PPF council. As Pozsgay recalls it in his memoirs, the meeting ended with his statement:

> from now on no one is going to believe you that everyone is free to speak openly before the CC ... As I see it, you are trying to push members of my generation to the fringes of political life ... In reality, it will be your doing that an orderly continuation of Kádárism through normal intergenerational change would not take place. From now on, you can expect only an anti-Kádár outcome."[73]

Kádár lived up to the bargain and gave a proper sendoff to the new secretary general of the PPF in July 1982. For the next six years, the PPF was Pozsgay's political base and, as shown below, the vehicle for the promotion of his personal and political agenda.

The PPF's role was that of a transmission belt to convey and gain acceptance of the party's policies by the country's noncommunist majority. In its original configuration, it had been the institutional vehicle that Imre Nagy sought to utilize in generating grassroots support for his short-lived New Course of 1953–4. Although it was generally regarded as a dumping ground for retired party notables, Pozsgay saw new possibilities in the PPF. The party's retreat from the political front lines and the onset of the HSWP's "rearguard" leadership left a void that the increasingly assertive industrial, agricultural, business (Chamber of Commerce), trade union, youth, and cultural policy lobbies and the emerging community of political dissidents tried to occupy.

Fortunately for Pozsgay, the PPF was not bound to any of these groups and was free to recruit and mobilize all those who were dissatisfied with the performance of their own "policy lobby." However, the PPF also proposed to reach out to those whose interests had not been served by any organized group. Thus, in terms of potential constituencies, Pozsgay had much of the country for himself. In speaking out for the interests of provincial Hungary, the intelligentsia, youth, women and families, the educational community, the religious minorities (including the Jewish community), the Populists, and the reform socialists, Pozsgay had a potential army of disgruntled citizens to enlist for his cause.

Indeed, from a review of the 117 articles, interviews, and published speeches by Pozsgay between mid-1982 and June 1988, it appears that he systematically cultivated every one of these nonparty constituencies. Although the details varied for each, his message may be paraphrased in a sentence: "There must be radical reforms in Hungary to shelter the people from the consequences of bad decisions, wrong priorities, and the loss of national purpose."

One of Pozsgay's unpublicized but politically crucially important activities was his regular visits with leaders of county and rural party organizations throughout Hungary. Though ostensibly consultations with local PPF and cultural notables, the visits helped strengthen his personal ties with local party elites. Pozsgay was a regular visitor in Borsod county as a guest of Károly Grósz. As Grósz recalled, "I was on very good terms with Pozsgay. I liked him and respected his intellect. His wide acquaintance with all kinds of social strata with which I had no contacts ... showed me new ways of getting to know them."[74] They were in agreement about their critical evaluation of the "old ones up there," but Grósz drew the line when it came to joining an "organized movement" to do something about the problem.[75] In any case, as one might infer from the fact that in the next six years Pozsgay managed to place only two articles in *Népszabadság*, Berecz was of no help in the spreading of Pozsgay's message to the one million readers of his newspaper.

Foreign travel was one of the perquisites of Pozsgay's position. Over the years, he somehow avoided spending any more time in the USSR than was necessary for the purposes of compulsory political education (a three-month stay in 1973–4) and protocol visits in Moscow. On the other hand, according to his friends, his visits in Poland in the early 1980s were "traumatic experiences," as was, in a rather different way, his one-month Washington-sponsored tour of the United States in September 1982. Frequent visits in Italy, Germany, Britain, and Scandinavia greatly contributed to his understanding of the workings of liberal democracies – particularly the importance of multiparty systems for the building and preserving of social consensus and political stability.

In a sense, Pozsgay was lucky that the issues came to him ready-made for his political purposes. The management of the admittedly artificial "public debates" preceding implementation of the new electoral law of 1983 was Pozsgay's responsibility, and so was providing a façade of legitimacy for the 1985 multicandidate elections for the Parliament. Although his good friend István Horváth – then CC secretary for law and public administration – was in charge of stage-managing the entire affair, Pozsgay made use of this opportunity to register his criticism of the way independent candidates were mistreated at nominating meetings.

His meeting on April 26, 1985 at an "alternative discussion forum" with the outraged supporters of independent candidates and his highly sympathetic speech marked his debut as a "samizdat author."[76] In his address, entitled (not by Pozsgay but by the editors of the samizdat publication) "Szavazás vagy választás?" (Voting or choosing?) Pozsgay openly admitted the "grave shortcomings" of the nominating process. Yet he urged his audience to make use of new opportunities for self-government in their communities and places of work, reminding them, "I am in the habit of trying to make full use of my opportunities ... be it the party congress ... or this Club. It does not matters where I speak, as long as I give my opinion with the maximum degree of candor and openness."[77] Indeed, no one could accuse Pozsgay of hiding his opinions. And that, at least in Kádár's book, might have been the posture that saved him from political repercussions at that time.

By 1986 the PPF had become a shelter for "civic initiatives," "alternative clubs," youth organizations, cultural societies, and reform intellectuals. Although operating on Grósz's turf – he took over the Budapest party committee in December 1984 – and under the watchful eyes of the central apparat, Pozsgay seemed to have become a one-man missionary society for "reform," "renewal," and "socialist democracy."

In the wake of the notorious July 1986 PB "opposition-equals-hostile-enemies" decision, Pozsgay was removed from circulation and sent off to a three-month party school in Moscow. As Pozsgay explained to me, he skipped most of the lectures and spent most of his time traveling in the Soviet Union. Although he denies having met with Gorbachev's people, one wonders whether his Soviet experiences were responsible for what happened at the December 1986 congress of the PPF.[78] In any case, it was this public forum where the party's March 1985 economic strategy of "accelerated development" came under open attack. The PPF-sponsored study "Turnabout and Reform" (see Chapter 4) supplied the necessary technical arguments that were further embellished in reports by similar PPF task forces on social welfare policies, *glasnost'*, and political democracy.[79]

Pozsgay's lone crusade changed form and substance in the summer of 1987. From his viewpoint, neither his program, nor his ambitions for a seat in the PB, could be realized as long as Kádár was at the helm. At the June 23, 1987 meeting of the CC, Rezső Nyers recommmended that Pozsgay be promoted to a position in the leadership. To this Kádár replied: "In principle, there is no objection to [Pozsgay's] joining the leadership. However, it is not appropriate at this time. If it were, you would have a recommendation from us by now. This is my reply."[80] On the other hand, the appointment of Grósz as prime minister, the promotion of István Horváth to deputy prime minister, and the naming of Miklós Németh as the new head of the CC's Department of Economic Policy were positive developments that were bound to strengthen Pozsgay's position in the coming months.

Imre Pozsgay had played a unique role in reshaping the regime's political agenda. Thanks to Pozsgay, some of the pragmatic *nomenklatura* elites were beginning to come to terms with the economic and social realities of the mid-1980s. In retrospect, it seems clear that Kádár intended to have Pozsgay and the PPF play the role of a co-opted "Hungarian *Solidarnosc*" – a combination of political safety valve and a social lightning rod. Pozsgay was not a Hungarian Wałesa, nor was Kádár a Hungarian Jaruzelski. As far as can be established, as head of the PPF, Pozsgay rarely spoke to factory workers, party activists, the military, and the police. That was Kádár's, Károly Németh's, Sándor Gáspár's, and János Berecz's job.

Pozsgay earned (and kept) his high position in the political hierarchy as the regime's "human face" in charge of rechanneling social discontent, particularly that of the intelligentsia, in the direction of evolutionary change. This role suited him well and at the same time helped make him useful and, in light of the further erosion of the party's authority, indispensable as the regime's principal liaison with the politicized intelligentsia. In the summer of 1987, with Grósz as prime minister and the politician best positioned to replace Kádár, Pozsgay's only option was to team up with him for realization of their shared interest in generational change in the HSWP.

János Berecz's appointment as editor of *Népszabadság* was a mixed blessing for all concerned. Other than his frequent radio and TV appearances, Berecz had no experience either as a journalist or as a working editor. In view of his modest training in Marxism–Leninism, philosophy, and sociology, his credentials as an ideologue left a great deal to be desired. His preoccupation with foreign affairs and interparty relations in the preceding fifteen years had left him largely unprepared to speak on domestic, particularly economic, issues with a degree of authority.

Berecz's ultimate boss was CC ideological secretary György Aczél. The latter, for reasons that are still inexplicable, had nothing but contempt for Berecz, and over the years Aczél went out of his way to discredit his young colleague. Professional jealousy may have been a part of the problem. As Berecz explained, he had been perceived as a "too-clever-by-half" "peasant intellectual" trying to encroach on the turf of professional ideologues and party elders. Moreover, his continued involvement in the CC Secretariat's weekly evaluation sessions of internal reports on the "mood of the party membership" often displeased Kádár. Once Berecz made the mistake of correcting Kádár on some minor point. Kádár did not forget or forgive and kept reminding Berecz for years of his breach of etiquette. In any event, the *gazda* was not interested in hearing bad news in the 1980s. Yet Berecz, as the recipient of thousands of letters – mainly of complaint – from the readers of *Népszabadság*, had no choice but to convey such adverse information to the party's leadership.[81]

In an effort to make himself useful to Kádár, Berecz urged him to cultivate the CPSU's young rising star Mikhail Gorbachev. In 1983 Kádár finally brought himself to call his old friend Yuri Andropov who promptly dispatched Gorbachev to Hungary. Although the visit was successful, it left Kádár unconvinced that he invited the right man, that is, a CPSU PB "comer" and future Soviet leader.[82]

In addition to two volumes of speeches and articles on international affairs and some uninspired prose in editorials on anniversaries and national holidays, Berecz's written work consisted of the re-publication of his conservative account of the 1956 revolution.[83] At any rate, whether it had been Berecz' performance at Népszabadság or his emerging public image as a tough and superloyal Kádárite, the first secretary must have been satisfied enough with his work to ask him to join the CC Secretariat with responsibility for ideological affairs.

Pozsgay, who received no promotion at the March 1985 party congress, called the newly appointed secretaries and PB members "Romanov's orphans." By this he referred to Kádár's wrong guess in the winter of 1984–5 that Grigory Romanov, the conservative Leningrad party boss, would be Konstantin Chernenko's successor as the next leader of the CPSU. Therefore, so Pozsgay asserts, Kádár had nominated (and cleared with Moscow) the appointment to leading positions of such cadres as would likely be on good terms with Romanov.[84] True or not, Aczél's replacement with Berecz was also seen as evidence of Kádár's determination to put in place a younger and more energetic person to deal with the dissidents, the writers, and the poorly managed press and electronic media.

In 1985–7 the top HSWP ideologue's lot was not a happy one. In his new position Berecz took on three projects in the next three years. The first involved a frontal attack on the dissident community's efforts to force the regime to own up to its past and rehabilitate the "events of 1956" and the regime's victims and call them a "popular uprising" and "martyrs," respectively. In his capacity as the party's resident expert on the 1956 "counterrevolution," Berecz orchestrated a major campaign to discredit both the revolution and its victims.[85] The affair culminated in a newspaper campaign and a heavily edited TV documentary on the events of October–November 1956. Much to the regime's surprise, Berecz's tough commentary and the film footage that accompanied it, generated widespread public outrage. The revulsion was particularly pronounced among young people, for whom 1956 had hitherto been an obscure historical event and one that their parents had tried not to remember. Thanks to Berecz, 1956 again became a topic of public attention.

The next propaganda disaster was precipitated by Berecz's bellicose speech to the December 1986 meeting of the Hungarian Writers'

Union. The writers, led by Sándor Csoóri and István Csurka, had been on the warpath with the regime since their last showdown in December 1981. Five years later there was no martial law in Poland. Moreover, *glasnost'* was supposed to be the new policy in Hungary. At any rate, the writers, who had been accustomed to Aczél's subtle methods, now threatened to bolt from their organization. From the renewed rivalry between the PB member Aczél and the "barefoot secretary" – Berecz's phrase to denote a CC secretary without a seat in the PB – the latter came out as poor second.

The third project involved a two-day high-level ideological conference of Hungarian social scientists in Szeged in February 1987. Although the meeting was stacked with conservatives, and even Berecz gave what he considered as a placatory concluding address, the conference was another fiasco. In fairness to Berecz, who followed Kádár's instructions to the letter, it was not his fault but that of the fundamental irrelevance of his (and Kádár's) message to Hungary's problems and to establishment intellectuals at the Szeged affair.[86]

The brand of ideology that Berecz was assigned to sell to the intelligentsia sounded like a collection of hoary anachronisms to the intended recipients. This, in terms of still-receptive audiences, left Berecz with his natural constituencies: the military, the police, the conservative apparat, trade union officials, and party pensioners. Support from these quarters seems to have been sufficient for Kádár to shoe, as it were, his "barefoot" propagandist with a seat in the PB in June 1987.

Berecz's "last hurrah" as an ideologue was his presentation on the subject of ideology and political change to the November 11, 1987 meeting of the CC.[87] Whether it was Kádár insisting on placing the long-neglected topic of ideology on the agenda, or Berecz trying to establish his authority as the party's chief ideologue, the outcome was yet another disaster. Speakers, ranging from the invited reform communist historian Iván Berend through Rezsző Nyers to György Aczél, tore Berecz's carefully crafted policy draft into shreds. All felt that ideology *qua* ideology had been perceived by the party membership as more of an irritant than a guide to action – let alone a source of inspiration to the party faithful.

Berecz's nonparty critics called him (unfairly, I think) the "Hungarian Ligachev." In politics perceptions often outweigh realities. Egor Ligachev's demotion in September 1987 may have emboldened Berecz's political enemies to destroy him at the November CC plenum, but although Berecz's trials had only begun, his performance sealed his fate as a serious contender for the position of secretary general of the HSWP.

The position of county first secretary was a long-term proposition in the Kádár era. Other than the volatile Budapest job, the average length of a county first secretary's service was about eight years. The longevity champions were Mrs Ferenc Cservenka of Pest county (twenty-two years), József K. Papp of Tolna county (twenty years), and János Pap of Veszprem county (twenty years).[88] As long as investment resources were plentiful, the county's political boss had little to do beyond doling out the funds to political clients in the factories, enterprises, and cooperative farms. However, for *Károly Grósz*, who was placed to run a county with loss-making smokestack industries and unprofitable mines, it was a challenging and, in the longer run, impossible assignment.

Faced with growing deficits and the threat of unemployment, Grósz came under pressure to make use of his political influence to obtain relief from Budapest. Although it was a predicament shared by the HSWP's nineteen county prefects, Grósz felt that his situation was becoming increasingly untenable. As he recalled,

> I could not accept that I as county first secretary had to hustle that the Soviets order 500 additional mortars from the Diósgyőr Engineering Works. If they do not place an additional order, the factory would shut down. I could not tolerate that I had to dispatch one of my deputies to sit in on the admission proceedings at the university to decide whether the applicants to the engineering faculty met certain political criteria while there were more places than applicants for admission to that faculty. It undermined [public respect for] legality when we were told to review results of valid judicial decisions with a view toward appealing these at a higher court.[89]

His frequent visitors from Budapest kept him abreast of developments at the party center. Some of them urged him to confront the leadership with the concerns of the party's field commanders. As Grósz recalled, "they were looking for a rogue elephant to break down the wall" that cloistered the leadership from the facts of life.[90] Being a "disciplined party worker," Grósz chose to share his concerns at the periodic conferences of county first secretaries rather than submit himself to futile confrontations with the PB. In his view, the conferences "were the most productive forums" for policy debates in those days.[91]

In the course of a three-day visit in Miskolc in the spring of 1983, Kádár asked Grósz whether he might be interested in an unspecified position in Budapest. In the belief that Kádár had his old agit-prop job in mind, Grósz declined the offer. Kádár then reminded Grósz that he, Berecz, and some others would have important roles to play in the "process of rejuvenation." Kádár also wanted to know whether Grósz was Jewish. Apparently, for twenty years he had nursed the idea that Grósz's firm stance in opposition to the proposed dismissal of Jewish staff members at the radio and TV had something to do with his religious background. Grósz (an ethnic German), though rather put off by this query, assured Kádár that he was not Jewish.[92]

A year later Kádár called Grósz to his office and offered him the position of first secretary of the Budapest party organization. Grósz again declined, saying that his habit of plain speaking had made him many enemies and that therefore Kádár should find a less controversial person. Kádár insisted, and Grósz, having no choice in the matter, accepted the offer. "Not coincidentally," as Grósz related the circumstances of his appointment to me, while still in Borsod, Egor Ligachev visited him for an "exchange of views."[93] This visit was followed by two groups of Soviet "party workers" – possibly for the further vetting of the future party chief of Budapest.

Grósz's arrival in Budapest in December 1984 was received with widespread alarm by the intelligentsia. The promotion of the reputed ideological hard-liner from Borsod was perceived as the first sign of a "leftist turn" at the forthcoming 13th HSWP congress in March 1985. Although neither Grósz's congressional speech nor his first year as Budapest party boss offered fresh evidence to support these concerns, his promotion was seen as a part of Kádár's last-ditch effort to forestall future reforms. This may well have been Kádár's intention but, as things turned out, Grósz chose not to accommodate either Kádár or the worried intellectuals.

For the next two years Grósz kept a remarkably low profile in Hungarian politics. Apart from some factual reports to the CC and a few obligatory articles in the party press, he gave no interviews, made few TV appearances and refrained from contributing to the ongoing reform debates in the media. In retrospect it appears that Grósz was biding his time and let his rivals be the ones to leave ideological and political footprints that might compromise their positions in the PB's eyes. In those days, as Budapest wit had it, when one turned on the water tap "either Pozsgay or Berecz came out of it." Grósz preferred to make his mark as a thoughtful party insider rather than as an ideologue.

To define his political persona as an open-minded party overseer of the capital yet remain a solid Kádár loyalist, Grósz had to steer cautiously in the treacherous waters of party politics. To his good fortune, as a newcomer to the PB, he had no part in and only residual responsibility for the maximalist policy goals of the 1985 party congress. As will be discussed in the next chapter, responsibility for those disastrous decisions lay with Kádár and those who failed to object in the PB. All this left Grósz with few issues on which to take an independent stand. This is probably why it was as late as September 1986 that he began publicly distancing himself from some aspects of the 1985 congressional guidelines.[94]

His criticism of the regime's egalitarian rhetoric and praise of the "underpaid and unappreciated" skilled workers and the technical intelligentsia could, if one so chooses, be seen as his belated rejection of the "workers'-opposition" line of the 1970s. His continued lip service to the "party's leading role," yet insistence on professionalism (*szakszerűség*) and tough work ethic, made him appear as an ideologically correct but down-to-earth pragmatist.[95] As the head of the Budapest apparat, Grósz wore many disguises so as not to jeopardize his standing with Kádár. The charade, if that is the word, paid off in the end. In June 1987 Kádár turned to him to replace György Lázár as prime minister. Thus, the stage was set for the last mile of the marathon for political succession in the HSWP.

(C)   The successor generation at the crossroads

In the foregoing discussion I sought to identify the systemic and national characteristics of leadership succession in communist party states and in Hungary. I endeavored to show that in Hungary the general process and the specific outcomes of political succession were determined by generational change, particularly the formative experiences of the potential successor generation, and by Kádár's personal choices. The elimination by the Rákosi regime of the first postwar generation of native radical intellectuals of the People's Colleges movement cleared the way for the regime's own young-peasant and working-class "Janissaries" – the graduates of the Lenin Institute and of Hungarian and Soviet higher party schools. The object was to train the party's own professional politicians to help and ultimately succeed Kádár's generation of professional revolutionaries, political survivors, and bureaucratic time-servers.

The incumbents of Kádár PBs were political actors in their own right, with ideas and policy preferences of their own. Regardless of their ideological differences, the middle-aged Jenő Fock, Lajos Fehér, Rezső Nyers, György Aczél, and Zoltán Komócsin were hardworking, on the whole capable, and at times daring policy managers. In the mid-1970s they were replaced by a group of mediocre apparatchiki who were typical products of the regime's *kontraszelekció* at its best. The ubiquitous György Aczél apart, Károly Németh, Pál Losonczi, György Lázár, Sándor Gáspár, and Miklós Óvári were modestly competent bureaucrats and intellectual nonentities. Until 1988 it was these senior cadres who stood between Kádár and his political successor, and some of them may have had leadership ambitions. Had Kádár died in 1982, any of them could have become a Hungarian Chernenko – and probably been overthrown in the next two or three years. In any case, none of them had the old autarch's charisma and his consummate political skills. Thus, for the want of an alternative and without opportunity for an honorable exit, they all served Kádár until the very end.[96]

My discussion of the parallel lives of Imre Pozsgay, János Berecz, and Károly Grósz focused on their social background, education, formative experiences, career paths, and ideological choices. Thanks to the cooperation of these retired and semiretired politicians, from their accounts of their childhood and adolescence one could reconstruct the social milieu and, at least in Pozsgay's case, the personal motivation that prompted them to choose politics as a career. In terms of formal education, notwithstanding his evening-school diplomas, Grósz, just like Kádár, was a self-made man, whereas Pozsgay and Berecz had been encouraged by their parents to better themselves through further education. Unlike the Lenin Institute, the Petőfi Military Academy trained ideological drill instructors rather than party intellectuals.

Of the three, only Grósz was in the political front line in the fall of 1956. Pozsgay and Berecz were bystanders at that time, but they saw enough to carry with them many unresolved questions that haunted them for the rest of their political lives. As a student in Moscow, Berecz tried to come to grips with his doubts, but in the end suppressed them for the sake of a political career and a fast-track job in the party apparat. Grósz paid a price for not deserting his post in October 1956. Unlike Kádár and the rest of the party leadership, he had nowhere to hide. He tried to cope the best he could and, for his troubles, was expelled from the party.

For Pozsgay, after a false start as a young propagandist, the meaning of the events of 1956 became an all-consuming intellectual dilemma: that of the reconciliation of socialism with democratic methods of political leadership. For him, it took the Prague Spring to understand what had happened in Hungary in 1956. In any case, until the mid-1980s the events of 1956 and their ideological labeling were not Pozsgay's, Berecz's, and Grósz's problem but the problem of Kádár and his fellow gerontarchs in the PB.

Pozsgay, Berecz, and Grósz were well-trained professionals with the necessary skills to do justice to their assignments in Kecskemét, Budapest, Miskolc, and Moscow, and at the party center. For them, their jobs as party workers were just that rather than parts of a lifelong ideological mission. All three were professional political communicators for whom articles in the party's ideological monthly, diplomatic negotiations, and the management of the electronic media were part of the day's work, rather than the ultimate fulfillment of career goals.

Of the three, it was only Grósz who, as county first secretary (twice) and Budapest party boss, ever had to "meet a payroll." There was no way of measuring the "productivity" of an ideologue or a party diplomat, but the party's county first secretaries had to account for the economic performance and the political stability of their districts. Managerial experience of this kind gave Grósz inestimable advantage over his rivals as Kádár's eligible successors.

Our protagonists were *native* Hungarian communists. Their attitudes toward the USSR were shaped, in Berecz's case, by extensive personal experiences, and in Pozsgay's, by only superficial contacts. Grósz, however, seemed to have developed a personal empathy with what he perceived as existing socialism in the Soviet Union. In addition to his several visits, he maintained extensive contacts with the CPSU (and possibly the military) apparat. It is a relationship that survived the collapse of the USSR and was still functioning in 1994. Of the three, Berecz was the best informed on Soviet foreign policies, and in his own way he helped Kádár protect Hungary's national interests from Soviet pressures to fall in line on issues of Eurocommunism and East–West relations. Notwithstanding his politically correct speeches at protocol occasions, Pozsgay was the least well connected with the Soviet party apparat. By the mid-1980s he came to share the Hungarian democratic opposition's dim view of the USSR: an empire on the brink of collapse.

Pozsgay, Berecz, and Grósz were finalists in Kádár's political obstacle course for aspiring young party executives. Over the years each of them had had to pass various loyalty tests and, above all, earn Kádár's personal esteem. Other than its statutes, the HSWP never had a code of ethics for its officeholders. As István Horváth explained it to me, one of Kádár's tests of personal fitness for *nomenklatura* notables was their conduct as members of elite hunting clubs. Though each county had one, the largest, with 700 members, was the Budapest-based *Egyetértés* (Concordia). Kádár believed that rules of good sportsmanship imposed standards of discipline that only a selected few could live up to.[97] Pozsgay and Grósz were avid hunters who comported themselves as proper sportsmen while engaged in such manly pursuits and thus were deemed clubable in higher party circles.

Kádár was conscious of his modest educational background and was always ill at ease in the company of intellectuals. This and his aversion to face-to-face confrontations with party colleagues made it difficult for him to meet and hold discussions with people like Pozsgay and Berecz. Among the younger cadres, perhaps Grósz was the only one with whom Kádár was comfortable enough to discuss his inner feelings about the party, the country, and, at the end, his own political succession. Still, the generational gap between Kádár and most of his political associates was wide enough for him to address all but a few in a formal manner (that is, *maga* or *Ön* [*Sie* or *vy*], rather than *te* [*Du* or *ty*] in Hungarian, German, and Russian).[98]

Károly Grósz was not a duplicitous intellectual but, like Kádár, a former factory worker, a journeyman printer – the most prestigious craft in the prewar labor movement – a problem solver, and a no-nonsense manager. Pozsgay and Berecz were useful to Kádár, and he may have been proud of them, but they were too obviously covetous of his job. From Kádár's viewpoint, ideologues like Pozsgay were loose cannons who could not be trusted with the ultimate responsibility of preserving his regime's social and political legacy. On the other hand, the brash Berecz made too many enemies and was a failure as a propagandist. These and his other personal problems disqualified him as a sound manager of human relations and as a maker of strategic decisions.

Among Kádár's aspiring successors only Imre Pozsgay – a man of considerable erudition and remarkable native intellect – had what one might properly call a program. As will be discussed in Part III, one can discern in the long paper trail of Pozsgay's articles and interviews published prior to 1988 the outlines of a postcommunist participatory political system and elements of democratic socialist values on social and cultural issues. Berecz was not given to intellectual introspection but was preoccupied with finding quick fixes for the regime's legitimacy problems that he never understood. Grósz's ideas and programs were focused solely on issues of political steering and resource management.

In terms of core beliefs, careers, and political goals, all three had a lifetime investment in the system that Kádár created from the ruins of the 1956 revolution. They called it socialism and believed that unless they, as responsible officers of the watch, removed the aged helmsman, they too would fall victim to what Pozsgay later called the "sailors' mutiny" and be thrown overboard. Thus, the issue in 1987–8 was not "treason" but the political survival of the party's successor generation.

PART III

From postcommunism to democracy

6 Political succession in the HSWP: issues, personalities, and strategies, 1984–1989

Since the early 1960s Hungary had witnessed the transformation of János Kádár from "reluctant hostage" to "risk-taking reformer," and, from there, to the "good king" of the 1970s. The party's leadership style and Kádár's shifting political personae were shaped by the changing structural and situational constraints. By the early 1980s, these constraints had become major obstacles to continued political stability, economic growth, and social consensus on the regime's political goals.

The Kádár regime found it extremely difficult to cope with the policy challenges posed by unanticipated changes in Hungary's international and domestic environment. The key processes were growing foreign indebtedness, heightened international tensions, and Moscow's refusal to lend a hand in the stabilization of the national economy. Internal challenges, such as the public's panicky reaction to price rises, unexpected criticism from younger party leaders, and the party membership's open dissatisfaction with the regime, were the first warning signs of a coming political crisis.

The main impediment to rapid change was the "enfeebled autarch" János Kádár and his growing difficulties in staying abreast of new developments. He had been accustomed to the luxury of long lead times, typically five years between party congresses, during which elaborate preparations for major policy decisions could be made. Kádár's sedate decision-making style and his grasp of the issues became woefully inadequate for management of the tasks at hand. By 1984–5 the most he could do was keep the PB in line, make a few new appointments, and trust his bankers to refloat the economy with the help of yet another round of borrowing abroad.

Rearguard leadership consisted of a series of stopgap measures to gain time for organizational self-examination, policy reassessment, and the deployment of party, military, and security personnel to the state and local governments. The principal beneficiaries of the party center's gradual surrender of its managerial prerogatives were the state bureaucracy, the interest-group and policy lobbies, and, as an unintended consequence, the citizens of Hungary. Professor János Szentágothai, a former president of the Hungarian Academy of Sciences, likened this process to the behavior of the frightened passengers on a troika pursued by wolves in the Siberian taiga. To survive, they began casting off their belongings and, when those were gone, one another.[1]

In this chapter I will consider the policy issues, the main turning points, and the key political actors of the five-year (1985–early 1989) process of Kádár's fall and his successors' attempts to keep the regime viable. The discussion will address the following topics: (A) rearguard leadership: adaptation and political space; (B) the politics of leadership succession in the HSWP: personalities and strategies; and (C) Kádár's successors: struggle for power and political survival.

(A)   Rearguard leadership: adaptation and political space

Political democratization was one of the ancillary objectives of the original NEM. A revised Constitution, steps toward functional differentiation between the party and the state, and the growing involvement of transmission-belt organizations, first in a consultative and later in an administrative capacity, in policy-making and implementation, were promising developments. Moreover, the invigoration of grassroots political participation by multicandidate elections and the granting by the Law on Local Councils of 1971 of greater fiscal and administrative autonomy to local governments were evidence of the regime's intent to make use of the NEM as a vehicle for evolutionary change in Hungary.

By the late 1970s the NEM had become the principal, if not the sole, device for the regime's self-legitimation. It was only then that the leadership realized that it had been a strategic blunder to hand over to the population a yardstick, that is, take-home pay and consumer prices, with which to measure the gap between the regime's political rhetoric and its economic performance. As long as the state had the resources to underwrite the costs of stable living standards, no one outside the party elites and small groups of dissident intellectuals took notice of the postponement of the contemplated political reforms. In any case, it was not the lack of political democratization but the stagnation and, by the mid-1980s, general deterioration of the economic system that fatally undermined Kádár's position.

The regime's poor economic performance between 1976 and 1988 was a necessary but not a sufficient precondition of the political crisis that brought Kádár down. As will be shown below, what made it happen was a combination of political, economic–social, and legitimacy factors that prompted the PB to set into motion a process of leadership change in November 1986.

The Hungarian Socialist Workers' Party

Over the years the HSWP became an ossified bureaucracy with a diminished capacity for policy innovation and effective leadership. The top party policy-making bodies were preoccupied with the daily administrative management of party and government affairs. The regime's centralized decision-making structure left the final say on thousands of issues in the hands of fewer than fifty top policy managers of the party center. As a result, the HSWP was frequently far behind events and could, at best, effect minor personnel changes and perform political fire-fighting functions, but not those of strategic policy planning. Thus, by default, the ostensibly omnicompetent but in fact decision-overloaded party leadership relinquished many of its economic managerial prerogatives to the National Planning Office and the government bureaucracy.

Rescue plans, such as the creation of an HSWP-sponsored multiparty system and the decentralization of the economy and public administration – though subjects of intense private discussions among leading members of the party's successor generation – could not be considered as long as Kádár was at the helm.[2] In Kádár's mind, the party was the only institution with the capacity to preserve political stability and to promote the values of socialism. He was willing to experiment with administrative changes but refused to accept the political consequences of administrative decentralization. For an old chess player, the wholesale upgrading of pawns to knights was a prescription for chaos and political unpredictability.

Still, the clock was ticking, and however much Kádár wanted to avoid the next move it was his. As can be inferred from the central party organs' policy-making record of 1981–3, Kádár's search for answers led to policy paralysis at the top. The unintended consequence was the creation of new political space both for the institutional actors "in place," such as the state bureaucracy and the policy lobbies, and for the newly emerging forces of Hungary's "second society" and second economy.

Over time, the CC's departments, its working teams, and other bodies of policy oversight became captives to nonparty interest groups that acquired *de facto* veto power over the party's resource-allocation agenda. The leadership, when confronted with competing demands of the YCL (for funds to underwrite the cost of a crash housing program for young people), the TUF (for inflation-indexed wages), and the county apparats (for investments in local industries and infrastructure) could satisfy none.[3] The regime was caught between pressures generated by societal expectations of higher living standards and by the various policy lobbies' "subcontractual" obligations to their own constituencies.

The government and state bureaucracy

The Hungarian government's essential task was policy implementation rather than policy initiation. The ideological-political mandate of the György Lázár-led Council of Ministers between 1975 and 1987 was, at best, ambiguous. The Lázár cabinet came into being as the direct result of Soviet contriving to thwart the unfolding of the "Hungarian model" into an ideologically unacceptable alternative path to building socialism in an East European client state.

Moscow's unhelpful posture on credits and energy prices left the Kádár regime at the mercy of Western markets, Western lending institutions, and the political vagaries of the Cold War. According to a declassified CIA study on Soviet–Hungarian relations in the 1970s, in March 1979 Brezhnev "publicly reminded Kádár that world economic conditions have an impact on the socialist community and also went out of his way to warn the Hungarians against excessive reliance on western trade by disparaging Western price fluctuations, inflation and fierce competition."[4] Although a year later the Soviets became more hospitable to economic-administrative experimentation in Hungary, adverse Western reactions to the invasion of Afghanistan in December 1979 placed new constraints on Hungary's ability to keep the economy afloat and improve its balance of payments with the country's foreign trading partners.[5]

The problem that neither the experts nor their principals could resolve was Kádár's obstinate refusal to face facts. While he was at the helm, Kádár did not permit free discussion in either the PB or the CC on policy options and possible remedies for the crisis at hand. In fact, according to the international finance expert Miklós Pulai, the auditors of the International Monetary Fund (IMF) had a more accurate picture of Hungary's budget and current account deficits than did the majority of the CC.[6]

The top government officials were caught in the crossfire between the PB's stifling hands-on management from above and bureaucratic-ideological sabotage from below.[7] Bureaucratic hostility to the party's – invariably cautious – policy innovations took many forms. Of these, vigorous ministry rule-making activity and the issuing of thousands of enabling regulations were the most important. Such measures sought to cushion the impact of PB directives on the party's and the government's political, social, and economic constituencies.[8]

The regime's resource-allocation dilemmas defied traditional remedies. As Kádár explained at the June 23, 1987 meeting of the CC, "the purely rational functioning of the economy runs counter to our social system, which is socialist and humane."[9] Hungary's capitalist and communist creditors in Basel, Tokyo, Frankfurt, and Moscow were not disoriented ideologues but pragmatic businessmen. Their message was the same: "Pacta sunt servanda."[10]

Policy lobbies and interest groups

Before June 1987 only the YCL, the TUF, and the National Council of Agricultural Cooperatives (NCAC) had the privilege of direct political representation in the HSWP PB. In 1980 these mass organizations were mandated to convey the party's policies to 855,000 young people, 918,000 cooperative farmers, and 4.3 million blue- and white-collar workers employed in the state sector.[11] The presence of László Maróthy (first secretary, YCL), Sándor Gáspár (chairman and secretary general, TUF), and Lajos Fehér (after 1985 István Szabó, president, NCAC) in the PB guaranteed that these constituencies' interests would be taken into account when decisions were made on social and economic issues.

Modest quotas for enterprise directors, county council chairmen, and various social and intelligentsia groups provided for a virtual representation of these constituencies in the party's CC.[12] The interests of the country's nonparty majority, and those of local governments, business groups, and the intelligentsia, were served by politically powerless bodies, such as the PPF, the Hungarian Chamber of Commerce, the Hungarian Academy of Sciences, and the Writers' Union.

Whether or not these interest groups actually served their constituencies is a moot question. The point is that since the early 1970s the largest ones had been given the authority to administer various social and welfare programs. The TUF had substantial income from member-ship dues, a full- and part-time staff of up to ten thousand, and the statutory right to administer a wide range of health, welfare, and recreation programs. The YCL, with a full-time staff of more than 1,500, had similar resources and entitlements. When we combine these numbers and resources with those of the other transmission-belt organizations, we have well over 15,000, mainly middle-level, *nomenk-latura* appointees with a vested interest in justifying their existence as indispensable parts of the political system.

The party's retreat into rearguard leadership helped upgrade the political power of these mass organizations. The statutory but rarely exercised consultative rights of the TUF, the YLC, and the NCAC were gradually transformed into preemptive veto power over income poli-cies, price rises, budget cuts, and agricultural price subsidies. The Polish events, particularly the awe-inspiring rise of Solidarity in 1980–1 as the powerful protector of the people's thitherto neglected interests, helped boost the stature of the TUF, the YCL, and of the intelligentsia organizations in Hungary.[13]

Each of these quasi-corporatist entities had the personnel, organiza-tional infrastructure, communications resources, and, above all, the bureaucratic survival instincts to fill the political void and begin to function as protoparties on behalf of sectorial interests. In the 1980s the Hungarian regime was in dire need of political buffers to shelter the incumbents from pressures from below. The mass organizations were ready-made components of a new style of political governance.

Political outcomes

A key goal of the party's rearguard strategy was the transformation of the HSWP from an interpenetrated party-state bureaucracy into a political movement: the restoration of the top incumbents' direct links with the rank-and-file membership. The leadership had two short-term objectives in mind. First, to empower the average party member, trade union activist, and member of the nonparty majority to have a greater say in the workings of the local and regional party and trade union apparats and those of the state bureaucracy. Second, with the help of such pressures from below, to transfer to the state and the mass organizations the fiscal and political responsibility for rising prices and bureaucratic unresponsiveness to citizen demands for improvements of various kinds. In ideological terms, these policy initiatives were to pave the way for the transformation of the HSWP into an "all-people's party" – a hegemonic force that *served*, rather than ruled the political community.[14]

The political center's decision to hand over some of its unwanted decision-making responsibilities to local and regional political authorities and mass organizations took many forms. These included:

1 the empowerment of the local governments to have a greater say in economic decisions affecting the local community;
2 the introduction of new forms of enterprise management, including the election of enterprise councils and their right to elect top managers;
3 the handing over to the county and local party organizations greater control over (lower-level) *nomenklatura* appointments;
4 the introduction of multicandidate elections for local and parliamentary elections.

These measures were later supplemented by the introduction – at only the local and regional level – of the secret ballot in the election of TUF and YCL officeholders, and initial steps toward limiting to two terms (typically five years each) the holding of low- and middle-level party offices.

The entire initiative was the domestic version of the regime's "escape-forward" strategy of seeking to develop external – mainly Western – diplomatic, trade, and financial links with which to prop up Hungary's ailing economy. The problem was that whereas the regime's external indebtedness could, up to a point, be finessed by import restrictions and depressed living standards, its "domestic indebtedness" – that is, the gap between political promises and economic performance – lacked the option to "reschedule" payment on accumulated debts.[15] A declaration of "insolvency" on the latter score would have called for a change *of* the political system, rather than *in* it. The stakes were high, for any tinkering with the existing power relationships among the party, the state, the interest groups, and the thitherto politically powerless nonelites entailed the risk of instability and loss of political control.

Local autonomy and community power

Hungary's Soviet-style highly centralized public administration left the county, municipal, and village governments with less than 20 percent of the locally extracted revenues, such as sales taxes and taxes on enterprise profits.[16] The cost of local administration, municipal services, and infrastructure have invariably exceeded locally available revenues. Central budgetary resources for rural electrification, road construction, schools, and health facilities had traditionally consisted of sums left over from cost-intensive priority allocations for military, heavy-industry, and other targeted prestige investment projects.

Imre Pozsgay's appeal at the December 3, 1981 CC meeting for the restoration of budget cuts for cultural, educational, scientific, and infrastructural projects sought to recapture a larger share of the central budget for Hungary's local governments. The state's industrial policies both deprived the local communities of needed resources for delivery on the regime's "social contractual" obligations, and helped perpetuate other inequalities as well. At issue were, on the one hand, the growing gap between the infrastructurally well-endowed capital city and the rest of the country, and, on the other hand, that between Hungary's more modern western region and the historically backward eastern, particularly northeastern, regions.[17]

The devolution of administrative decision-making authority found the local governments utterly unprepared to respond to community pressures for delivery on long-overdue promises of investments for paved roads, water and sewer lines, health facilities, new schools, waste disposal plants, and the containment of industrial pollution.[18] The principal actors in the local councils' executive committees – senior administrators and co-opted top officials from the party, and the legal, educational, and industrial agricultural sectors of the community – were confronted with new tasks but were bereft of new resources to pay for them. These problems were particularly acute in villages that had been forcibly "consolidated" in the 1970s, in smaller cities, and in counties that had not had a "native son" in the Politburo to deliver bail-out monies to his "home district."[19]

With the regime's local power structures in disarray, the thitherto latent forces of Hungary's "second society" – clubs, neighborhood groups, ad hoc action committees, and other PPF-sheltered nonparty cultural entities – came to the fore as aggressive petitioners for action of some kind. The political incumbents had neither the answers nor the money to satisfy such demands.

Ultimately, political responsibility for the central government's abandonment of the communities of provincial Hungary belonged to the ruling party. This, as Grósz explained to me, put the county first secretaries on the spot. Each of them, as the "first man" in the county, had been the recipient of increasingly shrill demands for action from many local constituencies. As an inevitable consequence, the party's regional commanders – though under the direct tutelage of Kádár's deputy, PB member Károly Németh – found themselves in an adversarial position *vis-à-vis* the PB and the government.[20]

Workplace democracy and self-management

Both Kádár and the socialist reform economists, each for different reasons, had since the mid-1970s been on the warpath with the "red barons" of Hungary's military–industrial complex. As Kádár saw it, the top management of the fifty major industrial enterprises had been the main beneficiaries of preferential budget allocations in view of their commitment to diversify and modernize the export industries and thus help improve Hungary's balance of payments.[21] Instead of improved efficiency, the smokestack industries and the mines proved to be financial sinkholes.

For the reform economists, the heavy-industry policy lobby represented the main obstacle to marketization and the expansion of the second economy from its semilegal status into a productive partnership with the state sector.[22] As the reformers saw it, the unholy alliance, within each enterprise, of party cadre director, incumbent trade union apparat, and conservative blue-collar "core group" on the shop floor helped perpetuate inefficiency. Moreover, the "enterprise triad" had a vested interest in preventing the transformation of informal bargaining relationships between labor and management into institutionalized venues of interest reconciliation between the two.

Beyond its economic rationale, the empowerment of the workers to elect enterprise councils and thereby have a say in the selection of a term-appointed manager made good political sense as a prophylactic measure to thwart the spread of Polish Solidarity-inspired labor activism in Hungary. A related objective was to pressure the incumbent and the new enterprise management to make provisions for the operation of new types of intraenterprise second-economy-type work teams. On balance, it was preferable to permit the efficient producers to earn substantial extra income "within the gates" than to see them leave the enterprise for greener pastures in the private sector.[23]

The reform of enterprise management established two types of mechanisms for the selection – reappointment or appointment by election – of managers. From a report by PB member Károly Németh on cadre policies and on the initial experiences of this innovation at the March 18, 1986 meeting of the CC, it appeared that, of the first thousand elections held, only sixty yielded a new enterprise director; the remaining directors had been duly reelected by the apathetic workers.[24] The ultimate protector of existing labor relations was Kádár himself. He explained to his PB colleagues, "As I see it, to work better is itself a sacrifice for the average man."[25] For him, a stable and inefficient labor force was preferable to political activism on the shop floor.

The decline of a mass party: membership views and organizational entropy

The *nomenklatura* system was one of the regime's key power resources. The leadership's responses to pressures for greater local autonomy in a "democratic centralist," yet "all-people's," party were issued in the form of various PB and CC decisions for the strengthening of intra-party democracy at the grassroots level.[26] To assess the local responses to these central directives, I reviewed monthly activity reports from several typical middle-level party organizations to the Departments of Agitation-Propaganda and of Party and Mass Organizations of the CC for the years 1981 through 1986.[27] What emerged from these reports may be summarized as follows:

1 The regional party organizations and those with "county rights" were overburdened with many kinds of mandated activities and reporting requirements. The first secretaries had neither the resources nor the inclination to mobilize the membership to implement the party center's ambiguous directives.

2 Because of the sheer size of Csepel Iron and Steel Works – the showplace of the regime's industrial policies – party officials therein had only bureaucratic contacts with the party cells. Their main functions seem to have been seeing to the fulfillment of production targets of military contracts and promoting periodic "socialist labor competitions" within the enterprise. The visceral issues of these years, such as absenteeism, conflicts between second-economy-type intraenterprise work teams and the regular labor force, and the local impact of the Polish events, were not discussed in the Csepel apparat's monthly reports.

3 The party's Budapest city-district and county-level "line" agencies were vastly overextended, most often economic, troubleshooting teams for crisis management and the transmitting of local grievances to higher party and state organs. Though their monthly reports were full of trivial statistics about the number of cell meetings held and people enrolled in ideological instruction and the like, nothing was said about the work of elected plenary bodies that nominally supervised the work of the full-time apparat.

4 With respect to the party membership's "mood," these reports offered a representative sampling of direct quotes and paraphrased statements made by members at meetings of local party cells. About three-fourths of the comments were about prices, shortages of consumer goods, and inflation. Even in a "sanitized" form, these comments bespoke disappointment, bitterness, and loss of faith in the national leadership. Over the years, as Kádár himself acknowledged at various CC meetings, the membership grew tired of the regime's lame excuses – oil prices, trade deficits, and imperialist intrigues against the socialist camp – and demanded positive action from above.

The seven-year process of the average party member's gradual estrangement from the HSWP and its leadership was complex and took many forms. However, as judged from opinion surveys and internal "mood reports," the main cause was a sense of betrayal and abandonment by the regime. As shown in Chapter 2, the regime tried, by way of economically unjustified boosts of social incomes, to stem the tide of public dissatisfaction. However, the party's internal reports on membership views demonstrated that these measures failed to assuage popular, especially blue-collar, concerns about declining living standards. In the end, even Kádár ceased to worry about complaints from below. He explained to the CC, "We have overinsured our society."

In sum, by the middle of the 1980s politics in Hungary had become "local" and "national" at the same time. On the one hand, there was a growing gap between the sense of gloom and the appearance of alarmist pathologies of socioeconomic difficulties in the *glasnost'*-driven media and the curiously detached soothing verbal placebos in the leadership's messages to the party membership. On the other hand, the tendency of the media to treat widely publicized instances of local problems as symptoms of a *national* malaise helped contradict and discredit official assessments of the same.

Choosing or voting? The elections of 1985

In 1967, more or less as an afterthought to the NEM reforms, the regime began experimenting with multicandidate elections in selected local and parliamentary electoral districts. Although there were several two-candidate elections in the coming years, the idea did not take root until the 1980s. Up to that point, the official slate had prevailed with 99 percent-plus majorities of the votes cast for the official nominees.[28] The

1985 elections for local councilors and parliamentary deputies were intended to be an experiment in expanded, yet controlled, political participation by the average citizen.

The introduction of *choice* between two candidates was designed to promote several regime objectives. Of these, the relegitimation and modest empowerment of the legislative branch was the most important. As István Horváth, then CC secretary for administrative, legal, and security affairs, explained to me, the PB had been anxious to revitalize the Parliament by the replacement of most of the incumbent MPs mainly with nonparty people, women, and younger cadres.[29]

Responsibility for the development of local slates of candidates was entrusted to special operative committees of the county party organizations. Each was given quotas (men/women, party/nonparty, worker, peasant, intellectual, young, and old) to fill from each county's share of Hungary's 352 parliamentary electoral districts. As a rule, the county operative committees delegated the task of candidate selection to the largest party organizations in each electoral district. Their task was to produce two candidates for each district and to ensure that both would have an "equal chance" to compete for the voters' support.

Thus, in most counties it was a combination of local apparat preferences, county-level "demographic adjustments" (see below), and the accommodation of "central cadres" (such as a PB member running in an individual district) that yielded the officially endorsed district slate. In addition, there was a "national" (noncontested) list of thirty-five parliamentary seats that the party center put together to spare busy public figures from the chore of attending nominating meetings. The national list was a corporatist assembly of party and state leaders, the clergy, token representatives of the main ethnic groups, top *nomenklatura* intellectuals, and a few political notables.[30]

With the regime's intentions in mind, let us consider how the regional party authorities and the voters responded to the challenge of the 1985 parliamentary elections. As it may be reconstructed from an in-house follow-up study on the election results that György Aczél commissioned at the CC Institute of the Social Sciences, the entire affair was a demonstration of the apparat's inability and apparent unwillingness to execute the PB's political will.[31] Moreover, contrary to original expectations, a remarkable number of voters made use of the ballot box to promote *local* issues and support candidates who pledged to act on behalf of local and regional interests. This is what happened:

1 Pursuant to central directives, the local party executives had to persuade most of the incumbent MPs to surrender their safe seats and retire from politics. The majority complied, but those who demurred and had support at the county level were allowed to run. Of the 172 incumbents who chose to run, ninety-eight were reelected, fifty-four were defeated in the first round – where it took 50 percent plus one vote to be elected – and twenty were forced into runoff elections in which about one-half regained a seat in the Parliament.[32]

2 The task of finding "running mates" for the incumbent MPs confronted the local selection committees with an unmanageable task. Giving the "other" official candidate an "equal chance" tended to cast doubt on the fitness of the incumbent and, more to the point, the incumbent's ability to lobby for local interests in the Parliament. More-over, the task of satisfying the party center's statistical expectations about nonmembers, women, and young people (at the expense of demographically nonconforming local political worthies) yielded local political standoffs that the county operative committees had to adjudi-cate. The eventual solution was the nationwide fielding of more than one hundred pairs of "two eggs," that is, two female physicians, two male schoolteachers, two nonparty lawyers, and so on) as candidates. The candidacy of artificially paired odd couples became yet another source of confusion for the apparat and party membership alike. The latter demanded to be told which candidate to support, but received no instructions from above.[33]

3 The April–May 1985 nominating meetings (typically, two were held in each district) were presented with 704 PPF-endorsed candi-dates. It was at this stage that the county party operative committees' bureaucratic scenarios fell apart. In one-seventh (fifty-four) of the electoral districts 152 additional nominations were made from the floor. Of these, six opposition candidates in Budapest and seventy-six spontaneous nominees elsewhere failed to obtain sufficient support at the nominating meetings to earn a place on the ballot. However, seventy of the "people's nominees" did get on the ballot. Among the latter were Zoltán Király and a dozen "dragon slayers" who eventually defeated the powerful incumbents in the first round or in the runoff elections.

4 For the first time since 1947 the Hungarian parliamentary elections were about *issues*. As a rule, the endorsed candidates' campaign speeches had been cleared with and approved by the local party committees. Each candidate offered a balance sheet of local accom-plishments and of the tasks that they, if elected, would support in the

Parliament. According to a survey on what the candidates at 574 nominating meetings said on these subjects, the balance sheet of "accomplishments versus tasks" showed an inordinate deficit: 833 to 69. Virtually all items on the "tasks" side of the ledger were in the area of infrastructure investments. Because of the relatively low share (152 out of 704) of non-prearranged and spontaneously chosen – that is, nominated by citizens from the floor, and therefore presumably more critical – candidates, the aggregate result of the tally of "tasks versus accomplishments" by *all candidates* must be seen as the local party elites' harsh condemnation of the regime's historic neglect of community needs.[34]

The issues behind the awakening and political radicalization of provincial Hungary are shown in Table 6.1. Citizens and political elites in three types of communities – "other cities and towns," "villages," and "small settlements" – were the main victims of the regime's resource allocation policies of the previous forty years that centered on Budapest and other large cities. Moreover, a growing number of enterprises and local councils began to take the party committees' *nomenklatura* recommendations as just that and went about their business as if they were autonomous entities. Thus, to survive, the local and regional party organizations had no choice but to "go native." The power elites of the small cities and village communities could now embrace local priorities and feel free to disregard the party center's political directives.

In terms of specific electoral outcomes, many of the local races turned out to be spontaneous plebiscites on the regime's policies and its politically vulnerable incumbents. The objects of the people's wrath were prominent politicians whom Kádár chose not to include in the sheltered national list. Among the losers were present and former CC members and government officials, six county first secretaries, several chairmen of county councils, top trade union officials, and senior media executives.

Of the top incumbents who *were* elected or reelected, three younger politicians – László Maróthy, 87.7 percent; Mátyás Szűrös, 85.7 percent; and János Berecz, 75.5 percent – each running in his native village, led the pack. Others, like György Aczél and Rezső Nyers, instead of the usual noncontested 99 percent majorities, had to settle for 70.3 and 63.7 percent respectively, against token opponents. Imre Pozsgay was on the safe national list and the farsighted Károly Grósz was granted his petition not to be nominated in an individual electoral district.

The real losers of the 1985 parliamentary elections were Kádár and

Table 6.1 *Frequency of issues candidates would support if elected to Parliament, by location of district, Hungary, 1985*[35]

Issue	Location of electoral district						
	A %	B %	C %	D %	E %	F %	G %
Sidewalks, roads, traffic	2	3	48	30	7	2	2
Sewage system, natural gas supply	2	2	37	35	11	9	4
Wells, drinking water	1	3	29	41	19	4	3
Schools, kindergartens, cultural centers	2	4	44	32	14	3	2
Health and social services	3	7	45	30	12	1	1
Electrification, street lights	0	0	75	25	0	0	0
Telephone service	4	4	43	35	4	4	4
Commercial services, retail trade	3	4	44	30	16	4	0
Other	1	9	43	31	12	3	2

Note: A = Budapest
   B = city with county status
   C = other city or town
   D = village
   E = small settlement
   F = urban periphery
   G = uncertain

the central party apparat.[36] From a review of the sociopolitical characteristics of MPs serving in 1980–5 and those elected in 1985, it appears that none of the PB's electoral policy targets was realized. Among the MPs elected to serve in the Parliament for the next five years the percentage of party members *increased* from 71.6 to 77, the share of women *decreased* from 30.1 to 20 percent and the ratio of MPs under 30 *declined* from 12.5 to 5 percent. Moreover, contrary to expectations for an increase in the number of well-educated legislators, that is, university or college graduates, the share of blue-collar workers (at best high-school graduates) *increased* from 23.6 to 34.3 percent.[37]

Most of the new MPs from professional and other white-collar backgrounds – including all those nominated from the floor – were members of local professional elites. The "people's choices" were not party hacks but respected community leaders, such as local physicians, lawyers, directors of small enterprises, engineers, and high-school teachers. Many of them were party members but, as judged from their conduct as national legislators in the next four years, their political loyalties belonged not to the party but to their home districts.[38]

The arrival of local notables on the national political scene marked the debut of Hungary's postcommunist political elites in the public arena. They were the first harbingers of a new kind of professional politician in Hungary. Their claim of representing the public interest rested on professional skills, aptitude for problem solving, and commitment to new principles of political legitimacy. Several of the spontanously nominated – elected and nonelected – candidates of the 1985 elections ran again in March 1990. Some of them were elected as newly minted "reform socialists" and "democrats" under the banner of the Hungarian Socialist Party (HSP), or of the Hungarian Democratic Forum (HDF) and the Alliance of Free Democrats (ADF).

The party's partial withdrawal from the public arena created new political space for the state, the regional party apparat, the organized interest groups, and increasingly for the politicized intelligentsia. These newly empowered political and social actors sought to protect their respective interests by making new claims on the political regime for resources, expanded mandates, and legal guarantees to secure their own space as semiautonomous participants in the political process. The essential requisite of an orderly and nondestabilizing devolution of power from the party center was, above all, firm leadership. The process also required a clearly articulated political vision of the future of socialism in Hungary and the country's prospects in the Soviet empire. Much, in fact far too much, depended on the septuagenarian János Kádár and his ability to reenergize the political system and to persuade citizens to remain loyal to the system that he had created in the previous three decades.

(B)   The politics of leadership succession in Hungary, 1984–8

Leadership succession is the supreme test of the capacity of a political system to manage the process of transition from one top incumbent to another. Precedents of previous succession scenarios, the outgoing leader's policy record, the regime's political legitimacy, the resiliency and adaptability of institutional structures to the management of new policies, and the next leader's strategic priorities are some of the instrumental components of this process.[39]

Political succession: actors, proxies, issues and venues of competition

János Kádár was the political leader, the embodiment of a paternalistic style of governance, and the bearer of personal political and moral responsibility for his record of strategic decisions since 1956. As most Hungarians saw it, Kádár *was* the political regime and, as an "ism," a way of life as well. As the economist László Lengyel in a perceptive essay on Hungarian leadership traditions explained, the three benevolent autocrats of the preceding 150 years – Emperor Franz Joseph, Admiral Miklós Horthy, and János Kádár – had left a legacy of a citizen quasi-fatalistic sense of dependency on the paramount leader.[40] Each began his reign with the bloody suppression of national aspirations for freedom and independence, yet, over time, each became synonymous with public perceptions of political stability and social peace. Franz Joseph's heir was assassinated in Sarajevo; Horthy's son died on the Russian front; and Kádár could never bring himself to name a successor. This, at least as much as the lost wars of his predecessors, was responsible for the fall of Kádár's regime.

The central issue of the entire process of leadership succession in Hungary was a search for answers to three principal policy dilemmas.

1 Political leadership. At issue were the devolution and redistribution among his associates of Kádár's political authority and the institutionalization of the same in the form of a collective leadership under a *primus inter pares* successor.

2 Principles of resource allocation. At issue were revision of the terms of the dysfunctional social contract and gaining social acceptance of new legitimating principles of socialism and welfare.

3 Political power and institutional restructuring. At issue was the organizational implementation of the Hungarian variant of *perestroika*, specifically the separation of party and state and the selective co-optation of policy lobbies and emerging social forces into a protopluralistic – or quasi-corporatist – political system.

Political actors who were salient to the process of political succession were top decision-makers and their proxies at the lower levels of the political hierarchy. To the former belonged the entire cluster of politically polarized and personally divided incumbent leadership. This, in turn, may be further divided into three groups:

1 János Kádár and the "Kádárist center" of longtime political allies in the PB and the central party apparat, such as Sándor Gáspár, György Lázár, Károly Németh, Miklós Óvári, László Maróthy, members of the Central Control Commission, a few CC secretaries and party veterans in the CC, and the heads of CC departments – particularly those of Party and Mass Organizations and Legal and Administrative (military, police, and foreign intelligence) Affairs.

2 An *ad hoc* alliance of putative successors (Károly Grósz, János

Berecz, Imre Pozsgay, and Rezső Nyers), "constituency representatives" in the PB (István Sarlós, Pál Losonczi, István Szabó), and CC secretary István Horváth, and their allies in the CC, the provincial party apparat.

3 "Swing voters" and "wait-and-see" types in the CC and the government. Individuals, such as the PB member Ferenc Havasi, foreign-trade expert József Marjai, party veteran Jenő Fock, CC foreign secretary Mátyás Szűrös, and the time-serving – and traditionally silent – majority of the CC belonged to this category. They were political lightweights, but their shared motivation was survival and the preservation of stability under *any* leader.

The second type of political actors who were salient to the politics of political succession included top *nomenklatura* leaders and the apparat of the policy lobbies, of the state bureaucracy, and of nonparty constituencies, particularly spokesmen of organized intelligentsia groups. Through complex clientelistic networks and personal access to senior politicians, these individuals and the groups they represented served as proxies for their principals above.

Although their respective priorities were quite different, the conservative and the proreform economic policy lobbies – the "red" and "green" barons and the Hungarian Chamber of Commerce, respectively – the print and the electronic media, and the unaffiliated reform intelligentsia were willing proxies of the contending leadership factions. All had a role to play as political auxiliaries of the main contenders in the process of succession. Moreover, at least two groups of influential – the reform socialist and the Populist – intelligentsia critics were, as Pozsgay's recruits, also parts of the political equation. So were, as uninvited guests to the Establishment's internal disputes, the democratic opposition and the restless intelligentsia.

The matter of political succession in the Hungarian party was also of concern to external constituencies. The most important of these were the the East European ruling parties, most prominently the CPSU and the Soviet government. Kádár and his much-publicized – mainly by the Western press – "Hungarian model" had been, since the early 1970s, a thorn in the side of the East German, Czechoslovak, and Romanian parties. Kádár's troubles again became the fodder of hostile *Neues Deutschland*, *Rude Pravo*, and *Scientiea* commentary throughout the 1980s. Such unwelcome attention counseled caution in Hungary and helped prolong the succession process.

Moscow's stakes in the outcome of political succession in Hungary were far more substantial than were those of Hungary's smaller neighbors. In any case, Khrushchev, Brezhnev, and Kádár's long-time political confidant Yuri Andropov considered him a trusted ally, a friend of the Soviet Union, and the personal guarantor of political stability in Hungary.[41] Although in September 1985 Gorbachev was anything but subtle in reminding Kádár of his earlier attempt to retire and of his advanced age, there is no evidence of Soviet pressures on Kádár to relinquish his position as secretary general of the HSWP.[42] On the other hand, Egor Ligachev's interview with Grósz in September 1984 was an obvious sign of Soviet interest in learning more about the personality and the ideas of the next party chief of Budapest. From this, however, it did not necessarily follow that Grósz was Moscow's early nominee for Kádár's job. As will be discussed below, the "selling" of Grósz to the Soviet leadership was Kádár's prerogative and one that, having little choice in the matter, he exercised in May 1988.

Kádár was a vehement opponent of wide dissemination of information that might upset the public. Real debates for real stakes took place not before large gatherings of rank-and-file trade union, youth, and PPF activists but in closed meetings of the mid- and upper-level party, government, and security apparat. "Consultations" and "special briefings" for selected audiences at the Ministry of Interior, the Ministry of Defense, and the Party Academy, and for hand-picked groups of senior enterprise managers, media executives, and important county party organizations, were special occasions for special purposes. It was there that Kádár, Aczél, Grósz, Berecz, and the rest of the PB felt free to speak their minds about the issues and, by way of oblique references to one another's alleged positions on policy problems, about one another.

The object of speech-making was building a constituency within the party apparat and enlisting of senior *nomenklatura* personnel to support the speaker's priorities on the tasks at hand. Paradoxically, unlike the PB members who had to clear their speaking engagements in advance with Kádár's administrative deputy, Károly Németh, a CC member, such as Pozsgay, was free to choose his audiences. Though these were mainly intelligentsia groups, Pozsgay was also a welcome visitor at county party organizations and small-town gatherings of the local political and cultural elites.

The media played a critically important role throughout the succession process. Although the national dailies and the electronic media were under direct CC and Department of AP control, the "pitch" of each became attuned to the perceived preferences of the various leadership groups. Whereas the party daily *Népszabadság* was directly supervised by the Politburo, *Magyar Hirlap* was the government's official newspaper; *Magyar Nemzet* belonged to the PPF; and *Népszava* spoke for the trade unions. On the other hand, the editors of (by the mid-1980s only *self*-censored) weekly and monthly publications were always on the lookout for an offbeat interview with some adventurous top officials and their quotable quotes on current policy issues.

Hungarian radio's hard-hitting "168 hours" Saturday afternoon fact-finding *cum* live interview program, became a much-sought-after outlet for the making of candid comments by frustrated officials. TV's "sectorial" (*réteg*) late-night interview programs, such as *Bagoly* (Night owl), were in effect proprietary forums of the reform intelligentsia. In any case, whatever happened behind closed doors among the top officials sooner or later found its way – with generous assists from Radio Free Europe and the BBC – into the Hungarian media. In fact, in June 1987 RFE "scooped" the Hungarian media by more than twenty-four hours in announcing the new lineup of the Grósz government. Toward the end, political succession became an increasingly transparent process in which the reporters of news and the moderators of talk shows became newsmakers themselves.

Political succession: personalities and strategies

Leadership succession in Hungary took place in five overlapping phases between April 1984 and May 1988. These were the collapse of the Kádárist center (April 1984 – November 1986); bureaucrats and technocrats ascendant (December 1986 – June 1987); the Grósz campaign (July 1987 – March 1988); conservative countermobilization (November 1987 – March 1988); and negotiated succession – a "leveraged buyout" (April–May 1988).[43]

The collapse of the Kádárist center

In early 1984 the Hungarian leadership was confronted with a set of policy decisions that ultimately sealed the fate of the Kádárist center. Foreign indebtedness, balance-of-payments deficits, the terms of Hungarian–Soviet trade, and, inevitably, domestic living standards were the principal items. After a shaky start in 1980–2, when the Hungarian National Bank barely escaped insolvency,[44] tough import restrictions, cutbacks in investments, and other corrective measures were introduced.

It was this background of what proved to be a "false dawn" that prompted Kádár to urge his colleagues to act before it was too late. As he put it at the April 17, 1984 meeting of the CC:

> the party, the government and the regime have earned some credit in the eyes of the people ... this is why they have been patient with us. [Yet] ... the two catch phrases – adverse international economic conditions and the preservation of living standards attained to date – are untenable ... [With these catch phrases] ... we cannot offer hope and a way out [of our difficulties]. The party and the regime have been unable to show new perspectives.
>
> Comrades, believe me that we cannot go on with one half of one per cent growth of national income. With that we cannot win the support of the masses ... we cannot go on like this! There must be more to this socialist system of ours. I know there is – a great deal more. I say to you, comrades, that we must aim for an annual growth of 2.5 to 3 percent of the national income.[45]

Yet, when it came to finding ways to effect needed changes with *internal resources*, Kádár shied away from strong-arm methods. He explained: "[In the Soviet Union] during the Andropov era they resorted to certain means – you know what kinds – and, as a result, the national income for 1983 doubled from the previous year. I know that a great deal could be done by shaking up things ... but I do not want to get into that sort of thing."[46]

Resources for new investments, and for wage and price subsidies, came from additional Western loans. Although the National Planning Office, CC secretary Ferenc Havasi, and prime minister György Lázár were vehemently opposed to incurring new financial obligations, Kádár forced the issue and in the end his preferences prevailed.[47] Kádár's desperate attempt to accommodate pressures for new investments and higher wages was codified in the economic policy resolutions of the 13th HSWP congress in March 1985.[48] Of the ten principal economic targets, only one was realized by the end of the year and none in 1986. On the other hand, between 1984 and 1987 Hungary's net foreign indebtedness in convertible currencies increased from $8.8 Bn to $17.7 Bn.[49]

In retrospect it is clear that in terms of leadership stability and drastic policy correction, the 13th party congress was the regime's last opportunity to set into motion a process of *controlled* change. The introduction of a balanced team of "succession managers" made up of Kádárists, government experts, and reformers could have preserved political stability yet signal Kádár's intention to step down some time before the next party congress. Instead, Kádár promoted himself to secretary general and named the 63-year-old Károly Németh as his deputy.

In the next eighteen months the infirmities of age and his declining health caught up with the secretary general. From 1986 on, Kádár started taking unannounced month-long vacations.[50] While he still held his own in informal meetings with his colleagues, Kádár's public speeches, particularly his improvised statements, struck his audiences as the confused and at times incoherent maunderings of an old man who was losing touch with realities.

Economic stagnation, policy paralysis at the top, and Kádár's deteriorating health were the main precipitants of a political sea change in Hungary between 1985 and 1987. Public beliefs in the myth of Hungary's invulnerability to the kinds of political and economic crises that beset Poland, Romania, and, increasingly, the USSR in the mid-1980s rapidly evaporated.[51]

Bureaucrats and technocrats ascendant, December 1986 – June 1987

The November 18–19, 1986 meeting of the CC marked the end of a protracted internal debate on economic policies and administrative reforms in the party center. The main conclusion was that looking for external scapegoats offered no solutions to the problems at hand. In the end, and for the first time since November 1972, the question of *political responsibility* for economic failures was placed on the agenda.[52] Posing the matter in this fashion had been prompted by the relentless pressures of an *ad hoc* coalition of economic experts, government officials, and assorted technocratic constituencies. Their main spokesman was the apparat's "favorite son" Budapest first secretary Károly Grósz.

Kádár, reporting to the CC on his meeting with Gorbachev in early November, admitted that the Soviet leader had been "deeply concerned" about Hungary's economic situation. Gorbachev was willing to help but insisted that such bilateral matters be handled solely through government channels.[53] Gone were the days when during a Crimean vacation Kádár could persuade Brezhnev to grant the personal favor of new loans and oil deliveries. Under Gorbachev such matters were strictly state business.

Ferenc Havasi, in his report on the economy, owned up to the party center's responsibility for contributing to the chaos in the economic sphere. The official diagnosis of Hungary's economic troubles was buried in the text of a curiously defensive yet in many ways unrepentant CC resolution on the economy. The key sentence, "The country has consumed more than it has produced," was Kádár's. The apparent intent was to apportion blame between the people and the regime.[54]

The real significance of the November CC meeting lay not in Kádár's maladroit formulations but in the unannounced decision to transfer the party's economic decision-making responsibilities to the government. This decision had originated with an unpublished policy paper of the CC's Department of Economic Policy of September 30, 1986, for the PB. The main thrust of the DEP's recommendations was the significant empowerment of the state bureaucracy and the reduction of the party's direct managerial role to that of political oversight and strategic priority setting.[55]

The next five months saw the radical rejuvenation of the CC's economic apparat and the appointment of younger experts to lead important party and government agencies. The promotion of the 38-year-old Miklós Németh to head the CC's Department of Economic Policy, the appointment of the 44-year-old Péter Medgyessy as minister of finance, and the naming of the 44-year-old László Maróthy to head the National Planning Office marked the beginning of this process.

With new people in strategic policy-planning positions came new ideas. The most important ones originated with Miklós Németh's team at the CC's Department of Economic Policy. Németh's policy papers for the PB dealt with the second economy (now called an "organic part of the national economy"), the semisamizdat "Turnabout and reform" (now called "a useful document"), and main components of the government's new "action program for economic development." Commenting on the latter, Kádár called it "our perestroika," though he hastened to add: "We will not call it that way."[56]

In April 1987 a draft version of the action program was forwarded for comments to thirty-eight organizations, policy lobbies, and government agencies. According to Miklós Németh's summary of the responses, "in the opinion of several recipient organizations, Hungarian society is confronted with the crises of institutional structure, economic policy and [political] ideology." Others were "critical of cadre policies and brought up questions of personal accountability and the inevitability of personnel changes."[57]

Grósz recalled that the circumstances of his selection as the new prime minister to implement the party's economic revitalization program had been "haphazard, improvised, chaotic, and had little in common with carefully thought out cadre policies."[58] Probably so, but by then he was the only senior party leader with a substantial following within the apparat and the only one with the image of a dynamic manager with no direct responsibility for the party's flawed record. This belief was also confirmed by Egor Ligachev during his meetings with Kádár, prime minister Lázár, and Grósz in late April 1987.[59]

Kádár was willing to field an aggressive young team to take over the government from Lázár, but he also needed guarantees to preserve his own authority at the party center. What he hoped to create was a solid Kádárist majority in the PB, a rejuvenated Secretariat, and the PB's dependable, however "remote," control over the government. The process of personnel redeployment involved four steps.

Informal consultations between Kádár and individual PB members. With Soviet approval at hand, it was not the choice of Grósz but the makeup of his team and that of the revamped PB and the Secretariat that were discussed in the first stage.

Formal decision on Grósz. In a closed PB meeting Grósz at first declined the appointment and recommended Rezső Nyers or Péter Medgyessy as suitable alternatives. Medgyessy was promptly rejected. Nyers received a few votes, but no action was taken on his nomination. A few days later the PB reconvened and decided on Grósz.[60]

Negotiations between Grósz and Kádár. As Grósz explained,

> even before my formal appointment I had a long conversation with János Kádár during which we came to terms on significant changes in the relationship between the party and the government. He made a promise that in all substantive policy matters the PB would refrain from making binding decisions on [government policies]. It was a major political concession on the part of János Kádár that helped solve the most important problem ... [that of] the right to make personnel decisions without [reference to] the party ... Thus, I had a free hand to put together the "Grósz team."[61]

The "selling" of the PB's personnel decisions to the CC. The June 23, 1987 meeting of the CC was the scene of the first open rebellion against Kádár's authority in party history. His most outspoken critics were former prime minister Jenő Fock and Rezső Nyers. Although he had been consulted about the personnel changes, Fock found that none of his recommendations had been accepted by the PB. He asked: "Do you call this rejuvenation?" and recommended that Kádár become the party's chairman and relinquish party leadership to someone else. He also hinted that the holding of a special party conference might be the occasion to complete the changing of the guard. Nyers concurred with Fock and recommended that Kádár become the head of state. To this

CC member István Hárs added: "this is not rejuvenation but a merry-go-round."[62]

Whereas the Kádár loyalists merely disputed Fock's and Nyers' case, Kádár himself flatly refused to be kicked upstairs either as head of state or as party chairman. As he put it, though he sympathized with the "discomfiture of the 83-year-old Deng-Xiaoping when preaching about rejuvenation," he was not about to surrender the helm to anyone else.[63]

The outcome of the June 1987 personnel reshuffle may be characterized as a complex game of musical chairs. The entire process struck the public, as a newspaper cartoon aptly depicted it, as a flock of birds suddenly taking flight from their tree – then returning there and each sitting on a different branch.

The Grósz campaign

As the new prime minister, Grósz inherited his predecessor's staff and cabinet members but was cut off from his own Budapest and Borsod county party clients. He could expect no help either from the PB or from the CC Secretariat dominated by Lázár, Óvári, and Berecz. Under the circumstances, Grósz had no choice but to mount an essentially one-man campaign to produce a "stabilization" and "recovery" program of his own.

Grósz had three immediate priorities: development of a realistic plan of action to halt the political drift that threatened the regime's survival; establishment of the government as *the* lead agency of the political system with the capacity to mobilize the country's human, political, and economic resources; and development of his personal authority as a pragmatic leader and as the *only* one who could restore order and stability from the chaos that the party left behind after the economic "counter reforms" of 1972–5.[64]

Grósz became the obvious alternative to Kádár when both delivered nationally televised speeches at the Parliament in mid-September. The Grósz speech and the government's economic program promised no easy or early solutions for Hungary's severe economic problems. However, what struck most people were Grósz's full and candid account of the regime's ideologically motivated mismanagement of the NEM and the fact that the text of the government program made only *one* reference to the party and said nothing about its possible role in its implementation.

By contrast, Kádár's speech was a rambling, defensive, and self-serving account. Two memorable statements – "Since I have served long enough in [policy-making] bodies, probably I too am responsible to a certain extent" and "On the Central Committee's behalf I can state that we never intended to halt the reform process" – helped cut Kádár down to size and demonstrated, for all to see, what he had become: a tired old man fighting for his political life. Kádár's advisors must have realized it because this was his last nationally televised speech for the next six months.[65]

Unlike his predecesssor, Grósz believed in delegating authority. Grósz's proxies were senior cabinet officers, heads of top government line agencies, expert policy advisors, and scores of university and Academy of Sciences experts in economics, business, law, and public administration. The proxies' task was to explain, justify, and sell to specific constituencies various components of the Grósz program. The hidden agenda was distancing the government and its administrative agencies from the party.[66]

Grósz's role as decision-maker, conciliator, and high-level trouble-shooter was reserved for specific policy fields and constituencies. In most cases, including foreign affairs, the central topic of his well-publicized meetings and visits was economics: credits, budgetary priorities, rescue packages, unemployment, and "safety nets."[67] Although he operated with finite resources, Grósz's greatest achievement was that he somehow made it appear that as far as the *government* was concerned, progress was being made on all fronts.

Conservative counter-mobilization

At the end of 1987 the Kádár leadership was under intense pressure from several directions. Gorbachev's vigorous efforts for institutional restructuring and party renewal in the USSR were a political challenge that the Hungarian party could no longer ignore. The Soviet party's call of June 26, 1987 for an extraordinary party conference in the summer of 1988 generated pressures for a similar emergency session in the Hungarian party. When in December 1987 the party center reluctantly decided to set May 1988 as the date for its conference, it also established a deadline for setting its house in order and acting on the issue of overdue leadership change.

The main components of this phase of the succession process were the November 11, 1987 CC meeting on ideology (see Chapter 5); the intraparty debate on ideology and party renewal; Grósz's declaration of his candidacy; and the Kádárists' attempts to restore stability and to silence critics.

Between mid-December 1987 and late January 1988, the PB-Secretariat theses on ideology and the party's leading role were forwarded to the party's 26,000 local, 3,600 intermediate, and scores of county-level organizations for discussion and written comments. To say that the ideological theses were irrelevant to the real concerns of the party membership is to understate the intended recipients' reactions to this document. The party conservatives were offended by the contradictory formulations on private property, payment according to work, the positive evaluation of expertise at the expense of political loyalty, and the party's continued retreat from direct management of the economy.

Berecz's team's theses on party renewal also abounded with contradictions. On the one hand, the party was to become a "movement" and a "servant of the people" rather than an agency of direct political oversight. On the other hand, the central apparat was to retain all of its traditional prerogatives, including – contrary to the "gentlemen's agreement" between Kádár and Grósz six months earlier – those over personnel matters. Though the party's "main task" was to be the strengthening of "democracy," its proposed implementation rested on the further strengthening of "centralism."[68]

In early February 1988, when reports on the party debate were tabulated by the central apparat, it became apparent, to paraphrase Brecht, that the party membership did not deserve the leaders' confidence. There were many signs of rank-and-file disapproval: mass resignations from the party; written demands for the dismissal of Kádár, Lázár, Németh, Óvári, and Aczél; and lengthy "countertheses" submitted by several intelligentsia constituencies.[69]

New Year's Day TV interviews with regime dignitaries usually had been ceremonial events in Hungary. The interview that Grósz gave on January 1, 1988 was different: it was a declaration of his candidacy for Kádár's position. In the course of an hour-long interview, Grósz presented himself as a man whose political career had been full of the kinds of pitfalls and frustrations that most Hungarians had experienced in the preceding thirty-two years. He made a point of relating, warts and all, his experiences in Miskolc in 1956–7, including the severe reprimand he had received for having collaborated with radical university students and for supporting the idea of a multiparty system in October 1956.

He was bitter about having been unfairly booted out of the central apparat in 1974, and blamed the party's traditions of "faceless leadership" and "artificial unanimity" for the lack of vigorous debates in the HSWP. He admitted that, until recently, in the area of bilateral trade Soviet interests had prevailed at Hungary's expense. However, he was confident that with "more courage," more equitable terms could be arranged with Moscow. In this connection, he called attention to the present institutional system that tended to "obliterate personal responsibility" for political mistakes of all kinds.[70]

The Grósz challenge and the disappointing outcome of the party debates reenergized the Kádárist center. After a month of (unannounced) rest at the Dobogókő party resort, Kádár took to the road on a campaign of county-by-county visits and consultations.[71] His theme was "trust the party and things will turn out right." Thereupon Grósz joined the fray. He went to the same counties and found himself openly contradicting his party's secretary general on many subjects.

When Kádár's statements failed to assuage the apparat's growing alarm over the rapidly deteriorating situation, or to prevent a remarkably high public turnout at the (unauthorized) March 15 demonstration of the democratic opposition, Kádár went on TV on March 17 and assured everyone that he "had not (as some had alleged) been out of touch with the workers," and that "there was no crisis" in Hungary.[72]

The selective intimidation and silencing of internal critics was another measure to restore stability in the party. At the end of February Pozsgay received a written reprimand from the Politburo for having spoken out of turn once too often. A month later Rezső Nyers was severely chastised by Óvári and Berecz for having agreed to lend his name to a new organization, the "New March Front," and was sentenced to two months of "silence" on all controversial subjects. And finally, the Kádár loyalists on the Central Control Commission – by then completely out of sync with the members' views – decided to expel four reform socialists from the party for having taken "positions that were contrary to the party's policies." In April 1988 no one seemed to know what these were.

Negotiated succession: deal-making for a leveraged buyout

In the present context, the term "deal" denotes a complex process of negotiations concerning alliance building, interest reconciliation, program development, strategy coordination, and covert cooperation among several players with a shared interest in leadership and policy change in Hungary. Because the incumbents controlled the political system's top personnel and power resources, they could be overcome, to borrow from the vocabulary of US corporate warfare, only by a strategy of a "leveraged buyout." In this case, the transaction involved, on the one hand, the incumbent chief executive officer (CEO) and his associates in control of the "Board of Directors," and on the other hand, insurgent Board members, regional executives, heads of corporate "subsidiaries" – that is, the policy lobbies – and party member "stockholders." The nonvoting disgruntled "employees" – that is, the Hungarian public – were observing the proceedings on their TVs' evening news program.

The object of the exercise was to obtain proxy votes from the normally passive stockholders and to raise additional "equity financing" from middle-management – that is, the regional party apparat – executives with which to force the incumbents either to resign *en masse* or to yield the majority of seats to the insurgents. The affair also involved "poison pills" for unpopular board members, a "golden parachute" for the deposed CEO, "white knights" in the persons of Imre Pozsgay and Rezső Nyers, and debt refinancing with ideological "junk bonds" in denominations of "renewal," "restructuring," and "stabilization" to serve as "collateral" for the *ex post facto* legitimation of the coup.

Though the business analogy might be worth pursuing as a useful analytical device, the point is that what took place in May 1988 was a negotiated "friendly takeover by insiders" rather than a "raid" by outsiders or by hostile nonparty interests. Because it was essentially an insider transaction – which took place with the full approval of the Soviet "holding company" of which the Hungarian "enterprise" was a heavily indebted subsidiary – the reconstruction of some of the events must, of necessity, be derived from interviews with key actors and nonattributable internal sources, and from the censored public record.

The main elements of the ten-month process between Grósz becoming prime minister and the ouster of Kádár may be characterized in terms of seven tasks addressed by the insurgents prior to the May 1988 "stockholders' meeting."

"To recruit allies"

When Grósz became prime minister, he needed committed allies to assist with the drafting and implementation of his government's program of "stabilization and renewal." Therefore, he sought to enlist constituencies with a demonstrated interest in radical economic reforms and institutional restructuring. His natural allies were the technical–scientific elites, proreform technocrats, senior government officials, the provincial apparat, and the PPF under Imre Pozsgay.

The precise sequence of alliance building, interest reconciliation, and strategy coordination has been reconstructed in a joint study by two colleagues and me.[73] It should suffice to say that by early 1988 the Grósz-led "corporate raiders" had managed to enlist the support of the regional party apparat, the main economic policy lobbies, and the technocratic intelligentsia. These constituencies played a key role in delivering the needed votes at the May 1988 party conference.

"To demoralize the incumbents"

In connection with the twentieth anniversary of the NEM, the Pozsgay "reform network"-controlled print media, and a half-dozen influential economic and literary journals mounted a concerted and, by all appearances, coordinated attack on the Kádár center's policy record since 1972 (November 1987 – January 1988).

"To divide the spoils"

Grósz recalled, "In the course of a one-on-one conversation with Imre Pozsgay in his villa on Lake Balaton, we tried to exchange opinions on the likely personnel changes in the next few years. It was in this context that I mentioned that, should my election as secretary general become inevitable, I would resign as prime minister. In response to Imre Pozsgay's question whether I could envisage him as my successor as prime minister, unfortunately I responded in the affirmative. This became the source of subsequent conflicts between us"[74] (Winter 1987 – Spring 1988).

"To neutralize the incumbents"

At the March 22–24 CC meeting Kádár's candidacy for the chairman-ship of the "operative committee" for the overall coordination of preparations for the May party conference was voted down. The task of preconference coordination was divided between Lukács (methods for the selection of conference delegates) and Berecz (draft theses for party debate and submission to conference).[75]

"To radicalize the stockholders"

In early April Pozsgay offered a radical reform program and declared his candidacy for a leadership position in a "reformed" party in a *Magyar Nemzet* interview.[76] This was followed by a national party debate on the CC's draft theses for the party conference. The Budapest, the Baranya, Komárom, and Borsod county party committees rejected, or substantially amended, the draft theses. So did the PPF, the Academy of Sciences, the TUF, and the YCL.[77]

"To set the terms for the takeover"

The CC meeting of May 10, 1988 was convened to take stock of the party membership's reaction to the conference draft theses. In the debate on the extent of personnel turnover at the party conference, Kádár's proposal for the replacement of one-third of the CC was defeated. A motion by István Tömpe – he had served as president of Hungarian radio and TV when Grósz was party secretary there in the 1960s – for a "complete renewal" of the CC, the PB, and the Secretariat was seconded by Aczél and Maróthy, and adopted by the Central Committee.

The "deal" proper, though several of its ingredients had been in place for some time, was firmed up at the May 10 CC meeting and in the days following. Its substance may be summed up as "political continuity and personnel change" – with compromises on both counts. The principal items were:

Kádár's future. When Kádár realized that he had to go in one way or another, he demanded and obtained guarantees he would not be made the scapegoat for three prominent items in the party's full closet of political skeletons. These were his complicity in the extraction of a confession of guilt from László Rajk in 1949; his role in the 1956 revolution and in the subsequent persecution of many of its prominent participants, especially Imre Nagy and associates; and his political responsibility for the "counterreforms" of the 1970s. The deal: Kádár becomes party chairman (with unspecified duties), retains his membership in the CC, but is excluded from the PB.

The new PB. The agreement called for the departure of Kádár, Aczél, Lázár, and Maróthy; the entry of Miklós Németh, Lukács, Ilona Tatai, Pozsgay, and Nyers; and the continued membership of the possible "swing voters" Szabó, Judit Csehák, and Hámori, and of the Kádárist rear guard: Károly Németh, Óvári, Gáspár, Havasi, and Berecz.

The Central Committee. Though Kádár's proposal for the replacement of one-third of this body had been defeated on May 10, the very same formula was adopted by the principals of the "leveraged-buyout" scheme. On the other hand, most new members came from the Grósz camp and replaced an identical number of Kádárist time servers in the CC.

Károly Grósz as party secretary general and prime minister. The combined resources of these two positions tended to confer exceptional and potentially dictatorial powers on one person. When confronted with this *fait accompli*, Kádár and his supporters in the "unreformed" PB had no choice but to consent to this arrangement.

"To secure approval of the holding company"

By mid-May an agreement was reached between Kádár and Grósz that called for Kádár's resignation and his nomination of Grósz as his successor. Kádár felt compelled to obtain Soviet consent to this agreement. Unwilling to put the matter in writing and insisting on complete secrecy, he asked Moscow that a Hungarian-speaking senior Soviet official come to discuss the matter. Gorbachev dispatched KGB General Vladimir A. Kriuchkov to meet with Kádár in Dobogókő. (Kriuchkov had served as press attaché at the Soviet embassy under Yuri Andropov in 1955–6 and was fluent in Hungarian.) At their meeting Kádár assured him that Grósz enjoyed his full confidence and that he was the right man to succeed him.[78] With Moscow's approval in hand, on May 19 Kádár submitted his resignation as secretary general to the PB. The PB also approved the makeup of the new PB, the Secretariat, the Central Control Commission, and the CC with a membership of 113, of whom thirty-seven would be newly elected.

The Third Conference of the HSWP, May 20–22, 1988

The party conference had three objectives: to facilitate and legitimate the transfer of political leadership from János Kádár to Károly Grósz; to provide an opportunity for the articulation of party elite opinions on current policy problems; and to rally the party membership behind the new leadership's short-term plans for party renewal, economic stabilization, and institutional transformation.[79]

The May conference had been carefully prepared by Grósz, Lukács, and their proxies in the party apparat. However, the original scenario was disrupted by Kádár. Instead of a graceful exit, the conference was treated to a defiant statement of ideological orthodoxy and a resuscitation by Kádár from the late 1950s of such code words as "enemy" and "class struggle" – terms that were thought to have been buried by Kádár himself twenty-five years ago.

The conference delegates' adverse reaction to Kádár's dissonant statements gave Grósz and his allies an opportunity to change, "*Putsch* style," the terms of the May 10 deal on the makeup of the new Politburo. Between late Saturday (May 21) evening and the following morning the Grósz forces contacted either in person or by telephone most delegates, urging them to cross out the names of Lázár, Gáspár, K. Németh, Óvári, and perhaps Havasi from the CC ballot. The majority of the delegates complied with this suggestion and denied a seat on the CC to these five Kádár allies.[80]

For all intents and purposes, the Kádárist party had fallen apart by the end of May 1988. The apparat and the hard-core membership were still there, but the local organizations and the counties were in total disarray.[81] The conference deliberations frightened the party conservatives. They had to be reassured and persuaded to go along with Grósz's new programs. Others in the party had succumbed to illusions of free speech, local autonomy, and other hopeful aspects of "intraparty democracy." They, too, had to be disciplined and brought back to the fold. Grósz and his fellow *Putschists* now had the party and the government and the state's economic resources under their nominal control. As it turned out, they inherited fewer of the assets and many more of the liabilities than they had bargained for.

(C)   Kádár's successors: struggle for power and political survival

The five-year process of internal and public contestation for leadership change and comprehensive reforms, though it achieved the desired political outcome, offered no clear alternative legitimating principles for the future course of Kádár's successors. The Grósz-led apparat insurgents' political dilemmas may best be summarized by citing Grósz's terse response in 1993 interview to a question about what he and his colleagues had hoped to accomplish after removing Kádár from power. As Grósz explained, "we rejected that which existed, but did not know what else might come to replace it."[82] This, as will be shown below, was not a completely truthful answer. What Grósz and his fellow *Putschists* had in mind was political survival by way of an immense salvage operation of the wreck of the old regime.

In what follows, I shall register and analyze the most important political, ideological, and personality components of this process between June 1988 and February 1989. The discussion will focus on the ruling party, on the political strategies of its leading personalities, and on the issues that contributed to the the collapse of the Grósz leadership in the spring of 1989.

The HSWP: reform options and policy priorities

The new leadership's reform strategies and policy priorities were first discussed at the June 14, 1988 (unpublicized) meeting of the PB.[83] The unprecedented number of more than one hundred individual items on the agenda included many subjects ranging from routine personnel decisions to enactment of policies of strategic importance. The main items pertained to the launching of four major task forces: for the drafting of new party statutes (under János Lukács); for economic rescue plans (under Miklós Németh); for a review of the "party's road" in the previous three decades (under Imre Pozsgay); and for the development of a new network of expert advisory groups to convey the views of various social (elite) constituencies to the party leadership (under Rezső Nyers).

Political revitalization and institutional change

All told, the PB set into motion twenty-nine projects for the overhaul of the HSWP, its internal organization, methods of public and intraparty communication, and assorted aspects of its *modus operandi* from the PB down to the local party cells. The PB also "recommended for consideration" eighteen administrative measures to the government, three items to the Parliament, and six projects to the major social organizations.[84] These recommendations, at least in the sense of policy intent, called for the complete reorganization and modernization of all aspects of Hungary's political, social, and economic institutions.

Unlike these medium- to long-term projects, the draft text – long in the works in the Ministry of Justice – of a new law on the freedom of assembly and of association received immediate attention.[85] At issue was formal implementation of the May 1988 party insurgents' vague notions about the institutionalization of "socialist pluralism." The official intent was to issue enabling legislation for Hungary's ratification, by way of a decree of the Presidential Council in 1976, of the Helsinki Final Act of 1975. However, the real question was drawing a line between permitting assorted social groups – be these already authorized policy lobbies, such as the TUF and the YCL, or informal citizen groups – to register with the courts as lawful and autonomous organizational entities and authorizing establishment of new political parties. Under the existing Constitution the HSWP was enshrined as the "leading force of the society," yet a new Constitution – in preparation since the mid-1980s – had not yet been adopted.

The outcome, as with many issues under PB consideration, was inconclusive. Whereas everyone agreed that new political parties were not covered by the ministry's draft, no one objected to the formation of "social groups for political purposes."[86] In any case, nothing was said about the "old," or "historic," political parties, such as the Social Democratic Party, the Smallholders' Party, the Peasant Party, and the rest that had never been formally banned either in the late 1940s or after their brief revival during the 1956 revolution.

To demonstrate the difference between forbidden and tolerated exercise of the right of peaceful assembly and orderly advocacy of political beliefs, the Grósz–György Fejti security team saw to it that some of the more outspoken demonstrators who attempted to commemorate in Budapest the anniversary of Imre Nagy's judicial murder on June 16, 1988 were brutally dispersed by the police.[87] On the other hand, twelve days later the regime stood by and tacitly encouraged a Hungarian Democratic Forum-sponsored mass demonstration with 60,000 participants against the Ceauşescu regime's human rights abuses in Romania.[88]

While the PB was still in the midst of discussing its plans for legal-institutional reforms, a group of fifteen independent MPs submitted to the Parliament's Committee on Law, Justice, and Public Administration what the press promptly labeled as a "democracy package plan."[89] The proposal, which was unanimously rejected by the committee, had been drafted by Pozsgay's reform socialist friends to call Grósz's bluff by showing what *real* democratization and institutional transformation were all about. The plan called for modification of the electoral law, revised parliamentary procedures, new laws on the office of the president of the Republic, the HSWP's constitutional position, the right of assembly and of association, the trade unions, human rights, national minorities, the citizens' initiatives and plebiscites, local self-government, the press, establishment of a constitutional court, office of the citizens' Ombudsman, and the drafting of a new constitution.

Economic strategies

As Miklós Németh explained to the PB and the CC, 1988 was a year of "do or die" for the Hungarian economy.[90] His economic rescue plan was one of several on the party's table.[91] Common to these blueprints and those that were subsequently submitted by the Council for Industrial Policy and the Hungarian Chamber of Commerce was the dual objective of protecting Hungary's external balance of payments and of drastically restructuring the domestic economy. The principal tools for the achievement of the desired results were "market," "monetary control," "decentralization," "deregulation," "privatization," "currency devaluation," and "hard budgetary constraints" on spendthrift enterprises.

An examination of the particulars of each plan reveals a number of unstated assumptions. These may be summarized under four headings:

1 The Hungarian political system was wholly without the will and administrative resources to regulate the economy in a "reform–conform" manner. Only "nonnegotiable" external pressures, such as IMF-mandated spending caps, could prompt the political authorities to act.
2 An effective program of economic stabilization had to be based on the principles of a free market and private enterprise. Neither of these was acceptable to the interpenetrated branch ministry-heavy industry and manufacturing policy lobby and their supporters in the party and state bureaucracy.
3 The state's economic role had to be confined to the amelioration of the social costs – unemployment, welfare, pensions, public health services – of the reform program.
4 Hungary's share of the costs of alliance maintenance – military, internal security, and uneconomical CMEA trade and investment obligations – represented critically important budgetary commitments of unknown magnitude that could thwart any reform program, no matter how well designed.

In political terms, the main consequence of the Hungarian economy's free fall toward insolvency and possible collapse was the complete withdrawal of the party from daily guidance of the economy and, with the passage of time, even from policy guidance. All of this left the government bureaucracy and economic policy lobbies to sort out, as best they could, the country's economic problems. The government opted for policy "liberalization" that included an eclectic package of minor budget cuts, deregulation, currency devaluation, and a free hand for the "red barons" to make the most of new opportunities for decentralization and various schemes of self-privatization.[92] These measures and the partial lifting of wage and price controls set into motion an inflationary cycle and, with it, the further erosion of living standards. As a result, the regime, with the help of yet another round of borrowing from the West, stayed afloat and gained desperately needed time to roll over Hungary's economic burdens to whatever political force might emerge after the next elections.

Foreign policy options

Leadership change in Hungary, though promptly endorsed by Moscow, evoked critical reactions from some of the still unreformed East European ruling parties. Bucharest's suspicions about the ideological soundness of Kádár's successors were soon confirmed by the regime-tolerated anti-Ceauşescu demonstrations in late June. The ready closing of the Hungarian consular office in the Transylvanian city of Cluj and expulsion of its diplomatic personnel were the opening salvo in what became an undeclared media war between the two regimes in the next several weeks. Pending Grósz's scheduled courtesy visits in those capitals, East Berlin, Prague, and Sofia withheld critical comments on Hungarian events.

It was against this background that Grósz's first official working visit with Gorbachev took place on July 4–5, 1988. At that point what Grósz needed was not yet another pat on the back but positive Soviet response to a long list of Hungarian requests for economic aid and foreign policy concessions. As may be gleaned from Grósz's official reports to the PB and the CC, he was cordially received in Moscow. He was told, so he declared, that the kind of transformation that had taken place in Hungary was "an objective phenomenon in the development of socialist states," regardless, as Gorbachev put it, of "what they might say in the GDR and however silent they chose to remain in Romania."[93]

The Hungarian wish list included the continued delivery, on current levels, of oil and gas supplies until 1995, the import of advanced Soviet machine tools, and the diminution of the growing Hungarian trade surplus with the USSR by the prompt delivery of goods in demand in Hungary. Grósz also pleaded for Soviet consent to substantial cuts in Hungary's projected defense budget for 1990 and expressed his appreciation for the improvement in the condition of Hungarian ethnic minorities living in western Ukraine. Gorbachev promised to look into these matters but, in return, asked for a favor. As he explained, he had been notified by Ceaușescu that the Romanian leader intended to go on record at the next WTO summit meeting about the USSR's alleged rightist political-ideological deviations. Gorbachev also expected Ceaușescu to try to force the CPSU to take sides in the Romanian–Hungarian dispute. The favor consisted of Grósz's consenting to meet with Ceaușescu to sort out their disagreements. Grósz agreed and cited Gorbachev's satisfaction with his "politically wise" response.[94]

Grósz also felt it necessary to inform the CC that Gorbachev had been aware of his plans to visit the United States and hinted that the trip enjoyed Moscow's support. By exhibiting a high profile in foreign affairs, Grósz was anxious to prove that the doors that had been closed to Kádár were open to him as Hungary's new leader. However, he failed to realize that he was about to walk into two traps – one in the United States, one in Romania – of his own making.

In the course of Grósz's visit in the United States in late July, he met both with officials – including President Reagan – and with representatives of the Hungarian community. To the latter, in a somewhat pathetic attempt to ingratiate himself, he made several statements that he had not cleared with his colleagues in the PB.[95] Among other matters, he consented to the reburial of Imre Nagy and agreed to look into the current relevance of certain historic problems, such as "the events of 1956."

Grósz's measure as national leader was taken at the end of August when he, armed with advice from the anxious PB and briefing material from the Foreign Ministry, accepted Ceausescu's invitation for a one-day meeting in the Transylvanian city of Arad. Among the several accounts of what took place on that day, even the most charitable would hold Grósz responsible for arrogance, ignorance, and lack of elementary prudence in his dealings with the wily Romanian leader. Instead of a businesslike exchange of ideas, Ceauşescu, in a brilliant display of diplomatic one-upmanship, browbeat the hapless Grósz and conceded nothing to his Hungarian comrade. Moreover, Grósz agreed to the exclusion of his own CC foreign secretary Szűrös, from a one-on-one dialogue with his host. At the end of the day, and subsequently on a Hungarian radio program, he proudly declared that there had been a meeting of minds. Unfortunately for Grósz, everyone understood that all this happened not on Grósz's but on Ceauşescu's terms.[96]

The Arad fiasco cost Grósz whatever prestige he may have had as head of the Hungarian government. He also lost (to Pozsgay) the support of the Hungarian Democratic Forum. As Grósz later recalled, the HDF leadership's stinging denunciation of his role at the Arad meeting put an end to a promising partnership between the HSWP's "pragmatic" leaders, that is, himself and György Aczél, who had been his go-between with the Populist intellectuals and the HDF.[97] Kádár would never have accepted Gorbachev's gambit, let alone agree to meet his long-time foe on Ceauşescu's terms and on Romanian soil. By early fall 1988 it became painfully obvious that the dual burden of party and government responsibilities well exceeded Grósz's modest talents as the nation's political leader.

Struggle for power: personal strategies, dissonant voices, and political realignment

Having issued a vast number of resolutions, decisions, and political instructions to the party, the government, the Parliament, and the policy lobbies, the new leadership left town for trips abroad and well-earned month-long vacations. However, none of these measures were seen as positive responses to widespread public expectations of immediate results. The apparat's "mood reports" on the (nonvacationing) rank-and-file party membership spoke of high initial hopes and growing impatience with the regime's lackadaisical responses to such burning issues as inflation and the threat of unemployment in the coming months.[98]

As far as it can be reconstructed from memoirs, interviews, and the published evidence, the leadership's real agenda had little in common with satisfaction of public demands for higher living standards and political stability. The real issue was the leaders' individual political survival between the summer of 1988 and the spring of 1990 when the mandate of the incumbent legislature would expire and new elections were to be held. The public, in effect, was written off and would be treated by the leadership as an object of manipulation rather than as politically empowered participants in "renewal," "transformation," and "democratization" in the next eighteen months.[99]

Each major player of the Kádár succession process – Károly Grósz, Imre Pozsgay, János Berecz, Rezső Nyers, and Miklós Németh – sought to carve out a niche for himself on the political map of Hungary. The object was to build a personal political power base for the inevitable *next* round of contestation for leadership and secure institutional sinecures. The principal actors' political strategies may be summarized as follows.

Károly Grósz was prudent enough to realize that, of the two main levers of power, he had to surrender one sooner or later. In his view, the state was a sinking ship, whereas the party, even if it were to lose one-fourth to one-third of its membership in the coming months, would still remain the largest organized political force in Hungary.[100] György Fejti's blueprints for electoral reforms, though they implicitly allowed for the involvement of other – preferably semi-coopted and politically tame – parties, still left the HSWP in a dominant position. Grósz also could depend on Gorbachev's continued support – his new emissary to Hungary was now Aleksandr N. Yakovlev instead of Egor Ligachev – to fend off anyone who might challenge the secretary general's authority. Moreover, Grósz held many political IOUs from the party's unreformed provincial apparat and, he hoped, from the military and the police as well.

Imre Pozsgay's position as a PB member and minister of state with line authority over the media and responsibility for official liaison with the dissidents and the reform intelligentsia may be likened to that of the fox in a chicken coop. On the one hand, as a PB member, he was now freed from backbiting by the apparat and criticism in the party press. On the other hand, he had a choice between "keeping [on the party's behalf] the dissidents on a leash" – as Jenő Fock had characterized Pozsgay's usefulness for a leadership position at the June 23, 1988 CC meeting – or going into business for himself by recruiting all nonparty constituencies behind his eventual candidacy for the position of president of the Republic.[101]

The job description for this position had been a part of the parliamentary independents' "democracy package." Pozsgay's carefully cultivated image as an "integrative personality" was confirmed by the opinion polls. According to an August 1988 survey, of the party's leaders he was, on a scale of 1 to 100, the most popular, at 73 points. He was followed by Berecz, 70; Grósz, 69; Kádár, 67; and Nyers, 65.[102] In any case, Pozsgay's strategy was to "transcend divisive party politics" and to eschew any state administrative responsibility. In doing so, he sought to avoid head-on confrontation with Grósz and to stay away from organizational tasks, for which, as will be shown in Chapter 8, he had no aptitude whatsoever.

János Berecz's share of the May insurgents' political booty consisted of the preservation of his dual PB membership and line secretary position and his assignment as the party spokesman (*szóvivő*), a fruit of Soviet *glasnost'* in the HSWP. Because of Grósz's preoccupation with affairs of state, the party apparat was left in Berecz's and János Lukács' care, as was the responsibility to reenergize the party faithful with the brave rhetoric of reform socialism. Similar to Grósz's, Berecz's survival strategy focused on keeping the party membership together – with the major difference that the logic of Berecz' scheme called for his hastening, and if that did not work awaiting, the collapse of the incumbent secretary general's position and replacing Grósz at the helm. In fact, Berecz's ambitions went beyond the party's leadership. At first, he argued for keeping both party and state top positions in one hand.[103]

Rezső Nyers' presence in the PB symbolized the Kádárist NEM reform genesis of the Grósz team. He was a low-key, amiable party veteran and a kind of self-appointed heir to the pragmatic traditions of the "historic" HSDP. Thus, he was ideally suited to legitimate the "reformed" HSWP in the eyes of the technocratic intelligentsia and those with a nostalgic yearning for the pretotalitarian days. With the help of his New March Front, another throwback to the Popular Front of the 1930s in Hungary, Nyers was well positioned to serve as an honest broker between the suspicious party apparat and the wishful public that hoped for the return of the era of low inflation, full employment, and "small freedoms" for the man in the street. In October 1988, Nyers became the hero of the reform intelligentsia when he, alone in the PB, chose to abstain from voting in the Parliament on the controversial Gabčikovo-Nagymaros Slovak–Hungarian hydroelectric project. (Pozsgay voted in favor of this measure – as he told me afterwards – "to remain as a part of the political leadership.")[104]

Miklós Németh was the junior member of the Grósz team. As he explained in a disarmingly candid biographical interview, as a junior faculty member at the Karl Marx University for Economics, he had found that he could not support his family on his university salary, and that was why he had accepted an offer to work in the CC apparat.[105] In terms of his political career, Németh was the valedictorian of the class of the "Dimitrov Square boys" (where the KMU was located). The point is that this well-spoken, highly intelligent – and partly Harvard-trained – economist never took a controversial ideological position and had no political enemies in the party and the government. Moreover, just like the reluctant Grósz in 1984, Németh professed to having no leadership ambitions beyond that of doing justice to the job that he was assigned by his administrative superior. He was the logical successor to Grósz as the next prime minister of Hungary.

In the summer and fall of 1988, each of these politicians gave speeches and interviews and went on record with his interpretation of the tasks and priorities facing the regime. The newly emancipated CC took notice of what the members perceived as a singular lack of unanimity among senior PB members on several fundamental policy issues and demanded an inquiry. Thereupon Grósz commissioned an in-house study by the CC Department of AP on public statements made by PB members in the preceding three months.

The 43-page collage of quotes from statements made by PB members and a 30-page analytical digest of what party members thought of their leaders' rhetoric was an alarming document. It revealed that the party's top officials held diametrically opposed views that neither party members nor the general public could reconcile with what they read in *Népszabadság* editorials.[106]

On the subject of ideologies, Grósz thought "it was not Marxism that proved to be a worthles doctrine ... but our ability to adapt it." He went on, "that which is capitalism in socialism is capitalism, and that which is communism is communism. These should not be confused with one another." In a less Delphic manner Csaba Hámori called communism "a utopia," whereas Németh considered the "coexistence of state, cooperative and private property and [unearned] income from capital" as the "essence" of socialism.

About the party, Grósz believed that it "should not belong to the workers alone," while Nyers characterized it as a "united workers' party" – unlike Pozsgay, who thought that it was an organization that "ought to be controlled by nonparty people." Whereas Grósz asserted that the party had "the right to dismiss the government," Berecz finessed the issue by calling attention to the new partnership of the party, government, the legislature, and the judiciary that he called "socialist pluralism." Standing apart from his less adventurous colleagues, Pozsgay submitted that a "multiparty system was not inconceivable in Hungary."

Whereas Grósz thought that the closing of the Hungarian consulate in Cluj and Hungarian cultural facilities elsewhere in Romania had been "matters of principle" for his Romanian colleagues, and thus "could not be helped," Pozsgay spoke of the "insane politics of Romania." In June 1988, speaking to an assembly of the Workers' Guards, Grósz still referred to the opposition as the "enemy"; three months later Pozsgay went on record extolling the possibilities of "cooperation between the HDF and the government."[107]

Perhaps the unkindest cuts sustained by the party faithful were statements made by the improbable trio of Imre Pozsgay, Csaba Hámori, and György Aczél at a political happening in mid-September. The affair was called "Reform Party Evenings," and was held before large crowds of students at the Technical University of Budapest.[108] Following a series of heretical radical reform statements by the three party notables, Hámori announced his resignation as the first secretary of the YCL and the forthcoming dissolution of this organization. Apparently, he had not cleared either announcement with the PB, of which he was a member, and to which, by party statutes, the YCL reported. In the fall of 1988 the CC had every reason to be concerned about the lack of unity in its top ranks.

The HSWP at the crossroads: "red terror" or political pluralism?

The regime's apparent free fall toward public confrontations among the leaders and political chaos was temporarily halted at the November 1–2, 1988 meeting of the CC. The party's premier deliberative body received and discussed the PB's theses on "the internal political situation and the party's tasks."[109] The bluntly worded document spoke of the "eroding legitimacy of the party and the government" and concluded that as far as the extent of institutional and policy changes was concerned, "the Stalinist model still existed in Hungary."[110] The real problem was the escalation of "reform rhetoric without structural change" whilst the party was still captive to "extreme centralization" and its provincial organs were crippled by "corruption cases" and conservative (in Hungarian: *fundamentalista*) resistance to internal reforms. Moreover, there were "daily tensions," on the one hand, between the party and the government, and between these two institutions and the TUF, the YLC, and the PPF, on the other.

Who governs? From "rearguard" to "dual power"

The proposed remedy, which the CC eventually endorsed, consisted of the regime's swimming with the tide and acceding to the inevitable. In specific terms, the CC accepted the *de facto* rebirth of political pluralism, the lifting of censorship, and the party's surrender of all but a few unspecified components of its political privileges to the government. Thus, with the exception of the three "security ministries" (Internal, Foreign Affairs, and Defense) the rest of the party center's traditional privileges of political decisions, including legislative initiatives, economic policies, personnel decisions – save about five hundred positions still under PB and CC *nomenklatura* control – now belonged to the government.

To become more responsive to the coming political changes, the central party apparat was reorganized and became, in effect, the secretary general's personal political machine. Grósz retained for himself direct authority over state administrative, legislative, internal security, and foreign affairs matters and hands-on control of the key mass organizations and the Workers' Guard. To assuage concerns about the concentration of the regime's coercive resources in one hand, the reorganization scheme also decreed that the "officers [that is, members of the PB and the secretaries] of the CC were sovereign politicians and not parts of the apparat."[111]

In case Grósz failed to understand that the majority of the CC was committed to *peaceful* methods of managing conflicts between the regime and the new "alternative" political organizations, Pozsgay's friend István Horváth, the minister of interior (and chair of the party-government National Defense Council), related an intriguing story to his fellow CC members. As Horváth explained, in early September Grósz had called him inquiring whether he would authorize the use of firearms by the police against environmental demonstrators before the Parliament building. No action was taken, but the entire affair prompted Horváth to offer an extended discourse on the regime's, as he put it, "prudent and restrained" traditional posture on nonviolent political dissent. His conclusion was that the reaching out to the nonparty masses and peaceful dialogue with the "alternatives" were the *only* methods of handling political dissent and social protest.[112]

As he had promised at the May conference, Grósz relinquished his position as prime minister in early November. For a successor, the PB recommended three candidates: Miklós Németh, Pál Iványi, and Imre Pozsgay. As Grósz explained to the closed November 22, 1988, session of the CC, he had taken two polls: one of the 95 members of the CC, and another of 264 party-member MPs. Miklós Németh came in first in both polls. Because Nyers received sixty-eight votes from the MPs – six more than Pozsgay – or because Pozsgay needed to be put in his place in the government, Nyers was also nominated as minister of state with unspecified responsibilities.[113]

Not to be outdone, two days later Pozsgay submitted to the Parliament, on the government's behalf, a legislative agenda of twenty items – including the independent MPs' entire fifteen-point "democracy package" of July 1988.[114] From then on, the initiation and implementation of public policy was in the hands of the Parliament and the Hungarian government.

Kto kogo? *Grósz's last stand*

In late November 1988 Lenin's classic question "Who shall prevail?" became the central issue of Hungarian politics. November 29 is an important date in the history of the old regime's collapse. On that day a group of party intellectuals in Szeged announced formation of the HSWP's first "Reform Circle."[115] It was also the day when Károly Grósz gave a major two-hour policy address at a mass rally of the Budapest party organization.[116] Unlike his usually carefully prepared speeches, this was an election-campaign-style diatribe that sought to appeal to the emotions of the frustrated middle-aged and elderly audience of party activists.

Grósz's main point was that the reform process had gotten out of hand and that the threat of "White terror" was looming on the horizon. Although a week earlier he had conceded to his PB colleagues that the one-party system was "untenable,"[117] Grósz assured his cheering listeners that the one-party system, albeit in a somewhat "pluralistic form," was there to stay. On the following day Berecz – ever anxious not to be left behind – declared to a group of 1,500 Tatabánya miners that there was a "revolutionary crisis" and that Hungary was at a "revolutionary crossroads."[118]

What happened? Why speak of "White terror" at a time when the rest of the leadership was on record as endorsing major political changes, including the *de facto* acceptance of noncommunist political parties? This was Grósz's reply five years later:

> At the time [of the November 29 speech] many of us knew that the party's disintegration was unavoidable. This speech merely sought to indicate the kinds of dangers that the change of regime would entail. It was a warning, if you will. I agree that I could have made my point in a more subtle fashion, but that would not have changed the essence of the situation. There was abundant evidence that the change of regime would be followed by tough showdowns (*leszámolás*). A politician must speak of this. I will not offer proof [of this likelihood] ... but speeches by [the HDF politician] Imre Kónya [in September, 1991(!)], Viktor Orbán [of Fidesz, in June 1989], the III/III affair [the exposure of the internal security organs in January 1990] and the way the 1956 shootings (*sortüzek*) were approached [by groups of veteran "freedom fighters" in 1989–90] were evidence that this part of my speech – even as cited out of context – was fully justified.[119]

Unlike Grósz, the party's reform wing, much of the rank-and-file membership, the intellectuals, and the country at large saw no justification for crying fire in the country's crowded political theatre. Therefore, an explanation of Grósz's conduct must be sought elsewhere. As Grósz explained in a letter and at a follow-up interview in June 1994, upon becoming prime minister in the summer of 1987, he had begun making two kinds of preparations for emergencies. The first included drafting measures to manage, by way of an economic-crisis regime, the worst-case scenario of a total economic collapse. The other standby plan pertained to the regime's political collapse and imposition of a martial law regime.

Although Grósz declined to elaborate on the details of these plans, the latter was to be prepared and managed by his "personal consultants" and György Fejti's staff at the CC's Department of Law and Public Administration. From this one could infer that the Grósz–Fejti team expected support from the Workers' Guards (perceived, incorrectly as it turned out, as the Hungarian version of the Polish ZOMOs), the "Revolutionary Battalions" of the riot police, and the socialist *Lumpenproletariat* of the factory- and mines-based "Ferenc Münnich Socialist Brigade" movement.[120]

In the end, the preparations came to naught. It appears that István Horváth's Ministry of Interior was aware of the plans and refused to join the cabal. Moreover, if Horváth's ministry knew, then the resident Soviet KGB advisors were also in the know.[121] By that time Gorbachev had enough problems on his hands not to condone a leftist coup in Hungary. In any case, since 1956 even the Soviet hard-liners had had a healthy respect for the volatile Hungarian public. The Hungarian military – quite demoralized, because of major internal corruption scandals in 1988–9 – was concerned mainly with the perceived threat posed by Romania and had no desire to reenact the role of the uniformed vigilante squads (*pufajkások*) of 1956–7.

The rest of the world was also keeping an eye on Hungarian developments. As Grósz explained, "from early 1989 on, I could not trust members of the party's [top] elected bodies," adding that "Miklós Németh felt aggrieved that he was denied a role in the preparations [for the introduction of a martial law regime] ... I told him that it would amount to my asking Mr. [Mark] Palmer, the American ambassador to Hungary, to join my team." Németh was Palmer's regular tennis partner and, as Grósz put it, "whatever went on in the PB, Palmer heard about it next morning."[122]

Grósz's belated attempt to tarnish Németh's reputation – since 1991 Németh has been serving as vice-president of the European Bank for Reconstruction and Development in London – may be a part of a personal feud between two semiretired communist politicians. However, the fact remains that Grósz's notorious November 29 speech introduced an element of uncertainty into the confused but otherwise peacefully unfolding process of Hungary's political transformation. The party's "fundamentalist" hard core was desperate and dangerous people who, if given a chance, might have turned the clock back to 1957–9.[123]

"Counterrevolution" or "popular uprising"? – showdown and compromise

According to CC protocol under Kádár, in the absence of the secretary general his deputy was in charge of political affairs, including preemptive censorship over policy statements made by senior officials. Grósz had no designated deputy, therefore in his absence such statements were left to the individual discretion of his colleagues. At the end of January 1989 Grósz was in Switzerland to attend the annual economic summit of the Western business community in Davos. On January 27 Pozsgay decided to take advantage of the unavailability of his party superior and arranged for an interview with Hungarian radio's popular "168 hours" program. Through some advance coaching of his interviewers, he had them ask about the preliminary findings of his CC-appointed committee to study the regime's history since 1956.[124] In the course of the interview Pozsgay made several provocative statements. Of these, two stood out and shook the regime to its very foundations.

Although he evaded the question about the role that Imre Nagy had played in 1956, he stated on his committee's behalf that what had taken place in October–November 1956 was a "popular uprising" rather – though he left it unsaid – than a "counterrevolution." To the question "Will the HSWP try to coexist with another party?" Pozsgay replied: "we must learn [to coexist] with not only one but two or several parties. The HSWP cannot, nor does it wish to, dictate as to what kind of partnership will come about, or what kind of opposition would emerge among those who do not wish to join a coalition."[125]

Opinions may differ on the wisdom and timing of these statements. However, there can be no doubt that it took a great deal of political courage to confront Grósz with the public rejection of two of the regime's core legitimating principles. If 1956 was *not* a counterrevolution, then much of the Kádárist record, especially the regime's bloody origins, were at best mistakes or at worst crimes against the Hungarian people and the party's best sons, who perished at the gallows. Moreover, if the HSWP was thus dethroned as the "leading force of the society," what was it? A criminal conspiracy, or the crumbling pillar of a vanishing "all-people's consensus"?

Upon his return to Hungary, the visibly nonplussed Grósz was faced with several dilemmas. Now that Pozsgay had called his bluff about the danger of "White terror," should he activate his scenario for a martial law regime? If so, would his senior associates support him? And, what is more important, how would the people react to a major attack, such as Pozsgay's expulsion from the CC and the party, on Hungary's most popular socialist politician? Although he had an armful of Telex messages from the party faithful condemning Pozsgay, at the January 31 meeting of the PB he chose to temporize by deferring action to the next meeting of the CC on February 11, 1989.[126]

In the meantime, several things happened that helped shape the eventual outcome of Pozsgay's "January surprise" in Hungarian politics.

Although most of Pozsgay's fellow historical fact finders on his committee chose to distance themselves from his terse "unscientific" characterization of the events of 1956, there was no one willing to stand up for the Kádárist epithet of "counterrevolution." However, those who took issue with Pozsgay's formulation on general political grounds included Miklós Németh, Rezső Nyers, and many fence-sitters from the political Establishment.

While Grósz was sorting out his options, Soviet ambassador Boris Stukalin and US ambassador Mark Palmer each paid publicized visits to the besieged secretary general. Grósz chose not to reveal what his Soviet comrade had in mind, but allowed that Palmer had urged him to refrain from taking hasty actions of unspecified nature. As Palmer recalled, "we personally advised Mr. Grósz and others with responsibility for security matters [in Hungary] as to the likely consequences of [coercive measures]. At [various] critical junctures, at the prodding of opposition leaders, I assured him that neither he nor incumbents like him would be jailed or persecuted in the future."[127]

With these assurances in hand, Grósz convened a strategy meeting in early February to discuss the regime's policy options. By that time, the leadership had about a dozen unsolicited and several officially commissioned detailed scenarios on ways to manage the policy dilemmas of the preelection (1990) period. Some of the unsolicited plans, such as the independent MPs' "democracy package," were quite specific. Others, such as those of the HDF, the democratic opposition, the New March Front, the "historic" parties, and assorted civic groups and critical statements by individual opposition politicians were mainly random lists of political hopes.

The regime's own rescue plans included lengthy legal-constitutional treatises, such as the one by law professors Géza Kilényi, Kálmán Kulcsár, and Tamás Sárközy,[128] and several studies commissioned from the party's Institute for the Social Sciences that had been coordinated, at Aczél's request, by the political scientist Csaba Gombár. Also there were policy drafts developed by the CC departments under Grósz, Berecz, and Lukács, as well as one from the CC's Party Academy that had been written under the supervision of its rector, CC member Pál Romány.[129] These internal documents covered contingencies ranging from a civil war to the regime's total surrender and the handing over of all power to the opposition.

The participants of the strategy meeting – Grósz, Berecz, Lukács,

Aczél, Pál Iványi, and their principal aides – tried to sort out the possibilities but could not reach agreement. In the end, Aczél came forth with what he asserted was a compromise solution. According to Romány's aide who represented his principal at the meeting, Aczél's version called for immediate reforms of the regime's "monolithic power structure." Aczél rejected any political backsliding (martial law?) and recommended that the incumbent leadership promptly implement the necessary reform measures. As this eyewitness put it, Aczél's blueprint, which the rest of the group chose to adopt, "called for the transfer of power" to the new political forces. In any case, this observer was convinced that the surrender of power to the opposition had been a "done deal" among the top leaders well before February 1989.[130]

The two-day, February 10–11, 1989, meeting of the CC was awaited with a sense of anxious anticipation by the Hungarian public. Because neither the people nor the majority of the CC had been privy to details of previous understandings, let alone "done deals" among the party leaders, there was widespread speculation as to the outcome of the Pozsgay affair. As the intellectuals saw it, after the January 29 bombshell not only Pozsgay's position but the future of the reform process was at stake.

The CC meeting consisted in part of well-rehearsed leadership rhetoric and in part of a spontaneous political morality play.[131] In his opening statement Grósz made it clear that the PB was seeking a compromise solution: Pozsgay would be taken to the CC's wood shed for a tongue-lashing and the thus chastised colleague would be kept on board as a valued member of the leadership. The secretary general was a keen student of opinion polls. Given Pozsgay's "sympathy" rating of 75, as against Németh's and Nyers' 66 and Grósz's 48, in a January 17–22 poll, it would have been an act of folly to expel the HSWP's top vote getter from the party.[132] Grósz accordingly concluded that "Comrade Pozsgay's announcement was premature" and asked that the CC share the PB's "political confidence" in him.[133]

Turning to substantive matters, Grósz submitted that the leadership chose to interpret the resolution of the May conference on "socialist pluralism" as a political mandate to open the gates for the development of a multiparty political system.[134] By the latter he meant a political matrix in which the HSWP would preserve its capacity "to shape a multi-party system that [will be] amenable to [our] influence."[135] Because Grósz and the PB were convinced that the HSWP could "retain its power in the coming years," they recommended that the party take the lead in effecting a "controlled division of power" with the noncommunist political forces on two conditions: the acceptance of "socialism" by all as a dominant ideological paradigm, and Hungary's continued adherence to the military alliance system to which the state, by valid treaty, belonged. As Grósz broadly hinted, these terms also enjoyed Gorbachev's support.

For the record, the leadership's timetable for implementation of the transition called for five steps: the enactment of a law on plebiscites (summer 1989); the enactment of a new Constitution and its public approval by plebiscite (winter 1989); election of the president of the Republic (spring 1990); national elections (summer 1990); and the holding of a party congress (fall 1990).[136]

In the course of the extended debate on Pozsgay's characterization of the events of 1956, the CC split into four groups. Of the forty-three speakers, only five (Ferenc Tőkei, Gyula Horn, Iván Berend, Rezső Nyers, and Miklós Németh) endorsed, with minor qualifications, Pozsgay's stance. The rest were divided into thirteen sharply critical, fifteen critical, and ten noncommittal speakers. The "morality play" aspect of the proceedings took the form of assorted party veterans – Gyula Kállai, István Sarlós, György Aczél, and others – offering ideological pieties to justify their personal conduct in 1956 and the succeeding thirty-three years. Well-rehearsed rhetoric came from Grósz's and Pozsgay's few supporters. They knew that what Pozsgay had said needed to be said sooner or later. They and the (mainly silent) PB also knew that the unreformed party was beyond redemption in early 1989.[137]

Throughout the heated discussion the unrepentant Pozsgay held his own and delivered solid counterpunches at his critics. Perhaps his best line was "I see nothing scandalous about our debates [today] ... What is a hundred times more scandalous is that all the mistaken decisions in the past fifteen years had been made by unanimous votes of elected bodies ... [including] those cast in the PB since 1974."[138] At least one-fourth of those present had, as CC members, gone along with the removal of Nyers, Fock, and Fehér from the leadership in 1974. With this comment, the potential CC lynching party was brought to heel.

In the end, Grósz had no difficulties in obtaining the CC's consent to a bland official statement on Pozsgay and to an equally matter-of-fact communiqué on the inauguration of the era of multiparty politics in Hungary. However, what was not made public included the appointment of a PB-CC negotiating committee to work with representatives of the new parties and of an internal work team to review "the working methods" of the party's leading organs. As will be shown in the next chapter, both had a critical role to play in the final few months of the ruling party's history.

Conclusions

The process of political succession in the HSWP was both the cause and the consequence of the ruling party's decline and subsequent disintegration in 1989. Once Kádár decided against the use of Andropov's methods to revitalize the economy and belatedly to reenact one of his neighbors' scenarios of "normalization," "systematization," or a martial law regime, the eventual political outcome was inevitable. Kádár's temporizing and the bureaucratic paralysis of the party and state organs gave way to halfhearted attempts at domestic "escape forward" strategies.

Political experiments, such as the 1985 multicandidate elections, the workers' involvement in the selection of enterprise managers, and the handing over of *nomenklatura* decisions to local party organizations, created space for new entrants into Hungarian politics. The policy lobbies, the political and social elites of provincial Hungary, and the regime's democratic, Populist, and reform socialist critics rushed in to fill the void. Each had an agenda of its own that was at odds with the Kádárist vision of building socialism in Hungary. Thanks to these new social forces, the thitherto dependably deferential social consensus of subject-citizens behind the "good king's" political goals was denied to the "autarch in decline." In a political sense, Kádár's burial took place not on July 14, 1989, but in December 1986 on the TV screen in the living room of the Hungarian citizen.

Kádár's greatest fault as a leader was that he considered himself indispensable, therefore irreplaceable. Some of his motives were self-serving; the rest were typical of the pathologies of ageing dictators. As the survivor of fratricidal struggles for power in his party, Kádár could ill afford the laying bare of his record while he still wanted to stay in power. It was only in the last months of his life that he owned up to the crushing psychological burden of his role in the deaths of László Rajk and Imre Nagy – he called it "my personal tragedy" – and of his error in summarily labeling the events of October 1956 as a "counter-revolution."[139] All of this, as contributing factors to a self-fulfilling prophecy, helped reinforce his tragic sense of personal destiny as a loyal party worker who must serve the cause of socialism until his dying day.[140]

Still, the person of János Kádár, both as a willful politician and as an "autarch in decline," was central to the timing, manner, and sequence of policy decisions that led to his downfall in May 1988. Whereas Kádár's choice of a successor was consistent with his personal values and ideological preferences, his reluctance to give up his power without a fight hinted at his deep-seated fear of having to account for his personal record to the party's successor generation. In the end, with the crumbling of the economic props under Kádár's "soft dictatorship" and of his confidence in the viability of socialism in the Soviet bloc, Kádár became a stranger to the system of his own creation. None of his successors, though they outclassed him as political tactician (Grósz) and ideological innovator (Pozsgay), had Kádár's sure grasp of what the working people of Hungary expected of the regime. Thus, as will be shown in the next two chapters, neither could profit from Kádár's legacy during the coming political struggles of 1989–90.

7   Negotiated revolution: from the Opposition Roundtable to the National Roundtable

The year 1989 has been called *annus mirabilis*. The phrase is apt but, like the labels "velvet," "stormy," and, indeed, "negotiated" that chroniclers have used to characterize the Czech, East German, and Hungarian events of that year, it can be misleading. Ascriptions of miraculousness ought to be treated with skepticism. According to Catholic Church traditions, claims of miraculous cures are investigated and verified by an *advocatus diaboli*. The proof of divine intervention lies, *inter alia*, in the full and permanent restoration of one's health. In the present context one would understand speedy replacement of the old regimes and the instauration of democratic pluralism, the rule of law, and a market economy. In the early 1990s the new democracies of Eastern Europe, Hungary included, were in the early stages of recovery from the ravages of communist rule. Five years later the prognosis is prolonged convalescence and a tendency to relapse into previous pathologies.

Founding myths are essential for the legitimation of a newly born political system. Tales of heroism by courageous individuals taking on the old tyrant, the drama of overcoming the oppressor on smoldering barricades, and the cathartic climax of the people's victory over the villainous despots are strands from which the fabric of myths is woven.[1] Whereas the fall of the Berlin Wall and the Romanian people's epic confrontation with the fleeing Ceauşescus' palace guard were moments of exultation, the collapse of the communist regimes elsewhere was protracted and anticlimactic. At the end, there was rejoicing in Wenceslas Square, in Kossuth Square, and throughout Poland. Yet, the psychological rewards of having become free peoples were soon dimmed by the hardships of daily life throughout the region. Therefore, instead of searching for miracles, the chronicler ought to extract facts from the mist of glowing accounts that still serve as explanations for what had occurred in that special year in East European history.

The general trends of systemic change in the 1980s in communist party-states showed unambiguous evidence of political entropy, economic stagnation, and rising social discontent. However, none of these symptoms of decline had been a conclusive predictor of the East European regimes' collapse by the end of 1989.[2] At that time the available political options for Hungary still provided for several possible outcomes, ranging from "more of the same" to sharp clashes between the people and the regime.

With respect to transition contingencies, the correlation of political and social forces in Hungary in the late 1980s included three constant and several variable, therefore inherently unpredictable, factors. What seemed a given was the incumbents' evident desire to share with the opposition political responsibility for the shortfalls of the Kádárist legacy of economic and social policies. On the other hand, the ruling party's endorsement of political pluralism and Grósz's offer to open negotiations with the "alternatives" contained no provisions for either good-faith negotiations or guarantees relative to the terms of future power sharing with the noncommunist political parties.

Another constant was the top Hungarian party leaders' divergent, yet at least at that time not necessarily irreconcilable, personal political ambitions. As Kádár's political and ideological heirs, Grósz, Pozsgay, Németh, Berecz, and Nyers had much in common. They had not been destined to find themselves at opposite ends of the political arena by the end of the year. Until mid-1989 there was still ample room for compromise among the incumbents.

The third constant was the shared objective of all opposition forces to avoid public confrontations with the regime and to come to terms with the powers that be at the bargaining table. As Péter Tölgyessy, one of the key negotiators at the National Roundtable, explained five years later, "The alternative to a negotiated transition would have been pressure from the streets. This form of mass pressure was alien to Hungary's political culture in the late Kádár era."[3] The tacit agreement between the outgoing and incoming political elites to exclude the "streets" from their negotiations made political sense. Above all, it permitted both sides to speak for their respective – the no longer and the not yet existing – constituencies without being second-guessed by the subjects of the exercise.

The principal variable of the Hungarian transition was the likely behavior of actors with the capacity to interfere with the secret and public negotiations between the old and new political elites. The internal actors were the several policy lobbies and their rank-and-file memberships that were denied either a seat or veto power at the bargaining table. As will be discussed below, the essential role of the "third side" at the National Roundtable (NRT) was that of symbolic representation of nonelite constituencies. The HSWP treated spokesmen of the "third side" not as the regime's natural allies but as nonvoting proxies of their vast but politically disenfranchised membership.

External actors that were salient to the outcome of the NRT negotiations included the Soviet Union, Hungary's neighbors, particularly Poland, Romania, and the GDR, and the Western political community, most prominently the United States. At critical junctures each of these external actors contributed, in one way or another, to the form and content of the NRT agreement of September 18, 1989. For example:

1 Without the initiation on February 6, 1989 and the successful conclusion on April 5, 1989 of the Polish National Roundtable, Grósz and the PB would have hesitated to initiate a similar process in Hungary.

2 Without Aleksandr Yakovlev's and the KGB's possibly uncoordinated but nevertheless maladroit meddling in the Grósz–Pozsgay–Nyers rivalry in the spring and summer of 1989, Grósz might have survived the reformers' challenge at the October party congress.

3 Without Nicolae Ceauşescu's incessant criticism of alleged nationalist tendencies in Hungary and his repressive policies against the Romanian people, including the Hungarian ethnic minority in Transylvania, the HDF's electoral support at the summer by-elections might not have been as decisive as it was

4 Without Mikhail Gorbachev's consent and Erich Honecker's resistance to Németh's and Pozsgay's decision in September 1989 to open the Iron Curtain for the East German citizens in Hungary, the Németh government might not have prevailed over the Workers' Guard a month later; and,

5 Without President George Bush's insisting on meeting publicly with the Hungarian opposition parties during his visit in Hungary, the Grósz–Fejti NRT negotiating team might have been tempted to terminate the regime's dialogue with the Hungarian "insurgents" in July 1989.

In early 1989 the fate of the Hungarian transition rested on the fragile pillar of the old and new elites' ambiguous consensus on the political essentials of this process. No one knew at that time what the desired outcome might be: a Czechoslovak- or a GDR-style token multiparty system under a reform communist hegemon; a Polish-style bicameral ersatz two-party system; or a combination of the two. The policy lobbies, the nonparty majority, and the world outside Hungary each claimed the right to have a say in what would take place between the regime and the opposition in 1989.

In what follows, I will examine the key events that played a decisive role in Hungary's transformation from one-party rule to political pluralism in the first nine months of 1989. The discussion will address four political processes and the social impact of landmark events: (A) From social movements to political parties – the rebirth of party pluralism in Hungary; (B) From party to political movement – the withering away of a ruling party; (C) The National Roundtable – strategies and outcomes; and (D) The HSWP – demise and resurrection.

(A)   From social movements to political parties – the rebirth of party pluralism in Hungary

At the end of 1988 in Hungary there were twenty-one new or recently founded political associations that identified themselves as "society," "league," "association," or "front" and the Independent Smallholders' Party (ISP).[4] The Opposition Roundtable (ORT) of March 22–June 10, 1989 included six political parties and two intelligentsia groups.[5] The three sides of the National Roundtable (NRT) of June 13–September 18, 1989 together comprised, in addition to the HSWP, six political parties, four policy lobbies, four social groups, and one organization as an observer.[6]

The process of party formation peaked in February 1990: sixty-six registered and nineteen nonregistered political parties and nine electoral coalitions. Thus, as will be shown in the next chapter, on the eve of the 1990 electoral campaign the full spectrum of organized groups with political ambitions included the reformed HSWP under the name of Hungarian Socialist Party (HSP) and several "new," "historic," "nostalgia," and "phantom" parties, and various "Trojan horse"-type electoral coalitions.[7] Of these, only a relative few played a substantive role in the lengthy political negotiations between the regime and the opposition. The process involved internal and external domestic participants. The key internal players were the HSWP, the Independent Lawyers' Forum (ILF), the Hungarian Democratic Forum (HDF), the Alliance of Free Democrats (AFD), and the League of Young Democrats (LYD, or Fidesz in Hungarian). The main external actors were the government and the state bureaucracy, the lame-duck Parliament, the HSWP's feuding policy caucuses, the Hungarian media, and the new parties' grassroots political activists. Public and informal interactions within and among these clusters of political actors were responsible for the outcome of the NRT negotiations.

The transformation in the mid-1980s of informal circles of politicized intellectuals into organized groups and, in some cases, into political minimovements was a complex process. Up to that point the "informal sphere" of the second society and official toleration of individual strategies of "interest realization" had helped ameliorate social pressures for organized interest articulation. Moreover, the Pozsgay-led PPF had recruited and promoted, as regime-sponsored social organizations, intelligentsia groups that agreed to abstain from explicitly political activities. Prior to 1988 the regime and Pozsgay's networks had succeeded in preventing all but a few social groups from joining the democratic opposition.[8] The local insurgents of the parliamentary elections of 1985 either became independent MPs or ended up in the camp of the Pozsgay-led loyal opposition.

Of the six parties and two intelligentsia groups that were the charter members of the ILF-coordinated ORT in March 1989, at least five had, in one way or another, been the regime's creations. On the other hand, the AFD and Fidesz were core components of the democratic opposition, and the Christian Democratic People's Party (CDPP), at least initially, was esssentially the "Catholic wing" of the HDF.[9] Let us briefly review the political origins of the ORT's constituent units.

The establishment of the HDF was in part the result of the HSWP successor generation's strategy to fill with nationalist, but proreform, provincial intellectuals the growing space between the rearguard party and the regime's established policy lobbies. The trade-off for the Populist intellectuals' support of the Grósz-led party insurgents was the regime's toleration of the HDF's low-key nationalism and its advocacy of the cause of Hungarian ethnic minorities in Romania and Slovakia. HDF-sponsored public meetings in early 1988, though quite self-restrained affairs, also helped articulate the critical socialist intellectuals' message.[10] For services rendered in assisting with Kádár's ouster, the HDF was rewarded by Grósz with the opportunity to be the first civic organization to organize a mass demonstration in behalf of human rights in Transylvania, in June 1988.

Early public exposure gave the HDF an inestimable advantage over its future rivals in the opposition camp. As long as Zoltán Bíró, a founder and chairman of the HDF, was at the helm, the movement's leaders sought to accommodate the increasingly radical demands of their national constituency and Pozsgay's current political needs at the same time. The two were still compatible in the spring of 1989 but ceased to be so by midsummer. In any case, as a political movement the HDF was more of a human rights lobby for ethnic Hungarians abroad than a champion of political democracy, social justice, and national self-determination for those at home.

The ISP was a "historic" party with a solid record of commitment to democracy and persecution by the Rákosi regime. Although never formally outlawed, in the 1980s very few of the party's former leaders were alive to "unfurl the flag" and to rally those who might have remembered what the ISP had stood for in the 1940s. With help from the PPF, the party reconstituted itself in the fall of 1988, first as a "political society" and later as a political party. The ISP's main problem – one that still haunts it seven years later – has been that of a modern identity. To stand up for the interests of small farmers after forty years of agricultural collectivization to bring about a new rural economy and new rural society was a daunting proposition. The elderly lawyers and middle-aged farm experts who came to speak for the party in the transition period were political novices. With the exception of the AFD-Fidesz plebiscite drive of October–November of that year, they played a minor role in the political arena in 1989–90.

The Hungarian People's Party (HPP) called itself the heir to the radical Hungarian Peasants' Party of the prewar era, as well as the successor to the Petőfi Party that the Populist intellectuals had created during the 1956 revolution. As a "movement," the HPP's immediate predecessor had been a society named after the Populist writer Péter Veres that the PPF helped establish in 1986.[11] In any case, the *old* HPP – at least its left wing, to which Veres belonged – had the dubious distinction of having been the Rákosi regime's first satellite party in the late 1940s. Now that the Populists had switched to the HDF, the historic shell of the old HPP was vacant and could be filled with younger people. The staffing, organization, and program were provided by Pozsgay's PPF. The latter had an ample supply of funds and well-spoken apparatchik intellectuals of rural background to carry the party's message to those not familiar with the HPP's checkered history.

The Hungarian Social Democratic Party (HSDP) was the "most historic," yet probably the least effective among the ORT and NRT parties in 1989. In 1948, upon the party's coerced merger with the communists, the moderate leaders had been driven into Western exile. Many of their followers had ended up in jails and, after 1956, on the gallows. The fellow-travelers and the renegades sought accommodation with the Rákosi and the Kádár regimes. Some of them turned out to be ruthless opportunists (György Marosán may be the best example), others faithful timeservers (György Lázár and István Sarlós); and a few, particularly Rezső Nyers, made important contributions to Kádár's reform programs.

The restoration of the HSDP in 1988 had benefited from Grósz's and Pozsgay's assistance.[12] The party proper had begun with the reunion of a few veterans (András Révész, Tibor Baranyai, and others) and a letter of registration with the government.[13] After a promising start, marked by Pozsgay advisor Mihály Bihari's short-lived tenure as the party's secretary general, the HSDP fell into several feuding factions. In July 1989, pending the resolution of internal conflicts, the HSDP was suspended from membership at the NRT. Though a signatory of the NRT agreement, the HSDP ceased to be a factor in Hungarian politics.[14]

The Endre Bajcsy-Zsilinszky Society (EBZS) was one of the two intelligentsia groups of the ORT.[15] The society had been established in 1986 as a PPF-sponsored discussion group to popularize Bajcsy-Zsilinszky's radical nationalist agenda (Bajcsy-Zsilinszky was a prominent politician in the 1930s) and to keep the Hungarian ethnic minorities' cultural aspirations in the forefront of public attention. The society and the HDF, both well connected with CC secretary György Fejti's office, had been the official cosponsors of the June 1988 anti-Ceausescu demonstration in Budapest.[16] The EBZS and the HDF were Pozsgay's *de facto* representatives in the ORT.

The Democratic Union of Scientific Workers (DUSW) was established in May 1988 as an "independent trade union" of white-collar workers and intellectuals.[17] The union had been founded by Pál Forgacs, a former Social Democrat and former official of the Prague-based World Federation of Democratic Trade Unions. The DUSW was assigned the status of observer at the ORT. However, three months later it was replaced by a broader and more authentic alliance of insurgent trade unionists, the Democratic League of Independent Trade Unions – or, for short, Liga in Hungarian – a bona fide economic pressure group that was given observer status at the NRT.

The AFD and LYD were the principal counterweights to Pozsgay's proxies at the ORT and the NRT later on that year. The AFD was the party of the democratic opposition. Its origins as a political movement date from the establishment of the Network of Free Initiatives (NFI).[18] The latter was an unstructured discussion forum and, in a way, the *Beszélő* circle's answer to the by then semilegitimate HDF. In November 1988 the NFI split between those who sought to advance the democratic opposition's agenda as a political party and those who chose to preserve its political independence.[19]

Unlike its political allies (and future rivals) at the ORT and the NRT, the ADF was a well-organized, well-financed and internationally well-connected opposition group. In addition to its formidable resources of expertise on most policy issues on the agenda, the ADF also enjoyed Western (mainly American) political and financial support. (The HDF's Western money came from Bavaria, France, and North America, and the HSDP's – that is, the faction headed by Anna Petrasovics – from the German Social Democrats.)[20] In any event, the ADF was the only Hungarian opposition group with a record of close cooperation with the Polish Solidarity and the Czechoslovak Charter '77 human rights activists.[21]

The LYD (Fidesz), though the latest arrival on the political scene, had the longest history as an informal political movement. Its origins lay in the simmering generational rebellion of university and college students that had begun in the late 1970s. The gradual collapse of the YCL, the "party's only youth organization" at Hungarian institutions of higher education, created a political vacuum that young radicals were ready to occupy. The spawning ground of Fidesz had been the residential colleges of Hungarian universities and, from 1985 on, summer conferences of young intellectuals.[22]

The interests of young people were an important casualty of the regime's rearguard strategy. The YCL bureaucracy did not care, and the PPF had no authority to recruit at the universities. In any case, the establishment of Fidesz by thirty-seven law and economics students and graduates on March 30, 1988 was the last nail in the coffin of the YCL – and the opening salvo of generational change in Hungarian politics. As will be shown below, as a political actor Fidesz was a unique phenomenon in both Hungarian and East European transition politics. The party's leaders were tough-minded young professionals with no ideological bonds or political debts to the Kádár regime.

The Independent Lawyers' Forum (ILF) was founded in November 1988 by 135 legal professionals.[23] Their goal was to assist – as they had, on a voluntary basis, the independent parliamentary MPs – those who sought to take advantage of new opportunities to form political clubs and associations. Among the members were law professors, attorneys, jurists, and legal experts in government ministries. The idea to bring together a representative group of the largest opposition parties to form the ORT was conceived by ILF. According to ILF spokesman Imre Kónya, the invitation to attend the inaugural meeting of ORT on March 22, 1989 was accepted by all eight groups.[24]

The ORT was the fourth attempt since the Monor conference of 1985 to bring all opposition groups together under the same political roof. The first was by the NFI in early 1988; the second was Pozsgay's notion for the creation of a Council of National Reconciliation on November 24, 1988; and the third was Rezső Nyers' New March Front trial balloon for a Hungarian National Committee (*Országos Nemzeti Bizottság*) in January 1989. Whereas the NFI's initiative had been premature, Pozsgay's and Nyers' proposals were obviously politically self-serving and therefore unacceptable to the regime's *real* opposition.[25]

The ORT groups' common goal was to initiate a dialogue and subsequently formal negotiations with the regime. The Pozsgay proxies, particularly the HDF, initially argued for negotiating with the government rather than with the HSWP. In the end, the lawyers' common sense prevailed and HSWP CC secretary György Fejti was notified of the ORT's intent to negotiate with the party on its constituents' behalf.

As discussed in András Bozóki's perceptive account of the history of seven weeks of negotiations between the HSWP and the ORT, Fejti and, behind him, Grósz sought to undermine the opposition in a variety of ways.[26] These attempts, such as the proposed exclusion of Fidesz from the negotiations and the unexpected bonus of the New March Front's abstention from the ORT–HSWP dialogue, helped strengthen the thitherto fragile unity of the opposition forces. Moreover, Fejti's broad hint that "the Polish Roundtable discussions serve as a model for us" sounded like a plausible proposition: the regime was willing to negotiate with a Solidarity-type "umbrella organization."[27] In any case, substantive negotiations between the two sides commenced in late April. The give-and-take between the ORT's designated negotiators – the lawyers and legal scholars Imre Kónya, László Sólyom, and Péter Tölgyessy – and Fejti's staff involved many critically important political and procedural trade-offs.

The ORT had no use for the "third side," but the HSWP insisted on its inclusion. The ORT sought to confine the agenda to the "fundamental" laws – the Constitution, electoral law, party law, law on the president of the Republic, the Criminal Code – but the HSWP insisted on discussing economic and social policy issues as well. Hoping to benefit from the "openness" of negotiations, the ORT argued for the public airing of its positions, but Fejti refused to share the spotlight with the opposition and preferred to negotiate behind closed doors. The two sides' respective objectives were different but not incompatible. On the one hand, the ORT sought to prevent the regime from submitting its version of transition laws to the Parliament, thus to confront the opposition with a political *fait accompli*. On the other hand, the HSWP was anxious not to lose a still-promising – and the *only* remaining – venue for coming to terms with the opposition at the negotiating table.[28]

The outcome was compromise on all substantive and procedural issues. The ORT was accepted as the sole negotiator of the Hungarian opposition. The "negotiating table," though generally referred to as "round," was – at the opposition's insistence – triangular, with the regime's proxies sitting at the third side. The agenda was to include both legal-political and socioeconomic issues. And the proceedings, except the ceremonial plenary sessions, were to be held behind closed doors.

The ORT was an *ad-hoc* alliance of Hungary's new political elites. Nearly all of them were intellectuals, but their ideological preferences and links to the incumbents were quite different. Common to them all was their virtual invisibility in the public arena. July 1989 was the first time when the names of opposition leaders registered in the "Do you know these politicians?" type of national surveys. And even then Viktor Orbán of Fidesz and András Révész of the HSDP were identified by only 33 and 27 percent of the respondents, respectively. Pozsgay, with 91 percent, Grósz, 92 percent, Németh, 90 percent, and Nyers, 92 percent seem to have had an unassailable lead at that time.[29]

The "alternative" groups' lack of money, office space, transportation, and telephones was another handicap. In the first three months of 1989, the opposition parties were still without clearly defined legal standing, and without the means to publicize their programs and recruit followers. Prior to joining forces in the ORT, the new parties subsisted in a twilight zone between the threat of police harassment and the hope of political toleration by the beleaguered incumbents.

(B)   From party to political movement – the withering away of a ruling party

The Central Committee's decision to embrace political pluralism and to empower scattered opposition groups as legitimate participants in the political process marked the end of the party's rearguard strategy and the beginning of a new era in Hungarian politics. The key feature of the February decisions was the regime's endorsement of the formulation of "popular uprising" to denote the events of the 1956 revolution. This major ideological turnabout introduced an element of "self-limitation" with respect to the state's coercive resources that might be deployed in the coming months to keep the "insurgents" off the streets and, if possible, to silence them as participants in confidential discussions at the negotiating table.

The management of the party's political devolution to a "movement" and an electoral party was a supreme challenge of the incumbents' administrative skills, political wisdom, and personal courage. Moscow's benign neutrality, Western encouragement, and the opposition parties' explicit commitment to peaceful methods and negotiated solutions, though helpful, could not compensate for the regime's lack of internal cohesion. In the spring of 1989, Grósz, Németh, Nyers, and Berecz tried to keep together a deeply divided mass party, its demoralized apparat, and such potentially violent constituencies as the Workers' Guard, the Ferenc Münnich Society, and the socialist *Lumpenproletariat*. Unlike his colleagues, Pozsgay marched to a different drummer. Though conscious of the threat from the Left, his priority was the creation of a "reform party" in the HSWP and drastic renewal of the system from within.

To realize their personal ambitions and to survive the exigencies of the transition period, the top incumbents needed for the time being the ruling party's political power and the state's resources behind them. However, the presence of five helmsmen on the bridge, though seemingly reassuring for the anxious public, offered no evidence that they had the same destination in mind. The "helmsmen" were the senior members of the HSWP PB: secretary general Károly Grósz, minister of state Imre Pozsgay, prime minister Miklós Németh, minister of state Rezső Nyers, and the "odd man still in" CC secretary for ideology János Berecz. They believed that the existing property relations, the regime's social and cultural achievements, and the old "expert" elites' positions were transferable assets, and therefore worth salvaging. None of them doubted that the HSWP would remain the largest party, or at least would become the dominant force in a coalition government after the next elections.[30] In any case, they all believed that the venue of peaceful negotiations was the only realistic option in 1989. As Grósz explained to the CC in March 1989,

> I believe that in creating a possibility for a multiparty system we have made the most important decision of the past decades. There have

been few instances in the history of politics that a party voluntarily surrendered its monopoly position while still in the possession of means with which to prevent it.

Is this a step forward or backward? In my view this has been an involuntary step (*kényszerlépés*). Today we cannot do anything else lest we cause an even greater catastrophe. We have a sad example before us: our Polish friends, who have had a formal but nonfunctioning multiparty system for some time, could not avert a crisis with political means, and thus had to resort to administrative methods [that is, a martial law regime on December 13, 1981]. And now consider the result – nine years later they have to start from scratch.[31]

The Polish precedent was compelling and, in a different way, so was Czechoslovakia's. According to the HSWP CC's internal newsletter for February 1989, the visiting Grósz was told by his fellow party chief Miloš Jakeš that "should the Czechoslovak party consent to the reevaluation of 1968 and the rehabilitation of its victims, the party would fall apart."[32] And all this, as Grósz's Czechoslovak informants claimed, with only "eighty active members of the Charter '77 opposition." By early 1989 the Hungarian "alternatives" had at least 5,000 signed-up members. The stakes were the same, but the chances of a negotiated outcome were much better in Hungary.

The withering away of the ruling party in Hungary took place in three overlapping phases between mid-February and late June 1989. These may be called: (a) an internal housecleaning and leadership reshuffle; (b) a showdown between the party and the government; and (c) the *de facto* dismissal of the CC and the rise of a caretaker "junta of four." Each phase involved the interaction of the party leadership, the opposition forces, the government, the old policy lobbies, grassroots party insurgents, the media, and, increasingly, the public as well. For the sake of brevity, I shall confine the following discussion to leadership strategies and the key events of this period.

The HSWP: toward an electoral party

The party's landmark decisions of February 10–11 set into motion a dual process. The first involved redefinition of the party's political identity; the second, an enormous cleanup operation of the regime's Augean stables and attempts at a speedy disposal of the political and legal debris of communist rule. Each task required CC review and political decision.

György Fejti's presentation and commentary on the draft text of a new Constitution was a traumatic experience to members of the legally untutored but politically alert Central Committee. The introduction of new politicial and judicial institutions, such as the replacement of the Presidential Council with the president of the Republic, the establishment of a constitutional court, and a state accounting office were seen by the bewildered members as a wholesale giveaway of the party's commanding positions.[33] Phrases such as "popular sovereignty" in a "free and democratic," albeit "socialist" Hungary, and the omission of the party as "the leading force of society" from the text of the Constitution evoked the specter of "bourgeois restoration" among members of the alarmed Central Committee.

In the end, the steamroller of the minister of justice Kálmán Kulcsár-led team of legal experts – the real authors of Fejti's text – prevailed. And so did, at another CC session, the proposal for abolition of the death penalty. The CC was in no position to protest. After all, some of the older members occupied seats that rightfully belonged to those whom this body had sent to the gallows in 1957–58.

By far the most sensitive item on the legal agenda was the official review of political show trials that had been held between 1949 and 1958. In addition to László Rajk and Imre Nagy and their codefendants, hundreds of thousands of party and nonparty people were also victims of Rákosi's reign. As Fejti explained, the latter category had been subjected to nine types of judicial and extra-judicial actions that took place between 1947 and 1953. These include (a) the trials of Smallholders MPs, (b) the "economic conspiracy" trials of enterprise managers, (c) the trials of military officers, (d) the trials of Social Democrats, (e) the "Church trials" of the Catholic hierarchy, (f) the trials of Catholic parish priests, (g) the "Yugoslav trials" of suspected Titoists, (h) the "sabotage trials" of industrial and railroad workers, and (i) the trials of thousands of peasants who resisted agricultural collectivization. This list did not include victims of the forced resettlement of tens of thousands from cities to villages nor of incarceration in forced labor camps in the Rákosi era.[34]

It was generally understood by those participating in the ensuing discussion that the August 1962 HSWP CC resolution on the party victims of Stalinist repression had been a whitewash. However, the reopening of these cases was, as Aczél cautioned, "a dangerous thing." He also added that the process of legal rehabilitation required tactful handling so that the survivors of "those who had been killed by our regime would not, yet again, be punished." Fejti conceded the point, but submitted that "we cannot make decent preparations for the future without the settling of accounts with the past."[35] The party had no choice but to act on this explosive matter. In July 1988 Grósz had promised his American audiences that the remains of Nagy and his fellow victims would be exhumed and, as a "humanitarian gesture," be handed over to the families for private interment. However, as the regime soon found out, the judicial murder of the leader of the 1956 "popular uprising" was no longer a private matter in 1989.

To prevent the opposition from making political profit from its planned public celebration of the anniversary of the outbreak of the revolution of 1848–49 on March 15, the regime invited everyone to march together on that day. Other than a few disoriented Social Democrats and an elderly ISP leader who joined the regime's official rally, the rest of the ORT groups had their own celebration – and a turnout five times larger than the crowd that the HSWP, the YCL, and the PPF mobilized for this purpose.[36] It was a fitting day for the opposition to make its political debut. The legacy of the March Youth of 1848 was a potent ideological weapon against tyrants old and new in Hungary.

The HSWP's hastily prepared electoral platform, "For our future – What are the goals of the HSWP?" was Berecz's handiwork. It was designed to present the HSWP as a political movement and an electoral party. Much of its nine-point "action program" was reform rhetoric with the obvious intent to preempt the opposition's slogans for March 15.[37] This document, like the party that issued it, was a victim of political disorientation. As the report of an internal CC advisory panel put it, it was a collection of tired slogans that roused no one and antagonized everyone.[38]

Next to the party center and the fledgling opposition, Imre Pozsgay was the "third force" in Hungarian politics in the spring of 1989. His January bombshell forced Grósz to make a choice between expelling him from the party and opening the floodgates to devastating historical truths and surrendering the party's monopoly of power. Though Grósz chose the latter, the outcome still left Pozsgay in political limbo. To prevent the apparat and the hostile CC from disposing of him at the first opportunity, Pozsgay had to go beyond his intelligentsia networks and present his case to the public.

In late February Pozsgay convened a group of supporters at the government's official guest house in the Buda hills to devise strategies for the next round of confrontations with the party center.[39] Though the possible utilization of the HSWP's Reform Circles (RC) was also discussed, the immediate task was to prepare a policy document to be distributed among the festive crowds on March 15. The result was a twelve-page one-time newspaper, *Márczius Tizenötödike*. It was a kind of modern replica of a March 15, 1848 feuilleton with the subtitle "Twelve pages [devoted to a] national search for a way out." The publication featured a lead editorial by Pozsgay and twenty-five articles by an unusual alliance of party and government officials and top reform intellectuals.

It was a remarkable testimony to Pozsgay's ability to attract followers to have Mátyás Szűrös (Speaker of the Parliament), István Huszár (president of the PPF), Imre Nagy (first secretary of the YCL), and Gyula Horn (state secretary in the Ministry of Foreign Affairs) join forces with the regime's leading reform socialist critics and go on record with unorthodox views. These officials sought to distance themselves from the party center's, to them outdated, policies and argued for bold new departures on many fronts.

Pozsgay's article, "The Chances for Freedom," was a seminal statement on the philosophical and moral roots of socialist reform initiatives in Hungary. In it Pozsgay appealed to the reason and conscience of the average party member and of the nonparty majority.

> The true custodian of political freedom is the citizen, its framework is the nation, and its means is the state. Behind all this lies the organic system of society in which the individual is capable of self-determination, and the collective is able to govern itself. The manner in which the state's tasks are performed, the quality of services it provides are controlled directly by the citizens or through their representatives. This interpretation of freedom is based not on the principle of usefulness but on humanistic considerations; it so happens, however, that in the European culture and civilization the most successful, and economically most efficient nations have always been those that have built their societies on political freedom and in accordance with the norms of human rights.[40]

For party members who had been traumatized by his characterization of the events of 1956, Pozsgay's message was equally straightforward: "Reestablishing the historical truth divests the dictatorship of its identity and the means of preserving its legitimacy; it sheds light on decisions that were never made and the consequences of inaction, and it presents the lessons of arbitrary decisions."[41] The intended recipients of Pozsgay's "truth" were mainly those who were prepared to work to change the party from within. The HSWP's RCs were such constituencies – and so were the restless rank-and-file members of the YCL and the socialist intellectuals throughout Hungary.

As far as it can be reconstructed from his memoirs and comments from his close advisors, Pozsgay believed that he had Grósz and Berecz on the run, and thus he had a chance to finish them off politically. In late March, during his visit in Italy, he saw two leaders. The first was the pope, with whom he had an audience – a first by a Hungarian politician since Kádár's audience in 1977 – where he obtained the pontiff's approval of his "man-centered" approach to political reforms. Pozsgay's public praise of the Hungarian Cardinal László Páskai was an astute move that signaled his support of the aspirations of the country's Catholic community.[42]

While in Rome, Pozsgay also met with the visiting Aleksandr Yakovlev at the Soviet embassy. There he submitted to the fellow cardinal of his "other Church" that "it would be helpful if they [that is, Moscow] obtained their information about Hungary not from ... the same Stalinist machine" but from him. Therefore, he proposed that he be invited to Moscow to meet with Gorbachev. This, as Pozsgay explained to Yakovlev, would demonstrate that Gorbachev meant what he had been saying about dismantling the legacy of Stalinism. Apparently, Yakovlev anticipated this request. At the end of their private dinner, he sternly advised Pozsgay that it was "the duty of the Hungarian comrades to support comrade Grósz." Pozsgay, however, refused to take no for an answer and angrily berated Yakovlev for the Soviet leadership's being "hostages to Stalinist traditions" in preferring "to work with agents rather than with allies." A few weeks later an invitation came, but, as will be shown below, Pozsgay's rivals saw to it that the visit never materialized.[43]

On March 23–24, the very time when Pozsgay was lobbying with Yakovlev in Rome, Gorbachev met with Grósz in Moscow. According to Grósz, his host consented to the inauguration of political pluralism in Hungary and "guaranteed" that the events of 1956 and 1968 "will not be repeated" in 1989.[44] Although Grósz made headway on the eventual withdrawal of Soviet troops from Hungary and even obtained minor trade concessions from Moscow, these were of no help against the next onslaught of the party reformers at the end of the month. The March 29 CC meeting saw the transfer of press and media supervision from the party center to a government committee chaired by Pozsgay. Moreover, it was decided that the government would take charge of the *public* reburial of Imre Nagy and his fellow victims later on that year.

Although minister of defense Ferenc Kárpáti assured the CC that "the army's job [was] to protect the country and support the present political system,"[45] and Grósz reiterated his commitment to keeping the party organizations "in the army, the police, and at the workplace," the object of support was falling apart. As CC secretary János Lukács reported, more than 120,000 people had left the party in the previous months. The remaining membership's concerns were aptly summarized in the CC's newsletter for March 1989: "can a party that has lost its prestige renew itself?"[46]

As Pozsgay saw it, the party's renewal under its current leadership was a hopeless proposition. Instead, he pointed to another institution and a different team of politicians that had the resolve to address the question of national renewal. As he explained in an interview "The Struggle Will Continue Until Purification Is Brought About" to the Austrian daily *Die Presse,*

> An inner cabinet has been formed within the government which, besides the premier, includes the ministers of state, the deputy premier, and the interior and the foreign ministers. This structure has increased our possibilities of pursuing policies, as opposed to the previous government, which was purely administrative and whose task it was to manage production ... As the result, the government can increasingly act as the political center. This means that it must also think about possible coalition partners.
>
> [The interviewer]: Does it mean in practical terms that this "inner cabinet" dissociates itself from the party?
>
> [Pozsgay]: Yes, this was the underlying idea: The so-called analogous system of decisions that in reality paralyzed the government's work can no longer be maintained. The practice was that the Politburo adopted a decision, which was then "nationalized" by the government[47]

Grósz's response to Pozsgay's challenge was presented in a major address to the April 12 meeting of the CC on the "working style of the CC and the PB," in which he summarized the findings of an internal task force on this subject. The author of the report was a Grósz ally, János Váncsa, who had canvassed the views of "over 500 CC members and other leading cadres" on what ailed the party in the spring of 1989. Though the report contained nothing that the CC members could not read in the party press, the concluding section recommended that the size of the PB be reduced by four and that the CC be increased by ten members. Thereupon, Grósz submitted his and the PB's resignation and asked for new nominations for these positions.[48]

The CC decided to support the key leaders and at the same time register its disapproval of Pozsgay. When the votes were counted,

Németh and Grósz, with 103 and 102 votes respectively, led the pack. Among those reelected, Pozsgay was the next to last, with 86 votes. The PB rejects were Lukács, Berecz, Judit Csehák, and István Szabó. Of these, Lukács was compensated by being appointed as the new head of the Central Control Commission. Berecz, though clearly on his way out, was allowed to keep his position as CC secretary. The new CC members were a mixture of young reformers and Grósz proxies. In any case, as Grósz submitted, "in the past ten months we have made the mistake of distancing ourselves from leftist tendencies, without clearly disassociating ourselves from attempts at rightist backsliding (*restau- rációs törekvések*). Since March 15 the [latter] tendency has gained strength in the party."[49]

Now it was Grósz's turn to call Pozsgay's bluff. Three days later the first national meeting of the HSWP RCs was to be held in Kecskemét. Pozsgay was widely expected to announce his leadership of this move- ment and to propose its secession from the HSWP. However, in the end, it was Pozsgay who "blinked" by announcing that he and Nyers would merely attend the conference, but take no action that would affect the party's unity.[50] One might, as did the hundreds of disap- pointed party insurgents at the Kecskemét meeting, ask, "Why?"

Pozsgay's public explanation is offered in his memoirs. There he argues that the disappointing outcome of his discussion with Yakovlev and the advice of Polish prime minister Mieczysław Rakowski to avoid a premature party split discouraged him from leaving the party.[51] However, his second explanation seems more convincing. As he put it,

> Had I initiated a party split in Kecskemét, I could have taken with me a part of the party's reform wing that was capable of rebellion, but not of leadership of political transformation. The HSWP's conserva- tive (*retrográd*) wing would have kept the party's infrastructure, property, and assets of public communication and reactivated the party's power resources. The well-meaning reform sheep, together with their shepherds, watchmen, and guard dogs, would have been devoured by the HSWP's post-Stalinist wolves. This would have created a new political situation and minimized the chances of a negotiated settlement [with the opposition].[52]

There is no point in second-guessing history. Pozsgay may have been right. Had he forced a showdown, he might have lost the support of the still vacillating Miklós Németh, that of his proxies at the ORT, and his PPF reform network. Moreover, he would have surrendered his freedom to continue, from a position of power, his "hit-and-run" tactics against Grósz and the party's still armed and dangerous

Neanderthals in the police, the army, and the Workers' Guards. By all apearances Grósz won this round. On the other hand, as Pozsgay had put it at the May 1988 party conference, "The clocks in Hungary are coming into sync with those of the rest of the world." The next round was only weeks away.

János Kádár: his last report

The party center's internal Donnybrook was brought to a temporary halt by the unscheduled appearance of János Kádár at the April 12 meeting of the CC. Although Grósz had tried to talk him out of it, Kádár was adamant about addressing, as it turned out for the last time, his comrades in the CC. Kádár's eighty-minute rambling and utterly disjointed speech was a pathetic performance. He was a gravely ill 77–year-old man. His mind wandered and most of what he said made no immediate sense to his audience. Yet, what emerged from his comments may, with due allowance for his frail condition, be called his political testament and an *apologia pro sua vita*.[53]

Kádár's recurring theme was his role in the events of 1956. As he explained, "When I was released (*szabadlábra kerültem*) [by the Soviets and upon his return to Hungary on November 4, 1956] ... there were two party newspapers" and order had to be restored. He kept repeating: "I was not a Soviet agent and I can prove it." Yet, he made a point of saying, "I will not name names." As for the characterization of the events of October 1956, he reiterated, "there was only one brief sentence in that declaration [that is, in the HSWP's official evaluation of December 5, 1956, on what had happened in October] ... and I only said that they opened the gates to counterrevolution."

Amidst many asides and *non sequiturs* Kádár raised some questions and tried to answer them as well. "What is my responsibility?" he asked. "I have only an eighth-grade education." "I am a scapegoat in the Biblical sense." "I have been a party member for fifty-seven years." He concluded: "From a distance of thirty years, I am sorry for everybody."

Kádár's speech was a deeply moving experience for his profoundly shaken audience. However, three weeks later the same audience unanimously endorsed a letter to Kádár in which the CC relieved him of his membership in that body.[54] Both the CC's decision and Kádár's official reply were written by Grósz. With this parting gesture, the "party's parliament," albeit "with the recognition of his merits," expelled Kádár from his political home of the past forty-three years.

In late May Grósz received a handwritten letter from János Kádár. It read as follows:

> To comrade Secretary General Károly Grósz. The undersigned requests the Central Committee of the HSWP to press for a judicial review of the Imre Nagy case. The historical review is already in progress.
> The 1958 sentence was handed down properly and according to the law thirty years ago. I request that you review my role in that case. Did I interfere with the investigation, did I interfere with the sentences etc.?
> If the court is willing to grant me a hearing, I will respond to all questions according to the best of my ability. Should the court consider me guilty, it should be so stated. If I am not [guilty], I request that the Central Committee see to it that gossip and insinuations about my person cease forthwith.
> I thank you for your efforts in advance.
> With comradely greetings:
> [different handwriting]: I reviewed the above, János Kádár P.S. The letter was written by the wife [a feleség irja][55]

János Kádár died on July 6, 1989. Though his wife and occasional visitors from the CC tried to comfort him, Kádár spent the last five weeks of his life imagining that he would be evicted from his home. At one point, Grósz had to rush to Kádár's villa to talk his delirious comrade, who was standing at the door with two suitcases and ready to leave, into returning to his bed.[56] Kádár was given a state funeral on July 14, and, at the end of a march with more than a hundred thousand mourners, was buried in the Budapest municipal cemetery in a section reserved for political leaders.

The HSWP: internal renewal and political retrenchment

The April 15 inaugural conference of the HSWP RCs was an important consciousness-raising experience for the assembled party insurgents. The main speakers held the secretary general responsible for the party's sluggish responses to internal reform initiatives, yet neither Pozsgay nor the three other PB members present rose to Grósz's defense.[57] The closing communiqué declared the RC as an independent policy caucus within the HSWP. It also called for a national RC conference in mid-May and for an all-party conference in the fall.[58]

The next prop to crumble under the party was the Young Communist League. Having lost half of its original membership of 800,000, the young apparatchiki decided to disband and restructure their organization into an independent entity called the National Council of Hungarian Youth Organizations.[59] Unlike his unmemorable speech to the assembled delegates of the YCL–NCHY meeting, Grósz's off-the-cuff remarks to a news reporter about the possible introduction of a "state of economic emergency" caused national consternation.[60]

As it happened, Miklós Németh was also watching the TV news. Instead of checking with Grósz about the accuracy of the quote, he called the TV station and explained that neither the prime minister nor his government had any intention of introducing such measures.[61] Two days later Grósz was forced to retract his statement by saying that, in view of the opposition of the prime minister and his two ministers of state (that is, Pozsgay and Nyers), he had elected not to force the issue by a majority vote, especially "when implementation [of this measure] depended on them."[62] Though Grósz chose "not to use Stalinist methods" to have his way, Németh made sure that a *faux pas* of this magnitude could not happen again.

In the next two weeks, Németh replaced six cabinet ministers.[63] Those dismissed included the ministers of industry, of finance, and of foreign affairs (Kádár's former personal assistant Péter Várkonyi), and Grósz's ally minister of food and agriculture Jenő Váncsa. The new appointees, such as Gyula Horn, who became foreign minister, were committed reformers. During the preceding months Horn had proven to be a valuable ally to Pozsgay and Németh. Next to Grósz's critic, the former CC secretary for international affairs Mátyás Szűrös – since March Speaker of the Parliament – Horn, for reasons best known to him, had become another vigorous advocate of radical reforms. Under Kádár, Horn had been a hard-working and self-effacing apparatchik with impeccable credentials of working-class background, Soviet university education, and volunteer service in the regime's *pufajkás* goon squads after the 1956 revolution. He was also a career diplomat with three decades of work abroad and in the CC's International Department apparat.[64] Therefore, when he argued that Moscow would "tolerate" and the West "expect" radical reforms in Hungary, not even the party conservatives could dispute that he was a credible source of policy advice.

The process of the government's emancipation from the party's tutelage was completed with the total surrender on May 8, 1989 of the PB's and the CC's *nomenklatura* prerogatives for nonparty appointments.[65] Thus, it seemed that Németh had become a master in his own house. To make certain that it would stay that way, the PB consented to the transfer of the 60,000-strong Workers' Guard to the government.

Henceforth the party's private army would operate as a part-time volunteer militia under the direct authority of the Ministry of Defense.[66]

The process of divestiture of the party's administrative powers to the state climaxed with Németh's May 10 address to the Parliament. He explained that

> a period in the relations between the HSWP leadership, the government, and Parliament has ended. Previously:
>
> government decisions were almost always based on party resolutions and thus the government played a limited executive role;
>
> the principle of the "least possible publicity" prevailed in government activity. Our formal communiqués on the sessions were published, and only a narrow circle of people learned about the majority of government decisions;
>
> instead of the government [that is, the Council of Ministers], government committees decided on sensitive issues, such as large-scale investments; and
>
> the government did not accept the Parliament either as a supervisory body or as an equal partner.[67]

The Németh cabinet called itself a "government of experts." The hidden message was that of a depoliticized caretaker state administration awaiting the instauration of political pluralism in Hungary. As Németh put it at the press conference following his address to the Parliament, "The situation today in the country is not yet of a coalition nature, no matter how much I personally would have liked to realize such an endeavor."[68]

To demonstrate that the government had become an independent political actor, Németh announced several overdue policy changes. These included abolition of the notorious State Office for Church Affairs and of the State Committee on Youth and Sports Affairs, establishment of the Office of Hungarian Minority Affairs, and suspension of work on the controversial Hungarian-Czechoslovak Gabčikovo–Nagyamaros hydroelectric and water-diversion project. Moreover, the government assumed full responsibility for the administrative management of the Imre Nagy case. While the Ministry of Justice and the procuracy were reviewing the documents of the 1958 trial, the Ministry of Interior began negotiations with the Committee for Historical Justice and other opposition groups. The subject was the planned June 16 memorial service and reburial of Imre Nagy and his fellow victims in Heroes' Square in Budapest and in the Rákoskeresztur cemetery, respectively. From May 1989 on, the government was in charge of Hungary.

Károly Grósz: showdown and defeat

In the face of the goverment's radical reform measures, the best that Grósz and Fejti could do was try to preserve the party's political infuence. This, in turn, necessitated making all kinds of "no-win" decisions. The holding of a party conference (or congress) was a case in point. On the one hand, as Fejti explained to the CC, the HSWP ought to have a national conference – if for no other reason than to present a program and an electoral platform. On the other hand, an early conference "would convey an image of disarray" that would cost "two-digit losses" at the ballot box in 1990.[69] In the meantime however, the draft text of the new party law that called for a thousand signatures to establish a party – the version that the apparat preferred – was flatly rejected by the opposition. Yet, without the consent of the latter to this and other "fundamental laws," there could be no elections.

Grósz and Fejti were also tempted to mount a law-making *blitzkrieg* in the Parliament to preempt the opposition's legislative reform package. However, there were no guarantees that even the party-member MPs were prepared to support such tactics. The opposition groups' recall campaign of unpopular MPs had sown seeds of confusion among the party's apprehensive parliamentary backbenchers. Anxious to be seen as "expert" legislators, many MPs in the summer of 1989 looked to the government for guidance and were beginning to abandon the party in its hour of need. CC member Béla Katona was probably on the mark when characterizing the situation as a "struggle between dwarfs with huge shadows and a prone clay giant."[70] Moreover, some of the "giant's" local clones had defected to the "dwarfs." As István Sarlós recalled, "I know a local couple. He is the vice-chairman of the [local] HDF and she is a secretary of the county party committee."[71]

To improve the terms of an eventual agreement with the opposition to the benefit of the HSWP, the party's only remaining option was to find allies among the opposition before negotiations commenced. As Fejti explained to the CC, "We are trying to find out whether any of the alternative organizations might be prepared to join us in an electoral alliance. [Such] inclinations can be detected among the historic parties" – that is, the HSDP, the ISP, and the HPP.[72] In any case, the optimistic

Fejti submitted that only "fear keeps [the ORT] together," and added, "The AFD is the only one with a well-developed bargaining position. Compared to the AFD, the HDF is quite unprepared, [while] the rest have no ideas [to put on the negotiating table]."[73]

Fejti's intelligence reports were quite accurate on the latter point. Yet, he greatly underestimated the personal and political courage of his political adversaries. He predicted that "if we persist for two [more] weeks, the ORT will fall apart."[74] However, when it came to authorizing Fejti to put pressure on the opposition, several CC members objected. They were more fearful of the party's own extremists than of the thus far businesslike ORT spokesmen. The CC majority's survival instincts counseled caution and against underestimation of political opposition of *any* kind.

By the end of May, Grósz's position in the CC had all but collapsed. The first national conference of the party's RCs had brought together representatives of one hundred local RCs and attracted an audience of 3,000.[75] Those present also included Pozsgay and Nyers. Németh and Szűrös could not come but sent letters of cordial support to the assembled party insurgents. The meeting resolved that a party congress rather than a party conference be held in the fall. The main task was to be the mandatory renewal of party leadership. Earlier that month a similar appeal had been issued by another party group at the opposite end of the ideologial spectrum. The group, which called itself the Marxist–Leninist Unity Platform, was led by the ultra conservative Róbert Ribánszki, a former personal assistant to Kádár. In the end, even the HSWP's archconservative Central Control Commission, chaired by Grósz supporter János Lukács, endorsed the idea.[76]

At the May 29 meeting of the CC Grósz bowed to the inevitable and reluctantly approved holding a party congress in late September 1989. He also conceded that what he chose to call the "Forum for National Reconciliation" would be held essentially on terms that had been proposed by the ORT.[77] His main accomplishment had been the recruitment of the ORT's own clients as the "third side" of the forthcoming negotiations. However, even this had been a dubious achievement. As the CC member and trade union chief Sándor Nagy put it in early May, "The party needs the trade unions more than the other way around." It was a sobering reminder that the old policy lobbies could no longer be taken for granted by the party center.[78]

Still refusing to see the handwriting on the wall, Grósz and Nyers tried yet again to have the Parliament act on laws that were to be parts of the NRT agenda. As Nyers put it, "If we give up our legislative initiative in the Parliament, we are done for."[79] However, owing to House Speaker Szűrös' dilatory tactics and to prime minister Németh's apparent unwillingness to submit drafts of the "fundamental laws" to the Parliament prior to commencement of the NRT process, Nyers' advice went unheeded.

The last item on the agenda of the May 29 CC meeting was a draft of a statement on the party's official position on Imre Nagy. The text had been fashioned by Grósz's staff and consisted of euphemistic and basically misleading statements about Imre Nagy's political career.[80] Thanks to impassioned speeches by Horn and others on Pozsgay's "historical subcommittee," the CC was forced to confront the truth about Nagy's actions and the Soviets' treacherous conduct in October–November 1956. This was also the moment of truth for people like Károly Grósz and János Berecz. As professional party propagandists, they had made a career in the previous three decades from their slandering of the memory of Imre Nagy and the nonparty victims of the Kádár regime's vendetta of 1956–9. In the course of the debate Grósz tried to explain his position by saying, "I am neither a reformist, nor a fundamentalist – I am a communist."[81] Precisely. In June 1989 communists were becoming politically endangered species in Hungary. Grósz, Berecz, and the CC conservatives were cornered and had nowhere to go.

The HSWP: catharsis and leadership realignment

In early June the center of political life was beginning to shift from the HSWP to the opposition parties and new social movements. Of the latter, two attracted public attention. The first was Movement for a Democratic Hungary. The initiative was Pozsgay's, and the objective to unite people on behalf of "national resurrection, European progress, and the values of democratic socialism."[82] The other was the refloating, yet again, of Rezső Nyers' New March Front.[83] In the coming months both of these trial balloons vanished without a trace. The principal sponsors' apparent purpose was to destabilize further the HSWP and to build up their own political stature.

The memorial service preceding the reburial of the earthly remains of Imre Nagy, Géza Losonczy, Miklós Gimes, Pál Maléter, and József Szilágyi, and of a sixth coffin representing all other victims of the 1956 revolution, was a historic event. The assembled crowd of 250,000 in Heroes' Square in Budapest on June 16 and the millions of viewers of the live TV broadcast were privileged to witness a complex political drama. The regime's reform spokesmen, Imre Pozsgay, Miklós Németh, Mátyás Szűrös, and deputy prime minister Péter Medgyessy, stood by the coffins as honorary pallbearers and, by their very presence, signaled a plea for national reconciliation. The homilies of the surviving veterans, such as Nagy's codefendant Miklós Vásárhelyi, spoke of historic justice, national unity, and the opportunity for "a peaceful transition to a free and democratic society."[84]

The memorial service also served as an opportunity for the drawing of some immediate political conclusions from the martyrdom of Imre Nagy and his associates. Sándor Rácz, onetime chairman of the Greater Budapest Workers' Council declared: "At present, there are many obstacles in the way of progress of the Hungarian people. One is the presence of Soviet troops in Hungary ... [and] the other is the communist party, which is not willing to release its grip on power, which forced Hungary into its present predicament."[85] However, the real meaning of the ceremonies was brought home by the Young Democrats' leader, Viktor Orbán:

> Remember: on October 6, 1956, on the day of László Rajk's reburial the party's daily *Szabad Nép* proclaimed in inch-high letters "Never again!" Three weeks later the communist party's armed thugs fired into crowds of unarmed demonstrators. In less than two years the HSWP, in the same kind of show trial as Rajk's had been, sent to the gallows hundreds of innocents, among them its own comrades. We are not satisfied with the promises of communist politicians that commit them to nothing; we must see to it that the ruling party can never again use force against us. This is the only way to avoid seeing new coffins and belated funerals like this one.[86]

Orbán's fiery speech achieved two objectives. It put his thitherto invisible party on the political map. It also served notice on the NRT negotiators that half-measures and Pozsgay-style fuzzy reform rhetoric were no substitutes for ironclad guarantees of the dismemberment of the communist party state. Orbán's message and harsh demand, "Out with the Soviet troops from Hungary!" outraged Pozsgay's timid proxies at the NRT.[87] By the same token, Orbán's speech helped the HWSP's "survivalists" to draw the appropriate conclusions from the events of June 16.

A few days after the reburial ceremonies, Pozsgay visited Grósz in his office and asked him to resign as secretary general "for the good of the country." Grósz refused.[88] In any case, Pozsgay's belief that Grósz had become a liability to the HSWP was not shared by what the in-house cynics called the "dead souls" (in Russian: *miortvye dushi*) of the

Central Committee. On the other hand, as it became apparent at the June 23–24 meeting of that body, the party's position had become untenable under its current leadership.

Each of the main speakers talked about the danger of the party's collapse, or worse, a formal split between the radical reformers and the Grósz-led central apparat. Grósz insisted that with the tightening of ranks, better discipline, and election of a new chairman, a party split was avoidable. Pozsgay hedged his arguments by delivering a blistering critique of the party's management and by reaffirming his commitment to party unity. Németh's and Szűrös' cases were similar, yet they, too, passed to the CC responsibility for making the necessary decisions. The charade came to an end with the presentation of a report by the party veteran Jenő Fock on behalf of a nominating committee for party chairman.[89]

Fock's report called not for a chairman but for establishment of a collective three-man presidency: Rezső Nyers as chairman and Pozsgay and Grósz as members, with the latter continuing as secretary general. Pozsgay was willing, but only if Németh agreed to serve in that body. With Németh's consent in hand, a four-man presidency was created. Thereupon Nyers proposed establishment of a twenty-one-person Political Executive Committee (PEC) to serve as "operative liaison" between the four senior leaders and the CC. The eventual task of this body was to coordinate the HSWP's electoral campaign in 1989–90.[90] Although purists complained that election of the PEC in fact would amount to the dismissal of the CC, the motion carried with eleven nays and one absention.[91] The votes cast for the individual candidates were: Nyers, 97; Grósz, 82; Németh, 78; and Pozsgay, 79.[92]

Immediately after the vote, the CC removed Grósz and appointed Nyers as the head of the HSWP negotiating team at the NRT. Pozsgay's reward for agreeing to be a loyal team player was Nyers' motion to endorse him as the party's nominee for president of the Republic. The prudent Nyers did not even bother putting this motion to a vote. The reason may have been, as one CC member tartly commented, because there was no such bill before the Parliament.[93] In any case, to remind Pozsgay that he was but a barely tolerated member of that body, the CC saw to it that his supporters, particularly Mátyás Szűrös and István Horváth, were left out of the PEC.[94]

The party's summer housecleaning was completed with the election of CC secretaries. The winning candidates were Jenő Kovács, ninety-five votes, and János Barabás, ninety-four votes. Also rans, with one vote each, were János Berecz and three CC nonentities.[95] Berecz's spectacular fall from the party's leadership and humiliating nomination as director of a yet-to-be-established party research institute may be seen as the new leadership's peace offering to the "wolves" of the Hungarian media. As Berecz explained, in November 1988 he had made the mistake of calling attention to an antiparty group at Hungarian radio. For this, he had ever since been pilloried, yet those who had instructed him so to act chose not to defend him.[96] (Berecz may have forgotten that as a "sovereign politician" he had acted on his own.) In any case, the "taiga" of Hungarian communist party politics thus claimed another victim. János Berecz's political career came to an end on June 24, 1989.

In sum, in terms of influence, leadership cohesion, and administrative power, the transformation of the ruling party into a political movement was a costly process. The party's perceived loss of prestige led to large-scale defections of party members. No one had an exact number, but the estimates ran from 120,000 to 200,000 by early September. Of the party's four nominal leaders, only Németh and Pozsgay had reliable followings among members of the public. With the abdication of its *nomenklatura* authority, the party became a top-heavy, politically powerless bureaucracy functioning under the aegis of the government and the legislature.

The HSWP's most keenly felt loss was the erosion of its political influence in the workplace and among the military and the police. The proposition that the workplace party cells be gradually transferred to the neighborhoods where the membership lived dealt a mortal blow to the regime's political influence at the grassroots level. With the disappearance of the party's political watchdogs from the personnel offices, the working people of Hungary were free to recapture their personal autonomy as citizens of a postcommunist state. The military and the police came under prime minister Németh's and minister of interior István Horváth's authority. The KGB advisors were sent packing. In the summer of 1989 it seemed that the rule of law was about to be restored in Hungary.

(C)   The National Roundtable – strategies and outcomes

The transitions from communist to postcommunist and, from there, to freely elected multiparty politics took many forms in Eastern Europe. In most cases the process of political transformation was a brief and essentially chaotic process marked by mass demonstrations – East Germany, Czechoslovakia, and Bulgaria – and, in Romania, by short periods of violence. In Poland and in Hungary political transformation was preceded by secret negotiations between the incumbents and the opposition.

Two Roundtables: Poland and Hungary

The main purpose of the Polish National Roundtable was to restore political normalcy by way of an extended dialogue between *Solidarność* and the post-martial-law Jaruzelski regime. The central issue of the Polish negotiations was limited power sharing between the old and new political elites and the outlining of the principles of socioeconomic reforms and trade union autonomy. The immediate political outcome was a quota-based system of national elections that gave legitimate standing to *Solidarność* representatives in the national legislature.[97]

The Hungarian NRT process was different from that which had taken place in Poland between the regime and its opposition. The differences lay in the respective powers, capabilities, and intentions of the incumbents; in the extent of a preexisting consensus reached by the regime and the opposition; and in the scope of the agenda that the Hungarian NRT participants addressed in the course of their deliberations. Much more so than the Polish regime, the Hungarian incumbents were sharply divided between an increasingly demoralized group of hard-liners and a cluster of politically well-positioned reformers. In fact, in terms of ideological preferences and political style, the latter had a great deal more affinity with the "insurgents" than with their rivals in the political leadership. Moreover, not as in Poland, the HSWP's reform elite was in complete control of the commanding heights power at the time when negotiations commenced between the two sides.

In Hungary the incumbents were anxious to divest themselves partly – and if need be fully – of responsibility for the regime's flawed record and were willing to face the political consequences of "non-quota," therefore free, elections. Similarly, the Hungarian NRT's agenda addressed only a partial spectrum (excluding foreign policies) of political, economic, and social issues that were parts of the nation's policy agenda in the summer of 1989. In Poland each of the National Roundtable's three main task forces – on political reforms, economic and social policy, and trade union pluralism – developed comprehensive agreements. In Hungary, however, the negotiators concentrated mainly on concrete legislative proposals that the regime, upon the reaching of a compromise agreement, was committed to enact into laws. No such *ex ante*, let alone public, commitment had been made by the Polish regime at the onset of the negotiations. For these reasons, the entire Hungarian NRT process should be seen as a unique, yet historically well-established, approach to political conflict resolution through negotiations among political elites.

The NRT negotiations were based on a "political agreement" between the HSWP and the ORT.[98] The signatories committed themselves to work for "an agreement according to the norms of European political culture" to facilitate transition "from one-party to representative democracy." Though the negotiations were, in theory, "open to all," the document precluded other partipants so as to preserve the "operability" (*működőképesség*) of the process. In any case, the object was to "draft bills" and to reach "political agreements" on the key issues on the table. The "third side" defined its role as that of "support of the two other sides' efforts to reach a consensus." In doing so, the regime's auxiliaries placed the political burden of coming to terms on the ORT and the HSWP.

The NRT process began with nationally televised formal opening statements by Károly Grósz, Imre Kónya, and the constitutional lawyer István Kukorelli (for the "third side") on June 13 in the Parliament building.[99] Speeches by the regime's spokesmen sought to summarize the HSWP's and the PPF's positive intentions, though the immediate motivation was obviously that of defusing political tensions that would arise at the Nagy reburial three days later. Kónya scored debating points by recalling the 1956 revolution and its martyrs but made one substantive point: "In the course of these talks it is not our intention to divide power with its present possessors ... over the heads of the people." This, as will be shown below, was a promise that neither the regime nor the opposition intended to honor either in the next three or in the next ten months.

The NRT began with the first plenary working session on June 21 and the bulk of its work was completed by September 18. The process involved 1,302 negotiators and expert consultants. They spent roughly 1,000 hours in 238 working sessions of the plenary group, of the two "mid-level" plenary groups, and of the twelve "working groups" hammering out an agreement.[100] All but a few plenary meetings were held behind closed doors in the Parliament building and most of the sessions were videotaped by the *Fekete Doboz* (Black Box) team of young journalists. To date (spring 1996), neither the tapes nor the 3,439-page transcript of the NRT negotiations have been made available to the Hungarian public.[101] A simplified version of the organization of the NRT process appears in Table 7.1.

Table 7.1 *National Roundtable, June–September 1989: organization and venues of decision-making*[102]

I	*Plenary Session** Committee for Conflict Resolution (*Jószolgálati Bizottság*)***
II	*"Midlevel" Plenary Sessions**
	Session I Legal and Political Affairs
	Session II Social and Economic Affairs
III	*Working Groups**

I/1 Constitutional Reform	II/1 Economic Crisis Management
I/2 Party Law and Party Financing	II/2 Social and Welfare Policies
I/3 Electoral Law	II/3 Property Reform
I/4 Principles of a Revised Criminal Code	II/4 Land and Agricultural Policies
I/5 Press and Media Policies and Regulation	II/5 Budgetary Policies
I/6 Peaceful Transition and Nonviolence: Substantive and Procedural Guarantees	II/6 Regulation of Economic Competition and of Business Monopolies

*Chaired, in rotation, by a representative of the HSWP, the ORT, and the "third side."

**An *ad hoc* committee between the working groups and the mid-level panels to assist with the development of consensus on disputed issues.

The National Roundtable: issues and participants

The ORT's negotiating priorities were spelled out in two statements of policy intentions.[103] The political document spoke of the electoral system and of constitutional changes: among other things, the establishment of a constitutional court and an office of the president of the Republic; of a revised criminal code and of criminal justice procedures, with emphasis on the protection of individual human rights; provisions guaranteeing equal chances for political parties during an electoral campaign; equal access to the print and electronic media; and disbanding the Workers' Guard.

The sociopolitical policy document was prefaced by the ORT's disavowal of political responsibility for the regime's bankrupt policies and the ORT's announcement of its disinclination to lend its name to last-minute rescue packages that the government might submit to stay afloat until the elections. On the other hand, the ORT proposed negotiations to limit the damage already caused by the Company Law that the Parliament had enacted earlier in the year. At issue were the early results of the privatization of various state-owned enterprises, specifically, the incumbent managers' government-assisted conversion of their political-administrative privileges into economic power.

The regime's plans, such as they were, had been described in Grósz's June 13 speech. He stated that "it would be sensible if we were to view the already worked-out draft laws that have been made public as a basis for talks," and added, "naturally, any of the negotiating sides can avail itself of [the opportunity to submit] new proposals."[104] The secretary general's final goal was a "future viable coalition and, later, political alliances, as well." In any case, the replacement of Grósz by Nyers as head of the HSWP's NRT delegation caused no visible changes in the regime's agenda. Apart from occasional appearances by Pozsgay, it was "Grósz's orphan" György Fejti who represented the regime at the ORT until the end of July.

As a process, the Hungarian NRT may be likened to a cooperative, yet competitive, multiplayer game. All players had a stake in a positive outcome, yet within each of the three sides there were clashing interests and objectives that were incompatible with the desired result. In the broadest sense, the HSWP, its allies on the "third side," and even some players within the ORT sought changes *in* the existing political model. The ORT's "hard core," that is, the AFD and Fidesz, and to a lesser extent the HDF, was committed to the changing *of* the political system.

The Pozsgay–Fejti and, later on, the Pozsgay-led regime negotiators were, with few exceptions, not party hacks but senior civil servants. They were either ministry department heads or key executives from various government agencies. Their task, especially of those from the ministry of justice, was to see to the reaching of agreements more or less along the lines of the current language of the government's draft bills on fundamental (*sarkalatos*) issues. Reform communist scholar-bureaucrats, such as deputy minister of justice Géza Kilényi, were the authors of all draft bills that the HSWP PB had heard and approved earlier in 1989; therefore, they had a personal stake in seeing their versions prevail at the end.

Most of the ORT negotiators were either academic experts or enthusiastic amateurs. A few, such as the HDF's József Antall, a former high-school teacher turned medical historian, and the AFD's Iván Pető (an economic historian) and Bálint Magyar (a sociologist), were both.[105] In any case, all ORT negotiators were playing with borrowed chips that had been handed to them by the regime. In practical terms, they enacted the role of an artificially empowered quasi-legislature. Unlike the lame-duck Parliament, the NRT had an open-ended agenda.

Moreover, the ORT was also endowed with veto power over proposals by the *actual* wielders of political power in Hungary. The stakes were high, and much depended on the wisdom and the political skills of these novice politicians. Their sudden elevation from political obscurity to the public limelight was a major test of the opposition forces' intellectual maturity and bargaining skills.

At the beginning of substantive negotiations with the regime, the ORT had two kinds of political assets with which to advance its case. One was its public identification with the emancipatory legacy of the 1956 revolution and the martyrdom of the regime's high- and low-status victims. The other consisted of a mixed record of opposition to the policies of the political incumbents. The AFD and Fidesz had solid programs, a compelling record of civil courage, and well-crafted alternative policy drafts. On the other hand, the HDF, while still under the leadership of the Lakitelek "founding fathers," was Pozsgay's ally, albeit increasingly restless. Moreover, its programs, though well articulated on some issues, were long on rhetoric and short on legal-political expertise. This deficiency was subsequently overcome by the switching to the HDF side of the top ILF legal experts Imre Kónya and László Sólyom. The rest of the ORT consisted of bright Liga experts, elderly lawyers of the "historic parties," and various self-styled democrats of the HPP and the EBZSS from Pozsgay's political stable.

With the exception of István Kukorelli – a noted legal scholar – and his team of lawyers from the PPF, the "third side" was represented by mid- to high-level apparatchiki from the regime's policy lobbies and by party veterans from the Anti-Fascist Resistance organization and the Ferenc Münnich Society. Except for vigorous declarations of good intentions in the socioeconomic working groups, the "third side's" representatives were generally ignored by the regime's and the ORT's principal negotiators at the legal-political sessions.

The National Roundtable: a cooperative game?

In terms of legal guarantees for an orderly transition from the political stalemate of the summer of 1989 to the holding of free elections in early 1990, the deliberations of three of the NRT's twelve working groups were of particular importance. The agendas of working groups I/1, I/2, and I/3 on the Constitution, the political parties, and the elections, respectively, were central to the entire process. What were the issues that each sought to resolve?

For working group I/1, the task was to reshape Hungary's much-amended Constitution of 1949 into a basic document to reflect the nation's political identity and institutional structure, and the citizens' new relationship to the state in a pluralistic political system. Because the new Constitution was deemed to be central to Hungary's future institutional structure, the ORT deployed its top experts at this negotiating table. Péter Tölgyessy (AFD), Imre Kónya (ILF, then HDF), Viktor Orbán (Fidesz), József Antall (HDF), and Imre Boross (ISP) were about the best people to guard the opposition's interests at this venue of political bargaining.

In addition to changing the language of the old Constitution and removing references to the HSWP from the text, decisions had to be made on the creation of new political institutions. In view of Imre Pozsgay's declared candidacy for the office of president of the Republic, both the powers of this office and the time and manner of election, or plebiscite to be held for this purpose, were matters of overriding importance. Everyone agreed that the popular reformer was preferable to the incumbent collective presidency. The ORT's dilemma was whether it was worth mortgaging the country's future for the premature election of a transition figure to oversee the national elections and to lead the nation therafter.

The establishment of a constitutional court represented another challenge to the ORT's political wisdom. Everyone seemed to agree that the upholding of the rule of law was best left in the hands of an independent judicial body. Still, it was unclear whether the initial appointees might not become the guardians of reform communist (that is, those of the top political incumbents such as Németh, Pozsgay, Nyers, and their deputies) notions of law and order and those of the proper balance of power among the Parliament, the government, and the president of the Republic. Few of the ORT negotiators had the expertise to amend the regime's draft text on the table.[106]

The political parties' legal status; the party membership of judges, prosecutors, and civil servants; and party finances were the subject of negotiations in working group I/2. Whereas the first two issues, particularly that of a nonpartisan judiciary and civil service, were quickly settled, the issue of party finances turned out to be difficult to resolve. Although the Németh government was willing to underwrite the initial expenses in connection with the launching of the new political parties, the HSWP refused to submit a detailed accounting of its assets.[107] After a four-week suspension of talks, the party relented but postponed publication of a report until the next congress of the HSWP in early October. Similarly, no agreement was reached on the contentious issue of party cells in the workplace. This, too, was rolled over to the next, post-NRT phase of political contestation between the regime and the opposition.

Changes in the electoral system were the subject of negotiations in working group I/3. The method of competing electoral lists of party nominees tended to favor the "historic" parties, whose candidates were unknown at the local level. On the other hand, elections held solely on the basis of contests in individual electoral districts favored the political incumbents and, so the AFD believed, the parties that could field nationally known prominent reform intellectuals in most electoral districts. Thanks to its early start, the success of its candidates at the summer by-elections, and confidence in its grassroots following, the HDF was in the position to propose a solution. The solution consisted of a compromise formula of filling the 350 parliamentary seats with MPs – half from party lists and half from individual districts.[108]

Other issues, such as the number of signatures required to put an individual candidate on the ballot (the NRT decided on 750) and the threshold of votes cast for party lists to count toward the election of candidates on such lists (4 percent was agreed upon), were resolved without particular difficulty. Similar consensus was reached on the potentially contentious technicalities of two-round elections in individual districts in which no candidate received 50 percent plus one of the votes cast in the first round.[109]

There is little information on the internal deliberations of five of the six working groups on socioeconomic issues. As András Bozóki (a Fidesz negotiator) put it, most participants were one of two types of reform economists: "those who left the HSWP in time" and "those who had forgotten to leave it in time."[110] However, thanks to the leading reform economist Erzsébet Szalai's insightful account of the issues and the personalities of the II/3 working group on privatization in which she participated, one can partly reconstruct what took place there in the summer of 1989.[111]

As Szalai explained, neither the regime nor the opposition had any ready-made policy positions on this subject. Therefore, each participant was free to develop his or her case as the work of the group progressed. Except for the articulate political emissaries of the "third side," negotiators for both the regime and the ORT were economists. They were the same people "who had been arguing with one another in the past few years – except that now they wore different hats."[112] Because the government refused to release information on the progress of privatization to date, the three sides joined forces to draft a statement demanding that "information on the performance and the contemplated transformation in the ownership of state assets be made public."[113]

It appears that both the "first side" and the AFD and Fidesz negotiators were in favor of starting the process of privatization of state assets as soon as possible. Moreover, the government's representative insisted that, irrespective of evidence of widespread abuses associated with many cases of self-privatization of state enterprises, the process had to continue. His explanation, "The suspension of privatization would provoke resistance from the directors of large enterprises and thus put at risk the economic foundations of the peaceful transformation of the political system," was the Németh government's official position in 1988–90.[114]

In citing this statement Szalai unwittingly pointed to the inherently flawed nature of the the entire NRT process. The government refused to make use of its legal resources to clear up the chaos surrounding the process of self-privatization by the incumbent managers. In doing so, the outgoing regime, in effect, gave a green light to the systematic embezzlement of state assets by the "red barons" of Hungary's industry and commerce.

While the government experts and the ORT's well-meaning democrats were arguing about subtle points of public law, the old regime's economic elites were busy transforming, through fairly simple legal tricks, state enterprises into "worker and management-owned" companies. Thanks to the Németh government's deliberately turning a blind eye to the quiet takeover of substantial portions of the country's productive resources by the incumbent captains of industry, banking, and commerce, much of the real power in Hungary remained in the hands of the Kádár regime's economic *nomenklatura* elite well beyond the 1990 elections.

Hungary's "red and green barons" were absent from the NRT, but their interests were well represented there. In a rare moment of candor, the "third side" of the II/3 working group sought to question the credibility of the AFD's negotiator. What they wanted to know was whether the distinguished economist was representing his party or Financial Research, Inc., of which he was the chief executive officer. What was left unsaid was that FRI had an extremely profitable consulting practice in its assisting state enterprises to become private firms.[115]

Szalai used the phrase "tryout for [future] roles" (*szereppróba*) to characterize the negotiators' and their sponsors' search for new roles in the public and business life of a postcommunist Hungary. As she explained, many of the ORT negotiators in the socioeconomic working groups made use of their experience to develop programs for their own parties and to make contacts among government bureaucrats. In fact, the process also worked the other way around. After the 1990 elections, several government negotiators, such as József Kajdi of the Ministry of Justice and György Szilvásy (one of Pozsgay's assistants), were promptly appointed by József Antall to serve as senior officials in the office of the prime minister.

The National Roundtable: the incumbents, the insurgents and the bystanders

The real agenda of the NRT negotiations was not the making of debating points and networking among negotiators but the distribution of political power among the old, the new, and the holdover elites. Decisions and nondecisions on each agenda item had bearing on the new balance of power among political parties, economic interests, and social forces of postcommunist Hungary. The incumbents and the insurgents had a shared interest in a mutually advantageous outcome. What came between them were Hungary's nonelites and their regime-sponsored spokesmen on the "third side."

According to a critical self-assessment of the "third side's" performance at the NRT, the constituent organizations had an eight-point program of negotiating objectives.[116] The key items were bread-and-butter issues, such as wages, workers' self-management, and the economic requisites of a social safety net. As negotiations progressed, it became apparent that neither the regime nor the ORT was willing to engage in substantive discussions on these issues.

At the end of August the regime's proxies on the "third side" found themselves bypassed at the mid-level negotiating sessions. One wrote in his diary, "This is how the French army's enlisted men must have felt at the Maginot Line during the Second World War. They were ready to give their lives to defend their country, but came to realize that behind their backs the [French] generals were cordially fraternizing with German officers."[117] To remind the "generals" that there was a war to be fought, the Trade Union Federation began preparations for strikes and work stoppages.[118] The old regime's favorites, the coal and uranium miners, led the way – only to find that the Németh government refused to accede to their demands.[119] And, when the

TUF's friends in the HSWP CC protested, Németh dismissed their complaints by saying that economic policies were not the party's but the government's responsibility.[120] In the summer and fall of 1989, neither the government-controlled media nor the key AFD-sympathizer press and media personalities were willing to take up the cause of the blue-collar workers.[121]

Some of the ORT's "officers," particularly the MDF's József Antall and the Christian Democrats, the Smallholders, and Pozsgay's proxies, were more willing to "fraternize" with the regime's representatives than were those of the AFD, Fidesz, and the Liga. In the summer of 1989 no one could foresee the collapse of the East German regime and the coming of the Czechoslovak "velvet revolution," nor could anyone predict how Gorbachev might react to the radicalization and drastic polarization of the Hungarian political scene. For these reasons, the HDF still thought in terms of an eventual coalition government between the HDF and a "reformed" HSWP.

The HDF's initial strategy, had it been implemented, would have left the Smallholders and the Social Democrats in limbo. On the other hand, the prospects of an HSWP–HDF electoral alliance posed a major threat to the AFD and Fidesz. The AFD-supporter János Kenedi's *bon mot* about the HDF–AFD rivalry was not far from the mark. To the question "Why hold negotiations behind closed doors?" his reply was "So the HDF could hide the absence of its experts and the AFD could hide the absence of its followers."[122] The HDF's clean sweep in the summer by-elections was an early indication of that party's strong electoral prospects in the spring of 1990. At that time the liberal democrats' mass support was nowhere on the horizon.

Confronted with the choice of either observing the NRT's ground rules and of finding itself at the periphery of the political arena or going to "the streets" to recruit new followers, the AFD chose the latter. The issue that presented the AFD with the opportunity to break ranks with the ORT had been the HSWP central apparat's amateurish attempts to "privatize" the party's assets in the form of several one-man "companies" and "foundations." Thanks to AFD lawyers and its supporters in the media, the news-starved public was shown incontrovertible evidence of the misappropriation of party assets for the benefit of a few enterprising apparatchiki.[123]

Not to be left behind, and to show that Fidesz was the most radical opposition group in Hungary, the Young Democrats mounted a different project. The party sent Tamás Deutsch and three other Fidesz activists to Prague to join the protest demonstration to commemorate the anniversary of the Soviet-led invasion of Czechoslovakia on August 21, 1968.[124] The detainment and the subsequent release – with the Hungarian government's help – of the Fidesz team was a courageous publicity stunt that kept the party in the political limelight in the coming months in Hungary.

Imre Pozsgay: a reform communist under crossfire

Imre Pozsgay was the designated leader of the regime's negotiating team at the NRT; however, most of the initial discussions were conducted by György Fejti, Grósz's deputy for legal and administrative affairs. Fejti (an engineer by training) was a competent and tough negotiator. His heavy-handed tactics ruffled feathers in the ORT camp. Pozsgay sought to avoid a showdown with the HSWP's new chairman, Rezső Nyers, on Fejti's unyielding stance at the negotiating table. Therefore, in mid-July he left town for a three-week vacation. His timing was right; in his absence the negotiations came to a standstill and were, at least for purposes of mid-level meetings, suspended until mid-August. At that point, Pozsgay was the only person who could rescue the HSWP–ORT dialogue from a premature collapse. As Pozsgay recalled, from then on he had a free hand to make the best deal he could with the opposition.[125] Still, as he came to realize in the coming weeks, his hands were tied in several ways.

Pozsgay found himself in an extremely difficult position during the last four weeks of the NRT negotiations. On the one hand, his party expected him to protect its local organizations in the workplace; to prevent the dissolution of the Workers' Guard; to shield the party's assets from outside scrutiny; and to keep the ORT divided on as many issues as possible. On the other hand, Pozsgay was convinced that the HSWP had no business in maintaining its intimidating presence in places of employment; he considered the Workers' Guard as the party conservatives' reserve army; and viewed the HSWP's assets as an unwanted burden for an electoral party.[126] In his view, these divisive issues tended to compromise his candidacy for the office of the president of the Republic. Moreover, Pozsgay wished to preserve his privileged relationship with the HDF, particularly with József Antall, who had emerged as his party's top negotiator and, in all probability, its future leader as well.[127]

Pozsgay's difficulties were, in part, exacerbated by the cooling off of his political relationship with Miklós Németh. Moreover, there was a growing distance between him and Rezső Nyers on fundamental issues of party politics – including his suspected ambitions to become the leader of a "reformed" HSWP after its October congress.[128] Németh's tough stance on labor issues, his public endorsement of Hungary's national values, and his appearance, as a private citizen, at Catholic religious services could be construed as his bid for support from Pozsgay's constituencies. Moreover, Németh refrained from publicly endorsing Pozsgay's candidacy for president and offered only lukewarm support to his beleaguered colleague before the party's hostile Central Committee.[129]

Pozsgay's differences with Nyers were ideological and tactical. Nyers sought to reshape the HSWP into a "united workers' party" yet preserve its dominant position in the workplace, in the military, and in the police. Pozsgay had a socialist party in mind with strong commitment to national values, rural interests, and the cultural intelligentsia. Nyers had his "private political movement" (the New March Front), and so did Pozsgay (Movement for a Democratic Hungary); both competed for the support of the same intelligentsia groups.[130] In any case, Nyers distrusted Pozsgay's leadership ambitions and had seen to it – probably during his meeting with Gorbachev in July – that Pozsgay's much-coveted invitation to Moscow would not be issued before the October party congress.[131]

In the last three weeks of the ORT negotiations, Imre Pozsgay had to do battle on three fronts. As the regime's chief negotiator, he had to persuade the skeptical ORT that a half loaf – essentially the regime's legislative package, as modified, in many cases quite substantially, by the opposition – was preferable to political chaos.[132] In the meantime he had to keep the HSWP's increasingly restless parliamentary caucus satisfied that neither he nor the ORT intended any disrespect to the party's parliamentary MPs whilst producing a ready-made legislative agenda for their approval. Although legislative liaison was Németh's and House Speaker Szűrös' responsibility, Pozsgay had to be certain that, should these fickle allies desert him, he still would have the MPs on his side. Németh's comment before the September 1 meeting of the HSWP CC, "If no agreement is reached at the NRT, the government should be empowered to submit the entire package to the Parliament," was an indirect threat against both Pozsgay and his friends at the ORT.[133] In any case, Pozsgay had to keep his presidential candidacy alive, including the critically important matter that elections for this office be held by a plebiscite *before* the national elections.

The HSWP's Central Committee was the third front where Pozsgay had to fight to gain this body's approval of his strategy at the ORT negotiations. At the September 1 meeting he reminded his listeners that the party's original intent had been "to resolve, in a negotiated manner, our differences at the [bargaining] table, rather than on the streets,"[134] and assured them that he had fully adhered to the secretary general's June 13 official statement on the HSWP negotiating objectives.[135] He went out of his way to point out that in the agreed-upon unicameral legislature only political parties rather than social organizations – such as the TUF and the PPF – would be present.

Pozsgay took pride in the compromise formula – "The Republic of Hungary is an independent democratic *Rechtsstaat* (*jogállam*) in which the values of bourgeois democracy and democratic socialism are realized equally" – that the NRT adopted as the introductory sentence of the revised Constitution.[136] In any case, he assured the CC that the NRT negotiations were well in hand. Moreover, he was pleased to report that:

> the ORT is not united and this helps improve the HSWP's negotiating position ... do not ask me for a [more] detailed report, for what we are involved in is a tactical [temporary?] situation ... [we] are participants in all kinds of informal, nonregulated and noninstitutional negotiations with the representatives of the opposition. In other words ... there is a great deal happening away from the negotiating table. We have frequent and sufficiently detailed information on the internal divisions of the opposition. Most recently, the ORT had a ten-hour non-stop debate on the Constitution and the presidency of the Republic. Even though they they came out with a consensus formula, we have exact knowledge that there is no real agreement among them ... we have access to internal information and this [enables us] to take advantage of the divisions among them.[137]

With the nearing of agreements on several parts of the NRT's expanded and, to some extent, improvised agenda, it fell to Pozsgay to sell the CC on the value of *its* "half of the loaf." He felt that the party's gesture of handing over to the state those of its assets that had come into the HSWP's possession since 1977 helped assuage public concerns on this subject. Though the final agreement was not yet in hand, he was confident that it would be reached within the next several days.[138]

In the course of the ensuing discussion the speakers, while more or less conceding defeat, made several points. The optimist István Horváth believed that parliamentary elections should be held in the following year. As he explained, "with longer lead time, the ORT will fall apart."[139] Fejti was chagrined by the media's coverage of the NRT negotiations. He said, "To me it is unacceptable that our own daily newspaper [*Népszabadság*] gives an objective account of the three sides' positions."[140] Németh submitted that "our defeat was almost complete when we sat down to negotiate" and added, "we had been unprepared." In a self-critical way, he also admitted that "the government had made a mistake when we suspended legislation [on issues] before [the commencement of] the trilateral negotiations. [The ORT] ... has held the government and the Parliament hostage."[141] He concluded by saying: "we need much better assessments about the opposition. Here and there we have some tools of our own and I even read some of these grade-school-level somethings [that are put on my desk]. What are they? Little pieces of paper."[142]

It appears that neither the prime minister's daily political intelligence reports nor transcripts of telephone taps of conversations among members of the opposition were of any help to the beset incumbents. The party tried but failed to outmaneuver the opposition. The CC did not like what it heard from its leaders. This, in turn, prompted Pozsgay to demand that the CC reconfirm his nomination as the party's standard-bearer for the office of president of the Republic. He reminded his colleagues that only trusted leaders, rather than the party, could turn the situation around. As he put it, "if we had ten times more air time and ten times more press coverage, we would be ten times more defeated."[143] On this melancholic note, the CC duly reconfirmed Pozsgay's candidacy for the highest office of the land.

The NRT agreement: mandate for peaceful transition?

The National Roundtable agreement of September 18, 1989 is a historic document in two senses of the word. As a compromise between the foreign-sponsored rulers and the indigenous elites, it was the last stage on the long road of coming to terms through negotiations between the political incumbents and the insurgent elites. The NRT agreement was also a symbolic capstone of the sheltering of individual and collective "little freedoms" that millions of Hungarian citizens had wrested from the regime since 1968. The ORT's negotiators built their case for temporary power sharing with the regime from the accumulated results of the people's quiet struggle for first-class citizenship through equitable representation of their interests in the political arena.

The agreement proper (see Appendix 7.1) was an open-ended document. On the one hand, it registered the few legislative items on which consensus had been reached by the negotiators. On the other hand, for the sake of peaceful transition to free elections, it unilaterally empowered the opposition parties to act as if they were the incumbents' political equals. Although much of the agreement is self-explanatory, the items listed in part 3 and the non-signers' position warrant two comments.

First, instead of being the domain of "expert NRT committees" that basically ceased to function after September 18, rule-making regarding the resolution and implementation of several transition measures became the government's and the Parliament's responsibility. The latter was no longer the party-state's voting machine but a collection of half-emancipated and half-bewildered lame-duck politicians with priorities of their own. Fortunately, the priorities largely coincided with those of the ORT's and the Németh government's policy intentions.

Second, it must be pointed out that the AFD and Fidesz, though refusing to sign the agreement, refrained from vetoing it.[144] In doing so, they chose to benefit, together with the rest of the ORT parties, from its positive achievements. At the same time, they thereby reserved the option to modify the objectionable points of the agreement by any legal means available to them.[145] In the liberals' view – one that the Smallholders and the Social Democrats came to share in the next two months – an early vote on the presidency would have put Pozsgay and his party in a position of dominant influence both before and after the 1990 parliamentary elections. Moreover, given the increasingly open collaboration between Pozsgay and Antall, and hence the HDF's vastly improved electoral chances, the left-of-center parties were at risk of political marginalization at the ballot box. The liberals' response to this challenge will be discussed in the next chapter.

(D)   The HSWP – demise and resurrection

According to *Népszabadság*, the dictatorship of the proletariat ceased to exist in Hungary on the second day of the 14th congress of the HSWP, at 10:24 p.m., October 7, 1989.[146] The time denoted the formal establishment of the Hungarian Socialist Party (HSP).[147] Although one-sixth of the 1,274 congressional delegates either did not vote or abstained, the birth of the HSP marked the end of an era and the beginning of the terminal phase of communist rule in Hungary. Befitting the first nonpremanipulated communist party congress in East European history, the transformation of the HSWP into the HSP was a complex, confusing, and chaotic process. The entire event was driven more by the delegates' desperate desire to escape the burden of the party's past than by their commitment to a coherent program of postcommunist politics.

"Revolt of the insecure new socialist middle class" may be one way to account for the congressional delegates' shared motivation to effect a radical change rather than renewal of the old political model. More than 85 percent of the delegates were university graduates and 83.1 percent were – mainly lower-level – party officials. They had had enough of the Kádár and Grósz regimes' ouvrierist demagogy and of the "iron law" of apparat gerontarchy. They refused to bear the burden of public disapproval of the old regime's corruption and of the top officials' brazen sabotage of much-needed reforms.

Many of the delegates spoke on behalf of frustrated provincial party constituencies. They had been stunned by the HSWP's disastrous electoral performance in the summer by-elections and demanded drastic changes at a high but still-tolerable political cost to the HSP. By this they meant the necessity of forgoing at the party congress a formal split into "conservative," "centrist," and "radical reformer" splinter parties and of desisting from the expulsion of adherents of the several policy platforms presented at the congress.

To finesse the matter of throwing the passive rank-and-file membership overboard, it was decided to "privatize" the procedure of transition from the old to the new party. Each HSWP member was given three weeks to decide whether to sign a pledge of adherence to the program and statutes, thus to join the HSP. This procedure made abandonment of the *new* party a private affair rather than a public gesture by the individual involved. The arrangement also suited the top leaders and the still-active party apparat. The former took legal title to the remaining and potentially vastly lucrative assets of the HSWP. The one-time "corporate raiders" paid off the latter from the proceeds and converted the rest into start-up reserves for the new party. In any event, for an average congressional delegate (91.9 percent of the delegates were men) it took courage to formally renounce his share of the power, privileges, and perquisites of the crumbling but not yet extinct party-state. The prospects of at best a minority share of governing power in a democratic pluralist political system were disconcerting to the assembled party faithful.

The endgame in the HSWP: leaders and policy platforms

The HSWP's interim four-man Presidium was rent by severe disagreements after its creation in late June. Though Pozsgay asserted that his nomination as the party's candidate for president of the Republic had been a trap laid by Grósz, the trap was of his own making.[148] Others considered it a peace offering to the HSWP's reform circles. However, none of this prevented Nyers from vetoing a number of Pozsgay-sponsored measures at the National Roundtable. Moreover, the Grósz-controlled apparat managed to embarrass Pozsgay by nominating him (without his knowledge), then arranging for his defeat, as a congressional delegate from the HSWP conservatives' Debrecen stronghold.

Németh, with his tough stance against the TUF and born-again Christian Socialist public rhetoric, was another odd man out. Nyers sought to play the role of peacemaker, but there was not any doubt that his sympathies lay more with the party's, by then quite hollow, center than with Pozsgay and Németh. Although Nyers and Pozsgay dutifully endorsed each other's private Popular Fronts – that is, Pozsgay's Movement for a Democratic Hungary and Nyers' New March Front – their words lacked conviction, and everybody knew it.

What kept the four men together was inertia – as much as their sense of fatalistically awaiting what the next day might bring. The dismantling of the Iron Curtain and the Hungarian leadership's management of the wholly unexpected East German refugee crisis is a case in point. The arrival in Hungary in August and September of thousands of East German tourists and their subsequent refusal to return home was an important test of the four leaders' political unity. The outcome is now history.[149] In any case, credit for having initiated the dismantling of the Iron Curtain at the Austrian border belonged to the former (Grósz) and the incumbent (Németh) prime ministers of Hungary – and whichever Western power *told* them to do it, and whoever in the Kremlin *let* them do it. Credit for co-sponsoring a "pan-European picnic" in late August when scores of GDR tourists first escaped through the Austrian border was Pozsgay's – and his deputy's (State Secretary László Vass) who stood in for him and witnessed the East Germans fleeing the coop. And the credit for rejecting the GDR party chief Erich Honecker's demands for the repatriation of the desperate East German citizens belonged to all four, as well as to Foreign Minister Gyula Horn whose job was to carry the leadership's messages between Budapest, East Berlin, and Bonn. In the end, the East Germans were free to go Austria. With their courageous stand, the HSWP's outgoing leadership earned the gratitude of the Federal Republic of Germany and the esteem of the Western political community. Oddly enough, this brave gesture, though it impressed the Hungarian military and the police, failed to earn political rewards from the Hungarian public.

In the waning weeks of the old regime, political courage and petty politics mixed easily. A case in point is Károly Grósz's last-ditch attempt to even the score with those in the leadership who had lent their presence, as honorary pallbearers, to Imre Nagy's reburial on June 16. Toward the end of the September 1 meeting of the HSWP CC, Grósz stood up and read his summary of a report on Imre Nagy that he had received from the KGB's archives.[150] According to the KGB documents, from his earliest days (1921–22) in the USSR, Imre Nagy was closely connected with the Cheka and later on with the OGPU. Upon his return to Moscow in 1930, he signed an agreement of cooperation with the political police. For the next ten years he was alleged to have supplied the authorities with names of Hungarian communist immigrants as suspected "enemies of the people." The report listed dozens of such people who had fallen victim to the Great Purges in the 1930s in the USSR.

At the end of his speech on this dismal business, Grósz asked: "Aren't we violating the memory of this reform politician and aren't we trying to debase (deheroizálni) the memory of one of the founders of the HSWP?" His reply: "I am convinced that what you heard is not decisive for the adjudication of Imre Nagy's career ... Of his activities, what we consider to be of value is what he did for [the cause of] democratic socialism and for a free, independent, socialist Hungary." Then why bring up this matter in the first place? No one had an answer, though his enemies in the CC called it behavior typical of a cornered carnivore. Political desperation and extreme psychological stress might be a more appropriate explanation for Grósz's conduct.[151]

Upon conclusion of the National Roundtable negotiations on September 18, Pozsgay and Nyers met to work out an agreement on their respective positions at the party congress. As far as can be reconstructed from information from those who were close to the two men, Nyers asked for and received a pledge from Pozsgay that the HSWP's Reform Circles, now renamed Reform Alliance (RA), would not precipitate a walkout or an open split during the congress. He also received Pozsgay's endorsement for the party's chairmanship and consented to the party's new name. In return, Pozsgay obtained Nyers' continued endorsement for the presidency of Hungary and his promise of full accommodation of the RA in the new party's leadership. The new party's program, statutes, and the substance of the HSWP's economic and foreign policy report were conceded, apparently without dispute, to Pozsgay's teams of reform intellectuals.

It was this compromise package that was presented by the party leadership to a meeting of the assembled delegates on the eve of the October 6–9 party congress. Last-minute efforts by Grósz to recast the congressional program and to amend the draft program documents were of no avail. His original report on party affairs was rejected by the outgoing Political Executive Committee. His only chance to address the congress was limited to his presentation of a revised general report, some of which may well have been written by someone else's staff.[152]

The HSWP: protoparties as policy platforms

By the end of September, the HSWP's internal divisions had come out into the open and begun coalescing into distinct policy platforms. The most visible ones may be characterized as those belonging to the extreme left, the left of center and the center of the ideological spectrum.

Because of its political-organizational links with the Workers' Guard, the extreme left's most important component was the Ferenc Münnich Society (FMS). The society's participation in the National Roundtable negotiations had been inconsequential. What mattered was that it had agreed to join this process in the first place. In doing so, the FMS had lost much of its conspiratorial character and its role was reduced to that of a symbol of the radical left's presence at these proceedings. The Workers' Marxist–Leninist Party, the Communist Party of Hungary, and the János Kádár Society – all established since the end of August – provided comic relief and indirectly helped legitimate the other pre-congress HSWP policy platforms that were closer to the ideological center.

The "Rally for the Renewal of the HSWP" and the "Unity Platform for the HSWP" had come about as the result of local and regional initiatives during the summer months. János Berecz lent his name to the latter but, as demonstrated by this group's performance at the party congress, it was successfully blocked by both the conservative apparat and the resurgent reform forces.

The HSWP's Reform Alliance was the most important new player in the political scene. The membership of a typical RA organization consisted of young professionals; lower-level party officials; particularly from the ideological and cultural apparat; assorted local Young Turks with political ambitions; and, in Budapest, sizeable contingents of reform intellectuals from all walks of life.

The RA's national conference of September 2–3, 1989 produced what may be called the reform camp's "maximum program."[153] It called for items that subsequently appeared, in a heavily watered-down form, in the HSP's own program, such as the abolition of the Workers' Guards, the return of party assets to the state, and the transfer of workplace party organizations to residential neighborhoods. The party congress failed to act on these issues.

Owing to poor coordination, resistance by the apparat, and apathy of the rank-and-file membership, the RA had peaked in mid-September and could not become the dominant force in early October. The RA's failure to effect a political breakthrough provides a key to an explanation for the ambiguous outcome of the HSWP's hoped-for rebirth as a "socialist" party. The very idea of drastic reforms, institutional restructuring, and the party's abandonment of the "commanding heights of power" had failed to win the support of the HSWP's passive and apprehensive majority. On the other hand, the party's semiactive minority was still dominated by the apparat. Therefore, it was all the more remarkable that the RA managed to gain the support of as many as 40 percent of the congressional delegates. The RA-pledged delegates had been winners, often by razor-thin majorities, of bruising local congressional nominating battles in Budapest and in the countryside.

At the beginning of the congress, the only open question was the delegates' likely affiliation with one or another policy platform. Whereas the RA arrived with 464 pledged delegates, the rest of the eight platforms had only about 200 committed supporters (see Table 7.2). Thus, it was the uncommitted 45 percent who, unless promptly recruited, could have posed a problem, such as rejecting the whole or parts of the Nyers–Pozsgay brokered agreement. From Nyers' viewpoint, the "bandwagon" to stop was Pozsgay's RA. To accomplish this, and because it was too late to start a new platform from scratch, an existing platform had to be found to serve as a vehicle for this purpose. By noon of the following day it became apparent that the People's Democratic platform (PD) – originally founded in September 1988 by a group of young Marxist intellectuals – was to be the chosen instrument to keep the RA at bay.

The HSWP: from rearguard to oblivion

October 6 was the first day of the HSWP congress. Apart from the unexpectedly uninspiring speeches by the leadership,[154] the only surprise was the appearance of speakers for the county caucuses. They were harshly critical of the leadership and demanded drastic changes.

Table 7.2   *Policy platforms, 14th HSWP/1st HSP congress*[155]

| Policy | Number of supporters | | |
caucus	Oct. 6 morning	Oct. 7 evening	Oct. 8 evening
People's Democratic	60	226	290
Unity*	30	20	14
Rally for the HSWP	35	27	23
Reform Alliance	464	474	511
Equal Opportunity for the Countryside**	43	56	62
Youth	26	29	32
Agriculture and Food Industries**	28	51	101
For a Healthy Hungary	–	32	38
Workers' Section	–	39	27
Total	686	954	1,098

* Dissolved, October 9
** Merged, October 9

These included a new deal for rural Hungary, the uprooting of systemic corruption, and local autonomy and semisovereign status for the local party organizations. Two speakers from Kecskemét and Zala county related the story of their electoral defeats as parliamentary candidates of a "700,000–strong party" at the hands of contenders sponsored by the Hungarian Democratic Forum, "a party of 20,000 members."

On October 7 the word was out that the PD platform was the group to sign up with if one wished to fall behind Nyers and his camp of cautious progressives. Many prescient delegates took the hint, and more than 160 joined the PD platform on that day. The apparat's Pavlovian reflexes were still in good working order. After all, it was Nyers who had decided on the amount of the party employees' severance pay.

The day climaxed with the formal establishment of the Hungarian Socialist Party. The event was announced by Nyers in a major policy speech.[156] One had to be present and understand Hungarian to appreciate the "out-of-character" nature of the speech. It was authoritative but also authoritarian. Nyers' gestures and intonation were vintage Kádár. He lashed out at Németh and Németh's so-called government of experts. He called for unity and discipline, and urged everyone, even Berecz, to stay in the new party. However, he remained silent about the party's electoral failures and about the controversial disposition of party assets and the Workers' Guard. Instead, he spoke of a new "social market economy" and a new synthesis of socialism and democracy in Hungary. Following this diatribe, Nyers met the international press. There he described himself as a "man with the habits of the 1930s," an "easygoing person," and a "reformer as early as 1953."[157] It was a pity that Kádár was not there to hear it. Even he could not have done a better job of dissembling and purveying disinformation.

The third day of the congress began with a severe "morning-after" ideological hangover for many RA delegates. The Nyers speech had shocked a goodly number into questioning the direction of the entire affair, particularly their role therein. By that time the RA leaders were locked in smoke-filled rooms with the PD negotiators. Spokesmen of each of the principal platforms had prepared lists of names of proposed HSP Executive Committee members. At that point, Pozsgay's and Nyers' lieutenants joined the fray. Insults and accusations were exchanged, and fairly soon the entire brokered behind-the-scenes nominating process collapsed.

It was at this juncture that Iván Vitányi – Nyers' man and Aczél's former errand-runner – called on the leaders to spell out their differences at a closed session. After a vote of 720 to 470 in favor of a closed session, it was held. Then the congress was recessed for four hours. During that intermission Pozsgay, Németh, and Horn had a private showdown with Nyers over the proposed exclusion of Horn from the party executive. Nyers relented, and the threatened walkout by the RA was thus averted.

Pozsgay's and Németh's negotiating position was strong but by no means decisive.[158] The PD platform was weaker, but, as the designated leader, Nyers had the capability to sway the rest of the platforms – save the truculent Grósz–Berecz camp of about 150 – and put down any nonprearranged motion by the RA.

The process of leadership selection resumed at 7:30 in the morning of the fourth day (October 9). Present were the RA and the PD negotiators but no one from the other platforms. The *modus operandi* was that of exchanging "closed lists" of names and letting the other side veto, or, as the negotiators put it, "to COCOM," a platform's proposed leadership list. The end result was the mutual annihilation of both side's top ideologues. Moreover, Mátyás Szűrös failed to get elected – an odd state of affairs for the Speaker of the Parliament and president pro tem of the Republic of Hungary. The most keenly felt loss was Pozsgay's, whose invitation to the leading socialist reform ideologues Mihály

Bihari and László Lengyel was promptly declined by these former allies.

According to congressional insiders, negotiators for the two platforms finally agreed on a list of twenty-one names, which they handed over to Nyers and Pozsgay, who crossed out some names and added a few. In the end a compromise was reached between the leaders and the platform managers on a list of twenty-four names. Those excluded from the final list became mortal enemies of their respective patrons, and after the congress very few of them chose to join the HSP.[159]

The roster of the new HSP Executive need not appear here. For the record: sixteen of the twenty-four members had belonged to the RA. However, the actual management of this body was in the hands of two "full-time party employees," one from the RA and one from the PD. The leaders – Nyers, Pozsgay, Németh, and Horn – remained the same. Grósz and Berecz disappeared,[160] but reemerged two months later as founding members of the new-old Hungarian Socialist Workers' Party.

Conclusions

The establishment of the HSP on October 7, 1989 was a historic step that marked the end of one-party dictatorship in Hungary. The new party discharged hundreds of thousands of its nominal members, internal fellow-travelers and true believers alike. It is remarkable that in the frenzy of casting off the HSWP's burdensome legacy, it never occurred to the Nyers–Pozsgay leadership to throw a lifeline and, with it, a sense of belonging, to the abandoned rank and file. Had they found a way to maintain, by whatever ideological chicanery, the average HSWP member's formal affiliation with a Pozsgay-led HSP, precongressional Western forecasts of 30-plus per cent electoral support might have materialized in 1990.[161] However, this was not to be.

Under its heterogeneous leadership the HSP was a disunited party, and in terms of its capacity to become a major electoral contender, it was severely handicapped as well. The party was disunited because the RA–PD compromise left the rest of the policy caucuses out in the cold. Each of the latter, particularly "countryside," "food and agriculture," and "youth" had been, as protoparties, emerging components of genuine political pluralism within the bowels of the defunct HSWP. As far as these constituencies were concerned, they had been dismissed by a handful of self-serving politicians from a yet-to-be-born democratic socialist political movement.

The party was also disunited because it lacked a dynamic leader with a credible program and broad national appeal. Nyers had neither. Under different circumstances, Pozsgay might have fitted the bill, but not in October 1989. After the party congress he struck most people as an exhausted, vacillating, and somewhat disoriented politician. He was visibly at a loss as to ways of meeting the dual challenge of presidential candidacy and party leadership. His precongressional campaign promised a radical break with the past, yet when it came to delivering on this commitment, he caved in and abandoned his followers to the mercy of Nyers and the unrepentant apparat. As a politician, he had built up his reform credentials as a man of vision, sincerity, and moral rectitude. In the end, however hard he tried, he could not recast his political image from that of an in-house reform communist rebel to that of socialist statesman.

Paradoxically, Miklós Németh's government and his adroit management of the now rudderless Parliament were the cause, as well as the effect, of a politically incompetent HSP. From early October on, the Hungarian government had no party, and "the party" had no government – at least none that it could control through the HSP Executive Committee. The management of the country's political agenda became the sole domain of the state bureaucracy and the Parliament. As will be shown in the next chapter, the kinds of decisions that Nyers' party dared not make on such matters as the disbanding of the Workers' Guard, workplace party organization, and the return of most of the HSWP's assets to the state were being made with seemingly effortless ease by these two *working* branches of the political system.

In October 1989 the Hungarian political scene was quite fluid, but the option of undoing the NRT agreement and the halting of the Németh government's legislative juggernaut was no longer available to the cashiered cadres of the old party state. The stage was set for the process of transition to a multiparty democracy.[162]

Appendix 7.1

Agreement on the termination of the June 13, 1989–September 18, 1989 phase of the National Roundtable negotiations

Representatives of the Hungarian Socialist Workers' Party, the organizations affiliated with the Opposition Roundtable, and the social organizations and movements that constitute the Third Side hereby agree that the three-month-long process of negotiations that commenced on June 13, 1989 has been successfully concluded.

The three sides submit that pursuant to their [respective] Declarations of Policy Intent, the negotiations have helped create legal and political conditions for a peaceful transition, have shaped the unfolding of a multiparty democratic *Rechtsstaat* (*jogállam*), and have aided the search for a way out of the [current] social and economic crisis.

1. The three sides submit that as a result of negotiations, there developed among them a political consensus with respect to substantive questions of a peaceful transition. These are embodied in six draft bills. To wit,

– a bill on modification of the Constitution;
– a bill on the Constitutional Court;
– a bill on political parties and party finances;
– a bill on elections of members of the Parliament;
– a bill on modification of the Criminal Code;
– a bill on modification of the Law on Criminal Procedure.

The three sides, pursuant to their shared political objectives, will forward these and attached documents to the prime minister with the request that he, in accordance with Law XI of 1987 on legislative procedure, submit them to the Parliament. Alternative formulations proposed in connection with [the development of] these bills by the Hungarian Socialist Workers' Party and the Third Side should be accurately presented [to the Parliament]. The HSWP and the Third Side acknowledge that of the different variants of each bill, the ones by the Opposition Roundtable are in the form of declarations.

The three sides reconfirm their resolve to have these agreements accepted by their respective organizations, to identify themselves with [their terms] in the public realm, and also to make use of all their political resources to see to their implementation.

2. Delegations of the three sides will make separate political agreements on any additional subjects that, by their nature, do not call for legislative action. The list below contains, in part, specific commitments undertaken by each of the three sides and, in part, recommendations to organs of the state and to those of the state's legal administrative agencies. The three sides take cognizance of, and/or recommend that

- the period of peaceful transition is deemed to have commenced with the beginning of [formal] negotiations and will have ended with the first session of a freely elected Parliament. The political agreements are in force for this period of time;
- the participants of the trilateral negotiations should enjoy political and personal immunity in connection with their activities as negotiators. For statements made at that venue they are responsible only to the organizations that delegated them. (The three sides request that the minister of interior, the minister of justice, the president of the Supreme Court, and the prosecutor general see to the [legal] immunity of all affected persons);
- any political discrimination in the workplace is deemed to be in violation of the spirit of [this] basic agreement, as well as that of the three sides' convictions on the rule of law and on the rights of [Hungarian] citizens;
- the suspension of the use of coercive measures by the police during the period of transition is an important confidence-building step. (The three sides request that the minister of interior see to the taking of appropriate measures);
- pursuant to the advisory opinion adopted by the [NRT's] Committee for Interest Reconciliation, it is necessary to alleviate pressures on the Parliament and its members. For this reason, to the extent possible, individual MPs ought to be spared from recall initiatives and demands that they resign;
- political transformation into a multiparty system may not place a greater financial burden on the society than did the one-party system;
- the acceleration of government measures for the creation of reasonable financial conditions for the operations of new and renewed social organizations and political parties. (The three sides request that the prime minister implement the necessary measures);

- the HSWP, as a demonstration of its financial self-limitation (*önmérséklet*), is handing over to the state from the assets at its disposal [several pieces of] real estate valued at HUF 2 billion for social utilization, including assistance with [the startup] costs of political parties; furthermore, from its current state budgetary support [the HSWP] returns a sum of HUF 50 million to the state;
- to cover the campaign expenses of candidates for the Parliament, approximately HUF 100 million will be necessary from the state budget. This sum should be distributed in a proportional way among the candidates and the sponsoring parties and organizations. (The three sides request that the minister of finance secure this sum for this purpose);
- nonpartisanship must prevail in the work of national institutions of the information media. For this reason, there should be established a committee for nonpartisan information by persons nominated by the three sides;
- for the sake of stability, it is desirable to elect the president of the Republic during the present calendar year.

3. The three sides agree that, on the basis of results achieved thus far, work must continue on still unresolved issues pertaining to the matter of peaceful transition. Expert committees ought to endeavor to work on agreements on the following subjects:
- the method of election of the president of the Republic;
- the electoral code of ethics;
- rules governing the openness (*nyilvánosság*) of elections;
- the new law on public communication (*tájékoztatási törvény*);
- the law on informatics [?];
- the law on public service employees;
- a ban on workplace discrimination in the Labor Code;
- questions concerning the transformation of the Workers' Guard (the ORT's recommendations for the devolution of the Workers' Guard); and
- the exclusion of coercive resolution of political questions.

Delegations at the [NRT's] plenary session have empowered the mid-level committee on questions of political transition to work out agreements on the above-listed subjects.

Representatives of the three sides declare that the [above-listed] principles and regulations together constitute their political agreement.

Furthermore, [the three sides] express their conviction that with the signing of the present document they have taken an important step on the road to the creation of parliamentary democracy in Hungary, as well as for betterment of the nation.

September 18, 1989, Budapest

SIGNATORIES

For the Hungarian Socialist Workers' Party:
Rezső Nyers, Imre Pozsgay
For the Opposition Roundtable:
Károly Vigh, Zsolt Zétényi
For the League of Young Democrats:
[no signatures]
For the Independent Smallholders Party:
Imre Boross, István Prepeliczay
For the Christian Democratic People's Party:
Tibor Füzessy, János Teleki
For the Hungarian Democratic Forum:
József Antall, György Szabad
For the Hungarian People's Party:
Csaba Varga, László Kónya
For the Hungarian Social Democratic Party:
István Baranyai, István Geskó
[Handwritten note: "We disagree with the election of the president of the Republic prior to free parliamentary elections."]
For the Alliance of Free Democrats:
[no signatures]
For Social Organizations and Movements of the Third Side:
For the Society of the Left Alternative:
Csaba Kemény
For the Patriotic People's Front:
Sándor Bugár
For the Hungarian Democratic Youth Association:
Imre Nagy
For the League of Hungarian Anti-Fascist Resistance Fighters:
Sándor Sárközi
For the League of Hungarian Women:
Judit T. Asbóth
For the Ferenc Münnich Society:
Ferenc Berényi
For the Trade Union Federation:
[no signatures]

Sources: *Népszabadság*, September 19, 1989, and photocopy of the typewritten original in Anna Richter, *Az Ellenzéki Kerekasztal. Portrévázlatok* (The Opposition Roundtable. Portraits) (Budapest: Ötlet Kft., 1990), pp. 310–15 (my translation).

8   The road to power: political mobilization, party formation, and free elections in Hungary, 1989–1990

The last phase of Hungary's transition to a parliamentary democracy began in the fall of 1989. It is difficult to assign a specific date to the commencement of this process. The NRT agreement of September 18, the dissolution of the HSWP on October 7, the enactment of the revised Constitution in mid-October, the proclamation of the Republic of Hungary on October 23, and the plebiscite of November 26 were important road markers. And so were the fall of the Berlin Wall, the Czechoslovak "velvet revolution," and the violent overthrow of the Ceauşescu regime in Romania. Agreements and understandings between Presidents Bush and Gorbachev at the Malta summit provided a stable international framework for East Europe's political transformation in the winter months of 1989–90.

Events at home and abroad helped define the internal and external contexts in which the main transition scenarios unfolded in Hungary. The critical components were the citizens' political mobilization, processes of party formation, and the final dismantling of the old regime's coercive institutions. The election campaign of February–March 1990, the two-round national elections of March 25 and April 8, and the complex negotiations that preceded the formation of an HDF–ISP–CDPP coalition government were the key elements of this general scenario.

The following discussion addresses five topics: (A) preparations for transition; (B) party formation and trends in public opinion; (C) electoral campaign; (D) founding elections; and (E) the governance of postcommunist Hungary.

(A)   Preparations for transition – issues and outcomes

The self-liquidation of the ruling party created a political void. The HSWP's abruptly discharged 700,000 members were given an opportu-

361

nity to rejoin one of the HSWP's successor parties, to join one of the new parties and movements, or to exit from the public arena. As a consequence, a vast but uncharted political space opened up for new entrants who sought to play a role in the transition process. Moreover, to "level the political playing field," the government extended direct financial subsidies to several new parties and political movements. By the end of October, fifteen political parties and associations had received sums ranging from from HUF 1 to 22 million and several were also provided with office space and communications equipment.[1]

The legislative implementation of the NRT agreements was a protracted process. Whereas the enactment of the "fundamental laws," such as the ones on the revised Constitution, the Constitutional Court, and the multiparty elections, was promptly dispensed with, many technical issues were formally resolved by the lame-duck Parliament in early 1990. The disbanding of the Workers' Guard, by the Law of 1989: XXX, was an important confidence-building measure that Prime Minister Németh personally supervised. On October 23, while the Republic of Hungary was being proclaimed by President pro tem Mátyás Szűrös, Hungarian army commando units raided the Workers' Guard's 180 ammunition depots and storage facilities. With the confiscation of 60,000 submachine guns, 53,000 handguns, and 5,300 machine guns, the old party center's private army was disarmed and its personnel were discharged by the government.[2]

The government's next step was to come to terms with the top Hungarian graduates of the Soviet elite military academies and find out where their loyalties lay after the fall of the HSWP. In wake of the decision by the Parliament's Committee on National Defense to launch an inquiry into allegations about corruption among former military leaders,[3] Németh met with the personnel of the Ministry of Defense. He thanked them for having taken the loyalty oath to the new Constitution and also briefed the generals on the army's place in the new world of multiparty politics.[4] A similar visit, though long overdue, did not take place at the Ministry of Interior. Therefore, the old regime's internal political counterintelligence bureaucracy still served its old masters until early January 1990.[5]

All opposition forces benefited from the disappearence of the HSWP, yet it was the HDF that gained most of new public support. The party's early start was one important factor. Another was its apparent leadership role among the signatories of the NRT agreement. According to a national poll taken in early November, to the question "If elections were held next Sunday, the candidate of which party would you vote for?" 27 percent of the respondents chose the HDF and 25 percent the HSP. The next two beneficiaries were the AFD and the LYD, with 9 and 8 percent respectively.[6]

As the Free Democrats and Fidesz saw it, unless something was done to catch up with their principal rivals, the electoral campaign was over before it had begun. These concerns were also shared by the Smallholders and the Social Democrats. These two parties had little in common, but the prospects of an HSP–HDF electoral landslide energized them to join forces with the liberals to prevent the emerging Pozsgay–Antall electoral coalition from making further headway. The issue to attack was Pozsgay's candidacy for president, and the means to stop him was a drive to gather signatures for the holding of a plebiscite on this matter.[7]

Thanks to a vigorous nationwide campaign, the four-party *ad hoc* coalition obtained 114,470 valid signatures in support of a plebiscite on four items on the legislative agenda.[8] Three – on the Workers' Guard, the withdrawal of communist party cells from the workplace, and the official accounting for the HSWP's assets – were resolved in the affirmative by the Parliament at the end of October. Added to these three "win-win" propositions was a fourth proposition. It pertained to the postponement of special elections for the office of the president of the Republic from January 7, 1990 (the date that the pro-Pozsgay Parliament preferred) until after the national elections.

The four-party initiative caught the HDF, the CDPP, the HSP, and Pozsgay's proxies by surprise. In the absence of any coordination – Pozsgay in the meantime had decided to take a long trip to the West – on this matter, the HDF nominated the historian Lajos Für as its candidate. Subsequently, the party switched signals and urged voters to boycott the November 26 plebiscite.[9] On the other hand, both the HSP and the "new/old" HSWP advised their adherents to take part in the plebiscite and "follow their conscience" at the ballot box. The perplexed prosocialist voters had been accustomed to be told whom to vote for. Moreover, the HDF's "go" and "stop" instructions to the party faithful tended to deprive Pozsgay of much-needed HDF grass-roots support.

The "four-question" plebiscite was held on November 26 and its outcome caused a drastic realignment of the political landscape. Of the 4,451,007 ballots (58.03 percent of the eligible voters) cast, the Parliament's stance on three questions was upheld by a 95 percent margin. On the other hand, the legislature's position on the holding of the presidential election in January 1990 was defeated by an extremely narrow margin of 6,101 votes.[10] The results of the plebiscite yielded several winners and two losers, and also catapulted József Antall into the center of the political arena.

By causing the postponement of the presidential elections, the opponents reaffirmed their individual political identities and gained an important boost as viable electoral contenders. The liberals, Small-holders, and Social Democrats crushed the putative "Populist-reform socialist Popular Front" as the front-runner in the forthcoming electoral campaign. Moreover, Miklós Németh became free of second-guessing about his partisan affiliation – and the monopolization of the political limelight – by a President Pozsgay. In fact, Pozsgay's defeat materially contributed to prime minister Németh's liberation from the burden of continued membership in the HSP. Three weeks after the plebiscite he resigned from the HSP's Presidium, and three months later he ran as an independent candidate in the national elections.[11]

Paradoxically, the HDF, too, was a winner. Pozsgay's defeat enabled the party to free itself from the political albatross of the old regime's last, albeit best, representative as its political partner. With Pozsgay – and his friend Zoltán Biró, who had stepped down as HDF chairman before the plebiscite – out of the picture, the HDF could reclaim its political birthright as a democratic party.

Upon discovering that less than 5 percent of the voters were ready to stand up for the Workers' Guard and the workplace party organizations, the Hungarian people also won in the plebiscite. The threat of a hidden conservative left-wing mass party vanished on November 26. Without an HSP president, there was no one to come between the political parties and the voters' free choice in the March elections.

The first loser was the resuscitated but ideologically unreconstructed HSWP.[12] Grósz and Berecz chose not to play a leadership role in this "Marxist–Leninist" and reform communist party. However, starting with the HSWP's refusal to lend moral support to the antiregime insurgents in Romania in December 1989, its leaders managed to make every possible political mistake in the next three months. In the end, they failed to garner enough votes – that is, 4 percent of votes cast in the first round of the March–April elections – from their hard-line constituencies to qualify as a parliamentary party.

The other loser was Imre Pozsgay. It appeared that his remarkable career as the old regime's courageous rebel and reform spokesmen left him unprepared to function as a truly autonomous risk-taking politician in the postcommunist public arena. Had he precipitated a formal split at the October party congress and walked out with his followers, or turned his "movement" into a political party by the end of that month, he could have won the plebiscite by a wide margin.

The "wolves" of the old regime were no longer a threat in Hungary in the fall of 1989. Németh, carried by the momentum of the government's GDR refugee decision – and closely watched by the West – would have done precisely the same things as far as the Workers' Guard and the army were concerned. Therefore, the issue was not the danger of a left-wing coup but the paralysis of Pozsgay's will to act and, for once, to take a *real* chance on his political future and material well-being. In his autobiography Pozsgay speaks of his sense of "peasant fatalism" in letting events unfold as they would.[13] As late as mid-November, his friends tried, but failed, to persuade him to "unfurl the flag" and start a party of his own. Imre Pozsgay was a free actor in the fall of 1989. Under these circumstances, a politician's place was at home, and his job was to put up a fight when his opponents were mobilizing the voters to stop him from becoming president of his country. Pozsgay's voters were not in London, Washington, Ottawa, and Helsinki but in Hungary.[14] And that is why he became a bystander rather than a central figure in Hungary's postcommunist politics.

The principal winner of the plebiscite was József Antall, the HDF's newly elected chairman. His meteoric rise from political obscurity to the center of the Hungarian transition process and, six months later, his election by the Parliament as head of the nation's freely elected government necessitate a brief detour on the life and early public career of this remarkable individual.

According to his official biography, József Antall was born on April 8, 1932, in Budapest.[15] His father, József Antall Sr, was a lawyer, a supporter of the parliamentary Independent Smallholders' Party, and a senior civil servant in the wartime government. Antall Sr served as government commissioner for refugees between 1939 and April, 1944, when the Gestapo arrested him. As government commissioner, he was credited with the care, sheltering, and, when possible, transit of hundreds of thousands of refugees, particularly those of the Polish Home Army. He was also a "Hungarian Raoul Wallenberg" who gave vital assistance to Jews – from both Poland and Hungary.[16] After the war he rejoined the Smallholders' Party and was elected to the Parliament. He served in three governments and held the position of minister for reconstruction in two. Upon the communist takeover in 1947–8 he retired from public life.[17]

The reason for detailing Antall's family background is to show – because Antall deemed it important when meeting with visitors and interviewers – that he viewed himself as heir to his distinguished father's legacy of public service, Christian values, moral rectitude, and commitment to political democracy. With these credentials in mind, let us return to József Antall. Upon graduating from the top academic Budapest Piarist *gimnázium* in 1950, he spent the next twelve years taking university courses and acquiring diplomas in history, literature, library science, and museum management. He wrote his diploma work on the role of the nineteenth-century statesman Baron József Eötvös in the political preparations that led to the Austro-Hungarian Compromise of 1867.[18] Thus, other than his fellow HDF negotiator Professor György Szabad, a distinguished scholar of nineteenth-century Hungarian history, Antall was the only one who had done his "homework" prior to joining the NRT in the summer of 1989.

The 24-year-old Antall's political activity during the 1956 revolution consisted of involvement in a Christian youth association in the high school where he taught history, and assistance in the drafting of a political position paper for the Smallholders' Party in mid-November 1956.[19] According to his biography, after the revolution he was detained by the authorities and, upon his release, came under police surveillance. He was also transferred to another high school, and in 1959 he was banned from teaching. From then on Antall's career continued first as an archivist and, from 1964 on, as a researcher at the Semmelweiss Museum of Medicine in Budapest. In the next twenty years he rose in rank to scientific associate, senior associate, deputy director, deputy director general, and, in 1984, director general of the museum.

Antall's scientific *œuvre* consisted of scores of short reports, essays on the history of medicine, and unpublished writings on history and world affairs. As László Lengyel explained in a brilliant, albeit somewhat vitriolic, obituary:

> Just like Antall, most of Hungarian society led a "submerged" life in the Kádár era ... They lived their everyday lives. They did not resist. They did not write and most of them did not even read samizdat journals. They did not sign [protest] petitions. They were not there in Monor and Lakitelek ... They complained at work. They laughed at political jokes. They told their family and friends that enough was enough. This is what Antall did too. His transformation and public appearance coincided precisely with that of the high-school teachers, ward physicians, design engineers, and ministry officials. Perhaps he was a few inches ahead of the rest so he could participate in the work of the National Roundtable.[20]

Lengyel's harsh assessment of Antall, however accurate it may be in sketching out the social milieu in which Antall lived and worked during the Kádár era, is incomplete in at least two respects. The account – like many others by socialist and liberal critics – fails to credit him as a widely read thinker and a courageous politician.[21] Few gave him credit for earnestly trying, even though ultimately failing, to reconcile the values of his intellectual patrimony with the realities of the Kádár era, and then craft a modern Christian democratic political agenda for a postcommunist Hungary. Although none of these unresolved conflicts impaired Antall's effectiveness as a negotiator and deal maker in the transition period, they would become fatal handicaps that marred his record as a national leader.

On the other hand, neither Antall's critics nor his apologists had enough respect for him to share with the uninitiated the full record, however modest, of Antall's political persona under the old regime. A nonparty intellectual, especially in a nonideological position, could go far, but only so far, even under the increasingly meritocratic Hungarian *nomenklatura* system of the 1970s. Therefore, it does not impugn Antall's personal integrity to say that he, too, had at least one, and probably two political "godfathers." One was a man of the party center: a former director of the party elites' hospital, and the deputy, and subsequently minister of health, Emil Schulteisz.

The other was minister of culture Imre Pozsgay, to whom Antall's museum reported in the late 1970s. At that time the positions of deputy director general and director general of major cultural institutions were subject to Politburo approval. It was this body, particularly the cultural-ideological *capo di tutti capi* György Aczél, who either initiated or endorsed such high-level appointments. Antall must have performed well as a senior cultural administrator because he was awarded – again with PB approval – the Gold Medal of Labor in 1982. The receipt of this and other official awards are duly registered in Antall's official biography.

Antall was absent from the Lakitelek conference of 1987, but he was enrolled as a charter member of the HDF when it became a political movement in September 1988. Although tempted to accept the leadership of the revived ISP and later that of the CDPP, he declined both offers and bided his time until the spring of 1989. As Grósz recalled, Aczél had volunteered to arrange for him a meeting with Antall, but because of the HDF's public rebuke of Grósz's performance at the August 1988 meeting with Ceaușescu, the meeting did not take place.[22] As far as one can tell, Antall's only contact with Grósz was a letter in which Antall protested his alarmist rhetoric ("White terror") in November 1988.[23]

In March 1989 Antall became tangentially involved in the work of the ORT as an HDF expert on constitutional history. It was partly in this capacity and on the strength of his family's political record that he rose high in the esteem of the HDF's inner circle of Populist intellectuals. Antall was a sparkling conversationalist, an impressive public speaker, a man of captivating personal charm and commanding presence.[24] These attributes served him well when he was named as a last-minute addition to the ORT's negotiating team at the National Roundtable. There, as discussed in Chapter 7, he soon emerged as a natural leader, a witty debater, and, more to the point, *the* opposition negotiator who enjoyed Pozsgay's respect and confidence. Indeed, this expert on the Compromise of 1867 acquitted himself well as a signatory, on his party's behalf, of the NRT agreement of September 18, 1989.

Thanks to Antall's rapport with Pozsgay, Németh, and the government's expert negotiators, he became the HDF's indispensable liaison person with the powers that be. Although still not a member of the HDF Presidium, he was invited by his friend the poet Sándor Csoóri to attend the meeting where Zoltán Biró tendered his resignation as party chairman. Biró felt that as a former, albeit expelled, member of the HSWP, he could become a political liability to the HDF.[25] Although no one questioned Biró's commitment to political democracy, he was Pozsgay's man – a reform socialist and a Populist ideologue rather than a born-again Smallholder or a Christian Democrat. Because the popular HDF Presidium member Lajos Für had already been committed as the party's presidential candidate, the somewhat disoriented party executive elected Antall as the new chairman of the HDF.[26]

The party could not have picked a better-qualified politician to lead it in the coming electoral campaign. On the other hand, as will be shown below, the party could not have picked a less appropriate person to carry the torch of the Lakitelek "founding fathers'" political agenda. With Antall, the HDF got a brilliant political strategist and a born leader. However, unbeknownst to the Presidium, the new party chairman was also a stubborn conservative ideologue dedicated to the values of Hungary's prewar "Christian-national" upper class. The *raison d'être* of Hungarian Populism in the 1930s had been a radical intelligentsia rebellion against the rule of the very class whose values Antall would attempt to resuscitate as prime minister. Antall's cards were not yet on the table in October 1989.

(B)   Party formation and trends in public opinion

Of the fifty-odd registered political parties, thirty-seven participated – mainly in single-member voting districts – in the March 25, 1990 national elections.[27] However, only twelve parties qualified to field national party lists. Of these only six received more than 4 percent of the votes to benefit from the votes cast for the party ballot and thus enter the Parliament. The twelve finalists that received 99.06 percent of the first-round votes are the subject of the following discussion.

Political parties: genesis, typology, and charter members

The process of party formation began in April 1988, when Fidesz was founded, and, at least for the twelve electoral finalists, was completed in October 1989, when the HDF declared itself to be an electoral party. These parties may be classified as "incumbent" and "incumbent-spinoff" parties (the HSP and the HSWP); "new" parties (HDF, ADF, and Fidesz); "historic" parties (ISP, SDP, and the CDPP); and "Trojan horse"-type parties and established policy lobbies running as electoral coalitions (the PEC [the Patriotic Electoral Coalition, formerly the PPF]; the Agrarian Alliance [formerly the NCAC]; and the Entrepreneurs' Party [a coalition of new entrepeneurs and old "red barons"]). With the exception of the new parties, the parties were, at least initially, beholden to the old regime. However, after October 1989 they were on their own and were in a position to define their "partisan" identity in electoral programs and political slogans.

From the record of documentable political activities of the historic and the new parties in 1988–9, we can reconstruct a general sequence of party formation in Hungary.[28] The typical stages were as follows:

1 *Ad hoc*, or regular meetings of affinity groups (professional, cultural, generational, or dissident); decision to formalize interaction by the establishment of groups, clubs, or associations;

2 Informal membership recruitment; to culminate in the holding of an event (rally, conference, "civic forum," or local roundtable); formal or informal identification of leaders and informal agreement on shared public concerns;

3 Determination of political objectives; agreement on plan of action; definition of group's political-ideological identity with reference to historical precedents and current policy issues;

4 Informal decision to transform group from a "movement" to a party, and to adopt a "party framework" for future activities;

5 Unofficial and word-of-mouth publicity to recruit participants for charter membership in the new party; the holding of first formal consultative conference;

6 Election of provisional party leadership; initiation of membership recruitment drive; and development of a network of local affiliates;

7 Formal establishment of the party at its first national conference or congress; adoption of party program and the launching of fund-raising and publicity campaigns for the popularization of the party's objectives;

8 Official registration as a political party; search for political allies among other political parties and nonparty or preparty groups; formation of intraparty interest groups and policy caucuses; (optional: departure of dissident elements for other parties or parties of their own);

9 Beginning of formal interaction with the government as actual or potential participant in formal negotiations between the opposition and the government.

The above process was foreshortened for the HSP, the HSWP, and the old regime's policy lobbies. In each case, whoever happened to have been left in charge of the party's or the "social organization's" assets became the designated party leader, and the top cadres were fielded – mainly on the regional and national lists – as candidates for seats in the Parliament.

The political parties' leadership was formed on the basis of incumbency or "inheritance" or merit. The electoral standard-bearers of the HSP and the HSWP were the survivor reform and conservative leaders and their handpicked associates from the old HSWP; those of the historic parties had been active either in 1945–7, or in 1956, or, as early joiners, were charter members; those of the new parties were selected on the basis of intellectual achievement, personality, and organizational skills; and those of the policy lobbies were, as indicated above, appointees of the old party center.

In the course of organization building the party leaderships sought to recruit new followers. The first wave came from among the local professionals and respected community leaders who had made their political debut at the 1985 elections. They were, like the new post-communist party elites elsewhere in Eastern Europe, mainly intellectuals – particularly educators, historians, and cultural notables – and other university graduates.[29] With the exception of Poland where *Solidarnosč* had ample opportunities to disseminate its programs, the main difference between the Hungarian "new democrats" and their neighbors was that they had more than a year as politically unrestrained actors in the public arena to organize their ranks, and to prepare and publicize their programs. Elsewhere in Eastern Europe – again, with the Polish exception – the time span between party formation and the first free elections was considerably shorter and had an adverse impact on the cohesion and political efficacy of the postcommunist parties.

In terms of membership recruitment, initially the decisive cleavage in Hungary – particularly in smaller towns and rural communities – was between the post-, new, or reform socialists/communists and the nonsocialists/communists. (The distinction between a "reform socialist" and a "reformc ommunist" – as may be inferred from the outcome of the November 26 plebiscite on Pozsgay's candidacy for president – was quite unclear for at least 49 per cent of the voting public in the winter of 1989–90.) The decision to join the HDF, the AFD, or the ISP was at first made not on the basis of programs – very few knew what they were – but on grounds of personal ties to one or another of the parties' local leaders. The November 1989 plebiscite that pitted two blocs of noncommunist parties against each other marked the beginning of party identification derived from *issues* rather than from local personal affinities.

Apart from those who benefited from incumbency or "inheritance," the new party leaders were self-selected early arrivals who staked out a part of the political turf in the name of their party, as much as in their own. As charter members, they had a decisive say in rank ordering their parties' candidates on the regional and national party lists. In doing so, they preselected certain types of individuals to win or lose at the elections. The same was also true for the socialist incumbents and for the "inheritors" of the historic parties. The point, which will be further discussed in the concluding chapter, is that the electoral system imparted substantial inbuilt advantages to incumbent party leaderships, regardless of how they had come to occupy their positions. The right to select the party's candidates and the possession of control over the disposal of state subsidies and the disbursement of political patronage – as backbenchers in the Parliament were soon to find out – made for the "iron law of oligarchy" in postcommunist Hungary.

Public opinion: dominant orientations and trends in party preferences

The regime's early decision to share power with other political parties and the HSWP's slow-motion collapse in the next seven months gave the public much-needed time to adjust to new political realities. The results of the sixty-odd polls taken in 1989–early 1990 reveal clear-cut as well as contradictory trends.[30] The main findings speak of the essential continuity, well into the fall of 1989, of public attitudes toward the political regime.

While the basic ratios of attentive/inattentive, political/prepolitical/apolitical, trust/distrust, optimism/pessimism, and so on were initially the same as those shown in polls of the mid-1980s, there was also evidence of minor shifts toward politicization and of the public's growing openness to change. Another constant was the ratio of "don't know" and "will not vote" respondents – about one-third of the samples – who came from the lower rungs of the social hierarchy. Moreover, the traditional spatial (Budapest–provincial city–village) and ideological (liberal–moderate–conservative) distribution of people and their beliefs did not seem to change until the summer of 1989. Unlike people in Budapest, villagers remained more supportive of the HSWP, and were less in favor of the two liberal parties than were Hungarians as a whole. And finally, the degree of partisanship among the educated and young respondents remained far more pronounced than that displayed by less-well-educated and older respondents.[31]

The underlying motivation behind the slow tempo of changes in the temporal, generational, educational, and spatial dimensions of attitudinal change was the public's fear of the unknown and deep anxiety about the danger of disorder. Patterns of the citizens' one-on-one "bargain culture" and the pursuit of individual life strategies by means of "back-door (*kiskapu*) negotiations" were habits that were difficult to change. The appearance of several political parties evoked contradictory responses. Whereas the majority of survey respondents were supportive of the general idea of having two, three, or several institutional alternatives to the ruling party, they were taken aback by the conflict potential and the inherent divisiveness of multiparty politics.[32]

In the first half of 1989 the notion of party pluralism was perceived by most as the consequence of the ruling party's involuntary devolution into several party-like political units that would eventually coalesce into an all-party national coalition government. This perception was reinforced by offers of political partnership with the incumbents in a "transitional government" by (the presumably most radical) AFD in the spring of 1989.[33] Thus, at that point the "Polish precedent," what we might call "self-limiting" or "attenuated" partisanship, was the accepted model of party politics for both the general public and the opposition.

Changing public attitudes toward political parties can be traced in thirteen opinion surveys on party preferences taken between March 1989 and March 1990.[34] To the question "If elections were held next Sunday, the candidate of which party would you vote for?" the responses of those who *had* a preference *and* intended to vote may be summarized as follows.

The HSWP started in March 1989 with a commanding lead at 32 percent. This level of support held; in fact it increased to 37 percent in mid-July. Public anticipation of a positive outcome of the October HSWP congress sustained public support until the middle of that month. From then on, – driven by the outcome of the November plebiscite, Imre Pozsgay's declining fortunes, and the "Danube-gate" scandal of January 1990 – the ex-communist HSP fell victim to a political landslide that bottomed out in early March 1990 at 8 percent public support, a figure quite close to the percentage of votes the HSP received on March 25.

The HDF started out with 13 percent in March 1989. However, thanks to its exceptional showing in the summer by-elections, the party was the choice of 24 percent of the would-be voters in September. The HDF's public support peaked on the eve of the November plebiscite at 27 percent. From then on, the HDF lost some ground, mainly to the parties of the proplebiscite coalition (AFD, Fidesz, ISP, HSDP). Its support leveled off at 21 percent in early March.

Because of its lack of visibility and the concentration of its followers in Budapest and five major cities, the initial public support of the AFD was a modest 6 percent in March 1989. The party's key role in the NRT negotiations was overshadowed by Pozsgay and later on by the Pozsgay–Antall duo; thus its image became that of a spoiler, scandal-monger (the exposure of the HSWP's shady business transactions), and obstructionist (as a nonsigner of the Roundtable agreement). Thereafter, as a payoff for public radicalization through preplebiscite political mobilization, the AFD's stock more than doubled and rose to 14 percent in December 1989. Then – thanks to growing visibility and a tough anticommunist posture in the election campaign – the AFD grew by 50 percent, finishing with preelection public support of 20.3 percent.

The Young Democrats' (Fidesz) initially high public support – due probably to the novelty of being seen as a "youth party," much beloved by young people and grandmothers alike – subsequently leveled off at 10 to 11 percent in the fall. When the AFD gained momentum in early 1990, Fidesz's suport declined to 6 to 7 percent. (At that point the public viewed Fidesz as the AFD's youth auxiliary: partly because of this inaccurate perception, Fidesz finished with 7.2 percent in March 1990.)

Mainly because of the party's slowly but surely growing rural support, the Smallholders rarely fell below 10 percent in party preference polls in 1989. The IPS's 15.7 percent on the eve of the elections was one of two cases in which the party fell *below* the survey results at the March elections. The other was the Hungarian Social Democratic Party, which started at 12 percent, peaked at 15 percent in November, and slid to 7.8 percent in March 1990 – only to fall below the 4 percent threshold on March 25. (The Christian Democrats' public support was 4 to 5 percent throughout and proved sufficient to assure the CDPP's parliamentary representation at the ballot box.)

Paradoxically, the public gave high marks to the six parties and electoral coalitions that did *not* receive 4 percent of the votes cast on March 25. Although the fault might have been that of the poll questionnaire (which yielded a total percentage of well over 100 percent), it is still remarkable how the respondents of this March 18–20, 1990 national survey with a sample of 5,000 could have over-estimated – for example the Social Democrats' – electoral support by more than 15 percent.[35] Yet, other than this miscue, party-preference polls proved to be reliable predictors of the electoral outcomes of 1990.

In sum, Hungarian public attitudes toward the phenomenon of party formation were hampered by latent fears of change, muted hostility toward partisan divisiveness, and a widely shared disinclination to participate in political activities. In general, the majority's evaluative judgments on political parties were based on incomplete and substantially distorted comprehension (other than being critical of the existing political system) as to what these parties were about. Moreover, it appeared that the respondents instinctively rejected or awarded low levels of support to parties that were seen as "extremist" at both ends of the ideological spectrum. As shown in the polls, Fidesz leader Viktor Orbán's vigorous anticommunist stance at the Nagy reburial subsequently ran into the same kind of public resistance as did the rhetoric by the spokesmen of the "fundamentalist" Ferenc Münnich Society.

To make informed choices among parties, the public needed time and opportunity to see, hear, and reflect upon the message of party spokesmen in the the print and electronic media. Though press censorship was nowhere in evidence in late 1989, access to TV – by far the most effective medium to help the citizen to combine names, faces, and party labels into a coherent image – was still controlled by a Pozsgay-appointed committee of media oversight. In fact, pictures of party spokesmen and programmatic statements of the new parties first appeared in the Christmas issue of *Népszabadság*.[36] By that time, much of the novelty of the affair was overshadowed by Hungarian TV's "demonstration-to-demonstration" coverage of Romanian events and year-end news roundups on the dramatic political changes in the region.

(C)   Electoral campaign – programs, issues, and political communication

The parties' electoral programs that were issued during the long (early December 1989 – mid-March 1990) campaign season as pamphlets, news releases, handbills, and media sound bites served to define each party's historical and ideological identity and place in the ideological continuum; to articulate (often impassioned) criticism of the old regime's policy record in human rights, and in cultural, economic, social welfare, and foreign policies; to specify and address the constituencies whose interests the party proposed to represent; and to offer a list of changes and policy innovations that the party promised to implement in the freely elected legislature and the government.

It is doubtful that, with the exception of the party-appointed authors of campaign documents, anyone in Hungary read in full and reflected upon the forty-odd party programs that reached the voters before March 25, 1990. However, a brief review of some of the programs reveals important similarities and differences.

The main differences among party programs lay in the degree and rapidity with which Hungary's transformation was proposed to be implemented by the various electoral contenders. In this respect there were important dissimilarities in the programs of the HSP and its clones (the PEC, the AA, and the HPP) and the five ORT parties that gained parliamentary representation in April 1990. The shared objective of the latter group was the dismantling and disposal of all political and ideological, some legal, and institutional remnants of communist rule. With few exceptions, such as the "new" HSWP, these policy preferences were also shared by even the finalist parties and electoral coalitions that failed to gain parliamentary representation in the March–April 1990 elections.

By contrast, the HSP held views that differed from those of most of the other parties on property relations, privatization, land ownership, wage and price controls, and social welfare policies. On the other hand, the socialists' foreign policy preferences were not appreciably different from those of the five other parliamentary parties. The HSP's stance on most issues was somewhat ambiguous and was a balancing act between paying lip service to the need for changes and eschewing radical solutions of any kind. The old party-state's reformist political heirs tended to advocate changes *in* the existing system as defined by the NRT agreement of September 18, unlike their electoral rivals, who insisted on a radical change *of* the old "political model" – including further revisions of the NRT pact.

As a demonstration of the old regime's commitment to "clean government," in February 1990 the Parliament enacted Law III/1990 that required all top officeholders since 1980 to account for their assets before a special parliamentary committee.[37] Of the 270 names listed, seventy-two were members of the Presidential Council or of the Lázár, Grósz, and Németh cabinets; sixty-six deputy ministers; forty chairmen of county councils; eighty-seven top central and county HSWP leaders; and nineteen trade union executives. Thus, the "troika" discharged the last of its passengers. The few hearings that were held, with elderly apparatchiki claiming penury, turned out to be a farce. Accordingly, the "wolves" ignored the bait and focused on the forthcoming elections.

Rhetoric, ideological pieties, and technical differences aside, the programs of *all* six parties that obtained parliamentary representation *were* compatible with reference to several areas of postcommunist policy priorities. There was substantial agreement among all concerned that Hungary was in deep economic trouble from which the country might not recover in less than five to ten years. All parties agreed that any of the proposed short-term remedies would entail painful social consequences in terms of unemployment, impoverishment, and a pronounced decline in the quality of life for those living on fixed wages or pensions.

Few disputed the need for privatization, but the parties parted ways on the degree to which the removal of subsidies for food and public services would be implemented. The HDF and the AFD had the courage to acknowledge that the social and political costs of economic transformation could be prohibitively high, yet no one spoke of "blood, sweat, and tears" during the electoral campaign. As far as it can be inferred from the two parties' economic programs, the difference between their proposed solutions was one of degree rather than kind.

Of the leading opposition parties, the AFD tended to assign greater urgency to economic crash programs than did the HDF. This was quite apparent in the areas of industrial privatization and the extent to which each party would allow foreign capital to acquire control over key manufacturing resources. The HDF's antimarket or, as the AFD called them, "anticommerce" biases were evident in campaign documents, as was the AFD's doctrinaire position on rapid marketization and privatization as main instruments to bring about early economic recovery.

The issue of reprivatization of land that had been forcibly collectivized and transferred to the cooperative sector in 1947–8 touched on raw nerves. Although the HDF was rather lukewarm about the necessity of prompt reprivatization, it could not afford to hand the rural vote over to the Smallholders on this issue. The latter stood foursquare for restoration of the precollectivization (but post-land-reform) property structure of the countryside. By contrast, the AFD counseled caution and gradualism in this politically volatile area of property relations.

For campaign purposes both the HDF and the ADF were opposed to the incumbent managerial elites' theft of state-owned industrial, trading, and service enterprises by privatization and through the abuse of legal loopholes for the rescuing of ill-gotten gains by means of fraudulent "joint ventures" with Western investors. On the other hand, through its spokesman at the NRT, the AFD was on record for proposing permissive policies with respect to the recovery of such purloined assets from the new owners.

All parties assigned the lion's share of economic responsibilities to the *state*. In this policy area the opposition parties' politicians and economists alike unabashedly embraced the redistributionist model of a modified welfare state. As heirs to etatist continental European traditions of state interference in economic affairs, the party experts' preferences largely coincided with the policy precedents of the presumably defunct socialist party-state. Although strongly opposed to central planning as such, no party program questioned the wisdom of assigning to the postcommunist state principal responsibility for the delivery of services in the fields of health, education, welfare, public transportation, culture, and environmental protection.

Most of the AFD's and some of the HDF's economists had been veteran expert consultants and policy advisors of the old regime. With the exception of the level-headed authors of the Fidesz program, they were still captives of a "let-the-state-do-it" mentality. Indeed, most parties' economic programs bore more than passing resemblance (with opposite ideological labels) to the doctrinaire policy papers – vintage "escape forward" of the late 1970s – that the old party center's in-house sages had prepared to guide the policy-makers.

Party programs also devoted generous amounts of space to postelection legislative priorities. At the top of the list was commitment to a strong Parliament, delegation of increased fiscal and administrative autonomy to the local governments, overhaul of the courts, and imposition of close legislative oversight on the army, police, and internal security agencies. The most provocative items concerned the proposed review of all holdover top state officials as to moral and professional fitness to serve in the public administration of a democratic Hungary.

In the politically overheated early months of 1990, electoral promises of "political justice" seemed like an attractive shortcut to gaining popular support for "jump-starting" postcommunist Hungary with a clean political slate. What gave a sense of urgency to electoral promises of this kind was the discovery – thanks to a defector from the Ministry of Interior's Department III/III (political counterintelligence) – that the Németh government had tolerated the practice of unconstitutional police surveillance of opposition politicians until late December 1989.[38]

The "Dunagate" affair led to the resignation of Minister of Interior István Horváth and to the commissioning of yet another parliamentary investigation committee on the government's internal security organs. Following a series of behind-closed-doors legislative hearings, the responsible officials were identified and pensioned off.[39] Five months later, most of the operational staff of the old regime's secret police was taken over by the new government, as were most of the senior civil servants of the old regime.[40]

The new parties' foreign policy programs were unanimous in endorsing the complete reorientation of Hungary from the Soviet bloc to the West. A key item in the "Christian-national" foreign policy platform was concerned with Hungary's responsibilities for the human rights and cultural autonomy of the 3.5 million ethnic Hungarians living in Romania, Czechoslovakia, and Yugoslavia. Hungary's withdrawal from the CMEA and military disengagement from the WTO were common objectives of all parties, as was joining the EEC with whatever status that a consensus of that community made available.

In sum, party programs, by the nature of the enterprise, were statements of intentions and not binding contracts between a party and its electoral supporters. At any rate, in the context of the forthcoming free elections, it was not the programs as such but the manner in which they were conveyed to the voters that warrants brief discussion.

Campaign '90 in Hungary

A political party's main objectives in an electoral campaign are to capture the voters' attention, to persuade them to accept and support the party's program, and to mobilize the public actually to vote on election day. In what follows, three aspects of the January–March 1990 campaign will be discussed: "equal chances" of political competition; aspects of "negative campaigning"; and the media and the electoral "message."

Parties: equals and "more equals"

The NRT agreement called for the creation of equal opportunity for all political parties to seek public support for their programs. It was an unrealistic proposition because it deliberately overlooked the vast disparity of resources at the disposal of the incumbents and of their noncommunist opponents. Government grants for campaign purposes allocated on a sliding scale according to registered membership were quite inadequate to overcome the new parties' multiple handicaps in the electoral campaign.

These inequalities were exacerbated by the resources the parties had available for newspaper, radio, and TV advertising in the still largely regime-controlled media.[41] The NRT agreement allowed the involvement of any number of new entrants into the campaign arena, but some of its provisions – such as the gathering of 750 signatures for individual candidates and the fielding of candidates in the majority of voting districts in several counties as a condition of having a national party list – quickly eliminated all but a dozen well-organized and well-financed contenders.

As an electoral competitor, the HSP enjoyed the advantages of incumbency and the benefits of its unreported wealth. The party's leaders were also members of the government, therefore the "nonpartisan" activities of Prime Minister Németh and Foreign Minister Horn received three to four times as much TV and radio exposure as did the HDF chairman József Antall and AFD chairman János Kis. In the four-week period between late January and late February 1990, the HSP as a *party* was on the TV screens on 218 occasions; the HDF and the AFD were seen on 142 and 116 occasions, respectively. A review of radio coverage of events in a two-week period put the HSP at the top with 298 news items, followed by the HDF and the AFD with 165 and 156 items, respectively.[42] Media coverage of this kind pertained to "straight news" as opposed to the officially allotted two five-minutes of free slots that were made available to each of the forty-three registered political parties to present their respective programs in January–February 1990.

On the other hand, the HDF, the AFD, and the Social Democrats received considerable amounts of Western financial support – probably well in excess of the amounts of their respective campaign allocations from the government. Western multinationals and individual investors were also anxious to see *their* playing field "leveled" by whichever party emerged victorious.[43] Another, obviously nonquantifiable, factor that helped equalize the opposition's chances was the regime's growing unpopularity and the widespread support among print, radio, and TV journalists that the opposition, particularly the AFD, enjoyed.

Campaign '90: the high road and the low road

The 1990 electoral campaign was a traumatic experience for the Hungarian people. Although the transition to democracy was meant to be "peaceful," no one could have anticipated the daily barrage of dramatic news from abroad – especially from Romania, where the fate of the Hungarian community hung on the outcome of that revolution – nor the startling revelations about continued secret police activity in Hungary. The old party-state died hard, and so did the burdensome psychological legacy of the totalitarian past that sowed seeds of distrust and dissension among the elites and the people.

As the campaign progressed, there developed a nearly complete breakdown of civilized communication among the new parties. The underlying causes were rooted in traditional antagonisms between "national" Populist and cosmopolitan "urbanist" values; in tensions between the presumed "winners" and "losers" of the old regime's cultural policies, and in the mutual distrust of motives of the "Christian-national" and "democratic opposition" camps. Public statements by demagogues and whispering campaigns by their followers concerning the other side's alleged anti-Semitic beliefs or latent Marxist sympathies helped poison the atmosphere and nearly succeeded in transforming the campaign into a shouting match between the Forum and the Free Democrats.

To ascertain the rhetorical balance between the parties' "positive" and "negative" attitudes toward one another, the content analysis, by the National Public Opinion Research Institute, of the parties' public "messages" sent by way of TV and radio campaign advertising in February 1990 is helpful. The institute sought to measure the positive and negative content of 644 TV and 679 radio comments, references, and messages that the top nine political parties had "sent" to one another.[44] It established two analytical categories; (a) how each party evaluated, in either a positive or negative way, the other parties and (b) how each party was characterized, in either a positive or negative way, by the other parties.

Concerning (a), which we can call an "aggressiveness index," the AFD led the list with an overall balance of −62; followed by the LYD, −53; the old/new HSWP, −50; the ISP, −23; the HDF, −12; the Social Democrats, −7; the HSP, −4; and the CDPP, +64. Concerning (b), which we can call a "threat perception index," the HSP was first with −52; followed by the old/new HSWP, −32; the Social Democrats, −28; the HDF, −10; the ISP, −5; the LYD, +2; the AFD, +5; and the CDPP, +8. The parties' radio advertising considered alone yielded similar results. In any case, the sum total of all TV and radio advertising by forty-three parties, when divided into "positive," "ambivalent," and "negative" party-to-party messages, yielded 27 percent positive, 11 percent ambivalent, and 62 percent negative.

The media and the message

The parties sought to promote their message through all available means of communication. Of these, TV was the most accessible to the voters. For this reason, and also to ascertain the ideological content of the parties' electoral propaganda, we shall refer to the main findings of another study on the "values," or ideational components, that the TV viewer could find in each of the two five-minute program presentations of the forty-three parties still in contention in February 1990.[45]

According to this study, in the 86 TV programs (43 × 2), the most frequently cited "values" were "Hungarianness," 132 instances; "nation," 84; "freedom," 70; "Europe," 59; "democracy," 58; "homeland," 48; and "Christianity," 42. In the next cluster there were such concepts as "enterprise," 32; "private property" and "security," 29 each; "solidarity," 24; "free elections," 22; "peace," 21; "children," 21; "morality," "environment," and "independence," 20 each; "self-government," 19; "rational taxation," 17; "happiness," 17; and "prosperity," 15.

Each of these terms may be placed in a "positive-affirmative," or "negative-critical" context, from which we can discover how *radical* a party tried to appear to the voters. The most critical comments came from the ultraradical Party of the Hungarian October (55 instances); followed by the AFD (50); the right-wing Homeland Party (46); the Party of the Nonparty People (44); and the clerical-monarchist Christian National Union (42). The *least radical* message came from the HDF: 10 critical references. The most positive comments came from the right-wing Freedom Party (108), followed by the LYD, the AFD, the CDPP, and the HDF.

The use of symbols and code words, and the intensity with which these were articulated in a political message, helped shape the Hungarian electoral campaign's cognitive and affective agenda. As the campaign unfolded, it soon became apparent that the message of the half-dozen communist and postcommunist political parties was overwhelmed and basically negated by the Christian-national "Eurocentric" programs of the other thirty-odd parties.[46] Whereas the AFD tried to persuade the voters by demonstrating its radical and uncompromising position on all policy issues and used strong language to make its case, the HDF used a low-key approach, though essentially making the *same* case. Of the two, the HDF's tone was more traditional, more reassuring, and a great deal less threatening to the voters' already precarious sense of security than was the AFD's harsh call for radical change. For these reasons, and given the actual electoral outcome, it can be argued that the parties' political style was at least as important as the programmatic content of their electoral message.

Voting decisions: symbols and substance

March 25, 1990 marked not only the end of a hard-fought electoral campaign but the political climax of a twenty-two-month period of a psychologically stressful transition from dictatorship to democracy in Hungary. The extended lead time was useful in mobilizing the citizenry to become conscious of the available political options. On the other hand, the protracted campaign exposed the voters to a crushing overload of new and old (and some half-forgotten) political ideas, new and traditional values, and new and old politicians.[47] Inevitably, exhaustion set in and, with it, a significantly reduced voter competence to make sophisticated judgments about their electoral choices.

A preelection Gallup survey on the Hungarian electorate's voting preferences asked respondents to give one-word reasons for why they would vote for one or another party.[48] The reasons for supporting the

AFD were "program," "radical," "expertise," and "future" and for the HDF, "balanced," "moderate," "well-being," and "security." ISP partisans offered "restoration of the land," "peasantry," "private property," and "family tradition." HSP voters mentioned "reform," "Left," "experience," and "party loyalty." These words represented the voters' decoding of both campaign rhetoric and images that appeared on campaign posters.

Some of the campaign posters turned out to be extremely effective in addressing particularly the inattentive and the affectively disengaged voter. In the war of graphics, subliminal messages of reassurance, such as the statesmanlike portrait of József Antall with the words "quiet strength"; group pictures of AFD leaders with the message "we know, we dare, we [will] act"; the CDPP's poster with the crucifix and the national colors; and the offbeat Fidesz poster depicting two kissing couples – Brezhnev and Honecker above, a young man and a woman below – left lasting impressions and garnered more votes than a dozen "talking heads" on paid political programs on TV.

In the end Hungarians chose on election day to support not impenetrable party programs but appealing political symbols and voted their core values and shared desire for radical political change. Much of this was typical of the way a vigorously fought electoral campaign ends in an established democracy. However, what Hungarians experienced in March–April 1990 was not a routine but a "founding" election that gave a popular mandate to parties that had promised to lay the foundations for a new political system. When seen in this light, elements of issue familiarity, the deliberate weighing of program alternatives, and faith in the outcome are critical factors by which to judge the political efficacy of the voting public. With these in mind, it is axiomatic that the outcome of Hungary's founding election was perhaps more the result of a collective temper tantrum (modified by second thoughts in the second round of voting) than of the voters' well-considered choosing among contending political parties.

(D)   Founding elections – winners and losers (round one)

On March 25, 1990, 5,083,086 Hungarians, or 65.77 percent of the eligible voters, took part in the national elections and cast their ballots on the regional party lists. A somewhat smaller percentage (about 61 percent) of the eligible voters cast a second ballot for an individual candidate of their choice in one of the 176 electoral districts.[49]

Twelve parties qualified to enter national slates. A somewhat greater number of parties managed to field county or regional slates. Any party that had obtained at least 750 signatures of endorsement on behalf of its candidate was free to place his or her name on the ballot in the individual electoral districts. All told, a total of 1,614 party-endorsed and independent candidates competed in the individual districts.

Over 90 percent of the candidates were men and, as can be inferred from the candidates' published campaign biographies, most were locally resident middle-aged male university graduates without previous membership in the old HSWP. To assure the election of key politicians, the larger parties in addition to (or instead of) entering their names in local contests, also placed their names on the county and national slates.[50] In any case, the March 25 elections mobilized more than 2,500 individuals with declared ambitions to serve in the Parliament, and at least ten times this number in terms of citizens who assisted with the balloting process.

As indicated in Chapter 7, the Hungarian electoral law was the product of a series of political compromises hammered out at the National Roundtable negotiations.[51] The final agreement, however, yielded a compromise consisting of (a) elaborate screening mechanisms, such as party registration and the collection of 750 endorsement slips for each candidate running in individual districts; (b) a complex process designed to separate parties, according to the number and distribution of successfully entered individual candidates into local, regional, and national levels; and (c) a hybrid system of direct (176 individual mandates) and indirect (152 "county" and 58 "national" list mandates) election of the candidates.[52]

The purpose of this electoral system – which calls for advanced mathematical skills to understand, let alone manage – was to balance local, regional, and national party interests and at the same time assure the governability of the country through elimination from the Parliament of parties that fail to receive 4 percent of votes cast for the party slates. Thanks to the patience and the goodwill of the Hungarian people and the Németh government's correct administration of the electoral process, the system worked. However, the outcome was very different from what anyone at the National Roundtable might have envisaged in the summer of 1989.

The March 25 elections yielded two immediate results. Sixty-five percent of the eligible voters cast 4,911,241 valid votes for nineteen parties and electoral coalitions on the party ballot (see Table 8.1). A smaller number of votes were cast for the individual candidates. (The

Table 8.1   *Votes for party ballot, first round, founding elections, Hungary, March 25, 1990*[53]

Political party or electoral coalition	Vote	
	N	%
Hungarian Democratic Forum	1,214,359	24.73
Alliance of Free Democrats	1,050,799	21.39
Independent Smallholders' Party	576,315	11.73
Hungarian Socialist Party	535,064	10.89
League of Young Democrats	439,649	8.95
Christian Democratic People's Party	317,278	6.46
Hungarian Socialist Workers' Party	180,964	3.68
Hungarian Social Democratic Party	174,434	3.55
Agrarian Alliance	154,004	3.13
Entrepreneurs' Party	92,689	1.89
Patriotic Electoral Coalition	91,922	1.87
Hungarian People's Party	37,047	0.75
Hungarian Green Party	17,951	0.36
National Smallholders' Party	9,944	0.20
Somogy County Christian Coalition	5,966	0.12
Hungarian Cooperative and Agrarian Party	4,945	0.10
Independent Hungarian Democratic Party	2,954	0.06
Freedom Party	2,814	0.06
Hungarian Independence Party	2,143	0.04
Total	4,911,241	100.00

difference stems from the number of voters who cast ballots outside their home districts, hence were ineligible to vote for the local candidates.)

Votes cast for the party lists defined the winners and losers in party terms; established the rank order of, and the initial balance of power among, the winners; and defined those segments of the electorate that, unless they changed their votes in the second round, would remain without parliamentary representation. Let us consider each of these propositions.

The top six "4-plus percent" parties received 84.69 percent of the party list vote. The old HSWP, the Social Democrats, the old regime's electoral alliances, and several small parties did not receive enough votes – the 4 percent "threshold number" was 196,449 – to qualify for parliamentary representation.

The relative share of first-round votes cast for the three Christian-national (HDF, CDPP, and ISP) parties was 42.92 percent; for the two liberal democratic parties, 30.34 percent; and for the socialists, 10.84 percent. This outcome became the voting public's new frame of reference for making electoral decisions about the political viability of party-endorsed individual candidates in the second round of voting on April 8. The initial balance of power among the three party clusters gave a preliminary indication of national party preferences and, in a "bandwagon-effect" sort of way, helped realign voter support in favor of the first-round winners. On the other hand, the relatively small 3.34 percent difference between the HDF and the AFD indicated that the race for first place among the former opposition (and the next governing) parties was far from over on March 25.

The outcome of the party vote left 777,000 voters and approximately 2.7 million nonvoters, or about 40 percent of the adult population, without direct parliamentary representation. What is of interest here is the attitudes of the voting but politically unrepresented public toward the six winners of the first round. Most of the losers were left-wing parties, while the rest were either right-wing or "single-issue" parties, such as the Hungarian Greens. From this, one might – erroneously, as it turned out – conclude that votes originally cast for the HSWP and the HSDP would be readily transferable to the HSP in the second round.

Another result of the March 25 elections was suggestive but far from conclusive as far as the eventual outcome of the second round was concerned. In the 176 contests in the individual districts only five candidates received 50 percent plus one vote and were, therefore, declared winners. Among the five were Zoltán Király (HDF), Speaker of the House and President pro tem Mátyás Szűrös (HSP), and prime minister Miklós Németh, who ran as an independent. What mattered, however, was that the results of the first round helped identify the two leading parties; which, in turn, helped make the second round primarily a "winner-take-all" (or -most) kind of contest between the HDF and the AFD.

The specific results of the first round of voting: the HDF led in 79 districts; the AFD, 63; the ISP, 11; the HSP, 3; the LYD, 2; the CDPP, 4; the AFD–LYD joint slate, 4; and the independents and others, 10. In 125 districts the first-round, first- or second-ranked candidates came from the HDF and the AFD, and the candidates of one of these two parties – the other either not on the ballot or in third place or below – were leading after the first round in twenty-one additional districts.

The outcome of the first round of voting prompts four observations about the broader implications of this event.

Judged by the balance of votes between those cast for the six parliamentary parties and the extra-parliamentary parties, the Hungarian people had voted, by a decisive margin, for the change of the system. Whether this should be considered a protest vote, a "collective temper tantrum," or a positive endorsement of the parliamentary parties' programs was unclear from the votes cast for the party slates. Another imponderable was whether the people had voted for or against the parties' political style or the substance of their message. The answer might be that they did both.

By refusing to hand first-round victories to the new parties' prominent personalities, the voters demonstrated a high level of party identification and, with it, their preference for political organizations over political personalities. Partisanship is a key attribute of democratic voting behavior. The Hungarian voters' reorientation from confusion and ambivalent attitudes toward political parties that they had displayed in the polls and in the by-elections of summer 1989 was evidence of the birth of an issue-conscious and increasingly competent electorate.

The voters' decisive rejection of the parties and the political symbols of the communist party-state went hand in hand with their endorsement, from a left-to a right-of-center political spectrum, of socialist, liberal-democratic, Christian-national, and conservative parties. To the extent these parties were on record as intending to rebuild Hungary's political institutions and restore its ailing economy, votes for them may be seen as evidence of widely shared commitment to political stability and peaceful socioeconomic change.

Hungary used to be a traditional society that defined legitimate political leadership and representation of the community's interests in terms of "maturity" and "experience." The public had not been in the habit of voting for young people to perform the "adult" task of political leadership. Then how should one interpret the decision of 439,649 Hungarian voters to support a political party whose leaders and paid-up members were 35 or younger? It appears that Fidesz's "new politics" – that of sincerity, plain speaking, and personal integrity – was mainly responsible for this psychological breakthrough.

(E)   Founding elections – winner and losers (round two)

On April 8, 1990, 3.5 million Hungarians, or 45.44 percent of the eligible voters, took part in the second round of the national elections, deciding the outcome of 171 contests in as many individual electoral

Table 8.2   *Parties, parliamentary seats after second round, founding elections, Hungary, April 8, 1990*[54]

| | Source of mandate | | | Total seats | |
Party	Individual district	County list	National list	N	%
HDF	114	40	10	164	42.49
AFD	35	34	23	92	23.83
SM	11	16	17	44	11.40
HSP	1	14	18	33	8.55
Fidesz	1	8	12	21	5.70
CDPP	3	8	10	21	5.44
Agrarian League	2	–	–	1	0.52
Independent	6	–	–	6	1.55
Jointly endorsed	2	–	–	2	0.52
Total	176	120	90	386	100.00

districts. The second-round vote also determined the eventual distribution of mandates in the regional and the national party slates (see Table 8.2).

For a balanced assessment of the rather startling outcome, it is necessary to reflect on the complex dynamics of the Hungarian electoral process, particularly on the way the voters perceived the results of the first round. The first round had narrowed the field of eligible political parties to six, and defined the HDF and the AFD as the principal competitors for voter support in the second round. With the initial results at hand, the nature of the political stakes changed. On March 25 the voters had completed their elite-guided task of deconstructing, with their free votes, the edifice of the postcommunist state. The next task was to build a new polity and to select a new leadership for realization of that objective.

As the Hungarian public saw it, system destruction and system building were related but different tasks. The AFD had distinguished itself as a vigorous foe of the old regime and its successor parties, including the HSP and its campaign manager Imre Pozsgay. However, once the reform socialist and the "new" HSWP were cut down to size, the AFD was seen in a different light regarding its fitness to lead the nation toward a new political system. This was certainly true of the thinking of the politically homeless 450,000 HSWP, Agrarian Alliance, Patriotic Electoral Coalition, and Hungarian People's Party voters. To a lesser extent, the same was true for the 535,000 voters who supported the HSP in the first round.

Between the two electoral rounds there was a politically uncommitted mass of about one million voters. Many, perhaps most of them, were parts of the "new social formation" that had come into being in the late Kádár era. (On this, see Chapter 3.) On April 8 they were confronted with the necessity of making a choice between two almost equally undesirable political alternatives. Although many of these first-round voters chose to stay home on that day, perhaps as many as 200,000 cast a vote – most of them for the "lesser evil," that is, the HDF, which received 1,460,838 votes, or 240,000 more than on March 25.[55]

The formation of electoral coalitions is a proven device for the maximization of two or more political parties' electoral assets. In addition to gaining votes, coalitions also help soften the individual parties' ideological posture by blending them into a composite image based on the lowest common denominators of the coalition members' respective electoral programs. The HDF, the ISP, and the CDPP, as these parties' joint statement pointed out after the first round, were "natural" coalition partners.[56] The common label "Christian-national" fitted them all, and also preempted the entire center of the ideological spectrum. As a consequence, the AFD was stuck with the unenviable task of defining its identity and the nature of its precarious second-round electoral coalition with Fidesz in terms that were other than "Christian-national" yet appealing to the voters. The HSP, more or less resigned to its fate as an undesirable coalition partner for the other five parties, had no problems on this score.

It was in the context of the HDF–AFD ideological squeeze play for the center ground, when the leaders of the two parties – whether by design or by default is still unclear – lost control over their followers. The two parties' loose cannons were well-met partnerships of party propagandists and rank-and-file extremists. The HDF's deniable-by-the-leaders propagandists began calling members of the AFD executive "former Maoists, Marxists, and children of communist parents." The AFD reciprocated by labeling their opponents "communist fellow-travelers, anti-Semites, and right-wing extremists." Although both sets of labels fit some of the intended recipients, from the voters' (remarkably mature) perspective, scurrilous campaign rhetoric was something to be largely ignored. Defaced election posters, swastikas, and the word "Jew" painted over the faces of AFD candidates were visible manifestations of "negative campaign" tactics. Such violations of the standards of civilized political discourse afforded a glimpse of the "dark side" of Hungarian politics: long-suppressed ideological passions and anti-Semitism on the one hand, and intolerance toward and contempt for the traditional values and beliefs of the Hungarian people on the other.

Most observers, including thoughtful AFD commentators on the outcome of the April 8 voting, agreed that smear tactics, though a factor, did not play a major role in the victory of the Christian-national coalition.[57] If not demagoguery, then what was responsible for the outcome?

In terms of socioeconomic background, there were no perceptible differences between the typical Forum and Free Democrat candidates running in individual electoral districts. The candidates of both parties tended to satisfy voter expectations with respect to eligibility for electoral support. According to a February 1990 poll, in order of importance the criteria of electability were "no previous HSWP membership"; "middle age"; "local resident"; "family man"; "university graduate"; "male"; "white collar, or intellectual"; and "candidate of a large party." The same poll, however, also established the overriding criterion of voter support: the candidate's party affiliation.[58]

Whereas in the first round a candidate's AFD affiliation was seen as a solid asset for the task of overthrowing the old regime at the ballot box, the main objective of the second round was construction of a new political system. And it was at this juncture where the two parties' coalition strategies and their leaders' political image came into play.

The Christian-national parties had no difficulties in defining their common ideological identity and had no problems with developing a second-round electoral alliance, including the making of several constituency-level agreements for vote swapping and mutual endorsements. By contrast, the AFD–Fidesz electoral coalition was a "marriage of necessity" between two parties without transferable blocs of voters. The problem was that unlike the ideologically roughly homogeneous, therefore interchangeable, Christian-national voting blocs, the AFD and Fidesz had two ideologically compatible – that is, both wanted radical change – but parallel and noninterchangeable first-round constituencies. These, as demonstrated by the results of the second round, were impossible to merge into a united voting bloc on behalf of either party. In the thirteen districts where one of the parties withdrew its candidate in favor of the other party, the outcome in only one instance was productive for the Fidesz candidate; in the other twelve districts either the HDF or the ISP won.[59]

To say that the HDF's program appealed to the voters' emotions and the AFD's message to their "reason" does injustice to the well-crafted HDF program, as well as to the genuine political passion of the AFD's ideological message. On balance, however, the AFD's program and campaign literature were seen by most people more as a well-reasoned unemotional "expert" critique of the old order than as a rousing call for the spiritual rebirth of the nation. The AFD offered polished policy alternatives, but the people expected moral uplift. Moreover, the voters needed assurances that the top parties would usher in a new age of normalcy rather than of radical changes. To the challenge of the AFD campaign slogan "We know, we dare, we will [get things done]," the HDF's response was "steady hand," "liberty," and "property." In the second round the public opted for a "steady hand" in overwhelming numbers. Thus the voters, in their collective wisdom, rewarded the AFD by giving it enough support to become the second-largest party, but punished the same party for its radicalism, aggressive political style, and its leaders' suspected lack of empathy with the aspirations of the common people.

Perhaps the most positive sign of the voter's growing political maturity was the outcome of individual second-round contests between local "favorite sons" and party dignitaries. In several races, top leaders, especially of the liberal-democratic parties, suffered humiliating defeats in the individual districts at the hands of unknown or younger opponents. The HDF got off lightly, with the defeat of national executive members Dénes Csengey, István Csurka, and Lajos Für (Antall did not deign to enter an individual race), but AFD executives Péter Tölgyessy, Miklós Szabó, Miklós Gáspár Tamás, and Ferenc Kőszeg were defeated in their respective districts. Also bested by political newcomers: Imre Pozsgay and Gyula Horn of the HSP, and Fidesz leaders Viktor Orbán, Gábor Fodor, and Tamás Deutsch. Although all of them have obtained parliamentary seats through their parties' regional or national lists, their rout served as an important reminder that it was the parties and not their "talking heads" on TV programs that the voters preferred on April 8.

In sum, on March 25 and April 8, 1990, the Hungarian voters removed the debris from the political playing field and, for the first time since November 1945, leveled it off for the country's political parties in the freely elected Parliament. The transition from the NRT agreement to the elections was peaceful, the communists were exiled into extraparliamentary oblivion, and the Németh government did all it could to hand over power to its successor in a businesslike way.[60]

Still, in the aftermath of the elections many issues remained unresolved and awaited action by the incoming government.

(F)   The governance of postcommunist Hungary – a negotiated transition

All parties, including the socialist, promised a "change of the system" in their electoral programs. Whereas the meaning of the first round of votes was an unambiguous "mandate for radical change," the message of the second round was "moderation" under the "steady hand" of József Antall. What was meant by "change"? The NRT agreement spoke of "fundamental laws" and procedural norms but left many legal-administrative and substantive policy issues – most prominently those in the area of economic, social, and welfare policies – in limbo. And what of the important precedent of the "all-elite" dialogue that had helped establish peaceful interaction among Hungary's elites? Could these be accommodated under the new rules of the political game? It was up to the parliamentary finalists in the transition marathon to find answers to such questions that faced the nation's new leaders in the spring of 1990.

The political-ideological foundations for implementing the transition from postcommunism to democracy rested on five pillars of uneven strength and stability: the parliamentary parties' choices regarding the balance of power among the principal institutions of democratic governance; the letter of the NRT agreement; the hidden agenda of elite consensus on political steering, principles of resource allocation and the nature of postcommunist society; political choices made by the two largest parliamentary parties about revising the terms of the NRT agreement; and strategic goals and policy choices of the people's freely elected government. Let us briefly discuss each of these propositions.

On the balance of power among the head of state, the legislature, and the government, Hungary's political traditions offered three modern precedents for the parliamentary parties in April–May 1990. The Horthy era provided a combination of an authoritarian leader, a series of governments led by political strongmen, and a one-party or government-coalition-dominated Parliament. The democratic interlude of 1945–7 was remembered as one with a weak president of the Republic, a nominally ISP-dominated (with 57 percent of votes in November 1945) Parliament, and coalition governments in which the communists, though with 17 percent of votes in a parliamentary minority, enjoyed veto power on all matters. And, apart from the fleeting moment of Imre Nagy's coalition government of October–November 1956, there was the current precedent of Miklós Németh's "government of experts" and a government-dominated lame-duck Parliament.

From the new parliamentary parties' viewpoint, each of these precedents left much to be desired on ideological and technical grounds. For the first time since 1848, there was no foreign hegemon to consider when making choices about assigning power to political institutions and defining the balance of power between the two principal – executive and legislative – branches of the government. Although the NRT agreement resuscitated the office of the president of the Republic, the Pozsgay precedent counseled caution about the powers that might be bestowed upon the first incumbent. The establishment of the Constitutional Court was essentially a gesture to modern Western traditions, and its main task of exercising quality control over legislative, executive, and judiciary law-making and rule-making was left subject to legislative approval.

The electoral outcome failed to yield an unambiguous distinction between winners and losers. The HDF was the largest party, but the two liberal parties' and, to a lesser extent, the socialist party's preferences had to be accommodated in one way or another. A combination of a "coalition," particularly a "grand coalition," and the "Németh" precedents would have been welcomed by most Hungarians. On the other hand, the overwhelmingly negative precedent of communist rule – including the tainted notions of a "Popular Front" and an "all people's party" – over the past forty years was utterly unacceptable to the new HDF–ISP–CDPP political center. In any event, the initial postelection AFD–Fidesz–HSP consensus (if that is the word) might be summed up as "Let the new incumbents make use, the best they can, of the existing political institutions under parliamentary supervision."

The NRT agreement's expiration date was April 8, 1990. The text included a great deal of useful language – as well as equally useful lacunae on economic and social welfare issues. In a positive sense, the agreement proper consisted of a series of recommendations for legislative action that the next legislature could alter at will. On the other hand, the "fine print" of the agreement introduced important precedents that were binding on whatever political regime emerged after the elections. The ban on workplace discrimination for political reasons had sheltered the noncommunists during the transition period, and now would protect former HSWP members. A budgetary subsidy for opposition parties was now made available to the extraparliamentary also-rans. The latter proved to be a farsighted move because it kept the 1990 electoral losers "off the streets" and, subject to good behavior, on the payroll of the postcommunist government. On the other hand, the glaring omission of agreed-upon measures on economic and social policies gave the new government the freedom (and responsibility) to act as it saw fit.

The NRT agreement was a politically binding contract between the old and the new elites – and two groups of university-trained intellectuals. The agreement, however, transcended the temporal confines of the designated transition period, and therefore could be seen as an informal yet solid framework for principles of a new relationship, in Edward Shils' terms, between "the intellectuals and the powers."[61] The NRT's political *raison d'être*, that is, sheltered exit and entry for the two elites, was discussed in Chapter 7. What is of interest here is the matter of unwritten understandings, mutual expectations, and the two elites' common hidden agenda. This, in my view, was made up of five main items:

First, that the intellectuals – not necessarily as a "class" in Szelényi's and Konrád's sense of the term – by virtue of their corporatist participation in the NRT negotiations, upgraded and legitimated their political standing as a major, or possibly *the*, logocratic (Csaba Gombár's term) interest group with claims for equal ideological status with, and privileged access to, postcommunist governments.

Second, that both elites agreed to distance themselves from the nonelites of the "streets" and from any drastic departure from the old regime's resource-allocation policies. Major macroeconomic changes due to rapid marketization, privatization, or any capitalist reform in redistribution priorities were widely perceived as a threat to them all. At risk was the intellectuals' economic security (and that of the Kádárist middle class, for whom most intellectuals spoke) and their vulnerability to measures that could result in declining incomes and white-collar unemployment.

Third, that the NRT negotiators had a shared interest in social stability and in the prevention of the nonelites' ideological passions interfering with the orderly unfolding of an intelligentsia-led postcommunist civil society. With the exclusion from the NRT and from the Parliament of left- and right-wing extremists, single-issue groups, associations of vintage-1956 radical "freedom fighters," monarchists, and representatives of the trade unions, the poor, and the unemployed, the contracting parties set the boundaries of politically salient interest articulation in postcommunist public policy.

Fourth, that beyond the unwelcome (or unauthorized) advocacy of nationalism, there was another tacit understanding on preventing political witch hunts on grounds of previous Communist Party membership and nonapparat civil service appointment (on this, see "Palmer's pledge" in Chapter 6). The AFD's acquisition of secret-police files in December 1989 alarmed oppositionists and incumbents alike. What if the AFD shared its opponents' files with the public? To everyone's relief, in the end the "rules of the game," that is, silence, were observed by the AFD executive. With the exception of prime minister Antall's publicly blackmailing his recalcitrant Smallholders coalition partners and the HDF's extremist ideologue István Csurka, no *public* use has been made of such incriminating material. (Antall was the only person in Hungary with total access to the files after his installation.)

Fifth, that in the spirit of the NRT agreement on "self-limitation" by the opposition and incumbents alike, the Németh government and the outgoing MPs under its control refrained from major rule making and legislative initiatives. On the other hand, the Németh regime had felt free since early 1988 to implement the government's economic reform agenda that it had initiated. The most prominent item was the Company Law and measures to facilitate privatization and self-privatization of state assets. Some of the "early starters" with good government connections found themselves to be multimillionaires (not in Forints, but in US dollars) in the early 1990s.

In addition to overlooking and assisting giveaways of valuable public assets (office buildings and well-appointed personal residences) to senior apparatchiki and executives of various policy lobbies, the government auditors gave ample time to the HSP to launder its liquid and fixed assets for the party's and its executives' benefit.[62] The government also turned a blind eye to – and the opposition remained silent about – the tremendous buying blitz by German and other Western press conglomerates of the Hungarian print media, particularly the HSWP–HSP's influential and lucrative national and county daily newspapers. Thanks to the Németh government, the old regime's agit-prop artists (also those in the state-controlled electronic media) kept their positions in their new role as "independent" journalists.

In sum, the "miracle" of Hungary's peaceful transition between two political systems had its origins in the terms of the unwritten agreements between the old and the new elites. Much of it was a "leveraged buyout," albeit a different kind. This time the now *voting* "stockholders" were promised freedom, democracy, and social justice. The first two were available to anyone but the third mainly to those who had "convertible" skills or were educated, healthy, lucky, or already provided for by the principals of the transaction. Therefore, the term *deus ex machina* seems more accurate than "miracle" to explain what happened in 1989–90 in Hungary.

The NRT agreement also served to constrain the incumbent legislators from altering virtually *any* recently enacted law to which the label "of constitutional standing" was attached. Without a two-thirds affirmative vote of the Parliament, such laws could not be amended or repealed. Although for the outgoing Parliament it had been the classical case of locking the barn after the horses were stolen, such impediments, unless reduced to manageable size, would have yielded permanent legislative stalemate for any government that had less than an overwhelming share of votes in the Parliament. The Antall-led HDF–ISP–CDPP coalition controlled 59 percent of the seats in the legislature.

Given the state of ideological and personal antagonisms between the three-party coalition and its future parliamentary opposition, unless the ground rules were changed, the Antall government was doomed to function at the sufferance of its political rivals. In any case, it was inconceivable that Antall or any noncommunist government would permit the election of the president of the Republic by plebiscite. Unless the law was changed, Pozsgay's failed gambit, ironically enough, would have put the outgoing prime minister, Miklós Németh, in the best position of being so elected by the grateful public. Antall, too, was appreciative of Németh's services, but he was not about to share power with his predecessor.[63]

Next to the removal of the threat of legislative paralysis, the two largest parties' national and international image was in need of repair. Campaign rhetoric left deep wounds, and also alerted the international financial community to the danger of legislative stalemate and the continued war of words between the winner and the runner-up in the 1990 elections. Thus, the HDF and the ADF had no choice but to come to terms before a government was formed.[64] There were four items on the table: the reduction in the number of "laws with constitutional standing" to only those having to do with truly fundamental issues and the fine-tuning of the language of the Constitution as amended in October 1989 by the old Parliament; the securing the country's governability by the introduction of a "constructive [parliamentary] vote of no confidence" to enable the prime minister to govern with a simple majority; an *ex ante* agreement on choice of president of the Republic who would be elected by a two-thirds majority of the Parliament; and the distribution of committee assignments in the legislature.

The HDF–AFD "pact" of April 29, 1990 addressed the first three issues.[65] The AFD, for its consent to a strong cabinet government, got the presidency (with somewhat strengthened constitutional powers over those that had been provided by the 1946 law) for the AFD backbencher Árpád Göncz and the position of deputy speaker of the Parliament for another AFD MP. The party fared better in the distribution of chairmanships of key parliamentary committees. By contrast, the HDF got a "governable" political system and more than a fair chance to implement its program. Moreover, both parties got a Constitution that drastically altered Pozsgay's NRT version of the preamble; it read: "The Republic of Hungary is an independent, democratic state of laws" – *jogállam* in Hungarian.

One of the great still-unsolved puzzles of the Hungarian transition is why the AFD did not hold out for either an HDF–AFD or for a "grand" coalition that the overwhelming majority of the voters hoped for in the spring of 1990. The Free Democrats' unilateral concessions may, at best, be seen as a courageous act of patriotism and a vote of confidence in the Antall government's adherence to the spirit of ORT consensus on national priorities and in the yet-to-be-written ground rules of democratic politics.[66]

The "pact makers" (János Kis, Péter Tölgyessy, and Iván Pető from the AFD; József Antall and four colleagues for the HDF) – though negotiated in total secrecy with the exclusion of their "natural" ideological allies – were not pragmatic (or Machiavellian) enough to give a cabinet post to Imre Pozsgay. Had they done so, the HSP would have split into a genuine reform-socialist minority and a "not-quite-reformed" majority – with the latter on its way to the periphery of politics for many years to come. Nor did they take advantage of Fidesz's interest in being part of the government coalition.[67] Though few in number, as a modern, pragmatic and socially aware leadership team, these brilliant *Wunderkinder* of Hungarian politics would have helped define Hungary's first postcommunist government. However, none of this came to pass.

What did happen was that József Antall recruited, to him an ideologically correct coalition that the label "Christian democratic" may generally, though not quite accurately, describe. The first Antall cabinet was at best a group of academic and, to a remarkable extent, humanistic intellectuals not tainted by previous membership in the HSWP. At worst, the cabinet was a handpicked collection of Antall loyalists, intellectually competent-to-mediocre survivors of the Kádár era without previous administrative experience, and with a vague understanding of the fuzzy policy agenda that Antall handed down to them. Though the government was certainly not of the "best and the brightest," it was an instrument that served the prime minister's purposes at that time.[68]

The last step in Hungary's epic journey "from revolution to liberty" was installation of a prime minister by the country's freely elected Parliament. Those who were privileged to witness this historic event were treated to a moving spectacle: a friendly handshake between the outgoing and incoming premiers, and József Antall's spirited delivery of his inaugural address.[69] The details of the address were incorporated in the government's action program that was published in the following days.

However, Antall's quote from Ferenc Deák's speech to the revolutionary Parliament of 1848 merits registration at this point. Deák said: "Those who are not friends of the recent transformation, we must make our friends. We shall reach our goals by holding each other's hands. Should we succumb to our feuds, we will not need external foes, for the country shall, on its own, annihilate itself."[70]

Two weeks later, at the national conference of the HDF, the party's chairman József Antall confronted, stared down, and dispatched the Lakitelek Populist "founding fathers" into political oblivion.[71] Two of them – the "founding father" Lajos Für and an ideological soulmate Bertalan Andrásfalvy – got a cabinet post each, and the rest were sent off to occupy politically harmless patronage jobs. Antall's cards were now on the table. A new age and a new (and probably very old) kind of politics was about to commence in Hungary.

9   Democracy in Hungary: toward a new model?

Hungary's first postcommunist government was different from yet in many ways similar to the governments of the "new democracies" that came into being in the wake of free elections throughout the region. József Antall's three-party Christian democratic coalition was one, and until the end of 1994 arguably the only, postcommunist regime that completed in full its originally stipulated term in office. Since 1989 Poland has seen a change of presidents and the rise and fall of governments; Czechoslovakia has been divided into two states; Slovakia has witnessed several political turnovers; and the Balkan states have experienced profound instability, including civil wars and unscheduled elections. Moreover, the Russian Federation and the rest of the successor states of the Soviet Union have been the scene of coups, countercoups, social turmoil, low- and high-intensity civil wars – with profound and not yet fully examined consequences for the stability of the outlying region.

By contrast, Hungary in the early 1990s seemed to be an island of manifest political stability, economic progress, and social contentment. The government governed, the Parliament made laws, foreign investments were pouring in, the intellectuals were restless, and the public disoriented. Hungary and its Central European neighbors were the first new democracies to sign Association Agreements with the European Union. As part of the "Visegrád Three" (and later with the split of Czechoslovakia into two states, "Four"), Hungary, too, became a sovereign actor in European politics.[1] Thus, by all appearances, the country was off to a promising start on the road to political democracy, a market economy, and the rebirth of civil society.

Yet, four years later Hungary could not escape the fate of its neighbors' first-round governments. In the May 1994 parliamentary elections the incumbent Christian democratic governing coalition was decisively repudiated by the public and swept out of office by the tide of resurgent ex-communist and liberal democratic forces. It seems that whatever initial advantages Hungary's own brand of "velvet revolution" might have imparted to the new regime, these were obliterated by the new iron laws of transition between posttotalitarian communism and parliamentary democracy in its part of the world.

In this chapter I shall briefly reflect on Hungary's experience since the electoral defeat of the old regime in the spring of 1990 and sum up the main findings of my reconstruction of that nation's path between its two revolutions. It is not my task to offer a detailed analysis of the complex record of postcommunist politics. It is the proper subject of another study addressing the full dimensions of the birth of democracy in Hungary in the broader context of the dynamics of systemic change in Eastern Europe.

(A)   Christian democrats at the helm

The Antall regime's record has been the subject of harshly partisan as well as of objective criticism.[2] The record warrants both, because Hungary's first postcommunist government was presented with some one-time choices and opportunities that could have set positive precedents for long-term political stability and orderly installation of democratic institutions and values in Hungary. József Antall's choice between an ideologically homogeneous Christian democratic and, with the inclusion of one or both liberal parties, a broader government coalition sowed seeds for the present lopsided bipolar left–right parliamentary configuration of party politics. Moreover, contrary to initial expectations, the fail-safe device of "vote of constructive no-confidence" helped deepen ideological cleavages between the right-of-center incumbents and the impotent and increasingly frustrated left-of-center liberal and socialist parliamentary opposition.[3] Instead of a precedent-setting confidence-building measure between the two largest democratic parties and the foundation of six-party consensus on the political essentials of Hungary's transition, the HDF–AFD pact and its perceived violations by both sides helped poison the wells of the body politic for the next four years.

Certain components of the new political architecture, particularly the president of the Republic, the Constitutional Court, and the newly elected (September–October 1990) local governments, performed rather differently from what the framers of the NRT agreement and the HDF and AFD "pact makers" had envisaged. As events unfolded, it appeared that President Árpád Göncz, instead of being a figurehead with a nonpartisan "integrative personality," had an ideological agenda of his own. To Antall's dismay, Göncz's political beliefs were about as close to those of his own party's (the AFD) social-liberal faction as to the HSP's political preferences on many issues.[4]

Contrary to expectations that the half reform communist and half "new democrat" Constitutional Court would be content with adjudicating technical issues of constitutional interpretation, this body became a highly active "third branch" of the government with a record of vigorous and, on the whole, constructive involvement in a wide range of issues.[5] Moreover, within six months of the national elections the central government had to contend with AFD- and Fidesz-dominated municipal governments (including that of Budapest), as well as with the crushing defeat of Christian democratic candidates by hold-over ex-HSWP independents as local administrators in 85 percent of Hungary's rural communities.[6] Antall may have controlled the central state bureaucracy, but the daily lives of four-fifths of the people were under the administrative control of local opposition politicians.

The result of these unexpected outcomes was multiple institutional stalemate rather than a workable system of constitutional checks and balances among the government, the Parliament, the president of the Republic, the Constitutional Court, and the local governments. Behind each of these institutions there were potentially volatile, and in terms of ideological preferences largely incompatible, interests of three sets of internally divided new, old, and holdover elite groups of the transition process.[7]

The new elites (former dissidents, local independents, and young intellectuals) were inexperienced party politicians occupying positions of power as cabinet officers, as parliamentary deputies, and as newly elected municipal officials. To convert their recently acquired power into political authority and to compensate for administrative inexperience, they sought to ideologize their policy stance in terms of traditional adversarial intelligentsia disputes rather than in the pragmatic language of law and public administration.

The old elites (*nomenklatura* notables in science, education and culture, the judiciary, the military, the red and green barons of industry and agriculture, trade union executives, media managers, and leaders of major religious groups) remained firmly ensconced in their respective institutional fiefdoms. Their shared objective was the preservation and consolidation, by way of *de facto* or legal recognition, of the old elites' pretransition corporatist entitlements *vis-à-vis* the entitlements of the new political incumbents. "Experience," "stability," and "European norms" were the operative terms of the old elites' collective self-legitimation, but the implicit agenda was the preservation of the status quo ante.

The holdover elites (mainly the middle- to lower-echelon public servants) were present throughout the vast state bureaucracy. In a very real sense, the Antall regime's political survival was in the hands of the tens of thousands of deputy department heads and low-ranking managers in government offices (including the military and the police), in administrative agencies, state-owned enterprises, and educational and cultural institutions. As the political regime's human face at the grassroots level, these denizens of the bloated state administration could make or break any government and any policy initiative that posed a threat to the well-being of the "silent middle" of Hungarian society.

The intellectuals – hitherto united in their quest to replace the Kádár regime – now found themselves between a rock and a hard place. Forces at work were policy initiatives of the new regime and a sullen opposition of the old and the holdover elites to radical change of any kind – particularly implementation of "political justice" by the new incumbents. In the belief that the NRT process automatically upgraded the intelligentsia to the status of spiritual-cultural counterweight to the postcommunist governments of the day, the humanistic intellectuals, particularly those in the print and electronic media, appointed themselves moral arbiters in public affairs. However, behind the façade of ideological posturing lay the literati's interest in preserving their collective immunity from accountability for their record in the Kádár era. In *this* sense, the intellectuals were very much part of the old elites.

In sum, the old and the holdover elites had a stake in the preservation of their previous power, status, income, and life prospects in a postcommunist Hungary. The old regime fell because it had neither the legitimacy nor the resources to satisfy the expectations of these constituencies of the new Hungarian middle class. The question was whether the now-legitimate institutional structures of the postcommunist polity were resilient enough to accommodate each of these interests.

Antall had little or no direct control over the behavior of the president of the Republic and the justices of the Constitutional Court, local politics and the politics of the embedded elite groups. However, the national government's policy agenda was his to shape, prioritize, and submit to legislative action. Here again, Antall had choices between embarking on a well-prepared long-term legislative program and the scoring of easy victories in the form of a "first-hundred-days" strategy of seeking enactment into law of the yes-able items of the HDF–AFD pact. In any case, instead of confronting the public – either in his inaugural speech or in the next several months – with the harsh facts of the country's economic inheritance from the old regime, Antall chose the path of least resistance and, as some critics put it, promised "pleasant dreams" and rapid progress to the citizens.[8]

It may have been impolitic to speak of crushing foreign indebtedness, of "blood, sweat, and tears," let alone "toil," and of the high price the nation had to pay for its freedom while the outgoing prime minister was still in the legislative chamber during the inauguration ceremonies. However, by failing to do so, the new government deprived itself of moral capital and of long-term credibility as the nation's responsible leader in its time of need for firm guidance to escape from the economic and political quagmire of the old regime. On the other hand – and we are still at the moment of *status nascendi* of the new Hungarian democracy – Antall in his first speech as duly elected prime minister *did* speak of tragic episodes in Hungarian history, specifically of the martyrdom of his earliest predecessor, prime minister Lajos Batthyány who had died on the gallows on October 6, 1849.[9]

What no one but Antall and his physicians knew in May 1990 was that he was an ill man with a treatable but terminal disease that would claim his life after three and a half years of courageous struggle to discharge his constitutional responsibilities as prime minister. Antall was aware that he lived on borrowed time. Yet, whether out of compassion for the people whom he wished to spare the pain of "radical therapies" or because he took personal pride in effecting the "most peaceful" of transitions in Eastern Europe, Antall chose not to act when timely action was both needed and politically feasible.

Antall's strategic choices as national leader were fundamentally constrained by what I in an earlier study called Münzer's dilemma.[10] The dilemma was spelled out in stark terms by Friedrich Engels in his classic treatise *The Peasant War in Germany*. Engels submitted:

> The worst thing that can befall a leader of an extreme party is to be compelled to take over the government in an epoch when the movement is not yet ripe for the domination of the class which he represents, and for the realization of the measures which that domination implies. What he can do depends not upon his will but upon the degree of contradiction between the various classes, and upon the level of development of the material means of existence, of the conditions of production and commerce upon which class contra-

dictions repose ... What he can do contradicts his previous actions, principles, and the immediate interests of his party, and what he ought to do cannot be done. In a word, he is compelled to represent not his party or his class, but the class for whose domination the movement is then ripe. In the interests of the movement he is compelled to advance the interests of an alien class, and to feed his own class with phrases and promises and with the asseveration that the interests of that alien class are its own interests. Whoever is put in this position is irrevocably lost.[11]

Antall was aware that it had been a fortuitous combination of circumstances, his serendipitous (and ideologically duplicitous) acquisition of party leadership, and a possibly onetime anticommunist protest vote of the public that launched him to the apex of political power. He was enough of a pragmatist to honor his political debts but not enough of a revolutionary to lead his people boldly on the uncharted paths of the postcommunist world.[12] In any case, in view of the limited time that was left to him (he died on December 12, 1993), he did not have a fair chance for a gradual implementation of his plans for Hungary.

Because the country or, as Engels put it, the "movement" was not "ripe" for the prompt instauration of democracy and a market economy, Antall's and his successor's (HDF MP and Minister of Interior Péter Boross served as prime minister between December 1993 and June 1994) policy choices were severely limited throughout their terms in office. On the one hand, Antall could insist on the full implementation of his original agenda (whatever that might have been) and run foul of widespread elite and mass resistance. On the other hand, he could try to accommodate the existing socioeconomic forces, but only at the cost of following his predecessor's policies. In practical terms it meant surrendering a great deal of his nominal powers to the old and holdover elites in the economy, business, public administration, and the media, and sharing the nation's ideological leadership with the politicized and traditionally antigovernment intelligentsia.

Although Antall and his coalition government were the ostensible political beneficiaries of Hungary's peaceful transition to a parliamentary democracy, his regime was captive to the logic of *ex ante* agreements that he and the ORT negotiators had entered into with the outgoing elites. On the one hand, the political, legal, and administrative provisions of the NRT agreement amounted to little more than a well-crafted rescue package for the outgoing elites and a bare-bones procedural blueprint for the launching of a postcommunist polity. On the other hand, the same document was an implicit charter for the preservation of the *ancien régime*'s economic power structure, and a strategic lever for subsequent conversion of the old managerial elites' custodial quasi-ownership prerogatives over state assets into private property and thence to political power.[13]

Much of the same was true for the whole cluster of social and welfare issues that the NRT negotiators chose not to address. It was one thing to boot out the trade unions from the NRT negotiations and to browbeat the third side into signing the September 18, 1989 agreement, but another to inherit the old regime's meager resources and be confronted with the people's heightened expectations for "more and better" of their freely elected government. It was a farsighted move to craft an electoral system that yielded a stable six-party-plus-independents distribution of parliamentary seats and that exiled the old HSWP into the political wilderness. However, the same electoral system created an instant prosocialist reserve army of disgruntled, politically nonrepresented voters and nonvoters with no stake in the preservation of the new postcommunist political status quo. In any case, the long-term political support of the protest voters of March–April 1990 was contingent on the new regime's delivery on the public's uninformed expectations for economic security and eventual prosperity in Hungary's "existing democracy."[14]

Well before his inauguration Antall was put on notice that Hungary's Western creditors, particularly the International Monetary Fund, expected the new government to live up to its predecessor's commitments with respect to domestic fiscal policies and the continued servicing of international debts. Although in per capita terms the most indebted among the former communist states, Hungary was denied the option of debt rescheduling or a debt-for-equity swap, an arrangement that Poland benefited from in the coming years. Antall was probably right in assuming responsibility for the old regime's reckless borrowing in the previous two decades. However, the burden he took on fatally handicapped the country's prospects of early economic recovery as well as those of his government to survive beyond its first term in office.[15] Ironically, the same Western loans that had paid for the "good king" Kádár's popularity in the 1970s, and that twenty years later were still being cherished by the former beneficiaries, became the principal obstacle to the fulfillment of the economic goals of the first freely elected government.

In sum, to claim the helm and to discharge the governing responsibilities for which he was elected, Antall had to honor by action or inaction the stated and unstated terms of previous political agreements. At the same time, he also had to satisfy unrealistic popular expectations for a new postcommunist social contract. Moreover, he was under irresistible pressures to reshape the nation into compliance with Western demands for the instauration of the rule of law, democratization, and a market economy. Unlike Münzer, Antall was an accidental beneficiary of a negotiated revolution; it had been crafted by two self-selected elite groups and was subsequently legitimated by a disoriented electorate.

Although nothing was "irrevocably lost" at the outset, to survive politically Antall had to serve two masters: the *Homo Kadaricus* of Hungary and the politically supportive but economically only marginally helpful Western political community. Between 1990 and 1994 Hungary was the recipient of over $8 billion (mainly cash but also in kind) in direct Western investments. In the same period the amount of Hungarian payments on external debts (principal and interest) was approximately $20 billion.[16] Who benefited from the fall of communism? The people of Hungary or Hungary's Western creditors? Probably both, but the initial loser was the country's first freely elected government.

(B)   Hungary at the crossroads: patterns of continuity and change

The five-year record of Eastern Europe's postcommunist transitions has been one of high hopes, remarkable achievements, and keen disappointments. The multiple challenge of implementing policies of the area's "dual transition" to democratization and marketization and the overcoming of societal resistance to the same proved to be a severe test of the new regimes' stability and political legitimacy. Indeed, the road from the exuberant "year of miracles" of 1989–90 to the seemingly effortless electoral comeback of the old, at best reform-communist, elites to power since 1994 tends to vindicate Engels' caveats about popular inertia and premature revolutions, and to serve as convincing explanation for the dashed hopes of present-day Münzers.

Like their immediate predecessors, these second- and third-round governments have become targets of public resistance to marketization and privatization, and the elites' disappointment in the performance of new political institutions.[17] Although yesterday's party apparatchiki with convertible skills have made an impressive comeback throughout Eastern Europe, the old-new incumbents are still servants to two masters. From this it follows that they are politically vulnerable to the same constraints that contributed to the downfall of the region's first-round governments. The imposition of new institutional architectures on the old foundations has yet to contain – let alone stabilize – the socioeconomic forces that caused the collapse of the old structures seven years ago.

The task at hand is not discussion of recent events but the identification of longitudinal trends that are still at work and are key determinants of continuity and change in Hungary. As discussed in the Introduction, the hypothesized six "mainsprings of political change" are analytical levers with which to develop explanations for the political outcomes of 1989–90. My initial objective was to identify and explain the contribution of each of these factors to the collapse of the old regime in 1989–90. Whereas the "Who?" "What?" "When?" and "How?" parts of the case were addressed in Chapters 6, 7, and 8 of this study, the continued salience of socioeconomic constraints on systemic change, that is, the "Why?" part of the case, requires further analysis.

Given the peaceful and elite-brokered nature of Hungary's political transformation, it is axiomatic that much of the old regime's unresolved social and economic agenda became the postcommunist governments' political responsibility. What changed and what has remained the same since 1990? For answers, I shall return to the six main themes of inquiry. The object is to provide a tentative balance sheet of continuity and change in Hungary's path between two revolutions and since the fall of the old regime.

Nation and progress

The terms of public discourse on Hungarian politics have been traditionally defined by contending elite ideologies on questions of economic backwardness, social justice, cultural modernization, and political empowerment. With the onset of communist rule and upon the defeat of the 1956 revolution, the complex issue of "nation and progress" was articulated by the participants in a protracted and at times highly confrontational dialogue between the regime and the intellectuals. The central topic was Hungary's domestic policy options under conditions of existing socialism in Soviet-controlled Eastern Europe.

Kádár's choice of native communist and radical agrarian socialist/ Populist ideas as *de facto* legitimating principles of modernization and consensus-building redefined the terms of official discourse on developmental priorities. By rejecting the maximalist formulation of

"Hungary as a socialist state" and eschewing Soviet-inspired *dognat' i peregnat'* (catch up and overtake) strategies of accelerated development, Kádár opted for a gradualist "people's democratic" model. The latter consisted of domesticist policies of evolutionary social change, selective economic modernization, and indigenous ways of building socialism.

Thanks to Kádár and György Aczél, the political requisites of "Hungary's road to socialism" were never fully elaborated in doctrinal terms. Instead, the regime's propaganda messages spoke of "community," "country and nation," "alliance policy," and "socialist democracy."[18] By extolling the virtues of hard work, family, and the acquisition of material possessions, the party sought to divert public attention from volatile issues of "nation and progress," such as the nationalist emancipatory legacy of the 1956 revolution. Thus, consumerism, as enhanced by "small freedoms" and the regime's retreat from the ideological arena, successfully preempted latent mass aspirations for national sovereignty and individual political rights. Under these circumstances, those intellectuals who were willing to buy into, or at least coexist with, the "good king's" regime had ample room to maneuver through the obstacle course of "support–toleration–ban" and still have their say about Hungary's place in the world.

The principal ideological achievement of the Kádár regime was the successful replacement of the Hungarian intellectual elites' traditional radical-libertarian, that is, potentially revolutionary, brand of nationalism with an inward-looking evolutionary paradigm that focused on the improvement rather than the overthrow of the institutions and policies of existing socialism in Hungary. Apart from the Populists' tolerated (and occasionally encouraged) concerns about the fate of conationals abroad, the mainstream intelligentsia consensus, including that of the democratic dissidents and socialist critics, sought changes from within the established power structure. In doing so, both the insurgents and the incumbents helped legitimate the etatist, redistributionist, and consensual essence of Kádár's model for Hungary's national survival (and progress of sorts) in Eastern Europe.

To make its way in the new postcommunist world, Hungary was expected to restructure its political institutions and transform its economic system. However, the elite-led negotiated transformation scenario made no provisions for either political or economic justice for the nonelites. The pact makers had neither the will nor the resources to satisfy public expectations associated with the change of regime. Instead, the incoming and the outgoing elites agreed to replace two old legitimating ideological abstractions with two new ones. Thus, the reform communists' NRT-sanctioned model of "rational governance by experts" was transformed by the electoral process into a "publicly accountable," albeit *de facto* irremovable, Christian democratic government, and the "people's (centrally planned *cum* second) economy" was renamed a "social market economy."[19]

These formulations were code words for incremental institutional change and for giving a new lease on life to an elite-managed posttotalitarian welfare state. This outcome has become a congenital legitimacy flaw in the postcommunist transition equation of "nation and progress." The preservation, under new labels, of elite governance and that of the state's role in the satisfaction of the public's traditional social-welfare expectations as indicators of the efficacy of newly democratized political institutions, has become a major obstacle to "progress" toward economic modernization and the rapid installation of a real market economy.

The task of effecting a dual breakthrough of democratization and rapid economic transformation while preserving elite consensus on the adverse social consequences of this process has been a no-win proposition for the new government. New legitimating principles were needed to build public confidence in the regime. The path of least resistance lay in Antall's swallowing the bitter pill of becoming hostage to the old and the holdover elites' vested interests, completing his predecessor's agenda of token reforms and paying lip service to political democratization. The alternative – quiet renegotiation of the terms of previous political agreements and the development of an all-elite survival pact to implement a tough economic program – was rejected by Antall.

Ideological mystification and political scapegoatism to cover up for economic shortfalls have been proven techniques of social-conflict prevention in Hungary. To bridge the gap between budgetary resources and public expectations, the HDF leadership opted for the revival of nationalist ideologies and the resuscitation of prewar notions on the nation's cultural hegemony in the region.[20] When these failed to impress either the public or the intellectuals – let alone the enraged nationalists in the neighboring states – the party's ideologues resorted to the selective rehabilitation of the Horthy regime's political personalities and the values of its Christian national middle class.

The Moscow *Putsch* of August 1991 evoked the specter of communist restoration in the minds of HDF officials. Some of these alarmed political novices, such as Imre Kónya the party's parliamentary leader, saw an opportunity to crack down on the old elites and finish the "spring housecleaning" the party had promised during the electoral campaign.[21] Antall stayed the course but, a year later, was powerless to prevent a major ideological split between the right-radical-Populist and the national-liberal wings of the HDF. In a fiery pamphlet the HDF MP and party vice president István Csurka demanded, on behalf of the social and economic losers of the transition process, a full accounting of the terms of previous elite pacts and a prompt return to the national roots of Hungarian politics. He also called for "housecleaning" of a different sort: with the use of right-radical and fascist code words "racial purity," he also evoked the specter of an international "Jewish conspiracy" as a threat to the *élettér* (*Lebensraum*) for the "national hinterland" of presumably like-minded Hungarians.[22]

Kónya's and Csurka's messages and their call for the instauration of a "law-and-order democracy," though eventually repudiated by Antall, energized the hitherto wait-and-see majority of the intelligentsia on many fronts. Of these, the "Democratic Charter" – an HSP- and AFD-led coalition of holdover intellectuals – proved to be the most effective instrument to take on the besieged incumbents. As the Charter's inaugural manifesto put it, "there will be democracy in Hungary when the legitimate government of the day refrains from trying to elevate, either openly or surreptitiously, any kind of belief system to the rank of state religion."[23]

The explicit assertion of the Kádárist precedent of ideological *laissez-faire* and the Charter critics' insistence that the political incumbents remain impartial guardians of the rule of law – that is, of earlier pacts and agreements – was an unassailable argument. It was also the beginning of the end of public support of the Christian democrats' right to define what Hungary ought to be for an intelligentsia-led postcommunist civil society.

Well before Antall's death his vision of "nation and progress" was shrugged off by the disenchanted public and replaced by the Chartists' HSP-AFD-promoted "social consensus." The key words were "constitutional democracy," "independent judiciary," "free press," (state-guaranteed) "social safety net," and, above all, "appointment of cultural executives by independent experts." Whether the HSP's landslide electoral victory of May 1994 was "Kádár's revenge" or a step toward a needed updating of elite notions of "nation and progress" is too early to tell. Since 1994–5, a new paradigm is being developed in intensive behind-closed-doors negotiations among the six parliamentary parties. The eventual terms of a new legal-ideological NRT II Agreement will be codified in a new constitution – possibly before the next scheduled elections in 1998.

Compromise and survival

During the past 450 years, save the Horthy era of 1920–44, Hungary was either occupied by or was the political appendage of a foreign power. The imposition of alien – Ottoman, Habsburg, and Soviet – rule left a deep imprint on the culture, values, and overt behavior of people and elites alike. The key to survival was adaptation, as well as the preservation of language, culture, and national identity. The elites of the day became the facilitators of interaction between the people and the powers that be. Their survival, albeit with reduced administrative, economic, and cultural autonomy, was essential to that of the nation as a whole. The people, as the Latin phrase aptly put it, *misera plebs*, took their cue from their native leaders and coped as best they could.

Over the centuries such patterns of adaptive behavior became embedded parts of the elites' quasi-participant and the people's traditional subject political culture. Common to both types of mindsets was pragmatism, a reduced sense of efficacy, and overt compliance with the givens of the political status quo. Mihály Babits' phrase cited in the Introduction, "lucid compromises ... [and] uninterrupted meditation on actual possibilities," points to the essence of the matter: however oppressed, the nation – nobles and commoners alike – have historically always retained a residual capacity for mental reservations about the legitimacy of foreign rule.[24]

At issue is the cumulative impact of the long history of alien, most recently Soviet, rule on the Hungarian people's ability rapidly to adapt to and make good use of opportunities that the instauration of political pluralism, parliamentary democracy, and rule of law have made available to the postcommunist public. Richard Rose, a critic of the political-culture approach to the study of East European transitions, called reasoning of this kind "static" and "historicist." He submitted, on the basis of rather inconclusive survey data, that "the contemporary political culture of these [East European] nations is *not* shaped by the distant past."[25] Although he acknowledges the salience of other factors, such as institutions, human nature, cultural consensus, and social cleavages, in his view it is the shared experience of "Sovietization" rather than precommunist traditions that "matters" in the 1990s.

My purpose is not to refute Rose's otherwise sensible propositions. Rather, it is to amend and, with the use of Harry Eckstein's postulates of cultural and cognitive change, reformulate them as warranted by the evidence of the Hungarian case.[26] To begin *in medias res*: under the communist regime there were two forces at work. The first was the party's effort to remold public consciousness and thereby effect rapid cognitive change. The second was the "orientational cumulativeness" of the public's core beliefs that served as "inertia in motivations" to protect and maintain each actor's cognitive balance between the old and the new. As Eckstein explains, "actors must often face novel situations with which their dispositional equipment is ill suited to deal."[27]

The regime sought to implement "externally imposed changes" of political mobilization, economic transformation, and social levelling that yielded "socially internal discontinuities." These, in Hungary's case, were exacerbated by the watershed event of a regionally unique experience of the 1956 revolution. The revolt proper was not merely "inertia in action" but a vigorous reaffirmation of the public's historically conditioned cumulative learning experience in dealing with cases of intolerable oppression. Policy premises of the Kádárist restoration included significant "culturalist" concessions to public expectations of normalcy and cognitive congruence concerning tolerated styles of political governance. On the other hand, though the regime tried to go native in some respects, its leadership was still committed to strategies of economic modernization and noncoercive policies of social engineering.

Strategies and policies of the system-management phase of political steering sought to promote change as well as to preserve, by way of an informal social contract and various group subcontracts, stability – as a new kind of ersatz continuity. It is axiomatic that both types of regime initiatives have made Hungarian society more complex, more modern, and more secular. From this it follows that "the more modern societies are, the more of the elements of their cultures will be general, thus flexible." To this Eckstein adds that

> the expectation of cultural flexibility ... should apply to *all* modern societies ... It thus pertains to polities initially based on rigid dogma (like communist societies) that have successfully pursued modernization. In such societies, the first expectation, that of cultural inertia, should hold. Old culture should resist new dogma. The expectation of pattern-maintaining change (or perceptual distortion) should hold as well. So one should expect also that as culture changes in such societies, it will change toward greater flexibility – and therefore to reinterpretation of dogma that make it increasingly pliable.[28]

The complex chemistry of the regime's ideological demobilization and the public's survival instincts – including a self-imposed collective amnesia with respect to the trauma of regime restoration – yielded, in

Eckstein's terms, to "cultural discontinuity" and a "highly formless" political culture. Discontinuity pitted the society's ingrained orientations against new experiences and prompted people to invest these with new meaning. Formlessness was due in part to general disorientation and in part to a cognitive healing process in people who tried to come to terms with new realities of the 1960s and the 1970s.

At issue here is the community's changed attitudes toward political incumbents, institutions, and legitimating symbols in the age of the "good king" János Kádár. A related concern is the way is which such attitudes and behaviors survived the fall of the regime and shape public orientations toward the postcommunist governments. As discussed in Chapters 2 and 3, the Kádár regime's economic strategy, particularly the NEM, and cultural policies gave birth to a differentiated, mobile, and well-educated hybrid society.

Official norms of public conduct placed a premium not on internalized beliefs but on outward conformity. The latter was accepted as evidence of citizen compliance with the regime's political and ideological expectations. Inevitably, the proposition entailed trade-offs between political efficacy and political infantilism. Society opted for the latter and retreated into the realm of private pursuits. This, in turn, helped create a normless void in which individual "strategies of interest realization" were given relatively free rein. The outcome made, at best, for a new kind of bargain culture in which groups and individuals sought to wrest economic concessions from the officials. At worst, this gray zone of tolerated and barely controlled social interaction became the scene of a *bellum omnium contra omnes*-style individualistic, amoral, and extralegal pursuit of personal gain.[29]

The cost, in terms of traditional standards of moral rectitude, civic probity, and personal decency, of social adaptation to existing socialism was very high. Ethical foundations of both the first and second societies rested on the incumbents' and the subject-citizens' relativized and reduced sense of moral competency. Much of this became manifest in officially tolerated and privately condoned forms of deviant behavior. With the exception of the behavior of the puritanical and the politically ostracized few, actions ranging from misuse or theft of state property and bribetaking to pathologies of amoral familism became accepted patterns of personal conduct in posttotalitarian Hungary.

Members of each "society" contributed to the morass: the apparat, when not busy with cutthroat politicking, helped enrich family and friends with patronage jobs and illegal real estate deals; *nomenklatura* notables amassed power and material possessions, and dispensed patronage; bureaucrats took bribes in money or reciprocal favors; health service professionals expected and received gratuities of both kinds; writers signed bogus publishing contracts; factory foremen and cooperative farm executives expected and received kickbacks; and those with no access to extra incomes retreated to self-destructive behavior and private despair. With respect to personal ethics and commitment to the welfare of the community, there did not seem to be discernible differences between members of the two societies. There is ample survey evidence to support the proposition that over time the values and norms of conduct in the public and private realms became fully interpenetrated and formed a symbiotic whole.[30]

The political orientations of the *Homo Kadaricus* were largely determined by various sociological attributes that defined one's position as a member of the elite or of the nonelite.[31] Although sharing core values of the same political culture, the elites had privileges to protect and social distance from the nonelites to maintain. To preserve these advantages, the elites met the regime more than halfway and became parts of an old-new sociopolitical matrix of power, privilege, and access to state resources.

The elites' preferential access to public goods by *de facto* class criteria bore uncanny resemblance to precommunist patterns of traditional socioeconomic hierarchy. In prewar Hungary, position, income, and social status were determined by birth, wealth, and educational credentials; under Kádár, by class background, *nomenklatura* status, and, from 1970 on, merit. The critical difference between the Horthy and the Kádár regimes was that the conduct of the former was bounded, however imperfectly, by the rule of law, and its style of governance was informed – again, however flawed – by meritocratic norms of its public administration. By contrast, the communist party-state muddled through by its voluntaristic and inherently chaotic rules that were seen as legitimate, hence valued, by neither the officals nor the public. Sharp cleavages in occupational-prestige surveys between the public officials' perceived "power" and "social usefulness" can only hint at the gap between official preferences and public consent to the new social hierarchy of existing socialism.

The public's retreat to small parochial units of family and closed intelligentsia circles gave a new lease on life to precommunist patterns of social interaction. The social and psychological context was amoral familism and politically infantile expectations of good, that is, caretaker government, traditional yearnings for law and order, predictable political outcomes, and authentic authority figures.[32] These were important parts of the society's hidden agenda that the Kádár regime could not satisfy.

For an interim summary of the case, let us return to Eckstein's propositions. As he explained,

> What of the long-run prospects of revolutionary transformation? I suggest the expectation that the long-run effects of attempted revolutionary transformation will diverge considerably from revolutionary intentions and resemble more the prerevolutionary condition of society. The expectation is not that little change in "content" will occur: in who holds power, gets privilege and so on. No inevitable Thermidorean Reaction is posited. The argument is less categorical: reconstructed culture patterns and themes will diverge widely from revolutionary visions and will tend to diverge in the direction of the old society and regime.[33]

The Kádárist civil society, such as it was, had a traditional inbuilt capacity for adaptation as well as for innovation by way of boring from within the political system and gradually reshaping the regime's *modus operandi* and the political culture of its successor generation. Too, the regime tried to adapt and innovate by way of ideological demobilization and administrative tinkering. However, the leadership's attempts, to use Rezső Nyers' *bon mot*, "to dance with both feet tied," were constrained by the society's "reconstructed culture patterns." In the ensuing stalemate the political regime became system-alien, the economy dysfunctional, the society privatized, and the elites quasi-autonomous.

The outgoing and the incoming political elites of 1989–90 had a shared political culture that defined the consensual essence of the NRT agreement. It was a "political artifice" (Eckstein's term) in the form of a well-made contract that preserved political stability, accommodated the nonelites' nascent autonomy, and rolled over the task of addressing the community's unfulfilled economic agenda to the next regime. The validity of the agreement was predicated on institutional change and sociocultural continuity. In the absence of a cathartic watershed event, such as a revolution, the latter rescued intact the whole range of social pathologies and political orientations of the *Homo Kadaricus* and reinserted these into the public life of postcommunist Hungary.[34]

In sum, the culturalist approach, when crafted from valid historical precedents and augmented with empirical evidence on elite and mass orientations in the period of the historically short-lived Sovietization of Hungary, can account for both continuity and change.[35] Alternative explanations, such as Rose's, deserve careful attention for what they tell us about public attitudes in the transition period. On the other hand, assertions as to which factors matter most must be supported by pretransition survey data of acceptable quality. With these at hand, the debate between the "anticulturists" and the "historicists" may be reopened. In the meantime, the culturalist case, however imperfect, should hold.

Revolution or evolutionary change?

According to Lenin, revolutions occur when people are no longer willing to obey the *ancien régime* and the latter is unable to rule in the old way. The Hungarian revolution of October–November 1956 satisfied both requirements. The overnight collapse of the Stalinist regime and its prompt replacement, with broad popular support, by Imre Nagy's reform communist government signaled a political sea change in that Soviet-occupied Central European nation. At issue is the ideological legacy and long-term salience of those thirteen days of liberty for the subsequent evolution of Hungarian politics. Specifically, what role did 1956 play in the collapse of the Kádár regime, and what, if any, residual effects might it have had on the political life of postcommunist Hungary?

From the perspective of four decades it is axiomatic that the revolution had a dual agenda: the recapturing of national sovereignty and the instauration of democratic socialism. These objectives were rooted in traditions of armed struggles for national independence and in widely shared aspirations for political participation, social justice, and the citizens' personal autonomy under socialism. The Nagy government's unilateral declaration of secession from the WTO implemented the first objective. The combined record of the nameless "freedom fighters," the Greater Budapest Workers' Council, and the courageous spokesmen of the Writers' Union fulfilled the second objective. Both were precedent-setting in defining the message of the revolution for the world, the Hungarian people, and the Kádár regime.

The Western powers' Cold War-driven strategic priorities could not accommodate Hungary's strivings for national independence. In 1956 neither Washington nor Moscow was ready to renegotiate, let alone alter unilaterally, the terms of the Yalta regime. The outcome – Soviet tanks in Budapest and Western hand-wringing in the United Nations – was responsible for the Hungarian people's sense of abandonment and the birth of a Munich syndrome that the people of Czechoslovakia had experienced after 1938. The absence of Western assistance brought home the futility of further resistance and helped attenuate the public's lingering moral doubts about coming to terms with the conquerors.

The local effects of global *Realpolitik* gave a decisive impetus to a regionally unique *rapprochement* between the people and the Kádár regime. The terms – trade-offs between the regime saying "never again" and the public's contingent consent to the political status quo – were discussed in the narrative. Over the years the revolution and its tragic aftermath receded into semioblivion. Yet, with the passage of time the dual agenda of 1956 acquired new salience and a life of its own. The matter resurfaced in various contexts, such as dissident programs, ideological dilemmas of the party's successor generation, and at key turning points in 1989–90.

Ferenc Donáth, the organizer of the Bibó Memorial Book project, was a respected left-wing intellectual and, as a surviving codefendant of Imre Nagy, a living symbol of the democratic socialist legacy of the revolution. The subject of *hommage* was István Bibó, another symbol of patriotism and personal integrity. Thus, the reexamined legacy of 1956 became a catalytic agent that helped define the individual contributors' ideological postures and recruit them into one of the three main clusters of organized dissent. The dissident intellectuals' supportive (the *Beszélő* circle), ambivalent (the Populists), and neutral (the socialist critics) attitudes toward the Polish events were evidence of the reexamined past that became a point of departure for the embracing of nonrevolutionary solutions to national problems.

At various points in their careers, each of Kádár's three potential successors was confronted with the intellectual and political necessity to take a stance on the revolution and its aftermath. To make their way in the HSWP, Grósz shrugged off his bitter personal experiences of 1957–8 and Berecz chose to betray what he as a participant of the Petőfi Circle debates in the summer of 1956 heard and agreed with. For Pozsgay – the only genuine intellectual of the three – democratic socialism was the essential political message of the revolution. For him, it was a valid solution to the legitimacy dilemmas of the late Kádár era. It was also a political lever with which to effect overdue generational change in the ruling party.

From his return to Hungary in November 1956 until his tearful farewell address to the Central Committe in April 1989, János Kádár's career as a politician may be described in terms of compensatory efforts to cover up for his complicity in the bloody crushing of the revolution and the betrayal of his comrades. From the moment when 1956 and the fate of Imre Nagy became parts of the dissidents' agenda, his days as leader were numbered. In one way or another, *glasnost'* in Hungary was about filling the blank pages of recent history with a truthful account of the revolution and its aftermath. At the end, only Kádár stood between his eager successors and the "truth" with which to effect reconciliation between the people and the regime.

The hidden agenda of the reform communists' "historic review of the past thirty years" was to demonstrate the Kádár regime's culpability for the bankruptcy of the political system. Once the review was put in motion, Pozsgay helped transform what might have ended up as exposure of past misdeeds by selected culprits into a public debate on political morality. By shedding light on the regime's birth defects, the party insurgents helped sever the ties that kept Kádár's amorphous mass party together. The dispirited rank and file was cast adrift. The political arena was cleared for the outgoing and incoming elites to bear witness to the symbolic rehabilitation of Imre Nagy, his codefendants, and the "unknown freedom fighter" of 1956.

The two elites' secret negotiations, commencing, as they did, on the eve of the martyrs' reburial, were thus perceived as a legitimate sequel to the unfinished revolution of thirty-three years ago. However, the NRT process was a political transaction designed to prevent a reenactment of armed confrontation with the regime. The political calendar of 1989 was driven by the regime's and the opposition's uncertainty as to what the "street" might do on October 23. To Hungary's good fortune, the elites understood what was expected of them. The NRT negotiators, the principals of the HSWP's burial party, and the lame-duck Parliament saw to it that the revolution's thirty-third anniversary would be a day of solemn remembrance and the joyful birth of the Republic of Hungary.

The bare-knuckled politics of the November 26, 1989 plebiscite and of the following electoral campaign had little to do with the "spirit of 1956." The radical Party of the Hungarian October fell by the wayside well before the campaign commenced. Some of the surviving veterans were put on party lists and gained seats in the Parliament. A few were given ceremonial positions or patronage jobs at new archives and research institutes. Árpád Göncz became president of the Republic – a position that he has reshaped to fit *his* understanding of the legacy of the 1956 revolution.

With national sovereignty restored, October 23 was declared an official holiday and a protocol event for speechmaking and showing the national colors. The anniversaries have been also occasions for elderly radicals to demand political justice and the indictment of those responsible for the massacre of unarmed demonstrators in several provincial towns in October–November 1956. These initiatives, just like those seeking to subject former officials to judicial lustration, came to naught. Other than a handful of old and ailing enlisted men of the 1956 firing squads (most of whose cases were dismissed for the lack of evidence), no one has been held accountable for the killing of hundreds of innocent men, women, and children almost forty years ago.

The message of the revolution, as it were, was laid to final(?) rest on October 23, 1994, in the Budapest municipal cemetery on a macabre note. The principal speaker at the official commemoration was newly elected prime minister Gyula Horn – a self-confessed and unrepentant veteran of the postrevolutionary *pufajkás* armed vigilante squads. He called for national reconciliation and shared honor for all, communist and anticommunist, victims of the revolt.[36] The honorees could not and the public did not object to this act of common absolution. In any case, thirty-eight years after the fact this eulogy seemed to be as good a way as any to dispatch the 1956 revolution, its heroes, and its villains to the history books.

Personality and leadership: János Kádár and József Antall

Next to Emperor Franz Joseph, who ascended to the throne in 1848 and died in 1916, János Kádár was Hungary's longest-serving leader in modern history. The era that bears his name has been the subject of this study. One of the main objectives was to review and replace journalistic labels, such as the "Kádár mystique," with documented facts and judicious interpretation of Kádár's political career. Although the narrative has accounted for much of the currently available evidence, it has not explicitly addressed the issue of Kádár's legacy in terms of public perceptions of benevolent leadership and attributes of legitimate personal authority.

According to Cecil A. Gibb, "leadership is basically a function of personality and social system in interaction."[37] It is axiomatic that in Hungary cycles of national history, the community's chronic sense of insecurity in an unstable regional environment, and consequent perceptions of vulnerability to external contingencies have had a decisive effect on public orientations to politics and political leadership. Such orientations have become manifest in fatalistic perceptions of national destiny and in the public's dependence on "firm," "courageous," or "heroic" political leadership.

At one time or another, Prince Ferenc Rákóczi, the Habsburg emperors, Lajos Kossuth, Mihály Károlyi, Béla Kun, Admiral Horthy,

Ferenc Nagy, Mátyás Rákosi, Imre Nagy, János Kádár, and József Antall were national leaders – and so are Árpád Göncz and Gyula Horn in the mid-1990s. They fulfilled, or have been trying to fulfill one or more of these public expectations in the discharge of their leadership roles. How do János Kádár and József Antall fit in with their predecessors? Have their personalities and styles of leadership made a lasting impact on the public? And, if so, what kind? Answers to these questions are difficult to come by. Yet, the issue must be raised if we wish, as we must, to account for the postcommunist public's complex relationship to political authority in the 1990s.

Kádár and Antall were both products of prewar Hungarian society. The dominant political issues of the Horthy era were the the Treaty of Trianon, the Great Depression, social justice, and the Second World War. The two men came from the opposite ends of the social hierarchy. Kádár's political beliefs were shaped by poverty, political persecution, and the vision of Hungary's revolutionary transformation under the Communist Party. Antall was a privileged offspring of a lawyer–politician–senior civil servant. He was brought up as a cautious progressive – sensitive to social problems but committed to Christian-national values and to the legitimacy of the political status quo.

Kádár's role models of political leadership were most likely the imprisoned underground party elite whom he perceived as selfless individuals and dedicated revolutionaries. Kádár was not an "internationalist" (he declined the party's invitation to volunteer to serve in the Spanish civil war) but a working-class radical. Other than his father, Antall's model of national leader was Count István Bethlen, a brilliant political tactician and prime minister in the 1920s. Bethlen was an ideological pragmatist who had come to terms with the social democrats but viewed the communists as Soviet agents. Antall may well have come to share this belief.

The roles of insiders and outsiders changed radically after 1945. Kádár's experiences as part of the HCP's top leadership were discussed in the narrative. His rise and fall as a junior member of Rákosi's team had as much to do with his non-Muscovite background as with inexperience as a political infighter. The negative example of Rákosi – a ruthless manipulator and clever dissembler – played a decisive role in Kádár's subsequent conduct as political leader. The scene of Kádár's mid-career training in political management was his prison cell, and his fellow students were his communist cell mates. Prisons, as Gramsci tells us, have a way of reminding the prisoner of his humanity and, as

Gramsci's prison diaries testify, of making him rethink his political beliefs.

Antall, even though the son of a sidelined bourgeois politician, suffered no persecution in the Rákosi years. Apart from his minor public roles in 1956 and short-term ban on employment thereafter, he got by – as did most prewar middle-class intellectuals. Although he declared that his years in the Kádár era were years of preparation for political leadership in a democratic Hungary, this notion may be safely dismissed as hubris and an attempt to shore up his political credentials as national leader. On the other hand, there is every reason to believe that, as a born politician, he was a keen observer of Kádár's leadership behavior. As a manor-born bureaucratic vassal of the "village shaman," Aczél's vassal (Emil Schulteisz), Antall had a major stake in the preservation of his privileged social status. In any case, he could not help but be impressed (and probably depressed) by the "village elder's" widespread popularity with the Hungarian public.

Kádár's evolving leadership styles and the operative substance of each phase were fully addressed in the narrative. What is of interest here is the way Kádár played the three main roles – those of guardian, provider, and normsetter – of his stewardship in Hungary after 1956. Each of these roles fulfilled leadership responsibilities of system maintenance, resource allocation, and preservation of ideological consonance.

The logic of Kádár's guardianship entailed his sense of loyalty to his class and the have-nots of the Horthy era and that of responsibility for his homeland. His rudimentary understanding of Marxism–Leninism and the political survival of his party demanded that the "people's power" be restored after the revolution by any and all means. With that accomplished, he sought to build a shelter to prevent Hungary from becoming a Soviet colony. His dealings with a succession of Soviet leaders, his tortured decisions in 1968, and the embracing of "escape-forward" domestic and foreign policy strategies are evidence of action on these objectives.

Kádár cultivated a public image of a reluctant leader – ready to serve but willing to step aside for the good of the cause. Yet, when challenged by political adversaries, he fought them off every time. His handling of opponents – giving them enough rope to hang themselves – was textbook Machiavelli, and so was his nonuse of incriminating material on his associates in his office safe. To remain "above politics" and yet to be in full control of the regime's power resources, Kádár assembled a formidable array of political prerogatives. Of these, the most important were his proprietary access to the Kremlin and, through long-term partnership with Yuri Andropov, to the KGB; hands-on management of foreign affairs; neutralization, as its *de facto* commander in chief, of the Hungarian military through a handpicked nonentity; and keeping the police on a short leash held by the hands of trusted subordinates.

Kádár's role of provider evolved in a series of leadership decisions regarding implementation of the regime's social contract. Food, clothing, shelter, and right to work were the principal components. The criterion of delivery on these commitments was Kádár's political sense as to what the people would put up with and find politically acceptable at a given point. Food security as a public entitlement was the foundation of what envious Soviet visitors dubbed "goulash communism." Yet, there was always more to the Kádár regime than subsidized food prices and shops well stocked with often shoddy but generally affordable merchandise.

When faced with choices between foreign indebtedness and the growing cost of ever-increasing social expenditures, Kádár did not hesitate to roll over the burden of repayment to his eventual successors. In doing so, he alone was responsible for the birth of a "premature welfare state" (János Kornai's term) with a pseudoegalitarian kept society of listless workers, corrupt bureaucrats, and parasitic intellectuals. The pragmatic Kádár saw to it that the hardworking farmers and the toilers of the second economy were left alone. Thus, the system, such as it was, worked – in fact, well enough to become a way of life that the society willingly embraced and still cherishes in the 1990s.

As a chronically unemployed (and often homeless and starving) victim of the Great Depression, Kádár was also conscious of the working men's aspirations for self-improvement and cultural betterment. The regime's educational and cultural policies set into motion a far-reaching process of social mobility and cultural modernization. The millions of beneficiaries have not forgotten and in 1994 endorsed again at the ballot box the political party to which they owe their skills, livelihood, and present social status. And this is probably the most durable aspect of Kádár's legacy as provider.

Kádár was a low-key nationalist, albeit one with a deeply pessimistic sense of history and dim vision of national destiny. He despised Ceauşescu and did not think much of the Slovak party's national communists, yet was enough of a realist not to write off the issue of Hungarian ethnic minorities beyond the national boundaries; instead, he put it on the political back burner. Indeed, unlike Antall, he had no delusions about being the secretary general of conationals in the neighboring states. Rather, Kádár tried to make the best of what there was at home. Thus, he became an apologist for second-best solutions – that of the country's reformed but still inefficient economy and of the society that was the *relatively* best fed and least regulated in the communist bloc.

Kádár's reformulation of his regime's ideological legitimacy in consumerist terms turned out to be a trap. What may have begun as a social experiment to produce a socialist man ended up creating a community of frustrated petty bourgeois consumers. Although consumerism successfully preempted nonsocialist ideologies, it could suppress neither individualism nor public instincts for the acquisition of material possessions. In any case, though the Hungarian "barrack" may have been the "jolliest" in the socialist camp, it was a barrack nonetheless. The denizens of the facility complied with the house rules and drowned their aspirations for a spiritually more fulfilling life in little freedoms, little apartments, little cars, and a great deal of alcohol.

Kádár was a frugal man and self-appointed member of the "party of pedestrians" (*gyalogosok*). His public identification with the non-car-owning majority was not a pose but represented inner conviction. Yet, the norms he tried to set for his party and his close associates were out of sync with the interests and lifestyles of the apparat and of the "dead souls" of the Central Committee. His older colleagues – Aczél, Fock, Nyers, and a few others – shared Kádár's puritanical values yet none had either the courage or Kádár's authority to enforce them. Andropov's failed attempts at cleaning up the Augean stables of the Brezhnev apparat were object lessons for Kádár and his fellow purists in the Hungarian leadership.

In sum, Kádár was the national leader and his party's "village elder." The term "paternalism" that Hungarian social scientists use to characterize the "good king's" and the old "autarch's" leadership style has the merit of brevity. However, its cognitive connotations help obscure the complexity of Kádár's multiple leadership roles as guardian, provider, and normsetter. Public opinion (December 1988) on Kádár's responsibility for the achievements and failures of his era credit the guardian and the provider for success and hold his creatures (the Politburo, the apparat, and the managers) responsible for failures.[38] Thus, Kádár's first two roles and Kádárism as a set of loosely enforced norms and a way of life have become powerful precedents for the Hungarian public's affective orientations toward political leadership and legitimate personal authority.

The Kádár precedent – far more so than the political record of other East European communist regimes – successfully delegitimated and replaced earlier, particularly the pre-1945 styles of governance. Among East European respondents to a 1992 survey question on "justice through history," on a scale of −100 to +100, Hungarians gave by far the lowest marks (−30) to the prewar regime and the highest to "communism" (+41). By contrast, the Czech respondents' ratings were +27 and −54, respectively.[39] Kádár thus "buried" the Horthy regime and, even in his grave, has been a tough act to follow.

Prime minister József Antall was a gentleman of the old school, a gifted politician, a conservative ideologue, and a typical Central European intellectual who died as a statesman. Some of these attributes were incompatible with effective discharge of the responsibilities he took on as the first leader of postcommunist Hungary. In any event, his conduct as leader ought to be measured by standards of the political system that he was mandated to install by the voters who put him in his office. As Lester G. Seligman explains,

> Generally, the democratic chief executive is legitimated by his identi-fication with the central values of his social system, both nonpolitical and political; by the manner in which he is recruited; by the symbolic and effective representation he bestows; and by his decision-making performance ... the political goals of the chief executive must conform to the traditional value system ... [he or she] must represent or appear to represent the public at large.[40]

These criteria of democratic leadership are compatible with, and may be analyzed by the roles – guardian, provider, and normsetter – that Antall sought to play as the country's freely elected chief executive. The first requisite of Antall's guardianship was to restore Hungary's political sovereignty by the severing of military and economic ties with the now-defunct Soviet bloc. With that accomplished, he initiated a long-term foreign policy to link up with the Western political and business community. This policy was augmented by Antall's efforts to craft a regional partnership of the three, later four, Central European states.

Unlike these successful undertakings, Antall's strategy to recast Hungary's links with Romania, Yugoslavia, and Czechoslovakia yielded meager results during his term in office. The fault was partly Antall's – his typically careless formulation of his role as prime minister, "in a spiritual sense," of 15,000,000 Hungarians haunted him to the very end – and partly that of the neonationalist regimes of these "new democracies." At any rate, it is doubtful that anyone else could have done a better job as guardian of the country's foreign policy interests. Domestic politics, however, was an altogether different proposition.

Antall's upbringing, personal values, and political experience made it virtually impossible for him to identify with the "central values" – political or nonpolitical – of the social system that he inherited from Kádár. Initially, he finessed the matter by taking the high road as conscientious executor of previous elite agreements. With the help of his government's parliamentary majority, he saw to it that the core institutions of a *Rechtsstaat* and the appropriate administrative regulations were established and implemented. Indeed, even his critics credit him for his unstinting efforts to lay and embed the legal-instutional foundations of political pluralism: parliamentary government and individual liberties in Hungary. The record is equally positive with respect to initial legislative steps for the reform of old and the creation of new laws and regulations with which to facilitate transition toward a market economy. Though he was personally in the forefront to implement needed measures, for Antall most of these were someone else's agenda.

To the extent that the record may be reconstructed, Antall had no intention to adapt to the post-Kádárist social system. Instead, he sought to remold it in the spirit of Hungary's nineteenth-century reform statesmen (his models were Ferenc Deák and Baron József Eötvös) and by the political techniques of his other role model, Count István Bethlen. Much of this was predicated on the restoration of a precommunist civil society and on the revival of its traditional social mainstay, that is, organized religion, specifically the Catholic Church. The designated vehicle of implementation was the HDF – with supporting roles by the other parties of the government coalition. To this end, Antall embarked on an ideological mission of designating his party as the bearer of what he called Hungary's main intellectual traditions – Populist radicalism, Christian democracy, and nineteenth-century liberalism.

The net result of Antall's ideological posturing was the return of the Catholic Church to public life and its high political profile therein; major concessions to the Smallholders' land reprivatization program; and the beginning of bruising ideological confrontations with the parliamentary opposition and its allies in the printed and electronic media. To protect his image as national leader, Antall tried to stay aloof from daily politics. His cabinet members and designated political lieutenants did his political fighting for him – often with disastrous results. Catholic religious services on prime-time TV in a country where the share of those attending church services had declined from 75–80 percent to 8 percent between 1950 and 1990, paralysis of agricultural production owing to litigation over land titles, and harsh public reaction to government attempts to staff the media with HDF loyalists helped discredit Antall's image as guardian of interests other than those of his rapidly shrinking national constituency.[41]

Antall's personal political style also contributed to what became a full-fledged crisis of his leadership in less than two years in office. Antall was a compulsive micromanager of all issues that came before the government cabinet. However, he soon discovered that this assembly of loquacious intellectuals had no more idea than he did about running a government. To make things happen, Antall retreated into the Office of the Prime Minister and there, with the help of bright staffers from the Németh government, he managed to re-create the working style, secretiveness, and unaccountability of Kádár's Central Committee apparat, vintage mid-1970s. By 1992, some parts of the government operated on the basis of top-secret executive orders rather than by laws duly enacted by the Parliament. It is unclear whether Antall regarded his associates as fools or incompetents, but his choice of trusted senior advisers (mainly scions of Hungarian aristocratic families living in the West) hints at both possibilities. In any case, Antall was not a self-effacing "village elder" but a short-tempered boss with seigneurial airs and the habits of a typical Budapest *Besserwisserei* intellectual. As an avid reader of old police files on friends and political foes, he had no illusions about the elites – new, old, and holdover – with whom he had to work as national leader.

The István Csurka-led intraparty rebellion against Antall's leadership served as reminder of Antall's dubious credentials as the HDF's chairman. As the Populists saw it, Antall was a discredited latecomer to the party who loaded his cabinet with deferential "liberals" at the expense of deserving Populists. With the help of incumbency, overdue political patronage, and strong-arm tactics, Antall weathered the storm but, with his declining health becoming public knowledge, his standing as national leader was beyond recovery well before his death in December 1993.

Paradoxically, Antall never received political credit and deserved public recognition for his role as provider. It is odd, because the Antall government continued, without missing a step, its reform-communist predecessor's generous social policies and even embellished the scope of some of the entitlements between 1990 and 1993. For example, in 1992 the Parliament approved a measure that forgave half of the outstanding indebtedness on housing mortgages of 800,000 lucky citizens at the cost of HUF 80 billion (about $1 billion according to 1992 rates of exchange) to the state budget.[42] Yet, neither then nor two years later at the ballot box did the voters choose to remember the government coalition that had been mainly responsible for this monetary windfall.

Antall's understanding, if that is the word, of the imperatives of a balanced budget for a workable market economy – "social" and otherwise – could readily accommodate Kádár's *après moi le déluge* approach to macroeconomic policies. When in doubt, just like Kádár, Antall went over the head of or fired his finance minister (he had three in three years) rather than upset the postcommunist social contract and risk awakening the public from its political stupor. The doubling of the (internal) state debt from about HUF 2 to 4 trillion and the growth of about $4 billion in Hungary's net foreign indebtedness in four years were the cost of maintaining the domestic status quo and keeping the unemployed and noisy intellectuals off the streets.[43]

The jury is still out on Antall's record as a normsetter. On the one hand, his attempts to resuscitate and gain public acceptance of the values of the prewar Christian-national middle class were flatly rejected by the intellectuals and were poorly received by the public. On the other hand, his staunch commitment to the institutionalization of the rule of law provided a solid framework for enhanced civil rights and personal liberties for the citizens of Hungary. In a sense, Antall was the victim of his success as provider of unconditional guarantees for the exercise of new citizen rights. However, his ill-tempered attacks on the media elites helped rally the *Homo Kadaricus* to the defense of his socialist and liberal critics and were mainly responsible for his party's electoral defeat in 1994.

As evidenced by Antall's declining ratings in the monthly political popularity polls after 1991, it appeared that he seriously misjudged what the postcommunist public expected of its leaders. In any case, it appeared that as a positive sign of growing social autonomy, the public chose to distance itself from wielders of substantive political power. As shown by President Göncz's stellar performance in the polls, the same public strongly endorsed symbolic authority figures and nonthreatening grandfather images that evoked and reinforced latent yearnings for paternalistic leadership. Antall made a major mistake in allowing his personal dislike of Göncz's left-wing ideological posturing to stir him to respond in kind.

A democratic chief executive must learn to live with internal dissent. From a series of acrimonious constitutional disputes between the prime minister and the president of the Republic, the latter emerged as clear winner. The ensuing vacuum of leadership yielded yet another instance of political *déja vu* that ushered in a postcommunist reincarnation of Miklós Németh's "government of experts" under HSP leader Gyula Horn in the summer of 1994. The HSP's landslide electoral victory was in many ways a protest vote against Antall's widely perceived attempts to turn back the clock to the prewar era. The semiofficial reburial of Admiral Miklós Horthy in September 1993 was an ominous sign for "Kádár's children." The public, as prompted by the holdover intellectuals, viewed this as a threat to legitimate governance. Thus, they cast their ballots to replace Antall's "quiet strength" with Horn's familiar hand at the helm.

Party and the state

The Comunist Party, under one of three names (HCP, HWP, and HSWP), and the state were the main institutional pillars of political power between 1948 and 1989. The party's evolution, *modus operandi*, and some aspects of its interaction with the state were discussed in the narrative. The party and the state were key facilitators of processes of socioeconomic modernization, ideological adaptation, and systemic change. The parallel evolution of the two institutions was driven by two conflicting imperatives. These were requirements of ideology, that is, the Leninist primacy of politics, and those of the state's genetic code, that is, its inbuilt propensity for institutional aggrandizement and striving for organizational autonomy.

Under "steady-state" conditions, requisites of political hegemony and administrative rationality are not incompatible as long as the regime's policy objectives are flexible enough to accommodate incremental administrative innovation by the state sector. However, when a ruling party chooses or is compelled to renew itself and embark on the path of system management, it must redefine the terms of its traditional working relationship with the state. At issue is the NEM and the way the Hungarian party went about implementing its peaceful revolution from above.

The NEM may have begun as a short-term, quick-fix economic experiment but became an open-ended political commitment to reinventing socialism in Hungary. The key to success or progress of any kind lay in revamping the party's working relationship with the administrative organs of the state. The process involved important trade-offs between the two bureaucracies. The party retained hands-on control over "politics," that is, the security ministries, foreign affairs, and political communication. The state was given, within a framework of broad political guidance by the party, a relatively free hand over the economy, regional development, and social-welfare matters. It was, as prime minister Fock and his successors never ceased to remind the PB, a flawed arrangement that yielded duplication of effort, waste of resources, and paralysis of administrative communications.

The state's administrative power entitlements were codified by laws, ministerial decrees, and the daily praxis of economy and society. This, in turn, gave birth to administrative pluralism and, in the 1980s, to political protopluralism. The first was made possible by the state's growing autonomy in setting priorities in the budgetary redistribution process that affected enterprises and wage earners alike. The Ministry of Finance, the National Planning Office, and the foreign-trade bureaucracy came to define, on a take it or leave it basis, the budgetary parameters for the HSWP, CC's economic policy groups to rubber stamp or to modify. Shrinking resources and growing foreign indebtedness meant there was less and less to modify and more to approve of in the government's numbers.

The HSWP was the owner of profitable newspapers and publishing houses. It was an unusual business firm that granted for itself exemption from corporate taxes and arranged in 1977 a long-term *pro bono* lease of more than 2,000 state-owned buildings and land for its own purposes. However, in an administrative sense, the party was but a (hidden) line item in the state budget for the disbursement of an annual apanage with which to balance its books. The ruling party's fiscal dependency on the state created an important precedent for party financing at the NRT negotiations. The granting of start-up capital (valuable real estate for party headquarters) and operating subsidies for postcommunist electoral winners and runners-up has its murky origins in the HSWP's decision to become a budgetary ward of the state.

Well into the 1980s the party clung to its role as a court of appeals for social and institutional participants of stalemated negotiations over wages, budgetary disbursements, and plan targets. The best the rear-guard party could do was to recommend rather than order state action of any kind. Such nondecisions helped deauthorize the party and upgrade the state, which came to be seen as the provider of last resort. The mobile party elites' flight to the state sector and the citizens' vigorous participation in the 1985 parliamentary elections to form a new partnership with the state through the legislative process were evidence of a major shift of elite and mass loyalties from the party to the state.

Political protopluralism originated with the granting of administrative entitlements and discretionary operating budgets to key policy lobbies in the early 1970s. This came to full bloom in the rearguard phase of the party's retreat as a visible actor in public administration. Entrants that rushed or, as the legislature, were reinserted by the party to fill the void in the political arena were, in an administrative sense, additional line items in the state budget. The state was pitted against new claimants on its shrinking resources. The industrial, agricultural, trade union, youth, and other social, such as the PPF, policy lobbies each staked out parts of the political turf. All demanded continued delivery on their constituencies' entitlements from the state budget. The gap between the economic targets of the 13th HSWP congress and the state's capacity to satisfy them defined the limits of the party's competency as guarantor of the regime's social contract.

Toward the end, apart from Delphic statements on a "new development path," "reform," and "fiscal prudence," the party was nowhere in evidence to arbitrate these conflicting claims. Thus it fell, as its principal task, to the Grósz government to salvage what it could from the fiscal-administrative wreck that the party bequeathed to the state. Upon relinquishing the government to Németh, Grósz belatedly sought to assert the situational logic of his new position as the *party's* chief executive officer. His showdown with Németh was a clash of two inherently incompatible methods of governance. It was also a classical case of locking the barn after the horses had migrated to the state's side of the fence. Final answer to the question "Who governs Hungary?" was provided in October 1989. In a fitting climax to the history of existing socialism, it was not the state but the party that withered away.

Much has been written both in this study and in the literature on political transitions about the emergence of civil society as a counterforce to the old regime. However, in Hungary's reform-driven public discourse on politics the main object of dissident criticism was the loose-cannon Communist Party rather than the Hungarian state. The latter, albeit in a radically modernized and democratized form, had always been seen as essential for the welfare of the community and the survival of the nation. The regime's socialist critics were not champions of a self-governing civil society but of a modern, possibly neocorporatist, state. Their scrutiny of the shortcomings of the legal and administrative system yielded valuable pathologies of the old regime's structural flaws. These, in turn, materially influenced the NRT's deliberations and helped lay the foundations for popular sovereignty and competent governance in a postcommunist state.

The fall of the old regime ushered in a new constellation of institutional actors in the political arena. Formal ground rules of the political game were derived from the NRT agreement, party pacts, and legislative exigencies of the first hundred days of the new government. These have been duly registered in the amended Hungarian Constitution. Informal norms of political interaction were another matter, which I will discuss below.

The locus of strategic decision-making shifted from the Politburo's ideologues to the new elites' ideologues in the government and the Parliament. The political system now rested on a new set of institutional checks and balances, and was also shaped by a complex interplay of party politics, policy lobbies, public opinion, and elite preferences as articulated in the media. What kept the process on an even keel were institutional inertia and the holdover administrative elites' contingent consent to the new political status quo.

The state is the main institutional survivor of the previous forms of governance. It is also a multipurpose instrument that is essential for the attainment of public aspirations for decent livelihoods and legally guaranteed personal autonomy in a postcommunist polity. The state is legitimate owner, guardian, and ultimate repository of the country's public assets. Moreover, the state is the employer of the vast majority of Hungary's wage-earning population. As guardian of the community's social safety net, the state is the provider of last resort.

It is axiomatic that the path to marketization lies in the state's divestiture of most of its assets to the private sector. And so is the proposition that the severance of the citizens' employee–employer hierarchical dependency on the state is indispensable for the public's emancipation from the tutelage of the political regime. In the given context, democratization and marketization may be conceptualized as outcomes of state-regulated competition for access to public goods. The citizens' nominal political equality and access to elective offices have thus far been adequately guaranteed by the Constitution and protected by the police, the procuracy, and the courts. However, public access to the state's economic resources and opportunities is a qualitatively different proposition.

At issue is the government's responsibility for delivery on the postcommunist state's social contract and provision of material guarantees for preservation of the citizens' personal autonomy. Answers to the question "Who got what, when, and how?" may be gleaned from state budgets and data on social incomes.[44] Since 1990 the Hungarian state did what it could – in fact, a great deal more than it could afford – to provide the basic necessities for most citizens. The question is not the provision of bare essentials for survival but of measures to help transform a society of state employees into owners of private property and possessors of tangible resources with which to protect their newly acquired personal liberties from the state.

The state's commitment to democratization without the transfer of most public assets to private hands is a hollow gesture. Property is political power. The process of denationalization by way of privatiza-tion and compensation-restitution vouchers and outright grants has been intensely politicized throughout the former communist world. The participants include claimants and gatekeepers, domestic and international actors, and, inevitably, winners and losers.

Michael McFaul's propositions aptly characterize the source of constraints on the economic deconstruction of the postcommunist state:

> Impetus for ... institutional destruction cannot be expected to come from social groups that benefited from the *ancien régime* ... Social groups of the old regime will therefore organize to resist fundamental economic transformation ... states designed to support one form of socioeconomic system do not have the capability to first create and then sustain a new socioeconomic order. "Capitalist" states cannot make a "socialist" economic system. "Socialist" states cannot create the conditions for the emergence of a "capitalist" economic system.[45]

It is axiomatic that in the short run the political incumbents and the state bureaucracy have little to gain and a great deal to lose from the unilateral economic empowerment of the public. Privatization, Hun-garian-style, has thus far yielded meager results. On the one hand, much progress has been made in the service sector, and compensation vouchers (which have depreciated by 65 percent since date of issue) have helped many people to buy shares in industrial firms and repurchase some of the affected families' collectivized land.[46] On the other hand, the state is still the outright owner or has controlling interest over much of the country's productive assets – including the banking sector and the major utilities.

As David Stark's excellent case study on industrial privatization in Hungary demonstrates, official data, such as share of national income derived from the private sector and employment in the same, are totally misleading.[47] To begin with, regardless of the method of legal incorporation, enterprises in which the state is a minority shareholder are for statistical purposes listed as parts of the private sector. Except for wholly foreign-owned firms in which, trade unions permitting, Western labor discipline obtains, employees in the state and the *de facto* state sector are also involved (on or off the job) in the thriving new second economy. Backdoor strategies of (mainly unreported) income enhancement could contribute to the acquisition of private property. Still, entrepreneurship of this sort is a far cry from state-supported programs to promote embourgeoisement and grassroots-level growth of private enterprise.

How to privatize yet retain the holdover economic elites' control over the state's productive assets? The answer, as Stark explains, lies in "recombinant property." It is

> a form of organizational hedging, or portfolio management, in which actors are responding to extraordinary uncertainty in the organizational environment in diversifying their assets, redefining and recombining resources. It is an attempt to have resources in more than one organizational form – or similarly – to produce hybrid organizational forms that can be justified or assessed by more than one standard of measure ... parallel to the decentralized reorganization of assets is a centralization of liabilities, and these twinned moments blur the boundaries of public and private: On the one hand, privatization produces criss-crossing lines of recombinant property; on the other, debt consolidation transforms private debt into public liabilities.[48]

Between early 1989 and mid-1994 the number of state enterprises declined by 60 percent; the number of incorporated shareholding companies increased from 116 to 2,679; and the number of limited liability companies increased from 450 to 79,000.[49] Most, mainly large, shareholding companies are legal successors of state-owned enterprises, and so are, as former subsidiaries, many of the limited-liability companies. Thus far it has been the state budget – by way of debt cancellation, subsidies, loan guarantees, bailout monies, and tax write-offs – much more than the market or direct Western investments that have kept the system afloat.

The above-described public/private economic hybrid has a collective will and a life of its own. The community of incumbent enterprise managers and their boards of directors have developed safety nets by cross-ownership and overlapping memberships in the management of satellite firms. The politically incestuous Japanese *keiretsu* model offers a reasonable analogy, except that the "Hungarian MITI" has neither the money nor the competency to turn this sector into a prosperous branch of the economy – let alone channel trickle-down benefits to the public.

Other forms of holdover- and new-elite expropriation of public resources for private gain include rigged bidding at auctions of denationalized state assets, the funneling of parts of the state budget and the laundering of untaxed profits into "private" or "public" foundations, and the extension of unsecured state loans to selected recipients. The flip side of the process is the use of corporate treasuries to finance local and national party organizations through foundations, political action committees, and the co-optation of senior public officials to membership on boards of directors. "Conflict of interest" has yet to become an actionable offense against the yet-to-be-developed code of ethics in Hungarian politics.

The postcommunist state is an organizational shell with the statutory authority and no apparent political will to lead Hungary's transformation into a market economy of autonomous citizen-entrepreneurs and self-organized employees in a predominantly private enterprise economy. Although irrevocable individual political rights are available to everyone, the holdover state bureaucracy's priority seems to be, to use Anatole France's *bon mot*, to bar the economic transition's winners and losers from sleeping under the Danube bridges. The state's role of night watchman has yet to address the day care of its citizens.

Sovereignty and interdependence

The Cold War and the Yalta regime sheltered the people but constrained Hungary's conduct in international affairs. The regime's affiliation with the WTO protected the country from overt hostilities and wars by proxy to which non-European communist states were exposed between 1949 and 1990. *Pax Sovietica* yielded forty-five years of peace – the longest period in the region's history uninterrupted by wars in the past two centuries. In any case, Hungary's role within a broader framework of Soviet strategic interests was defined by its geographic location, economic capabilities, and the outcomes of the 1956 revolution.

The terms of Hungary's relationship with the USSR changed over time. The politico-economic imperatives of the NEM process compelled Kádár to embark on an "escape-forward" strategy of foreign-trade-led opening to the West. From the late 1970s on, the conduct of Hungary's external relations and the setting of foreign policy priorities were increasingly motivated by Kádár's pragmatic understanding of national interests. Moscow's default on aid and trade commitments helped undermine Budapest's political confidence in the regime's hitherto steadfast ally. Soviet military adventurism in Afghanistan, the Kremlin's ambiguous responses to the Polish challenge, and the buildup of conventional and nuclear capabilities in the European theater sent conflicting signals to Budapest. Much of this spelled new East–West tensions and posed threats to the process of Hungary's cautious economic and diplomatic opening to the West.

In so far as it can be established, Gorbachev would have preferred to see Kádár replaced as early as 1986. Grósz may have begun as Ligachev's man, but he soon became Gorbachev's creature, and heir to the Andropov–KGB–Kriuchkov–Kádár network. However, beginning with Grósz's trip to the United States in the summer of 1988, Hungarian foreign policies took a new turn. The Kremlin's benign neglect, the assertive Western diplomatic posture in Eastern Europe, and the preoccupation of Kádár's heirs with domestic affairs helped widen the state's foreign policy options. International affairs professionals at the party center seized the opportunity to decouple party-to-party links from interstate relations and develop a new *Spielraum* for the advancement of Hungary's national interests.

It is axiomatic that East–West *rapprochement*, the positive outcome of superpower dialogue on winding down the Cold War, and sophisticated Western diplomacy were responsible for preparing the ground for the "year of miracles" in Eastern Europe. What may have been less apparent was that at the July 14–16, 1989 Paris G-7 summit, the assembled political leaders declared Poland, Czechoslovakia, and Hungary as the countries with the best chances of success in effecting peaceful transitions to a postcommunist world. In doing so, the Western political community made an explicit bid to become active participants in the areawide process of Central Europe's forthcoming political realignment.

The Arc de Triomphe declaration and many others in the following eighteen months registered in various multilateral treaties the results of Western efforts to bring about desirable political changes in Eastern Europe. With the withdrawal of Soviet troops and the establishment of freely elected political regimes in the area, the Cold War came to an end and a new chapter began in European politics. It is against this background that some questions concerning the Western powers' role, particularly that of the United States in the Hungarian transition, ought to be raised. At issue are the short- and long-term effects of Western involvement in Hungarian affairs in the late 1980s and since 1990.

The United States and to a lesser extent the Federal Republic of

Germany were the key Western players in Hungary between the late 1970s and 1989. Diplomacy and trade were the main tools of pressuring the Hungarian regime to promote liberalization at home and take a low political-ideological profile abroad. Though US involvement in domestic affairs was nowhere as vigorous as it was in Poland, Washington had a stake in the preservation of political stability in Hungary. On balance, Kádár was vastly preferable to Honecker, Jakeš, and Ceausescu. And so were the anxious-to-please Grósz and the accommodating bright technocrat Miklós Németh.

With respect to the Hungarian dissident community, Washington tried to remain an impartial friend to all. Still, inevitably it was far more comfortable with the pro-Western multilingual democratic opposition than with the (mainly monolingual and monocultural) Populists. The latter, with or without proof, were viewed with suspicion as potentially uncontrollable nationalists. At any rate, other than with Pozsgay, neither Washington nor Bonn had any contacts with, or the slightest idea about the policy agenda of, the regime's socialist critics.

The West was mainly concerned about the ways and means of effecting peaceful transition in Hungary and elsewhere in Eastern Europe. To this end, Washington extended explicit guarantees to the incumbents (on "Palmer's pledge," see Chapter 6) of their personal immunity during and after the political transition. Chances are that similar pledges were made to other East European leaders. In doing so, the winners of the Cold War set the terms for the administration, by way of lustration and review of the incumbents' criminal culpability for past acts, of political justice in postcommunist Eastern Europe. Bonn was not bound by such pledges, hence the large-scale exposure of Stasi agents and informers in the former GDR.

With the collapse of the USSR, the West, both as a main direction of foreign policy orientation and as a domestic (mainly economic) reality, has become an embedded factor in postcommunist Hungarian politics. The Antall and Horn governments' foreign policy dilemmas are beyond the purview of this study. However, to complete the discussion on the influence of external determinants on internal political outcomes, four observations ought to be be made.

1 Hungary is a part of Eastern Europe that, as Andrew János submitted, "has never been more economically backward and underdeveloped compared to the West than it is today."[50] The West has been a model that became a moving target and ultimate yardstick of success. With the fall of the Iron Curtain, what used to be an island of relative prosperity in the Soviet bloc has become a threadbare outpost

of an affluent Europe. The demonstration effect of Hungary's relative backwardness has had a major and still not fully examined impact on the Hungarian public. A few take it as a challenge, but the majority still wait for miracles and early admission to NATO and the European Union.

2   Political incumbents of a small state are compelled to legitimate their position by demonstrating the regime's good standing with the regional hegemon and the great powers of the world. In this sense, Kádár and Antall were in the same position. No gratuitous comparisons are necessary between "Eastern" and "Western" brands of international approval. Though the most recent electoral returns do not quite show it, the latter is more compatible with the public's political beliefs in Hungary today. On the other hand, at least economically and culturally, Western influences are far more intrusive than were those of the USSR even in the Stalinist years.

3   Thanks to Hungary's free press, reports on the country's total dependence on the goodwill of a wide range of external agencies from the European Union to IMF and on individual Western governments have helped foster two types of public reaction. On the one hand, writings by István Csurka and like-minded critics that depict Hungary as a victim of Western cultural trash and overpriced imported merchandise also cast aspersions on Western political values. On the other hand, the proposed remedy, that is, withdrawal into a shell of righteous patriotism, is only a step away from waging ideological *Kulturkampf* on foreigners, particularly on Hungary's immediate neighbors.

4   Politicians of all parties are on record in support of "European norms" of good government and a market economy. Words and deeds are still far apart. In the belief that this is all that the West expects of them, the incumbents have been going through the motions of relinquishing some of the state's powers to the citizens. It is both important and necessary to review thousands of laws and decrees relative to their compatibility with Council of Europe guidelines. However, the retraining of state bureaucrats to become servants of the public is a different proposition. It is not likely to happen any time soon. The same is true for managers of "recombinant property." These captains of private/public corporations are often "Wild East" quasi-entrepreneurs of questionable probity. Caught in the netherworld between state socialism and state capitalism, they have a long way to go before becoming pillars of a democratic civil society.

In sum, as Hungarian folk wisdom has it, the distance between realities and hopes can be as great as that which separates the proverbial town of Makó from the city of Jerusalem. Europe is much closer than that. When the politicians cease telling the public that the West has a moral debt to pay Hungary for helping win the Cold War, and when the West chooses to act on its security interests and agrees to the widening of EU and NATO by the admission of East European states, the present gap could narrow substantially. The proof of admissibility lies in nonreversible progress in Hungary's fulfillment of the Atlantic community's ideological, political, and economic expectations. The state's newly won political sovereignty and the economy's interdependence with the global markets are assets as well as opportunities that still await full utilization by the people and government of Hungary.

Conclusions: toward a new model?

This study was prompted by my dissatisfaction with existing accounts on the Kádár era and misgivings about labels attached to 1989 as the "year of miracles," or worse yet, "refolutions." As I see it, understanding the regional ripples of the global sea change of 1989–90 calls not for hyperbole and clever oxymorons but careful review of facts. The appearance of assessments by Latin American and southern European experts with a new interest in postcommunist politics somewhat reinforced these concerns. With the help of secondhand East European evidence these works propose comprehensive explanations for both Latin American cum southern European and East European political outcomes. Although the explanations raise important questions of conceptualization, I find the academic transitologists' "acontextual extrapolations" (Ken Jowitt's phrase) unhelpful for my purposes. One need not go to Chile or Spain to explain what happened in Eastern Europe.

My case for Hungary is built on six themes of inquiry that I characterized as mainsprings of political change. The components were ideology, political culture, revolution, leadership, policy-making, and the external environment. I sought to test these by studying interaction among political actors and among political, economic, and social processes from a developmental perspective of modernization and institutional change. The research objective was to identify the unique and generic characteristics of Hungary's road between two revolutions and to show, in so far as data permitted, the salience of continuity and change prior to and since 1989–90.

Embedded elements of continuity, such as elite dominance, preparticipant political culture, relative economic backwardness, and a weak civil society, and incremental institutional change have been the defining characteristics of Hungary's evolution between 1956 and 1996. Within this timespan the net assessment of the confluence of continuity and incremental change may, in my view, be summed up as a quantum leap from communism to a new kind of democracy. My way of resolving the analytical dilemma posed by the prevalence of socio-economic continuity in the context of incremental institutional change has been to call the critical intervening factor, that is, the NRT agreement, negotiated, yet denote the result as revolution. Thus, the phrase "negotiated revolution" is both a descriptive label and a metaphor to call attention to the political ambiguity of the outcome.

Hungary's place in the universe of regional and global transitions is difficult to establish with any degree of precision. The regime was communist, and Kádár thought he was building socialism. Throughout the narrative, I sought to juxtapose what was generic and what I believed was unique about the regime and the way it went about its tasks. At any rate, it appears that in most respects the country was very much like its communist-dominated neighbors.

From a half-century perspective what seems unique about Hungary is the exceptionally widespread use of terror in the Rákosi era, the 1956 revolution, the NEM, the political leadership of János Kádár, patterns of regime–dissident interaction, and the way the NRT agreement was arrived at and has been implemented to date. In my view, pending the publication of works of similar scope, these six factors, in combination with the postulated mainsprings of political change, do explain Hungary's place in the context of Eastern Europe.

The change of the political regime in 1990 set into motion a process of daunting complexity. Under its second-round government, Hungary is still a democracy – in fact, in some ways more so than it was six years ago. What is less clear is whether we are witnessing a country in transition between two political systems or one that is in the midst of transformation. The difference between transition and transformation is not one of labels, but one of perspectives. From a political-institutional viewpoint there has been a by-now-completed transition between communism and democracy. From the perspective of economic and social change there has been, as part of Hungary's "long wave" of overall modernization, significant transformation from a traditional to a modern society. The two – completed and ongoing – processes have given birth to what George Schopflin calls "a sui generis system."[51]

Schopflin submits, and I agree, that Eastern Europe today is something new under the sun. Transitional features have coalesced with slowly unfolding long-term changes and created a new reality, one that is likely to remain the same for some time to come. It is a variegated political landscape, much of which fits Schopflin's characterization of the area dominated by "semi-authoritarian system[s] by consent." Cautiously optimistic reading of recent polling data suggests that the Czech Republic, Poland, and Hungary may be more democratic than semi-authoritarian. In any case, it is a dynamic reality in which instances of a few states' national bootstrap strategies of accelerated economic change and vigorous efforts to enforce the rule of law coexist with stubborn resistance to the same right next door. Whether "progressive" or "retrograde," all new democracies have shared problems and shared objectives.

With the exception of three ethnically more or less homogeneous states (Lithuania, Poland, and Hungary), issues of ethnocultural identity impinge on and at times paralyze peaceful progress toward adherence to "European norms" of human rights and personal autonomy. Here Schopflin's labeling of postcommunist polities as "democratic in form and nationalist in content" may be somewhat off the mark. Reckless rhetoric and prudent *Realpolitik* mix easily in postcommunist legislatures and the media. Western pressures have helped alleviate some of the more notorious instances of human rights violations. Still, the negative demonstration effect of the same West's inability to put an end to the Balkan wars is a needed reminder that democracy and human rights cannot be imposed from without but must be nurtured from within.

The lessons of Sarajevo, Chechnya, and other unreported venues of ethnic violence seem to have penetrated public awareness in East Central Europe. Postcommunist societies are searching for security, predictability, and a new kind of normalcy. These expectations will be difficult to satisfy. Whether it will be liberal democracy or a new semiauthoritarian model, the public is entitled to a period of respite to recover from the misguided half-century-long adventure of building socialism in this part of the world. The next step is internal self-examination and the free peoples' reinvention of democracy and civil society. For the first time in modern history, this is a feasible undertaking for both Hungary and its Central European neighbors.

Notes

Introduction

1 Many of these issues have been discussed in the general literature on the politics of the Kádár era in Hungary. See Paul Ignotus, *Hungary* (New York: Praeger, 1972); Bennet Kovrig, *Communism in Hungary from Kun to Kádár* (Stanford: Hoover Institution, 1979); Hans-Georg Heinrich, *Hungary* (Boulder, CO: Lynne Rienner, 1986); and Thomas F. Robinson, *The Pattern of Reform in Hungary* (New York: Praeger, 1973).

2 The principal sources are published collections of decisions, resolutions, statements, and advisory opinions of the leading bodies of the HSWP. These include:

A MSZMP Központi Bizottságának Párttörténeti Intézete, *A Magyar Szocialista Munkáspárt határozatai és dokumentumai, 1956–1962* (Resolutions and documents of the HSWP, 1956–1962) (Budapest: Kossuth, 1964), and subsequent volumes for 1963–66, 1967–70, 1971–75, 1975–80, 1980–85, 1985–86, and 1987 that were published in 1968, 1974, 1978, 1983, 1988, 1987, and 1988, respectively (cited hereinafter as *HSWP Decisions, 1956–1962*, etc.).

A Magyar Szocialista Munkáspárt Országos Értekezletének Jegyzőkönyve, 1957 junius 27–29 (Stenographic minutes of the national conference of the HSWP, June 27–29, 1957) (Budapest: Kossuth, 1957) (cited hereinafter as *HSWP Conference, 1957*); *A Magyar Szocialista Munkáspárt VII. Kongresszusának Jegyzőkönyve, 1959 november 30 – december 5* (Seventh congress of the HSWP, stenographic minutes) (Budapest: Kossuth, 1960), stenographic minutes of the Eighth (November 20–24, 1962), Ninth (November 28 – December 3, 1966), Tenth (November 23–28, 1970), Eleventh (March 17–22, 1975), Twelfth (March 24–27, 1980), and Thirteenth (March 25–28, 1985) congresses that were published in 1963, 1967, 1971, 1975, 1980, and 1985, respectively (cited hereinafter as *HSWP Seventh etc. Congress*); *A Magyar Szocialista Munkáspárt Országos Értekezletének Jegyzőkönyve, 1988 május 20–22* (Stenographic minutes of the national conference of the HSWP, May 20–22, 1988) and, in a separate volume, written contributions to the same (Budapest: Kossuth, 1988); and *Kongresszus '89* (Background documents, in 32 parts, to the Fourteenth Congress of the HSWP, October 5–9, 1989)

(Budapest, 1989) (cited hereinafter as *Congress '89*). Text of congressional speeches may be found in the daily press, especially in the October 6–10, 1989 issues of *Népszabadság*; and László Soós, ed., *A Magyar Szocialista Munkáspárt Központi Bizottságának 1989. évi Jegyzőkönyvei* (Stenographic minutes of the meetings of the CC, HSWP in 1989). 2 vols. (Budapest: Magyar Országos Levéltár, 1993) (cited hereinafer as *HSWP CC Minutes, 1989*); and collected speeches and writings of thirty-six HSWP leaders published between 1957 and 1989, as well as memoirs by, and volumes of interviews with, incumbent and retired party and government officials. These will be cited, when appropriate, as footnotes to the following chapters.

3 By "internal records" I refer to secret (*titkos*) and top-secret (*szigorúan titkos*) agendas and transcripts of HSWP Politburo (PB) and Central Committee (CC) meetings, drafts of policy proposals to the PB from CC Secretariat departments and background materials and reports submitted by regional and local party organizations to these (Agitation and Propaganda [AP], Party and Mass Organizations [PMO], Public Administration [legal-security and military affairs] [PA], Economic Policy [EP], Cultural-Scientific-Educational [CSE] and International [INT]) departments. With the exception of PA, certain EP and CSE and most INT materials, access to these documents, originally classified at the level of "confidential" (*bizalmas*) or "strictly confidential" (*szigorúan bizalmas*), may be obtained by special permission from the MDP-MSZMP (HWP-HSWP) Depository of the Hungarian National Archives (Országos Levéltár – OL). PB materials are archived as "288 f5/1,2,3 ...", CC stenographic minutes as "288 f4/1,2,3 ..." (cited herafter as OL 288 f5/xxx (month, day, year) and OL 288 f4/xxx (month, day, year). Other internal HSWP materials will be cited in a similarly identifiable form.

4 It must be emphasized that the available HSWP archive material represents but the "visible part of the iceberg." Much of the substantive internal communication was verbal and informal rather than written and fully transcribed. The most keenly felt gap is the absence of full transcripts of the PB's deliberations for 1969–89. For this period only the annotated agendas and, occasionally, the transcribed text of János Kádár's summary remarks are available. The rest is on audiocasettes and is unavailable for research purposes.

5 For the text of the programs of the top twenty political parties for the 1990 elections, see Sándor Kurtán *et al.*, eds., *Magyarország Politikai Évkönyve, 1990* (Hungarian Political Yearbook, 1990) (Budapest: Aula, 1990), pp. 491–618.

6 For example, András Bozóki, "Post-communist transition: political tendencies in Hungary," in András Bozóki, *et al.*, eds., *Post-Communist Transition: Emerging Pluralism in Hungary* (London: Pinter Publishers, 1992), pp. 13–29.

7 Cf. George Schopflin, "The Political Traditions of Eastern Europe" *Daedalus* 119, 1 (1990), 55–90. See also Gale Stokes, "The Social Origins of East European Politics," *East European Politics and Society* (hereinafter *EEPS*) 1, 1

(1987), 30–74; Daniel Chirot, ed., *The Origins of Backwardness in Eastern Europe: Economics and Politics from the Middle Ages until the Early Twentieth Century* (Berkeley and Los Angeles: University of California Press, 1989).

8 Cf. Ernest Gellner, *Nations and Nationalism* (Ithaca: Cornell University Press, 1974), Hans Kohn, *The Idea of Nationalism: a Study of Its Origins and Background* (New York: Macmillan, 1944) and John A. Armstrong, "Toward a Framework for Considering Nationalism in East Europe," *EEPS*, 2, 2 (Spring, 1988) pp. 288–305.

9 On the political ideas of Hungary's "first reform generation," see George Bárány, *Stephen Széchenyi and the Awakening of Hungarian Nationalism, 1791–1841* (Princeton: Princeton University Press, 1968) and Andrew C. János, *The Politics of Backwardness in Hungary, 1825–1945* (Princeton: Princeton University Press, 1982), pp. 35–83.

10 Gyula Szekfű, *Három nemzedék és ami utána következik* (Three generations and that which follows) (Budapest: Magyar Szemle, 1934).

11 Béla Faragó, "Magyar liberalizmus" (Hungarian liberalism) *Századvég* 6–7 (1988), 41–54; Máté Szábo et al., "Symposium on liberalism," in *Válság és reform* (Crisis and reform) (Budapest: Magyar Politikatudományi Társaság, 1987), 125–74; and Andrew C. János, *Politics of Backwardness*, pp. 84–148.

12 In making this distinction I rely on the considered opinion of the great Hungarian historian György Ránki on this subject. He wrote: "In 1927 [prime minister István] Bethlen called this system 'democracy based on corporative correctives'. It probably would have been more correct to speak about a corporative system with democratic trappings. If these fascist [i.e., corporatist] features are compared with the classical, but nevertheless most extreme type of fascism found in Germany and Italy, then this system cannot be called fascist." See György Ránki, "The Problem of Fascism in Hungary," in Peter F. Sugár, ed., *Native Fascism in the Successor States, 1918–1945* (Santa Barbara, CA: ABC-Clio, 1971), p. 69.

13 See C. A. Macartney, *October Fifteenth: A History of Modern Hungary, 1929–1945* (Edinburgh: Edinburgh University Press, 1957) and István Deák, "Hungary," in Hans Rogger and Eugene Weber, eds., *The European Right* (Berkeley and Los Angeles: University of California Press, 1965), pp. 364–407.

14 Zoltán Horváth, *A magyar századforduló: a második reformnemzedék története, 1896–1914* (The Hungarian fin de siècle – a history of the second reform generation, 1896–1914) (Budapest: Gondolat, 1961); Zsuzsa L. Nagy, *The Liberal Opposition in Hungary, 1919–1945* (Budapest: Akadémiai Kiadó, 1983); and Gyula Schopflin, *Szélkiáltó* (A migrant bird) (Budapest: Magvető, 1991).

15 Gyula Borbándi, *A magyar népi mozgalom* (The Hungarian Populist movement) (New York: Püski, 1983), and Daniel Chirot, "Ideology, Reality and Competing Models of Development in Eastern Europe between the Two World Wars," *EESP* 3, 3 (1988), 378–411.

16 István Bibó, *Harmadik ut: politikai és történelmi tanulmányok* (The third road: political and historical studies) (London: Magyar Könyves Céh, 1961). See

also, Rudolf L. Tőkés, "The 'Third Road': Three Case Studies on the History of Hungarian Populist Ideologies." (Unpublished MA thesis) Columbia University, 1961.

17 The political record and the leading personalities of these "Marxist-internationalist" periods are discussed in Tibor Hajdu, *A Magyarországi Tanácsköztársaság* (The Hungarian Soviet Republic) (Budapest: Kossuth, 1969) and Rudolf L. Tőkés, *Béla Kun and the Hungarian Soviet Republic* (Stanford: Hoover Institution, 1967).

18 On this see, George Schopflin, "Hungary: An Uneasy Stability," in Archie Brown and Jack Gray, eds., *Political Culture and Political Change in Communist States* (London: Macmillan, 1977), pp. 131–58.

19 The Hungarian sociologist László Bruszt in his perceptive essay, "1989: The Negotiated Revolution in Hungary," *Social Research* 57, 2 (1990), 365–88, uses the term "negotiated" (*tárgyalásos*) to denote the process of official and informal interaction between the regime and the opposition in the spring and summer of 1989 without reference to earlier (1970–88), or historic precedents of interest reconciliation through bargaining in Hungary.

20 Cf. László Péter, "Montesquieu's Paradox of Freedom and Hungary's Constitutions 1790–1990," *New Hungarian Quarterly* 32, 123 (1991), 3–14.

21 The use of geopolitical factors as key determinants in the evolution of Hungarian politics and public administration may also be inferred from Immanuel Wallerstein's "center–periphery" propositions in his *The Modern World System* (New York: Academic Press, 1974) as applied for Hungary by Andrew C. János in his *Politics of Backwardness*. See also Jenő Szücs, *Vázlat Európa három történeti régiójáról* (A sketch on the three historic regions of Europe), in Ferenc Donáth et al., eds., *Bibó Emlékkönyv* (Bibó Memorial Book) (Budapest: Samizdat, 1980), pp. 184–254.

22 Cited in François Fejtő, "Hungarian Communism," in William E. Griffith, ed., *Communism in Europe* vol. I (Cambridge, MA: MIT Press, 1964), p. 191.

23 On this see, Béla Köpeczi et al., eds., *Erdély Története*, 3 vols. (Budapest: Akadémiai Kiadó, 1986).

24 Bálint Hóman and Gyula Szekfű, *Magyar történet* (Hungarian history), vol. IV, 7th edn (Budapest: Királyi Magyar Egyetemi Nyomda, 1943), pp. 317–65 and 486–576.

25 István Deák, *The Lawful Revolution: Louis Kossuth and the Hungarians, 1848–1849* (New York: Columbia University Press, 1979).

26 See György Szabad, *Hungarian Political Trends Between the Revolution and the Compromise, 1849–1867* (Budapest: Akadémiai Kiadó, 1977) and János, *Politics of Backwardness*, pp. 84–148.

27 See Oscar Jaszi, *The Dissolution of the Hapsburg Monarchy*, 2nd edn (Chicago: University of Chicago Press, 1958) and Francis Deák, *Hungary at the Paris Peace Conference* (New York: Columbia University Press, 1942). See also Robert W. Seton-Watson, *Racial Problems in Hungary* (London: Constable, 1908).

28 Gyula Juhász, *Hungarian Foreign Policy, 1919–1945* (Budapest: Akadémiai Kiadó, 1979); Miklós Horthy, *Memoirs* (London: Hutchinson, 1956); and

Mario D. Fenyő, *Hitler, Horthy, Mussolini* (New Haven: Yale University Press, 1972).

29 Magda Ádám *et al.*, eds., *Magyarország és a második világháború* (Hungary and the Second World War) (Budapest: Kossuth, 1959); György Ránki, *1944 március 19* (Budapest: Kossuth, 1968); and Randolph L. Braham, *The Politics of Genocide: The Holocaust in Hungary*, 2 vols. (New York: Columbia University Press, 1981).

30 György Ránki, ed., *Hungarian History – World History* (Budapest: Akadémiai Kiadó, 1984) and Stephen D. Kertesz, *Diplomacy in a Whirlpool* (Notre Dame: Notre Dame University Press, 1953).

31 Of the voluminous literature, consisting of several thousand books, articles, memoirs, and documentary collections on the Hungarian revolution, five studies are exceptionally useful. These are Ferenc Vali, *Rift and Revolt in Hungary* (Cambridge, MA: Harvard University Press, 1961), Paul Kecskemeti, *The Unexpected Revolution: Social Forces in the Hungarian Uprising* (Stanford: Stanford University Press, 1961), Paul E. Zinner, *Revolution in Hungary* (New York: Columbia University Press, 1962), Bill Lomax, *Hungary 1956* (London: Allison and Busby, 1976), and Bill Lomax, *Hungarian Workers' Councils in 1956* (New York: Columbia University Press, 1990).

32 These interactions, conceptualized as those taking place between the "second" (private sphere) and "first" (public sphere) societies are discussed in Elemér Hankiss, *East European Alternatives* (Oxford: Clarendon Press, 1990), especially pp. 50–103.

33 See Miklós Haraszti's *Worker in a Workers' State* (London: Penguin Books, 1977) and Miklós Haraszti, *The Velvet Prison: Artists under State Socialism* (New York: Basic Books, 1987) on the workers' and the intellectuals' situation and bargaining leverage, respectively.

34 For an inside commentary, see Emil Kimmel, *Végjáték a Fehér Házban* (Endgame in the White House) (Budapest: Téka, 1990). See also, Csaba Gombár, "Kormányzati kérdéseken tünődve" (Reflections on questions of governance), in Györgyi Várnai, ed., *Logosz* (Budapest: ELTE Szociologiai és Szociálpolitikai Intézet, 1990), pp. 47–62.

35 This point is made in Rudolf L. Tőkés, "Hungary's New Political Elites: Adaptation and Change, 1989–1990," in György Szoboszlai, ed., *Democracy and Political Transformation* (Budapest: Hungarian Political Science Association, 1991), pp. 226–86.

36 Data on Hungarian casualties are in *Statisztikai Szemle* 10 (1990), 3–5 and in Péter Gosztonyi, "Az 1956-os forradalom számokban" (Statistics on the 1956 revolution), *Népszabadság*, November 3, 1990. On Soviet casualties, see Valeri Musatov, "Szovjet politikai beavatkozás és katonai intervenció Magyarországon 1956-ban" (Soviet political intereference and military intervention in Hungary in 1956), *Multunk* 36, 4 (1991), 168. Musatov gives the number of Hungarian victims of the Soviet invasion at 4,000.

37 János Balassa *et al.*, eds., *Halottaink*, 2 vols. (Our dead) (Budapest: Katalizátor, 1989); Mária Ormos, "A konszolidáció problémái 1956 és 1958

között" (Problems of consolidation between 1956 and 1958), *Társadalmi Szemle* 44, 8–9 (1989), 48–65,

38 For contemporary official Soviet assessments on the Hungarian events in 1956–57, see Vyacheslav Sereda and Aleksandr Stikhalin, eds., *Hiányzó lapok 1956 történetéből: dokumentumok a volt SZKP PB levéltárából* (Missing pages from the history of 1956: documents from the archives of the Politburo of the former CPSU) (Budapest: Zenit, 1993) and Éva Gál et al., eds., *A "Jelcin dosszié" Szovjet dokumentumok 1956-ról,* (The "Yeltsin dossier" – Soviet documents on 1956) (Budapest: Századvég Kiadó, 1993).

39 The fate of Imre Nagy and his associates, who were executed on June 16, 1958, and of those who were sentenced to prison terms has generated voluminous literature. Although the full text of the trial transcripts is not yet available, the most important documentary evidence and scholarly interpretation include the following: *The Truth about the Nagy Affair* (New York: Praeger, 1959); Miklós Molnár, *Imre Nagy, réformateur ou révolutionnaire?* (Geneva: Droz, 1972); György Litván, "A Nagy Imre per politikai háttere," *Világosság* 10 (1992), 743–57; János M. Rainer, "Nagy Imre életútja" (Imre Nagy – a biographic sketch) *Multunk* 4 (1992), 3–14.

40 The regime's early actions and policy dilemmas are well summarized by Levente Sipos in his introductory essay in K. V. Németh and Levente Sipos, eds., *A Magyar Szocialista Munkáspárt vezető testületeinek jegyzőkönyvei* vol. I. (November 11, 1956 – January 14, 1957) (Stenographic minutes of the [deliberations of] the leading organs of the Hungarian Socialist Workers' Party) (Budapest: Interart, 1993), pp. 7–24.

41 There are two book-length biographies of János Kádár. The first is by László Gyurkó, "Introductory Biography," in János Kádár, *Selected Speeches and Interviews* (Oxford: Pergamon Press, 1985), pp. 3–168 and had been commissioned by the HSWP. The second is by William Shawcross, *Crime and Compromise: János Kádár and the Politics of Hungary since the Revolution* (New York: E.P. Dutton, 1974).

42 Kádár's activities between 1945 and October 1956 are covered in the standard literature on Hungary's postwar politics. New evidence is provided in his 1989 in-depth interview on his political career in András Kanyó, *Kádár János: végakarat* (János Kádár – last will and testament) (Budapest: Hirlapterjesztő, 1989) and in Gábor Koltay and Péter Bródy, eds., *El nem égetett dokumentumok* (Unburned documents) (Budapest: Szabad Tér, 1990).

43 Anastas Mikoyan's cabled report of July 20, 1956, to members of the CPSU, CC, Presidium, provides a penetrating account on the outcome of the HSWP CC's plenary session. See, V. Sereda and A. Stikhalin, eds., "Missing pages," pp. 59–65.

44 Jenő Györkei, "Kádár vesszőfutása Moszkvába és vissza" (Kádár: running the gauntlet to and from Moscow), *Uj Magyarország*, April 8, 1993. Kádár's only semipublic reference to this trip was made in his last farewell speech to the HSWP CC on April 12, 1989.

45 The text of Kádár's police confession is in Kanyó *Kádár*, pp. 61–6.
46 Firsthand information from the young Kádár's contemporaries is difficult to come by. However, I was extemely fortunate to have met and conducted several in-depth interviews with Mr. Pál Demény between November 1984 and February 1985. Mr. Demény had been the leader of the "native" dissident faction of the underground Hungarian communist movement between the two world wars and was well acquainted with János Kádár. Before his death in Janury 1991, Mr. Demény had served as a parliamentary deputy for the Hungarian Socialist Party.
47 On this, see Tibor Hajdu, "Farkas és Kádár Rajknál. Az 1949 junius 7-i beszélgetés hiteles szövege" (Farkas and Kádár at Rajk. The authentic transcript of the conversation) *Társadalmi Szemle* 4 (1992), 70–89.
48 Kádár's personal responsibility for the execution of Imre Nagy and four of his codefendants is beyond dispute. As Kádár explained it to members of the CC: "The people accept and approve that Imre Nagy and a few of his colleagues were hanged, because they knew that the party [had the courage] to forgive the half million crazies [i.e., average Hungarians] who had gone astray [in October–November 1956]. To forgive the small trespasses, the main culprits had to be destroyed." OL 288 f4/45 (February 9, 1962), p. 14.
49 Stenographic minutes of the November 11, 1956 meeting of the Provisional CC of the HSWP, in K. V. Németh and L. Sipos, eds., *A Magyar Szocialista*, p. 25.
50 On this see, Judit Ember, *Menedékjog 1956: a Nagy Imre csoport elrablása* (Right to asylum – 1956: the abduction of the Imre Nagy group) (Budapest: Szabad Tér, 1989).
51 See Péter Tölgyessy, "Célegyenesben" (In the home strech), *Népszabadság*, April 16, 1994, and László Lengyel, "Kádár János és kora" (János Kádár and his era), *Népszabadság*, July 6, 1994.
52 In the present context, both terms refer to efficiency deflators from the declared, but inherently unattainable, optimal levels of the ruling party-state's managerial performance. These are only preliminary benchmarks because, as Anthony Downs explains, "The merits and efficiency of bureaucratic organizations can be considered only in relation to specific social functions and specific forms of organization suitable for carrying out those functions." Anthony Downs, *Inside Bureaucracy* (Boston: Little, Brown, 1964), p. 40.
53 Martin Malia, "From Under the Rubble, What?" *Problems of Communism* 41, 1–2 (January–April, 1992), 105.
54 Cf. Paul G. Lewis, ed., *Eastern Europe: Political Crisis and Legitimation* (New York: St. Martin's Press, 1984), and T. W. Luke and C. Boggs, "Soviet Subimperialism and the Crisis of Bureaucratic Centralism," *Studies in Comparative Communism* 15, 1–2 (1982).
55 An earlier version of the following argument was presented as a paper of mine, "From Vanguard to Rearguard: The Hungarian Party in Transition," at the conference "Before the Storm Breaks: The Extent, Limits and Dangers

of Reform in Communist Hungary" held at the Pennsylvania State University, State College, April 14–17, 1988.

56 On other requisites of successful leadership, see, Lester G. Seligman, "Leadership – Political Aspects," in David L. Sills, ed., *International Encyclopedia of the Social Sciences* vol. IX (New York: Macmillan and The Free Press, 1968), pp. 107–13. (Cited hereinafter as *IESS*.)

57 The terms "manner," "style," and "mode" of party leadership are used to indicate the way in which a Marxist–Leninist ruling party makes use of the resources of the state to advance its policy agenda over time. The labels "vanguard," "system management," and "rearguard" are inferred from the efforts of ruling-party elites at self-legitimation by way of ideological messages "on the nature of the present epoch" to internal (the cadres) and external (the nonparty majority) constituencies. These three leadership styles are causally related to the amount – high, medium, low – of coercion that the party expends to preserve the scope of its shrinking authority as ultimate maker of public policies. Some of these points have been developed from Richard Lowenthal's seminal study "Development vs. Utopia in Communist Policy," in Chalmers Johnson, ed., *Change in Communist Systems* (Stanford: Stanford University Press, 1970) pp. 33–116.

58 Cf. Lowenthal, "Development," p. 34.

59 Cf. Alfred Meyer, "Legitimacy of Power in East Central Europe," in S. Sinaian *et al.*, eds., *Eastern Europe in the 1970s* (New York: Praeger, 1972), p. 56.

60 *HSWP Decisions, 1956–1962*, pp. 14–16.

61 As Béla Biszku explained in a 1991 interview: "for us [the phrase] 'cult of personality' was a codeword for lawlessness." After Khrushchev's fall in October 1964, Kádár demanded that the Soviet party reconfirm its commitment to the "spirit of the 20th [CPSU] congress." After two days of tense negotiations with Mikhail Suslov and Ponomarev the Soviet Politburo conceded the point. László Vitézy [director and editor], "A legvidámabb barakk" (The jolliest barrack in the camp of peace). Unpublished transcript of TV interview program with former HSWP leaders, 1991–92), pp. 251–2.

62 Although the precise scope of the HSWP's direct administrative oversight over nonparty agencies, such as the government bureaucracy, was always ambiguous, in 1970 the HSWP PB made a major effort to stabilize the jurisdictional boundaries between the party and the government, the legislature, the courts, and the procuracy. On this see OL 288 f5/523 (July 14, 1970), OL 288 f5/524 (July 28, 1970), pp. 7–33 and pp. 37–79. See also "[Magyar Országgyűlés] A Honvédelmi Bizottság 1989 októberi ülésszakán létrehozott vizsgálóbizottság 1989 december 11-i (1990 január 3-i, 1990 január 15-i, 1990 február 6-i) ülése jegyzőkönyvének nyilt részlete" ([Hungarian Parliament] Declassified excerpts from hearings before the Investigative Subcommittee – established at the October 1989 meeting of the Parliament's Committee on National

Defense – held on December 11, 1989, and on January 3, January 15, February 6, and February 12, 1990), 5 vols. (cited hereinafter as "Military Hearings, 1989–1990"). My thanks to Dr. Péter Tölgyessy, MP and former Chairman of the AFD, for his kind assistance to my review of these documents.

63 "This term denotes a recurring trend in Soviet history characterized by the emergence of *incipient bipolarity* in party–state relations (1939–1954, 1962, and since 1966) and by the ascendancy of the state and its encroachment on some of the party's decision-making prerogatives, particularly in economics, science and national defense." Rudolf L. Tőkés, "Dissent: Politics for Change in the USSR," in Henry W. Morton and Rudolf L. Tőkés, eds., *Soviet Politics and Society in the 1970s* (New York: Free Press, 1974), p. 42.

64 Richard Lowenthal conceptualizes the party's and the state's respective claims for leadership in terms of built-in conflicts between the "reds" and the "experts," in Lowenthal, "Development," pp. 55–73.

65 The writings of Antonio Gramsci, particularly his notions on hegemony and civil society in Antonio Gramsci, *Selections from the Prison Notebooks, 1929–1935* (New York: International Publishers, 1971), were quite influential in Hungarian party intelligentsia circles in the early 1980s.

66 There are haunting similarities between the HSWP's rearguard strategies and survival scenarios of "organizations in decline." The outcome of a typical confrontation between the taxpayers and a beleaguered board of education of a American community may, according to the consultant's report, be best managed for the survival of the latter, in five steps: 1. "Frame the perception of others – share information," 2. "Structure the activities that others will pursue – anticipate needs, issue new challenges," 3. "Lead without directly supervising – offer increased opportunities for participation," 4. "Deal with politics – anticipate conflicts – channel political forces into newly created formal structures," and 5. "Accept and promote a model of shared governance." See Zehava Rosenblatt *et al.*, "Toward a Political Framework for Flexible Management of Decline," *Organization Science* 4, 1 (1993), 86–9.

67 On this see Raymond C. Taras, ed., *Leadership Change in Communist States* (Boston: Unwin Hyman, 1989).

68 Peter Wiles, "Capitalist Triumphalism in Eastern Europe, or the Economics of Transition: An Interim Report," in Armand Clesse and Rudolf L. Tőkés, eds., *Preventing a New East–West Divide: The Economic and Social Imperatives of the Future Europe* (Baden-Baden: Nomos, 1992), pp. 389–407.

69 See Alex Pravda, ed., *The End of the Outer Empire: Soviet–East European Relations in Transition, 1985–1990* (London: The Royal Institute of International Affairs, 1992).

70 See Valerie Bunce, "Decline of the Regional Hegemon: The Gorbachev Regime and Reform in Eastern Europe," *EEPS*, 3 (1989), 395–430.

71 Michael R. Beschloss and Strobe Talbott, *At the Highest Levels: The Inside Story of the End of the Cold War* (Boston: Little, Brown, 1993).

1 From vanguard to rearguard

1 András Hegedüs, *A történelem és a hatalom igézetében* (Under the spell of history and power) (Budapest: Kossuth, 1988), pp. 317–32. See also István Feitl, "A moszkvai emigráció és az MSZMP. Rákosi Mátyás 1956 és 1958 között" (The Moscow emigrants and the HSWP. Mátyás Rákosi between 1956 and 1958), *Multunk* 36, 4 (1991), 3–31.

2 Iván Szenes, *A Kommunista Párt ujjászervezése Magyarországon, 1956–1957* (The reorganization of the Communist Party in Hungary, 1956–1957) (Budapest: Kossuth, 1981), p. 26.

3 Paul E. Zinner, ed., *National Communism and Popular Revolt in Eastern Europe* (New York: Columbia University Press, 1956), pp. 464–7.

4 Zinner, *National Communism*, p. 466.

5 OL 288 f4/273 (September 25, 1989), pp. 56–101.

6 K. V. Németh and L. Sipos, eds., *A Magyar Szocialista*.

7 Ágnes Ságvári, *Mert nem hallgathatok* (I cannot remain silent) (Budapest: Magyar Hirlapkiadó, 1989), p. 146.

8 Yehezkel Dror, *Public Policymaking Reexamined* (Scranton, PA: Chandler Publishing Company, 1968) and Yehezkel Dror, *Policymaking Under Adversity* (New Brunswick, NJ: Transaction Books, 1986).

9 James A. Robinson, "Decision Making: Political Aspects," in Sills, ed., *IESS* vol. IV, p. 55.

10 Harold Laswell, "Policy Sciences," in Sills, ed., *IESS* vol. XII, p. 181.

11 Dror, *Public Policymaking*, p. 12.

12 *Ibid.*, p. 34.

13 *Ibid.*, p. 16.

14 OL 288 f4/198 (April 17, 1984), p. 34/3.

15 Kanyó, *Kádár*, p. 139. See also Ságvári, "I cannot remain silent," p. 215.

16 Soviet advisors were withdrawn in 1960, but in the Ministry of Defense and in the Ministry of Interior they were replaced by Soviet military (GRU) and political (KGB) "liaison personnel."

17 Ságvári, "I cannot remain silent," p. 216. This was not exactly the way Khrushchev recalled the terms of his dialogue with Kádár.

> "Comrade Kádár," I said, "have you given any thought to the presence of our troops in Hungary? ... [W]e rely on your judgment and we'll do whatever you recommend." Kádár: "Comrade Khrushchev, I think you'd best decide this for yourself. There is no resentment in our country against the presence of your troops on our territory. I say this very frankly."
> Strobe Talbott, ed., *Khrushchev Remembers: The Last Testament* (Boston: Little, Brown, 1974), p. 216.

18 Party insiders dispute this point. Some maintain that once his conservative patrons, as members of the CPSU "antiparty group" of June 1957, were swept out of power, Rákosi's chances of returning to Hungary were nil. I find this unconvincing (after all, Rákosi had served Khrushchev, too) and

would put his "date of no return" well after the 22nd CPSU congress of 1961 – in fact, as late as 1967.

19 Ferenc Münnich served as prime minister between January 28, 1958 and September 13, 1961. József Bölöny, *Magyarország kormányai 1848–1972* (Hungarian governments, 1848–1972) (Budapest: Akadémiai Kiadó, 1978), pp. 81–2.

20 Ságvári, "I cannot remain silent," p. 215. According to former minister of defense Lajos Czinege, in 1956–57 more than 8,000 officers – among them many Hungarian graduates of top Soviet military academies – were dismissed from the Hungarian army as politically unreliable. See "Military Hearings," December 11, 1989, p. 261.

21 János Radványi, *Hungary and the Superpowers* (Stanford: Stanford University Press, 1972).

22 "Military Hearings" held on January 3, January 15, and February 6, 1990 and testimonies by Béla Biszku, György Lázár, and Jenő Fock on January 3 (pp. 47–58), January 15 (pp. 93–183), and February 6 (pp. 81–272), respectively.

23 Bálint Magyar, "1956 és a magyar falu" (1956 and the Hungarian villages), *Medvetánc* 2–3 (1988), 207–12.

24 *Társadalmi Szemle* 24, 1 (1959), 1–12; *HSWP Decisions, 1956–1962*, pp. 353–65; *Népszabadság*, February 14, 1960; *HSWP Decisions, 1956–1962*, pp. 417–26 and 461–71; and *Népszabadság*, February 19, 1961.

25 William F. Robinson, *The Pattern of Reform in Hungary* (New York: Praeger, 1972), pp. 38ff. Apparently, agricultural policies were also of interest to the Soviet Union. In 1991 Sándor Gáspár recalled that in early 1958 Soviet Ambassador Bromov called the entire HSWP PB to his office and harshly criticized the members for the way they proposed to restore agricultural cooperatives in Hungary. Kádár said: "it is not the CPSU but we who are responsible for this country." Shortly thereafter Bromov was recalled to Moscow. Vitézy, "The jolliest barrack," p. 185.

26 *Népszabadság*, February 17, 1961.

27 On the regime's farm policies, see Lajos Fehér, *A szocialista mezőgazdaságért* (For a socialist agriculture) (Budapest: Kossuth, 1963) and Lajos Fehér, *Sorsfordító évtizedek* (Crucial decades) (Budapest: Kossuth, 1987).

28 András A. Gergely's *A pártállam varázstalanítása* (The demystification of the party state) (Budapest: Institute of Political Science, Hungarian Academy of Sciences, 1991).

29 OL 288 f4/51 (August 14–15, 1962), pp. 114–16.

30 György Marosán, *Fel kellett állnom* (I was compelled to leave) (Budapest: Hirlapkiadó, 1989), pp. 117–32.

31 Károly Grósz, who succeeded Kádár as secretary general in May 1988, was the only person with access to Kádár's personal papers – and the only one who visited him during the last six weeks of his life in late May–early July 1989. As Grósz explained in an unpublished interview in 1992, Kádár, for the most part, had been disappointed in his subordinates. Once Grósz

asked him: "Why do you tolerate them?" Kádár replied: "You see, they knew that I knew what kind of people they were. Therefore, it was easier for me to work with them." Interviewer to Grósz: "In other words Kádár had them by the short hair?" Grósz: "I would not put it this way, but he created a psychological, political and interpersonal sense of dependent relationships ... He knew their weaknesses ... It is not that they stole something and had too much for dinner, but he knew their political vulnerabilities." Vitézy, "Interview with Karoly Grósz," pp. 112–13.

32 *Népszabadság*, August 17, 1962.

33 According to a top-secret memorandum of October 18, 1954 from attorney general Kálmán Czakó to prime minister Imre Nagy on the "operative scope" of the Hungarian political police, the AVH (National Security Authority) had more than 1.5 million names on file as suspected political enemies. Of these, 758,611 individuals benefited (release from jail, reduction of sentence, cancelation of court-imposed fines or criminal proceedings, and so on) from the Imre Nagy government's amnesty programs of 1953. Ibolya Horváth *et al.*, eds., *Iratok az igazságszolgáltatás történetéhez* (Documents on the history of justice in Hungary) vol. I (Budapest: Közgazdasági és Jogi Kiadó, 1992), pp. 498, 430–1.

34 The text of Marosán's letter to Kádár is in OL 288 f4/58 (August–September 1962), pp. 21–101. Kádár's letters to Marosán and the CC are in *ibid.*, pp. 102–51.

35 Marosán, *ibid.*, p. 271.

36 After 1962, when visiting in the Soviet Union, Kádár took with him the prime minister and the minister of defense (Warsaw Treaty Organization summits) and, depending on the occasion, the CC secretary for agitation and propaganda, or for foreign affairs, or for economic policy. Béla Biszku, Kádár's (then) trusted deputy, between 1964 and 1967 did accompany Kádár on three visits to Moscow.

37 *HSWP Seventh Congress* (November 30 – December 5, 1962), pp. 545–56.

38 One way of estimating the proximity of Kádár's associates to the general secretary might be the position they occupied in the rank order of fourteen groups of people who were listed as honorary pallbearers at his funeral on July 14, 1989. Members of the "iron brigade" were at the top of the list. See *Népszabadság*, July 15, 1989.

39 "Interview with Tibor Zinner," *Népszabadság*, February 29, 1992.

40 The evidence on Kádár's role in the invasion of Czechoslovakia is drawn from eleven HSWP CC and PB meetings held between January and mid-September, 1968.

41 Interview with Mihály Korom in Vitézy, ed., "The jolliest barrack," p. 340. Korom was Dubček's classmate at a Soviet party academy in 1956.

42 OL 288 f5/444 (January 23, 1968), p. 15.

43 *Ibid.*, pp. 19–20.

44 OL 288 f5/445 (February 6, 1968), p. 19.

45 OL 288 f5/448 (March 4, 1968), pp. 11–17.

46 OL 288 f4/90 (February 8–10, 1968), pp. 209–20.

47 As Fock recalled, "The decision to invade or not to invade [Czechoslovakia] had been made months before the fact ... when we were in Dresden ... the preparations for the invasion were already under way ... they [that is, the Soviets] were trying to coerce us to sign a document that we were unwilling to sign ... The way Dubček remembers it, he was the only one under pressure. Actually, he never said a word – we spoke for him. In fact, it was I who persuaded Dubček not to sign, so neither of us would sign ... What kind of document? [One] which criticized Dubček et al., following which there would have been an invasion in May [1968]. In the end, only a brief communiqué appeared." See testimony by Jenő Fock, "Military hearings," February 6, 1990, pp. 153–61. See also, Secretariat, General Staff, Hungarian People's Army, "Jelentés a Politikai Bizottságnak az Egyesitett Fegyveres Erők Főparancsnoka által vezetett SUMAVA parancsnoki és tőrzsvezetői gyakorlatokról" (Report to the PB on the command and staff exercise code named SUMAVA held under the authority of the commander in chief of the WTO Unified Command. July 5, 1968), Társadalmi Szemle 50, 2 (February 1995), 88–94.
48 OL 288 f5/452 (April 2, 1968), p. 15.
49 Ibid., p. 17.
50 OL 288 f5/455 (May 14, 1968), p. 29.
51 OL 288 f5/457 (June 11, 1968), p. 48.
52 Ibid., p. 83.
53 OL 288 f5/460 (July 9, 1968), p. 20.
54 OL 288 f5/463 (July 18, 1968), p. 4.
55 OL 288 f4/93 (August 7, 1968), pp. 22–3.
56 OL 288 f4/93 (August 7, 1968), p. 37.
57 Interview with Kádár's interpreter Mrs. István Bartha (Nadia Rabinovics) in Vitézy, ed., "The jolliest barrack," p. 375.
58 OL 288 f4/93 (August 7, 1968), p. 79.
59 OL 288 f4/94 (August 23, 1968). As Fock recalled, "A few days after the invasion Kádár asked Brezhnev what would have happened if we had not caved in two days prior to [August 21] ... It would have been terrible and it would have been a catastrophe ... the way I sensed it, the [Soviet army] would have crushed (keresztülmennek) us too ... that after administering a side-blow (oldalvágás) to us, they would have entered Czechoslovakia." He added: "János Kádár was worried about the country, rather than about himself." See "Military Hearings," February 6, 1990, pp. 163–4.
60 Rudolf L. Tőkés, "Hungarian Intellectuals' Reaction to the Invasion of Czechoslovakia," in E. J. Czerwinski and J. Piakalkiewicz, eds., The Soviet Invasion of Czechoslovakia: Its Effects on Eastern Europe (New York: Praeger, 1972), pp. 139–58.
61 OL 288 f5/471 (September 13, 1968), pp. 20 and 47.
62 Ibid., p. 16.
63 Jiri Valenta, Soviet Intervention in Czechoslovakia, 1968 (rev. edn) (Baltimore: Johns Hopkins University Press, 1991), p. 178.
64 These "universals" pertained to the communist parties' use of "general

methods (1) of reorienting the party after coming to power ... (2) organization building ... (3) of resolving political problems of agricultural nationalization and collectivization; (4) of structuring political life ... (5) of target-setting ... and (6) irregular replacement of personnel, e.g., purges." Chalmers Johnson, ed., *Change in Communist Systems*, pp. 27–8.

65   András Nyirő et al., eds., *Segédkönyv a Politikai Bizottság tanulmányozásához* (Handbook for the study of the Politburo) (Budapest: Interart, 1989), p. 1.

66   Their findings were published in a symposium, Rudolf L. Tőkés, ed., "Hungary: Anatomy of a Party-State," *The Journal of Communist Studies* 8, 3 (1992), 27–75.

67   Mihály Bihari, "A hatalom csúcsán" (At the pinnacle of power) in Nyirő et al., "Handbook," pp. xi–xx.

68   Cf. *HSWP Decisions, 1971–1975*, pp. 131–6.

69   Although a Soviet Army intelligence (GRU) veteran, with the exception of the brief period between November 12, 1956 and March 1, 1957, Ferenc Münnich had no command responsibilities in the Hungarian army. For short periods of time PB members Miklós Óvári and Dezső Nemes also served as ideological secretary and foreign secretary, respectively.

70   George Schopflin, Rudolf L. Tőkés, and Iván Völgyes, "Leadership Change and Crisis in Hungary," *Problems of Communism* 37, 5 (1988), 23–46.

71   Nyirő et al., eds., "Handbook," pp. 31–2.

72   In the realm of policymaking on national security issues, there existed one top (and secret) and two public groups. The top group was a "Coordinating Commission" for military and security policies within the CC apparat. With Kádár as ex officio chair, the committee was probably coordinated by the CC secretary for administration and its members were senior party and government officials. See testimony of retired deputy prime minister János Borbándi "Military Hearings," January 15, 1990, pp. 3–183.

73   See József Kozári and Mátyás Tóth, heads, Department of Party Finances and Administration (PFA) and the Department of PMO, "Submission to the PB on the status of cadre positions in the party," in OL 288 f5/523 (July 14, 1970), pp. 80–91.

74   OL 288 f5/724 (August 9, 1977), pp. 16–22.

75   OL 288 f5/353 (July 14, 1970), pp. 89–90.

76   OL 288 f5/529 (October 20, 1970), p. 34.

77   *Ibid.*, p. 35.

78   *Ibid.*, p. 142. However, as a PB task force on "questions of party guidance of the state" pointed out, "the party cannot relinquish its right to consider any matter because, under certain circumstances, anything could become of sociopolitical importance." OL 288 f5/529 (October 20, 1970), p. 23. György Lázár, Jenő Fock's successor as prime minister, voiced the same complaints in his testimony before the (postcommunist) Hungarian Parliament's Investigative Committee on Military Affairs. See, "Military Hearings," January 15, 1990, pp. 183–202.

79   András Nyirő, "The Leading Bodies of the Party in the Mirror of their Resolutions," *The Journal of Communist Studies* 8, 3 (1992), 69.

80 These figures do not include the CC department heads' quota of 475 positions and pertain to the party center's *nomenklatura* authority as of June 1, 1971. See György T. Varga and István Szakadát, "Ime a nomenklatura! Az MDP es a volt MSZMP hataskori listai" (Voilà! the nomenclature system. The lists of personnel competency of the HWP and the HSWP), *Társadalmi Szemle* 47, 3, (1992), 73– 95.

81 *HSWP Decisions 1957–62, 1963–6, 1967–70, 1971–5, 1975–80, 1980–5, 1985–6, 1987* and issues of *Népszabadság*, for January 1, 1989 – October 10, 1989.

82 OL 288 f5/1002 (June 30, 1987), pp. 66–7.

83 In fact, one can make a case for arguing that as policy initiators, the little-known CC department heads had at least as much to do with influencing strategic decision-making in Hungary as did Kádár, or any combination of PB members, or cabinet ministers between 1957 and 1989.

84 Other than Kádár's *modus operandi* of "when in doubt, don't" kind of postponing, as long as possible and, at times, well beyond, the making of politically difficult decisions, the gestation period of any new policy tended to be excruciatingly long in cases when the party center sought to "test the waters" in the apparat and in the government bureaucracy prior to making a decision.

85 Mária Tamáska, or "Aunt Mária" to those close to her, was said to be a tough, no-nonsense working-class woman. She divorced her first husband in 1946 and married Kádár in 1949. As Kádár's wife and as one of the senior censors in the Office of Public Information of the Council of Ministers, she had firm views and pronounced personal and ideological likes and dislikes on cadre policies and political issues. The only biographic sketch on Mária Tamáska is her obituary "Akit soha nem láttak first ladynek" (She has never been seen as the First Lady), *Magyar Hirlap*, April 1, 1992.

86 As Gyula Kállai put it: "The essence of Kádárism was that ... nothing happened without his consent. Even in his absence, his views were stated at the outset which, in turn, decided the outcome." Vitézy, ed., "The jolliest barrack," p. 381.

87 Personal communication from Dr. István Horváth, former HSWP CC secretary for administrative and security affairs (March, 1985 – June, 1987) and minister of interior (June, 1987 – January, 1990). Interview with István Horváth, Budapest, June, 1993; and László Vitézy, "Interview with Károly Grósz," p. 118.

88 See, for example, comments by Béla Háry, Gyula Kállai, Béla Biszku, and Károly Németh in Vitézy, ed., "The jolliest barrack," pp. 268, 298–9, 323, 474, and 502.

89 *Magyar Hirlap*, May 23, 1988, and Nyirő *et al.*, eds., "Handbook," *passim*.

90 Vitézy, ed., "The jolliest barrack," p. 488.

91 Cf. "György Aczél," in Nyirő, *et al.*, eds., "Handbook," p. 261; Interviews with György Aczél, May 1988 and June 1989, Budapest. See also György Aczél, *Culture and Socialist Democracy* (Budapest: Corvina Press, 1975) and György Aczél, *Socialism and the Freedom of Culture* (Budapest: Corvina Kiadó, 1984).

92 *HSWP Thirteenth Congress*, pp. 600–1.
93 Nyirő *et al.*, eds., "Handbook," pp. 337–41.
94 As Béla Háry, former first secretary of the Győr-Sopron county party committee, explained, "the county [first] secretaries never had a chance to get together [for fear of] being labeled factionalists." Vitézy, ed., "The jolliest barrack," p. 455.
95 Interview with Rezső Nyers, November 1984, Budapest.
96 *HSWP Decisions, 1967–1970*, pp. 138–40, 451–5; *HSWP Decisions, 1975–1980*, pp. 671–93; *HSWP Decisions, 1980–1985*, pp. 97–100; and OL 288 f4/211 (April 29, 1985), pp. 16– 17.
97 As related by Béla Biszku in Vitézy, ed., "The jolliest barrack," p. 255.
98 OL 288 f4/265 (June 23–24, 1989), p. 244.
99 Interview with György Aczél, May 1988, Budapest.

2 Economic reforms

1 Of the literature of economic reforms in communist states, I found the following particularly useful: David Granick, *Enterprise Guidance in Eastern Europe: A Comparison of Four Socialist Economies* (Princeton: Princeton University Press, 1975); Wlodimierz Brus and Kazimierz Laski, *From Marx to Market* (Oxford: Clarendon Press, 1989); János Kornai, *The Socialist System: The Political Economy of Communism* (Princeton: Princeton University Press, 1992); and Alexander Eckstein, "Economic Development and Political Change in Communist Systems," *World Politics* 22, 4 (1970), 475–95. For Hungary, I relied mainly on Paul Marer's seminal study "Economic Reforms in Hungary: From Central Planning to Regulated Market," in John P. Hardt and Richard F. Kaufman, eds., *East European Economies: Slow Growth in the 1980s* vol. III. Country Studies on Eastern Europe and Yugoslavia. Joint Economic Committee, US Congress (Washington DC: USGPO, 1986), pp. 223–98.
2 Cf. Wlodimierz Brus, "Political Pluralism and Markets in Communist Systems," in Susan Gross Solomon, ed., *Pluralism in the Soviet Union* (London: Macmillan, 1983), p. 113.
3 R V. Burks, "Technology and Political Change in Eastern Europe," in Chalmers Johnson, ed., *Change in Communist Systems*, pp. 265–312.
4 Iván Pető and Sándor Szakács, *A hazai gazdaság négy évtizédenek története, 1945–1985: I. Az ujjáépités és a tervutasitásos irányitás időszaka, 1945–1968* (The history of four decades of the Hungarian economy, 1945–1985: vol. I. The period of economic reconstruction and of the centrally planned economy, 1945–1968) (Budapest: Közgazdasági és Jogi Kiadó, 1985), p. 11. For a different method of rank-ordering countries according to levels of economic development see Éva Erlich, *Országok versenye, 1937–1986: Fejlettségi szintek, struktúrák, növekedési ütemek, iparosodási utak* (The competition of nations, 1937–1986. Levels of development, structures, phases of growth and paths of industrialization) (Budapest: Közgazdasági és Jogi Kiadó,

1991), pp. 69ff. My thanks to Professor Paul Marer for calling my attention to this important work.

5 Cf. Iván T. Berend and György Ránki, *Underdevelopment and Economic Growth: Studies in Hungarian Economic and Social History* (Budapest: Akadémiai Kiadó, 1979).

6 Iván T. Berend and Miklós Szuhay, *A tőkés gazdaság története Magyarországon, 1848–1944* (History of the capitalist economy in Hungary, 1848–1944) (Budapest: Kossuth Könyvkiadó, 1973), pp. 253–6.

7 György Ránki, *Magyarország Gazdasága az Első Hároméves Terv Időszakában* (Hungarian economy during the first Three Year Plan) (Budapest: Közgazdasági és Jogi Kiadó, 1963).

8 Imre Vajda, *Az első ötéves terv. Beszéd az MDP Központi Vezetőségének 1949 április 2-i ülésén* (The first Five Year Plan. Address before the April 2, 1949 meeting of the Central Committee of the HWP) (Budapest: Szikra, 1949).

9 Pető and Szakács, "Hungarian economy," pp. 18–19.

10 *Ibid.*, p. 22.

11 *Ibid.*, p. 39.

12 *Ibid.*, p. 103.

13 *Ibid.*, p. 169.

14 *Ibid.*, p. 168.

15 Cf. E. H Carr and Robert W. Davies, *Foundations of the Planned Economy* (New York: Macmillan, 1947) and Maurice H. Dobb, *Soviet Economic Development since 1917* (London: Routledge and Kegan Paul, 1947).

16 See, Tamás Bauer, *Tervgazdaság, beruházás, ciklusok* (Planned economy, investment, cycles) (Budapest: Kőzgazdasági és Jogi Kiadó, 1981); János Kornai, *Economics of Shortage* (Amsterdam: North Holland, 1980); János Kornai, *Erőltetett vagy harmonikus növekedés* (Forced or harmonious growth) (Budapest: Akadémiai Kiadó, 1972); Iván Major, "Kifulladási periodusok a magyar gazdaság fejlődésében" (Periods of exhaustion in the development of the Hungarian economy), in Robert Hoch and Iván Major, eds., *Gazdaságunk helyzetéről és fejlődésének problémáiról* (On the situation of our economy and problems of its development) (Budapest: Kossuth, 1985), pp. 214–40.

17 This periodization is one of several that was developed by Hungarian economists. Of these I found László Bogár's version that he proposed in his chapter, "Economic Structure," in Rudolf Andorka, Tamás Kolosi, and György Vukovich, eds., *Social Report* (Budapest: Tarki, 1992), pp. 155–78, the best suited for my purposes.

18 *Ibid.*, p. 160.

19 *Ibid.*, p. 163.

20 Tamás Bauer, "A második gazdasági reform és tulajdonviszonyok" (The second economic reform and property relations), *Mozgó Világ* (November 1982).

21 Ágnes Ságvári, "I cannot remain silent," p. 185.

22 Pető and Szakács, "Hungarian economy," pp. 372–3.

23 *Ibid.*, p. 389.

24 *Ibid.*, pp. 391–3.
25 *HSWP Eighth Congress*, p. 579.
26 OL 288 f4/50 (August 12–14, 1962), p. 17.
27 Pető and Szakács, "Hungarian economy," p. 405.
28 *Ibid.*, p. 409.
29 Cf. Moshe Lewin, *Political Undercurrents in Soviet Economic Debates* (Princeton: Princeton University Press, 1974); Michael Gamarnikow, *Economic Reforms in Eastern Europe* (Detroit: Wayne State University Press, 1968).
30 László Szamuely, ed., *A magyar gazdasági gondolat fejlődése, 1954–1978* (The development of economic theories in Hungary, 1954–1978) (Budapest: Közgazdasági és Jogi Kiadó, 1986), pp. 57–154 and W. T. Robinson, *Pattern of Reform*, pp. 16–48.
31 Rezső Nyers, "Visszapillantás az 1968-as reformra" (A look back at the reforms of 1968), *Valóság* 31, 8 (1988), 11.
32 Rezső Nyers' loyalty to Kádár had been demonstrated on December 21, 1957, when he, too, voted at that meeting of the CC HSWP in favor of the leadership's proposal to "release" Imre Nagy from his *nomenklatura* immunity and hand him over to the Hungarian judiciary. On this, see Zoltán Ripp, ed., "Döntés a Nagy Imre csoport ügyében. A KB zárt ülése 1957 december 21-én" (Decision on the case of the Imre Nagy group. The closed session of the CC on December 21, 1957) *Multunk* 35, 4 (1990 [April, 1991]), 163–80.
33 *HSWP Decisions, 1963–1966*, pp. 94–109.
34 All quotes from this meeting will be taken from the original transcript, OL 288 f4/76 (November 18–20, 1965), rather than from the censored version of the Nyers report that appeared only in 1968.
35 OL 288 f4/76 (November 18–20, 1965), p. 75.
36 *Ibid.*, pp. 60–1.
37 *Ibid.*, pp. 65–78.
38 *Ibid.*, pp. 91–97.
39 *HSWP Decisions, 1963–1966*, pp. 233–64.
40 OL 288 f4/80 (May 25–27, 1966) and *HSWP Decisions, 1963–6*, pp. 301–450.
41 OL 288 f4/80, p. 32.
42 *Ibid.*, pp. 64–5.
43 The best source on this subject is W. T. Robinson, *Pattern of Reform*, and several Radio Free Europe (RFE) Research Reports authored by him between 1967 and 1972.
44 OL 288 f4/80, p. 96
45 OL 288 f4/76, p. 108.
46 *Magyarország Nemzeti Számlái. Főbb Mutatók, 1988–1990* (National Accounts, Hungary. Main Indicators, 1988–1990) (Budapest: Hungarian Central Statistical Office, 1992), p. 148.
47 Pető and Szakács, "Hungarian economy," p. 685.
48 Cited in Brus and Laski, *From Marx to Market*, p. 67.
49 Pető and Szakács, "Hungarian economy," p. 678.

50 *HSWP Decisions, 1963–1966*, p. 448.
51 See contributions by György Sik and Sándor Kopátsy to the NEM debates in Szamuely, "Economic Theories," pp. 429–39 and 500–5.
52 See *HSWP Decisions, 1967–1970*, pp. 138–40 and 451–5.
53 The practice of soliciting written comments from these bodies on the HSWP CC's "mid-term" and precongressional draft policy papers began in the mid-1960s and became a part of the predecisional consultative process on major policy items after 1972.
54 OL 288 f4/119 (November 14–15, 1972).
55 Cf. Judy Batt, *Economic Reform and Political Change in Eastern Europe* (New York: St. Martin's Press, 1988), pp. 267–75; and Iván T. Berend, *The Hungarian Economic Reforms, 1953–1988* (New York: Cambridge University Press, 1990), pp. 201–31.
56 On this see Jenő Fock's statement to the CC on the occasion of his resignation, for reasons of health, from the office of prime minister. OL 288 f4/138 (May 15, 1975), p. 42.
57 OL 288 f5/424 (May 9, 1967), p. 124.
58 *Ibid.*, pp. 41–3.
59 *Ibid.*, p. 38.
60 *Ibid.*, pp. 122–3.
61 OL 288 f4/102 (November 26–28, 1969), pp. 198–202.
62 My review of the Soviet press was through the issues of the *Current Digest of the Soviet Press*, for 1965–7.
63 For a review of Hungarian and Soviet commentaries in the Soviet press in 1968 and early 1969, see "Hungary's NEM: A Documentary of Soviet Views and Magyar Hopes," RFE *Research*, East Europe, Hungary/25 (May 30, 1969).
64 Vitézy, ed., "The jolliest barrack," p. 338.
65 Cited in William F. Robinson, "Hungarian–Soviet Relations: Reading the Signs," RFE *Research*, East Europe, Hungary/12 (July 14, 1972), p. 1.
66 *Ibid.*, p. 2.
67 Radio Budapest, March 29, 1972, as cited in Robinson, "Hungarian–Soviet Relations," p. 2.
68 For the text of Kádár's letters and the transcript of the June 15, 1972 secret CC meeting, see Koltay and Bródy, "Unburned documents," pp. 75–104. Thirteen years later, in the course of his first formal secretary general to secretary general meeting with Mikhail Gorbachev, Kádár admitted that he had sent a copy of his letter of resignation to Brezhnev. According to Kádár, "He was very upset. He did not like my reasoning. At our next meeting he angrily told me 'your Central Committee had been right.'" In "Dokumentum. Kádár János és M. Sz. Gorbacsov találkozója Moszkvában 1985. szeptember 25-én" (Document. [Transcript of] meeting between János Kádár and M. S. Gorbachev in Moscow on September 25, 1985), *Történelmi Szemle* 34, 1–2 (1992), 142.
69 Vitézy, ed., "The jolliest barrack," p. 315.
70 *Ibid.*, p. 313.

71 *Ibid.*, p. 320.
72 Katalin Ferber and Gábor Rejtő, eds., *Reform évfordulón* (Reform anniversary) (Budapest: Közgazdasági és Jogi Kiadó, 1988).
73 On this, please see Chapter 4.
74 The ideological platform of the "workers' opposition" was summarized in Béla Biszku's report on the "Situation of the working class" to the CC HSWP. OL 288 f4/125 (March 19–20, 1974), pp. 32–45 and 139–44. On Grósz's position see, Vitézy, "Interview with Károly Grósz," pp. 29–30.
75 Nyers, "A look back," p. 19.
76 *Ibid.*, pp. 19–20.
77 For Kádár's views on the HSWP's political-ideological dilemmas, see 288 f4/124 (November 28, 1973), pp. 9–47. For a rather different and, in my view more authentic, perspective on Kádár's ideological priorities, the following excerpt from his birthday speech of May 26, 1972 is of considerable interest. As Kádár explained,

> the relationship between Marxism–Leninism, socialism and communism does not consist of the fact that we possess an excellent theory that we are trying out, let's say, on 10 million guinea pigs, so that we can see if the theory is a good one and therefore must work. I believe that it is the other way around: Marxism–Leninism and the entire communist ideological system exist for the purpose of giving these 10 million Hungarians a better life. For, if it were not for this purpose, and if something were wrong in this respect, then we would not be doing a good job.
>
> Translation of text from the June 1972 issue of *Társadalmi Szemle*, in RFE *Research*, East Europe, June 23, 1972, p. 8.

78 Interview with Rezső Nyers, November 1984, Budapest.
79 OL 288 f4/125 (March 19–20, 1974).
80 OL 288 f4/137 (March 22, 1975).
81 Rumor and facts about the alleged "plot of 1977" are difficult to separate. Concerning Biszku, rumor had it that he prepared a long memorandum on corruption and poor leadership in the HSWP and tried to forward it to Brezhnev. The Hungarian ambassador to Moscow, József Marjai, intercepted the message and informed Kádár. Fact *and* rumor: the Soviets had attempted to approach Károly Németh (he promptly informed Kádár and was therefore absolved) and, as Béla Háry explained, later Biszku, by extending to him unspecified courtesies during his visits there, to which, in protocol terms, only a foreign first secretary was entitled. Vitézy, ed., "The jolliest barrack," pp. 328–9.

  In making the announcement on "cadre redeployment" to the CC, Kádár made oblique references to the matter by saying that "no one should try to present himself that he is a friend of the Soviet Union in a certain field" and that "no one should try to be more Catholic than the pope." 288 f4/156 (April 19–20, 1978), pp. 32, 81.
82 Paul Marer, "Hungary's Balance of Payments Crisis and Response, 1978–1984," in Hardt and Kaufman, eds., *East European Economies*, vol. III, p. 300.

83 Joan Parpart Zoeter, "Eastern Europe: The Hard Currency Debt," in John P. Hardt and Richard F. Kaufman, eds., *Eastern European Regional Assessment,* Part II. Regional Assessments. Joint Economic Committee, US Congress (Washington DC: USGPO, 1981), p. 720. The size of losses, due to adverse terms of trade with the USSR and CMEA trading partners was 6 billion Rubles between 1973 and 1983. On this, see Gábor Koltay and Péter Bródy, *Érdemei elismerése mellett: beszélgetések Havasi Ferenccel* (With the recognition of merits: conversations with Ferenc Havasi) (Budapest: Szabad Tér, 1989), p. 62.

84 By early 1977 it became obvious to Hungarian banking experts that, unless drastic remedial actions were taken, Hungary would not be able to service its Western indebtedness beyond 1979. A report to this effect was prepared by three senior managers of the Hungarian National Bank and forwarded to the National Planning Office and (several months later) from there to Ferenc Havasi, the recently appointed CC secretary for economic policy. After lengthy delays, Havasi finally gathered the courage to confront Kádár with this news. In the end, Kádár consented to the initiation of some of the recommended remedial measures. (Personal communication from Professor Tamás Bácskai, Budapest University for Economics and the Social Sciences, and former Vice President and Managing Director of the Hungarian National Bank.) See also, Rita Bozzai and Zoltán Farkas, eds., *Hitelválság: adósságunk története* (Credit crunch: the story of our indebtedness) (Budapest: Codex, 1991).

85 See Béla Balassa and Laura Tyson, "Policy Responses to External Shocks in Hungary and Yugoslavia: 1974–1976 and 1979–1981," in Hardt and Kaufman, eds., *East European Economies,* vol. I, pp. 57–80.

86 On the case of the fifty "priority enterprises," see Erzsébet Szalai, *Gazdasági mechanizmus, reformtörekvések és nagyvállalati érdekek* (Economic mechanism, reform endeavors and large enterprise interests) (Budapest: Közgazdasági és Jogi Kiadó, 1989), pp. 27–67. For data on the demographic, political, and educational attributes of the full-time party apparat in 1976, see OL 288 f5/ 523 (July 28, 1977), pp. 64–8. For data on party member executives in industry, agriculture, and public administration, see OL 288 f5/714 (March 22, 1977), p. 49.

87 One way of measuring the importance the regime attached to "scientific and cultural workers" might be by considering the size of the quota of government honors and medals that the PB assigned to people belonging to this occcupational cluster. Of the 5,500 medals awarded by the Presidential Council in 1978 for meritorious contributions in all fields to the building of socialism in Hungary, the intellectuals' share was 5.5 percent. Those in "economic fields" were allocated 50.2 percent and cadres in the party and the mass organizations 21.8 percent. OL 288 f5/733 (December 13, 1977), p. 22.

88 OL 288 f5/722 (July 2, 1977), pp. 36–49.

89 *Ibid.,* p. 49.

90 OL 288 f4/156 (April 19–20, 1978), pp. 33, 36.

91 *HSWP Decisions, 1975–1980,* p. 765.
92 Much of the decision-making scenario described below is based on two studies, one unpublished and one published, by Judit Fekete, "Puccsszerü döntéshozatal és jogszabályalkotás" (*Putsch*-style decision- and rule-making) (Budapest, January, 1988) and *Adalékok a kisvállalkozás jelenségrend-szeréhez* (Data on the phenomenon of small enterprises) (Budapest: Social Science Institute, CC, HSWP, 1984). I am grateful to Dr. Fekete, formerly of the Department of Political Science, Faculty of Law, The Loránd Eötvös University, Budapest, for sharing the results of her case studies with me.
93 Cf. István Latos, ed., *Szervezeti kérdések a Magyar Szocialista Munkáspártban* (Organizational questions in the Hungarian Socialist Workers' Party) (Budapest: Kossuth, 1984).
94 See Rudolf L. Tőkés, "Hungarian Reform Imperatives," *Problems of Communism* 33, 7 (1984), 3–24.

3   Social change

1 Mary E. McIntosh and Martha Abele MacIver, "Coping with Freedom and Uncertainty: Public Opinion in Hungary, Poland and Czechoslovakia, 1989–1992," *International Journal of Public Opinion Research* 4, 4, (1992), 375–91; William Mishler and Richard Rose, *Trajectories of Fear and Hope: The Dynamics of Support for Democracy in Eastern Europe* (Glasgow: Centre for the Study of Public Policy, University of Strathclyde, 1993).
2 Piotr Sztompka, "The Intangibles and Imponderables of the Transition to Democracy," *Studies in Comparative Communism* 24, 3 (1981), 295–312.
3 Linda J. Cook, *The Soviet Social Contract and Why It Failed* (Cambridge, MA: Harvard University Press, 1993), p. 3.
4 *Ibid.,* pp. 6ff.
5 In a substantive sense, the particulars of the "subcontracts" composed the essential agenda on interest-group politics in communist states. This proposition does not deny the importance of *policy* priorities that interest groups might choose to promote from time to time, but calls attention to the underlying, most often "bread-and-butter" issues of group autonomy and related demands for the enhanced redistribution by the party and state of various material (investments and subsidies) and nonmaterial (medals, prizes, foreign travel, and so on) benefits and privileges for the members and the wider constituencies of such groups.
6 Daniel Lerner, "Modernization, Social Aspects," in Sills, ed., *IESS* vol. X, p. 387.
7 Cf. George Barany, "Hungary: From Aristocratic to Proletarian Nationalism," in Peter F. Sugár and Ivo J. Lederer, eds., *Nationalism in Eastern Europe* (Seattle: University of Washington Press, 1969), pp. 259–309.
8 See George Schopflin, *Politics in Eastern Europe* (Oxford: Blackwell, 1993), pp. 66–8.
9 *Hungarian Statistical Yearbook, 1990* (Budapest: Central Statistical Office, 1991), pp. 29–30.

10 Rudolf Andorka and Tamás Kolosi, eds., *Stratification and Inequality* (Budapest: HSWP Institute for the Social Sciences, 1984), p. 288.

11 Iván Szelényi *et al.*, *Socialist Entrepreneurs*, especially pp. 78–90.

12 Gábor Vági, *Magunk, uram: válogatott irások a településekről, tanácsokról, önkormányzatról* (It is up to us, kind Sir: selected writings on settlements, local councils and self-government) (Budapest: Gondolat, 1991).

13 See Paul Shoup, ed., *The East European and Soviet Data Handbook: Political, Social and Developmental Indicators, 1945–1975* (New York: Columbia University Press, 1981).

14 *Hungarian Statistical Yearbook, 1990* (Budapest: Central Statistical Office, 1991), pp. 56–7.

15 *Magyarorszag 1985. Statisztikai évkönyv* (Hungarian statistical yearbook, 1985) (Budapest: KSH, 1985), p. 16.

16 *Népesség és társadalomstatisztikai zsebkönyv* (Demographic and social statistical handbook) (Budapest: KSH, 1987), p. 255.

17 Tamás Kolosi, *Tagolt Társadalom* (Stratified society) (Budapest: Gondolat, 1987), p. 315.

18 See János Pelle, *A diplomák inflációja* (Diploma inflation) (Budapest: Gondolat, 1986).

19 Cf. Hungarian Central Statistical Office, *Foglalkoztatottság és kereseti arányok, 1982, 1983, 1984* (Employment and income ratios, 1982, 1983, 1984) (Budapest: KSH, 1985).

20 The ultimate "micromanager" was Kádár himself. Most of his concluding comments at PB meetings with social and economic policy items on the agenda were divided between exhortations on the absolute necessity of improving living standards and expressions of doubt about the factual accuracy of policy submissions on these matters.

21 Thad Alton *et al.*, "Money Income of the Population and Standard of Living in Eastern Europe, 1970–1982" (New York: International Financial Research, Inc., 1983), cited in Elizabeth M. Clayton, "Consumption, Living Standards, and Consumer Welfare in Eastern Europe," in Hardt and Kaufman, eds., *East European Economies* vol. I, p. 253.

22 Mária Rédei *et al.*, "A fiatalok anyagi-jövedelmi és lakáshelyzete" (Young people's income and housing situation), in Zoltán Békés, ed., *A magyar ifjuság a nyolcvanas években* (Hungarian youth in the 1980s) (Budapest: Kossuth, 1984), p. 155.

23 See Tamás Kolosi, "Az ipari dolgozók életkörülményeinek néhány eleme" (Certain aspects of the industrial workers' living conditions), in Tamás Kolosi, *Struktura és egyenlőtlenség* (Structure and inequality) (Budapest: Kossuth, 1983), p. 236.

24 Mária Rédei *et al.*, "Young people's income," p. 164.

25 On the travails of private housing construction in Hungary, see János Kenedi, *Do It Yourself: Hungary's Hidden Economy* (London: Pluto Press, 1986).

26 Iván Szelényi, *Városi társadalmi egyenlőtlenségek* (Urban social inequalities) (Budapest: Akadémiai Kiadó, 1990), p. 62.

27 Mária Rédei et al., "Young people's income," p. 162.
28 Ágnes Vajda and János E. Farkas, "Housing," in Rudolf Andorka, Tamás Kolosi, and György Vukovich, eds., Social Report, 1990 (Budapest: TARKI, 1992) (Hereinafter SR '90), p. 93.
29 National Accounts, Hungary 1988–1990 (Budapest: Central Statistical Office, 1992), pp. 152–3.
30 György Vukovich, "Health," in SR '90, p. 125. See also, Nicholas Eberstadt, "Health and Mortality in Eastern Europe, 1965 to 1985," in John P. Hardt and Richard F. Kaufman, eds., Pressures for Reform in the East European Economies vol. I. Joint Economic Committee, US Congress (Washington DC: USGPO, 1989), pp. 97–119.
31 Hungarian Statistical Yearbook, 1990, p. 236.
32 Cf. Ágnes Losonczy, A kiszolgáltatottság anatómiája az egészségügyben (The anatomy of dependency and the delivery of health services) (Budapest: Magvető, 1986).
33 Ágnes Bokor, Szegénység a mai Magyarországon (Poverty in Hungary today) (Budapest: Magvető, 1987), p. 35.
34 Ibid., p. 47.
35 Rudolf Andorka et al., Társadalmi beilleszkedési zavarok Magyarországon (Disturbances in social adaptation in Hungary) (Budapest: Kossuth, 1988), p. 44.
36 SR '90, p. 146 and Hungarian Statistical Yearbook, 1990, p. 246.
37 Tamás Kolosi, Struktura és egyenlőtlenség (Structure and inequality) (Budapest: Kossuth, 1983), p. 125.
38 Antal Örkény, "A társadalmi mobilitás történelmi perspektivái" (Historic perspectives on social mobility), Valóság 22, 4 (1989), 24.
39 Walter D. Connor, Socialism, Politics and Equality: Hierarchy and Change in Eastern Europe and the USSR (New York: Columbia University Press, 1979), p. 139.
40 Márta Szénai, "Az ifjúság helyzete az oktatás tükrében," in Ifjúság és társadalom: tanulmányok (Youth and society: studies) (Budapest: KSH, 1985), pp. 92–3.
41 Ibid., p. 90.
42 Kolosi, "Structure and inequality," p. 153.
43 Rudolf Andorka, A társadalmi mobilitás változásai Magyarországon (Changes in social mobility in Hungary) (Budapest: Gondolat, 1982).
44 R. Andorka, I. Harcsa, R. Kulcsár, and A. Motoricz, "A társadalmi mobilitás alakulása és összefüggése a társadalom szerkezetével" (Trends in social mobility and linkages with social mobility), in Tibor Halay, ed., Rétegződés, mobilitás és egyenlőtlenség (Stratification, mobility and inequality) (Budapest: Institute for the Social Sciences, 1979), p. 33.
45 Péter Róbert, "Social Mobility," in SR '90, pp. 251–2.
46 Szelényi, Socialist Entrepreneurs, pp. 146–58. The main findings of a 1992 national survey on social mobility tend to confirm most of these generalized statements on the dynamics of social mobility between 1973 and 1983. However, what the 1992 survey shows quite conclusively is that the year

1983 marked the exhaustion of NEM-generated mobility opportunities for most wage earners. From 1983 on, it was mainly those who were linked to the second economy who experienced economic gains but no changes in terms of status and occupational mobility. See also E. Büködi, I. Harcsa, and L. Reisz, ed., *Társadalmi tagozódas, mobilitás az 1992 évi mobilitás vizsgálat alapján* (Social stratification and mobility: a summary of results of a 1992 national survey) (Budapest: Központi Statisztikai Hivatal, 1994).

47 Milovan Djilas, *New Class* (New York: Praeger, 1957). See also Zygmunt Bauman "Officialdom and Class: Bases of Inequality in Socialist Society," in Frank Parkin, ed., *The Social Analysis of Class Structure* (London: Tavistock, 1972), pp. 129–48, and Alvin Gouldner, *The Future of Intellectuals and the Rise of New Class* (New York: Seaburg, 1979).

48 Cf. Ted Robert Gurr, *When Men Rebel and Why* (Princeton: Princeton University Press, 1971), pp. 22–122; Gerald E. Lenski, *Power and Prestige* (New York: McGraw Hill, 1966), pp. 87–8; Tamás Kolosi, "Státus csoportok és életmód" (Status groups and way of life), in Miklós Szántó, ed., *Hogyan Élünk?* (The way we live) (Budapest: Közgazdasági és Jogi Kiadó, 1984), p. 177; and Tamás Kolosi, "A státusinkonszisztencia mérése" (The measurement of status inconsistency), *Szociológia* 1 (1987), 1–20.

49 The issues were addressed in four sets of publications. These included: (a) nine volumes of studies on "models of stratification," published between 1984 and 1988 under the general editorship of Tamás Kolosi; (b) three volumes of studies on the "development of the social structure of Hungary," published in 1981, under the general editorship of Tibor Halay; (c) twelve research bulletins, with several studies in each, on the "transformation of social structure, way of life and consensus in Hungary," published between 1983 and 1985; and (d) several major monographs and topical symposia on social mobility, social stratification, inequality, and the second economy that were published in the 1980s.

50 András Klinger, "Az osztály és a rétegszervezet változásai" (Changes in the structure of classes and strata), in Tibor Halay and Tamás Kolosi, eds., *Társadalom, szerkezet és rétegződes* (Society, structure and stratification) (Budapest: Kossuth, 1982), p. 188.

51 Kolosi, "Stratified society," pp. 242–3.

52 Ágnes Utassi, "Life styles, demand levels and Hungarian elite," in Rudolf Andorka and Tamás Kolosi, eds., *Stratification and Inequalities* (Budapest: HSWP CC Institute for the Social Sciences, 1984), pp. 152ff.

53 Kolosi, "Stratified society," p. 153.

54 *SR '90*, pp. 223–4. See also Tamás Kolosi, "Status and Stratification," in Rudolf Andorka and Tamás Kolosi, eds., *Stratification and Inequality* (Budapest: HSWP CC Institute for the Social Sciences, 1984), p. 55, and Kolosi, "Stratified society," p. 130.

55 See note 48 above.

56 István Harcsa and Rózsa Kulcsár, *Társadalmi Mobilitás és Presztizs* (Social mobility and prestige) (Budapest: Központi Statisztikai Hivatal, 1986), pp. 373–5.

57 William H. Form, "Occupations and careers," in Sills, ed., *IESS* vol. XI, p. 247.
58 Harcsa and Kulcsár, "Social mobility," p. 87.
59 OL 288 f5/714 (March 22, 1977), p. 47; *HSWP Twelfth Congress*, pp. 9–11 and *HSWP Thirteenth Congress*, pp. 9–11.
60 OL 288 f5/622 (October 23, 1973), pp. 88–9.
61 Department of Party and Mass Organizations, CC, HSWP, "Statistics on party membership according to current occupation, 1974, 1975, 1976," OL 288 f5/714 (March 22, 1977), p. 48.
62 The most perceptive pathologies on the quality of Hungarian public administration may be found in István Bibó's writings on this subject. See István Bibó, "A magyar közigazgatásról II. (Jellegzetes kórformák) (On Hungarian public administration – typical pathologies) and "A magyar közigazgatási reform problémái" (Reforming Hungarian public adminis-tration – issues and problems), in István Kemény and Mátyás Sárközi, eds., *István Bibó összegyüjtött munkái* vol. II (István Bibó, collected works) (Berne: EPMSZ, 1981), pp. 658–64 and 673–94. See also László Belley, "A szocialista bürokráciáról" (On socialist bureaucracy), *Szociológia* 3–4 (1989), 221–36 and Gábor Vági, "Az iróasztalok túloldalán" (On the other side of the desk), in Vági, "It is up to us," pp. 441–62.
63 Data on then-current disciplinary action against those in the executive category of state administration are in the survey "Hungarian Executives and Top Managers in the 1980s." Data are on disks at the Institute of Social Inquiry, the University of Connecticut, Storrs.
64 Data on Hungarian *nomenklatura* elites in the 1980s have been derived from (a) extracts from the 1980 and 1990 census in István Harcsa, Ferenc Kesedi, János Kisdi, and Miklós Lakatos, *Vezetők a nyolcvanas években* (Hungarian executives and top managers in the 1980s) (Budapest: Központi Statisz-tikai Hivatal, 1991), pp. 9–18; (b) data (basic distribution tables) and commentary by István Harcsa *et al.* on the results of three surveys (commissioned by the Department of PA, CC, HSWP and the Executive Secretariat of the Council of Ministers and administered by the National Statistical Office in 1983, 1985, and 1987) on the Hungarian *nomenklatura* elites with samples of 14,000 to 15,000 each; (c) my calculations from the data base; and (d) data and secondary analysis of results of two surveys (1981, 1989) on full-time HSWP officials by Ferenc Gazsó, published as "Cadre Bureaucracy and the Intelligentsia" in a symposium, Rudolf L. Tőkés, ed., "Hungary: Anatomy of a Party-State," *Journal of Communist Studies* 8, 3 (1992), 76–90.
    I am indebted to Dr. György Vukovich, president, The Hungarian Central Statistical Office; Dr. István Harcsa, head, Main Department of Social Statistics, HCSO; Mr. János Kisdi, MDSS, HCSO; and Professor Ferenc Gazsó, Department of Sociology, Budapest University for Eco-nomics and the Social Sciences, for their help with the acquisition and interpretation of the Hungarian *nomenklatura* survey. Mr. Tamás Fellegi, a former graduate student at the Department of Political Science, University

of Connecticut, provided assistance with the recoding and with the preparation of cross-tables from this material.

65 The elite survey (described above), however useful, is incomplete in several respects. Whereas it includes 219 and 142 (!) parliamentary deputies in 1983 and 1987 as evidence of "social activity" by members of this sample, possible membership in the CC, HSWP was not among the questions asked. Government ministers, members of the Presidential Council, and the Hungarian Academy of Sciences were not included in the survey. Moreover, there are no data on the top military, police, internal security, and foreign service personnel. For example, the inclusion of all members of the Parliament would have necessitated the consideration of much of the HSWP Politburo, including János Kádár. Data on these power elites were kept in the Department of PMO, CC, HSWP and are still unavailable for scrutiny.

66 Harcsa et al., "Hungarian executives," p. 17.

67 Ibid., pp. 23–4. On the specific occupational components, such as job titles, of each cluster see Appendix 3.1.

68 Ibid., pp. 55–6.

69 Vitézy, "Interview with Károly Grósz," p. 90.

70 Gazsó, "Cadre Bureaucracy."

71 Ibid., p. 87.

72 Ibid., p. 86.

73 Congress '89, 23 (October 6, 1989).

74 György Konrád and Iván Szelényi, The Intellectuals on the Road to Class Power (New York: Harcourt Brace Jovanovich, 1979).

75 Zygmunt Bauman, "Intellectuals in East-Central Europe: Continuity and Change," EEPS 1, 2 (1987), p. 174.

76 The travails of former expert advisors to policy-makers are well described in a volume of in-depth interviews in József Farkas, Szürke zóna (Grey zone) (Budapest: Társadalmi Konfliktusok Kutató Központja, 1992).

77 Harry Eckstein, "On the Etiology of Internal Wars," History and Theory 4, 2 (1965), 133–63.

78 Csaba Gombár, Boritékolt politika (On politics) (Budapest: Pénzügyi Kutató, RT., 1989), p. 12.

79 Elemér Hankiss, East European Alternatives (Oxford: Clarendon Press, 1990), pp. 82–111.

80 Ibid., p. 87.

4 Opposition

1 For a typology of dissident interest articulation, see Rudolf L. Tőkés, "Varieties of Soviet Dissent: An Overview," in Rudolf L. Tőkés, ed., Dissent in the USSR (Baltimore and London: The Johns Hopkins University Press, 1974), pp. 11–16.

2 Frederick C. Barghoorn, "Factional, Sectoral and Subversive Opposition in Soviet Politics," in Robert A. Dahl, ed., Regimes and Oppositions (New Haven: Yale University Press, 1973), p. 39.

3 George Schopflin, "Opposition and Para-Opposition: Critical Currents in Hungary," in Rudolf L. Tőkés, ed., *Opposition in Eastern Europe* (London: Macmillan, 1979), pp. 142–86.

4 Rudolf L. Tőkés, "Dissent: The Politics for Change in the USSR," in Henry W. Morton and Rudolf L. Tőkés, eds., *Soviet Society and Politics in the 1970s* (New York: Free Press, 1974), p. 31.

5 Robert A. Dahl, *Polyarchy* (New Haven: Yale University Press, 1971), p. 15.

6 See András Vágvölgyi, "A falu társadalmi strukturájának és a falusi életmódnak a változásai" (Changes in the the way of life and social structure of villages. A preliminary research report on a subject recommended by the Department of AP, CC, HSWP) (Directors of research: Iván Szelényi and Győző [*sic*] Manchin) (Budapest: Institute of Sociology, HAS, 1974) in OL 288 f22/1974/49, pp. 1–111; Department of Economic Policy, CC, HSWP, "Memorandum on the Activities of the Consultative Committee at the CC's Committee for Economic Policy, June 23, 1988," in Gábor Koltay and Péter Bródy, *Érdemei elismerése mellett ... beszélgetések Havasi Ferenccel* (With the recognition of his merits ... conversations with Ferenc Havasi) (Budapest: Szabad Tér, 1989), pp. 220–7.

7 See Rudolf L. Tőkés, "The Czechoslovak Invasion and the Hungarian Intellectuals," in E. Czerwinski and J. Piekalkiewicz, eds., *The Soviet Invasion of Czechoslovakia: Its Effects on Eastern Europe* (New York: Praeger, 1972), pp. 139–58.

8 Miklós Haraszti, *A Worker in a Worker's State: Piece-Rates in Hungary* (New York: Penguin Books, 1977).

9 OL 288 f4/124 (November 28, 1973), pp. 38–40.

10 In his report to the CC on his recent audience with the pope, Kádár was pleased to convey the Vatican's approval of the Hungarian regime's management of church–state relations, including the active role of László Cardinal Lékai in the work of the PPF. See OL 288 f4/150 (June 22, 1977), pp. 65–8. See also "Open letter of Catholic priests to Cardinal Lékai" (October 13, 1983), in *Hirmondó* 4 (1984), 37.

11 Levente Sipos, "MSZMP dokumentum az ellenzékröl, 1980-ból" (A HSWP document on the opposition, 1980), *Társadalmi Szemle*, May 1992, p. 82.

12 Among the Hungarian dissidents it was mainly Miklós Haraszti, a superb investigative journalist, who reported on police affairs and on cases involving the involuntary psychiatric confinement of local troublemakers in provincial cities and towns of Hungary. See Miklós Haraszti, "Politikai pszichiátria Magyarországon" (Political psychiatry in Hungary), *Magyar Füzetek* (Paris) 1 (1982), 73–82.

13 *Magyar Nemzet*, September 8, 1957.

14 Tibor Gyurkovics, "Mi ellen tiltakozott 216 magyar iró 1957-ben?" (Against what did 216 Hungarian writers protest in 1957?), *Uj Idő* 1, 3 (1989), 4–8.

15 For a detailed, albeit partisan, history of the Populist movement, see Gyula Borbándi, *A magyar népi mozgalom* (The Hungarian Populist movement) (New York: Puski, 1983).

16 On the genesis of Populist ideologies, see Rudolf L. Tőkés, "The 'Third

Road' – Three Case Studies on Hungarian Populist Ideologies" (Master's thesis, Columbia University, 1961), and Éva Kovács, "Indulatok a népi-urbánus vitában" (Passions in the Populist-urbanist dispute), *2000* 6, 8 (1994), 15–22.

17 *HSWP Decisions 1956–1962*, pp. 196–223.

18 László Németh, "Ha én miniszter lennék. Levél egy kulturpolitikushoz" (If I were a minister. Letter to a cultural politician) *Valóság* 29, 6 (1986), 1–45. In 1973 Németh gave Aczél the original manuscript as a Christmas present with the dedication: "To György Aczél, my old friend in agreements and in disagreements, with fondest regards. László Németh," *ibid.*, p. 45.

19 Interviews with András Hegedüs, October–December, 1984, Budapest. See also András Hegedüs, *Élet egy eszme árnyékában* (Life in the shadow of an ideology) (Vienna: Zoltán Zsille, 1985).

20 András Hegedüs, *A történelem és a hatalom igézetében* (Under the spell of history and power) (Budapest: Kossuth, 1988), especially pp. 333–52.

21 Of the vast amount of secondary literature on Lukács, I found three works to be particularly useful. Mary Gluck, *George Lukacs and His Generation, 1910–1918* (Cambridge, MA: Harvard University Press, 1985); Andrew Arato and Paul Breines, *The Young Lukacs and the Origins of Western Marxism* (New York: The Seabury Press, 1979); George Lichtheim, *George Lukacs* (New York: The Viking Press, 1970).

22 Yet, none of this prevented him from saying, "in my opinion, even the worst socialism is better than the best capitalism" (*Népszabadság*, December 24, 1967), and from giving highly contradictory interviews on Marxism and on his constantly shifting private beliefs.

23 Iván Szelényi, "Notes on the Budapest School," *Critique* (Glasgow) 8 (1977), 67.

24 Ervin Csizmadia, "Kis János – A Filozófia Intézettől a *Beszélő* szer-kesztőségéig" (János Kis – from the Philosophy Institute to the editorial offices of *Beszélő*. An interview), *Valóság* 31, 12 (1988), 88–108. See also Miklós Gáspár Tamás, "Ecsetvonások Kis János arcképéhez" (Brush strokes for a portrait of János Kis) in Miklós Gáspár Tamás, *Másvilág: politikai esszék* (Otherworld: political essays) (Budapest: Uj Mandátum Kiadó, 1994), pp. 326–36.

25 György Bence, János Kis, and György Márkus, *Hogyan lehetséges kritikai gazdaságtan?* (How can there be a critical [political] economy?" (Budapest: Samizdat, 1970–2). I am indebted to Professor György Bence for his gift of one of the original copies of this manuscript.

26 Csizmadia, "János Kis," p. 97.

27 OL 288 f22/1973/45, pp. 27–31, 37–59.

28 Marc Rakovski (pseud. for György Bence and János Kis), *A szovjet tipusu társadalom marxista szemmel* (Soviet-type society from a Marxist perspective) (Budapest: Samizdat, 1981), p. 200. This text does not appear in the English-language version of this work. Cf. Marc Rakovski, *Towards an East European Marxism* (New York: St. Martin's Press, 1978).

29 Csizmadia, "János Kis," p. 101.

30 Personal communication from Professor George Schopflin, November 1994.
31 János Kenedi, "Emberekről, eszmékről, politikáról" (Of people, ideas and politics), *Valóság* 33, 4 (1990), 33–51.
32 Collections of "unpublishable" writings was the preferred format of samizdat publication in the late 1970s. See *Marx a negyvenes években* (Marx in the forties); *Profil*; and *0.1%*. I am indebted to Professor János Kis for his gift of several volumes of samizdat writings from 1977 to 1982.
33 In the absence of a full-scale intellectual biography, Zoltán Szabó's introductory essay on Bibó's life in István Kemény and Mátyás Sárközi, eds., *István Bibó összegyűjtött munkái* (István Bibó, collected works), 4 vols. (Berne: EPSZM, 1981) vol. I, pp. 8–35 is an excellent substitute.
34 See, "Bibó István 1911–1979," Special Memorial Issue of *Magyar Füzetek* (Paris) 4 (1979).
35 Ferenc Donáth *et al.*, eds., *Bibó Emlékkönyv* (Bibó Memorial Book) (Budapest: Samizdat, 1980).
36 In a 57-page evaluation, "H.T." [Professor Tibor Huszár], the publisher's politically reliable expert reader, was in favor of publication after the omission of several controversial chapters. See OL 288 f22/1981/46, pp. 224–81.
37 The text of the report from which this is cited was available until late 1994 in the Hungarian archives of Radio Free Europe's Research Division in Munich.
38 OL 288 f5/815 (December 9, 1980).
39 Above the journal's masthead a frame resembling iron bars over the window of a prison cell was superimposed over the word "Beszélő." In this visual context the meaning of "beszélő" was not "speaker" but that of the occasion for a supervised conversation between a prison inmate and a visitor. Between 1981 and 1989 twenty-seven samizdat issues of the journal appeared. In late 1989 *Beszélő* went public as a weekly journal of liberal opinion. Material cited from *Beszélő* will be from Fanny Havas *et al.*, eds., *Beszélő összkiadás, 1981–1989* (*Beszélő* – annotated edition, 1981–1989), 3 vols. (Budapest: AB Beszélő Kiadó, 1992) (cited hereafter as *Annotated Beszélő*).
40 *Annotated Beszélő* vol. I, 1 (1981), pp. 11–12.
41 Miklós Haraszti, "A helsinki giccs" (The Helsinki *Kitsch*) *Annotated Beszélő*, vol. II, 15 (1985), pp. 272–4.
42 *Annotated Beszélő* vol. I, 9 (1982), pp. 551–7.
43 János Kis, "A reformtól a továbbfejlesztésig vagy a reformig?" (Toward the "further development" of reforms, or toward [real] reforms?) *Annotated Beszélő* vol. I, 10 (1984), pp. 590–4.
44 For comprehensive coverage, from the dissidents' viewpoint, of the 1985 elections, see *Választási Almanach, 1985* (Electoral Almanac, 1985) (Budapest: Samizdat, 1985).
45 "Electoral Almanac", pp. 153ff.
46 The text of the major presentations and comments by designated discus-

sants is in *Monori tanácskozás, 1985 junius 14–16* (The Monor conference, June 14–16, 1985) (Budapest: Samizdat, 1985).

47 *Ibid.*, p. 57.

48 *Ibid.*, p. 64.

49 Mihály Bihari, "Reform és demokrácia" (Reform and democracy), *Társadalomkutatás* 2 (1986), 108.

50 Csaba Gombár and László Lengyel, "A társadalmi reform kérdéseihez" (On the questions of social reform), *Társadalomkutatás* 1 (1986), 98.

51 George Konrád and Iván Szelényi, *Intellectuals*.

52 Some of the most important titles were Mihály Bihari, *Politikai rendszer és szocialista demokrácia* (Political system and socialist democracy) (Department of Scientific Socialism, Faculty of Law, University of Budapest, 1985); István Csillag and László Lengyel, *Vállalkozás, állam, társadalom* (Enterprise, state, society) (Budapest: Közgazdasági és Jogi Kiadó, 1985); Zsuzsa Ferge, *Társadalom-politikai tanulmányok* (Studies on social policies) (Budapest: Gondolat, 1980); Csaba Gombár, *Egy állapolgár gondolatai* (Thoughts of a citizen) (Budapest: Kossuth, 1984); János Kornai, *Contradictions and Dilemmas: Studies on the Socialist Economy and Society* (Budapest: Corvina, 1985); Tamás Sárközy, *Egy gazdasági szervezeti reform sodrában* (In the midst of reforms of the economic structure) (Budapest: Magvető, 1986).

53 Mihály Bihari, "Politikai kultúra és demokratikus reformok" (Political culture and democratic reforms), *Társadalomkutatás* 2 (1985), 50–63.

54 On this, see speeches by János Kádár, Károly Grósz, and György Lázár at the Hungarian party's 13th congress in March 1985 in *HSWP Thirteenth Congress*, pp. 183–201 and 552–64, 210–17 and 263–71.

55 See Csaba Gombár, "Demokratikus rendezőelvek" (Democratic organizing principles) in György Szoboszlai *et al.*, eds., *Anarchizmus és rendezőelvek* (Anarchism and organizing principles) (Yearbook of the Hungarian Political Science Association, 1986) (Budapest: HPSA, 1986), pp. 5–19.

56 Csaba Gombár, "A helyi hatalom hermeneutikája" (The hermeneutics of local power), in Gombár, "Thoughts of a citizen," pp. 32–47.

57 Géza Kilényi, "A kormányzati tevékenység továbbfejlesztéséről" (On the further development of governing functions) *Társadalmi Szemle* 8–9 (1987), 54–63.

58 Csaba Gombár, "A demokrácia kérdéseiről" (On the questions of democracy), in Gombár, "Thoughts of a citizen," pp. 139–96.

59 Z. Breitner, "Jogállamiságért" (For a *Rechtsstaat*), *Figyelő*, October 8, 1987, p. 22.

60 These points were made most sharply in "Social contract," pp. 13ff.

61 OL 288 f5/972 (July 1, 1986), pp. 107–107/c/1.

62 Interview with György Aczél, June 1988, Budapest.

63 Zoltán Biró, *Elhervadt forradalom* (The withered revolution) (Budapest: Püski, 1993), pp. 9–10.

64 *Ibid.*, p. 11.

65 János Kenedi, "Of people, ideas and politics," p. 42.

66 The conference proceedings were first published in samizdat as *Lakitelek*.

1987 szeptember 27. A magyarság esélyei (Lakitelek, September 27, 1987. Hungary's chances) (Budapest, 1987) and later in printed form by Püski Publishers in 1993.
67 *Ibid.*, p. 12. Except as indicated, the following citations will be taken from the samizdat version.
68 *Ibid.*, pp. 22ff.
69 *Ibid.*, p. 75.
70 *Ibid.*, p. 147.
71 *Ibid.*, p. 132.
72 *Ibid.*, pp. 177–8 (book version).
73 *Ibid.*, p. 364 (samizdat version).
74 Biró, "The withered revolution," pp. 16ff.
75 Interview with Károly Grósz, May 1994, Gödöllő.
76 June 1987 (samizdat).
77 *Ibid.*, pp. 4–5.
78 *Ibid.*, pp. 52–3.
79 *HSWP Resolutions, 1980–1985*, p. 859.
80 *Népszabadság*, April 9, 1988.
81 Zoltán Ács, ed., *Kizárt a párt* (Expelled from the party) (Budapest: Primo, 1988).
82 László Lengyel, "Adalékok a Fordulat és Reform történetéhez" (Background to the history of Turnabout and Reform), *Medvetánc*, Supplement to No. 2 (1987), 137.
83 *Ibid.*, pp. 140–1.
84 The work appeared both in samizdat and in a printed version. For the latter, see *Medvetánc* 2 (1987), 5–46.
85 "Fordulat és reform" (Turnabout and reform). This is a truncated and partly rewritten version with a preface by Establishment economists. *Közgazdasági Szemle* 6 (1987).
86 Ács, "Expelled from," pp. 63–124.
87 Mihály Bihari, *Reform és demokrácia*, (Reform and democracy) (Budapest: Institute of Sociology, HAS, August, 1987) (Manuscript).
88 Zoltán Biró, *Saját ut* (My road) (Budapest: Eötvös Kiadó, 1988).
89 Ács, "Expelled from," pp. 127–80 and Biró, "The withered revolution," pp. 21–2.
90 "Expelled from," pp. 185–255.
91 On March 18, 1988, Professor Mihály Bihari invited me to join him at the informal monthly meeting of critical Budapest intellectuals in the home of Dr. László Levendel. (Dr. Levendel, a reform socialist advocate of public health and environmental issues, had been hosting such gatherings since the mid-1980s.) That evening's program included the reading of a paper by Miklós Szabó (a historian and the founder of the "Flying University" of the late 1970s) on *glasnost'* in Eastern Europe and a freewheeling discussion by the guests. The latter included Rezső Nyers, Szilárd Ujhelyi (one of Imre Nagy's surviving codefendants), Sándor Csoóri, János Kis, the prominent historian Péter Hanák, and others. (Pozsgay intended to come, but had

other commitments that evening.) At the end, Kis – one of the public speakers three days earlier at the March 15 demonstration – gave a concise account of the events of that day. The guests' businesslike discourse and crisp analysis of the issues gave me the feeling that I was in the presence of Hungary's next postcommunist leadership. On Dr. Levendel, see László Levendel, *A túlélő* (The survivor) (Budapest: Főnix Alapitvány, 1993).

92 OL 288 f4/198 (April 17, 1984), p. 153.
93 Some of these may be found in Bihari, "Reform and democracy."
94 OL 288 f4/190 (April 17, 1984), p. 36.

5 Party elites in transition

1 See István Bodzabán and Antal Szalay, eds., *A puha diktaturától a kemény demokráciáig* (From soft dictatorship to tough democracy) (Budapest: Pelikán Kiadó, 1994).

2 Letter from Károly Grósz, April 1994. The term *in petto* is mine, and it refers to the pope's prerogative to name new cardinals without formally advising the affected individual. Thus, the nomination is held *in petto*.

3 On this, see Mária Csanádi, "A döntési mechanizmus szerkezetéről" (On the structure of decisional mechanisms) *Társadalomkutatás* 4 (1987), 5–26.

4 Gyula Horn, *Cölöpök* (Pillars. Memoirs) (Budapest: Zenit Könyvek, 1991), p. 14.

5 Lajos Czinege, the longest-serving (1960–84) Hungarian minister of defense in history, may have been an exception. Apparently, the Soviets liked him and so did Kádár – for different reasons. See Imre Bokor, *Kiskirályok mundérban* (Petty tyrants in uniform) (Budapest: Uj Idő Kft., 1989).

6 On the history of generational clashes in the Hungarian party see Rudolf L. Tőkés, *Béla Kun and the Hungarian Soviet Republic* (Stanford, CA: The Hoover Institution Press, 1967); György Borsányi, *Kun Béla: egy politikai életrajz*, (Béla Kun: a political biography) (Budapest: Kossuth, 1979); Pál Demény, *A párt foglya voltam* (I was the party's prisoner) (Budapest: Medvetánc, 1988); Pál Demény, *Zárkatársam, Spinoza* (My cellmate, Spinoza) (Budapest: Akadémiai Kiadó, 1989).

7 Mária Tamáska (1912–91) was Kádár's second (?) (whether his relationship with a fellow underground party activist Piroska Döme had been formalized by way of marriage is unclear) wife and Kádár was her second husband. They met in 1943 when Kádár was a lodger in her and her first husband's apartment and were married in 1947. Prior to Kádár's arrest she had worked in the Ministry of Interior and held the rank of captain in the political police (AVH). From the 1960s until her retirement in 1981 she worked as head of a main department at the Office of Public Information at the Council of Ministers.

8 In the end, and after a fashion, the apparat compensated the high-ranking victims of Rákosi's "cult of personality" in Hungary. In 1956 the surviving victims and the widows were awarded monetary compensation in sums ranging from 75,000 to 150,000 Forints (HUF), or about $7,500 to $15,000 at

the 1956 HUF/US$ exchange rates. Kádár (163,000) and Aczél (132,000) were paid off, and so were Mrs. László Rajk (132,500) and several of Imre Nagy's political friends, including Ferenc Donáth (135,000) and Géza Losonczy (125,000). "Ennyit kaptak a káderek" (What the cadres received), *Magyar Hirlap*, February 13, 1990.

9 Unlike Kádár's contemporaries (György Marosán, Gyula Kállai, and others) in the HSWP PB and Secretariat who did not have a kind word for him in their public statements after his death on July 6, 1989, Imre Pozsgay and János Berecz have written and spoken about him with affection and personal respect.

10 Jenő Fock, in response to the question whether he had been one of those with the greatest influence on Kádár's personnel decisions, said: "Unfortunately, this had not been the case. In such matters György Aczél had the greatest influence. They met socially quite frequently because Mrs. György Aczél was the personal physician of comrade Kádár's wife." *Népszabadság*, July 8, 1989.

11 As Berecz explained to me, "Aunt Mária" disapproved of his marriage to the free-spirited (nonparty) actress Anikó Sáfár in 1986, and this helped undercut his standing with Kádár. Interview with János Berecz, June 1993, Budapest.

12 See Karl Mannheim, "The Problem of Generations," in Karl Mannheim, *Essays on the Sociology of Knowledge* (New York: Oxford University Press, 1952), pp. 276–320.

13 On this, see Marvin Rintala, "Political Generations," in Sills, ed., *IESS* vol. VI, pp. 92–6.

14 István Szakadát, "Karriertipusok a magyar kommunista párt vezető testületeiben, 1945–1988" (Career types in the leading organs of the Hungarian Communist Party, 1945–1988), in András Nyirő, ed., *Politikai szociológiai tanulmányok a kommunista bürökrácia vezérkaráról* (Studies in political sociology on the General Staff of the communist bureaucracy) (Budapest, 1990), pp. 39–54.

15 László Lengyel pointed out that classification of Politburo incumbents along generational lines may not be the best device to account for the personality dynamics of this body. In his view, the 1985 PB included people who symbolized ideological-administrative continuity (Aczél, Gáspár, Benke, and Óvári); who represented the state administration (Lázár or the prime minister of the day); the "peasantry" as titular head of state (István Dobi in the 1950s and Pál Losonczi in the 1970s and the early 1980s); the "agrarian lobby" (Lajos Fehér in the 1960s and 1970s and István Szabó after 1980); the county apparat (Károly Németh and Ferenc Havasi, western Hungary; Károly Grósz, northeastern Hungary); the "Social Democrats" (Marosán, Nyers, and István Sarlós); the YCL (László Maróthy and Csaba Hámori); and "women" (Valéria Benke). Letter from László Lengyel, January 1995.

16 Tamás Fricz, "Generációk és politikai értékek" (Generations and political values), *Valóság* 33, 4 (1990), 8–17.

17 On the People's Colleges see László Kardos, ed., *Sej a mi lobogónkat fényes szellők fujják* ... *Népi Kollégiumok, 1939–1949* (People's Colleges, 1939–1949) (Budapest: Akadémiai Kiadó, 1977); László Kardos, ed., *A fényes szelek nemzedéke: Népi Kollégiumok, 1939–1949* (Generation of the bright winds: People's Colleges, 1939–1949), 2 vols. (Budapest: Akadémiai Kiadó, 1980); János Illés, ed., *A népi kollégisták utja, 1939–1971* (The People's Collegians: paths and careers, 1939–1971) (Budapest: Central Statistical Office, 1977).

18 Hungary's premier residential college for top university students was the Eötvös Kollégium. Established in 1895 and patterned after the French Ecole Normale Supérieur, it was Hungary's elite yet merit-based "school for excellence" and the academic home of the country's leading humanistic intellectuals between 1900 and 1947. The Rákosi regime perceived this institution as an elitist hotbed of reactionary intellectuals and disbanded it in 1949. See Imre Szász, *Ménesi ut: regény és dokumentum* (Ménesi Street: a novel and a document) (Budapest: Magvető, 1985).

19 Most of the People's Collegians were hard-working students preoccupied with their studies and the challenge of making ends meet from their modest stipends. However, the activist minority had an ultraradical political agenda and the potential of becoming a kind of "Red Guard" of young political zealots. See Szász, "Ménesi Street," pp. 237–377.

20 In the mid-1970s the regime decided to "rehabilitate" the People's Colleges movement. This, in turn, gave new impetus to the establishment of residential colleges of the various university faculties. The László Rajk College of the Karl Marx University of Economics and the István Bibó College of the Faculty of Law, Loránd Eötvös University became centers of radical student politics in the 1980s. The founders of the League of Young Democrats (Fidesz) were students and tutors at the Bibó College.

21 Information on Imre Pozsgay, János Berecz, and Károly Grósz has been derived from: (a) interviews (Pozsgay, June and August 1989; Berecz, June 1993 and May 1994; Grósz, June 1994); (b) correspondence with Pozsgay, 1990–3; letter from Grósz (April 1994) and tape-recorded autobiographical statement by Berecz (March–April 1994); (c) published autobiography of Imre Pozsgay, *1989 Politikus pálya a pártállamban és a rendszerváltásban* (1989 – a political career in a party state and during the change of the regime) (Budapest: Püski, 1993); (d) published biographical interviews with Pozsgay, Berecz, and Grósz, especially Zoltán Biró, *Októberi kérdések: Pozsgay Imrével beszélget Biró Zoltán* (The questions of October: conversation with Imre Pozsgay) (Budapest: Eötvös Kiadó, 1988), János Berecz, "Az utókor a tényeket latja" (The posterity sees only the facts), in János Berecz, ed., *Visszaemlékezések 1956* (Remembering 1956) (Budapest: Zrinyi, 1986), pp. 339–69 and RFE/RL *Research Report* November 5, 1986 (a report on a radio interview with Károly Grósz on September 8, 1986); (e) biographical summaries on, and chronology of appointments held by, top HSWP officials in András Nyirő *et al.*, eds., "Handbook"; (f) statements at meetings of the CC and PB, HSWP; and (g) books, articles, and speeches by

Pozsgay, Berecz, and Grósz. These sources will be cited separately to document specific points in the narrative.

22 The Lenin Institute was called by its critics a "school for Janissaries." (The reference is to military schools for orphaned boys who went on to serve in elite units in the armies of the Ottoman Empire.) The Gorky School that János Kis attended and the Oleg Koshevoi program for Hungarian scholarship applicants to Soviet universities that Gyula Horn attended were parts of the Rákosi regime's training programs for academically promising and politically reliable young cadres.

23 Pozsgay needed the job to supplement his stipend from which he also supported his mother and sister. Moreover, he did not have a dark suit to take his fiancée (a classmate) to "cultural events." Pozsgay, "1989 – a political career," p. 25.

24 Her son, even though then a member of the HSWP PB, was respectful enough of his mother's beliefs to arrange for a church funeral when she died in 1987.

25 Her father, a physician, had been a Hungarian communist émigré in the Soviet Union since 1919. See Olga Lányi, *Moszkoviták* (Muscovites) (Budapest: Hevesi Gyula Alapitvány, 1992).

26 The Köztársaság Square building housed both the YCL and the Budapest party committee – and this is where the headquarters of the Hungarian Socialist Party has been located since 1990. It was the scene of one of the few well-publicized and -photographed (for example, on the front page of *Life* magazine) atrocities by the insurgents against party and police officials in Hungary in the fall of 1956.

27 Berecz owed his good fortune to CC member and YLC first secretary Zoltán Komócsin, who finally understood what Berecz's mission had been – and possibly may have supported the notion of a separate youth organization for university students. In any case, Komócsin protected Berecz from his political enemy Árpád Prandler, a two-fisted conservative YCL executive.

28 On Grósz's early career, see published biographic interviews cited in note 21(c) above.

29 Vitézy, "Interview with Károly Grósz," p. 25.

30 *Ibid.*, p. 17.

31 Imre Pozsgay, "Forradalom vagy ellenforradalom?" (Revolution or counterrevolution?), *Petőfi Népe*, December 15, 1957, p. 5.

32 Pozsgay, "1989 – political career," p. 29.

33 Imre Pozsgay, "A szocialista demokrácia és politikai rendszerünk tovább-fejlesztésének néhány kérdése" (Some questions of the further development of socialist democracy and of our political system), dissertation for the degree of Candidate of Sciences in Philosophy, Hungarian Academy of Sciences, 1969 (unpublished). I am indebted to Professor Imre Pozsgay, Department of Political Science, Lajos Kossuth University, Debrecen, for making a copy of this work available to me.

34 *Ibid.*, p. 3.

35 *Ibid.,* p. 90.

36 *Ibid.*

37 *Ibid.,* pp. 110–11.

38 *Ibid.,* p. 117.

39 *Ibid.,* p. 173.

40 Pozsgay, "1989 – a political career," p. 30.

41 Information on János Berecz's career between 1957 and 1972 is derived from Berecz, "Autobiographical statement."

42 János Berecz, *Ellenforradalom tollal és fegyverrel, 1956* (Counterrevolution with pens and weapons) (Budapest: Kossuth, 1969, 1981, 1986).

43 Grósz chose not to respond to my queries about these years. However, he did say that he had made an effort to master the Russian language. Although he was never sent for any of the prestigious one- or three-year programs in Moscow, over the next twenty-five years he visited the Soviet Union five times, for several months each time. His fluency in Russian proved to be a major asset in his meetings with high-level Soviet visitors such as Egor Ligachev and Mikhail Gorbachev in the 1980s.

44 Vitézy, "Interview with Károly Grósz," p. 28.

45 Although Grósz was reticent on the subject of his various political "godfathers," it appears that Sándor Nógrádi – a Comintern and Soviet military intelligence veteran; a manager of the military show trials of 1949–50; Rákosi's critic; after 1957, Hungarian Ambassador to Peking and Hanoi; and after 1959 head of the HSWP's Central Control Commission – had a friendly interest in Grósz's advancement.

46 Critics suggest that for a high-level cadre, such as Grósz, it was sufficient to know that Engels was *not* Marx's first name to earn a diploma from this program.

47 Vitézy, "Interview with Károly Grósz," pp. 32–3.

48 Background information on the workings of CC departments are from former staff members who requested anonymity as sources of information on this subject.

49 Most of these were reprinted in Imre Pozsgay, *Demokrácia és kultúra* (Democracy and culture) (Budapest: Kossuth, 1980), pp. 29–178.

50 Imre Pozsgay, "Társadalmi konfliktus és érdekegyeztetes" (Social conflict and interest reconciliation), *Népszabadság*, February 27, 1972.

51 See Pozsgay, "Democracy and culture," pp. 179–216.

52 In the 1980s Berecz made frequent TV appearences but, at least in intelligentsia circles, gained few converts to his clipped but often tough and didactic prose.

53 One of his first actions as minister was pensioning off the wife of Béla Biszku from her sinecure as the head of one of the ministry's main departments. In so doing, Pozsgay helped Aczél to get even with the (now-defeated) "workers' opposition" and became the hero of the intelligentsia.

54 Imre Pozsgay, "A régi világ rothadt gyümölcse. Gondolatok a nacionalizmusról" (The rotten fruit of the old regime. Thoughts on nationalism),

Petőfi Népe, November 10, 1957, and Imre Pozsgay, "A hazát szeretni …" (To love one's country), *Petőfi Népe*, March 15, 1958.

55 Imre Pozsgay, "A NÉKOSZ-ra emlékezünk" (Remembering the National Association of the People's Colleges), in Pozsgay, "Democracy and culture," pp. 217–32. On cultural policies see pp. 223–90.

56 As Pozsgay recalled this event, Nemes read the names from a crumpled piece of paper that Kádár had handed to him ten minutes earlier. Pozsgay, "1989 – a political career," p. 40.

57 Information on Berecz's activities between 1972 and 1982 was derived mainly from Berecz, "Autobiographical statement."

58 Moscow objected to Kádár's presence at the official ceremonies surrounding the return by the US government of St. Stephen's Crown in January 1978. Kádár stayed away from the public receptions, but he received secretary of state Cyrus Vance anyway.

59 Grósz letter, April 1994.

60 To protect himself from backbiting on this score, Berecz, although he had ample opportunities to do so, did not take a private Western vacation until 1986, when he took his three children to Cyprus after his wife's death.

61 Berecz, "Autobiographical statement."

62 Information on Grósz's activities in the 1970s is from his letter of April 1994 and personal interview in May 1994.

63 *Ibid.*

64 *Ibid.*

65 *Ibid.*

66 Interview with János Berecz, June 1994.

67 My thanks to Dr. László Vass, state secretary and chief of staff of minister of state Imre Pozsgay's office in 1988–9, for making copies of Mr. Pozsgay's publications available to me.

68 Clashes between the two involved not budgets but the authority to appoint protégés to key positions in Pozsgay's ministry. For reasons best known to him, Aczél conducted a vendetta against Pozsgay's confidant Zoltán Biró. Aczél prevailed, but the knives were out. Pozsgay complained to Kádár but received no response to his memorandum. See Pozsgay, "1989 – a political career," pp. 46–7.

69 *Ibid.*

70 Text of the draft version is in Pozsgay, "1989 – a political career," pp. 193–8.

71 From a comparison of the original text of Pozsgay's speech and the version in the CC's offical minutes, it appears that several passages were deleted from the original version. The CC version is in OL 288 f4/183 (December 3, 1981), pp. 153–82. The original text is in Pozsgay, "1989 – a political career," pp. 198–208.

72 His involvement in Havasi's committee brought him into a working relationship with Hungary's top economists and gave him the opportunity to meet with Miklós Németh, a rising star in the CC's Department of Economic Policy and his future political partner in 1988–9. Pozsgay, "1989 – a political career," pp. 60–1.

73 Pozsgay, "1989 – a political career," p. 67. Kádár always took his time in giving a reply to difficult questions. However, this was his public reply to Pozsgay's question:

> We can encounter notions that in the life of the country a certain generation should run things for twenty years after which they are "discharged" by the next one. Generational change does not happen the same way as two military divisions relieving one another of duty. This is a gradual process in society.

János Kádár, "Előadói beszéd a Központi Bizottság április 12–13-i ülésén" (Speech at the April 12–13, 1983 meeting of the Central Committee), *Pártélet*, May 1983.

74 Vitézy, "Interview with Károly Grósz," p. 43. In response to my direct question, Pozsgay confirmed in June 1993 that he had approached Grósz with this idea, but nothing came of it until 1986–7, when they resumed their dialogue on this subject.

75 *Ibid.*, p. 41.

76 Pozsgay's talk was published in *Választási Almanach* (Electoral Almanac) (Samizdat, 1982).

77 *Ibid.*, p. 131.

78 Interview with Imre Pozsgay, August 1989.

79 The PB ordered Pozsgay to prepare a written explanation on the role that he had played in having the PPF sponsor the controversial study by reform economists. In a seven-page memorandum, written in impeccable bureau-cratese, Pozsgay proved that the PPF had done nothing wrong. In fact, it had successfully co-opted those reform intellectuals who otherwise would have succumbed to the temptation of publishing by means of samizdat. Imre Pozsgay, "Feljegyzés A fordulat és reform cimű tanulmányról" (Memorandum [to comrade István Petrovszki, head, CC Department for Party and Mass Organizations] on a study entitled "Turnabout and reform," March 13, 1987) in OL 288 f5/991 (April 21, 1987), pp. 83–9.

80 OL 288 f4/255 (June 23, 1987), p. 83.

81 Interview with János Berecz, June 1993.

82 János Berecz, "Autobiographical statement."

83 See János Berecz, *Harc és együttmüködés* (Struggle and cooperation) (Budapest: Akadémiai Kiadó, 1979); János Berecz, *Vitáink és egységünk* (Our disputes – our unity) (Budapest: Akadémiai Kiadó, 1980); János Berecz, ed., *A néphatalom védelmében* (In defense of the people's power) (Budapest: Zrinyi Katonai Kiadó, 1984); János Berecz, *Folyamatosság és megujúlás az MSZMP politikájában* (Continuity and renewal in the policies of the HSWP) (Budapest: Kossuth, 1985); János Berecz, "A nemzeti és nemzetközi érdekek dialektikájáról" (On the dialectics of national and international interests), in Tibor Polgár, ed., *Politikatudományi tanulmányok* (Studies in political science) (Budapest: Kossuth, 1981), pp. 188–202; and János Berecz, "A kapitalizmus korunk nemzetközi rendszerében" (Capitalism in today's international system), in György Szoboszlai, ed., *Biztonság és együttmüködés* (Security and cooperation) (Budapest: Hungarian Political Science Association, 1985), pp. 151–68.

84 Pozsgay, "1989 – a political career," p. 73.
85 As a part of this exercise, the third edition of Berecz's "Counter-revolution with pens and weapons" was serialized in the Hungarian press.
86 See János Berecz, *A szocializmusról gondolkodva* (Thoughts on socialism) (Budapest: Kossuth, 1988), pp. 69–108.
87 On this see OL 288 f4/228 (November 11, 1986), pp. 26–59. Comments are in pp. 65–118.
88 See Nyirő *et al.*, eds., "Handbook," pp. 345–7.
89 Vitézy, "Interview with Károly Grósz," p. 47.
90 *Ibid.*, p. 44. The truthfulness of this account is open to doubt. For one thing, Kádár knew *everything* about his colleagues, including their drinking habits, womanizing and unguarded comments – let alone their ethnic and religious backgrounds. Moreover, Grósz has been cited by party insiders as a man in the habit of introducing himself to party audiences by saying: "I am Grósz – but I am not from *Dob utca*" (a street in the Jewish district of Budapest).
91 Grósz letter, April 1994.
92 *Ibid.*
93 Interview with Károly Grósz, June 1994.
94 "Our concerns and opportunities. Interview with Károly Grósz," *Siker*, September 1986.
95 Unlike his colleagues who "lost touch with the masses," Grósz knew what was happening in his district. He was probably the first local party boss in Hungary to commission weekly opinion polls to stay abreast with what the people thought of the regime.
96 However careful Kádár was in making suitable postretirement arrangements for his senior associates, he could not overcome the prevailing perception among the attentive publics that loss of one's high- or middle-level position caused the person involved to become a "fallen man" (*bukott ember*). Thus, an "honorable exit" was sought by many, but was granted to few in the Kádár era in Hungary.
97 Organized hunting and hunting clubs were strange throwbacks to the era of the landed gentry in Hungary. Except for the devotees of killing animals in the Hungarian military's fenced-in game preserves, hunting parties served as occasions for socializing, heavy drinking, lavish meals, and stag parties in hunting lodges throughout Hungary. Trophies of Kádár's, Aczél's, and the PB's hunting prowess were (as late as 1993) displayed in the Budapest Agricultural Museum. Kádár saw to it that the party elite behaved even when inebriated. Grósz recalled that in 1983 or 1984 a group of top YCL leaders on the eve of a hunting party in Somogy county had made some unprintable comments about the party elders. The following morning a full transcript of the young lions' comments was on Grósz's desk. As county first secretary he was on the distribution list of daily counterintelligence reports. He did not recall what happened to the culprits. Interview with Károly Grósz, May 1994.
98 Interpersonal communication, specifically the matter of addressing one

another by first or last names, has always been a perplexing problem in Hungary. Age, gender, official position, shared experiences – whether in prison, in the military, or in school – play a role in mode of address. The ambiguity of the matter was further compounded when an older and a younger politician, such as Aczél and Grósz, once on first-name basis, found themselves at loggerheads over an issue, such as the dismissal of TV personnel in the 1960s. As Grósz recalled, for the next twenty years Aczél insisted on the formal mode of address. Aczél relented when both found themselves as full members of the PB in 1985. Kádár was said to be on first-name basis with few people, such as Rajk, Aczél, Nyers, Marosán, Münnich, former prison-cell mates, and old comrades from the prewar communist movement.

6   Political succession in the HSWP

1 Interview with Professor János Szentágothai, January 1989, Budapest. The quote is from his statement on the floor of the Hungarian Parliament on January 9, 1989.
2 Interview with Károly Grósz, June 1994, Gödöllő, Hungary.
3 Personal communication from Dr. László Vass, August 1993. See also Péter Tölgyessy, *Gazdasági érdekképviseletek Magyarországon* (Economic interest groups in Hungary) (Budapest: Institute for the Social Sciences, CC, HSWP, 1988).
4 "The USSR and Hungary: An Uneasy Relationship," FBIS *Analysis Report*, May 24, 1979, FB 79–10008, p. 5 (material obtained from the Central Intelligence Agency under the Freedom of Information Act).
5 "The Hungarian Variant: Soviet Reactions to Hungary's Economic Reform," National Foreign Assessment Center, CIA, July 1980, PA 80–10309, p. 16 (material obtained from the Central Intelligence Agency under the Freedom of Information Act).
6 István Bodzabán and Antal Szalay, eds., *A puha diktaturától a kemény demokráciáig* (From soft dictatorship to tough democracy. Interviews) (Budapest: Pelikán, 1994), pp. 70–7.
7 Koltay and Bródy, "With the recognition," p. 69.
8 Typically, each CC economic policy decision was followed by a flurry of decrees issued by the Council of Ministers and the relevant ministry, or ministries.
9 OL 288 f4/255 (June 23, 1987), p. 79.
10 Cf. Rezső Nyers (Jr), ed., *Külső eladósodás és adósságkezelés Magyarországon* (External indebtedness and debt management in Hungary) (Budapest: Hungarian National Bank, December 1992).
11 *HSWP Twelfth Congress*, pp. 23–7.
12 Charles Kovács, "The New Hungarian Central Committee," RFE *Research*, August 1, 1980.
13 See "Interview with Sándor Gáspár," in Katalin Ferber and Gábor Rejtő,

eds., *Reform évfordulón* (Reform anniversary) (Budapest: Közgazdasági és Jogi Kiadó, 1988), pp. 219–31.

14 The HSWP was declared to be an "all people's party" at the 13th congress in March 1985.

15 The formulation of the concept of "internal (political) indebtedness" was first advanced by the Hungarian reform economist Mária Zita Petchnig in an unpublished commentary on the economic policy decisions of the November 1986 meeting of the CC, HSWP.

16 On this, see Gábor Vági, *Versengés a fejlesztési forrásokért* (Competition for investment resources) (Budapest: Közgazdasági és Jogi Kiadó, 1982).

17 András A. Gergely, *A pártállam varázstalanítása* (The demystification of the party-state) (Budapest: MTA Politikai Tudományok Intézete, 1991), pp. 188–206.

18 *Ibid.*, p. 17.

19 PB members were assigned one or more counties for the holding of periodic inspection tours. One of these was usually a "home" district (Budapest XIIIth district for Kádár, Baranya county for Aczél, Vas county for Károly Németh, Borsod county for Grósz, Komárom county for Ferenc Havasi, and so on), where the "native son" was expected to deliver additional budgets, new buildings, roads, and cultural facilities.

20 Letter from Károly Grósz, April 1994.

21 The heavy-industry sector's unresponsiveness to preferential resource allocations and other incentives for improved efficiency was a recurring theme of Kádár's summary statements following CC deliberations on industrial policies between 1968 and 1984.

22 Erzsébet Szalai, *Gazdasági mechanizmus, reformtörekvések és nagyvállalati érdekek* (Economic mechanism, reform initiatives and large enterprise interests) (Budapest: Közgazdasági és Jogi Kiadó, 1989), especially pp. 139–78 and 248–56.

23 *HSWP Decisions*, 1980–1985, pp. 407–13.

24 *HSWP Decisions, 1985–1986*, pp. 144–55.

25 OL 288 f5/998 (June 3, 1987), p. 204.

26 *HSWP Decisions, 1980–1985*, pp. 97–100, 172–83, 453–62, 582–604, and 768–70.

27 From the forty-five regularly reporting local and regional party organizations, I selected five to represent a cross-section of county-level party constituencies: the Technical University of Budapest, the Budapest VIth district, the Csepel Iron and Steel Works, and the Baranya and Borsod county organizations for the months of March and November between 1980 and 1986. On these, see OL 288 f22/1980, 1981, 1982, 1983, 1984, 1985, 1986 under miscellaneous font numbers.

28 *HSWP Decisions, 1980–1985*, pp. 515–17 and 777–81. As Kádár envisaged it, "neither the dual nor the multiple candidacy system will alter the fact that socialism is the political foundation of the electoral system. It will not be possible to have candidates who stand for an alternative view to socialism ... Voting and choosing a candidate is the same thing – that of

taking a stand in support of our political system." OL 288 f4/194 (July 6, 1983), p. 3.

29 Interview with István Horváth, June 1993, Budapest.

30 *Magyar Nemzet*, April 12, 1985.

31 György Szoboszlai, ed., *Az 1985. évi országgyűlési választások politikai tapasztalatai* (On the political experiences of the 1985 parliamentary elections) (Budapest: Institute for the Social Sciences, HSWP, 1985).

32 *Magyar Nemzet*, June 10, 1985.

33 OL 288 f22/1985/9 and 10. The PB's April 9, 1985 meeting was devoted to the subject of political coordination of the forthcoming elections. With respect to "look-alike" candidates, a "hands off" policy was adopted. OL 288 f5/937 (April 9, 1985), pp. 16–153.

34 Ildikó Kováts and János Tölgyesi, "Az 1985 évi parlamenti képviselői es tanácsválasztások sajtóvisszhangja. Tartalomelemzés" (Content analysis of press coverage of the 1985 parliamentary and local council elections) (Budapest: Mass Communications Research Institute, 1985) (unpublished), p. 106.

35 *Ibid.*, p. 107.

36 This was the consensus of the CC meeting devoted to evaluation of the results of the 1985 elections. Kádár shrugged off the results by saying, "some of the [defeated county first secretaries] lacked the aptitude to make a case for our policies." OL 288 f4/212 (June 26, 1985), p. 177.

37 *Magyar Nemzet*, June 29, 1985.

38 Cf. Gábor Halmai, "Az országgyűlés szerepének módosulása az ügyrendek tükrében" (Changes in the role of the Parliament in the light of new House rules), *Medvetánc* 2 (1987), 51– 82.

39 For an excellent overview of the succession issue in communist party states, see Raymond Taras, "Political Competition and Communist Leadership: A Historiographical Introduction," in Raymond Taras, ed., *Leadership Change in Communist States* (Boston: Unwin Hyman, 1989), pp. 1–23.

40 László Lengyel, "Három öreg" (The three old ones), in László Lengyel, *Magyar alakok* (Hungarian personalities) (Budapest: 2000/Pénzügykutató, 1994), pp. 12–17.

41 Andropov called Kádár "a tested leader of socialist Hungary and a good friend of the Soviet Union." Quoted in Alfred Reisch, "Kádár policies get nod of approval from new Soviet leaders?" RFE *Research*, Hungary Background 195/1983 (August 11, 1983), p. 3.

42 "Dokumentum. Kádár János es M. Sz. Gorbacsov találkozója Moszkvában 1985. szeptember 25-én" (Document. [Transcript of] meeting between János Kádár and M. S. Gorbachev in Moscow on September 25, 1985) *Történelmi Szemle* 34, 1–2 (1992), 142ff.

43 Parts of the discussion on the Kádár–Grósz succession are based on my contribution to George Schopflin, Rudolf L. Tőkés, and Iván Volgyes, "Leadership Change and Crisis in Hungary," *Problems of Communism* 37, 5 (1988), 27–39.

44 Cam Hudson, "Hungary staves off liquidity crisis with IMF loans" RFE *Research*, Hungary Situation Report 19/1982 (December 27, 1982), pp. 6–10.

45 OL 288 f4/198 (April 17, 1984), p. 156.
46 *Ibid.*
47 Interview with János Barabás (CC Secretary for Ideology, June–September 1989), June 1994, Budapest.
48 *HSWP Thirteenth Congress*, pp. 575–84.
49 "Hungary: Economic Performance in the 1980's Prospects for the 1990's," in *Pressures for Economic Reform in East European Economies* vol. II, Study Papers submitted to the Joint Economic Committee, US Congress (October 27, 1989) (Washington, DC: USGPO, 1989), p. 34.
50 The prolonged absences, due mainly to illness and exhaustion, of Kádár and his senior colleagues from their respective offices were formalized by the PB that awarded additional months and weeks of vacation to Kádár, Lázár, Gáspár, and Károly Németh. OL 288 f5/991 (April 21, 1987), p. 5.
51 László Lengyel, *Végkifejlet* (Endgame) (Budapest: Közgazdasági és Jogi Kiadó, 1989), p. 141.
52 OL 288 f4/220 (November 19–20, 1986).
53 *Ibid.*, p. 54.
54 *Ibid.*, pp. 245–52.
55 OL 288 f5/980 (October 7, 1986), pp. 22–52.
56 OL 288 f5/995 (April 17, 1987), p. 31.
57 OL 288 f5/998 (June 3, 1987), pp. 96–113.
58 Károly Grósz, letter of April 1994.
59 Interview with János Berecz, May 1994.
60 Károly Grósz, letter of April 1994.
61 *Ibid.*
62 OL 288 f4/225 (June 23, 1987), pp. 43–6.
63 Pp. 87–8.
64 "Interview with Károly Grósz," *Képes 7*, September 12, 1987.
65 The text of each speech was published in *Népszabadság*, September 17, 1987. László Lengyel, in a brilliant essay on the impact of the electronic media on Hungarian politics, contrasted Kádár's and Grósz's performance on TV. Kádár's TV appearance in December 1986 was a disaster due, in part, to unfriendly camera angles that focused on his shaking hands, and, after a Kádár *bon mot*, on the stone-faced audience, then on Kádár – the only one who laughed at his jokes. Grósz, as Lengyel explained, seemed to have taken his clues for his stage persona from the Italian newsreels of the 1930s that showed a dynamic, smiling, sincere Mussolini. This image impressed the party faithful but not Gorbachev who, on another televised occasion, refused to be embraced by Grósz. László Lengyel, "Üvegszem" (Glass eye), *Filmvilág*, March 1990, pp. 9–11.
66 "Interview with Imre Pozsgay," *Heti Világgazdaság*, October 24, 1987; "Interview with Rezső Nyers," *Magyar Ifjuság*, December 18, 1987; "Interview with József Bognar, Rezső Nyers and Tamás Sárközy," *Figyelő*, December 3, 1987. See also "Statement by Peter Medgyessy, September 17, 1987," in FBIS, *Daily Report – EEU*, October 5, 1987, pp. 28–40.
67 "Interview with Károly Grósz," *Magyar Hirlap*, December 3, 1987.

68 OL 288 f5/1015 (December 15, 1987), pp. 16–154.
69 See Information Subdepartment, Department of Agitation and Propaganda, CC, HSWP, "Excerpts from background reports of December 17, 1987 for the Department of Party and Mass Organizations," OL 288 f22/1987/23, pp. 43–8 (December 18, 1987); Information Subdepartment . . ., "Excerpts . . . of January 14, 21, and 28, 1987 . . . for the Department of PMO," OL 288 f22/1988/17, pp. 1–4, 1–9, and 1–9; and Department of Agitation and Propaganda, CC, HSWP, "Excerpts from background reports on frequently asked questions" (Prepared from reports of the Budapest party committee, county party committees, directly reporting party committees, the CC, Young Communist League, and the National Councils of the Trade Union Federation and the Patriotic People's Front) (February 1988), OL 288 f22/1988/17, p. 23.
70 *Magyar Hirlap*, January 2, 1988.
71 János Berecz, biographical statement, April 1994.
72 Text in FBIS, *Daily Report* – EEU, March 18, 1988, pp. 18–21.
73 See note 43.
74 Károly Grósz, letter of April 1994.
75 The following quotes help illustrate the CC members' views on current problems: "Today it is not enough to say that who is not against us is with us" (István Tömpe); "A multiparty system is not necessary for the representation of different interests" (György Lázár); "The conference delegates will receive their mandate from the local party committees" (János Lukács); "Administrative measures are still available [to handle] dissent" (János Berecz); "There is no unity in the party" (Imre Katona); "A party that has been in power for forty years should not talk about its lack of experience" (György Vajda); "How should those 600,000 party members who do not have a university degree understand the HSWP's views?" (Sándor Borbély); "The 'Gorbachev effect' has become a source of tensions in Hungary" and "The YCL does not represent the youth and the TUF does not represent the workers" (Rezső Nyers). The prospect of these comments coming through in the offical communiqué prompted an exasperated Kádár to ask: "Why bypass the Secretariat [that is, his own office] when drafting published resolutions? We might as well rename the HSWP the [British] Labour Party." In OL 288 f/232 (March 23, 1988), pp. 61–284.
76 *Magyar Nemzet*, April 2, 1988.
77 *Népszabadság*, April 25, 1988.
78 Interview with János Berecz, May 1994.
79 *Az MSZMP Országos Értekezletének Jegyzőkönyve* (Stenographic Minutes of the [Third] National Conference of the HSWP, May 20–22, 1988) (Budapest: Kossuth, 1988). In English: FBIS, *Daily Report* – EEU Supplement, May 23, 1988.
80 A total of 133 names were on the list of nominees for membership in the CC; 994 delegates cast valid votes, and 50 percent plus one vote was necessary for election. Kádár received 911 votes; Grósz, 971; Pozsgay, 970; Nyers, 835; Berecz, 936; and Miklós Németh, 966. Those not elected

included Sándor Gáspár, 249; György Lázár, 355; Károly Németh, 433; Miklós Óvári, 459; and Ferenc Havasi, 485. See, Gábor Koltay and Péter Bródy, eds., "With the recognition," pp. 250–8. The cashiered party elders' state of mind is well illustrated by a postconference exchange between Kádár and Havasi. Kádár: "And what about us? Shall we meet again?" Havasi: "You have my telephone number. At any rate, it is certain that you will die before me. I'll come to your funeral. Should I die first, I am sure that you will not come to my burial. So this is how we parted." Vitézy, ed., "The jolliest barrack," p. 502.

81 Information Subdepartment, Department of AP, CC, "Excerpts from reports [from local party organizations] of June 2, 7, 9, 16 and 23 for the Department of PMO, CC" in OL 288/22/1988/18 and 19.
82 Bodzabán and Szalay, eds., "From soft dictatorship," p. 114.
83 OL 288 f5/1028 (June 14, 1988).
84 Ibid., pp. 151–68.
85 Ibid., pp. 34–44.
86 Ibid., p. 39.
87 Grósz justified the use of force in "self-defense" by law-abiding policemen. Interview with Károly Grósz, Newsweek (International Edition), July 18, 1988.
88 Although the PB urged the party and youth organizations to stay away from the planned demonstration, nothing was said about party penalties for those who chose to join the protest march. See OL 288 f5/1029 (June 23, 1988), pp. 4–5.
89 Péter Szalay, "Mi van a demokrácia csomagtervben?" (What is in the democracy package plan?), in Sándor Kurtán, Sándor Péter, and László Vass, eds., Magyarország Politikai Évkönyve, 1988 (Hungarian Political Yearbook, 1988), pp. 254–64.
90 OL 288 f4/240 (July 13–14, 1988), pp. 7–28 and 223–32.
91 For a useful overview of the regime's economic problems in 1988, see István Csillag et al., Mélyfúrások: tanulmányok a 80-as évek magyar gazdaságáról (Deep probes: studies on the Hungarian economy in the 1980s) (Budapest: Pénzügykutató Rt., 1988).
92 Zita Mária Petschnig, "Gazdaság a politikai változások árnyékában" (Economy in the shadows of political changes), in Kurtán et al., "Hungarian Political Yearbook," pp. 79–85.
93 Károly Grósz, "Report to the Political Committee," in OL 288 f5/1031 (July 12, 1988), p. 22.
94 OL 288 f4/241 (July 13–14, 1988), pp. 156–66.
95 The meeting that I attended took place on July 25, 1988 in New York City.
96 Tiszatáj, June 1990, pp. 75–110 and Tamás Forró and Henrik Havas, eds., Arad után (After Arad) (Budapest: Háttér, 1988).
97 Letter from Károly Grósz, April 1994.
98 Department of AP, CC, Excerpts from reports [from party orgnizations] of July 14, August 4, 11, 25, and September 1, 1988 to the Department of PMO, CC. OL 288 f22/1988/19.

99 Attila Ágh, "A félfordulat éve" (The year of half-turn); Mihály Bihari, "Változások a politikai intézményrendszerben" (Changes in the structure of political institutions); László Lengyel, "Ezerkilencszácnyolcvannyolc" (Nineteen hundred and eighty-eight), in Kurtán et al., "Hungarian Political Yearbook, 1988," pp. 23–34, 53–60, and 81–9.

100 "Keeping the party together" was a constantly recurring theme in Grósz's political statements in 1988–9.

101 OL 288 f4/238 (June 23, 1988), p. 199.

102 Népszabadság, August 10, 1988.

103 Magyar Nemzet, November 8, 1988. Berecz's frantic quest for power proved to be his undoing. According to János Barabás, at the end of July 1988 Berecz forwarded a written statement to Aleksandr Yakovlev in which he denounced (feljelentette) Grósz for alleged political mistakes. Because neither Yakovlev nor Gorbachev had any intention to remove Grósz from leadership, they dispatched Kriuchkov with the Berecz missile to Budapest to incur yet another IOU with the secretary general. Thus, as of August 1988, Berecz was politically dead – a fact, that did not dawn on him until April 1989. Telephone interview with János Barabás, February 1995.

104 Interview with Imre Pozsgay, June 1989, Budapest. See also Zoltán Biró, Októberi kérdések (The issues of October, conversation with Imre Pozsgay) (Budapest: Eötvös-Püski, 1988), p. 13.

105 "Interview with Miklós Németh," Magyar Hirlap, March 23, 1990.

106 OL 288 f5/1040 (October 18, 1988), pp. 137–208.

107 All quotes in ibid.

108 Reformpárti esték (Reform Party evenings), 3 vols. (Budapest: KISZ, 1988).

109 OL 288 f4/245 (November 1, 1988) pp. 13–46.

110 Ibid., p. 16.

111 OL 288 f5/1044 (November 21, 1988), pp. 18ff.

112 OL 288 f4/244 (November 1–2, 1988), pp. 86–98.

113 OL 288 f4/246 (November 22, 1988), pp. 220–40.

114 Imre Pozsgay, "1989 – a political career," p. 86.

115 Délmagyarország, November 29, 1988.

116 Népszabadság, November 30, 1988. See also OL 288 f22/20 (December 1 and 8, 1988).

117 The precise quote: "somehow I do not believe that the one-party system can be sustained in the long run." OL 288 f4/246 (November 22, 1988), p. 149.

118 Cited in Alfred Reisch, "Hard-Pressed Party Leader Launches Political Offensive," RFE Research (Hungary/20) (December 15, 1988), p. 28.

119 Letter from Károly Grósz, April 1994. See also Bodzabán and Szalay, "From soft dictatorship," pp. 112–13.

120 I am indebted to Professor Attila Ágh of the Department of Political Science, Budapest University for Economics and the Social Sciences, for calling my attention to the Ferenc Münnich Socialist Brigades as potential auxiliaries for a "Leftist turn" in Hungary in 1988–9.

121 According to Dr. Horváth, Soviet advisors had been among the routine recipients of daily intelligence and counterintelligence reports at the Ministry of Interior until "they were left off the list." Dr. Horváth did not specify the latter date. Interview with István Horváth, June 1993, Budapest.

122 Letter from Károly Grósz, April 1994, and interview, June 1994, Gödöllő.

123 Imre Pozsgay and his friends were convinced of this in the winter of 1988–9.

124 Imre Pozsgay, "1989 – a political career," p. 95.

125 For the transcript of Pozsgay's radio interview, see ibid., pp. 222–7.

126 OL 288 f5/1050 (January 31, 1989), pp. 5–39.

127 Bodzabán and Szalay, "From soft dictatorship," p. 130.

128 Excerpts from this 400-page study were published in Népszabadság, November 23–8, 1987.

129 Bodzabán and Szalay, "From soft dictatorship," p. 115.

130 Ibid., p. 119.

131 OL 288 f4/250 (February 10–11, 1989). See also László Soós, ed., A Magyar Szocialista Munkáspárt Központi Bizottságának 1989. évi Jegyzőkönyvei (Steno-graphic minutes of the meetings of the CC, HSWP in 1989), 2 vols. (Budapest: Magyar Országos Levéltár, 1993) vol. I, pp. 1–194. (Cited hereafter as HSWP CC Minutes, 1989.)

132 Magyar Nemzet, February 1, 1989.

133 OL 288 f4/250, p. 20.

134 Ibid., p. 24.

135 Ibid., p. 36.

136 Ibid., pp. 26ff.

137 Only three days earlier the PB had been presented with a report on the status of the county and major city party organizations. In many places cut-throat power struggles between the pro- and antireform apparatchiki and the spread of local corruption scandals paralyzed the regime's local power elites. OL 288 f5/1051 (February 7, 1989), pp. 141–9. See also György Czippán, ed., Botránykrónika '88 (Chronicle of scandals, 1988) (Budapest: Laude Kiadó, 1989).

138 OL 288 f4/250 (February 10–11, 1989), pp. 70–1.

139 János Kádár, Végakarat (Last will and testament) (Budapest: Hirlapkiadó, 1989), p. 137.

140 As he put it at the June 23, 1987 meeting of the CC, "I am beginning to doubt that I will ever be free of full-time work. It seems that I have to fall off the chair before I am believed that I cannot go on working like a pack mule." OL 288 f4/225 (June 23, 1987), p. 87.

7 Negotiated revolution

1 The mythologies of the East European revolutions of 1989–90 were recorded in, and to some extent promoted by, Timothy Garton Ash's brilliant accounts of these events. See Timothy Garton Ash, The Magic Lantern: The Revolution of '89 Witnessed in Warsaw, Budapest, Berlin and

Prague (New York: Random House, 1990). My goal is to transcend awkward neologisms, such as Garton Ash's "refolution," and to reconstruct what actually happened in 1989 in Hungary and to show, in so far as possible, why.

2 For a stimulating critique of Western writings on the continued stability or collapse of communist-type systems, see Walter Laqueur, *The Dream That Failed* (New York: Oxford University Press, 1994), pp. 50–130.

3 Cited in László Kasza, *Metamorphosis Hungariae, 1989–1994* (Budapest: Századvég, 1994), p. 31.

4 These groups and parties are listed in Sándor Kurtán, Péter Sándor, and László Vass, eds., *Magyarország Politikai Évkönyve, 1988* (Hungarian Political Yearbook, 1988) (Debrecen: R-Forma Kiadó, 1989), pp. 699–799. (These volumes are cited hereafter as "Hungarian Political Yearbook, 1989, 1990," etc.)

5 These were the Hungarian Democratic Forum, the Independent Smallholders' Party, the Hungarian Social Democratic Party, the Hungarian People's Party, the Christian Democratic People's Party, the Alliance of Free Democrats, the League of Young Democrats, the Endre Bajcsy-Zsilinszky Society and the Democratic Trade Union of Scientific Workers which was replaced by the Democratic League of Independent Trade Unions. See Anna Richter, ed., *Az Ellenzéki Kerekasztal: portrévázlatok* (The Opposition Roundtable: portraits) (Budapest: Ötlet, 1990) and "Alternativ arcképcsarnok" (Alternative portrait gallery), *Képes 7*, June 24, 1989.

6 Organizations participating in the National Roundtable of June 14 – September 18, 1989 were, in addition to the ORT parties and two intelligentsia groups, the Hungarian Socialist Workers' Party, the Patriotic People's Front, the Trade Union Federation, the Ferenc Münnich Society, the Association of Hungarian Women, the League of Anti-Fascist Resistance Fighters, the National Council of Hungarian Youth Organizations (formerly the Young Communist League), and the Alliance for a Leftist Alternative). *Magyar Nemzet*, June 14, 1989.

7 These are listed in "Hungarian Political Yearbook, 1991," pp. 523–31.

8 Exceptions to this were a handful of very small groups of environmental, human rights, religious, peace, and antipoverty activists that wielded negligible influence in 1989–90.

9 The CDPP was the political heir to the Hungarian Democratic People's Party of 1947–8 under the prominent Catholic layman István Barankovics. See Richter, "The Opposition Roundtable," pp. 235–53.

10 The HDF sponsored a meeting at the Jurta theatre on January 30, 1988. The organizers of this affair denied the request of Sándor Rácz, the former president of the Greater Budapest Workers' Council, of November–December, 1956, to address the audience.

11 Péter Veres (1897–1970) was an agrarian socialist-Populist writer and an active participant in prewar left-wing politics. It was Veres who coined the phrase "Frigidaire socialism." Text of the charter of the Péter Veres Society is in "Hungarian Political Yearbook, 1988," pp. 785–87.

12 As Grósz recalled, "I met with the potential leaders of the Social Democratic Party in my office. We gave them financial support. We paid for automobiles and salaries." In László Vitézy, "Interview with Károly Grósz," p. 62.

13 Interview with András Révész, *Magyar Hirlap*, January 13, 1989.

14 A combination of the older leaders' proximity to Grósz and Nyers, generational clashes within the party, disputes over the distribution of financial support from the Socialist International and political ineptitude were responsible for the HSDP's poor electoral performance (3.55 percent of the votes) in the 1990 elections.

15 On the origins of the Endre Bajcsy-Zsilinszky Society, see Richter, "The Opposition Roundtable," pp. 201–15.

16 Katalin Bossányi, *Szólampróba: beszélgetések az alternativ mozgalmakról* (Voice rehearsal: conversations on the alternative movements) (Budapest: Láng Kiadó, 1989), p. 17.

17 On the DUSW, see *ibid.*, pp. 268–79. On the Liga, see Richter, "The Opposition Roundtable," pp. 105–32.

18 See Bossányi, "Voice rehearsal," pp. 208–19.

19 Alliance of Free Democrats *Elvi Nyilatkozat* (Declaration of Principles), October 24, 1988, in *Annotated Beszélő*, vol. III, pp. 654–5.

20 Western support came mainly from liberal sympathizers, from educational and cultural foundations established by the Hungarian-American philanthropist George Soros, and the US government-funded National Endowment for Democracy. The latter also extended support to the League of Young Democrats, as did the AFL-CIO to the League of Democratic Trade Unions.

21 Contacts between the Polish opposition and the *Beszélő* group were established in 1977–8 and were maintained in the following years by the leaders of the democratic opposition and of *Solidarnosč*.

22 Full documentation on the history of LYD may be found in András Bozóki, ed, *Tiszta lappal: a FIDESZ a magyar politikában, 1988–1991* (With a clean slate: Fidesz in Hungarian politics, 1988–1991) (Budapest: Fidesz, 1992).

23 On the establishment of the ILF, see Richter, "The Opposition Roundtable," pp. 11–26.

24 Károly Vigh, "Az Ellenzéki Kerekasztaltól a Nemzeti Kerekasztalig" (From the Opposition Roundtable to the National Roundtable), in "Hungarian Political Yearbook, 1990," pp. 231–2.

25 András Bozóki, "Az Ellenzéki Kerekasztal (első) Története" (An early history of the Opposition Roundtable), *Beszélő*, March 3, 1990, pp. 12–13; Imre Pozsgay, Speech to the Hungarian Parliament, November 24, 1988; *Népszabadság*, January 14, 1989. I am indebted to the late Hungarian prime minister Dr. József Antall for sharing with me, in the course of an interview in January 1989, those parts of Imre Pozsgay's speech that he had written for Mr. Pozsgay.

26 Bozóki "An early history," in *Beszélő*, March 10 and 15, 1990.

27 "Fejti Discussed Concluded Warsaw Talks," MTI, 18 March, 1989. FBIS-EEU, *Daily Report*, March 21, 1989, p. 30.
28 *HSWP CC Minutes, 1989*, pp. 914–15, 916 and 1083–4.
29 "Hungarian Political Yearbook, 1990," p. 451.
30 *HSWP CC Minutes, 1989*, p. 386.
31 *Ibid.*, p. 648.
32 OL 288 f11/4507 (February 1989), p. 173.
33 See Kálmán Kulcsár, minister of justice, "Submission to the PB on an unicameral, or a bicameral Parliament" (April 10, 1989), in OL 288 f5/1062 (April 19, 1989), pp. 55–65.
34 *HSWP CC Minutes, 1989*, pp. 391–3.
35 *Ibid.*, pp. 394–5.
36 *Annotated Beszélő*, vol. III, pp. 775–91.
37 *A jövőnkért: fellendülést, demokráciát, szocializmust! Mire törekszik a Magyar Szocialista Munkáspárt?* (For our future: prosperity, democracy, socialism! What are the goals of the HSWP?) (Budapest: Kossuth, 1989).
38 OL 288 4/256 (March 7, 1989) pp. 27–9.
39 Imre Pozsgay, "1989 – a political career,", p. 111.
40 FBIS-EEU, *Daily Report*, April 6, 1989, p. 20.
41 *Ibid.*, p. 22.
42 *Magyar Nemzet*, March 22, 1989.
43 Pozsgay "1989 – a political career," pp. 121–2.
44 OL 288 f4/257 (March 29, 1989), pp. 13–24.
45 *HSWP CC Minutes, 1989*, pp. 645–7.
46 OL 288 f11/4508 (March 1989), p. 88.
47 *Die Presse* (Vienna), March 24, 1989. In FBIS-EEU, *Daily Report*, March 27, 1989, p. 21.
48 *HSWP CC Minutes, 1989*, pp. 578–9 and 720–57.
49 *Ibid.*, p. 713.
50 On this, see *ibid.*, pp. 747–8 and "Interview with Imre Pozsgay and Rezső Nyers on the Hungarian radio's '168 hours' program," in FBIS-EEU, *Daily Report*, April 18, 1989, pp. 27–30. See also "Interview with Károly Grósz," *Népszabadság*, April 13, 1989.
51 Pozsgay, "1989 – a political career," p. 126.
52 *Ibid.*, p. 127.
53 *HSWP CC Minutes, 1989*, pp. 758–63.
54 Grósz justified Kádár's removal from the CC and his forced resignation as party chairman by saying that "in view of [Kádár's] health we would have had to make a decision sooner or later ... if we were to make a decision to this effect after June 16th [the date of Imre Nagy's public reburial] ... it would appear as if our action had been the result of public pressure that would inevitably surface during the [reburial] demonstration. *HSWP CC Minutes, 1989*, p. 881. Why did Kádár put up with this humiliating charade? As his widow explained, "because the poor thing was a good[-natured] idiot (*mert a szegény egy jó marha volt*) ... [he was] a disciplined person who never put himself ahead of others." "Jóban – rosszban" (In

sickness and in health. Interview with Mrs. János Kádár), *Magyarország*, December 8, 1989.

55 OL 288 f4/263 (May 29, 1989), pp. 12–14.

56 Cf. "Kádár János utolsó napjai" (The last days of János Kádár), *Magyar Hirlap*, September 12, 1990.

57 At the next CC meeting Grósz bitterly complained about unnamed CC members who had failed to stand up for the secretary general. OL 288 f4/260 (May 8, 1989), p. 45.

58 *Magyar Nemzet*, April 17, 1989.

59 Radio Budapest 1000 GMT, April 23, 1989, in FBIS-EEU, *Daily Report*, April 26, 1989, pp. 36–7.

60 The actual quote: "My own Politburo voted down my proposal a few weeks ago, therefore I did not submit it to the CC. I believe the situation is ripe for the introduction of an economic state of emergency ... In the government Miklós Németh had similar ambitions; that is why he created his [new] cabinet." FBIS-EEU, *Daily Report*, April 25, 1989, p. 22.

61 Budapest Television Service 1730 GMT, April 22, 1989, in FBIS-EEU, *Daily Report*, April 24, 1989, p. 23.

62 *Ibid.*

63 Text of announcement in FBIS-EEU, *Daily Report*, April 26, 1989, p. 30.

64 On this see Gyula Horn, "Pillars," and *HSWP CC Minutes, 1989*, p. 920.

65 *Magyar Nemzet*, May 10, 1989. This, however, was not the case. As will be shown below, Grósz as secretary general was still the commander in chief of the armed forces. He kept his (secret) statutory grip on the levers of coercion until he surrendered the "keys to the panic button" to Rezső Nyers or Miklós Németh on October 10, 1989.

66 The Hungarian professional military never thought much of what they called a "second-class hunting club" of submachine-gun-toting weekend civilian warriors. Until March 1989, when the HSWP PB disbanded the elite *Egyetértés* (Concordia) hunting club, lower-status cadres with such sporting ambitions had limited access to the elites' reserved hunting grounds. The Workers' Guard had a full-time bureaucracy of three thousand and assets valued at HUF 9 billion, or about $150 million at 1989 exchange rates. See *Népszabadság*, December 14, 1989.

67 *Magyar Hirlap*, May 11, 1989.

68 FBIS-EEU, *Daily Report*, May 12, 1989, p. 32.

69 OL 288 f4/260 (May 8, 1989), p. 20.

70 *Ibid.*, p. 88.

71 *Ibid.*, p. 151.

72 *Ibid.*, p. 185.

73 *Ibid.*, p. 188.

74 *Ibid.*, p. 220.

75 FBIS-EEU, *Daily Report*, May 20, 1989, p. 20.

76 *Ibid.*, May 22, 1989, pp. 31–2.

77 OL 288 f4/260 (May 8, 1989), pp. 54ff.

78 *HSWP CC Minutes, 1989*, p. 863.

79 *Ibid.*, p. 858.
80 Draft version of the HSWP's official statement on Imre Nagy, *HSWP CC Minutes, 1989*, pp. 1079–80.
81 *Ibid.*, p. 1031.
82 *Népszabadság*, June 8, 1989.
83 *Népszabadság*, June 11, 1989.
84 Hungarian press reports, June 17, 1989. One of the macabre aspects of the Nagy reburial had been the judicial authorities' efforts to locate the victims' bodies. Some of the bodies had been dumped in unmarked sites in the potter's field of the Budapest municipal cemetery. In any case, Nagy's executioners had observed the legal guidelines that were in force in 1958 concerning disposal of the remains of certain types of individuals. According to a secret decree (No. 1105/1954 XII. 17) of the council ministers, the remains of those executed for political crimes were not to be surrendered to their relatives. The decree was signed by prime minister Imre Nagy. See "Emberiességi okokból" (For humanitarian reasons), *Magyarország*, January 2, 1989, p. 25.
85 FBIS-EEU, *Daily Report*, June 19, 1989, p. 34.
86 András Bozóki, ed., "With a clean page," pp. 154–6.
87 Károly Vigh, "A temetés után" (After the funeral), *Magyar Nemzet*, June 24, 1989.
88 Pozsgay, "1989 – a political career,", p. 150.
89 *HSWP CC Minutes, 1989*, pp. 1184–6.
90 *Ibid.*, p. 1215.
91 *Ibid.*, p. 1221.
92 *Ibid.*, p. 1234.
93 *Ibid.*, p. 1256.
94 *Ibid.*, p. 1265.
95 *Ibid.*, p. 1234.
96 *Ibid.*, p. 1266.
97 Text of the Polish Roundtable agreement is in *Trybuna Ludu*, April 7, 1989, in FBIS-EEU, *Daily Report*, May 5, 1989, pp. 19–35. For the full text and appendices, see *Poruzumenia Okrałego Stolu* (The Roundtable agreement) (Warsaw, 1989). According to the signed documents, between February 6 and April 5, 1989, three task forces, nine auxiliary task forces, and two working groups, for a total of 128 negotiators and fourteen experts, participated in this historic enterprise.
98 Richter, "The Opposition Roundtable," pp. 294–300.
99 Text of Grósz's statement is in Budapest Domestic Service, 1500 GMT, June 13, 1989, FBIS-EEU, *Daily Report*, June 14, 1989, pp. 33–5; Kónya's statement is in Richter, "The Opposition Roundtable," pp. 302–3; Kukorelli's remarks are in *Magyar Nemzet*, June 14, 1989.
100 *Magyar Hirlap*, September 18, 1990.
101 Although all political parties consented to the release of the material, some of the individual participants, in the exercise of their "personality rights" (to privacy), vetoed the idea. By the process of elimination, the

wielders of veto power may be tentatively identified as those, then incumbent, government officials who later became justices of the Constitutional Court or served as subcabinet-level officials in the Antall and Boross governments of 1990–4.

102 Reconstructed from data in András Bozóki, "Út a rendszerváltáshoz: az Ellenzéki Kerekasztal" (Road to the change of the system: the Opposition Roundtable), *Mozgó Világ*, 8 (1990), 23–37 and from NRT working documents that Dr. László Bruszt (a Liga observer) was kind enough to make available to me. I am also indebted to several Hungarian colleagues from all three sides of the NRT for sharing their experiences and insights with me.

103 Richter, "The Opposition Roundtable," pp. 304–9.

104 FBIS-EEU, *Daily Report*, June 14, 1989, p. 34.

105 Biographies of the key ORT negotiators are in Richter, "The Opposition Roundtable," and in József Kiss, ed., *Az 1990–ben megválasztott Országgyűlés almanachja* (Almanac of the Hungarian legislature elected in 1990) (Budapest: A Magyar Országgyűlés Kiadása, 1992).

106 I am indebted to Dr. Géza Kilényi, Justice of the Hungarian Constitutional Court (then of the Institute of State and Law, the Hungarian Academy of Sciences), for making copies of background studies on legal reforms available to me.

107 As it turned out, the party had a great deal to hide. According to its official accounting of late September 1989, in the previous four decades the HSWP had accumulated assets worth more than HUF 10 billion – appraised at book value as of the mid-1950s. The current 1989 market value of these assets, including 2,641 buildings, was estimated to be twelve to fifteen times higher than the amount stated in the original appraisals. A preliminary report on the HSWP's assets was submitted by Pál Iványi to the last (September 25, 1989) meeting of the CC, HSWP. Text in *HSWP CC Minutes, 1989*, pp. 1851–77.

108 In late September, upon conclusion of the NRT discussions, József Antall, prime minister Németh, and minister of justice Kulcsár altered the agreement by adding thirty-six additional seats to the previously agreed-upon 350. On this, see Kálmán Kulcsár, "A 'jog uralma' és a magyar alkotmánybíráskodás" (Rule of the law and the record of the Hungarian Constitutional Court, 1990–1992) (First draft of MS, 1992). This useful information was omitted from the published version in *Politikatudományi Szemle* 1 (1993), 5–38.

109 For a "mid-course" progress report on the deliberations of the I/3 working group, see "Az I/3. számú munkabizottság javaslata a középszintű egyeztető bizottságnak a választási törvénnyel kapcsolatos vitás kérdések eldöntésére" (Recommendations of the I/3 working group to the mid-level reconciliation committee (*egyeztető bizottság*) for the resolution of disputed questions on the electoral law), August 24, 1989.

110 András Bozóki, "Intellectuals and Democratization in Hungary," Paper read at the 26th National Convention of the AAASS, Philadelphia, PA, November 17–20, 1994, p. 31.

111 Erzsébet Szalai, "Szereppróba" (Tryout for a role), *Valóság* 12 (1990), 14–29.

112 *Ibid.*, p. 18.

113 *Ibid.*, p. 25.

114 *Ibid.*, p. 24.

115 *Ibid.*, pp. 26–7. To the question "Do you see anything objectionable in the transformation of state enterprises to [private] companies?" the AFD expert's response was unequivocal: "Much of the outcry about this matter is without merit. Many people fail to realize that the transformation of state property into private property is likely to be more beneficial than will be the losses incurred due to suspicious transactions." See "Interview with Márton Tardos," *Heti Világgazdaság*, September 30, 1989. See also, "Privatizáció – 1989–1990" (Privatization, 1989–1990; interviews), *Mozgó Világ*, January 1991, pp. 3–33.

116 József Szekeres, "Fegyverletétel. A Politikai Egyeztető Tárgyalások Történetéből" (Surrender – [pages from] the history of the the National Roundtable), *Szabadság*, February 16, 1990.

117 *Ibid.*

118 *Népszava* [the TUF's daily], "Special Issue for a Strike Fund, August, 1989."

119 *Népszabadság*, August 31, 1989.

120 As an angry Németh put it: "Let's have the government have its say, if you don't mind." OL 288 f4/270 (September 12–13, 1989), p. 42.

121 On this, see András Végvári, "Szerepzavar" (Role confusion), *Valóság*, March 1991, p. 94.

122 János Kenedi, "Emberekről, eszmékről, politikáról" (Of people, ideas, and politics), *Valóság*, April 1990, p. 48.

123 All such objectionable transactions involved the surreptitious transfer of titles to party-owned real estate to trusted low-level party officials in about eight locations. See *Népszabadság*, August 29, 1989. In the end, even the HDF joined the AFD's position on this matter. See *Népszabadság*, September 6, 1989. Pál Iványi, CC secretary for economic affairs, admitted before the CC that "our efforts to preserve our assets by transferring them to [private] companies failed." On the other hand, he believed that transferring such assets through private companies "into a joint venture with a foreign investor would make the property disappear." OL 288 f4/268 (September 1, 1989), p. 172. See also "Csillapithatatlan pártvágy a magántulajdon iránt" (Unquenchable party thirst for private property), *Magyar Nemzet*, September 20, 1989.

124 András Bozóki, "Vencel téri képeslap" (Greeting card from Wenczeslas Square), *Világ*, August 31, 1989. According to foreign minister Gyula Horn's report to the HSWP CC, prior to his official intercession on their behalf, the Czechoslovak authorities had been planning to hold a show trial for the two detained Fidesz activists. They were to receive a prison sentence of six months – to be served in Hungary. OL 288 f4/268 (September 1, 1989), pp. 7–8.

125 Pozsgay, "1989 – a political career," pp. 158ff.
126 Interview with Imre Pozsgay, August 26, 1989, Balatonarács, Hungary.
127 Pozsgay and Antall were in daily contact throughout the NRT negotiations. Because neither elected to divulge the subject of their discussions, these private meetings gave rise to various conspiracy theories about the agreements (if any) concluded between these politicians and, at least in 1988–9, personal friends.
128 Although Pozsgay's memoirs speak about Németh in positive terms, there was a great deal of petty rivalry between the two. According to Gombár, Németh took offense when in the fall of 1988 Pozsgay dismissed the importance of the office of prime minister as one that was fit for a "clerk" (*hivatalnok*). (By contrast, in an interview with a Polish newspaper Pozsgay described himself as a "statesman.") On the other hand, Pozsgay found it galling that Németh had pirated some phrases and passages from his speeches without attribution. See Csaba Gombár, "Kormányzati kérdéseken tünődve" (Reflections on governance), in György Várnai, ed., *Logosz* (Budapest: ELTE Szociológiai és Szociálpolitikai Intézet, 1990), p. 54; Grzegorz Woczyk, "Fever Pitch," *Życie Warszawy*, April 18, 1989 in FBIS-EEU *Daily Report* May 9, 1989, p. 35, and Interview with Imre Pozsgay, August 26, 1989, Balatonarács, Hungary.
129 OL 288 f4/270 (September 12, 1989), pp. 42 and 72ff.
130 Commenting on Movement for a Democratic Hungary, the AFD's Bálint Magyar remarked, "this was an odd creature ... it was like a frozen dish – it was precooked, then put in the freezer ready to be warmed up when needed. This is what Pozsgay did ... but failed to realize that a dish, when taken in and out of the freezer, becomes spoiled at the end." See Richter, "The Opposition Roundtable," p. 33. The same was true for Nyers' New March Front. Both the MDH and the NMF disappeared from public view at the end of September 1989.
131 Interview with Imre Pozsgay, August 26, 1989. On Nyers' visit with Gorbachev, see "Interview with Rezső Nyers," Budapest Television Service 1700 GMT, July 30, 1989, in FBIS-EEU, *Daily Report*, July 31, 1989, pp. 16–17.
132 As is shown in Appendix 7.1, the size of the ORT's "half loaf" was quite substantial. In terms of legal reforms, the ORT's lawyers succeeded in producing a revised Constitution, the text of which was 80 percent new. See Gábor Halmai, "Alkotmány és alkotmánybiráskodás" (Constitution and the Constitutional Court), in "Hungarian Political Yearbook, 1991," pp. 149–55.
133 OL 288 f4/268 (September 1, 1989), p. 209.
134 *Ibid.*, p. 24.
135 *Ibid.*, p. 29.
136 *Ibid.*, p. 38.
137 *Ibid.*, pp. 58–60. It took monumental hubris for Pozsgay to imagine that the AFD and Fidesz had been oblivious to the existence of his proxies and

political informants within the ORT. Moreover, by that time the ORT's liberals had *their* informants among the HSWP's central apparat.

138 OL 288 f4/270 (September 12, 1989), pp. 8–23.

139 *Ibid.*, p. 24.

140 *Ibid.*, p. 35.

141 *Ibid.*, pp. 40–1.

142 *Ibid.*, p. 45.

143 *Ibid.*, p. 68.

144 At the nationally televised signing ceremony, the AFD and Fidesz declined to sign the NRT agreement. As Pozsgay recalled, this "caught the rest of the unsuspecting particiants [himself included] by surprise." He added that "for the first time in three months of negotiations, I lost my temper and, looking straight into the cameras, I said what I thought of the entire procedure." In Pozsgay, "1989 – a political career," pp. 164–5. Pozsgay need not have been surprised. Had he, as a member of the party Presidium, read the government's daily intelligence digests, or asked his friend, minister of interior István Horváth, whose Department III/III was in charge of domestic political counterintelligence, he could easily have learned about the liberals' impending coup. In any case, as late as December 5, 1989, in addition to the prime minister, minister of state Rezső Nyers, foreign minister Gyula Horn, and HSP secretary Jenő Kovács [!], Imre Pozsgay was one of the fourteen recipients of reports from the Ministry of the Interior, Department III/III (political counter-intelligence) shown on the "distribution list" (*elosztó*). On this, see statement by Gáspár Miklós Tamás, MP (AFD) to the Parliament (broad-cast live on Hungarian radio), in "Report on Security Service," Budapest Domestic Service 1323 GMT, March 2, 1990 in FBIS-EEU, *Daily Report*, March 5, 1990, pp. 44–5; and "A BM Belső Biztonsági Szolgálat Tevékeny-ségét Vizsgáló Bizottság, 655. számú bizottsági jelentés a BM belső biztonsági szolgálat tevékenységéről" ([Parliamentary] Investigation Committee on the activities of the counterintelligence service of the Ministry of Interior, Committee Report No. 655 on the activities of the counterintelligence service) (February 28, 1990) [Attachment No. 2; List of recipients of reports from the Ministry of Interior, p. 2].

145 The Law on Plebiscites (Law XVII of 1989), which the Parliament had enacted on June 15, made provisions for citizens' initiatives. Upon the submission of 100,000 verified signatures to the Ministry of Interior, the Parliament was legally bound to authorize the holding of a plebiscite on the issue addressed by the initiative. An earlier law on the recall of MPs by petition of registered voters in their constituencies had been an effective tool in the hands of the opposition parties in 1989. By the end of that year, twenty-six MPs had been recalled, and up to one-fourth threatened by such grassroots initiatives.

146 *Népszabadság*, October 8, 1989.

147 Sources utilized for the analysis of the on- and off-the-record deliberations of the HSWP's 14th and the HSP's first congress include *Kongreszus '89*

(Congress '89) Documents of the congress in 32 parts, August 14–October 8, 1989; reports in the Hungarian national press for October 6–11, 1989; and miscellaneous handouts by representatives of various congressional policy caucuses. I am indebted to the BBC's Hungarian Service for the opportunity to assist, as an expert commentator, with its coverage of this event.

148   Pozsgay, "1989 – a political career," pp. 150–2.

149   The East German refugee crisis was fully covered by the international press in September 1989.

150   Earlier in the year KGB chief Kriuchkov had tried to plant some of this material on Rezső Nyers, but Nyers turned him down. The text of Grósz's remarks does not appear in the minutes of the September 1, 1989 meeting of the HSWP CC, but was subsequently published in the "new" HSWP's daily, *Szabadság*, June 15, 1990.

151   Grósz's wife, whom he married when he was a young military officer in the early 1950s, died after a long illness in early July. According to Grósz's associates, his wife's death and the pressure of intraparty feuds had been too much for him to cope with.

152   As Grósz explained, "The failure [to precipitate] a party split was my fault. My congressional speech was the product of a bad compromise. It was written the previous night. I tried to come up with a balance between my earlier position and what I heard from the Political Executive Committee. I knew that my rivals in the party did not want a split that would have put them on a collision course with the rank-and-file membership. I was hoping that the congress would reject the RA's position and that they would leave the party after the congress. My meetings with delegates from the counties helped reinforce this belief ... Because my original report was rejected by the PEC, the alternatives that I presented in my congressional speech never reached the party membership. I will never forgive myself for my conduct at that time. Although the social outcome [that is, the election results of 1990] would not have been different ... a much stronger party would have emerged from this dispute." Letter From Károly Grósz, April 1994.

153   *Reformkörök és reform alapszervezetek budapesti tanácskozása, 1989 szeptember 2–3* (The Budapest conference of Reform Circles and reform party cells, September 2–3, 1989) (Budapest: Kossuth, 1989).

154   There was one memorable sentence in Miklós Németh's speech: "Comrades, we do not care how many [party] members we will have, but we do care about how many votes we will get" (my notes).

155   Data are from various issues of "Congress '89."

156   "Congress '89," no. 27 (October 28, a.m.), pp. 2–3.

157   My notes.

158   Cf. "A kormányfő nem érzi helyét a pártelnökségben" (The prime minister is uncomfortable in the party Presidium), *Népszabadság*, September 26, 1989.

159   On this, see "Kétségek és kérdőjelek" (Doubts and question marks. Interview with Ferenc Gazsó), *Magyar Nemzet*, November 6, 1989.

160 The denouement of Grósz's exit from the regime took place on the last day of the HSP congress. As Grósz recalled, he and some of his friends were having a conversation in his suite in the same building (Hotel Novotel) in which the congress was being held. Then "I received a telephone call from the minister of defense Ferenc Kárpáti – right from the meeting of the Council of Ministers [also held in the same hotel]. He informed me that Miklós Németh recommended that we should be arrested ... for organizing a *Putsch*. I asked Kárpáti to come over and see for himself ... He came and when he saw what we were doing, he left. Later on that evening he called and told me that the government had given up on the idea of my arrest. I was annoyed and told him that to be arrested would have been politically the best thing that could have happened to me. Németh knew ... that there existed a [standby] scenario for implementation of a martial law regime, but did not know what was in it and was worried that we might want to set it into motion." See Bodzabán and Szalay, eds., "From soft dictatorship," pp. 142–3.

161 "Hungary: a fatal split," *Eastern European Newsletter* (London) September 11, 1989, p. 3. For Pozsgay's second thoughts on this matter, see "Sikerült a pártot letaglózni" (The party was successfully bludgeoned to the ground. Interview with Imre Pozsgay), *Beszélő*, September 26, 1992, pp. 16–18.

162 See Rudolf L. Tőkés, "Beyond the party congress. Hungary's hazy future," *The New Leader*, October 30, 1989, pp. 5–7. See also David K. Shipler, "Letter from Budapest," *The New Yorker*, November 20, 1989, pp. 74–101.

8   The road to power

1 *Heti Világgazdaság*, October 28, 1989.
2 *Népszava*, November 16, 1989 and *Reform*, November 24, 1989. Unlike laid-off workers and employees, each member of the Workers' Guard received severance pay equal to one year's wages. See "Military Hearings," January 15, 1990, p. 241.
3 *Magyar Hirlap*, November 10, 1989.
4 "Hungarian Political Yearbook, 1990 "p. 330.
5 *Magyar Nemzet*, January 9, 1990.
6 *Magyar Nemzet*, October 22, 1989.
7 The matter could be referred to either as a "referendum," that is, "the submission of a law, proposed or already in effect, to a direct vote of the people," or as a "plebiscite," that is, "an expression of the people's will by direct ballot of all eligible voters on a political issue." My sense is that in the given context, the word "plebiscite" conveys the *political* essence of that which took place on November 26, 1989 in Hungary. The definitions are from *Webster's New World Dictionary of the American Language* (Cleveland and New York: The World Publishing Company, 1959), pp. 1221 and 1122.
8 "Hungarian Political Yearbook, 1990," p. 321.

9 Text of the statement by the HDF's Presidium, p. 328. The HDF's anti-plebiscite slogan, "Whoever is a Hungarian stays home!" was seen by the promoters of the plebiscite as an attack on their patriotism. Chances are that the HDF's verbal innuendo offended enough people and thus helped increase the turnout on November 26.

10 *Népszava*, November 30, 1989.

11 *Magyar Nemzet*, December 21, 1989. Six weeks later the gloves were off as far as the HSP was concerned. An author in the party's weekly put it this way: "Miklós Németh's government is not the HSP's but the International Monetary Fund's government." Attila György Kovács, "Baloldaliság, záró-jelben?" (Leftist identity: should it be hidden?), *Uj Forum*, February 9, 1990, p. 10.

12 "Interview with Gyula Thürmer, President of the HSWP," *Népszabadság*, December 19, 1989. See also Tamás Fricz, "Vándorkommunisták" (Wandering communists), *Világ*, November 16, 1989, pp. 18–21; and "Regardless of our mistakes, we are not turncoats." Interview with János Berecz, *Hajdu Bihari Napló*, November 21, 1989.

13 Pozsgay, "1989 – a political career," p. 7.

14 On October 25, Pozsgay embarked on a three-week trip to Great Britain, Canada, the United States and Finland. *Ibid.*, pp. 173–84.

15 József Antall, *Modell és valóság* (Model and reality), 2 vols. (Budapest: Athenaeum, 1994), pp. 645–50.

16 József Antall, Sr., was the recipient of official honors from the Polish and Israeli governments, and of a Certificate of Merit from General Mark Clark, U.S.A., for personal and official assistance rendered to American prisoners of war (US Air Force personnel) in Hungary.

17 József Antall, Sr., died in 1970.

18 See "Modell és valóság. Eötvös József a kiegyezési politika sodrában" (Model and reality. [Baron] József Eötvös in the midst of [pre-]Compromise politics), in Antall, "Model and reality," pp. 19–40.

19 Text of position paper, pp. 467–73.

20 László Lengyel, "Az Antall rejtély" (The Antall mystery), *Magyar Hirlap*, December 13, 1993.

21 A signal exception to this was the obituary by the AFD leader Péter Tölgyessy, who had been Antall's fellow ORT negotiator at the National Roundtable. See Péter Tölgyessy, "Tette, mint lehetett" (He did what he could), *Népszabadság*, December 18, 1993.

22 Károly Grósz, letter of April 1994.

23 This letter is a remarkable document and evidence of civilized discourse between the regime and its high-status nonparty *nomenklatura* critics in the winter of 1988–9. Antall's letter and the replies from Grósz's secretariat were published in *Uj Magyarország*, January 9, 1992. See also József Antall, "Letter to Tivadar Pártay, editor-in-chief of *Heti Kis Ujság*," in *Heti Kis Ujság*, January 24, 1992.

24 My notes on an interview with József Antall, January 1989, Budapest.

25 Biró was also opposed to the MDF's fielding a candidate against Imre

Pozsgay for the presidency. See "Interview with Zoltán Biró" *Komárom Megyei Dolgozók Lapja*, November 28, 1989.

26 Biró, "The withered revolution," pp. 33–5. See also *Népszabadság*, October 24, 1989.

27 For a listing of 250 parties and quasi-political associations in Hungary in 1989, see *Politikai Bedekker* (Political Baedecker) (Budapest: Credit Kiadó, 1990); *Lel-Tár I, II* (Inventory – catalogues of new social organizations) (Budapest, 1988, 1989); and "A guide to political parties," *Heti Világgazdaság*, November 11, 1989.

28 For a comprehensive account of processes of party formation, see Bihari, ed., "The development," and "Hungarian Political Yearbook, 1990," *passim*. See also Rudolf L. Tőkés, *Vom Post-Kommunismus zur Demokratie: Politik, Parteien und die Wahlen 1990 in Ungarn* (Bonn: Konrad Adenauer Stiftung-Forschungsinstitut, 1990).

29 For biographical information on the parliamentary MPs elected in 1990, see József Kiss, ed., *Az 1990–ben megválasztott országgyűlés almanachja* (Parliamentary almanac, 1990) (Budapest, 1992).

30 Hungarian Institute of Public Opinion Research, "Közvélemény 1989-ben" (Public opinion in 1989), in "Hungarian Political Yearbook, 1990," pp. 433–63.

31 *Ibid.*

32 *Ibid.*

33 János Kis, "A visszaszámlálás megkezdődött" (The countdown has begun), *Annotated Beszélő*, vol. III, p. 803.

34 *Hang-Súly* 1, 5 (1989), 18; *Magyar Nemzet*, November 22, December 23, 1989; February 17 and March 13, 1990.

35 Ágnes Bokor, "Public Opinion Concerning the Process of Regime Change," in *SR '90*, p. 435.

36 On the Pozsgay media committee, see "Tizenkét honap krónikája, november 23" (Chronicle of twelve months, [events of] November 23 [1989]), in "Hungarian Political Yearbook, 1990" pp. 331–2. See also Zoltán Farkas, "Hadijelentés. Harcok a sajtó körül – adalékok egy vitához" (War report. Press war, addenda to a dispute), *Mozgó Világ*, July 1990, pp. 12–32.

37 "Idézés a vagyonelszámoltató bizottság elé" (Warrant to appear before the assets-review committee), *Magyar Hirlap*, February 21, 1990.

38 The cashiered counterintelligence chief's recollections offer novel perspectives on this affair. See József Horváth, *A lehallgatástól a kihallgatásig* (From wiretapping to [parliamentary] hearings) (Budapest: Holding Kiadó, 1991). See also József Végvári and Zoltán Lovas, "Szomorújáték" (Melodrama), *Magyar Narancs*, February 5, 1990. On the Ministry of Interior's network of 16,500 secret informants, see "Nincs teljes lista" (There is no complete list), *Népszabadság*, September 4, 1990.

39 Parliamentary committee to investigate the activities of the counterintelligence service of the Ministry of Interior, Károly Mezey, Chair, "655. számú bizottsági jelentés a BM belső biztonsági szolgálatának tevékenységéről; 1990 február 28" (Report no. 655 on the activities of the counterintelligence

service of the Ministry of Interior; February 28, 1990). A list of twenty-three parties (including the HSP itself) and social organizations under police surveillance until late December 1989 is in Appendix 3 of this report. For Miklós Németh's justification of his government's conduct, see "Speech by Premier Miklós Németh at the National Assembly session," FBIS-EEU, *Daily Report*, March 5, 1990 (1300 GMT March 2, 1990), pp. 41–4. For AFD MP Miklós Gáspár Tamás' rebuttal of the same, see *ibid.*, pp. 44–5.

40 Cf. Rudolf L. Tőkés, "Hungary's New Political Elites: Adaptation and Change, 1989–90," *Problems of Communism* 39, 6 (1990), 61.

41 The subject of party and campaign financing did not, for understandable reasons, benefit from much *glasnost'* in Hungarian party publications. The year-end 1989 financial statements of the HDF, the AFD, the ISP, and the HSP were given in *Világ*, April 12, 1990, pp. 30–1.

42 *Népszabadság*, March 23, 1990.

43 According to Hungarian election law, all campaign contributions must be reported by the recipients. Cf. Tibor Bogdán *et al.*, *Pártok és választások* (Parties and elections) (Budapest: Közgazdasági és Jogi Kiadó, 1990), pp. 53–60. According to Western business executives active in Hungary since 1989, this rule was ignored by both the foreign donors and the domestic recipients.

44 *Népszabadság*, March 23, 1990.

45 Ágnes Kapitány and Gábor Kapitány, "The parties' values," *Magyar Hirlap*, March 8, 1990. See also Anna Zelenay, "The viewers, the parties and the media," *Világ*, April 5, 1990, p. 101.

46 Ágnes Kapitány and Gábor Kapitány, "The structure of electoral values," *Első Kézből*, 2, 13 (1990), 10–15.

47 Cf. László Kéri, "Kérdések a választás elött" (Questions before the elections. Twenty-four theses on the electoral chances). Unpublished MS (February 1990).

48 Preelection poll by Gallup Budapest, February–March 1990.

49 *Magyar Nemzet*, March 28, 1990.

50 For a list of independent and party-endorsed candidates, see *Népszabadság*, February 10, 1990. For a full roster (1,007 names) of the twelve top parties' national slates, see *Magyar Nemzet*, March 2, 1990.

51 On this, see György Szoboszlai, "Választási rendszer és politikai tagoltság" (Electoral system and political stratification), in György Szoboszlai, ed., *Parlamenti választások, 1990* (Parliamentary elections, 1990) (Budapest: Társadalomtudományi Intézet, 1990), pp. 12–26.

52 See John R. Hibbing and Samuel C. Patterson, "A Democratic Legislature in the Making: The Historic Hungarian Elections of 1990," *Comparative Political Studies* 24, 4 (1992), 430–53.

53 Hungarian press reports, April 3, 1990.

54 *Heti Világgazdaság* April 14, 1990; *Népszabadság*, April 10, 1990; András Körösényi, "The Hungarian Parliamentary Elections, 1990," in András Bozóki *et al.*, eds., *Post-Communist Transition: Emerging Pluralism in Hungary* (New York: St. Martin's Press, 1992), p. 79.

55 Körösényi "The Hungarian Parliamentary Elections."

56 József Kiss and Éva Kovács in Bihari, ed., "The development," pp. 261–2.

57 Sándor Csizmadia, "Why did the Free Democrats lose?" *Magyar Hirlap*, April 13, 1990 and Tamás Bauer, "Why did we lose?" *Magyar Hirlap*, April 23, 1990.

58 *Magyar Nemzet*, March 14, 1990.

59 *Népszabadság*, April 10, 1990.

60 *Beszélő*, April 14, 1990, pp. 5, 20.

61 Cf. Edward Shils, *The Intellectuals and the Powers and Other Essays* (Chicago: University of Chicago Press, 1972).

62 The political ethics of the Németh government's last-minute actions, such as the tranfer of valuable real estate to the successor organizations of the YCL and the Young Pioneers, left a great deal to be desired. Some of the beneficiaries, such as YCL first secretary Imre Nagy, ended up four years later with a publishing empire from the management of assets bequeathed to him by the outgoing Németh government. See also Endre Babus, "A hatalmi, politikai infrastruktúra és rendszerváltás" (Change of regimes: power and infrastructure), "Hungarian Political Yearbook, 1991," pp. 156–86.

63 Németh's payoff was Antall's recommendation and US support to his nomination for a vice-presidency of the European Bank for Reconstruction and Development. As of early 1996, Németh is still employed there.

64 See János Kis, "Megállapodás" (The agreement), *Beszélő*, May 5, 1990, pp. 4–5.

65 Text in *Magyar Hirlap*, May 5, 1990. For an English translation, in FBIS-EEU, *Daily Report*, June 14, 1990, pp. 26–30.

66 For a perceptive commentary on the HDF–AFD pact, see Zoltán Lovas, "No reconciliation. Only an agreement," *Magyar Hirlap*, May 3, 1990, in FBIS-EEU, *Daily Report*, June 14, 1990, pp. 25–6.

67 On this, see Viktor Orbán, "A paktum" (The pact), *Magyar Narancs*, May 17, 1990, p. 2. On Pozsgay's reaction, see "Interview with Imre Pozsgay," *Magyar Hirlap*, May 5, 1990.

68 Tamás Korányi, "A rendszerváltás kormánya" (The new government), *Világ*, May 24, 1990.

69 Text in Bihari, "The development," pp. 267–94.

70 *Ibid.*, p. 292.

71 On this, see Károly Alexa, "Az MDF és a hatalom" (The HDF and [political] power), *Népszabadság*, June 18, 1990.

9 Democracy in Hungary

1 Rudolf L. Tőkés, "From Visegrad to Cracow: Security and Cooperation in Central Europe," *Problems of Communism* 40, 6 (1991), 100–14.

2 The first comprehensive assessments of the Antall–Boross government's record are Csaba Gombár *et al.*, eds., *Balance: The Hungarian Government, 1990–1994* (Budapest: Centre for Political Research, 1994), and "Mérleg –

1990–1994" (Balance – 1990–1994), Special Issue, *Társadalmi Szemle* 49, 8–9 (1994).

3 István Schlett, "A politika nyelvezetének alakulása a rendszerváltás után" (The language of politics and its evolution since the change of the regime), in "Mérleg – 1990–1994," pp. 28–34.

4 Although Árpád Göncz's political beliefs have not received the attention they deserve, his key policy statements are registered in post-1990 volumes of the "Hungarian Political Yearbook." For a pro-Göncz account, see István Kukorelli, "The Government and the President of the Republic: The Head of State in the Line of Fire," in Gombár, *et al., Balance*, pp. 97–116.

5 Kulcsár, "The 'rule of law,'" pp. 5–38.

6 Zoltán Tóth, "Önkormányzati választások, 1990" (Local elections, 1990), "Hungarian Political Yearbook, 1991," pp. 195–206.

7 On the three elites, see Rudolf L. Tőkés, "Hungary's New Political Elites: Adaptation and Change, 1989–1990," *Problems of Communism* 39, 6 (1990), 44–65.

8 Cf. Attila Ágh, "The Year of Incomplete Changes," "Hungarian Political Yearbook, 1991," pp. 16–31.

9 József Antall, "Model and reality," vol. I, pp. 72–5.

10 Rudolf L. Tőkés, "Democracy in Hungary: The First Hundred Days and a Mid-term Assessment," in Peter M. E. Volten, ed., *Bound to Change: Consolidating Democracy in Central Europe* (Boulder, CO: Westview, 1991), pp. 151–90.

11 Lewis S. Feuer, ed., *Marx and Engels: Basic Writings on Politics and Philosophy* (New York: Doubleday, 1959), p. 435.

12 For a judicious commentary on Antall's options see J. F. Brown, *Hopes and Shadows: Eastern Europe after Communism* (Durham, NC: Duke University Press, 1994), pp. 83ff.

13 Of the various social strata and occupational groups surveyed in 1994 on whether they were better off than they had been in 1989–90, former party-member economic experts and managers gave by far the most positive responses. See György Lengyel, "Ébredő káderdzserek?" (Awakening cadre-managers?) *Heti Világgazdaság*, December 24, 1994, pp. 105–11.

14 Béla Márian, ed., "A politikai közvélemény a Médián kutatások tükrében, 1991–1994" (Public opinion in the mirror of surveys by Médián, Inc., 1991–1994), in "Hungarian Political Yearbook, 1994," pp. 719–56.

15 Cf. István Hetényi, "Public Finances in the early 1990s," in Gombár *et al.,* eds., *Balance*, pp. 182–211; Paul Marer, "Hungary during 1988–1994: A Political Economy Assessment," in John P. Hardt and Richard F. Kaufman, eds., *East-Central European Economies in Transition: Study Papers Submitted to the Joint Economic Committee, Congress of the United States* (Washington: USGPO, 1994), pp. 480–505; Paul Marer, ed., *Financial Sector Reform and Enterprise Restructuring in Hungary* (Indianapolis: Hudson Institute, 1994). See also Jeffrey Sachs, "Postcommunist Parties and the Politics of Entitlements," *Transition* 6, 3 (1995), 1–4.

16 Cf. Károly Okolicsányi, "Macroeconomic Changes in Hungary, 1990–1994," *RFE Research Report* 3, 24 (1994), 21–6.

17 Richard Rose, *Between State and Market: Key Indicators of Transition in Eastern Europe* (Glasgow: Centre for the Study of Public Policy, University of Strathclyde, 1991), especially pp. 55–80.

18 László Reisz, *Gazdasági és társadalmi koncepciók a politikai propagandában, 1962–1980* (Economic and social concepts in political propaganda, 1962–1980) (Budapest: KSH Könyvtár és Dokumentációs Szolgálat, 1988), p. 122.

19 In the Hungarian politicians' minds the term *Sozialmarktwirtschaft* evoked the attractive precedent of Ludwig Erhardt's policies in the shaping of the German "economic miracle" in the 1960s.

20 The Christian democrats' nationalist message was articulated by members of the government (particularly József Antall, minister of defense Lajos Für, minister of culture Bertalan Andrásfalvy, and foreign minister Géza Jeszenszky), designated HDF MPs, party ideologues (István Csurka and Sándor Csoóri), village radicals (Sándor Lezsák), and government-appointed mouthpieces, such as István Pálffy, in the regime-controlled TV.

21 Text in *Magyar Hirlap*, September 9, 1991.

22 Text in *Magyar Fórum*, August 20, 1992.

23 Text in "Hungarian Political Yearbook, 1992," pp. 570–1.

24 Cited in François Fejto, "Hungarian Communism," in William E. Griffith, ed., *Communism in Europe* vol. I (Cambridge, MA: MIT Press, 1964), p. 191.

25 Richard Rose and Christian Haerpfer, *New Democracies Between State and Market: A Baseline Report on Public Opinion* (Glasgow: Centre for the Study of Public Policy, University of Strathclyde, 1992), p. 66.

26 Harry Eckstein, "A Culturalist Theory of Political Change," *American Political Science Review* 82, 3 (1988), 789–804.

27 *Ibid.*, p. 793.

28 *Ibid.*, pp. 795–6.

29 See Elemér Hankiss, Róbert Manchin, László Füstös, and Árpád Szakolczai, *Kényszerpályán? A magyar társadalom értékrendszerének alakulása 1930 és 1980 között* (On a forced path? Changes in the value structure of Hungarian society between 1930 and 1980) (Budapest: Sociology Institute, Hungarian Academy of Sciences, 1982). See also Elemér Hankiss, "Társadalompatológia" (Social pathology), in Elemér Hankiss, *Diagnózisok 2* (Diagnoses 2) (Budapest: Magvető, 1986), pp. 99–218, and Elemér Hankiss, *Hongrie diagnostiques: essai en pathologie sociale* (Geneva: Georg Eshel, 1990).

30 Lajos Géza Nagy, *Történelem képek és jövő-képek* (Images of history and ideology. The stratification of ideological beliefs in the early 1980s), unpublished dissertation for the degree of Candidate of Sociological Sciences, Budapest, 1989, p. 155. My thanks to Dr. Nagy for making a copy of his work available to me.

31 *Ibid.*, pp. 189–201 and György Csepeli and Rudolf L. Tőkés, "Our Place in the World: National Identity and National Consciousness in Hungary" (1985), unpublished MS.

32 Guy Lázár, ed., *Társadalmi-gazdasági fejlődésünk ideológiai kérdései közgondolk-*

odásban (Ideological questions of sociopolitical development in public opinion) (Budapest: MCRI, 1986), p. 83.

33 Eckstein, "A Culturalist Theory," p. 800.

34 Guy Lázár, "Állampolgári vélemények a politikai rendszerről" (Citizens' opinions about the political system) (Budapest: Social Science Institute, CC, HSWP, 1987), p. 11, and data calculated from responses to a follow-up national survey of March 1989.

35 See László Bruszt and János Simon, *A lecsendesitett többség* (The silenced majority) (Budapest: Társadalomtudományi Intézet), especially pp. 5–32.

36 Hungarian press reports, October 23 and 24, 1994.

37 Cecil A. Gibb, "Leadership – Psychological Aspects," in Sills, ed., *IESS* vol. IX, p. 95.

38 Géza Lajos Nagy, "A másik társadalom. A lakosság, a párttagság és az értelmiség képe a pártról" (The other society. Views of the public, party members and of the intellectuals on the party) (1989, unpublished MS) pp. 13, 16.

39 Jan Hartl, "Perceptions of Social Safety in the Czech and Slovak Republics, Hungary and Poland," in András Bozóki, ed., *Democratic Legitimacy in Post-Communist Societies* (Budapest: Twins, 1994), pp. 272–3.

40 Lester A. Seligman, "Leadership – Political Aspects," in Sills, ed., *IESS* vol. IX, p. 109.

41 See Miklós Tomka, "Changes in Religious and Church Policy," in Gombár *et al.*, eds., *Balance: The Hungarian Government, 1990–1994* (Budapest: Centre for Political Research, 1994).

42 Ibolya Jakus, "Leépülés" (Build-down), *Heti Világgazdaság*, April 8, 1995, pp. 103–6.

43 Zoltán Farkas, "The Antall Government's Economic Policy," in Gombár *et al.*, eds., *Balance*, pp. 162–81.

44 Katalin Tausz, "The Government and the Welfare of the Citizens," in Gombár *et al.*, eds., *Balance*, pp. 251–66.

45 Michael McFaul, "State Power, Institutional Change, and the Politics of Privatization in Russia," *World Politics* 47, 2 (1995), 216–17.

46 On privatization in Hungary, see "Hungary," in Roman Frydman *et al.*, *The Privatization Process in Central Europe* (London: Central European Press, 1993), pp. 95–147; "Privatizáció" (Privatization), special supplement *Népszabadság*, November 30, 1994, and four studies on privatization by Tamás Szabó, Bertalan Diczházi, and János Szabó Hatvani in "Hungarian Political Yearbook, 1994," pp. 826–53.

47 David Stark, "Recombinant Property in East European Capitalism," *Public Lectures*, No. 8 (Budapest: Institute for Advanced Study, Collegium Budapest, 1994).

48 *Ibid.*, p. 7.

49 *Ibid.*, p. 12 and *Népszabadság*, November 30, 1994.

50 Andrew C. János, "Continuity and Change in Eastern Europe: Strategies of Post-Communist Politics," *East European Politics and Societies* 8, 1 (1994), 3.

51 George Schopflin, "Post-communism: A Profile," *Javnost* 2, 1 (1995), 63–74.

Select bibliography

Ács, Zoltán, ed. 1988. *Kizárt a párt* (Expelled from the party). Budapest: Primo.

Aczél, Tamás, ed. 1967. *Ten Years After: The Hungarian Revolution in the Perspective of History*. New York: Holt, Rinehart and Winston.

Aczél, György. 1974. *Szocialist kultúra – közösségi ember* (Socialist culture and man of the community). Budapest: Kossuth.

1975. *Culture and Socialist Democracy*. Budapest: Corvina Press.

1984. *Socialism and the Freedom of Culture*. Budapest: Corvina Kiadó.

Ádám, Magda *et al.*, eds. 1959. *Magyarország és a második világháború* (Hungary and the Second World War). Budapest: Kossuth.

Ágh, Attila. 1989. *A századvég gyermekei* (Children of the *fin de siècle*). Budapest: Közgazdasági és Jogi Kiadó.

Ágh, Attila, ed. 1994. *The Emergence of East Central European Parliaments: The First Steps*. Budapest: Hungarian Centre for Democracy Studies.

Andorka, Rudolf. 1982. *A társadalmi mobilitás változásai Magyarországon* (Changes in social mobility in Hungary). Budapest: Gondolat.

Andorka, Rudolf, and Tamás Kolosi, eds. 1984. *Stratification and Inequality*. Budapest: HSWP Institute for the Social Sciences.

Andorka, Rudolf, *et al.* 1988. *Társadalmi beilleszkedési zavarok Magyarországon* (Disturbances in social adaptation in Hungary). Budapest: Kossuth.

Andorka, Rudolf, Tamás Kolosi, and György Vukovich, eds. 1990. *Social Report, 1990*. Budapest: TARKI.

Antall, József. 1994. *Modell és valósag* (Model and reality), 2 vols. Budapest: Athenaeum.

Armstrong, John A. 1988. "Toward a Framework for Considering Nationalism in East Europe." *East European Politics and Societies* 2, 2: 288–305.

Augusztinovics, Mária. 1982. "A makrostruktúra változása Magyarországon, 1950–2000" (Changes in the economic macrostructure in Hungary, 1950–2000). *Közgazdasági Szemle* 28, 9: 1026–43.

Balassa, János *et al.*, eds. 1989. *Halottaink* (Our dead), 2 vols. Budapest: Katalizátor.

Balogh, Sándor, and Lajos Izsák, eds. 1977. *Pártok és pártprogramok Magyarországon, 1944–1948* (Parties and party programs in Hungary, 1944–1948). Budapest: Tankönyvkiadó.

Balogh, Sándor and Árpád Pünkösti. 1992. *Rákosi a hatalomért* (Rákosi's road to power). Budapest: Europa.

Bárány, George. 1968. *Stephen Szechenyi and the Awakening of Hungarian Nationalism, 1791–1841*. Princeton: Princeton University Press.

Batt, Judy. 1988. *Economic Reform and Political Change in Eastern Europe*. New York: St. Martin's Press.

Bauer, Tamás. 1979. "Investment Cycles in Planned Economies." *Acta Oeconomica* 21, 3: 233–50.

1981. *Tervgazdaság, beruházás, ciklusok* (Planned economy, investment, cycles). Budapest: Közgazdasági és Jogi Kiadó.

Bauman, Zygmunt. 1972. "Officialdom and Class: Bases of Inequality in Socialist Society." In Frank Parkin, ed., *The Social Analysis of Class Structure*. London: Tavistock. 129–48.

1987. "Intellectuals in East-Central Europe: Continuity and Change." *East European Politics and Societies* 1, 2: 162–86.

Belley, László. 1989. "A szocialista bürökráciáról" (On socialist bureaucracy). *Szociológia* 3–4: 221–36.

Bence, György, János Kis and György Markus. 1970–2. *Hogyan lehetséges kritikai gazdaságtan?* (How can there be a critical [political] economy?). Budapest: Samizdat.

Berecz, János. 1969, 1981, 1986. *Ellenforradalom tollal és fegyverrel, 1956* (Counter-revolution with pens and weapons). Budapest: Kossuth.

1979. *Harc és együttmüködés* (Struggle and cooperation). Budapest: Akadémiai Kiadó.

1980. *Vitáink és egységünk* (Our disputes – our unity). Budapest: Akadémiai Kiadó.

Berecz, János, ed. 1984. *A néphatalom védelmében* (In defense of the people's power). Budapest: Zrinyi Katonai Kiadó.

Berend, Ivan. 1990. *The Hungarian Economic Reforms, 1953–1988*. New York: Cambridge University Press.

Berend, Ivan T. and György Ránki. 1979. *Underdevelopment and Economic Growth: Studies in Hungarian Economic and Social History*. Budapest: Akadémiai Kiadó.

Berend, Ivan T., and Miklós Szuhay. 1973. *A tőkés gazdaság története Magyarországon, 1848–1944* (History of the capitalist economy in Hungary, 1848–1944). Budapest: Kossuth Könyvkiadó.

Beschloss, Michael R., and Strobe Talbott. 1993. *At the Highest Levels: The Inside Story of the End of the Cold War*. Boston: Little, Brown.

Bibó, István. 1961. *Harmadik ut: politikai és történelmi tanulmányok* (The third road: political and historical studies). London: Magyar Könyves Céh.

Bihari, Károly. 1916. *Báró Eötvös József politikája* (The politics of Baron József Eötvös). Budapest: Magyar Tudományos Akadémia.

Bihari, Mihály. 1985. *Politikai rendszer és szocialista demokrácia* (Political system and socialist democracy). Budapest: Department of Scientific Socialism, Faculty of Law, University of Budapest.

1987. *Reform és demokrácia* (Reform and democracy). Budapest: Institute of Sociology, HAS.

Bihari, Mihály, ed. 1992. *A többpártrendszer kialakulása Magyarországon, 1985–1991* (The development of the multiparty system in Hungary, 1985–1991). Budapest: Kossuth.

Biró, Zoltán. 1988. *Saját ut* (My road). Budapest: Eötvös Kiadó.

1988. *Októberi kérdések: Pozsgay Imrével beszélget Biró Zoltán* (The questions of October: conversation with Imre Pozsgay). Budapest: Eötvös Kiadó.

1993. *Elhervadt forradalom* (The withered revolution). Budapest: Püski.

Biszku, Béla. 1972. *A párt és az állam szolgálatában* (In the service of the party and the state). Budapest: Kossuth.

Body, Paul. 1972. *József Eötvös and the Modernization of Hungary, 1840–1870: A Study of Ideas of Individuality and Social Pluralism in Modern Politics.* Philadelphia: American Philosophical Society.

Bodzabán, István, and Antal Szalay, eds. 1994 *A puha diktaturától a kemény demokráciáig* (From soft dictatorship to tough democracy). Budapest: Pelikán Kiadó.

Bogár, László. 1992. "Economic Structure." In Rudolf Andorka, Tamás Kolosi, and György Vukovich, eds., *Social Report.* Budapest: Tárki. 155–78.

Bogdán, Tibor et al. 1990. *Pártok és választások* (Parties and elections). Budapest: Közgazdasági és Jogi Kiadó.

Böhm, Antal, and László Pál. 1979. *Bejáró munkások* (Commuting workers). Budapest: MSZMP Társadalomtudományi Intézet.

1987. *A helyi hatalom működése* (Local governance). Budapest: MSZMP Társadalomtudományi Intézet.

Bokor, Ágnes. 1987. *Szegényseg a mai Magyarországon* (Poverty in Hungary today). Budapest: Magvető.

Bokor, Imre. 1989. *Kiskirályok mundérban* (Petty tyrants in uniform). Budapest: Uj Idő Kft.

Bölöny, József. 1978. *Magyarország kormányai 1848–1972* (Hungarian governments, 1848–1972). Budapest: Akadémiai Kiadó.

Borbándi, Gyula. 1983. *A magyar népi mozgalom* (The Hungarian Populist movement). New York: Püski.

Bossányi, Katalin. 1989. *Szólampróba: beszélgetések az alternativ mozgalmakról* (Voice rehearsal: conversations on the alternative movements). Budapest: Láng Kiadó.

Botos, János et al. 1988. *Magyar hétköznapok Rákosi Mátyás két emigrációja között, 1945–1956* (Everyday life in Hungary while Mátyás Rákosi was not an emigrant abroad, 1945–1956) Budapest: Minerva.

Bozóki, András, ed. 1992. *Tiszta lappal: a FIDESZ a magyar politikában, 1988–1991* (With a clean slate: Fidesz in Hungarian politics, 1988–1991). Budapest: Fidesz.

Bozóki, András, et al., eds. 1992. *Post-Communist Transition: Emerging Pluralism in Hungary.* London: Pinter Publishers.

Bozzai, Rita, and Zoltán Farkas, eds. 1991. *Hitelválság: adósságunk története* (Credit crunch: the story of our indebtedness). Budapest: Codex.

Braham, Randolph L. 1981. *The Politics of Genocide: The Holocaust in Hungary.* 2 vols. New York: Columbia University Press.

Bródy, András. 1981. *Ciklus és szabályozás* (Cycle and regulation). Budapest: Közgazdasági és Jogi Kiadó.

Brown, Archie H., and Jack Gray, eds. 1977. *Political Culture and Political Change in Communist States.* London: Macmillan.

Brown, J. F. 1994. *Hopes and Shadows: Eastern Europe after Communism.* Durham, NC: Duke University Press.

Brus, Wlodimierz, and Kazimierz Laski. 1989. *From Marx to Market.* Oxford: Clarendon Press.

Bruszt, László. 1987. "The Political Organization of Business Interests in Hungary." *EUI Colloquium Papers 261/87.* Florence: European University Institute.

Bruszt, László, and János Simon. 1990. *A lecsendesitett többseg* (The silenced majority). Budapest: Társadalomtudományi Intézet.

Brzezinski, Zbigniew K. 1971. *The Soviet Bloc: Unity and Conflict.* (Rev. edn) Cambridge, MA: Harvard University Press.

Brzezinski, Zbigniew, and Samuel Huntington. 1965. *Political Power: USA/USSR.* New York: Viking.

Büködi, E., I. Harcsa, and L. Reisz, eds. 1994. *Társadalmi tagozódás, mobilitás az 1992 évi mobilitás vizsgálat alapján* (Social stratification and mobility: a summary of results of a 1992 national survey). Budapest: Központi Statisztikai Hivatal.

Bunce, Valerie. 1989. "Decline of the Regional Hegemon: The Gorbachev Regime and Reform in Eastern Europe." *East European Politics and Societies* 3: 395–430.

1995. "Should Transitologists Be Grounded?" *Slavic Review* 54, 1: 111–27.

Burawoy, Michael. 1985. *The Politics of Production.* London: New Left Books.

Central Intelligence Agency. 1980. "The Hungarian Variant: Soviet Reactions to Hungary's Economic Reform." National Foreign Assessment Center. PA 80–10309.

Chirot, Daniel. 1988. "Ideology, Reality and Competing Models of Development in Eastern Europe between the Two World Wars." *East European Politics and Societies* 3, 3: 378–411.

Chirot, Daniel, ed. 1989. *The Origins of Backwardness in Eastern Europe: Economics and Politics from the Middle Ages until the Early Twentieth Century.* Berkeley and Los Angeles: University of California Press.

Clayton, Elizabeth M. 1985. "Consumption, Living Standards, and Consumer Welfare in Eastern Europe." In Paul Hardt and Richard F. Kaufman, eds., *East European Economies: Slow Growth in the 1980s* vol. I. Economic Performance and Policy, Joint Economic Committee, US Congress. Washington, DC: USGPO.

Connor, Walter D. 1979. *Socialism, Politics and Equality: Hierarchy and Change in Eastern Europe and the USSR.* New York: Columbia University Press.

Cook, Linda J. 1993. *The Soviet Social Contract and Why It Failed.* Cambridge, MA: Harvard University Press.

Csanádi, Mária. 1987. "A döntési mechanizmus szerkezetéről" (On the structure of decision mechanisms). *Társadalomkutatás* 4: 5–27.

Dahl, Robert A. 1971. *Polyarchy*. New Haven: Yale University Press.

Dahl, Robert A., ed. 1973. *Regimes and Oppositions*. New Haven: Yale University Press.

Dávid, János *et al.* 1990. *Forradalom, sortüz, megtorlás* (Revolution, firing squads, retaliation). Budapest: Progresszió.

Deak, Francis. 1942. *Hungary at the Paris Peace Conference*. New York: Columbia University Press.

Deák, István. 1965. "Hungary." In Hans Rogger and Eugene Weber, eds., *The European Right*. Berkeley and Los Angeles: University of California Press. 364–407.

1979. *The Lawful Revolution: Louis Kossuth and the Hungarians, 1848–1849*. New York: Columbia University Press.

Demény, Pál. 1988. *A párt foglya voltam* (I was the party's prisoner). Budapest: Medvetánc.

1989. *Zárkatársam, Spinoza* (My cellmate, Spinoza). Budapest: Akadémiai Kiadó.

Dér, Ferenc, and Lajos Kovács, eds. 1989. *A Nagy Imre vonal* (The Imre Nagy line). Budapest: Reform.

Donáth, Ferenc. 1969. *Demokratikus földreform Magyarországon, 1945–1947* (Democratic land reform in Hungary, 1945–1947). Budapest: Akadémiai Kiadó.

Donáth, Ferenc. *et al.*, eds. 1980. *Bibó Emlékkönyv* (Bibó Memorial Book). Budapest: Samizdat.

Downs, Anthony. 1964. *Inside Bureaucracy*. Boston: Little, Brown.

Dror, Yehezkel. 1968. *Public Policymaking Reexamined*. Scranton, PA: Chandler Publishing Company.

1986. *Policymaking Under Adversity*. New Brunswick, NJ: Transaction Books.

Dunmore, Timothy. 1980. *The Stalinist Command Economy: Soviet State Apparatus and Economic Policy, 1945–1953*. London: Macmillan.

Eckstein, Alexander. 1970. "Economic Development and Political Change in Communist Systems." *World Politics* 22, 4: 475–95.

Eckstein, Harry. 1965. "On the Etiology of Internal Wars." *History and Theory* 4, 2: 133–63.

1988. "A Culturalist Theory of Political Change." *American Political Science Review* 82, 3: 789–804.

Ember, Judit. 1989. *Menedékjog 1956: a Nagy Imre csoport elrablása* (Right to asylum – 1956: the abduction of the Imre Nagy group). Budapest: Szabad Tér.

Erlich, Éva. 1991. *Országok versenye, 1937–1986: fejlettségi szintek, strukturák, növekedési ütemek, iparosodási utak* (The competition of nations, 1937–1986: levels of development, structures, phases of growth and paths of industrialization). Budapest: Közgazdasági és Jogi Kiadó.

Faragó, Béla. 1988. "Magyar liberalizmus" (Hungarian liberalism). *Századvég* 6–7: 41–54.

Faragó, Klára, and Anna Vári. 1988. "Tárgyalásos módszerek környezeti konfliktusok kezelésére" (Negotiating techniques for the management of enviromental conflicts). (Internal publication). Budapest: Magyar Közvéleménykutató Intézet.

Farkas, József. 1992. *Szürke zóna* (Grey zone). Budapest: Társadalmi Konfliktusok Kutató Központja.

Fehér, Ferenc, and Ágnes Heller. 1983. *Hungary 1956 Revisited: The Message of a Revolution – A Quarter of a Century After*. London: Allen and Unwin.

Fehér, Lajos. 1963. *A szocialist mezőgazdaságért* (For a socialist agriculture). Budapest: Kossuth.

1987. *Sorsforditó évtizedek* (Crucial decades). Budapest: Kossuth.

Feitl, István. 1991. "A moszkvai emigrácio és az MSZMP. Rákosi Mátyás 1956 és 1958 között" (The Moscow emigrants and the HSWP. Mátyás Rákosi between 1956 and 1958). *Multunk* 36, 4: 3–31.

Fejto, François. 1964. "Hungarian Communism." In William E. Griffith, ed., *Communism in Europe* vol. I. Cambridge, MA: MIT Press.

1986. *Mémoires de Budapest à Paris*. Paris: Colmann-Levy.

Fekete, Judit. 1984. *Adalékok a kisvállalkozás jelenségrendszéréhez* (Data on the phenomenon of small enterprises). Budapest: MSZMP Társadalomtudományi Intézet.

1988. "Puccsszerű döntéshozatal és jogszabályalkotás" (*Putsch*-style decision- and rule-making). (Unpublished manuscript.)

Felkay, Andrew. 1989. *Hungary and the USSR, 1956–1988*. New York: Greenwood Press.

Fenyo, Mario D. 1972. *Hitler, Horthy, Mussolini*. New Haven: Yale University Press.

Ferber, Katalin, and Gábor Rejtö, eds. 1988. *Reform évfordulón* (Reform anniversary). Budapest: Közgazdasági és Jogi Kiadó.

Feuer, Lewis, S., ed. 1959. *Marx and Engels: Basic Writings on Politics and Philosophy*. New York: Doubleday.

Fock, Jenő. 1972. *A szocializmus épitésének gazdaságpolitikája* (Economic policies of the building of socialism). Budapest: Kossuth.

Földes, György, and László Hubai, eds. 1994. *Parlamenti képviselőválasztások, 1920–1990* (Parliamentary elections, 1920–1990). Budapest: Politikatörteneti Alapitvány.

Fricz, Tamás. 1990. "Generációk és politikai értékek" (Generations and political values). *Valósag* 4: 8–17.

Frydman, Roman *et al.*, eds. 1993. *The Privatization Process in Central Europe*. London: Central European Press.

Gál, Éva *et al.*, eds. 1993. *A "Jelcin dosszié" Szovjet dokumentumok 1956-ról* (The "Yeltsin dossier" – Soviet documents on 1956). Budapest: Századvég Kiadó.

Galasi, Péter, and György Szirácki, eds. 1985. *Labor Market and Second Economy in Hungary*. Frankfurt: Campus Verlag.

Garton Ash, Timothy. 1985. "The Hungarian Lesson." *New York Review of Books*, 5 December 1985.

1990. *The Magic Lantern: The Revolution of '89 Witnessed in Warsaw, Budapest, Berlin and Prague.* New York: Random House.

Gáspár, Sándor. 1973. *A munkáshatalom szolgálatában* (In the service of the workers' power). Budapest: Táncsics.

Gazsó, Ferenc. 1988. *Megujuló egyenlőtlenségek: társadalom, iskola, ifjúság* (Renewed inequalities: society, school and the youth). Budapest: Kossuth.

Gellner, Ernest. 1974. *Nations and Nationalism.* Ithaca: Cornell University Press.

Gergely, András A. 1991. *A pártállam varázstalanitása* (The demystification of the party state). Budapest: Institute of Political Science, Hungarian Academy of Sciences.

Gerő, Ernő. 1952. *A vas, az acél, a gépek országáért* (For a country of iron, steel and machines). Budapest: Szikra.

Giddens, Anthony. 1973. *The Class Structure of the Advanced Societies.* London: Hutchinson.

Gluck, Mary. 1985. *George Lukacs and His Generation, 1910–1918.* Cambridge, MA: Harvard University Press.

Gombár, Csaba. 1984. *Egy állampolgár gondolatai* (Thoughts of a citizen). Budapest: Kossuth.

1987. "A helyi hatalom hermeneutikája" (The hermeneutics of local power). In Zsuzsa Pápay, ed., *Helyi hatalom – helyi társadalom* (Local power and local society). Budapest: MSZMP Társadalomtudományi Intézet. 31–40.

1989. *Boritékolt politika* (On politics). Budapest: Pénzügyi Kutató, RT.

1990. "Kormányzati kérdéseken tünődve" (Reflections on questions of governance). In Györgyi Várnai, ed., *Logosz.* Budapest: ELTE Szociológiai és Szociálpolitikai Intézet. 47–62.

Gombár, Csaba *et al.*, eds. 1994. *Balance: The Hungarian Government, 1990–1994.* Budapest: Centre for Political Research.

Gombos, Gyula. 1966. *Szabó Dezső.* Munich: Aurora Könyvek.

Gonzalez, Carmen Enriques. 1993. *Crisis y cambio en Europe del Este. La transición húngara a la democracia.* Madrid: Centro de Investigaciones Sociológicas.

Gosztonyi, Péter. 1990. "Az 1956–os forradalom számokban" (Statistics on the 1956 revolution). *Népszabadsag,* 3 November.

Gouldner, Alvin. 1979. *The Future of Intellectuals and the Rise of New Class.* New York: Seaburg.

Gramsci, Antonio. 1971. *Selections from the Prison Notebooks. 1929–1935.* New York: International Publishers.

Granick, David. 1975. *Enterprise Guidance in Eastern Europe: A Comparison of Four Socialist Economies.* Princeton: Princeton University Press.

Gratz, Gusztáv. 1934. *A dualizmus kora* (The age of dualism). Budapest: Magyar Szemle.

Gulácsi, Gábor. 1987. "Egy struktúrafeszegető intézmény és egy politikai kampány a nyolcvanas években: A tehó" (A structure-stretching institution and political campaign in the 1980s: the case of voluntary levy for community infrastructure development). *Szociológia* 3 (1987), 361–94.

Gurr, Ted Robert. 1971. *When Men Rebel and Why*. Princeton: Princeton University Press.

Győrffy, Sándor et al., eds. 1983. *Szárszó – 1943* (Szárszó, 1943). Budapest: Kossuth.

Györkei, Jenő. 1993. "Kádár vesszőfutása Moszkvába és vissza" (Kádár: running the gauntlet to and from Moscow). *Uj Magyarország*, 8 April.

Gyurkó, László. 1985. "Introductory Biography." In *János Kádár, Selected Speeches and Interviews*. Oxford: Pergamon Press. 3–168.

Hajdu, Tibor. 1969. *A Magyarországi Tanácsköztársaság* (The Hungarian Soviet Republic). Budapest: Kossuth.

　　1992. "Farkas és Kádár Rajknál. Az 1949 junius 7–i beszélgetés hiteles szövege" (Farkas and Kádár at Rajk. The authentic transcript of the conversation). *Társadalmi Szemle* 4: 70–89.

Hankiss, Elemér. 1986. *Diagnózisok 2* (Diagnoses 2). Budapest: Magvető.

　　1990. *East European Alternatives*. Oxford: Clarendon Press.

　　1990. *Hongrie diagnostiques: essai en pathologie sociale*. Geneva: Georg Eshel.

Hankiss, Elemér et al., 1982. *Kényszerpályán? A magyar társadalom értékrendszerének alakulása 1930 és 1980 között* (On a forced path? Changes in the value structure of Hungarian society between 1930 and 1980). Budapest: Sociology Institute, Hungarian Academy of Sciences.

Haraszti, Miklós. 1977. *Worker in a Workers' State*. London: Penguin Books.

　　1987. *The Velvet Prison: Artists under State Socialism*. New York: Basic Books.

Harcsa, István. 1993. "A közelmult hatalmi elitjének főbb csoportjai" (Main groups of the *ancien régime*'s power elites). *Statisztikai Szemle* 71, 2: 101–17.

Harcsa, István, and Rózsa Kulcsár. 1986. *Társadalmi mobilitás és presztizs* (Social mobility and prestige). Budapest: Központi Statisztikai Hivatal.

Harcsa, István, et al., 1991. *Vezetők a nyolcvanas években* (Hungarian executives and top managers in the 1980s). Budapest: Központi Statisztikai Hivatal.

Hare, P. G. et al., eds. 1981. *Hungary: A Decade of Economic Reform*. London: George Allen and Unwin.

Hartl, Jan. 1994. "Perceptions of Social Safety in the Czech and Slovak Republics, Hungary and Poland." In András Bozóki, ed., *Democratic Legitimacy in Post-Communist Societies*. Budapest: Twins. 267–92.

Havas, Fanny et al., eds. 1992. *Beszélő Összkiadás, 1981–1989*. (Beszélő – annotated edition, 1981–1989), 3 vols. Budapest: AB Beszélő Kiadó.

Havasi, Ferenc. 1982. *Uj fejlődési pályán* (On a new development path). Budapest: Kossuth.

Hegedüs, András. 1988. *A történelem és a hatalom igézetében* (Under the spell of history and power). Budapest: Kossuth.

Hegedüs, András, and Mária Márkus. 1966. *Ember, munka, közösség* (Man, work, community). Budapest: Közgazdasági és Jogi Kiadó.

Hermann, István et al., eds. 1983. *A magyar filozófiai goldolkodás a két világháború között* (Hungarian [schools of] philosophy between the two world wars). Budapest: Kossuth.

Héthy, Lajos, and Csaba Makó. 1972. *Munkásmagatartások és társadalmi szervezet* (Workers' behavior and social organization). Budapest: Akadémiai Kiadó.

Hibbing, John R., and Samuel C. Patterson. 1992. "A Democratic Legislature in the Making: The Historic Hungarian Elections of 1990." *Comparative Political Studies* 24, 4: 430–53.

Hóman, Bálint, and Gyula Szekfű. 1943. *Magyar történet* (Hungarian history) vol. IV, 7th edn Budapest: Királyi Magyar Egyetemi Nyomda.

Horn, Gyula. 1991. *Cölöpök* (Pillars. Memoirs). Budapest: Zenit Könyvek.

Horthy, Miklós. 1956. *Memoirs*. London: Hutchinson.

Horváth, Ibolya *et al.*, eds. 1992. *Iratok az igazságszolgaltatás történetéhez* (Documents on the history of justice in Hungary) vol. I. Budapest: Közgazdasági és Jogi Kiadó.

Horváth, József. 1991. *A lehallgatástól a kihallgatásigig* (From wiretapping to [parliamentary] hearings). Budapest: Holding Kiadó.

Horváth, Tamás M. 1988. "A kisvárosok politikai viszonyai" (Politics in small towns). *Valóság* 31, 7: 89–98.

Horváth, Zoltán. 1961. *A magyar századforduló: a második reformnemzedék története, 1896–1914* (The Hungarian *fin de siècle* – a history of the second reform generation, 1896–1914). Budapest: Gondolat.

Huntington, Samuel P. 1991. *The Third Wave: Democratization in Late Twentieth Century*. Norman: University of Oklahoma Press.

Huszár, Tibor. 1978. "White-Collar Workers, Intellectuals and Graduates in Hungary." In Tibor Huszár *et al.*, eds., *Hungarian Society and Marxist Sociology in the 1970s*. Budapest: Corvina. 159–75.

1979. *Történelem és szociológia* (History and sociology). Budapest: Magvető.

Hutchings, Robert L., ed. 1989. "Symposium on 'Leadership Drift' in the Communist Systems of the Soviet Union and Eastern Europe." *Studies in Comparative Communism* 22, 1: 5–56.

Ignotus, Paul. 1972. *Hungary*. New York: Praeger.

Illés, János, ed. 1977. *A népi kollégisták utja, 1939–1971* (The people's collegians: paths and careers, 1939–1971). Budapest: Központi Statisztikai Hivatal.

Janos, Andrew C. 1982. *The Politics of Backwardness in Hungary, 1825–1945*. Princeton: Princeton University Press.

1991. "Social Science, Communism and the Dynamics of Political Change." *World Politics* 44, 1: 82–112.

1994. "Continuity and Change in Eastern Europe: Strategies of Post-Communist Politics." *East European Politics and Societies* 8, 1: 1–31.

Jones, T. Anthony. 1976. "Modernization Theory and Socialist Development." In Mark G. Field, ed., *Social Consequences of Modernization in Communist Societies*. Baltimore: The Johns Hopkins University Press. 19–49.

1986 "Models of Socialist Development." In Gerhard Lenski, ed., *Current Issues and Research in Macrosociology*. Leiden: Brill. 86–99.

Jowitt, Ken. 1992. *New World Disorder: The Leninist Extinction*. Berkeley: University of California Press.

Juhász, Gyula. 1979. *Hungarian Foreign Policy, 1919–1945*. Budapest: Akadémiai Kiadó.

1983. *Uralkodó politikai eszmék Magyarországon, 1939–1944* (Dominant political ideas in Hungary, 1939–1944). Budapest: Kossuth.

Kádár, János. 1975. *A fejlett szocialista társadalom épitésének utján* (On the path of building a developed socialist society). Budapest: Kossuth.
1985. *Selected Speeches and Interviews.* Oxford: Pergamon Press.
Kállai, Gyula. 1971. *Szocializmus, népfront, demokrácia* (Socialism, Popular Front, democracy). Budapest: Kossuth.
Kanyó, András. 1989. *Kádár János: Végakarat* (János Kádár – last will and testament). Budapest: Hirlapterjesztő.
Kardos, László, ed. 1977. *Sej a mi lobogónkat fényes szellők fujják ... Népi Kollégiumok, 1939–1949* (People's Colleges, 1939–1949). Budapest: Akadémiai Kiadó.
1980. *A fényes szelek nemzedéke: Népi Kollégiumok, 1939–1949* (Generation of the bright winds: People's Colleges, 1939–1949). 2 vols. Budapest: Akadémiai Kiadó.
Kasza, László. 1994. *Metamorphosis Hungariae, 1989–1994.* Budapest: Századvég.
Kecskemeti, Paul. 1961. *The Unexpected Revolution: Social Forces in the Hungarian Uprising.* Stanford: Stanford University Press.
Kecskés, Gyula. 1988. *Vezéráldozatok – avagy mit tesznek a kiskirályok pánikban* (Kings and pawns, or the little tyrants in panic). Budapest: Tornado-Damenija.
Kemény, István, and Mátyás Sárközi, eds. 1981. *Bibó István összegyüjtött munkái* (Istvan Bibó: collected works). 4 vols. Berne: Europai Protestáns Magyar Szabadegyetem.
Kenedi, János. 1986. *Do It Yourself: Hungary's Hidden Economy.* London: Pluto Press.
Kimmel, Emil. 1990. *Végjaték a Fehér Házban* (Endgame in the White House). Budapest: Téka.
Király, Béla, and Paul Jonas, eds. 1977. *The Hungarian Revolution in Retrospect.* New York: Columbia University Press.
Kis, János. 1988. "Az 1956–57–es restaurácio" (Restoration in 1956–1957). *Medvetánc* 2–3: 229–78.
Kiss, József, ed. 1992. *Az 1990–ben megválasztott Országgyülés almanachja* (Almanac of the Hungarian legislature elected in 1990). Budapest: A Magyar Országgyülés Kiadása.
Kiss, József, and Zoltán Ripp. 1993. "Három dokumentum a Nagy Imre per 1958 februári elhalasztásáról" (Three documents on the February 1958 postponement of the Imre Nagy trial). *Társadalmi Szemle* 4: 82–95.
Kohn, Hans. 1944. *The Idea of Nationalism: A Study of Its Origins and Background.* New York: Macmillan.
Kolosi, Tamás. 1983. *Struktura és egyenlőtlenség* (Structure and inequality). Budapest: Kossuth.
1987. *Tagolt társadalom* (Stratified society). Budapest: Gondolat.
Koltay, Gábor, and Péter Bródy. 1989. *Érdemei elismerése mellett: beszélgetések Havasi Ferenccel* (With the recognition of merits: conversations with Ferenc Havasi). Budapest: Szabad Tér.

Koltay, Gábor, and Péter Bródy. eds. 1990. *El nem égetett dokumentumok* (Unburned documents). Budapest: Szabad Tér.

Konrád, György, and Iván Szelényi. 1979. *The Intellectuals on the Road to Class Power*. New York: Harcourt Brace Jovanovich.

Köpeczi, Béla *et al.*, eds. 1986. *Erdély története* (History of Transylvania). 3 vols. Budapest: Akadémiai Kiadó.

Kornai, János. 1972. *Erőltetett vagy harmonikus növekedés* (Forced or harmonious growth). Budapest: Akadémiai Kiadó.

1980. *Economics of Shortage*. Amsterdam: North Holland.

1985. *Contradictions and Dilemmas: Studies on the Socialist Economy and Society*. Budapest: Corvina.

1992. *The Socialist System: The Political Economy of Communism*. Princeton: Princeton University Press.

Körösényi, András. 1995. "The Reasons for the Defeat of the Right in Hungary." *East European Politics and Societies* 9, 1: 179–94.

Kővári, György, and György Szirácki. 1984. "Béralku az üzemben" (Wage bargaining in the workshop). *Közgazdasági Szemle* 31, 2: 155–67.

Kovrig, Bennet. 1979. *Communism in Hungary from Kun to Kádár*. Stanford: Hoover Institution.

Kukorelli, István. 1988. *Így választottunk: adalékok a választási reform és az 1985. évi általános választások történetéhez* (On electoral reforms and the elections of 1985). Budapest: Department of Political Science, Faculty of Law, ELTE.

Kulcsár, Kálmán. 1993. "A 'jog uralma' és az alkotmánybíráskodás" (The "rule of law" and the Hungarian Constitutional Court). *Politikatudományi Szemle* 1: 5–38.

Kun, Béla. 1958. *A Magyar Tanácsköztársaságról* (On the Hungarian Soviet Republic). Budapest: Kossuth.

Kun, Gábor, ed. 1989. *Kádár János 1912–1989* (János Kádár Memorial Book). Budapest.

Kurtán, Sándor, Sándor Péter, and László Vass, eds. 1989. *Magyarország Politikai Évkönyve, 1988* (Hungarian Political Yearbook, 1988). Debrecen: R-Forma Kiadó.

1990. *Magyarország Politikai Évkönyve, 1990* (Hungarian Political Yearbook, 1990). Budapest: Aula.

1991. *Magyarország Politikai Évkönyve, 1991* (Hungarian Political Yearbook, 1991). Budapest: Ökonomia Alapitvány.

1992. *Magyarország Politikai Évkönyve, 1992* (Hungarian Political Yearbook, 1992). Budapest: Demokrácia Kutatások Magyar Központja Alapitvány.

1993. *Magyarország Politikai Évkönyve, 1993* (Hungarian Political Yearbook, 1993). Budapest: Demokrácia Kutatások Magyar Központja Alapitvány.

1994. *Magyarország Politikai Évkönyve, 1994* (Hungarian Political Yearbook, 1994). Budapest: Demokrácia Kutatások Magyar Központja Alapitvány.

1995. *Magyarország Politikai Évkönyve, 1995* (Hungarian Political Yearbook, 1995). Budapest: Demokrácia Kutatások Magyar Központja Alapitvány.

Lackó, Miklós. 1975. *Válságok – választások* (Crises and choices). Budapest: Gondolat.

Lányi, Olga. 1992. *Moszkoviták* (Muscovites). Budapest: Hevesi Gyula Alapit-vány.

Látos, István, ed. 1984. *Szervezeti kérdések a Magyar Szocialista Munkáspártban* (Organizational questions in the Hungarian Socialist Workers' Party). Budapest: Kossuth.

Lázár, Guy, ed. 1986. *Társadalmi-gazdasági fejlődésünk ideológiai kérdései közgon-dolkodásban* (Ideological questions of sociopolitical development in public opinion). Budapest: Tömegkommunikációs Kutatóintézet.

Lázár, György. 1983. *A nép támogatásával a szocializmus utján* (With the people's support on the path to socialism). Budapest: Kossuth.

Lengyel, László. 1989. *Végkifejlet* (Endgame). Budapest: Közgazdasági és Jogi Kiadó.

1992. *Útfélen* (At the roadside). Budapest: Századvég.

1994. "Kádár János és kora" (János Kádár and his era). *Népszabadság*, 6 July.

1994. *Korunkba zárva* (Locked into our age). Budapest: Pénzügykutató.

1994. *Magyar alakok* (Hungarian profiles). Budapest: Pénzügykutató.

Lenski, Gerald E. 1966. *Power and Prestige*. New York: McGraw Hill.

Levendel, László. *A túlélő* (The survivor). Budapest: Főnix Alapitvány.

Lewin, Moshe. 1974. *Political Undercurrents in Soviet Economic Debates*. Prin-ceton: Princeton University Press.

Lewis, Paul G., ed. 1984. *Eastern Europe: Political Crisis and Legitimation*. New York: St. Martin's Press.

Lichtheim, George. 1970. *George Lukacs*. New York: The Viking Press.

Lindblom, Charles E. 1977. *Politics and Markets*. New York: Basic Books.

Litván, György. 1992. "A Nagy Imre per politikai háttere" (Political back-ground of the Imre Nagy trial). *Világosság* 10: 743–57.

Lomax, Bill. 1976. *Hungary 1956*. London: Allison and Busby.

1990. *Hungarian Workers' Councils in 1956*. New York: Columbia University Press.

1993. "Eastern Europe: Restoration and Crisis: The Metamorphosis of Power in Eastern Europe." *Critique* 25: 7–84.

Lőrincz, Lajos. 1981. *A közigazgatás kapcsolata a gazdasággal és a politikával* (Public administration – linkages with economics and politics). Budapest: Közgaz-dasági és Jogi Kiadó.

Losonczy, Ágnes. 1986. *A kiszolgáltatottság anatómiája az egészségügyben* (The anatomy of dependency and the delivery of health services). Budapest: Magvető.

Lowenthal, Richard. 1970. "Development vs. Utopia in Communist Policy." In Chalmers Johnson, ed., *Change in Communist Systems*. Stanford: Stanford University Press. 33–116.

Lukács, György. 1919. *Taktika és ethika* (Tactics and ethics). Budapest: Közokta-tási Népbiztosság.

Macartney, C. A. 1957. *October Fifteenth: A History of Modern Hungary, 1929–1945*. Edinburgh: Edinburgh University Press.

McCagg, William O. 1972. *Jewish Nobles and Geniuses in Modern Hungary*. New York: Columbia University Press.

McClelland, David C. 1961. *The Achieving Society*. Princeton: Princeton University Press.

McFaul, Michael. 1995. "State Power, Institutional Change, and the Politics of Privatization in Russia." *World Politics* 47, 2: 210–43.

Magyar, Bálint. 1988. "1956 és a magyar falu" (1956 and the Hungarian villages). *Medvetánc* 2–3: 207–12.

Magyar Demokrata Forum. 1987. *Lakitelek. 1987 szeptember 27. A magyarság esélyei* (Lakitelek, September 27, 1987. Hungary's chances). Budapest: Samizdat.

Magyar Országgyülés (Hungarian Parliament). 1994. "A Honvédelmi Bizottság 1989 októberi ülésszakán létrehozott vizsgálóbizottság 1989 december 11–i (1990 január 3–i, 1990 január 15–i, 1990 február 6–i, 1990 február 12–i) ülése jegyzőkönyvének nyilt részlete" (Declassified excerpts from hearings before the Investigative Subcommittee – established at the October 1989 meeting of the Parliament's Committee on National Defense – held on December 11, 1989, and on January 3, January 15, February 6 and February 12, 1990). 4 vols.

Major, Iván. 1985. "Kifulladási periódusok a magyar gazdaság fejlődésében" (Periods of exhaustion in the development of the Hungarian economy). In Robert Hoch and Iván Major, eds., *Gazdaságunk helyzétéről és fejlődésének problémáiról* (On the situation of our economy and problems of its development). Budapest: Kossuth. 214–40.

Makó, Csaba. 1985. *Munkafolyamat: a társadalmi viszonyok erőtere* (The labor process: an arena of social power relations). Budapest: Közgazdasági és Jogi Kiadó.

Malia, Martin. 1992. "From Under the Rubble, What?" *Problems of Communism* 41, 1–2: 89–106.

Marer, Paul. 1981. "Economic Performance and Prospects in Eastern Europe: Analytical Summary and Interpretation of Findings." In *East European Economic Assessment*, Part 2. Regional Assessments. A Compendium of Papers, Joint Economic Committe, US Congress. Washington, DC: USGPO. 19–95.

  1986. "Economic Reforms in Hungary: From Central Planning to Regulated Market." In *East European Economies: Slow Growth in the 1980s*, vol. III. Country Studies on Eastern Europe and Yugoslavia. Joint Economic Committee, US Congress. Washington, DC: USGPO. 223–98.

  1994. "Hungary During 1988–1994: A Political Economy Assessment." In John P. Hardt and Richard F. Kaufman, eds., *East-Central European Economies in Transition: Study Papers Submitted to the Joint Economic Committee, Congress of the United States*. Washington, DC: USGPO. 480–505.

Marer, Paul, ed. 1994. *Financial Sector Reform and Enterprise Restructuring in Hungary*. Indianapolis: Hudson Institute.

Marjai, József. 1984. *Egyensúly, realitás, reform* (Balance, reality, reform). Budapest: Kossuth.

Mannheim, Karl. 1952. "The Problem of Generations." In Karl Mannheim,

Essays on the Sociology of Knowledge. New York: Oxford University Press. 276–320.

Marosán, György. 1989. *Fel kellett állnom* (I was compelled to leave). Budapest: Hirlapkiadó.

Meyer, Alfred. 1972. "Legitimacy of Power in East Central Europe." In S. Sinaian *et al.*, eds., *Eastern Europe in the 1970s.* New York: Praeger.

Miller, R.F., and F. Feher, eds. 1984. *Khrushchev and the Communist World.* London: Croom Helm.

Mishler, William, and Richard Rose. 1993. *Trajectories of Fear and Hope: The Dynamics of Support for Democracy in Eastern Europe.* Glasgow: Centre for the Study of Public Policy, University of Strathclyde.

Molnar, Miklós, 1972. *Imre Nagy, réformateur ou révolutionnaire?.* Geneva: Droz.

1990. *From Béla Kun to János Kádár: Seventy Years of Hungarian Communism.* New York: St. Martin's Press.

MSZMP Központi Bizottsága. 1957. *A Magyar Szocialista Munkáspárt Országos Értekezletének Jegyzőkönyve, 1957 junius 27–29* (Stenographic minutes of the national conference of the Hungarian Socialist Workers' Party, June 27–29, 1957). Budapest: Kossuth.

1960. *A Magyar Szocialista Munkáspárt VII. Kongresszusának Jegyzőkönyve, 1959 november 30–december 5* (Seventh congress of the HSWP, stenographic minutes). Budapest: Kossuth.

1963. *A Magyar Szocialista Munkáspárt VIII. Kongresszusának Jegyzőkönyve, 1962 november 20–24* (Eighth congress of the HSWP, stenographic minutes). Budapest: Kossuth.

1967. *A Magyar Szocialista Munkáspárt IX. Kongresszusának Jegyzőkönyve, 1966 november 28–december 3* (Ninth congress of the HSWP, stenographic minutes). Budapest: Kossuth.

1971. *A Magyar Szocialista Munkáspárt X. Kongresszusának Jegyzőkönyve, 1970 november 23–28* (Tenth congress of the HSWP, stenographic minutes). Budapest: Kossuth.

1975. *A Magyar Szocialista Munkáspárt XI. Kongresszusának Jegyzőkönyve, 1975 március 17–22* (Eleventh congress of the HSWP, stenographic minutes). Budapest: Kossuth.

1980. *A Magyar Szocialista Munkáspárt XII. Kongresszusának Jegyzőkönyve, 1980 március 24–27.* (Twelfth congress of the HSWP, stenographic minutes). Budapest: Kossuth.

1985. *A Magyar Szocialista Munkáspárt XIII. Kongresszusának Jegyzőkönyve, 1980 március 25–28* (Thirteenth congress of the HSWP, stenographic minutes). Budapest: Kossuth.

1988. *A Magyar Szocialista Munkáspárt országos Értekezletének Jegyzőkönyve, 1988 május 20–22* (Stenographic minutes of the national conference of the HSWP, May 20–22, 1988). Budapest: Kossuth.

1989. *Kongresszus '89* (Background documents, in 32 parts, to the Fourteenth congress of the HSWP, October 5–9, 1989). Budapest: Samizdat.

MSZMP Központi Bizottságának Párttörténeti Intézete. 1964. *A Magyar Szocialista Munkáspárt határozatai és dokumentumai, 1956–1962* (Resolutions and documents of the Hungarian Socialist Workers' Party, 1956–1962). Budapest: Kossuth.

1968. *A Magyar Szocialista Munkáspárt határozatai és dokumentumai, 1963–1966* (Resolutions and documents of the Hungarian Socialist Workers' Party, 1963–1966). Budapest: Kossuth.

1974. *A Magyar Szocialista Munkáspárt határozatai és dokumentumai, 1967–1970* (Resolutions and documents of the Hungarian Socialist Workers' Party, 1967–1970). Budapest: Kossuth.

1978. *A Magyar Szocialista Munkáspárt határozatai és dokumentumai, 1971–1975* (Resolutions and documents of the Hungarian Socialist Workers' Party, 1971–1975). Budapest: Kossuth.

1983. *A Magyar Szocialista Munkáspárt határozatai és dokumentumai, 1975–1980* (Resolutions and documents of the Hungarian Socialist Workers' Party, 1975–1980). Budapest: Kossuth.

1988. *A Magyar Szocialista Munkáspárt határozatai és dokumentumai, 1980–1985* (Resolutions and documents of the Hungarian Socialist Workers' Party, 1980–1985). Budapest: Kossuth.

1987. *A Magyar Szocialista Munkáspárt határozatai és dokumentumai, 1985–1986* (Resolutions and documents of the Hungarian Socialist Workers' Party, 1980–1985). Budapest: Kossuth.

1988. *A Magyar Szocialista Munkáspárt határozatai és dokumentumai, 1987* (Resolutions and documents of the Hungarian Socialist Workers' Party, 1987). Budapest: Kossuth.

Musatov, Valeri. 1991. "Szovjet politikai beavatkozás és katonai intervenció Magyarországon 1956–ban" (Soviet political interference and military intervention in Hungary in 1956). *Multunk* 36, 4.

Nagy, Ferenc. 1948. *The Struggle Behind the Iron Curtain*. New York: Macmillan.

Nagy, Lajos Géza. 1989. "Történelem képek és jövő-képek" (Images of history and ideology: the stratification of ideological beliefs in the early 1980s). Budapest: Magyar Tudományos Akadémia. Dissertation for the degree of Candidate of Sociological Sciences (unpublished).

Nagy, Zsuzsa L. 1983. *The Liberal Opposition in Hungary, 1919–1945*. Budapest: Akadémiai Kiadó.

Németh, Károly. 1974. *Tettekkel, felelőséggel* (With responsible deeds). Budapest: Kossuth.

1986. *Párt, társadalom, politika* (Party, society, politics). Budapest: Kossuth.

Németh, K. V., and Levente Sipos, eds. 1993. *A Magyar Szocialista Munkáspárt vezető testületeinek jegyzőkönyve*, vol. I (November 11, 1956 – January 14, 1957) (Stenographic minutes of the [deliberations of] the leading organs of the Hungarian Socialist Workers' Party). Budapest: Interart.

Nyers, Rezső. 1988. *Utkeresés – reformok* (Search for a path – reforms). Budapest: Magvető.

Nyers, Rezső [Jr.] ed. 1992. *Külső eladósodás és adósságkezelés Magyarországon* (External indebtedness and debt management in Hungary). Budapest: Hungarian National Bank.

Nyirő, András *et al.*, eds. 1989. *Segédkönyv a Politikai Bizottság tanulmányozásához* (Handbook for the study of the Politburo). Budapest: Interart.

Odom, William E. 1992. "Soviet Politics and After: Old and New Concepts." *World Politics* 45, 1: 66–98.

Ormos, Mária. 1989. "A konszolidáció problémái 1956 és 1958 között" (Problems of consolidation between 1956 and 1958). *Társadalmi Szemle* 44, 8–9: 48–65.

Országos Statisztikai Hivatal. 1992. *Magyarország nemzeti számlái: főbb mutatók, 1988–1990* (National Accounts, Hungary: main indicators, 1988–1990). Budapest: Hungarian Central Statistical Office.

Papp, Zsolt. 1987. "Adalékok a tervezés demokratikus legitimaciójához" (Data on the democratic legitimation of planning). In Antal Böhm and László Pál, eds., *A helyi hatalom működése* (Local power, the way it works). Budapest: MSZMP Társadalomtudományi Intézet. 37–1.

Péter, László. 1963. "A magyar nacionalizmus" (Hungarian nationalism). In Sándor Németh, ed., *Eszmék nyomában* (Ideas and ideologies). Munich: Hollandiai Mikes Kelemen kör. 186–224.

　　1991. "Montesquieu's Paradox of Freedom and Hungary's Constitutions 1790–1990." *New Hungarian Quarterly* 123: 3–14.

Pető, Iván, and Sándor Szakács. 1985. *A hazai gazdaság négy évtizedének története, 1945–1985. I. Az ujjáépites és a tervutasitásos irányitás időszaka, 1945–1968* (The history of four decades of the Hungarian economy, 1945–1985, vol. I. The period of economic reconstruction and of the centrally planned economy, 1945–1968). Budapest: Közgazdasági és Jogi Kiadó.

Pozsgay, Imre. 1969. "A szocialista demokrácia és politikai rendszerünk továbbfejlesztésének néhány kérdése" (Some questions of the further development of socialist democracy and of our political system). Dissertation for the degree of Candidate of Sciences in Philosophy, Hungarian Academy of Sciences (Unpublished).

　　1980. *Demokrácia és kultúra* (Democracy and culture). Budapest: Kossuth.

　　1993. *1989 Politikus pálya a pártállamban és a rendszerváltásban* (1989 – a political career in a party state and during the change of the regime). Budapest: Püski.

Pravda, Alex, ed. 1992. *The End of the Outer Empire. Soviet–East European Relations in Transition, 1985–1990.* London: The Royal Institute of International Affairs.

Przeworski, Adam. 1991. *Democracy and Market: Political and Economic Reforms in Eastern Europe and Latin America.* Cambridge: Cambridge University Press.

Radványi, János. 1972. *Hungary and the Superpowers.* Stanford: Stanford University Press.

Rainer, János M. 1992. "Nagy Imre életútja" (Imre Nagy – a biographic sketch). *Multunk* 4: 3–14.

Rákosi, Mátyás. 1947. *A magyar demokráciáért* (For Hungarian democracy). Budapest: Szikra.

Rakovski, Marc. 1978. *Towards an East European Marxism.* New York: St. Martin's Press.

Ránki, György. 1963. *Magyarország gazdasága az első hároméves terv időszakában* (Hungarian economy during the first Three-Year Plan). Budapest: Közgazdasági és Jogi Kiadó.

1968. *1944 március 19* (19 March 1944). Budapest: Kossuth.

Ránki, György, ed. 1984. *Hungarian History – World History*. Budapest: Akadémiai Kiadó.

Révai, József. 1949. *Élni tudtunk a szabadsággal* (We made good use of freedom). Budapest: Szikra.

Richter, Anna ed. 1990. *Az Ellenzéki Kerekasztal. portrévázlatok* (The Opposition Roundtable – portraits). Budapest: Ötlet.

Rigby, H. T., and Ferenc Fehér, eds. 1982. *Political Legitimation in Communist States*. New York: St. Martin's Press.

Ripp, Zoltán. 1990. "Döntés a Nagy Imre csoport ügyében. A KB zárt ülése 1957 december 21–én" (Decision on the case of Imre Nagy and his group at the closed session of the CC, HSWP on December 21, 1957). *Multunk* 4: 163–80.

Róbert, Péter. 1988. "A származási egyenlőtlenségektől a státuszkülönbségekig" (From unequal social backgrounds to status inequalities). In Ágnes Bokor et al., *Egyenlőtlen helyzetek* (Unequal conditions). Budapest: Kossuth. 89–125.

Robinson, James A. 1968. "Decision Making: Political Aspects." In David L. Sills, ed., *International Encyclopedia of the Social Sciences* vol. IV. New York: The Free Press and Macmillan.

Robinson, Thomas F. 1973. *The Pattern of Reform in Hungary*. New York: Praeger.

Romsics, Ignac. 1982. *Ellenforradalom és konszolidáció* (Counterrevolution and consolidation). Budapest: Gondolat.

Rose, Richard. 1991. *Between State and Market: Key Indicators of Transition in Eastern Europe*. Glasgow: Centre for the Study of Public Policy, University of Strathclyde.

Rose, Richard and Christian Haerpfer. 1992. *New Democracies Between State and Market: A Baseline Report on Public Opinion*. Glasgow: Centre for the Study of Public Policy, University of Strathclyde.

Rosenblatt, Zehava et al. 1993. "Toward a Political Framework for Flexible Management of Decline." *Organization Science* 4, 1: 86–9.

Ságvári, Ágnes. 1989. *Mert nem hallgathatok* (I cannot remain silent). Budapest: Magyar Hirlapkiadó.

Schmidt, Péter, ed. 1985. *Állam, közgazdaság és érdekviszonyok* (State, economy and interest relations). Budapest: MSZMP Társadalomtudományi Intézet.

Schmitter, Phillippe C. 1994. "The Conceptual Travels of Transitologists and Consolidationists: How Far to the East Should They Attempt to Go?" *Slavic Review* 53, 1: 173–85.

Schopflin, George. 1977. "Hungary: An Uneasy Stability." In Archie Brown and Jack Gray, eds., *Political Culture and Political Change in Communist States*. London: Macmillan. 131–58.

1979. "Opposition and Para-Opposition: Critical Currents in Hungary." In

Rudolf L. Tőkés, ed., *Opposition in Eastern Europe*. London: Macmillan. 142–86.

1990. "The Political Traditions of Eastern Europe." *Daedalus* 119, 1: 55–90.

1993. *Politics in Eastern Europe*. Oxford: Blackwell.

1995. "Post-communism: A Profile." *Javnost* 2, 1: 63–74.

Schopflin, George, Rudolf L. Tőkés, and Ivan Volgyes. 1988. "Leadership Change and Crisis in Hungary." *Problems of Communism* 37, 5: 23–46.

Schopflin, Gyula. 1991. *Szélkiáltó* (A migrant bird). Budapest: Magvető.

Seligman, Lester G. 1968. "Leadership – Political Aspects." In David L. Sills, ed., *International Encyclopedia of the Social Sciences* vol. IX. New York: Macmillan and The Free Press. 107–13.

Sereda, Vyacheslav, and Aleksandr Stikhalin, eds. 1993. *Hiányzó lapok 1956 történetéből. Dokumentumok a volt SZKP PB levéltárából* (Missing pages from the history of 1956. Documents from the archives of the Politburo of the former CPSU). Budapest: Zenit.

Shawcross, William. 1974. *Crime and Compromise: János Kádár and the Politics of Hungary since the Revolution*. New York: E.P. Dutton.

Shils, Edward. 1972. *The Intellectuals and the Powers and Other Essays*. Chicago: University of Chicago Press.

Shipler, David K. 1989. "Letter from Budapest." *The New Yorker*, 20 November: 74–101.

Shoup, Paul, ed. 1981. *The East European and Soviet Data Handbook: Political, Social and Developmental Indicators, 1945–1975*. New York: Columbia University Press.

Solt, Pál *et al.*, eds. 1992. *Iratok az igazságszolgaltatás történetéhez* vol. I (Documents on the history of judicial and quasi-judicial trials, hearings, and political justice in Hungary). Budapest: Közgazdasági és Jogi Kiadó.

Soós, Attila Károly. 1986. *Terv, kampány, pénz* (Plan, campaign, money). Budapest: Kossuth.

Soós, László, ed. 1993. *A Magyar Szocialista Munkáspárt Központi Bizottságának 1989. évi Jegyzőkönyvei* (Stenographic minutes of the meetings of the Central Committee, Hungarian Socialist Workers' Party in 1989). 2 vols. Budapest: Magyar Országos Levéltár.

Stark, David. 1985. "The micropolitics of the firm and the macropolitics of the reform – new forms of workplace bargaining in Hungarian enterprises." In Peter Evans *et al.*, eds., *States versus Markets in the World-System*. Beverly Hills: Sage.

1994. "Recombinant Property in East European Capitalism." *Public Lectures* 8. Budapest: Institute for Advanced Study, Collegium Budapest.

Stokes, Gale. 1987. "The Social Origins of East European Politics." *East European Politics and Societies* 1, 1: 30–74.

Sugar, Peter, F. ed. 1971. *Native Fascism in the Successor States, 1918–1945*. Santa Barbara, CA: ABC-Clio.

Szabad, György. 1977. *Kossuth politikai pályája* (Kossuth's political career). Budapest: Kossuth.

1977. *Hungarian Political Trends Between the Revolution and the Compromise, 1849–1867*. Budapest: Akadémiai Kiadó.

Szabó, Miklós *et al.* 1988. "Symposium on Conservatism." In *Változás és alternatívák* (Change and alternatives). Budapest: Magyar Politikatudományi Társaság. 213–90.

1991. *Politikai kultúra Magyarországon, 1896–1986* (Political culture in Hungary, 1896–1986). Budapest: Medvetánc könyvek.

Szakadát, István. 1992. "Káderfo(r)gó" (The cadre trap and musical chairs). *Társadalmi Szemle* 47, 8–9: 97–120.

Szalai, Erzsébet. 1989. *Gazdasági mechanizmus, reformtörekvések és nagyvállalati érdekek* (Economic mechanism, reform initiatives and interests of large enterprises). Budapest: Közgazdasági és Jogi Kiadó.

Szamel, Katalin. 1988. *Közigazgatás az állampolgárokért vagy az állampolgár a közigazgatásért?* (Public administration for the citizen, or the citizen for the public administration?). Budapest: Közgazdasági és Jogi Kiadó.

Szamuely, László, ed. 1986. *A magyar gazdasági gondolat fejlődése, 1954–1978* (The development of economic theories in Hungary, 1954–1978). Budapest: Közgazdasági és Jogi Kiadó.

Szekeres, József. 1990. "Fegyverletétel. A Politikai Egyeztető Tárgyalások történetéből" (Surrender – [pages from] the history of the the National Roundtable). *Szabadság*, 9 February.

Szekfű, Gyula. 1934. *Három nemzedék és ami utána következik* (Three generations and that which follows). Budapest: Magyar Szemle.

Szelényi, Iván. 1990. *Uj osztály, állam, politika* (New class, state, politics). Budapest: Europa.

1990. *Városi társadalmi egyenlőtlenségek* (Urban social inequalities). Budapest: Akadémiai Kiadó.

Szelényi, Iván *et al.* 1988. *Socialist Entrepreneurs. Embourgeoisement in Hungary*. Madison: The University of Wisconsin Press.

Szenes, Iván. 1981. *A Kommunista Part ujjászervezése Magyarországon, 1956–1957* (The reorganization of the Communist Party in Hungary, 1956–1957). Budapest: Kossuth.

Szoboszlai, György, ed. 1985. *Az 1985. évi országgyülési választások politikai tapasztalatai* (On the political experiences of the 1985 parliamentary elections). Budapest: MSZMP Társadalomtudományi Intézet.

1990. *Parlamenti választások 1990* (Parliamentary elections, 1990). Budapest: MTA Társadalomtudományi Intézet.

Talbott, Strobe, ed. 1974. *Khrushchev Remembers: The Last Testament*. Boston: Little, Brown.

Tamás, Miklós Gáspár. 1994. *Másvilag: politikai esszék* (Otherworld – political essays). Budapest: Uj Mandátum Kiadó.

Taras, Raymond C., ed. 1989. *Leadership Change in Communist States*. Boston: Unwin Hyman.

Timár, Mátyás. 1973. *Gazdaságpolitika Magyarországon, 1967–1973* (Economic policies in Hungary, 1967–1973). Budapest: Közgazdasági és Jogi Kiadó.

Tobiás, Áron, ed. 1989. *In Memoriam Nagy Imre*. Budapest: Szabad Tér.

Tőkéczki, László, ed. 1993. *Magyar liberalizmus* (Hungarian liberalism). Budapest: Századvég.

Tőkés, Rudolf L. 1961. "The 'Third Road': Three Case Studies on the History of Hungarian Populist Ideologies." (Unpublished MA thesis) Columbia University.

1967. *Béla Kun and the Hungarian Soviet Republic.* Stanford: Hoover Institution.

1974. "Dissent: Politics for Change in the USSR." In Henry W. Morton and Rudolf L. Tőkés, eds., *Soviet Politics and Society in the 1970s.* New York: Free Press.

1984. "Hungarian Reform Imperatives." *Problems of Communism* 33, 7: 3–24.

1990. "From Postcommunism to Democracy: Politics, Parties and the 1990 Elections in Hungary." *Internal Studies* 18. Bonn: Konrad Adenauer Stiftung-Forschungsinstitut.

1991. "From Visegrad to Cracow: Security and Cooperation in Central Europe." *Problems of Communism* 40, 6: 100–14.

1991. "Hungary's New Political Elites: Adaptation and Change, 1989–1990." In György Szoboszlai, ed., *Democracy and Political Transformation.* Budapest: Hungarian Political Science Association.

1991. "La 'segunda transicion' en Hungria: Perspectivos de los elites y campos de batallo politica." *Revista de Estudios Politicos* (Madrid) 72: 7–44.

Tölgyessy, Péter. 1988. *Gazdasági érdekképviseletek Magyarországon* (Economic interest representation in Hungary). Budapest: MSZMP Társadalomtudományi Intézet.

1994. "Hosszú átmenet" (The long transition). *Népszabadság*, 18 June.

Vági, Gábor. 1982. *Versengés a fejlesztési forrásokért* (Competition for investment resources). Budapest: Közgazdasági és Jogi Kiadó.

1991. *Magunk, uram. Válogatott irások a településekről, tanácsokról, önkormányzatról* (It is up to us, kind Sir. Selected writings on settlements, local councils and self-government). Budapest: Gondolat.

Valenta, Jiri. 1991. *Soviet Intervention in Czechoslovakia, 1968* (rev. edn) Baltimore: Johns Hopkins University Press.

Vali, Ferenc. 1961. *Rift and Revolt in Hungary.* Cambridge, MA: Harvard University Press.

Varga, György T., and István Szakadát. 1992. "Ime a nomenklatúra! Az MDP és a volt MSZMP hatásköri listái" (Voilà! the nomenclature system. The lists of personnel competency of the HWP and the HSWP). *Társadalmi Szemle* 47, 3: 73–95.

Varga, Eugène. 1922. *La Dictature du prolétariat: problèmes économiques.* Paris: L'Humanité.

Vermes, Gábor. 1985. *István Tisza: The Liberal Vision and Conservative Statecraft of a Magyar Nationalist.* New York: Columbia University Press.

Vitézy, László. 1992. "Interjú Grósz Károllyal" (Interview with Károly Grósz). (Unpublished text.)

Vitézy, László, ed. 1991–92. "A legvidámabb barakk" (The jolliest barrack [in the camp of peace]. Transcript of TV interviews with former political leaders). 5 vols. (unpublished).

Voszka, Éva. 1984. *Érdekek és kölcsönös függőség* (Interests and mutual dependency). Budapest: Közgazdasági és Jogi Kiadó.

Wallerstein, Immanuel. 1974. *The Modern World System*. New York: Academic Press.

Ward, Benjamin. 1967. *The Socialist Economy: A Study of Organizational Alternatives*. Berkeley, CA: University of California Press.

Wiles, Peter. 1992. "Capitalist Triumphalism in Eastern Europe, or the Economics of Transition: An Interim Report." In Armand Clesse and Rudolf L. Tőkés, eds., *Preventing a New East–West Divide: The Economic and Social Imperatives of the Future Europe*. Baden-Baden: Nomos. 389–407.

Yanov, Alexander. 1984. *The Drama of the Soviet 1960s: A Lost Reform*. Berkeley, CA: Institute of International Studies, University of California Berkeley.

Zinner, Paul E. 1962. *Revolution in Hungary*. New York: Columbia University Press.

Index

Cambridge Russian, Soviet and Post-Soviet Studies